Research in Criminology

Series Editors
Alfred Blumstein
David P. Farrington

Research in Criminology

Understanding and Controlling Crime: Toward A New Research Strategy
D. P. Farrington, L. E. Ohlin and J. Q. Wilson

The Social Ecology of Crime
J. M. Byrne and R. J. Sampson (Eds.)

The Reasoning Criminal: Rational Choice Perspectives on Offending
D. B. Cornish and R. V. Clarke (Eds.)

The Social Contexts of Criminal Sentencing
Martha A. Myers and Susette M. Talarico

Predicting Recidivism Using Survival Models
Peter Schmidt and Ann Dryden Witte

Coping, Behavior, and Adaptation in Prison Inmates
Edward Zamble and Frank Porporino

Prison Crowding: A Psychological Perspective
Paul B. Paulus

Off School, In Court: An Experimental and Psychiatric Investigation of Severe School Attendance Problems
I. Berg, I. Brown and R. Hullin

Policing and Punishing the Drinking Driver: A Study of General and Specific Deterrence
Ross Homel

Judicial Decision Making, Sentencing Policy, and Numerical Guidance
Austin Lovegrove

Criminal Behavior and the Justice System: Psychological Perspectives
H. Wegener, F. Lösel and J. Haisch (Eds.)

Criminal Behavior and the Justice System

Psychological Perspectives

Edited by
Hermann Wegener
Friedrich Lösel
Jochen Haisch

With 26 Illustrations

Springer-Verlag
New York Berlin Heidelberg
London Paris Tokyo

Hermann Wegener
Institute of Psychology, University of Kiel, New University,
Building N 30, Olshausenstraße 40, 2300 Kiel, FRG

Friedrich Lösel
Institute of Psychology I, University of Erlangen-Nuremberg,
Bismarckstraße 1, 8520 Erlangen, FRG

Jochen Haisch
Department of General Medicine, University of Ulm, Am Hochsträß 8,
7900 Ulm, FRG

Series Editors
Alfred Blumstein
School of Urban and Public Affairs, Carnegie-Mellon University,
Pittsburgh, Pennsylvania 15213, USA

David P. Farrington
Institute of Criminology, University of Cambridge, Cambridge CB3 9DT, England, UK

Library of Congress Cataloging-in-Publication Data. Criminal behavior and the justice system: psychological perspectives / edited by Hermann Wegener, Friedrich Lösel, Jochen Haisch. p. cm. – (Research in criminology) Bibliography: p. Includes index.
ISBN 978-3-642-86019-5
1. Criminal behavior – Cross-cultural studies. 2. Psychology, Forensic – Cross-cultural studies. 3. Criminal justice, Administration of – Cross cultural studies. I. Wegener, Hermann, 1921– . II. Lösel, Friedrich. III. Haisch, Jochen. IV. Series. HV6080.C73 1989 364.3'01'9 – dc19 88-29488 CIP

Printed on acid-free-paper

Softcover reprint of the hardcover 1st edition 1989

Typeset by K+V Fotosatz GmbH, 6124 Beerfelden, FRG.

9 8 7 6 5 4 3 2 1

ISBN 978-3-642-86019-5 ISBN 978-3-642-86017-1 (eBook)
DOI 10.1007/978-3-642-86017-1

Preface

Although psychology has long been one of the essential reference disciplines in jurisprudence and criminology, this has, for example in comparison to sociology, not always been clearly visible. Recently, however, there has been a noticeable change that we wish to document with this book.

The background to this publication was a conference on psycholegal research in Braunschweig, Federal Republic of Germany. To this conference, the editors, as chairmen of the Division of Psychology and Law in the German Psychological Society, invited experts from six countries. During the discussions, we decided to publish the contributions to this conference together with further papers on psychological research into criminal behavior and the justice system. The Division of Psychology and Law, like the corresponding divisions of the English and American Psychological Associations founded in 1977 and 1981, respectively, was established in 1984. One of its major goals is to develop and strengthen international collaboration within this special field of research.

In Germany, as long ago as the turn of the century, university professors began tackling problems with which they were confronted by the courts. Thus, at that time, W. Stern, H. Münsterberg, C.G. Jung, and M. Wertheimer, for example, examined the conditions and sources of error in witness testimonies. Following a period of varying research activities, after World War II there was a renaissance of "Forensic Psychology" in Germany. This was reflected, for example, in Undeutsch's (1967)[1] *Handbook of Forensic Psychology.* Then, in the 1970s and parallel to similar developments in other countries (see Monahan & Loftus, 1982[2]; Chapman, Müller & Blackman, 1984[3]), at several German universities there was an increase in experimental research in psycho-

---

[1] Undeutsch, U. (Ed.). (1967). *Handbuch der Psychologie: Vol. 11. Forensische Psychologie.* Göttingen: Hogrefe.

[2] Monahan, J., & Loftus, E.F. (1982). The psychology of law. *Annual Review of Psychology, 33,* 441–475.

[3] Chapman, A.J., Müller, D.J., & Blackman, D.E. (Eds.) (1984). Some applications of psychology to law [special issue]. *International Review of Applied Psychology, 33* (1).

logy and law, which was later supplemented by qualitative research methods. In the process, this branch of applied psychology ceased to be restricted to assessing witnesses and the accused; rather it was expanded to encompass various other aspects of psychology. The present volume aims to document the results of this development for the field of criminal law[4].

Up until the 1960s, scientific interest was dominated by the activities of psychologists as expert witnesses. As a result, this specialized area was named "Forensic Psychology". Its primary goal was the development of psychodiagnostic procedures and theories for application in court settings. Later, this was supplemented by research in criminal psychology, that mainly studied deviant behavior. During the last 15 years, jury, juror, and judicial decision-making, the effects of sanctions, social-psychological aspects of police activities, and the development and control of norms have become topics of psychological research. The field is now termed psychology and law, legal psychology, or psycholegal research.

The former procedure of ad hoc selection and eclectic combination of general psychological knowledge (used to solve practical problems) has nowadays been expanded by theoretically guided research. This involves examining and suggesting improvements to the actual functioning of the legal system, but also includes more basic research on the legal system with its norms and control mechanisms, its theories of human action, and its psychological foundations. We consider the present volume as a contribution to psychology and law in this broader sense.

The structure of this volume reflects four traditional key areas of psychological research within the framework of criminal law, which were also the major themes at the Braunschweig conference[5]:

- Prediction and explanation of criminal behavior
- Legal thought, attribution, and sentencing
- Eyewitness testimony
- Correctional treatment: clinical and organizational aspects

Since there is no general theory of legal psychology, the contributions represent different theoretical perspectives. We hope that this volume demonstrates that psychology and law is no longer merely applied psychology in the pragmatic sense, but instead, as a consequence of the enlargement of its research focus and its various relations to basic research, has developed into a significant and independent area of psychology.

We would like to express our gratitude to Professor Elisabeth Müller-Luckmann, our host in Braunschweig. The conference was funded by the German

---

[4] For earlier reviews see, e.g., Wegener, H. (1981). *Einführung in die Forensische Psychologie.* Darmstadt: Wissenschaftliche Buchgesellschaft; Lösel, F. (Ed.) (1983). *Kriminalpsychologie.* Weinheim: Beltz.

[5] The Division has held since a second conference that dealt especially with the psychological aspects of civil law.

Research Council (DFG) and the Minister of Justice of Niedersachsen. The editors would like to thank Robert Goldsmith and Jonathan Harrow for translations and "native speaker" advice. We are further indebted to Thomas Thiekötter, Janet Hamilton, and Bärbel Wehner from Springer for their kind support and patience during the publishing process.

The Editors

Contents

Contributors

Norman H. Anderson Department of Psychology, University of California, San Diego, La Jolla, CA92093, USA

Wolfgang Bandilla Waldhofstraße 2, 6800 Mannheim 1, FRG

Maya Bar-Hillel Department of Psychology, The Hebrew University, Jerusalem 91905, Israel

Hans Werner Bierhoff Department of Psychology, University of Marburg, Gutenbergstraße 18, 3550 Marburg, FRG

Thomas Bliesener Special Research Unit 227, University of Bielefeld, P.O. Box 8640, 4800 Bielefeld 1, FRG

Ernst Buck Department of Psychology, University of Marburg, Gutenbergstraße 18, 3550 Marburg, FRG

Noel K. Clark Institute of Social and Applied Psychology, The University of Kent at Canterbury, Kent CT2 7LZ, England, UK

Ronald V. Clarke School of Criminal Justice, Rutgers, The State University of New Jersey, 15 Washington Street, Newark, New Jersey 07102, USA

Derek B. Cornish Department of Social Science and Administration, London School of Economics and Political Science, Houghton Street, London WC2A 2AE, England, UK

Hans F. M. Crombag Faculty of Law, State University of Limburg, P.O. Box 616, 6200 MD Maastricht, The Netherlands

Ingrid M. Deusinger Institute of Psychology, University of Frankfurt, Kettenhoferweg 128, 6000 Frankfurt 11, FRG

John P. J. Dussich Department of Sociology, Western Michigan University, Kalamazoo, Michigan 49008-3899, USA

David P. Farrington University of Cambridge, Institute of Criminology, 7 West Road, Cambridge CB3 9DT, England, UK

Robert W. Goldsmith Department of Applied Psychology, University of Lund, Paradisgatan 5, 223 50 Lund, Sweden

Jochen Haisch Department of General Medicine, University of Ulm, Am Hochsträß 8, 7900 Ulm, FRG

Albert R. Hauber Faculty of Law, State University of Leiden, Hugo de Grootstraat 27, P.O. Box 2520, 2300 RA Leiden, The Netherlands

Wilfried Hommers Institute of Psychology, University of Würzburg, Domerschulstraße 13, 8700 Würzburg, FRG

Renate Klein Department of Psychology, University of Marburg, Gutenbergstraße 18, 3550 Marburg, FRG

Bromley H. Kniveton Department of Social Science, Loughborough University, Loughborough, Leicestershire LE11 3TU, England, UK

Peter Köferl Institute of Psychology I, University of Erlangen-Nuremberg, Bismarckstraße 1, 8520 Erlangen, FRG

Günter Köhnken Institute of Psychology, University of Kiel, New University, Building N30, Olshausenstraße 40, 2300 Kiel, FRG

Helmut Kury Max-Planck-Institute of Foreign and International Penal Law, Güntherstalstraße 73, 7800 Freiburg i. Br., FRG

Waldemar Lilli Faculty of Social Sciences, University of Mannheim, A5, 6800 Mannheim 1, FRG

Elizabeth F. Loftus Department of Psychology, University of Washington, Seattle, Washington 98195, USA

Friedrich Lösel Institute of Psychology I, University of Erlangen-Nuremberg, Bismarckstraße 1, 8520 Erlangen, FRG

John Monahan School of Law, University of Virginia, Charlottesville, Virginia 22901, USA

Pär-Eric Nilsson Department of Applied Psychology, University of Lund, Paradisgatan 5, 22350 Lund, Sweden

David C. Raskin Department of Psychology, University of Utah, Salt Lake City, Utah 84112, USA

Bernd Schünemann Department of Criminal Law, University of Freiburg, Erbprinzenstraße 17, 7800 Freiburg i. Br., FRG

A. Philip Sealy Department of Social Psychology, London School of Economics and Political Science, Houghton Street, London WC2A 2AE, England, UK

Willi Seitz Institute of Special Education, University of Mainz, Hegelstraße 59, 6500 Mainz, FRG

Siegfried Ludwig Sporer School of Law/Criminology, University of Marburg, Universitätsstraße 6, 3550 Marburg, FRG

Max Steller Department of Forensic Psychiatry, Free University of Berlin, Spandauer Damm 130, 1000 Berlin 19, FRG

Egon Stephan Institute of Psychology, University of Cologne, Herbert Lewin-Straße 2, 5000 Cologne 41, FRG

Geoffrey M. Stephenson Institute of Social and Applied Psychology, The University of Kent at Canterbury, Kent CT2 7LZ, England, UK

Gunilla Throfast Department of Applied Psychology, University of Lund, Paradisgatan 5, 22350 Lund, Sweden

Hermann Wegener Institute of Psychology, University of Kiel, New University, Building N30, Olshausenstraße 40, 2300 Kiel, FRG

Werner Wippich Department of Psychology, University of Trier, P.O. Box 3852, 5500 Trier, FRG

1
When Law and Psychology Meet

HANS F. M. CROMBAG

A Technology for Controlling Behavior

Psychologists working in the field of law and psychology tend to think that there is a special relationship between the two disciplines. The law, as a system of rules and a practice of applying these rules, is a human, perhaps an all too human, enterprise. The rules of law, however, are not only invented and applied *by* men; they are also meant to apply *to* men. As a device for the control of human behavior, the law is subject to empirical constraints of a psychological nature. In order to be successful, the law must take into account the possibilities and impossibilities of human behavior. The rules can only prescribe what is humanly possible; they cannot forbid what is humanly unavoidable. As an institution it should only take measures that can successfully affect behavior. There is no moral issue here; it is merely a matter of practicalities. If the law disregards the constraints of empirical psychology, it simply becomes ineffective. Whether that would be morally wrong is at best a secondary question.

There is yet another reason why law and psychology are intricately connected. Every legal qualification – with very few exceptions, if any at all – depends not only on factual conditions but also on psychological conditions. In criminal law this is most prominent: *Actus non facit reum nisi mens sit rea* (an act is not guilty without a guilty mind). In civil law things are not different: No liability without fault, and no contract without the intention of parties to enter into it. This being the case, one may think that every judicial decision is at least in part a psychological one, i.e., a decision on the presence or absence of a particular state of mind. Now one may hold, as John Fleming does (1967, p. 27), that "negligence is not (...) a state of mind, but conduct," but even then the question of which conduct deserves the qualification of negligence seems to have strong psychological overtones.

If the law is a technology for controlling behavior, then the law is a branch of applied psychology, and an important one at that. Quite possibly it is more:

perhaps it is also and even primarily the expression of an ideal, a social philosophy describing what constitutes "the good life" for man. But in daily practice it is a technology through which we regulate our social behavior, and there the more prominent question seems to be whether it works. Leaving aside whether the rules of law are an adequate expression of our social philosophy and even more so, whether our social philosophy is the best possible one, the question of whether the rules and the way we apply them are actually capable of affecting human behavior is a profoundly psychological one.

If this is true, why were psychologists so late in turning their eye towards the law? Psychiatrists, sociologists, and even economists preceded us. Why were we so late?

A Brief History

We were not particularly late, but for a long time we were rather one-sided in our interests. For many years psychologists have been working in criminology, turning this field of study into what may be called "the psychology of the criminal mind." The psychology that went into this was predominantly differential psychology, i.e., psychology which stresses individual differences, while overlooking the ways in which people resemble each other. Of the "two disciplines of psychology," as Lee Cronbach (1957) called them, only one payed attention to the law and produced a brand of correlational research on personality traits of criminals, which only now is becoming recognized as remarkably unsuccessful.

But there were other psychologists who approached the law with a broader view than that of differential psychology. For the German-speaking world the largely forgotten book of Sturm (1910) merits mention in this context. In the Anglo-Saxon world Hugo Münsterberg's *On the Witness Stand* (1908) seems to mark a psychological approach to the law which is not primarily inspired by differential psychology. Incidentally, in the last chapter of his book Münsterberg explicitly warns against the idea that personal characteristics of criminals may explain and predict their behavior; a chapter apparently overlooked by generations of criminologists to come.

Despite Münsterberg's prestige and influence, his book did not start a new branch of applied psychological research. During the first half of this century many psychologists applied their knowledge of human behavior to schools and education, to industrial organizations and work, and even to armies and the conduct of war. All these activities led to separate branches of applied psychology. The work in law and psychology always remained of an accidental nature. It was done by psychologists who bumped into some legal problem or other. Psychologists making the law their major field of study over a longer period of time are a relatively new phenomenon. Law and psychology only emerged as a separate field of study during the last decade. June Tapp's contribution to the 1976 *Annual Review of Psychology* (Tapp, 1976) may be seen as a starting point of this new development. The subtitle of her article, "An Overture," suggests as much, although some think that Hans Toch (1961) may claim the honor of having turned "legal psychology" into a distinct field of applied psychology.

The list of references of Tapp's 1976 review article contained 199 titles and that list was not exhaustive [e.g., John Hogarth's (1971) landmark book was conspicuously absent]. Only since then has the field gained momentum. By now there must be several thousands of studies in the field[1]. New as the field may be, it already appears impossible for any one person to know it all.

I shall not even try to give a state of the art review. Instead I shall argue that the relationship between law and psychology is still very ambiguous. When psychologists address the law and its practice, they sometimes overstate their case, criticizing the law and lawyers on insufficient grounds and making inappropriate recommendations; I think this is the case for a good deal of work done by psychologists on judicial decision-making. On other topics, however, they are too modest and agree too easily with *opinions chics* in legal circles that run counter to strong psychological evidence. It seems to me that a case in point is the failure of psychologists to stick to their guns when lawyers, politicians, and the media tell us that punishment does not work. I shall argue both points in greater detail.

Decision-Making Under Uncertainty

We are told that judicial decision-making "most surely is a social invention for deciding between disputed alternatives *under conditions of uncertainty*" (Saks & Kidd, 1980/1981). This seems to me an exaggeration considering the many criminal cases with confessing defendants and cases where offenders were caught in the act. But in the majority of civil cases and in a small but significant portion of criminal cases adjudication is indeed decision-making under uncertainty. The uncertainty may originate from various sources: the facts of the case can be uncertain; the degree and distribution of liability (criminal or civil) can be uncertain; it can be uncertain which rule applies and what the rule means; it can be uncertain which measure is the most appropriate; and, finally, any combination of these uncertainties can occur. The third source mentioned, that pertaining to the applicable rule of law, is typical of civil disputes but only

---

[1] An overview of work done in the Federal Republic of Germany was given by Jochen Haisch during the 33. Kongreß der Deutschen Gesellschaft für Psychologie in Mainz, 1982, an extract of which was published in Lüer (1983). An overview of work done in my own country (The Netherlands) was recently given by Van den Heuvel (1985).

rarely occurs in criminal cases. In criminal cases typical sources of uncertainty are the facts and the degree of liability. In handling both these sources of uncertainty, psychologists have tried to be of help to laywers. Let us consider these attempts in somewhat greater detail and see how successful they have been.

Establishing Facts

Courts establish the facts of a case on the basis of evidence put before them. In a civil dispute each party has to present proof of its own contentions. In addition each party is allowed to present evidence challenging the opponent's contentions. In a criminal case the prosecution must present proof of its allegations. The defence does not have to prove anything, but is allowed to present any evidence that contradicts the prosecution's allegations.

Evidence offered in proof may be anything, but a major category of evidence is eyewitness testimony. The reliability, or rather the unreliability, of eyewitnesses has been a major concern of psychologists. Most of Hugo Münsterberg's classic book (1908) was on this subject. Other significant names are those of Udo Undeutsch (1967), Arne Trankell (1972), and Elizabeth Loftus (1979), but many, many others have contributed. The work in this field is a showcase for the relevance of psychology to legal matters. I shall not review this work as I think it is sufficiently known.

Another issue which attracted the interest of psychologists is that in establishing the facts of a case by means of evidence there is always a margin of uncertainty. There is no such thing as a fact, we are told, "all information is really probability information" (Saks & Kidd, 1980/1981, p. 153). That being so, the accuracy of judicial decision-making depends heavily on human ability to handle probabilistic information. Since the seminal work by Amos Tversky and Daniel Kahneman (Kahneman, Slovic & Tversky, 1982; Nisbett & Ross, 1980) we know that people are very poor intuitive statisticians. We use such simplifying heuristics as representativeness and availability, which in many instances lead us astray in our conclusions. We ignore base rates, we fail to combine correctly prior and posterior probabilities and probabilities in general, we appreciate insufficiently the effects of sample size, and we detect correlations in data that are not there and overlook those that are. I shall not illustrate each of these mistakes, as such examples seem common knowledge and part of the stock of anecdotes which psychologists employ to amuse their students and lay audiences. "Decision makers' intuitive, common-sense judgments depart markedly and lawfully (in the scientific sense) from *the actual probabilities*," Michael Saks and Robert Kidd say, and this also applies to adjudication, which they name "trial by heuristics" (Saks & Kidd, 1980/1981, p. 127; italics added).

How do we know what "the actual probabilities" are? We can calculate them, assuming there is sufficient information, by applying mathematical probability theory as originally developed by Pascal and Fermat, taken up by Leibniz and Bernoulli, and varied upon by the Reverend Bayes. In order to avoid the erroneous conclusions which in many instances are sure to result from "trial by heuristics," we should bring mathematical probability theory into the courtroom and start practicing "trial by mathematics" [the expression used by Tribe (1971)]. This is advocated by Finkelstein and Fairly (1970) with respect to Bayesian methodology, and in more general and stronger terms by Saks and Kidd (1980/1981). The latter authors state: "It has been well established for some time that when the same information is available to intuitive humans or a *good* mathematical model, the human's decisions are consistently less accurate" (p. 146; italics added). Since we know that "a good mathematical model" is mathematical probability theory, let us use it.

Laurence Tribe (1971) disagrees, but chiefly on practical grounds. If the probabilities involved were measurable, he would agree that they would "obey the principles of the mathematical calculus" [quote from L. Jonathan Cohen (1977, p. 53)], but he thinks that in most legal disputes the probabilities involved cannot be established with any rigor. Tribe may have a point here: in a case where an eyewitness testifies that the offender had a red beard, what is the probability that any one person has a red beard? What percentage of males in a population have red beards? In which population: a particular town, a country, or the world? There is no way we can put an accurate number on so simple a question. What, then, is the point of applying a strong mathematical model to weak, intuitive data? The only excuse may be that in psychology we have a long history of doing just that. There is no reason, however, why the lawyers should follow suit.

All this does not exclude the possibility of using probability calculus in those rare cases where accurate numerical values can be put on likelihoods involved. Tribe would concede this. But conceding this has implications which Tribe cannot possibly accept. Let me, for reasons of brevity, mention only one of those implications.

The overwhelming majority of cases brought before the criminal courts result in convictions. The reason for this is obvious: only sure cases are actually prosecuted. I do not have the exact figure for my country, but I am convinced that the conviction rate is well in excess of 90%. As soon as a suspect is brought to trial, the base rate is overwhelmingly against him. But no court in the world would convict on this basis alone[2]. Why not? Because doing so would violate a basic legal principle known as "the presumption of innocence." It states that prior to the presentation of evidence the probability of guilt is zero. But Saks and Kidd think differently. They think lawyers are stupid not using such a solid piece of evidence. "Like it or not," they say (p. 154), "base-rate information

[2] Not consciously that is. Still, this is what Saks and Kidd (1980/1981) recommend in a comparable case (see p. 152).

can be helpful to a decision maker." So long as psychologists are willing to consider a principle that lawyers hold sacred in their trade, as a sign of stupidity and bad logic, the dialogue between the two is going to be very awkward indeed.

Models of Rationality

If Pascalian probability theory and its derivations is the unique and unquestionable model for rationality, then prior probabilities cannot be ignored. Is it? Some think differently, the most notable among them being the Oxford philosopher Jonathan Cohen (1977). According to him there is another theory of probability, which he calls "Baconian." This theory of inductive probability is less well developed than Pascalian probability theory, but it has as long a history as the Pascalian variety and provides a theoretical explanation for most of our intuitive practices in experimental design. It is concerned with the detection of cause-effect relationships, not merely with empirical covariations and predictions. It has different rules for combining probabilities and its negation principle is not complementational. It seeks to justify induction, i.e., how we proceed from specific instances to general causal laws. This is a problem of long standing, which many consider unresolved. Whether this is true or not, two things must be clear: we constantly, both within and outside science, make inductions and Pascalian theory cannot accommodate this practice.

Jonathan Cohen claims to have formalized Baconian logic, which previously was only an intuitive practice. I am not competent to judge whether his very complex formalization is adequate, but he has convinced me that the way in which Tversky and Kahneman criticize the stupidity of their experimental subjects because they violate the rules of Pascalian logic may have been rash, even more so since they themselves admit that there may be a rival model (Shafer, 1976) to the standard Pascalian calculus, a "central feature" of which is "its deliberate nonutilization (or heavy discounting) of the base rate in many problems where the Bayesian insists on its full employment" [quotation taken from Nisbett and Ross (1980, p. 265)]. Their reply to Cohen's critique of their work (Cohen, 1979, 1980) is not free of flippancy (Kahneman & Tversky, 1979).

There may be more than one valid model for making inferences. Each may be valid in its own universe of discourse. Something similar was recently said by Jerome Bruner in an invited address during the 1984 APA convention (Bruner, 1984). He proffered the hypothesis that "there are two irreducible modes of thought": *the paradigmatic or logico-scientific mode*, concerned with context-free and universal knowledge of the world, which is subject to formal verification and empirical proof, leading to falsifiability; and *the narrative mode*, concerned with context-sensitive and particular information, subject to tests of verisimilitude, and leading to believability. According to Bruner, these two modes of thinking are "irreducible to one another;" their outcomes can "neither contradict nor corroborate" one another; "each is a version of the world." Perhaps Amos Tversky and Daniel Kahneman are trying to contradict the outcomes of a narrative mode of thought with arguments from a paradigmatic mode of thought, the very thing that Bruner considers impossible. Maybe Jonathan Cohen (1979) is right when he says that they "misclassify certain human reasoning processes." Possibly a legal dispute is indeed a conflict of narratives and a judicial decision is indeed a test of the believability of two versions of a narrative. We should consider this hypothesis and its implications. Flippant criticism of judicial stupidity for not adhering to Pascalian probability theory, while brushing aside basic legal principles, is not going to be very productive for the dialogue between psychologists and lawyers.

Attribution of Liability

Let us move on to the other source of uncertainty in judicial decision-making: the distribution of liability. Liability depends on the presence of *mens rea*, which comes in degrees ranging from intent, via recklessness, to negligence[3]. *Mens rea* is commonly defined as "knowledge of circumstances " and "foresight of consequences" (Hart, 1968, p. 90). Knowledge is something which is *in* the person and since courts are no more able to read minds than anybody else, they have developed their own peculiar way of attributing *mens rea* to the people appearing before them. To this purpose they created the fiction of "reasonable man": *mens rea* is assumed if "any responsible person in his (i.e., the defendant's or the suspect's) place and with his knowledge would have known" that the consequences of his actions would be harmful (Denning, 1961, p. 17).

Some psychologists have thought that they could do better than this and have offered attribution theory as a rational model for attributing guilt and liability. Jochen Haisch (1980), in one of his contributions to the field, speaks of "*Attributionstheorie als normatives Modell*" (attribution theory as a normative model). Now, that is a surprising claim for what I thought was a descriptive theory.

What is attribution theory? According to one of its founders, Harold Kelley, it is a theory of "social perception" and a particular form of social perception at that: it deals with "how people make causal explanations" of behavior (Kelley, 1973). From these simple statements it follows that attribution theory is not a theory about the causes of behavior but about the perceptions of those causes. The latter would coincide with the first if and only if our perceptions on the subject are accurate, i.e., if people may be assumed to know what moves themselves and others.

---

[3] I skip over a host of complications here, as I have discussed them elsewhere (Crombag, 1984).

There are reasons to doubt this. First of all there is Kelley's own remark that "the answers of interest are those given by the man in the street." And he adds: "Thus, attribution theory concerns what Heider has called 'naive psychology'." Is there reason to believe that the way in which "naive" people think and talk about the causes of behavior has much connection with psychological reality? One does not have to be a rabid behaviorist to have some serious doubts here; all the more so because attribution theorists themselves, most notably Edward Jones (1976), have pointed out that people are given to making many mistakes in this context. The most common among these is called the "fundamental attribution error." The error is said to be made by observers when drawing inferences about the causes of the behavior of others. Then we are inclined to overestimate dispositions of actors as causes of their behavior while underestimating the role of situational factors.

How do we know that observers overestimate the role of dispositional factors? Because actors attribute more to situational factors (Jones & Nisbett, 1972). Actors are supposed to know, which makes the observers wrong. I believe they are indeed, but that does not follow from the empirical result. The actors may be wrong too. There is empirical evidence showing that actors frequently fail to report factors that can otherwise be shown to have affected their behavior, or erroneously report factors as influential that can otherwise be shown not to have affected their behavior. Richard Nisbett and Lee Ross (1980, Chap. 9), who review the available evidence, conclude that people have no privileged or direct access to "the workings of their mental machinery," though they have an edge over observers in that they have more information about their personal histories. It would, however, be imprudent to assume that the actor is always right about the causes of his own behavior and the observer, when deviating from the actor's statements, always wrong.

I am aware that attribution theorists, Kelley in particular, have developed a set of criteria – distinctiveness, consistency, and consensus – meant to help in making attributions about causes of behavior in such a way as to avoid making the fundamental attribution error. Incidentally, together those criteria constitute a Baconian method for establishing causal relationships, although most attribution theorists trace their method back to John Stuart Mill. I understand why they are tempted to present their method for causal attributions as a model for judicial decision-making. But they overstate their case as long as they have not demonstrated that the unarmed human eye, admittedly helped by their method for attributional analysis, has direct access to all or the most significant causes of human behavior. And that position, although popular even among psychologists, is not uncontested. If it were, our whole psychological machinery could, once again, be reduced to asking people questions and classifying their answers. We would be back at the old "*Bewusstseinspsychologie*". Is that what we want? If not, I see no justification for advising courts to model their decision-making after attributional analysis. Attribution theory may well serve as a descriptive theory of judicial decision-making. It may more or less explain what happens in our courts, i.e., describe the psychology which is apparently used. Let us find out[4]. If next we want to criticize what is going on, we shall need a bigger slice of psychology than attribution theory.

Effects of Punishment

After these two examples of instances in which psychologists, to my mind, tend to overstate the case they have against lawyers, let me turn to an area where I think psychologists tend to understate their case. This concerns the effects of punishment and the threat of punishment.

Nowadays one can frequently hear lawyers and politicians involved in making legal policy say that punishment does not work. Of course, courts still impose punishment and lawmakers do not fail to attach sanctions to the rules they proclaim, so one may well wonder whether they really believe what they are saying. But they tell us they keep doing this for lack of anything better. If possible they want alternatives to punishment. Psychologists have been eager to agree and to offer help in finding alternatives, e.g., rehabilitation programs and psychotherapeutic measures.

Why? Punishment is one of the better studied subjects in experimental psychology. In our laboratories we have punished thousands of rats and pigeons and cats and monkeys and humans in different ways, in varying intensities, given after varying intervals and according to different schedules, for experimentally induced and spontaneous behaviors, and we have found that punishment is a powerful response suppressor. We know that punishment is most effective as a response suppressor when it is immediate, inescapable, severe, and given on an FR 1 schedule, i.e., each time the forbidden response is given (see, e.g., Walters & Grusec, 1977). Whether this is so because of Thorndike's original formulation of the Law of Effect (Thorndike, 1911, Chap. 6), involving one single learning mechanism, or because Guthrie's competing-response theory (Guthrie, 1935), assuming two separate learning mechanisms, is the better explanation, need not bother us here, although there seems to be a growing consensus that Thorndike's original position was right (see Van Houten, 1983). What counts is that it works.

As always, some confusing phenomena turned up in many of the experiments, such as habituation and spontaneous recovery, which may blur, but not undo the main effect. Moreover, under certain conditions punishment may lead to unintended effects such as escape and even aggression. And apart from all this, punishing someone is not a nice way to behave: it raises aesthetic and ethical questions. All this is true.

[4] As, for example, was done by Fincham and Jaspers (1980). However, Fincham and Jaspers did not analyze actual court decisions, but the way in which legal theorists such as Hart and Honoré (1959) reason about causation and responsibility. The fact that on p. 96 of their paper they speak of those notions as "commonsense notions of responsibility in legal philosophy" suggests that they too have more than descriptive aspirations.

However, when applied in the proper way and with the proper controls, punishment suppresses behavior. Or does it not? One of the most frequent objections to punishment is that it produces no *permanent* effects. You punish a particular response for some time until it is suppressed. Then you turn your back and after a while the suppressed behavior reappears. When the suppressed behavior, if unpunished, is of itself rewarding, of course it does. A response learned through reinforcement is subject to extinction when the reinforcing contingency that brought it about is no longer in force. The effects of rewards are as temporary as the effects of punishment. The mechanism involved in both instances is the same: adaptation to environmental contingencies. One cannot reap the harvest of adaptation only half the time. The only punishment with lasting effects is capital punishment. So long as there is life, adaptation works, because that is what keeps life going. The objection that punishment does not produce lasting effects is silly. Psychologists should not be moved by it.

Punishment in the Real World

Punishment may work in the psychological laboratory, but does it work in real life and particularly in criminal law enforcement? In view of the ever-rising crime rates (see, e.g., Van den Haag, 1975), apparently not quite. Before addressing some of the real problems involved in the practice of criminal law, let me first mention that in thinking about the matter we tend to be led astray by the availability heuristic. Most people in our society are still more or less law-abiding, i.e., they do not come into contact with the police for anything more serious than a traffic ticket and they restrict their mischief to what is not forbidden by the law or is not effectively prosecuted. For the overwhelming majority of citizens the threat of punishment works.

Of those who at one point in time do run into trouble with the law, again the vast majority turn out to be one-time offenders. It is the relatively small group of recidivists that is, by the salience of the behavior of its members, highly available to our minds when we think about crime and criminals. While the vast majority of citizens are effectively deterred by the threat of punishment and actual punishment, a relatively small group of recidivists, which is responsible for most of the offenses committed, appears to be entirely insensitive to punishment. Let me first mention that even if it were true that they are totally insensitive to punishment, this would not justify the generalization that punishment does not work and that our psychological data are merely experimental artifacts.

Let me next remind the reader that crimes are not committed out of irrational malice, but because crime, if unpunished, pays; it serves a purpose for those who commit it. You can grow rich by pushing drugs, driving your competitors out of the market through violence, or by robbing banks and burglarizing houses, shooting possible witnesses in the process. We may not share the purposes of rapists and hooligans, but they do commit their mischief for a purpose. Trying to fight this as a society, we run into a number of principled and practical problems. I shall briefly discuss one of each and their interconnection.

A principled problem is, that many crimes are so advantageous to their committers that we cannot possibly meet these crimes with punishments that would make the outcome negative on balance. The reason for this is ethical: we think there are limits to the amount of pain that civilized society can inflict on people, whoever they are. The drug-pusher who assaults a rival and brutally mutilates him goes to jail for several years, but he is not mutilated in turn. We think that, in order to preserve a minimum of civility in society, there are strict limits to what we can do to others, even criminals. There are, however, criminals who do not care for any minimum of civility. They take or do what they want at whatever cost to their victims or even themselves. Thus they put themselves outside our range of effective control.

A practical problem is connected with this. Recidivists are by definition repeat players: they can calculate their gains and losses over many instances. The price a recidivist pays when caught is easily outweighed by the profit made through the many times he got away. There is a type of burglar who robs family homes. The profit each time may not be very large, but it is easy and not very risky. Eventually almost all of these petty burglars are caught[5] and tried for one or a few of their burglaries which can easily be proven in court. But the total amount of their profits over tens or even hundreds of cases may be quite substantial indeed. Are we going to fine them to the amount of their profits over the years? Are we going to put them in jail for as many years as it would have taken them to earn these profits honestly? No, we shall not, for ethical and practical reasons. So crimes with a low risk of being caught and brought to justice, pay and that is another reason why many recidivists are outside our range of effective control.

If we cannot live with this, we must lower our ethical standard as to the amount of pain we are willing to inflict on others if necessary, and we must considerably tighten police control. What we are up against is a group of criminals who are on fixed ratio schedule of reinforcement of close to 1, and a variable ratio schedule of punishment of much higher value. If we want to change this, there is a terrible price to pay: a police state operating a brutal criminal justice system. I am not advocating that we pay that price, I am simply trying to clear up the issue. And I am criticizing psychologists who, for reasons of professional modesty or personal comfort, refuse to do the same. Psychologists sometimes do have something to say to lawyers, but the message is not always a pretty and a happy one.

---

[5] See *Interimrapport van de Commissie Kleine Criminaliteit* (1984). Den Haag: Staatsuitgeverij, p. 83 ff.

References

Bruner, J. (1984). Narrative and paradigmatic modes of thought. (Invited Address), Division 1, APA Annual Convention, Toronto, August 25.

Cohen, L. J. (1977). *The probable and the provable.* Oxford: Clarendon.

Cohen, L. J. (1979). On the psychology of predication: Whose is the fallacy? *Cognition, 7,* 385–407.

Cohen, L. J. (1980). Whose is the fallacy? A rejoinder to Daniel Kahneman and Amos Tversky. *Cognition, 8,* 89–92.

Crombag, H. F. M. (1984). Some psychological observations on *mens rea.* In D. J. Müller, D. E. Blackman, & A. J. Chapman (Eds.), *Psychology and law* (pp. 55–65). Chicester: Wiley.

Cronbach, L. J. (1957). The two disciplines of scientific psychology. *American Psychologist, 12,* 671–684.

Denning, L. (1961). *Responsibility before the law.* Jerusalem: Magnes.

Fincham, F. D., & Jaspers, J. M. (1980). Attribution of responsibility: from man the scientist to man the lawyer. In L. Berkowitz (Ed.), *Advances in experimental social psychology*: Vol. 13 (pp. 81–138). New York: Academic.

Finkelstein, W. O., & Fairly, W. B. (1970). A Bayesian approach to identification evidence. *Harvard Law Review, 83,* 489–517.

Fleming, J. G. (1967). *An introduction to the law of torts.* Oxford: Clarendon.

Guthrie, E. R. (1935). *The psychology of learning.* New York: Harper and Row.

Haisch, J. (1980). Anwendung von Attributionstheorie als normatives Modell für eine rationale Strafzumessung: experimentelle Überprüfung eines Trainingsprogrammes. *Zeitschrift für Experimentelle und Angewandte Psychologie, 27,* 415–427.

Hart, H. L. A. (1968). *Punishment and responsibility.* Oxford: Clarendon.

Hart, H. L. A., & Honoré, A. M. (1959). *Causation in the law.* Oxford: Clarendon.

Hogarth, J. (1971). *Sentencing as a human process.* Toronto: University of Toronto Press.

Jones, E. E. (1976). How do people perceive the causes of behavior? *American Scientist, 64,* 300–305.

Jones, E. E., & Nisbett, R. E. (1972). The actor and the observer: divergent perceptions of the causes of behavior. In E. E. Jones et al. (Eds.), *Attribution: Perceiving the causes of behavior.* Morristown, NJ: General Learning.

Kahneman, D., & Tversky, A. (1979). On the interpretation of intuitive probability: a reply to Jonathan Cohen. *Cognition, 7,* 409–411.

Kahneman, D., Slovic, P., & Tversky, A. (Eds.). (1982). *Judgment under uncertainty: heuristics and biases.* Cambridge: Cambridge University Press.

Kelley, H. H. (1973). The process of causal attribution. *American Psychologist, 28,* 107–128.

Loftus, E. (1979). *Eyewitness testimony.* Cambridge, MA: Harvard University Press.

Lüer, A. (Ed.). (1983). *Bericht über den 33. Kongress der Deutschen Gesellschaft für Psychologie in Mainz 1982.* Göttingen: Hogrefe.

Münsterberg, H. (1908). *On the witness stand. Essays on psychology and crime.* New York: Doubleday, Page.

Nisbett, R., & Ross, L. (1980). *Human inference: strategies and shortcomings of social judgment.* Englewood Cliffs, NJ: Prentice Hall.

Saks, M. J., & Kidd, R. F. (1980/1981). Human information processing and adjudication: trial by heuristics. *Law and Society Review, 15,* 123–160.

Shafer, G. (1976). *A mathematical theory of evidence.* Princeton: Princeton University Press.

Sturm, A. (1910). *Die psychologische Grundlage des Rechts.* Hannover: Helwigsche Verlagsbuchhandlung.

Tapp, J.L. (1976). Psychology and law: an overture. *Annual Review of Psychology, 27,* 359–404.

Thorndike, E.L. (1911). *Animal intelligence: experimental studies.* New York: Macmillan.

Toch, H. (Ed.). (1961). *Legal and criminal psychology.* New York: Holt, Rinehart and Winston.

Trankell, A. (1972). *Reliability of evidence.* Stockholm: Beckmans.

Tribe, L.H. (1971). Trial by mathematics: precision and ritual in the legal process. *Harvard Law Review, 84,* 1329–1393.

Undeutsch, U. (Ed.). (1967). *Forensische Psychologie.* Göttingen: Verlag für Psychologie.

Van den Haag, E. (1975). *Punishing criminals.* New York: Basic Books.

Van den Heuvel, G.A.A.J. (1985). Psychologie en recht: variaties op een thema. *Nederlands Tijdschrift voor de Psychologie, 40,* 196–207.

Van Houten, R. (1983). Punishment: from the animal laboratory to the applied setting. In S. Axelrod, & J. Apsche (Eds.), *The effects of punishment on human behavior.* New York: Academic.

Walters, G.C., & Grusec, J.E. (1977). *Punishment.* San Francisco: Freeman.

Part One Prediction and Explanation of Criminal Behavior

Introduction

FRIEDRICH LÖSEL

Models that predict and explain criminal behavior have a more or less direct influence on nearly all the procedures and decisions in the criminal justice system. According to the logic of science, the problems of explanation and prediction can be differentiated through the following structure: in the case of explanation, the explanandum – a fact of crime or criminality – is given. A search is made for the antecedent conditions and a deterministic or probabilistic scientific law from which the problematic issue can be derived as a special case. In prediction, the antecedent condition is given, and a search is made for a scientific law from which future facts can be derived. For criminal predictions, whether they are individual or collective predictions, no explicit theories of criminality are necessary. A substantial, repeatable empirical correlation between predictors and criterion is sufficient. However, the selection of predictors is to some extent already implicitly codetermined by theoretical assumptions, that is, there is no observation that is free of theory. And, vice versa, a valid prediction is the strongest methodological support for the utility of a theory. Models of explanation and prediction in criminology should therefore, on the one hand, be differentiated according to their logic and content, while, on the other hand, they cannot be strictly separated from one another.

In criminology, there is a great number of explanations of criminal behavior which are only loosely interrelated. It can be seen that there is no *single* psychological perspective for the explanation of crime, but a great number of hypotheses that are derived from very different theories, such as (1) biopsychological theories, (2) trait theories from personality psychology, (3) (cognitive-social) learning theories, (4) theories of informal social control, (5) action and decision-making theories, (6) theories of moral development, and (7) self-concept and attribution theories.

In many explanations, several fields of theory are integrated, as in, for example, the hypotheses from Eysenck (1977) and Wilson and Herrnstein (1985) that are derived from personality psychology, learning theory, and (partially) physiology; or the assumptions regarding interpersonal bonds, learning processes, and informal social control in Hirschi (1969) and Elliott, Huizinga, and

Ageton (1985). However, otherwise the theories only partially compete with one another. The situation is far more that each theory appears to be either more or less suitable for different phenomena of criminality (cf. Warren & Hindelang, 1979).

In the same way that there is a general overlap in the areas studied by the human sciences, there are also ties, overlaps, and complements between the *psychological* explanations of crime and those from other disciplines. This particularly applies for sociology. In comparison to the sociological explanations, the psychological ones tend to relate more strongly to levels of analysis that cover the criminal, his or her crime, and interactions in small groups (family, peers). Less attention is paid to historical and societal or macro-level aspects of criminality. However, this does not reflect a basic "blindness" in psychology, but rather a necessary and traditional division of labor. The question whether, for example, sociological explanations can be reduced to psychological ones, and these back to psychophysiological ones, cannot be answered at this time. For neither are the theoretical relations between different levels of analysis sufficiently elaborated, nor are integrative empirical data available. Putting aside the problem of reductionism, the way in which the experiencing subject interrelates and interacts with his or her environment – that is, the topic of *psychological* research (Traxel 1976) – in any case takes an intervening position. Following this path, there are very promising approaches to the integration of micro- and macro-level criminological theories (e.g., Pearson & Weiner, 1985).

The supporters of the labeling approach or the social reaction perspective have particularly spoken out against the focus on the crime and the criminal in explanations of criminality. For example, criticism is directed against the medical model of deviance, in which criminality is regarded as an expression of psychological deficits, traits, conflicts, disorders, or a "criminal personality". In contrast, the social science model of deviance stresses that "crime" is not a category that is intrinsic to the respective activity, but is historically and societally attributed in a relatively variable way within the frameworks of interaction processes (for a recent discussion of the related "language problems" see Wilkins, 1987). The decision-making, selection, and stigmatization processes from the institutions of social control are of particular significance for the social construction of crime.

To what extent the dichotomy between the "medical" and the "social science" model of deviance is actually suitable for the majority of empirical research is an open question. Assumptions about the different nature of criminals, which are rightly criticized by, for example, Sarbin (1979) when he refers to the "criminal type", are often more differentiated, even in those theories that are close to the medical concept of sociopathy [cf., e.g., Trasler's model (1962), which is a development of Eysenck's personality theory]. Nevertheless, the labeling approach has contributed to an important broadening of perspectives in criminal psychology. Thus, recent research, for example, pays more attention to attributions and decisions within the framework of the criminal justice system or is methodologically more critical of the traditional comparisons between official criminals and noncriminal contrast groups. However, it must be remembered that the labeling approach, even in the conceptions of its fundamental authors (e.g., Lemert, 1967), cannot replace crime- and criminal-related explanations. It is mainly an interpretation framework for the reaction of society to primary deviance, which is by no means equally distributed. In addition, the selection and stigmatization processes of official social control that contribute to secondary deviance have not been as empirically consistent as has sometimes been postulated (cf. Gove, 1980). Despite these differences in perspective, from today's viewpoint it would appear to be meaningful to conceive of research into crimes and criminals and research into social definitions and reactions less as opposites but more as complementary approaches. For example, such integrations can be operationalized empirically according to MacNaughton-Smith's (1968) concept of the primary and secondary code (Lösel, 1978).

While the labeling perspective had a strong influence on the discussion of criminological theory during the 1960s and 1970s (cf. Kaiser, 1985), recent developments are less unified. Nevertheless, some general trends can be seen. For example, there is more differentiation than before between various types of crime, and there is a clear separation between the explanation of long-term and serious crime compared to casual and petty crime (cf. Wilson & Herrnstein, 1985). There is also a movement to work out more or less homogeneous crime structures (e.g., Chaiken & Chaiken, 1984) that transcend the former attempts to develop psychological typologies of criminals. As far as research into the socialization background of (persistent) criminals is concerned, characteristics of the multiproblem milieu in particular still retain great significance for explanation and prediction (cf. Farrington, Ohlin, & Wilson, 1985; Loeber & Dishion, 1983; Lösel, 1982). However, less emphasis is now placed on relatively static causal chains in which characteristics of socialization lead to fixed personality characteristics that, in turn, are responsible for a disposition to criminal activity. The individual is now seen more as an active participant in the shaping of his or her own relatively flexible development [see, e.g., concepts such as effective coping, invulnerability, or resilience (Lösel, Bliesener, & Köferl, in press; Rutter, 1985; Werner, in press)]. In accordance with this perspective, it is on the one hand accepted – as longitudinal studies show – that there is a certain consistency and stability of problem behavior in the field of delinquency (Farrington, 1986; Wolfgang, Figlio, & Sellin, 1972). On the other hand, even relatively persistent offenders and career criminals can only be predicted in a rather limited way (Petersilia, 1980), though at the same time persistent dispositions can be most readily assumed in that small circle of offenders who are apportioned a disproportionately large number of all crimes (for a controversial discussion of the concepts of "career criminals, criminal careers, selective incapacitation," etc., see Blumstein, Cohen, & Farrington, 1988a, b; Gottfredson & Hirschi, 1986, 1987).

In accordance with the general theoretical development in personality psychology, in recent times criminal behavior has also increasingly been seen from the perspective of the actual interaction between person and situation. In this field, we can mention, for example, the research into the "reasoning criminal," the structure of crime opportunities, or victimology (Cornish & Clarke, 1986; Schneider, 1987). Likewise, more attention is also being paid to context characteristics and victim situations in prediction and prevention (Lösel, 1987; Monahan, 1981). However, personality dispositions for subareas of criminality must also not be neglected in an interactional perspective, but can be integrated with situation-related psychological constructs. This is shown, for example, in the cognitive social learning reconceptualization from Mischel (1973). Mischel stresses that cognitive and behavioral construction competences, encoding strategies and personal constructs, behavior-outcome and stimulus-outcome expectancies, subjective stimulus values, and self-regulatory systems and plans also have to be taken into account (when applied to criminal behavior, see Lösel, 1985).

The contributions in the first part of this volume represent essential aspects of the recent developments sketched above. In the first chapter, *Dave Farrington* reports new findings from the Cambridge Study in Delinquent Development. This prospective longitudinal survey in Great Britain has, together with the work of Glueck and Glueck (1950) among others, and the cohort study from Wolfgang et al. (1972), become one of the most significant and most cited empirical investigations in criminology. In the present chapter, Dave Farrington deals with the long-term prediction of adult offending, social failure, and other life outcomes. The predictors are data from the 8th to the 12th years of life. The findings show that, on the one hand, there is a striking continuity between ages 8 and 32, but, on the other hand, many boys from criminogenic backgrounds go against the prediction. Additionally, there are differences in the structures of the relationships in juvenile delinquency and in adult offending, so that different theories are required to explain early versus later, or the beginning versus the persistence of offending. This differentiated finding posts many challenges to researchers and policy-makers, regarding, for example, the effect of protective factors or the scientific background of selective incapacitation.

Whereas Dave Farrington deals with the early prediction of offenders, the chapter from *John Monahan* addresses the prediction of violence or dangerousness within the framework of US criminal law and civil law. Although the commitment to mental hospitals and release from prison are organized differently in all countries, and there are also differences regarding sentences of unspecified duration, the scientific problem is rather similar. John Monahan describes several phases in the approach to the problem: After an initial phase of naive trust in the clinical predictions of psychiatrists and psychologists, a "first generation" of research in the 1970s seriously questioned the validity of these expert predictions. In a still young, third phase of "pragmatic resurgence," there is a stronger attempt to include actuarial or statistical devices. Account should be taken of both the seriousness of the person's offences in the past and the probability that he or she will commit another crime in the future. John Monahan presents empirically founded decision algorithms and analyzes case examples. He also gives research perspectives: For example, in the group of mentally disordered persons, it is necessary to differentiate according to subgroups so that the focus can be placed on the potential victims as well as on the offenders.

In the third chapter, *Egon Stephan* deals with prediction in offenders with drunken driving offences in the Federal Republic of Germany. Here, too, the question of the prediction of recidivism is closely tied to that of prevention. Egon Stephan briefly explains the legal treatment of drunken driving offences in West Germany, and compares it with that in other countries. He uses his own studies to show that the majority of the population in this offence area is probably more norm-conforming than is frequently supposed. The drivers who have been caught and particularly those who are recidivists in no way appear to be the more or less randomly caught "tip of the iceberg," but a subpopulation with a particularly high undetected offence rate and frequent alcoholism. The empirical data suggest that the normal legal reaction is not sufficient for this particular high risk group. While, for example, the normal or, if need be, an increased density of control and corresponding sanctions are a suitable means of prevention for the sections of the population who are not threatened with alcoholism, it would appear that a more exact psychological diagnosis of the problem, treatment measures, or a restrictive policy in the returning of driving licenses is required for this high risk group.

The chapter from *John Dussich* addresses the explanation of juvenile delinquency. He first undertakes a critical analysis of the concept of juvenile delinquency in the United States and the problem of the status offender. The situation in West Germany, for example, where, as with adults, only offences against criminal law are regarded as delinquency, appears to be criminologically less ambiguous. The theoretical approach presented by John Dussich is tied to Hirschi's (1969) control theory. This theory and its further developments (e.g., Elliott et al., 1985) belong to the most promising interdisciplinary explanations of juvenile delinquency. John Dussich's concept of significant spacerounds stresses the quality of the bonds and relationships to others involving both different social institutions (family, peers, school, work, community) and also various interaction characteristics (participation, exchange, control). As in coping theories, the individual takes a relatively active role in his or her relationship to the environment. John Dussich has also made an international test of his approach, for example, with subjects in West Germany who were on probation. If this approach holds up to further empirical investigation, the consequence for crime policy would be not to apply preventive measures in an isolated way, but, in the sense of spaceround integration, to apply them to several locations in the adolescents' networks of relationships.

The chapter from *Robert Goldsmith, Gunilla Throfast*, and *Pär-Eric Nilsson* concerns adolescent delinquency. The authors attempt to provide a theoretical explanation for the decisions to carry out delinquent acts, by testing the effect of moral goals, moral reasoning, and personal constructs. The previous applications of Kohlberg's theory of moral development (1984) among others, to the field of delinquency have been subject to controversial discussion. The present work clearly goes beyond this controversy by including various other theoretically important factors. In a comparison of delinquents with officially nondelinquent Swedish adolescents, and with the help of self-reports on delinquency, the authors show that the moral development level is only tied to delinquency in an indirect way (over goal priorities and evaluations). It is more the case that the willingness to perform delinquent acts appears to depend not only on other cognitive personality constructs but especially on situative and offence-specific factors. In contrast to the studies by Yochelson and Samenow (1976) on typical criminovalent thinking patterns of serious criminals, Robert Goldsmith, Gunilla Throfast, and Pär-Eric Nilsson suggest a more individualized approach to the field of adolescent delinquency. The authors also deal with methodological problems involved in moral development research.

The chapter from *Derek Cornish* and *Ronald Clarke* contains an application of rational choice theory to problems in criminality. This is one of the most important perspectives in recent criminology (cf. Cornish & Clarke, 1986). The focus of the explanation is particularly guided toward variables of the opportunities, costs, and benefits which are also the basis of theories of deterrence (cf. Beylefeld, 1979; Lattimore & Witte, 1986). Derek Cornish and Ronald Clarke not only present general characteristics of the rational choice approach, but also tackle the problems of crime specialization and crime displacement that are of great practical significance. The question of specialization, which has been dismissed at least for adolescents under the slogan "cafeteria style delinquency" (Klein, 1984), is, among others, significant for the detection of criminals through their modus operandi (cf. Oevermann, Schuster, & Simm, 1985). The question of displacement particularly arises for the long-term locational and temporal effectivity of measures of situational prevention (cf. Lösel, 1987). Derek Cornish and Ronald Clarke offer answers to both problems that go beyond the usual conceptions. They show that only "deeper" psychological analyses of decision-making structures can provide a suitable answer to the questions of displacement and specialization.

While Derek Cornish and Ronald Clarke address the basic theoretical questions in the decision to commit deviant behavior, *Ingrid Deusinger* reports an empirical study into a specific field of application. Her study investigates whether and, if this is the case, which features of homes are perceived to be particularly favorable crime opportunities for burglaries (low risk, high spoils, etc.). Ingrid Deusinger systematically varied features of homes, which were then judged by imprisoned burglars, police officers, and a sample from the normal population. Thus, in contrast to the original concept of defensible space (Newman, 1972), direct and offence-specific ecological factors were studied. The study is closer in context to the investigations into crime opportunities for shoplifting (Carroll & Weaver, 1986) or bank robberies (Servay & Rehm, 1986). Ingrid Deusinger's findings show that offenders have clear concepts of favorable offence opportunities. Their estimations differ in their "expert knowledge" from those of the normal population, but are closer to those of the police officers. This pragmatically designed study points to concrete starting points for prevention by using the knowledge of "cooperative" persons from the other side. Nevertheless, as in all crime policy, single approaches should not be overrated. Flexible offenders, for example, can use feedback to adjust their perception of offence opportunities in line with publicly recognizable prevention strategies.

Such considerations on the dynamics of crime phenomena do not just apply to the field of prevention. In that, crime is essentially constituted by social conditions that are subject to cultural and historical change, models of explanation and prediction should not only be conceived of as quasinatural laws, but as attempts to explicate time- and context-specific regularities.

References

Beylefeld, D. (1979). Identifying, explaining and predicting deterrence. *British Journal of Criminology, 19,* 205–224.

Blumstein, A., Cohen, J., & Farrington, D.P. (1988a). Criminal career research: Its value for criminology. *Criminology, 26,* 1–35.

Blumstein, A., Cohen, J., & Farrington, D.P. (1988b). Longitudinal and criminal research: Further clarifications. *Criminology, 26,* 57–74.

Carroll, J., & Weaver, F. (1986). Shoplifter's perception of crime opportunities: A process-tracing study. In D.B. Cornish, & R.V. Clarke (Eds.), *The reasoning criminal.* (pp. 19–38). New York: Springer.

Chaiken, M.R., & Chaiken, J.M. (1984). Offender types and public policy. *Crime and Delinquency, 30,* 195–226.

Cornish, D.B., & Clarke, R.V. (Eds.). (1986). *The reasoning criminal. Rational choice perspectives of offending.* New York: Springer.

Elliott, D.S., Huizinga, D., & Ageton, S.S. (1985). *Explaining delinquency and drug use.* Beverly Hills, CA: Sage.

Eysenck, H.J. (1977). *Crime and personality* (2nd ed.). London: Routledge & Kegan Paul.

Farrington, D.P. (1986). Age and crime. In M. Tonry & N. Morris (Eds.), *Crime and justice: An annual review of research* (Vol. 7, pp. 190–250). Chicago: The University of Chicago Press.

Farrington, D.P., Ohlin, L.E., & Wilson, J.Q. (1985). *Understanding and controlling crime: Toward a new research strategy.* New York: Springer.

Glueck, S., & Glueck, E. (1950). *Unraveling juvenile delinquency.* Cambridge: Harvard University Press.

Gottfredson, M., & Hirschi, T. (1986). The true value of lambda would appear to be zero: An essay on career criminals, criminal careers, selective incapacitation, cohort studies and related topics. *Criminology, 24,* 213–234.

Gottfredson, M., & Hirschi, T. (1987). The methodological adequacy of longitudinal research on crime. *Criminology, 25,* 581–614.

Gove, W.R. (Ed.). (1980). *The labeling of deviance. Evaluating a perspective* (2nd ed.). Beverly Hills: Sage.

Hirschi, T. (1969). *Causes of delinquency.* Berkeley: University of California Press.
Kaiser, G. (1985). *Kriminologie* (7th ed.). Heidelberg: Müller, C. F.
Klein, M. W. (1984). Offence specialisation and versatility among juveniles. *British Journal of Criminology, 24,* 185–194.
Kohlberg, L. (1984). *Essays on moral development: Vol. 2. The psychology of moral development.* San Francisco: Harper & Row.
Lattimore, P., & Witte, A. (1986). Models of decision making under uncertainty: The criminal choice. In D. B., Cornish, & R. V. Clarke (Eds.), *The reasoning criminal* (pp. 129–155). New York: Springer.
Lemert, E. M. (1967). The concept of secondary deviation. In E. M. Lemert (Ed.), *Human deviance, social problems and social control* (pp. 40–64). Englewood Cliffs: Prentice-Hall.
Loeber, R., & Dishion, T. (1983). Early predictors of male delinquency: A review. *Psychological Bulletin, 94,* 68–99.
Lösel, F. (1978). Über elementare Konzepte sozialer Devianz und ihre Beziehung – Ein Beitrag zur Explikation und ein empirischer Prüfversuch. *Zeitschrift für Sozialpsychologie, 9,* 2–18.
Lösel, F. (1982). Prognose und Prävention von Delinquenzproblemen. In J. Brandtstädter & A. von Eye (Eds.), *Psychologische Prävention* (pp. 197–239). Bern: Huber.
Lösel, F. (1985). Täterpersönlichkeit. In G. Kaiser, H.-J. Kerner, F. Sack & H. Schellhoss (Eds.), *Kleines kriminologisches Wörterbuch* (2nd ed., pp. 471–479). Heidelberg: Müller, C. F.
Lösel, F. (1987). Psychological crime prevention: Concepts, evaluations, and perspectives. In K. Hurrelmann, F.-X. Kaufmann & F. Lösel (Eds.), *Social intervention: Potential and constraints* (pp. 289–313). Berlin: de Gruyter.
Lösel, F., Bliesener, F., & Köferl, P. (in press). On the concept of "invulnerability": Evaluation and first results of the Bielefeld Project. In M. Brambring, F. Lösel, & H. Skowronek (Eds.), *Children at risk: Assessment and longitudinal research.* Berlin: de Gruyter.
MacNaughton-Smith, P. (1968). The second code. Toward (or away from) an empiric theory of crime and delinquency. *Journal of Research in Crime and Delinquency, 5,* 189–197.
Mischel, W. (1973). Toward a cognitive social learning reconceptualization of personality. *Psychological Review, 80,* 252–283.
Monahan, J. (1981). *Predicting violent behaviour.* Beverly Hills. CA: Sage.
Newman, O. (1972). *Defensible space.* New York: Macmillan.
Oevermann, U., Schuster, L., & Simm, A. (Eds.). (1985). *Zum Problem der Perseveranz in Delikttyp und modus operandi* (pp. 129–188). Wiesbaden. Bundeskriminalamt.
Pearson, F., & Weiner, N. A. (1985). Toward an integration of criminological theories. *Journal of Criminal Law and Criminology, 76,* 116–150.
Petersilia, J. (1980). Criminal career research: A review of recent evidence. In N. Morris & M. Tonry (Eds.), *Crime and Justice: An Annual Review of Research* (Vol. 2, pp. 321–379). Chicago: The University of Chicago Press.
Rutter, M. (1985). Resilience in the face of adversity. *British Journal of Psychiatry, 147,* 598–611.
Sarbin, T. R. (1979). The myth of the criminal type. In T. R. Sarbin (Ed.), *Challenges to the criminal justice system: The perspectives of community psychology* (pp. 1–27). New York: Human Science.
Schneider, H.-J. (1987). *Kriminologie.* Berlin: de Gruyter.

Servay, W., & Rehm, J. (1986). *Bankraub aus der Sicht der Täter.* Wiesbaden: Bundeskriminalamt.

Trasler, G. (1962). *The explanation of criminality.* London: Routledge, & Kegan Paul.

Traxel, W. (1976). Der Gegenstand der Psychologie als Produkt und Problem des psychologischen Denkens. In G. Eberlein, & R. Pieper (Eds.), *Psychologie – Wissenschaft ohne Gegenstand?* (pp. 105–139). Frankfurt a. M.: Campus.

Warren, M. Q., & Hindelang, M. J. (1979). Current explanations of offender behaviour. In H. Toch (Ed.), *Psychology of crime and criminal justice* (pp. 166–182). New York: Holt, Rinehart, & Winston.

Werner, E. E. (in press). Vulnerability and resiliency: A longitudinal perspective. In M. Brambring, F. Lösel, & H. Skowronek (Eds.), *Children at risk: Assessment and longitudinal research.* Berlin: de Gruyter.

Wilkins, L. T. (1987). Making criminology policy relevant? In M. R. Gottfredson, & T. Hirschi (Eds.), *Positive criminology* (pp. 154–172). Beverly Hills, CA: Sage.

Wilson, J., & Herrnstein, R. J. (1985). *Crime and human nature.* New York: Simon, & Schuster.

Wolfgang, M. E., Figlio, R. M., & Sellin, T. (1972). *Delinquency in a birth cohort.* Chicago: University Press.

Yochelson, S., & Samenow, S. E. (1976). *The criminal personality: Vol. I. A profile for change.* New York: Aronson, J.

2
Long-Term Prediction of Offending and Other Life Outcomes

DAVID P. FARRINGTON

Many of the best predictors of juvenile offending are well known. Farrington (1987a, b) reviewed numerous research projects showing the predictive power of: (1) early troublesome, dishonest, aggressive, or antisocial behavior; (2) poor parental child-rearing methods, such as cruel, passive, or neglecting attitudes, harsh or erratic discipline, and poor supervision; (3) criminal parents and delinquent siblings; (4) broken homes and early separations caused by divorce or parental conflict; (5) social deprivation, as reflected in low family income, large family size, poor housing, and an erratic parental employment record; and (6) school failure, as indexed by low intelligence, poor educational achievement, and truancy.

Glueck and Glueck (1950) carried out the most famous early study of the prediction of delinquency, by comparing 500 institutionalized male delinquents in Massachusetts with 500 unconvicted boys in ordinary schools. However, their research attracted a great deal of criticism because of its retrospective and cross-sectional nature. Their interviewers' ratings could have been biased by the knowledge of who was or was not a delinquent, and hence their reported level of predictive efficiency (98.1% delinquents among those in the highest scoring category) is misleadingly high. Prospective longitudinal surveys are needed to investigate the true ability of early individual, family, and school features to predict later offending. Farrington, Ohlin, and Wilson (1986) have reviewed such surveys of crime and delinquency, and the present chapter describes one longitudinal survey – the Cambridge Study in Delinquent Development.

Many years ago, Toby (1961) distinguished between "circumstantial" and "extrapolative" predictions of delinquency. In other words, delinquency can be predicted on the basis of either social circumstances that might cause offending or early antisocial behavior that eventually escalates into offending.

Several important theoretical issues arise from further consideration of this distinction. It may sometimes be difficult to determine whether a predictor is circumstantial or extrapolative. For example, if early aggression predicts later delinquency, is this because aggressiveness causes offending or because aggressive behavior escalates into delinquency? Another problem is that two kinds of extrapolative relationship can be distinguished. For example, early aggression may predict later delinquency because both measure the same underlying theoretical construct (e.g. antisocial behavior) which tends to remain constant over time (either relatively, so that people tend to have the same relative ordering over time, or absolutely). Alternatively early aggression may be a stepping stone in a developmental sequence leading to offending, so that the construct underlying aggression leads to a different construct underlying offending (see Farrington, Loeber, & van Kammen, 1988, for a discussion of these issues as applied to hyperactivity).

There are always problems in deciding what theoretical constructs underlie any empirical measures. For example, in regard to offending, is there only one underlying theoretical construct (e.g., criminal tendency) which influences the age of onset, the frequency of offending, the seriousness of offending, the persistence of offending, and so on? If so, the predictors of one of these measures of offending should be the same as the predictors of others.

West and Farrington (1977) argued that the usual type of offending that led to conviction (a crime of dishonesty) was only one element of a larger syndrome of "antisociality" which also included drinking, gambling, drug use, sexual promiscuity, reckless driving, violence, vandalism, erratic job histories, and poor relationships with parents. If so, the predictors of offending should be the same as the predictors of other kinds of antisocial behavior. In agreement with the idea of a single syndrome, Farrington (1986) showed that the best predictors of a composite measure of antisociality at age 18 (that did not include offending) were earlier official and self-report measures of offending.

Rather than using the terms "circumstantial" and "extrapolative", this chapter will distinguish between "explanatory" and "predictive" research. Explanatory research is concerned about theoretical constructs underlying empirical variables, often takes steps to ensure that each theoretical construct is measured by only one empirical variable, and investigates the extent to which one variable predicts *independently* of others. Predictive research, on the other hand, is primarily concerned with maximizing the efficiency of prediction, does not ensure that predictor variables are theoretically independent, and investigates the extent to which variables can predict *in combination*. Both approaches can lead to predictions of offending and both have been used in the Cambridge Study in Delinquent Development.

The Cambridge Study in Delinquent Development

This is a prospective longitudinal survey of 411 males. At the time they were first contacted in 1961–1962, they were all living in a working-class area of London, England. The vast majority of the sample was chosen by taking all the boys who were then aged 8–9 and on the registers of six state primary schools within a 1-mile radius of our research office. In addition to 399 boys from these six schools, 12 boys from a local school for the educationally subnormal were included in the sample to make it more representative of the population of boys living in the area. The boys were overwhelmingly white, working class, and of British origin. The major results of this survey can be found in four books (West, 1969, 1982; West & Farrington, 1973, 1977), and a concise summary has been produced by Farrington and West (1981).

The aim in this survey was to measure as many factors as possible that were alleged to be causes or correlates of offending. The boys were interviewed and tested in their schools when they were aged about 8, 10, and 14, and they were interviewed in our research office at about 16, 18, and 21. They were then interviewed in their homes at age 24, and recently (1984–1986) they have again been interviewed in their homes, at age 32. The tests in schools measured intelligence, attainment, personality, and psychomotor coordination, while information was collected in the interviews about such factors as living circumstances, employment histories, relationships with females, and leisure activities such as drinking, fighting, and drug taking. On all occasions except at ages 21 and 24, the aim was to interview the whole sample, and it was always possible to trace and interview a high proportion. For example, at age 18, 389 of the original 411 at age 8 (94.6%) were interviewed.

In addition to the interviews and tests with the boys, interviews with their parents were carried out by female social workers who visited their homes. These took place about once a year from when the boy was about 8 until when he was aged 14–15 and in his last year of compulsory education. The primary informant was the mother, although many fathers were also seen. The parents provided details about such matters as family income, family size, their employment histories, their child-rearing practices (including attitudes, discipline, and parental agreement), their degree of supervision of the boy, and his temporary or permanent separations from them.

The boys' teachers also completed questionnaires, when the boys were aged about 8, 10, 12, and 14. These provided information about the boys' troublesome and aggressive school behavior, their school attainments, and their truancy. Ratings were also obtained from the boys' peers when they were in their primary schools, about such topics as their daring, dishonesty, troublesomeness, and popularity.

In addition, repeated searches have been made in the central Criminal Record Office in London to try to locate findings of guilt sustained by the boys, by their parents, by their brothers and sisters, and (in recent years) by their wives and cohabitees. Convictions were only counted if they were for offenses normally recorded in the Criminal Record Office. The majority of offenses were thefts, burglaries, and taking vehicles. We were not entirely dependent on the official records for our information about offending, however, since we also asked the boys at each age from 14 onwards to tell us about offenses that they had committed which had not necessarily come to the notice of the police.

This chapter reports data collected in the recent interview at age 32. Up to this age, 8 of the men had died and 20 had emigrated permanently. Of the remaining 383 who were alive and in the United Kingdom, 360 were interviewed personally (94.0%). Seven of the emigrated men were also interviewed, either abroad or during a temporary return visit that they made to the United Kingdom, giving a total number interviewed of 367. In addition, 9 emigrated men filled in self-completion questionnaires, and two cooperative wives of refusers filled in questionnaires on behalf of their husbands, at least in one case with the husband's collaboration and assistance. Therefore, interviews or questionnaires were obtained for 378 of the 403 men still alive (93.8%). For ease of exposition, I will refer to 378 men interviewed at age 32.

Explanatory and Predictive Research

In searching for explanations of juvenile delinquency, West and Farrington (1973) reduced about 200 measured variables at age 8–10 to about 20 key factors which, they believed, were measuring theoretically distinct constructs. This reduction was achieved by identifying clusters of variables that were interrelated empirically and theoretically, and then either choosing one variable as the best representative of a cluster or combining a number of variables into a composite measure. They were reluctant to use parametric techniques such as factor analysis because their data violated the underlying assumptions of such methods.

They then investigated whether each key factor was significantly related to delinquency independently of each other key factor, using matching analyses. For example, delinquents and nondelinquents differed significantly in intelligence when matched for parental criminality, and they differed significantly in parental criminality when matched for intelligence. Hence, it was concluded that intelligence and parental criminality were independent predictors of delinquency. Only five nonbehavioral (and possibly causal) factors proved to be independent predictors of delinquency: low family income, large family size, convicted parents, low nonverbal intelligence (on the Progressive Matrices test), and poor parental child-rearing behavior. The best predictor of all was a behavioral measure: troublesomeness in the primary school, as rated by peers and teachers.

West and Farrington (1973) then identified 63 boys who had adverse ratings on at least three of the five nonbehavioral predictors, and found that about half (31) were convicted as juveniles (between ages 10 and 16), in comparison with 53 of the remaining 348 (15.2%), a highly significant difference ($\chi^2 = 35.81$, 1 *df*, $P<0.001$; all χ^2 values in this chapter have 1 *df*). For ease of exposition, scores (out of 5) on this 5-point scale will be termed "E5" scores, the "E" indicating that the scale was derived in explanatory research. A later analysis (Farrington, Gallagher, Morley, St Ledger, & West, 1988a) investigated which factors predicted those of the 63 boys who were "false positives" and went against the prediction, remaining free from conviction. The major conclusion was that the unconvicted boys tended to have few or no friends at age 8, and that this social isolation may have acted as a protective factor.

These early matching analyses were undoubtedly rather crude. Farrington (1986) carried out more sophisticated explanatory analyses, using log-linear and logistic techniques to investigate how far one variable predicted measures of offending independently of others. These analyses helped in the development of a theory to explain the key results of this survey.

The major predictive analyses in the Cambridge Study in Delinquent Development were described by Farrington (1985). He compared five methods of selecting and combining variables into a prediction index: the Burgess points score method, the Glueck method (weighting by percentages), least-squares multiple regression, predictive attribute analysis, and logistic regression. The total sample of 411 boys was divided at random into one subsample used to construct the prediction device and another used to validate it. Farrington found that the more sophisticated techniques were, if anything, worse than the simpler Burgess and Glueck methods. Similar conclusions have been reached in research on the prediction of recidivism (Farrington & Tarling, 1985).

Farrington (1985) developed a 7-point Burgess-type scale to predict juvenile delinquency, based on the seven best predictors in the construction subsample. Three of these variables were measures of bad behavior: troublesomeness, conduct disorder rated by teachers and social workers, and acting out, which was a combined variable including poor conduct, unpopularity, and a neurotic-extravert personality. One variable reflected a deprived background: social handicap, which was a combination of low family income, low social class, poor housing, large family size, and physical neglect of the boy. Acting out and social handicap were both derived in advance of knowledge about delinquency (West, 1969). The other three variables were: convicted parents, low intelligence, and poor parental child-rearing behavior.

Because of the primary interest in this analysis in maximizing predictive efficiency, no attempt was made to ensure that these variables were theoretically independent. Of 56 boys with four or more of these seven predictors, about half (29) were convicted as juveniles, in comparison with 55 of the remaining 355 (15.5%), a highly significant difference ($\chi^2 = 36.98$, $P < 0.001$). For ease of exposition, scores (out of 7) on this 7-point scale will be termed "P7" scores;, the "P"indicating a scale derived in prediction research.

Blumstein, Farrington, and Moitra (1985) investigated how far the P7 score predicted the chronic offenders: the 23 men who between them accounted for half of all the convictions of this sample up to the 25th birthday (see Farrington, 1983). Each of these "chronics" had at least six convictions. Excluding men who had died, the 55 men scoring 4 or more on P7 included the majority of the future chronics (15 out of 23), 22 of the 132 nonchronic offenders (with between one and five convictions), and 18 of the 265 unconvicted men. These results showed that many of the chronics could have been predicted in advance.

While a great deal is known about the factors that predict juvenile offending, less is known about the prediction of adult offending. Similarly, not much is known about the prediction of antisocial behavior that often co-occurs with offending. West and Farrington (1977) studied the prediction of offending and antisociality at age 18, using the E5 score. As already mentioned, this significantly predicted juvenile convictions. It almost significantly predicted, out of those who were not convicted as juveniles, those who went on to be convicted as young adults (25.0% of identified men scoring 3 or more, in comparison with 11.1% of nonidentified men: $\chi^2 = 3.34$, $P < 0.10$).

The antisociality score was based on 11 interrelated factors (heavy gambling, heavy smoking, driving after drinking, use of prohibited drugs, sexual promiscuity, unstable job record, spending time hanging about, involvement in antisocial groups, most aggressive in behavior, antiestablishment attitudes, and tattooed). The E5 score significantly predicted antisociality (65.5% of 58 identified men interviewed at age 18 being antisocial, in comparison with 21.8% of 331 nonidentified men: $\chi^2 = 44.48$, $P < 0.001$).

The main aim of this chapter is to investigate the long-term predictive power of two scales: the E5 scale, which identified 63 boys, and the P7 scale, which identified 56. It is now possible to compare these measures, taken at age 8–10 before any boy had been convicted, with offending and antisocial behavior at age 32. As might have been expected, in view of the fact that three variables contributed to both scales, the two scales overlap somewhat: 35 boys were identified by both scales, 28 only by E5, 21 only by P7, and 327 by neither. Hence, in spite of their different methods of derivation, the two scales might have comparable predictive efficiency.

Prediction of Offending

Up to the interview at age 32, 152 men (37.0%) were convicted of criminal offenses. Of these, 24 were first convicted after their 21st birthday, and will be termed the "latecomers to crime." Of 124 men first convicted before their 21st birthday and still alive after age 21, 65 (52.4%) committed further offenses, and will be termed the "persisters." The "chronics" at age 32 were the 22 men (5.4% of the sample, and 14.5% of the offenders) who each had at least nine offenses leading to conviction, on at least seven separate occasions of conviction. They accounted for 310 of the 679 offenses of this sample that led to convictions up to age 32 (45.7%), an average of 14 each. The "current offenders" at age 32 were the 45 men who had been convicted for offenses committed in the 5 years preceding the interview, out of 404 still alive at age 27 (11.1%).

Table 2.1 shows the extent to which the E5 and P7 scores predict offending. For example, 24.0% of 154 men scoring 0 on E5 (i.e., having none of the five

TABLE 2.1. Explanatory and prediction scores

	% convicted (37.0)	% latecomers to crime (8.5)	% persisters (52.4)	% chronics (14.5)	% current offenders (11.1)
E5 score (n)					
0 (154)	24.0	5.6	40.0	8.1	5.9
1 (120)	33.3	11.1	32.1	2.5	6.8
2 (74)	39.2	2.2	74.1	17.2	16.7
3 (30)	66.7	23.1	52.9	20.0	23.3
4–5 (33)	78.8	30.0	68.2	34.6	28.1
0–2 (348)	30.5	6.9	48.2	8.5	8.5
3–5 (63)	73.0	26.1	61.5	28.3	25.8
Significance	0.001	0.01	–	0.005	0.001
P7 score (n)					
0 (152)	21.1	4.0	34.6	6.3	4.6
1 (107)	32.7	11.1	46.2	0.0	8.5
2 (54)	33.3	7.7	57.1	0.0	7.5
3 (42)	64.3	21.1	65.2	25.9	27.5
4–5 (42)	66.7	12.5	56.0	28.6	22.0
6–7 (14)	85.7	33.3	70.0	41.7	38.5
0–3 (355)	31.5	8.0	49.4	8.0	8.9
4–7 (56)	71.4	15.8	60.0	32.5	25.9
Significance	0.001	–	–	0.001	0.001

Notes:
% convicted, % current offenders out of whole sample
% latecomers to crime out of those not convicted before 21
% persisters out of those convicted before 21
% chronics out of all offenders

adverse factors at age 8–10) were convicted up to age 32, in comparison with 33.3% of 120 men scoring 1, 39.2% of 74 men scoring 2, 66.7% of 30 men scoring 3, and 78.8% of 33 men scoring 4 or 5. Nearly three-quarters of the 63 identified men scoring 3 or more (73.0%) were convicted, in comparison with only 30.5% of the 348 nonidentified men scoring 2 or less, a highly significant difference ($\chi^2 = 39.65$, $P<0.001$). Similarly, 71.4% of 56 men identified on the P7 scale (scoring 4 or more) were convicted up to age 32, in comparison with 31.5% of the 355 nonidentified men ($\chi^2 = 31.32$, $P<0.001$).

E5, but not P7, predicted latecomers to crime out of all those who were unconvicted up to their 21st birthday (26.1% of identified men on E5, as opposed to 6.9% of nonidentified ones: $\chi^2 = 7.68$, $P<0.01$). Neither score significantly predicted the persisters out of those who had offended before the 21st birthday. However, because the value of χ^2 increases directly with sample

TABLE 2.2. Component variables at age 8 – 10

	% convicted (37.0)	% latecomers to crime (8.5)	% persisters (52.4)	% chronics (14.5)	% current offenders (11.1)
Low income (93)	51.6	8.2	66.7	27.1	16.5
Remainder (318)	32.7	8.5	45.1	8.7	9.6
Significance	0.005	–	0.05	0.01	0.10
Large family size (99)	56.6	15.7	63.0	21.4	17.5
Remainder (312)	30.8	6.9	46.2	10.4	9.1
Significance	0.001	0.10	–	–	0.05
Convicted parent (104)	58.7	14.0	59.3	21.3	24.3
Remainder (307)	29.6	7.3	47.1	9.9	6.6
Significance	0.001	–	–	0.10	0.001
Low intelligence (103)	53.4	17.2	58.1	21.8	16.8
Remainder (308)	31.5	6.2	49.4	10.3	9.2
Significance	0.001	0.025	–	0.10	0.10
Poor child-rearing (96)	47.9	7.4	57.5	21.7	16.1
Remainder (300)	32.3	9.0	50.7	11.3	9.1
Significance	0.01	–	–	–	0.10
Social handicap (55)	65.5	17.4	64.5	36.1	18.5
Remainder (356)	32.6	7.7	48.4	7.8	10.0
Significance	0.001	–	–	0.001	–
Troublesome (92)	62.0	12.5	57.1	28.1	22.1
Remainder (319)	29.8	7.8	49.3	6.3	8.2
Significance	0.001	–	–	0.001	0.001
Conduct disorder (83)	59.0	15.0	65.9	22.4	23.8
Remainder (328)	31.4	7.4	45.8	10.7	8.0
Significance	0.001	–	0.10	0.10	0.001
Acting out (77)	58.4	15.8	62.2	24.4	21.6
Remainder (334)	32.0	7.3	48.3	10.3	8.8
Significance	0.001	–	–	0.05	0.005

Notes:
% convicted, % current offenders out of whole sample
% latecomers to crime out of those not convicted before 21
% persisters out of those convicted before 21
% chronics out of all offenders

size, it is difficult to achieve statistically significant results in a comparison such as this, based on only 124 people. Both E5 and P7 predicted the chronics out of all offenders, and both predicted the current offenders out of the whole sample. The prediction of current offending (between ages 27 and 32) shows the long-term predictive power of these scores, based on variables measured at age 8–10.

Table 2.2 shows the relationship between these five measures of offending and the nine individual variables that contribute to the two scores. The first five variables contribute to E5, while the last seven contribute to P7. For example, 51.6% of 93 boys from low income families at age 8 were convicted up to age 32, in comparison with 32.7% of the remaining 318, a statistically significant difference ($\chi^2 = 10.24$, $P<0.005$). All nine variables significantly predicted conviction; the weakest predictor was poor parental child-rearing behavior, which had been quite a strong predictor of juvenile offending ($\chi^2 = 6.99$, $P<0.01$), and the strongest was troublesomeness ($\chi^2 = 30.35$, $P<0.001$).

Only one variable – low intelligence – significantly predicted the latecomers to crime, although large family size was almost significant. Similarly, only one variable – low family income – significantly predicted the persisters, although conduct disorder was almost significant. Troublesomeness, social handicap, low income, and acting out significantly predicted which of the offenders would go on to become chronics. Convicted parents, troublesomeness, conduct disorder, acting out, and large family size significantly predicted the current offenders.

Prediction at Age 32

Of the 62 men identified by E5 and still alive at age 32, 56 were interviewed (90.3%), in comparison with 322 of the remaining 341 (94.4%). Similarly, of 54 men identified by P7 and still alive, 50 were interviewed (92.6%), in comparison with 328 of the remaining 349 (94.0%). Table 2.3 shows differences in social circumstances between identified and nonidentified men at age 32. For example, 91.1% of 56 men identified by E5 at age 8–10 were not home owners at age 32, in comparison with 44.7% of the remaining 322, a highly significant difference ($\chi^2 = 39.20$, $P<0.001$). In the whole sample of 378 interviewed, 51.6% were not home owners.

The variables "unsatisfactory accommodation," "unsatisfactory cohabitation," and "difficulties with children" are composites based on the preceding three variables, while "unsatisfactory employment" is a composite based on the preceding four variables. For example, a man was rated unsatisfactory on accommodation if he had at least two of the preceding three adverse factors (not a home owner, poor home conditions, four or more addresses in the previous 5 years), and the same principles applied with other composites. (For more details of these measures, see Farrington, Gallagher, Morley, St Ledger, &

TABLE 2.3. Social circumstances at age 32

	E5 score			P7 score		
	Ident. (56)	Not (322)	Sig.	Ident. (50)	Not (328)	Sig.
Not home owner (51.6)	91.1	44.7	0.001	76.0	47.9	0.001
Poor home conditions (27.6)	40.9	25.5	0.10	40.5	25.6	0.10
4 or more addresses[a] (13.3)	16.1	12.8	–	10.0	13.8	–
Unsat. accommodation (31.0)	51.8	27.3	0.001	36.0	30.2	–
Living in London (51.6)	71.4	48.1	0.005	70.8	48.8	0.01
Not currently employed (11.9)	32.1	8.4	0.001	26.5	9.8	0.005
Social class IV-V (25.3)	42.9	22.8	0.005	42.9	22.6	0.005
Take-home pay < £ 120 pw (25.8)	55.0	21.7	0.001	52.6	22.2	0.001
Unemployed 10 m +[a] (17.0)	35.7	13.8	0.001	34.7	14.4	0.001
Unsat. employment (24.0)	57.1	18.2	0.001	51.0	19.9	0.001
No wife or cohabitee (23.5)	23.2	23.6	–	26.0	23.2	–
Divorced/separated (19.6)	28.6	18.0	0.10	18.0	19.8	–
Doesn't get on well with wife/cohabitee (7.6)	16.3	6.1	0.05	21.6	5.6	0.005
Unsat. cohabitation (25.4)	28.6	24.8	–	28.0	25.0	–
Has hit wife/cohab. (14.5)	30.2	11.8	0.005	29.7	12.3	0.025
Child elsewhere (22.4)	33.3	20.3	0.10	26.3	21.7	–
Child has real problem (30.3)	31.4	30.1	–	31.0	30.2	–
Doesn't agree with W/C about children (18.1)	38.9	14.0	0.001	30.3	15.9	0.10
Difficulties with children (23.6)	28.6	22.6	–	23.7	23.5	–
Doesn't get on well with mother (15.3)	30.6	13.3	0.025	35.3	12.8	0.005
Doesn't get on well with father (19.5)	29.0	18.2	–	27.6	18.5	–

Abbreviations: Ident., identified; Unsat., unsatisfactory; pw, per week; W/C, wife/cohabitee

[a] In the previous 5 years

West, 1988b). It can be seen that E5, but not P7, significantly predicted unsatisfactory accommodation at age 32.

All the measures of unsatisfactory employment, including unemployment, low social class (on the Registrar-General's scale of occupational prestige), and low take-home pay, were significantly predicted by both scores. Similarly, both predicted the men who did not get on well with their wife or cohabitee or who had hit her. (Men with no wife or cohabitee were excluded from these comparisons.). Only E5 significantly predicted those who did not agree with their wife or cohabitee about how to control the children. (Men with no children

TABLE 2.4. Deviant behavior at age 32

	E5 score			P7 score		
	Ident. (56)	Not (322)	Sig.	Ident. (50)	Not (328)	Sig.
4 or more evenings out pw (17.2)	14.3	17.7	–	16.7	17.2	–
Heavy smoker (27.2)	32.1	26.4	–	31.3	26.6	–
Involved in fights[a] (37.1)	53.6	34.3	0.01	55.1	34.5	0.01
Drunk driver[a] (52.6)	62.5	51.1	–	48.5	53.0	–
Heavy drinker (19.7)	30.4	17.9	0.05	30.6	18.1	0.10
Taken marijuana[a] (18.4)	25.0	17.2	–	24.5	17.4	–
Taken other drug[a] (9.5)	16.1	8.4	–	10.2	9.5	–
Substance abuser (11.7)	19.6	10.3	0.10	16.3	11.0	–
Theft from work[a] (24.1)	25.0	23.9	–	22.0	24.4	–
Tax evasion[a] (50.3)	44.6	51.3	–	36.7	52.3	0.10
Other SRO act[a] (22.2)	30.4	20.8	–	28.0	21.3	–
GHQ score 5 or more (23.8)	33.9	22.0	0.10	24.0	23.8	–
% Failure over 33 (24.3)	50.0	19.9	0.001	42.0	21.6	0.005

Abbreviations: Ident., identified; SRO, self-reported offending; GHQ, General Health Ouestionnaire; pw, per week

[a] In the previous 5 years

were excluded from comparisons involving children.) Both scores significantly predicted the men who did not get on with their mother.

While E5 and P7 often predicted accommodation, employment, and relationship difficulties, they did not often predict deviant behavior at age 32 (Table 2.4). Both scores significantly predicted the men who had been involved in fights (in which blows had been struck) in the previous 5 years, and the E5 score significantly predicted heavy drinking (consuming 20 or more units of alcohol in one session in the last month, where one unit of alcohol corresponds to one half-pint of beer or one single whisky). However, neither score significantly predicted driving after drinking at least 10 units of alcohol, taking marijuana or other drugs, or committing other offenses (all in the last 5 years). Similarly, neither predicted a high score on the General Health Questionnaire, which detects nonpsychotic psychiatric disorder (Goldberg, 1978).

A composite measure of general social failure at age 32, based on nine criteria, was developed before any of the data was available for analysis. Consequently, it is not designed to maximize the strength of relationships between predictor and outcome variables. The nine criteria are as follows:

1. Unsatisfactory accommodation
2. Unsatisfactory employment
3. Unsatisfactory cohabitation
4. Difficulties with children

5. Substance abuser (heavy current drinking, or drug use in the last 5 years)
6. Involved in fights in the last 5 years
7. General Health Questionnaire score 5 or more
8. No self-reported offenses in the last 5 years, other than theft from work or tax evasion
9. No convictions for offenses committed in the last 5 years

Each man was scored according to the percentage of these nine criteria on which he was considered a (relative) failure. Where a man was not known on one criterion, for example if he had no children, the percentage score was based on eight criteria. Our previous work showed that men with a failure score of 33 or less were also, independently, considered to be leading successful lives by our interviewers (Farrington, et al. 1988a). Table 2.4 shows that both E5 and P7 at age 8–10 significantly predicted social failure at age 32. For example, 50.0% of men identified by E5 were general social failures, in comparison with 19.9% of nonidentified men, a significant difference ($\chi^2 = 21.90$, $P<0.001$).

The extent to which the component variables of the E5 and P7 scales predicted the various measures of life success or failure at age 32 was also investigated. Low family income, large family size, and social handicap all significantly predicted unsatisfactory accommodation. All the variables except poor parental child-rearing behavior significantly predicted unsatisfactory employment. Conduct disorder, troublesomeness, acting out, and social handicap significantly predicted involvement in fights. Only convicted parents significantly predicted substance abuse and self-reported offending. No component variable significantly predicted unsatisfactory cohabitation, difficulties with children, or a high General Health Questionnaire score.

The best predictor of general social failure was low family income; 41.2% of boys from low income families at age 8 were considered social failures at age 32, in comparison with 19.5% of the remainder, a highly significant difference ($\chi^2 = 15.72$, $P<0.001$). Other significant predictors of social failure were social handicap ($\chi^2 = 13.36$, $P<0.001$), conduct disorder ($\chi^2 = 11.22$, $P<0.001$), convicted parents ($\chi^2 = 11.17$, $P<0.001$), acting out ($\chi^2 = 9.64$, $P<0.005$), large family size ($\chi^2 = 8.42$, $P<0.005$), and troublesomeness ($\chi^2 = 3.93$, $P<0.05$). The other two variables – low nonverbal intelligence and poor parental child-rearing behavior – did not significantly predict social failure.

Conclusions

It is important to draw a distinction between explanatory and predictive research. Both types have been carried out in the Cambridge Study in Delinquent Development, which is a prospective longitudinal survey of 411 London males from age 8 to age 32. The explanatory research led to the E5 scale, while the predictive research led to the P7 scale. Three-quarters of boys identified by either E5 or P7 at age 8–10 were later convicted up to age 32, in comparison with less than one-third of those not identified. Both scores significantly predicted current offenders (those convicted between ages 27 and 32) and the small number of chronics who accounted for a nearly half of all offenses.

E5 and P7 at age 8–10 predicted several aspects of life success or failure at age 32, especially employment, accommodation, and relationship difficulties. However, with the exception of fighting and heavy drinking, they did not predict deviant behavior at age 32 (such as self-reported offending or drug abuse).

The individual variables measured at age 8–10 also had long-term predictive power. Low nonverbal intelligence predicted the latecomers to crime, low family income predicted the persisters, and several variables predicted chronics and current offenders. Similarly, several variables predicted employment and accommodation difficulties and fighting, but only convicted parents predicted self-reported offending and drug abuse at age 32. Low family income at age 8 was the best predictor of general social failure at age 32.

These results pose many challenges to researchers and indeed to policymakers. It is important to elucidate the links in the causal chain, or the stepping stones in the developmental sequence, leading from social deprivation at age 8 to social failure at age 32. It is only after such explanations are developed and tested that firmly based ameliorative proposals can be made about how to interrupt this progression. Different theories may be needed to explain early as opposed to later offending, and the onset as opposed to the persistence of offending. Different theories may also be needed to explain difficulties in accommodation and employment at age 32, as opposed to deviant behavior and offending, despite the interrelationships between all these factors.

The present analyses are in some sense preliminary, because the data collected at age 32 have only just been checked and corrected and hence become available for analyses. More work is needed to investigate empirical relationships between variables at age 32, and therefore to see if better summary measures of difficulties in different areas of life, and a better overall social failure score, can be developed. However, the long-term predictive power of early variables such as low family income and convicted parents is likely to remain impressive. While the continuity between age 8 and age 32 is striking, many boys go against the prediction. Further research is needed to investigate why predictions fail, and to establish which factors protect boys from criminogenic backgrounds from becoming social failures, and which encourage such boys to become social successes.

References

Blumstein, A., Farrington, D.P., & Moitra, S. (1985). Delinquency careers: innocents, desisters and persisters. In M. Tonry & N. Morris (Eds.), *Crime and justice: An annual review of research*: Vol. 6 (187–219). Chicago: University of Chicago Press.

Farrington, D.P. (1983). Offending from 10 to 25 years of age. In K.T. van Dusen & S.A. Mednick (Eds.), *Prospective studies of crime and delinquency* (pp. 17–37). Boston: Kluwer-Nijhoff

Farrington, D.P. (1985). Predicting self-reported and official delinquency. In D.P. Farrington & R. Tarling (Eds.), *Prediction in criminology* (pp. 150–173). Albany: State University of New York Press.

Farrington, D.P. (1986). Stepping stones to adult criminal careers. In D. Olweus, J. Block & M.R. Yarrow (Eds.), *Development of antisocial and prosocial behavior: research, theories and issues* (pp. 359–384). New York: Academic.

Farrington, D.P. (1987a). Early precursors of frequent offending. In J.Q. Wilson & G.C. Loury (Eds.), *From children to citizens:* Vol. 3. *Families, schools, and delinquency prevention* (pp. 27–50). New York: Springer.

Farrington, D.P. (1987b). Predicting individual crime rates. In D. M. Gottfredson & M. Tonry (Eds.), *Crime and justice: An annual review of research:* Vol. 9. *Prediction and classification* (pp. 53–101). Chicago: University of Chicago Press.

Farrington, D.P., & Tarling, R. (Eds.). (1985). *Prediction in criminology.* Albany, NY: State University of New York Press.

Farrington, D.P. & West, D.J. (1981). The Cambridge study in delinquent development. In S.A. Mednick & A.E. Baert (Eds.), *Prospective longitudinal research: an empirical basis for the primary prevention of psychosocial disorders* (pp. 137–145). Oxford: Oxford University Press.

Farrington, D.P., Ohlin, L.E., & Wilson, J.Q. (1986). *Understanding and controlling crime: toward a new research strategy.* New York: Springer.

Farrington, D.P., Gallagher, B., Morley, L., St Ledger, R., & West, D.J. (1988a). Are there any successful men from criminogenic backgrounds? *Psychiatry, 51,* 116–130.

Farrington, D.P., Gallagher, B., Morley, L., St Ledger, R., & West, D.J. (1988b). A 24-year follow-up of men from vulnerable backgrounds. In R.L. Jenkins (Ed.), *The abandonment of delinquent behavior: promoting the turnaround.* New York: Praeger (in press).

Farrington, D.P., Loeber, R., & Van Kammen, W. (1988) Long-term criminal outcomes of hyperactivity-impulsivity-attention deficit and conduct problems in childhood. In L.N. Robins & M. Rutter (Eds.), *Straight and devious pathways from childhood to adulthood.* Cambridge: Cambridge University Press. (in press).

Glueck, S., & Glueck, E.T. (1950). *Unraveling juvenile delinquency.* Cambridge, MA: Harvard University Press.

Goldberg, D. (1978). *Manual of the general health questionnaire.* Windsor: NFER-Nelson.

Toby, J. (1961). Early identification and intensive treatment of predelinquents: a negative view. *Social Work, 6,* 3–13.

West, D.J. (1969). *Present conduct and future delinquency.* London: Heinemann.

West, D.J. (1982). *Delinquency: its roots, careers, and prospects.* London: Heinemann.

West, D.J., & Farrington, D.P. (1973). *Who becomes delinquent?* London: Heinemann.

West, D.J., & Farrington, D.P. (1977). *The delinquent way of life.* London: Heinemann.

3
Prediction of Criminal Behavior: Recent Developments in Research and Policy in the United States

JOHN MONAHAN

The great American philosopher and psychologist William James once remarked that we should not attempt to write biographies in advance. Yet much of American law – and perhaps the law of other countries as well – is concerned with doing just that: predicting who will commit a violent or criminal act, and then intervening to prevent the predicted harm.

It would be accurate to divide the recent history of American policy in regard to the prediction of violence into three stages. The first stage, ending perhaps 10 years ago, might be called the stage of Naive Reliance upon psychological and psychiatric predictions of violence.

Naive Reliance

Ten years ago, a national movement was underway in the United States to revise the criteria for civil commitment to mental hospitals away from an assessment of a paternalistic "need for treatment" and toward a prediction of "dangerousness" to others or to self. So appealing to the legal mind was the logic of what came to be known as the "dangerousness model" that by the mid-1970s virtually every American state had, if not entirely thrown over need for treatment in favor of dangerousness, at least grafted dangerousness on to its existing standards for commitment (Monahan, 1984).

Also, a decade ago, indeterminate prison sentences were the rule throughout much of the United States. Persons convicted of crime were sent to prison with brief minimum and lengthy maximum sentences – 1–20 years, for example – and the decision about when within those broad constraints they were to be released was given to parole boards. These administrative agencies relied largely upon their own intuitive clinical judgments, sometimes aided by psychological and psychiatric reports, to decide the moment at which rehabilitation had been achieved and the offender could be released without danger.

It is important to emphasize that there was no empirical basis for the reliance upon professional expertise in predicting violent behavior. The law simply *assumed* that psychologists or psychiatrists, as "experts" on human behavior, were accurate in their predictions, or, at least, were accurate enough to be useful in forming mental health and criminal justice policy.

Empirical Retreat

These trends in American mental health and criminal law were suddenly called in question by what might be called the "first generation" of research on the prediction of violent behavior. This research, consisting of perhaps five studies conducted in the early 1970s, seemed to show in a very dramatic way that psychiatrists and psychologist were vastly overrated as predictors of violence. The data, from Monahan (1981), are presented in Table 3.1. Even in the best of circumstances – with lengthy multidisciplinary evaluations of persons who had already manifested their violent proclivities on several occasions – psychiatrists and psychologists seemed to be wrong at least twice as often as they were right when they predicted violence. Dark clouds began to form in our crystal balls. The next stage in policy toward violence prediction had begun. It might be called the stage of Empirical Retreat.

So it was now claimed that scientific research had conclusively demonstrated that reliance upon predictions of dangerousness in involuntary commitment was, in my own unfortunate phrase, "doomed" (Monahan, 1976). Some took such dire assessments as empirical support for the proposition that involuntary hospitalization should be abolished. Others took this research as empirical support not to end commitment but to change the criteria by which it was invoked. In the debate between proponents of commitment standards based on

TABLE 3.1. Validity studies of the clinical prediction of violent behavior

Study	Percent true positive	Percent false positive	Percent true negative	Percent false negative	Number predicted violent	Number predicted nonviolent	Follow-up (years)
Kozol, Boucher, & Garofalo (1972)	34.7	65.3	92.0	8.0	49	386	5
Steadman & Cocozza (1974)	20.0	80.0			967		4
Cocozza & Steadman (1976)	14.0	86.0	84.0	16.0	154	103	3
Steadman (1977)	41.3	58.7	68.8	31.2	46	106	3
Thornberry & Jacoby (1979)	14.0	86.0			438		4

dangerousness and commitment standards based on the formerly discredited "need for treatment", the prediction research became a weapon in the hands of the advocates of treatment. "Whatever the appropriate criterion is for civil commitment," they could say, "we know from research that it is not dangerousness."

As influential as this first-generation research was in the mental health system, it had an even more profound impact on criminal justice in the United States. How could we send offenders to prison for indefinite periods in the belief that they would be let out when they were "safe," when in fact prison psychologists, psychiatrists, and parole boards had been shown to have little ability to distinguish the safe from the violent? Would it not be better to focus our attention backward, on the offender's moral blameworthiness in having chosen to commit a crime in the first place, rather than forward, on his or her likelihood of doing it again? While many factors underlie the current move in the United States to abolish indeterminate prison sentences and, as it were, rehabilitate retribution as the guiding principle for allocating punishment, the research on the prediction of violent criminality has figured prominently among them.

Pragmatic Resurgence

In the past several years, American policy regarding the prediction of violent behavior has entered a third phase, which might be called "Pragmatic Resurgence." There have been no major breakthroughs in prediction research. Yet everywhere there is a new acceptance that prediction is here to stay. Part of the reason for this dramatic change of heart may be traced to a reevaluation of the empirical studies I mentioned earlier (Monahan, 1984).

Unquestionably, a great deal can be learned from the existing research on prediction, particularly from the carefully designed studies of the sociologist Henry Steadman. But for a topic of such fundamental importance, the existing research base is remarkably shallow. The five studies that form the core of the knowledge base all demonstrated that clinical predictions of violent behavior among institutionalized mentally disordered people are accurate at best about one-third of the time. While several methodological criticisms can be leveled against these studies, I believe that they can withstand critical scrutiny reasonably well.

The most telling criticism of the existing prediction research does not concern its methods; it concerns its scope. The studies deal with only one form of prediction, clinical prediction, and with only one setting for prediction, long-term custodial institutions. Other forms of prediction, emphasizing actuarial or statistical methods, and other settings for prediction, such as short-term community settings, have been largely unexplored. Yet it is precisely these other forms of and settings for prediction that are the most promising candidates for a workable level of predictive accuracy.

There is a growing awareness that the last word is not in on the ability of psychologists and others to predict violent behavior. We know less than we thought about how accurate predictions can be made in many settings.

But the major factor accounting for the resurgence of interest in predicting violent behavior in the United States has nothing to do with the research literature. Rather, it has to do with the pragmatic fact that when you take prediction out of many public policy decisions, there is very little to take its place. There is coming to be a realization that the issue is not whether it is good or bad, on some absolute scale, to base public policy on predictions of violence. Rather the issue is: how do public policies based on prediction compare with public policies based on something else? And the view of many is that, inadequate as predictions are, they may be all we have.

With this as a general background, I will address two specific areas in American policy where prediction of violence is becoming increasingly influential: prediction used in the sentencing and release of criminal offenders, and prediction in tort law.

Parole prediction is the area of criminal identification in which psychologists and others are most heavily involved. This takes one of two forms. Correctional psychologists, and psychiatrists, sometimes perform evaluations of prisoners for the purpose of offering clinical predictions of the likelihood of recidivism. Their reports are used by parole boards to help identify those among the prison population with the highest probability of offending again – for whom release will be denied – and those with the lowest probability of offending again – for whom release will be granted.

In addition to applying clinical techniques to the task of identifying those who will violate the law in the future, psychologists and other social scientists are heavily involved in developing actuarial or statistical devises for accomplishing the same end. Surely the best known and most influential work in this area is that of the United States Board of Parole. The actuarial device or "Salient Factor Score" they have developed consists of six items. Research studies have found that within 2 years after their release, 49% of the prisoners who score poorly on the Salient Factor Score are rearrested (for any crime, not necessarily a violent one) and reincarcerated, while of those who score well, only 12% are rearrested and sent to jail or prison. Those who score poorly, therefore, are 4 times more likely to be rearrested than those who score well. Note that this is more accurate than the "best" clinical prediction studies. The relevant information is presented in Tables 3.2 and 3.3.

It is important to note that the parole predictions offered by psychologists – either as clinical practitioners or as statistical researchers – are not the only things that determine the length of time an offender spend in an American prison. The *seriousness* of the crime for which he or she was convicted in the past, as well as the probability that he or she will commit another crime in the future, is also relevant. Until 1987, in the federal system, for example, the length of an offender's sentence was determined by a "matrix" which had two factors: the seriousness of past crime, and the probability of future crime. The

TABLE 3.2. Salient Factor Score (Monahan and Walker, 1985)

Item A:	Prior convictions/adjudications (adult or juvenile)		____
	None	=3	
	One	=2	
	Two or three	=1	
	Four or more	=0	
Item B:	Prior commitment(s) of more than thirty days (adult or juvenile)		____
	None	=2	
	One or two	=1	
	Three or more	=0	
Item C:	Age at current offense/prior commitments		____
	Age at commencement of the current offense:		
	26 years of age or more	=2 *	
	20–25 years of age	=1 *	
	19 years of age or less	=0	
	* Exception: If five or more prior commitments of more than thirty days (adult or juvenile) place an "x" here ____ and score this item	=0	
Item D:	Recent commitment free period (three years)		____
	No prior commitment of more than thirty days (adult or juvenile) or released to the community from last such commitment at least three years prior to the commencement of the current offense	=1	
	Otherwise	=0	
Item E:	Probation/parole/confinement/escape status violator this time		____
	Neither on probation, parole, confinement, or escape status at the time of the current offense; nor committed as a probation, parole, confinement, or escape status violator this time	=1	
	Otherwise	=0	
Item F:	Heroin/opiate dependence		____
	No history of heroin/opiate dependence	=1	
	Otherwise	=0	
	Total score		____

intersection of where an offender's past crime fell on the seriousness scale, and where his or her likelihood of future crime fell on the actuarial prediction device determined the presumptive sentence the offender would serve, as demonstrated in Table 3.4. (This system was revised on November 1, 1987: see United States Sentencing Commission, 1987.)

Many state prison systems have developed their own actuarial devices for use in identifying future criminal offenders. The State of Michigan, for example, uses an actuarial table, which they call the Assaultive Risk Screening Sheet (see Figure 3.1), that has been empirically shown to be capable of identifying, on the one hand, a group of prisoners 40% of whom will be rearrested and

TABLE 3.3. Released prisoners with unfavorable outcome (Monahan and Walker, 1985)

Risk category	Unfavorable outcome (%)
Poor (3 – 0)	49
Fair (5 – 4)	39
Good (7 – 6)	25
Very good (10 – 8)	12

TABLE 3.4. Customary total time to be served before release (in months) – adults (Monahan and Walker, 1985)

Severity of offense behavior	Salient Factor Score			
	Very good (10 – 8)	Good (7 – 6)	Fair (5 – 4)	Poor (3 – 0)
Category One (e.g., draft evasion, sale of 10 lbs. of marijuana)	0 – 6	6 – 9	9 – 12	12 – 16
Category Two (e.g., assault without injury, wire tapping)	0 – 8	8 – 12	12 – 16	16 – 22
Category Three (e.g., tax evasion of $ 20000, selling obscene material by mail)	10 – 14	14 – 18	18 – 24	24 – 32
Category Four (e.g., involuntary manslaughter, threat to kill)	14 – 20	20 – 26	26 – 34	34 – 44
Category Five (e.g., robbery, burglary of home)	24 – 36	36 – 48	48 – 60	60 – 72
Category Six (e.g., arson of a home, theft of $ 500000)	40 – 52	52 – 64	64 – 78	78 – 100
Category Seven (e.g., voluntary manslaughter, rape)	52 – 80	64 – 92	78 – 110	100 – 148
Category Eight (e.g., murder, kidnapping)	100+	120+	150+	180+

returned to prison for a *violent* crime (murder, rape, robbery, or assault) within 1 year after release, and, on the other hand, a group of prisoners only 2% of whom will commit similar acts within that period.

Despite the rise in recent years of the "just deserts" model of sentencing (e.g., von Hirsch, 1976), which holds that only factors relating to the crime committed in the past, rather than predictive factors, should be taken into account in determining the length of a prison term, the courts have been very kind to the use of social science in identifying offenders most likely to offend again. In case after case, the legality of actuarial prediction devices in setting prison sentences has been upheld. Indeed, I think it fair to say that the role of social science in identifying future criminals is beyond dispute, at least beyond dispute in the American courts.

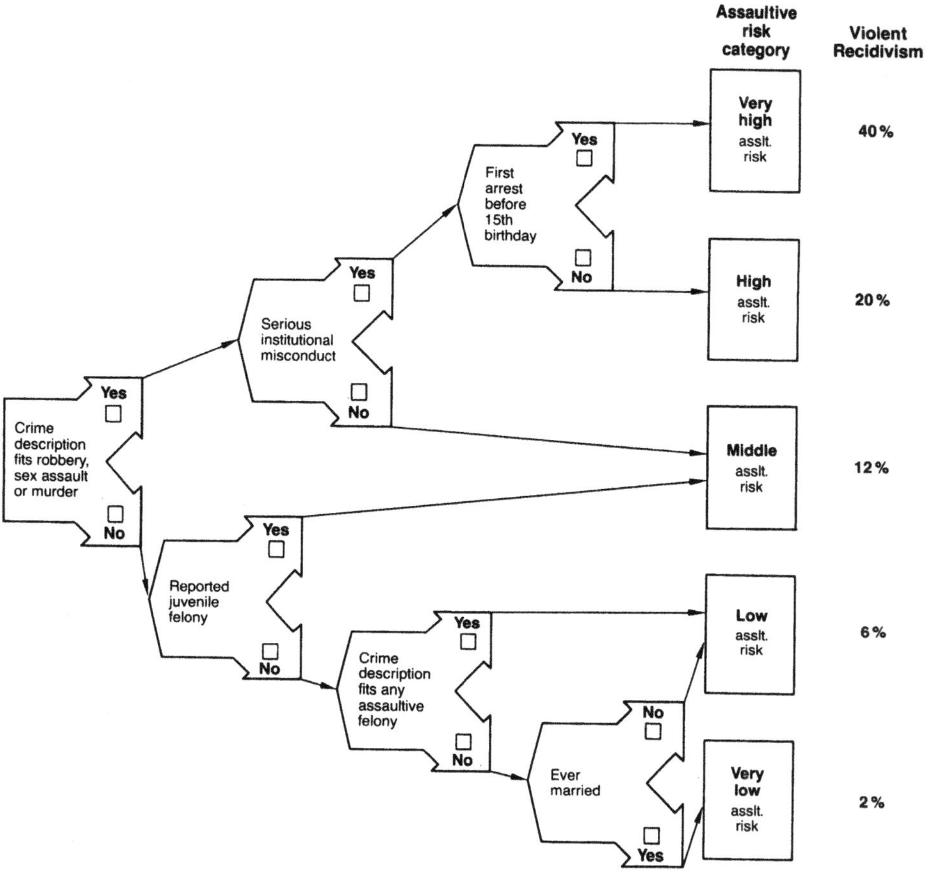

FIGURE 3.1. Assaultive risk screening sheet

If there was any doubt about whether social science has a predictive role in criminal sentencing, those doubts were definitely dispelled by the U.S. Supreme Court in its 1983 *Barefoot v. Estelle* decision [103 S.Ct. 3383 (1983)]. The issue in this case was whether the American constitution's prohibition against cruel and unusual punishment and its guarantee of due process were violated by a statute in the state of Texas that gave us the criterion for imposing the death penalty on certain kinds of murder a jury judgment that "there is a probability that the defendant would commit criminal acts of violence that would constitute a continuing threat to society."

The state had presented as expert witnesses two psychiatrists, neither of whom had ever examined Barefoot, the defendant, who had been convicted of killing a police officer. In response to hypothetical questions, both testified that "within reasonable medical certainty" Barefoot would commit new acts of violence. One of the psychiatrists, Dr. James Grigson (often referred to as the "Killer Shrink" or "Doctor Death," given his penchant for predicting violence in the 8000 persons he has personally evaluated for the Texas courts), testified that on a scale of sociopathy of 1 to 10, Barefoot was "above ten." (One hopes that Dr. Grigson knows more about sociopathy than he knows about scale construction.) He further said that there was a "one hundred percent and absolute" chance that Barefoot would commit future acts of violence if not executed. When on cross-examination the defense attorney confronted Dr. Grigson with the empirical validity studies mentioned earlier finding that psychiatrists and psychologists were most often wrong when they made clinical predictions of violent behavior, indeed were wrong on average at least twice as often as they were right, studies that a psychologist had testified to at an earlier hearing in the case, Dr. Grigson stated that he had not read most of the studies and that only a "small minority" of psychiatrists agreed with them anyway.

It took the jury only one hour to agree with the expert witnesses and to sentence Barefoot to death.

In a brief filed by the American Psychiatric Association when the Barefoot case was appealed to the U.S. Supreme Court, the empirical research on predictions of violence was reviewed with great care and considerable sophistication. The American Psychiatric Association concluded that "the unreliability of psychiatric predictions of long-term future dangerousness is by now an established fact within the profession." It agreed with the psychologist who had testified earlier in the case that the best accuracy rate (the best true positive rate) for clinical predictions of violence was one-in-three. But a majority of the U.S. Supreme Court did not see it that way. The Court upheld Barefoot's sentence of death. It stated that "Acceptance of [Barefoot's] position that expert testimony about future dangerousness is far too unreliable to be admissible would immediately call into question those other contexts in which predictions of future behavior are constantly made," and gave civil commitment to mental hospitals as an illustration.

In a genuinely remarkable display of a virtually complete lack of understanding of the nature of probability, Justice White wrote:

> Neither [Barefoot] nor the [American Psychiatric] Association suggests that psychiatrists are always wrong with respect to future dangerousness, only most of the time. [Parenthetically, I would point out that if psychiatrists were *always* wrong, you could then achieve perfect predictive accuracy by simply taking their recommendations and then doing the opposite.] Yet the submission is that this category of testimony should be excised entirely from all trials. We are unconvinced, at least as of now, that the adversary process cannot be trusted to sort out the reliable from the unreliable evidence and opinion about future dangerousness.

The jury, Justice White said, will be able to determine which prediction of violence is the one-out-of-three that will turn out to be accurate and which are the two-out-of-three that will turn out to be inaccurate. Barefoot was executed several months ago. So given that the highest American court has held that it is acceptable to use clinical predictions of violence for imposing the death penalty, there is little doubt that predictions can be used in many other contexts as well.

The second rapidly developing area of American law that involves the prediction of violent behavior is *tort law.*

In 1976, the Supreme Court of California stunned the psychological and psychiatric community when it held that a therapist could be liable for damages when his or her patient committed a violent act that the therapist "should have" predicted [Tarasoff v. Regents of the University of California, Sup. 131 Cal. Rptr. 14 (1976)]. The offender in this case, a graduate student at the University of California named Poddar, believed that he had been jilted by a woman named Tarasoff. Poddar was in outpatient treatment with a psychologist at the University. He told the psychologist that he intended to kill the woman when she returned from vacation. The psychologist called the police and tried to have Poddar involuntarily hospitalized. But by the time the police found him, they said that Poddar was not mentally disordered enough to be hospitalized. So they left him remain free. No one warned the woman, and Poddar, true to his word, killed her 2 months later.

Tarasoff's parents sued the psychologist's employer, the University of California. The trial court dismissed the case, saying that the psychologist had no duty to protect the public. But the California Supreme Court reversed the decision. As the California Supreme Court stated:

> When a therapist determines, or pursuant to the standards of his profession should determine, that his patient presents a serious danger of violence to another, he incurs an obligation to use reasonable care to protect the intended victim against such danger.

More recent cases have expanded the *Tarasoff* decision. In Hedlund v. Wilson [194 Cal. Rptr. 805 (1983)], the California Supreme Court addressed the question of "whether a therapist who negligently fails to fulfill his duty to warn an identifiable victim that a patient has threatened violence may be liable not only to the person against whom the threat is made, but also to [other] persons who may be injured if the threat is carried out." In this case, a patient "told" two psychologists "of his intent" to commit serious bodily injury upon a woman the patient knew. The woman was not warned. She was later seriously injured when the patient fired on her with a shotgun. The woman had a 2-year-old son who was seated next to her at the time of the assault. She threw herself over her son, thereby saving his life and preventing physical injury to him. The boy was alleged to have suffered emotional injury and psychological trauma as a result of the shooting, however. The court held, by a vote of 4 to 3, that not only the mother but also the young son had a cause of action against the psychologists: "it is [f]oreseeable when a therapist negligently fails to warn a mother of a patient's threat of injury to her and she is injured as a proximate result, that her young child will not be far distant and may be injured or, upon witnessing the incident, suffer emotional trauma."

Justice Mosk, in dissent, stated that "[t]he majority opinion unfortunately perpetuates the myth that psychiatrists and psychologists inherently possess powers of clairvoyance to predict violence. There is no evidence to support this remarkable belief, and, indeed, all the credible literature in the field discounts the existence of any such mystical attribute in those who practice the mind-care professions."

To evaluate the effects of the *Tarasoff* decision on the practice of psychotherapy, the Stanford Law Review surveyed 1200 California psychologists and psychiatrists (Wise, 1978). The respondents indicated that they saw an average of more than one case per month that they believed to be "potentially dangerous." One-quarter of those responding to the survey said that they now gave more attention in their therapy sessions to the possibility of their patients' violent behavior. Almost as many said that the ruling led them to focus more frequently on their patients' less serious threats. One-third of the psychiatrists and psychologists surveyed had increased the frequency with which they consulted colleagues concerning cases in which violence was an issue. Over half reported an increase in their own anxiety concerning the entire topic of "dangerousness" as a result of the *Tarasoff* decision. The survey also revealed that, as a result of *Tarasoff*, almost one-fifth of the respondents had decided to avoid asking questions that could yield information bearing on the likelihood of violent behavior by their patients. Even more reported that they had changed their record-keeping procedures in an effort to avoid legal liability they might otherwise incur as a result of *Tarasoff*. Some therapists ceased keeping detailed records; others began keeping more detailed records, including information that might justify any decisions they made, thereby trying to create a favorable evidentiary record for future litigation.

Most bothersome to psychologists and psychiatrists is the possibility that they will be held liable to the victims of their patient if the patient commits a violent act, and will be held liable to their patient for breaching confidentiality if they warn others. In at least one case, a psychiatrist was successfully sued for "negligent warning." In Hopewell v. Adebimpe [130 Pittsburgh Legal Journal 107 (1982)], a patient sued her psychiatrist for breaching the confidentiality provisions of the state Mental Health Procedures Act. The psychiatrist had sent the following letter to the patient's employer, without the patient's consent,

RE: Rebecca Hopewell
Dear Sir:

In the course of a psychiatric interview which took place in my office on October 2, the above-named reported feelings of being so enraged about her work situation that she "will blow up and hurt somebody very seriously if the harassment does not stop."

This information is being relayed to you because there is a legal precedent requiring it and is not to be taken as an estimate of the probability that the threat will actually be carried out. It is, however, important that the person or persons at risk be notified. In this case I believe that her immediate supervisor should know of this letter.

In light of the great publicity the *Tarasoff* decision had received in the United States, the psychiatrist evidently thought it was the law in his home state of Pennsylvania as well as in California. He found out that in Pennsylvania, however, the law held that the confidentiality of psychotherapy was believed to be more important than public protection.

In the past several years, during the period I have referred to as the Pragmatic Resurgence, the policy question has shifted from *whether* to predict violence at all to *how* predictions of violence should best be made. This is obviously a task that only research can address.

Let me conclude by mentioning one research project that I believe has promise for advancing our knowledge of a key issue in violence prediction: the relationship between violence and mental disorder. There has always been a strongly held public perception that violence and mental disorder are clearly linked (Monahan & Steadman, 1983a).

Research on the actual, as opposed to the perceived, relationship between mental disorder and violent behavior, however, yields a much different picture. Reviewing nearly 100 studies on the topic, Monahan and Steadman (1983b) concluded:

> The overarching impression that remains after reviewing the vast array of existing epidemiological data on crime and mental disorder is that, when one makes the appropriate controls for demographic and anamnestic factors (e.g., prior patterns of institutionalization), rates of true and treated criminal behavior vary independently of rates of true and treated mental disorder. ... Put another way, the correlates of crime among the mentally ill appear to be the same as the correlates of crime among any other group: age, gender, race, social class, and prior criminality.

Contrary to public opinion, therefore, the mentally disordered do not appear any more prone to violence than nondisordered persons of comparable age, prior arrest history, etc. We went on to note, however, that this conclusion applied only to mentally disordered persons *in the aggregate* and that such aggregation may mask the fact that some *subgroups* of the mentally disordered may indeed be prone to violence by virtue of mental disorder while other subgroups may be inhibited from violence by virtue of mental disorder (thereby cancelling each other out when the subgroups are aggregated). Nonetheless, empirical research has yet to identify subgroups of sufficiently high risk of violence to warrant institutional intervention.

A principal task for research, then, is to identify the characteristics of those specific subgroups of the mentally disordered which are especially prone to violence, rather than to focus on the relationship between violence and mental disorder "in general."

One way of approaching this task is to adopt an *offender focus*, i.e., to take a sample of mentally disordered persons, observe who among them commits a violent act and who does not, and compare the groups on such characteristics as psychiatric symptomatology and diagnosis. Unfortunately, the research adopting this offender focus has not been able to identify any diagnostic or other psychological characteristics useful for classifying the mentally disordered into violent and nonviolent subgroups.

An alternative approach to studying the relationship between violence and subgroups of the mentally disordered has been proposed: *a victim focus*. There is some theoretical reason to believe, and some anecdotal evidence to support, the notion that *those mentally disordered persons prone to violence tend to choose certain identifiable types of victim.* Put another way, some types of victim may disproportionately attract offenders who are mentally disordered. If this is so, research that approaches the problem by focusing initially on "high risk victims" might yield fruitful insights into the characteristics of the persons who offend against them, if only because the base rate of mental disorder among the offenders might be high enough to permit useful analysis.

It may be that the most promising candidates for such a victim-focused approach to the relationship between mental disorder and violence are *victims who are public figures.* There is some reason to believe that at least one highly public figure, the President of the United States, has been the target victim of persons among whom the disordered are disproportionately represented. Greenstein (1965), for example, has advanced the theory that "at least for a portion of the population, the President is the unconscious symbolic surrogate of childhood authority figures" and thus serves as "an outlet for affect" among some groups in the population.

Anecdotal evidence for the proposition that the President is often the target of mentally disordered persons is provided by the picture of the "archetypal assassin" painted by the President's Commission on Violence as a "lonely, demented man." Indeed, a diagnosis of mental disorder has been suggested for 12 of the 13 persons who have assassinated or attempted to assassinate a U.S. President or Presidential Candidate. As well, the Institute of Medicine report "Behavioral Science and the Secret Service" (1981), noted, "Approximately 90 percent of all persons the Secret Service presently considers dangerous to protected persons [i.e., the President, the Vice-President, their spouses, etc.] gave some indication of mental disorder before coming to the attention of the Service."

It may be that the President is simply the most highly public figure in the country and that this claimed overrepresentation of the mentally disordered among those who threaten, attempt, or succeed in assassination would apply equally when other public figures are victims. In other words, the psychological processes that underlie presidential assassination (e.g., a pathological need for "fame") may also underlie the choice by a subgroup of the mentally disordered of other public figures as their victims. In this regard, "public figures" would include nonpresidential politicians (e.g., Senators, Governors, Mayors) and others with high media exposure, such as motion picture and television personalities and sports figures.

While there has been no systematic analysis of cases of violence against public figures other than the President, some well-known examples would lend plausibility to the view expressed above. It might be noted in this regard that John W. Hinckley, Jr., debated at several points killing the actress Jodie Foster rather than Ronald Reagan (Transcript of U.S. v. Hinckley).

A promising research project supported by a U.S. National Institute of Justice grant to Dr. Park Dietz is investigating the process by which mentally disordered people go about choosing high-publicity victims. The results of this project may tell us much about the relationship between violence and mental disorder, and may ultimately help us better target our predictive efforts.

Acknowledgments. Preparation of this paper was supported by a National Institute of Justice grant (83-N1-AX-0005) to Park E. Dietz, M.D., Ph.D. and a grant by the Guggenheim Memorial Foundation to the author.

References

Cocozza, J., & Steadman, H. (1976). The failure of psychiatric predictions of dangerousness: clear and convincing evidence. *Rutgers Law Review, 29*, 1084–1101.
Greenstein, F., (1965). Popular images of the President. *American Journal of Psychiatry, 122*, 523–529.
Institute of Medicine (1981). *Behavioral science and the secret service* [Report]. Washington: National Academy.
Kozol, H., Boucher, R., & Garofalo, R. (1972). The diagnosis and treatment of dangerousness. *Crime and Delinquency, 18*, 271–392.
Monahan, J. (1976). The prevention of violence. In J. Monahan (Ed.), *Community mental health and the criminal justice system.* New York: Pergamon.
Monahan, J. (1981). The clinical prediction of violent behavior. Washington: Government Printing Office.
Monahan, J. (1984). The prediction of violent behavior: towards a second generation of theory and policy. *American Journal of Psychiatry, 141*, 10–15.
Monahan, J., & Steadman, H. (1983 a). Mentally disordered offenders: perspectives from law and social science. New York: Plenum.
Monahan, J., & Steadman, H. (1983 b). Crime and mental disorder. An epidemiological approach. In N. Morris, & M. Tonry (Eds.). *Crime and justice: an annual review of research.* Chicago: University of Chicago Press.
Monahan, J., & Walker, L. (1985). *Social science in law: cases and materials.* Mineola, NY: Foundation.
Monahan, J., & Wexler, D. (1978). A definite maybe: proofs and probability in civil commitment. *Law and Human Behavior, 51*, 527–654.
Steadman, H. (1977). A new look at recidivism among Patuxent inmates. *Bulletin of the American Academy of Psychiatry and the Law, 5*, 200–209.
Steadman, H., & Cocozza, J. (1974). *Careers of the criminally insane.* Lexington, Mass.: Lexington Books.
Thornberry, T., & Jacoby, J. (1979). *The criminally insane: a community follow-up of mentally ill offenders.* Chicago: University of Chicago Press.
United States Sentencing Commission. (1981). Federal sentencing guideline manual. St. Paul, Minn.: West.
Von Hirsch, A. (1976). *Doing justice: the choice of punishment.* New York: McGraw Hill.
Wise, T. (1978). Where the public peril begins: a survey of psychotherapists to determine the effects of Tarasoff. *Stanford Law Review, 31*, 165–190.

4
The Prediction of Drunken Driving Offences

EGON STEPHAN

The present study considers from a psychological point of view criteria in the Federal Republic of Germany (FRG) for the prediction of drunken driving. The following topics will be discussed: (1) the legal framework within which predictions are made and the psychologist's role within this framework; (2) how drunken driving is viewed by offenders, by authorities, and by the public; (3) the scientific basis for predictions; and (4) possibilities for improving prognosis through dynamic links between prediction and intervention.

Human behavior can be considered as the result of interactions between personal dispositions and situational conditions. Predicting behavior is difficult since it requires that situational conditions be anticipated and prognoses made of changes in personal dispositions. Thus, predictions are always probabilistic.

The potential contribution of psychology to the area of predicting the later behavior in traffic of those who have been found to have committed a drunken driving offence is to help such predictions to be made and to become as accurate as possible. Problems in this connection, as seen within the framework of the legal and judicial systems of the FRG, will be discussed.

The Legal Framework and the Role of Psychologists

Legal Framework

When a driver in the FRG becomes conspicuous in traffic under the influence of alcohol, a temporary prohibition to drive can be imposed for a period of 1 – 3 months (see §25 of the Road Traffic Act and §44 of the Penal Code), the length of the period depending upon the level of blood-alcohol concentration (BAC) found; in serious cases the individual's driver's license can be suspended without being reissued until a period of at least 6 months has elapsed. Being temporarily prohibited to drive is a penalty imposed in addition to the principal form of punishment (see Himmelreich & Hentschel, 1986), whereas suspension of the license is a measure taken with the aim of both security and improvement (see Himmelreich & Hentschel, 1986).

Lawmakers assume that a driver who participates in traffic under the marked influence of alcohol (0.8‰ or more, see §24 of the Road Traffic Act) is not qualified to drive. Suspension of the license aims at allowing the qualification to drive to be reestablished.

Not the court but the traffic authorities are responsible for reissuing the license when the period of its suspension has elapsed (see §4 of the Highway Code of the Road Traffic Act and §15b of the Road Licensing Regulations). The termination of the period which the court has imposed during which the license cannot be reissued is a necessary but not a sufficient condition for the driver's license to be reissued (see also Hentschel, 1986). It is the duty of traffic authorities before reissuing the license to evaluate all those aspects of the personality and behavior relevant to driving performance (see Himmelreich & Hentschel, 1986). The qualifications as a driver the person is seen to possess can be expressed in terms of the assessed probability of a new offence, although neither the legislature nor the courts have fixed any universal criterion for this:

- The Higher Administrative Court of Baden-Württemberg [in case Az.: Mannheim –x 1665/75 (note that Az., which stands for the German word *Aktenzeichen*, means reference number)] assumed that a driver with a recurrence risk 6 times the rate of occurrence of drunken driving offences among drivers generally (this would be a 30% probability of recurrence during the ensuing 10 years) is unqualified to drive.
- The Administrative Court in Düsseldorf (in case Az.: –6 K 291/77) set the qualification limit at 20%–25%.
- The Higher Administrative Court NRW Münster (in case Az.: 19 A 1110/82) assumed the qualification limit to be a recurrence risk of between 5% and 6%.

One should note that the courts considered only officially registered offences in fixing these limits. However, from the standpoint of traffic safety, only the probability of the driver again driving under the influence of alcohol is of relevance, regardless of whether such an offence is registered and the delinquent punished or not (see Fürst, 1970).

In major judicial commentaries it has been proposed that the criterion for considering a person unqualified to drive be a "predominant probability" of a new offence, which supposedly means a probability of over 50% (see Himmelreich & Hentschel, 1986). In view of the possibility of a driver's committing offences that escape detection, this suggestion could be interpreted as meaning that the judge should suspend the person's license for whatever period of time is deemed necessary for the person's qualification to drive to be reestablished – that is, for the probability of a new offence (whether detected or not) to drop to less than 50%. After the period during which the license could not be reissued had elapsed, traffic authorities would need to determine how effective this measure and any other measures the court had taken had been in reestablishing the person's qualification to drive. Whenever in doubt about this, traffic authorities can demand that the person undergo a medical and psychological examination (see §15b of the Road Traffic Licensing Department).

The Role of Psychologists

As an aid in determining the length of the period for which the license should be suspended or in determining whether the qualification to drive has been reestablished, a report by a psychological expert may be called for. However, neither the court nor the traffic authorities are bound by this report; rather, it provides a potential basis for a decision. The task of the psychologist here is to establish – on the basis of his or her professional knowledge and competence – those individual characteristics and relevant facts allowing a prediction of the person's future behavior to be made. The psychologist can present a recommendation *expressis verbis*, but the court and the traffic authorities are free to decide whether or not to follow it. The major question the psychologist's report is to address may be whether the probability of recurrence is greater or less than 50%. To what extent the knowledge at a psychologist's disposal permits him or her to take a position concerning this question is a matter which will be discussed below. Regarding legal practice one can note that judges tend to be primarily concerned not with the personality of the offender but with certain features of the offence, for example whether anyone has been injured, in determining the length of the period for which the license is to be suspended. Consequently, a report by a psychologist is often not requested. Such emphasis on the effects of criminal or delinquent acts is evident in legislation and in legal practice generally (see Jescheck, 1978; Jakobs, 1983; Schönke, 1986; Lackner, 1987; for critical comments see Kaufmann, 1968; Horn, 1973; Zielinski, 1973). As a result, despite the fact that the suspension of a license is conceived not as a punishment but as a measure leading to improvement, the length of the period it is to last may depend to a considerable extent upon factors of a purely coincidental character – hardly justified in view of the aim such a measure is intended to have.

As a rule, whenever a driver is caught for drunken driving with a BAC of 2.0 or more, or after having previously had his or her license suspended for drunken driving, a medical and a psychological report are demanded, in accordance with a decree of the Ministry of Transportation.

Views Regarding Drunken Driving

Views of the Public, of Legislative and Traffic Authorities, and of the Court

How drunken driving offences tend to be viewed generally can be seen as having an important bearing on the probability of such offences occurring. The courts and the traffic authorities, as well as the public at large, appear to assume that those caught for drunken driving display in a certain sense "normal" behavior, behavior which is not approved but is also not condemned entirely. The public in general seems to feel that those who become conspicuous on account of drinking are a random sample of those drivers who fail both to live abstinently and to separate in a strict way their consumption of alcohol from their driving of a vehicle (cf. Karstedt-Henke & Kretschmer-Bäumel, 1984). Thus, such drivers are thought not to be seriously deviant and not to be driving drinkers but drinking drivers. Some 50% of those who drive also do combine alcohol consumption with driving to some extent (INFAS, 1982, Table 55). Many drivers believe too that they often drive with as much as 0.8‰. However, such levels appear to be reached only by a small portion of them (cf. Karstedt-Henke & Kretschmer-Bäumel, 1984).

Since drunken drivers tend not to be viewed as particularly deviant, reestablishing their qualification to drive through use of such sanctions as a fine or suspension of the license is seen as sufficient (cf. §69 of the Penal Code). Neither prediction of the person's future driving behavior nor more individual intervention with the aim of bettering such behavior is regarded as necessary for those caught the first time.

Views of Offenders

The author had some 275 drivers whose licenses had been suspended because of drunken driving fill out a questionnaire sent to them by mail. The following results are of particular interest:

- These drivers did not tend to view themselves as outsiders with respect either to their consumption of alcohol in comparison with the group of all other drivers or to their proneness to drunken driving as compared with drivers generally. According to their statements more than 80.4% of them had shown BACs of more than 1.3‰ and some 24.4% of them levels of over 2.0‰. Nevertheless, some 50% of them considered their consumption of alcohol as being average and 24% even thought it to be below average! In light of results of drinking experiments (see below) such statements can be clearly viewed as self-deceptive.
- Some 63.6% of those with self-reported levels less than 1.6‰ stated that they "often" had family problems because of alcohol. Of those with levels

above 1.6‰, only 48.6% were in this category. This can be interpreted as suggesting more active suppression by those persons with the more pronounced alcohol problems. On the other hand, 74.6% of those with levels above 1.6‰ stated that they had already gone through periods of abstinence of up to 1 month, whereas in the group with lower levels the figure was only 63.5%. However, from research on alcoholism it is known that just such statements of maintaining limited phases of abstinence tend to be used by problem drinkers to reassure and deceive themselves.

- Assessments by the group as a whole of how law abiding drivers generally tend to be, are interesting. In response to the question of what percentage of drivers tend at weekends to participate in traffic with unlawful BACs, 75.3% estimated it to be more than 15% and 28.3% believed it to be over 50%.

Although the estimates subjects made can be seen as enormous overestimates, they indicate what little effect punishment and suspension of the driver's license can be expected to have on driving behavior when the persons in question perceive themselves as randomly selected "victims."

The Scientific Basis for Predictions

The "General Probability of Becoming Conspicuous"

Müller (1976) found that during the 10 years following their acquisition of a driver's license, some 5 persons out of 100 become conspicuous in traffic because of a drunken driving offence. This figure is often cited by the courts as representing the "general probability of becoming conspicuous" when the qualification to drive of those who have been caught for drunken driving is evaluated. Use of such a probability can be seen as inappropriate, however, since it is the probability for the individual driver which is of relevance. This is evident when one notes that 92.5% of the officially registered offenders are males and only 7.5% females (Ziegler, 1987), which, considered in conjunction with the overall figure of 5% for the population as a whole, means that the figure for males should be 9.3% and for females 0.7%. Bearing this in mind, it becomes evident that a verdict such as that of the Administrative Court in the German state of Nordrhein-Westfalen (Münster, Az.: 19 A 1110/82) – in which a person who has been found to be drunk while driving is only considered to be qualified to drive if the probability of behaving in this way again is equal to that of a driver who has never been found with a BAC of 0.8‰ or more – is nonsensical, for it would mean, if he were a male, that he would already be disqualified because of his sex, for that alone would yield a probability of becoming an offender again of 9.25%.

Obviously then, the "general probability of becoming conspicuous" is not a suitable criterion for prediction. It appears to make more sense to rely on recurrence rates obtained for the category of drivers who have already become conspicuous one or more times previously, since the individual offender will probably be closer to this group than to an average group of drivers as regards the risk of recurrence. In support of such an approach it will be shown that those caught for drunken driving tend to differ in a characteristic way from the general population of drivers.

Recidivism Rates

In view of the extremely large number of undetected cases of drunken driving and of the 44% official rate of recidivism for detected cases, it can be assumed that more than half (and possibly even nearly 100%) of those who are convicted of drunken driving for the first time are recidivists, a considerable portion of whose offences have been undetected. This means that for the average offender with a record of one or more offences there is a predominant probability of recurrence. According to this and the definition of being qualified to drive suggested above, the average offender must be considered unqualified to drive.

An analysis we carried out of a sample of drivers convicted of drunken driving (sample "D" of the Federal Traffic Office, cf. also Stephan, 1986) revealed that 44% of them were convicted again during the subsequent 10 years. One should note that the recidivism rate here applies to the period between 1973 and 1982, during which no medical or psychological investigation was required for reissue of the license after the period of suspension of the license set by the court had expired.

Factors Affecting the Distribution of Blood-Alcohol Concentration Values Obtained

According to criminological findings generally, offences usually show a so-called J-curve dispersion in that relatively minor offences are committed more frequently and relatively serious ones more rarely. Under conditions of most drunken driving offences being registered one might analogously expect the frequently occurring offences to be those with BAC levels of between 0.8‰ and 1.3‰, with a relatively small frequency for those above 2.0‰. However, every empirical study we know of in the FRG (cf. e.g., Toffel-Nadolny, 1981; Müller, 1984) has found not a J-dispersion but rather a normal dispersion with means of between 1.5‰ and 1.8‰.

The range between 0.8‰ and 1.0‰, which corresponds to a disqualification to drive (see Hentschel & Himmelreich, 1984), shows a percentage of occurrence of less than 10%, although BACs of this level should theoretically be more frequently found than extremely high values.

The results obtained can probably be essentially attributed to restrictions being placed on the possibilities for police to order blood alcohol tests. In Sweden, where no well founded suspicion is necessary to order a blood test, mean BAC values (cf. Valverius, 1985) are only half of what they are in the FRG.

Müller (1984) found, for example, that in only 8% of the cases of lethal accidents involving pedestrians were the drivers in question ordered to undergo a blood alcohol test! The curve of BAC values found in a study carried out during a 1-year period in a North American town (Borkenstein et al., 1964), involving registration of the BAC values of all drivers involved in accidents, indicated the curve, as expected, to differ only slightly from a classical J-dispersion (cf. also Müller, 1984, Fig. 3).

Not only the normal dispersion but also the high mean obtained in studies in the FRG indicates those persons officially registered as drunken drivers to be persons with an alcohol consumption far exceeding the average.

Relation Between Drinking and Blood-Alcohol Concentration Levels

Numerous studies show that "social drinkers" (for the discussion of this term, see Kunkel, 1985) usually do not show BAC values of over 1.0‰ (see Birrell, 1965, 1975; Pryor, 1966; Camps & Robinson, 1968; Harvard, 1975; Shortt & Vogelsprott, 1978; Rüdell et al. 1981; Blick & Liebhard, 1981; Kunkel, 1985). Both Müller (1976) and Kunkel (1985) argue that "normal" drinkers usually do not have levels exceeding 1.3‰. The present author (Stephan, 1986) considers 1.6‰ to mark the beginning of a "pathological alcohol tolerance," indicative of a permanent abuse of alcohol (Stephan, 1986). The U.S. Department of Transportation takes a BAC of 1.5‰ to be the mark of a problem drinker (1969). The National Council on Alcoholism (1972) in the United States designates a BAC of 1.5‰ or more without distinct symptoms of drunkenness as being a criterion of alcoholism.

In a study of our own we examined the amounts consumed under "favorable" conditions by a group of persons "able to carry a lot," what BAC levels resulted from particular amounts, and how driving performance was affected. A total of 43 men (judges, prosecutors, and traffic authority employees) took part. All participants consumed as much alcohol as they wished. More than half (23 persons) drank at least 3 liters of beer, or an amount of wine and liquor of equivalent alcohol content. Despite these amounts, only five participants exceeded levels of 1.3‰, the maximum value being 1.69‰ after 3.8 liters of beer (consumed within less than 5 h). Thus, the maximum was clearly less than the value of 1.8‰ which Toffel-Nadolny (1981) found to be the average (!) for drivers generally. This seems to indicate clearly that the Widmark formula, used to calculate the BACs which given amounts of alcohol produce, leads to values that are far too high. This can be explained by the historical origin of the formula, which was developed for appraising ability to have a guilty conscience. In accordance with the principle "in dubio pro reo," the values were so calculated that no estimate would be too low.

Our investigation showed impairments in efficiency and capabilities such as could be expected after the amounts of alcohol consumed. According to the reports of driving instructors in the cars the subjects then drove, as well as of observers placed outside while driving tests were conducted, numerous situations evolved which could have been extremely dangerous in normal traffic. Thus, the study strongly suggests that the average drunken driving offender has drinking habits out of the ordinary.

Results of Studies of the Alcohol Consumption of Traffic Participants Generally

Numerous investigations have been carried out to determine what portion of drivers have unlawfully high BACs through checking at some point every driver who comes past. As a rule, less than 1% of the drivers have been found to have inadmissibly high BACs. Such has been the case both in the FRG and in several other European countries (cf. Kerner, 1985). An investigation of our own yielded the following results:

- On a Friday between 11.30 p.m. and 0.45 a.m. 14 policemen conducted a traffic check on an arterial road of a big city. Every car coming from the city was stopped and the driver checked, no criterion of safe or unsafe driving being employed. Altogether, 100 drivers were tested. While checking usual things (registration card, warning triangle, first-aid box, etc.), the policemen also tried to determine whether any of the drivers had too high a level of BAC. Some 12 drivers were suspected and were required to take the breath test. Only once did the tube became stained so strongly that the car had to be put in safekeeping and a blood alcohol test ordered.
- With the other 11 persons a gas chromatographic analysis (infrared analysis) of their breath was carried out, but none led to a value of over 0.3‰. In a countercheck, the breath analyses of 11 persons who were classified as inconspicuous indicated 0.0‰ for all of them.

It can be noted that the presumed exceeding of 0.8‰ by only one driver was found on a day and at a time of day when a relatively high number of "alcohol sinners" could be expected. The result also fails to correspond with the self-perceptions of the drivers. Several of them appeared to assume that they had a BAC of more than 0.8‰.

These findings, then, provide further evidence that drunken drivers represent a particular population with unusual drinking habits. Against this background, it seems appropriate to consider what bearing the findings of research on alcoholism have on the prediction of drunken driving.

Findings of Research on Alcoholism

Epidemiological Data

The results of studies of relations between drinking and BAC levels, on the one hand, and the dispersion of BAC values of officially registered offenders on the other, suggest that more than 90% of officially registered offenders have a "pathological alcohol tolerance," since they "dare" to participate in road traffic with a BAC of 1.3‰. This pathological alcohol tolerance hints at permanent alcohol abuse and possible alcohol addiction. To further clarify this matter, epidemiological data from alcohol addiction research are useful.

It is generally acknowledged that in West Germany at least 5% of the male population older than 14 years suffers from alcohol abuse or excessive alcohol consumption (see Brakhoff, 1985). Insofar as we can judge, groups of persons with particularly active traffic participation tend to be overrepresented among persons who suffer from alcohol abuse or are in danger of it. Above all, men in the age group 20–50 are involved. It is also the case that approximately 90% of this group consume alcohol predominantly outside their place of abode, which means that they are often forced to drive after excessive consumption of alcohol (see Solms, 1975; Reuband, 1980). According to Wieser (1973), some 5% of the population consume 36% of the alcohol consumed. In view of the fact that the annual consumption of pure alcohol in the FRG is 12 liters per capita (see Ziegler, 1987), this suggests there to be an annual per capita consumption of about 84 liters of pure alcohol on the part of the 5% of the male population most strongly afflicted. This represents a consumption of 66.36 kg alcohol/year or a daily per capita consumption of over 180 g alcohol. At a very cautious estimate this means that the group in question tends regularly to reach BAC levels of 1.8‰ at the end of their daily consumption of alcohol. These figures can be substantiated by numerous empirical data (Schuster, 1980; Troschke, v. & Stünzner, v., 1983; Püschel, 1985; Jakobsen & Stallmann, 1985).

Since it is the heavy drinkers who tend most to underestimate the danger to traffic safety resulting from the consumption of alcohol (see, e.g., Karstedt-Henke & Kretschmer-Bäumel, 1984), it can be assumed that these persons cannot be prevented from driving after excessive drinking by any general appeal to reason and good sense, and that they thus strongly jeopardize traffic safety. This also explains the discrepancies between the BAC levels shown by normal persons in studies of the effects of drinking and those shown by persons conspicuous in traffic for drunken driving.

Findings in a Drug Clinic

In view of the fact that drunken drivers appear mainly to be problem drinkers and serious misusers of alcohol, it was felt that investigating patients of an alcohol and drug clinic regarding their use of alcohol in conjunction with drinking, and their possible loss of the driver's license at some time for drunken driving, would illuminate problems here. Interviews of 336 persons who were patients in such a clinic yielded the following results:

- Some 91% of those patients who had at some time acquired a driver's license declared themselves to have participated in road traffic with an unlawful BAC frequently. Of these persons, only 45% had ever lost their license because of driving while intoxicated!
- Of the 1976 persons questioned, 32% reported having been checked by police without it being detected that they were under the influence of alcohol!

The results of the interviews confirmed the hypothesis that persons with a problematic consumption of alcohol often retain the driver's license, that they very often participate in traffic under an unlawfully high influence of alcohol, and that they have good chances of remaining undetected permanently despite numerous offences.

Linking Findings of Research on Alcoholism with Those Concerning Drunken Driving

Statistical links between findings of research on alcoholism and those concerning drunken driving can be shown. The most extensive longitudinal study of alcohol abuse carried out in the FRG thus far (Schreiber, 1985), relating to the federal and state program for the prevention and treatment of alcohol abuse, indicated that about 15% of men between 31 and 57 years of age are permanently endangered by alcohol. More precisely, results of the Manson scale indicated 13.1% and those of the shortened version of it 18.5%, which averages to 15.8%.

If our assumption is correct that drivers who are caught with more than 1.3‰ are problem drinkers, then the proportion of those drivers who at some time are drunk at the wheel should correspond with this figure of 15.8%. Taking Müller's (1976) figure (see also Müller & Weiler, 1987) of 5% of those who acquire a driver's license becoming conspicuous at the wheel because of alcohol consumption, and Ziegler's (1987) figure of 92.5% of those who receive a drunken driving sentence being men, which results (see above) in a 9.25% probability of a male driver becoming conspicuous, one can note that about 90% of these 9.25% – thus, about 8% of male license holders – are caught with BAC levels of 1.3‰ or more. Taking the figure obtained at the alcohol clinic of only about half of those drivers who combine driving with heavy drinking being caught, one can conclude that the 8% figure should be doubled, which would yield a figure of 16%. This is indeed very close to the 15.8% figure mentioned above which epidemiological data yielded.

This makes obvious the need for a more precise definition of "problem drinkers" so as to include not only those persons ill with alcoholism in the narrow sense (see Jellinek, 1946; Feuerlein, 1978) but also that whole portion of the population endangered by alcohol on account of permanent excessive consumption. These truly ill with alcoholism (in the narrower sense) thus represent a subgroup of problem drinkers. It should be emphasized very strongly that a person who drives with more than 1.3‰ is not a "social drinker," whether he himself and his social environment believe this or not. [Regarding complexities of diagnostic categories here, see Antons & Schulz (1976)].

In summary, the following can be stated regarding the prediction of drunken driving:

- Neither the drunken driver nor society infers a problematic consumption of alcohol from a drunken driving offence. It can be assumed, however, that drivers who have been convicted for the first time will commit the offence again if no intervention takes place. Because of a lack of problem consciousness, they see no reason to change their drinking habits.
- Drunken drivers are recruited from that group of the population having "problematic" drinking habits.
- The aim of a psychological examination here is to find evidence of whether or not the examinee differs in a definite way from the average drunken driver.
- Differing in this way would tend to involve a genuine problem consciousness (perception of own problems with alcohol) and, as a consequence thereof, a change in behavior (as a rule an abstinence from alcohol). To achieve such a state, a combination of diagnosis and intervention can be highly useful.

An Interactionistic Approach to Prediction and Diagnosis

The conclusion which the facts and empirical results presented here imply – that persons registered as having committed drunken driving offences tend to be permanent abusers of alcohol who not only have drinking habits out of the ordinary but also violate the law frequently – should be taken into account in predicting the future driving behavior of persons caught for drunken driving. The diagnostic task here is in a sense a simple one as compared with, say, that of vocational counseling, since it can be limited to the attempt to answer the following two questions: (1) whether the person has a genuine consciousness of the problem, and (2) whether he or she has abstained from alcohol and whether this tendency has become stabilized. Another aspect of the diagnostic task which facilitates its solution is the fact that both anamnestic and catamnestic data can be used in prediction. In connection with question (1), it can be noted that the extent to which the person is able to separate an excessive consumption of alcohol from traffic participation is of central importance. The results which have been cited indicate that this is usually not the case due to a high blood alcohol level having become a permanent condition in the person, making traffic participation with a BAC of below 0.8‰ either impossible or difficult. This is aggravated by the intoxication tolerance which has been acquired, impeding the person's perception of his or her blood alcohol level.

Additional results to be presented underline the importance of how the frequency of checking by the police (that is, the risk of detection) is perceived. The actual frequency of checking (checking density) varies considerably from one place or region to another and can be seen as affecting, in conjunction with the other factors that have been mentioned, the readiness to drive while drunk. In a study of our own, two bodies of data were utilized: (1) cross-sectional data obtained in the investigation of a random sample of 50000 drunken driving offences which had been registered at the Federal Traffic Office during 1981 and 1982; (2) longitudinal data from 10000 persons from seven cities of differing size whose trustworthiness in traffic during the 10 years following receipt of their license (from 1973 to 1983) was investigated.

The data of (1) indicated the following: The checking densities by the police in the various geographical areas could be compared on the basis of the percentage of accidents in which the driver was found to be drunk. This was based on the fact that accidents are statistically rare events. The variations in checking density obtained, which appear representative for West Germany generally, were considerable. A North-South and a city-rural gradient were also found.

Various cities of similar size also exhibited marked differences. The proportion of drunken driving offences in which an accident was involved varied in cities with a population greater than 100000 between 29.8% and 63.6%.

A comparison of two large cities suggested that a high checking density affected the behavior of drivers. Faced with the possibility of losing the driver's license owing to drunken driving, people apparently tend to let the least intoxicated person drive, or they use public transport. It was also found that in the city with the higher checking density both alcohol offences as a whole and accidents involving alcohol occurred less frequently than in the city with the lower checking density.

With a portion of the longitudinal data in (2) it was possible to examine the trustworthiness in traffic of 1000 drivers in two cities of differing checking density over the 10 years following the receipt of their license. According to the data of the cross-sectional study, a higher percentage of drivers conspicuous in traffic due to their consumption of alcohol, and higher BAC values generally, could be expected in the city with the lower checking density. Such was found to be the case. In the city in which the checking density was low, 24% of those caught had a BAC of 2‰ or more, whereas in the city in which it was high, only 6% of them did. In the city with low checking density, 7% had been registered for drunken driving offences during the 10-year period, whereas in the city with high checking density only 4% had been.

Thus, not only does checking density by the police vary substantially but traffic participants also appear to react to this with changes in behavior.

The situation in the two cities can be characterized as follows: In the city with lower checking density, drivers apparently feel that they are only in danger of their BAC being checked if they are involved in an accident and/or show a BAC higher then they usually have (cf. the higher percentage of values over 2.0‰). Thus, drivers with problematic consumption of alcohol readily participate in traffic while intoxicated. In the course of 10 years they at some time have the "misfortune" of being involved in an accident or of driving with a very high BAC while being stopped for other reasons (e.g., malfunction of headlights).

If this line of argumentation is correct, it means that in the city with lower checking density the population of drivers registered for drunken driving the first time consists of at least two groups: those who are able to separate consumption of alcohol from the driving of a vehicle and to possibly choose other alternatives (e.g., letting someone else drive), and those who are not able to do so, the former having a rather favorable prognosis.

In the city with high checking density it is probable that particularly those persons are registered for drunken driving, who, despite the high checking density, are unable to separate drinking from driving and who must thus be assumed to be in particular danger of serious alcoholism. In addition, the data regarding persons who repeatedly violate the law support the interpretation that in such a city it is almost entirely persons with pronounced alcohol problems who become conspicuous.

A comparison of two randomly selected samples of 100 persons showed the percentage of persons with a BAC over 2.0‰ to be higher in the city with higher checking density. There, those caught for drunken driving appear to represent a selection of persons for whom the prognosis is particularly unfavorable.

These data appear to indicate that those officially registered for drunken driving in West Germany represent, at least at the time of committing the offence, a highly selected, rather homogeneous population as far as their serious abuse of alcohol is concerned. Bearing this in mind, it is not astonishing that the legal measures taken for purposes of security and improvement – withdrawal of the driver's license and use of various sanctions – are insufficient. With a low checking density, the one conviction in the course of several years is experienced as a "misfortune." With a high checking density, only those who are unable to separate drinking from driving tend to be caught anyway. In either case, there appears to be no perception among those caught of a connection between delinquency and personal alcohol problems. This is due both to the supression of the problem by the person concerned and to traffic safety propaganda tending to mislead the public.

In view of these considerations, there is obviously no point in basing a criterion for the qualification to drive on the "general probability of becoming conspicuous" in traffic. The empirical data cited suggest that those caught for drunken driving represent a particular population whose probability of committing a new offence, whether it is detected or not, is nearly 100% and whose probability of being detected committing a new offence is approximately 44% (cf. also Stephan, 1984).

The judiciary view (see Himmelreich & Hentschel, 1986) that a driver should not be considered qualified if there is a predominant probability – that is, a probability of a new offence (whether detected or not) of more than 50% – would imply, against this background, that the average driver caught for drunken driving for the first time is unqualified to drive. Judging whether the person in question differs significantly and in a positive way from the average drunken driver is thus vital. Two questions are important here: (1) whether consciousness of the problem and the motivation to live abstinently are present, and (2) at the behavioral level, whether abstinence can be sustained over a long period, possibly with some form of continuing treatment or of participation in self-help groups. Thus, abstinence must be stabilized.

Since, when interviewed, nearly 90% of those examined stated that they had already maintained prolonged periods of abstinence or of very frugal consumption of alcohol, the diagnostic aim should be to separate credible statements about abstinence and problem consciousness from those not worthy of belief. Adequate differential diagnosis of the problem drinker and conclusions regarding the type of intervention called for (which may range anywhere from training aimed at improving the ability to separate the consumption of alcohol from driving to treatment in a hospital ward) are needed. Since drunken driving offences tend to be misconceived both by society and by the offenders themselves, the individual motivational and behavioral prerequisites for adequate improvement are usually lacking when the person in question is first tested. It is possible, however, both upon initial contact with the person and in the report which is submitted, to make suggestions on how the qualification to drive can be reestablished through abstinence and therapy, and whatever. In a later examination the attempt should be made to determine whether the person has followed the recommendations provided and whether the necessary changes at the cognition and behavioral levels have occurred.

The interactionist approach proposed here should not only consider antecedent conditions but also yield a prediction of what will happen during the period following the initial examination. In the individual case either a positive or a negative assessment of the person's chances of becoming qualified to drive may be made.

Such a temporal stretching of the diagnostic process is already possible within the present legal framework (*de lege lata*). The term "limited qualification" is used in §15b of the Road Licensing Regulations. The law states that – given "limited qualification" – reissue of the driver's license can involve certain requirements (e.g., a regular check-up on liver function) and restrictions (e.g., being allowed to drive a truck only if the offence was committed during leisure time while driving a car), which the traffic authority is recommended to make reissue of the license dependent upon. Also, it is possible to limit being deemed qualified to drive to a certain period (e.g., 6 or 12 months), after which a reassessment of the qualification to drive is required. Prediction and intervention can thus be combined.

Diagnosis of this sort goes beyond the area of mere selection and prediction, taking account of psychological insight into the interaction between situational factors and personal dispositions. Through utilizing the current legal framework to its full extent, it is possible not only to improve prediction through combining diagnosis and intervention but also to allow for a compromise between individual interests and the justifiable demands for traffic safety on the part of the public.

References

Antons, K., & Schulz, W. (1976). *Normales Trinken und Suchtentwicklung.* Göttingen: Hogrefe.

Birrell, J.H. (1965). Blood alcohol levels in drunk drivers, drunk and disorderly subjects and moderate social drinkers. *Medical Journal of Australia, 2,* 949–999.

Blick, U., & Liebhard, E. (1981). Trinkbeobachtungen in Münchner Weingaststätten. *Blutalkohol, 18,* 10–16.

Borkenstein, R.F., Crowther, R.F., Shumate, R.P., Ziel, W.B., & Zylman, R. (1964). *The role of the drinking driver in traffic accidents.* Bloomington: Department of Police Administration, Indiana University.

Brakhoff, J. (1985). Ambulante Behandlung Alkoholabhängiger in der Bundesrepublik. In Deutscher Caritasverband e.V. (Ed.). *Caritas '85: Jahrbuch des Deutschen Caritasverbandes.* Freiburg: Deutscher Caritasverband.

Bund gegen Alkohol im Straßenverkehr e.V. (without year). *Wieviel darf ich trinken? Eine Promille-Fibel.* Hamburg: Steintor.

Camps, F.E., Robinson, A.E. (1968). Experiments designed to establish the amount of alcohol in the blood under social drinking conditions. *Medicine, Science and the Law, 8,* 153–160.

Feuerlein, W. (1975). *Alkoholismus – Mißbrauch und Abhängigkeit.* Stuttgart: Thieme.

Fürst, W. (1970) Beweiswert und Beweiswürdigung psychologischer Gutachten im verwaltungsgerichtlichen Verfahren. *Kraftfahrt und Verkehrsrecht, 9,* 175–186.

Gerchow, J. (1971). Zum 0,8-Promille-Gefahrengrenzwert. *Suchtgefahren, 17,* 1–5.

Harvard, J.D.J. (1975). Cross-national comparisons of drinking-driving laws. *Proceedings of the Sixth International Conference on Alcohol, Drugs and Traffic Safety* (pp. 637–654). Toronto.

Hentschel, P. (1986). Probleme der Praxis des Führerscheinentzugs in der Bundesrepublik Deutschland. *Blutalkohol, 23,* 1–14.

Himmelreich, K., & Hentschel, P. (1986). *Fahrverbot, Führerscheinentzug: mit Eignungsrichtlinien* (5th ed.). Düsseldorf: Werner.

Horn, E. (1973). *Konkrete Gefährdungsdelikte.* Köln: Schmidt.

Infas (1982) Untersuchungen zur Beurteilung der Wirksamkeit des Verkehrszentralregisters. Bonn - Bad Godesberg. Acc. to: Menken, E. (1985). Die Abschreckung alkoholisierter Kraftfahrer: Trugbild oder Wirklichkeit? Einige häretische Ansichten. *Drogalkohol, 9,* 16–43.

Jakobs, G. (1983). *Strafrecht: Allgemeiner Teil.* Berlin: de Gruyter.

Jakobsen, G., & Stallmann, M. (1985). Alkoholkonsum von Berliner Jugendlichen. *Suchtgefahren, 31,* 394–401.

Jellinek, E.M. (1946). Phases in the Drinking History of Alcoholics. *Quarterly Journal of Studies on Alcohol, 7,* 1–88.

Jescheck, H.-H. (1978). *Lehrbuch des Strafrechts: Allgemeiner Teil.* (3rd ed.). Berlin: Dunker & Humblot.

Karstedt-Henke, S., & Kretschmer-Bäumel, E. (1984). *Alkohol am Steuer: Orientierungen und Verhalten von Kraftfahrern. Ergebnisse einer Befragung.* Köln: Bundesanstalt für Straßenwesen. (Untersuchungen zu „Alkohol und Fahren", Vol. 12).

Kaufmann, A. (1968). Die Dogmatik im Alternativentwurf. ZStW, *80* (34), 50–51.

Kerner, H.J. (1985). *Gesetzgebung, polizeiliche Überwachung und Strafgerichtsbarkeit in der Bundesrepublik Deutschland: Dokumentation und Perspektive.* Bergisch-Gladbach: Bundesanstalt für Straßenwesen. (Bericht zum Forschungsprojekt 7612/4 der Bundesanstalt für Straßenwesen – Bereich Unfallforschung, Vol. 13).

Kunkel, E. (1977). Bedeutung der Dunkelziffer für das Eignungskriterium bei alkoholauffälligen Kraftfahrern. *Blutalkohol, 14,* 81–93.

Kunkel, E. (1985). Angaben zum Trinkverhalten, soziales Trinken und Blutalkoholkonzentration. *Blutalkohol, 22,* 341–356.

Lackner, K. (1987). *StGB: Kommentar.* (17th ed.). München: Beck.

Müller, A. (1976). *Der Trunkenheitstäter in der Bundesrepublik Deutschland.* Frankfurt: Lang. (Beiträge zur empirischen Kriminologie, Vol. 3).

Müller, A. (1984). Bei wieviel Prozent der Straßenverkehrsunfälle in der Bundesrepublik Deutschland ist Alkoholeinfluß ursächlich beteiligt? *Blutalkohol, 21,* 501–528.

Müller, A., & Weiler, C. (1987). Ergebnisse einer Untersuchung über Alkoholiker als Kraftfahrer. *Blutalkohol, 24,* 109–125.

National Council of Alcoholism – Criteria Committee, New York. (1972). Criteria for the Diagnosis of Alcoholism. *Annals of Internal Medicine, 77,* 249–258.

Pryor, W.J. (1966). Social drinking and blood alcohol levels. *New Zealand Medical Journal, 65,* 689–690.

Püschel, K. (1985). Blutalkoholbefunde bei Arbeitsunfällen. *Suchtgefahren, 31,* 31–37.

Reuband, K.-H. (1980). Alkoholkonsum in der Bundesrepublik: Eine empirische Bestandsaufnahme. In H. Berger, A. Legnaro & K.-H. Reuband (Eds.), *Alkoholkonsum und Alkoholabhängigkeit* (pp. 26–53). Stuttgart: Kohlhammer.

Rüdell, E., Bonte, W., Sprung, R., & Frauenrath, C.L. (1981). Anflutungssymptomatik nach exzessivem Trinkverhalten. *Blutalkohol, 18,* 326–330.

Schönke, A. (1986). *StGB: Kommentar* (22nd ed.). München: Beck.

Schreiber, M. (1985). Längsschnittuntersuchungen zum Alkoholkonsum. In H. Ziegler (Ed.), *Jahrbuch zur Frage der Suchtgefahren,* (pp. 22–31). Hamburg: Neuland.

Schuster, E. (1980). Fakten zum Alkoholmißbrauch. *Das öffentliche Gesundheitswesen, 42,* 31–36.

Shortt, R., & Vogelsprott, M.D. (1978). Social drivers' self-regulation of alcohol intake. J Stud Alc *39,* 1290–1293.

Solms, H. (1975). Die Ausbreitung des Alkoholkonsums und des Alkoholismus: Soziokulturelle, wirtschaftliche und geographische Verschiedenheiten. In W. Steinbrecher, & H. Solms (Eds.), *Sucht und Mißbrauch,* pp. 3/1–3/73. Stuttgart: Thieme.

Stephan, E. (1984). Die Rückfallwahrscheinlichkeit bei alkoholauffälligen Kraftfahrern in der Bundesrepublik Deutschland. *Zeitschrift für Verkehrssicherheit, 30,* 28–30.

Stephan, E. (1986). Die Legalbewährung von nachgeschulten Ersttätern in den ersten zwei Jahren unter Berücksichtigung ihrer BAK-Werte. *Zeitschrift für Verkehrssicherheit, 23,* 2–9.

Toffel-Nadolny, P. (1981). Zur alkoholischen Beeinflussung der Verkehrsteilnehmer in West-Berlin 1980. *Blutalkohol, 18,* 253–260.

Troschke, J. von, & Stünzner, W. von (1983). Alkoholkonsum von jungen Soldaten als Versuch der Bewältigung emotionaler Spannungen im Zusammenhang mit der Wehrdienstzeit. *Suchtgefahren, 29,* 1–17.

U. S. Department of Transportation (1969). Alcohol and highway safety countermeasures. *Proceedings of the National Highway Safety Bureau Priorities Seminar* (Vol. 2). Fredericksburg, Virginia, Washington, DC.

Valverius, M. (1985). Punishment and/or treatment for driving under the influence of alcohol and other drugs. In M. Valverius (Ed.), *Proceedings of the International Workshop,* (pp. 7–11). 19–20 October 1984, Stockholm, Sweden.

Wagner, H.-J. (1977). Mißbrauch und Sucht im Hinblick auf die Arbeits- und Verkehrssicherheit. In W. Steinbrecher, & H. Solms (Eds.), *Sucht und Mißbrauch* (pp. 3/50–3/65). Stuttgart: Thieme.

Widmark, E.M.P. (1938). *Die theoretischen Grundlagen und die praktische Verwendbarkeit der gerichtlich-medizinischen Alkoholbestimmung.* Berlin: Urban & Schwarzenberg.

Wieser, S. (1973). *Das Trinkverhalten der Deutschen. Eine medizinisch-soziologische Untersuchung.* Herford: Nicolai.

Ziegler, H. (Ed.). (1987). *Jahrbuch '87 zur Frage der Suchtgefahren.* Hamburg: Neuland-Verlagsgesellschaft.

Zielinski, D. (1973). *Handlungs- und Erfolgsunwert im Unrechtsbegriff: Untersuchung zur Struktur von Unrechtsbegründung und Unrechtsausschluß.* Berlin: Dunker & Humblot.

5
Juvenile Delinquency: Definitions, Character, and Theory

JOHN P. J. DUSSICH

The purpose of this paper is to present a brief overview of juvenile delinquency, primarily in the United States, with comments on how juvenile delinquency is defined, a discussion on the character of delinquency, and finally, a theoretical statement explaining delinquency.

Definition

Juvenile delinquency is an ambiguous concept mingled with many different criteria, especially those concerning age, sex, race, and nature of offense. In the broadest sense, juvenile delinquency means behavior by nonadults that violates the formal norms. In a more narrow sense, juvenile delinquency is any behavior by those persons designated as nonadults that would make them subject to the juvenile court. Thus, officially, a person is not considered a juvenile delinquent unless he or she has been adjudicated as such.

The term juvenile is defined differently in the United States among the 50 states and the District of Columbia. Most have accepted the common-law age minimum of 7 years, below which a child may not be held criminally responsible; four states have fixed the lower age limit at 10 years (Cavan & Ferdinand, 1975, p. 25; Task Force on Juvenile Justice and Delinquency Prevention, 1977, p. 297). With regard to the upper limits of the definition of juvenile, 32 states have set it at 18 years, 12 at 17 years, and 6 at 16 years (Cavan & Ferdinand, 1975, p. 25; Sari & Vinter, 1975, p. 4). If a youth commits a serious crime, the usual criteria for age may change. In all but two states (New York and Vermont), youths who have committed serious crimes may be tried in adult criminal courts. In New York and Vermont the upper age limit for being tried in juvenile court is 16 years, and regardless of the offense, persons under this age limit may not be tried in an adult court (Task Force Report, 1977, p. 303). Recently there has been a trend to lower the upper age limit from 18 to 16 or 17 years. The region with the lowest upper limit is New England and the region with the highest upper limit is the Far Western states (Cavan & Ferdinand, 1975, p. 25).

The Children's Bureau of the U.S. Department of Health, Education, and Welfare (DHEW) defines delinquency in the following way:

Juvenile delinquency cases are those referred to courts for acts defined in the statutes of the State as the violation of a state law or municipal ordinance by children or youths of juvenile court age, or for conduct so seriously anti-social as to interfere with the rights of others or to menace the welfare of the delinquent himself or of the community. This broad definition of delinquency includes conduct which violates the law only when committed by children, e.g., truancy, ungovernable behavior, and running away (DHEW, 1972).

This official definition by DHEW is the one principally used in all Federal Government dealings. It is general enough to cover most of the definitions used for research as well as for delinquency projects, and specific enough to be close to most of the legal definitions used in the many jurisdictions of the United States.

Alongside the broad American concept of juvenile delinquency is the often elusive concept of the status offender. Status offenders are generally those who, if adults, would not be arrested for their acts. These include: those who run away from home, are incorrigibly disobedient, refuse to attend school, violate local curfew regulations, and commit similar acts prohibited only for the young (Kobrin, Hellum, & Peterson 1980, p. 203). Perhaps one of the most disturbing aspects of this category of delinquency is that it means youths are often incarcerated for noncriminal behavior: behavior which may in fact be a normal and often necessary response to family and community situations. Based on recent research, most status offenders have never committed even status offenses before and will probably never commit an offense again, and if they do, they are usually limited to further status offenses (Kobrin et al. 1980).

When considering nonlegal definitions, Cavan and Ferdinand (1975, p. 28) developed a definition appropriate for this category: "any child who deviates from normal behavior so as to endanger himself, his social career, or the community." Perhaps the primary reason for the need of a nonlegal definition is to focus on behavior that is similar to the legal definition of delinquency and that can be operationalized for purposes of conducting research and developing theories.

Thus, it can be seen that defining juvenile delinquency is often an exercise in relativity. How one defines it depends on the intended use of the definition and one's point of reference.

Character

According to national statistics (Uniform Crime Report – UCR), the nature of criminal behavior became more violent during the 1970s. Since most criminal activity has been attributed to persons between the ages of 16 and 24 years, this increase in violence has developed into a popular assumption that most of the serious crime was perpetuated by juveniles. However, this assumption is not supported by the data (Snyder & Hutzler, 1981). Based on the 1977 UCR arrest rates, juvenile delinquency in the United States primarily involved property crime. The age of 16 appears to have been the "peak" for serious property crimes. With regard to the four violent crimes (murder, forcible sexual intercourse, aggravated assault, and robbery), the UCR arrest rates show that juveniles were involved in only 1% of all arrests for criminal offenses. The trend between 1964 and 1977 indicated that juveniles were continuing to commit the property crimes of burglary and larceny-theft; however, the proportion of juveniles involved in the more violent crimes of robbery and aggravated assault had increased since 1964. The juveniles most accountable for the index crimes were males, even though females had been arrested at an increasing rate during the period 1964–1977. It was also noted that even though black youths were not arrested for most of the juvenile offenses, they were overrepresented in each of the index offense categories, especially the violent crimes (Smith & Alexander, 1980, pp. 13–15).

Thus, the typical profile of the American delinquent has been a white, 16-year-old male whose main interest is in material gain. The recent trends indicate that both property and violent crime rates are leveling out (and in some instances declining) from when they peaked in the mid-1970s. The overall trend seems to indicate that in the near future juvenile crime will be lower than in the 1970s.

Theoretical Statement

The three dominant theoretical traditions developed for delinquency have been strain theories, cultural deviance theories, and control theories. Strain theories (also called anomie theories, anomie being a concept first developed in the early 1900s by Emile Durkheim in France) claim that a person is forced into delinquency in order to satisfy legitimate desires that are not met through conformity to society. Perhaps the best example of a strain theory is that of Robert K. Merton espoused in his book *Social Theory and Social Structure* (1957).

Cultural deviance theories claim that delinquency is a middle-class perspective which views deviance as conformity to another set of norms. One of the classic cultural deviance theories was propounded by Edwin H. Sutherland and is known as "differential association" (1966, pp. 77–83).

Control theories claim that delinquents are amoral beings whose bond to society is broken. The most explicit statement of this theoretical tradition was made by Travis Hirschi (1969) with the publication of his book *Causes of Delinquency*. In this author's opinion, the theoretical approach that best captures the social reality of delinquency behavior is control theory. In Hirschi's statement of control theory he focused on the importance of the bond between delinquents and the conventional social order. Looking at the traditional institutions of family, school, and work, as well as peers, Hirschi identified four elements which significantly affected the bond between juveniles and society. These elements of the bond were: attachment, commitment, involvement, and belief. When these elements strengthened the bond, high conformity resulted.

The major formulations of Hirschi's control theory have been supported by numerous research efforts (Conger, 1976, pp. 17–40; Hindelang, 1973, pp. 471–487; Hirschi, 1969; Lyerly & Skipper, 1981, pp. 385–399; Pode & Regoli, 1979, pp. 188–193). While Hirschi's theory stressed the individual's bond as the key element, another control theorist, Paul C. Friday, went further by focusing on significant role relationships as the main component in determining the extent of social integration (Friday & Hage, 1976). Friday's work refers almost exclusively to juvenile delinquents and recognizes the interdependence of the various social levels (structural, institutional, and individual) as they operate through the traditional institutions on juveniles to produce conditions for delinquency or nondelinquency (nonintegration or integration). The vital statement of this theory in explaining conforming behavior is the relation between the development of significant role relationships as a process of social integration and the resulting manifestation of deviant behavior: "as the intimacy (in relationships) declines..., the youth is less integrated into society and more likely to be involved in various kinds of crime" (Friday & Hage, 1976, p. 350).

Friday contends that for relationships to be effective they must be intimate. Intimacy is affected by four factors: frequency, scope, choice, and overlap. Of all these factors, one of the main pillars of Friday's theory is overlap. He contends that overlapping relationships exert strong pressures in the direction of conformity and have the effect that the juvenile's exposure to diverse norms is constrained.

The main difference between Hirschi and Friday is that Hirschi asks how close the bonds of youth are to the norm structures of society, while Friday asks how many role relationships exist within the different institutional areas and how intimate these relationships are.

Hirschi and Friday, in their development of control theory, limited themselves primarily to the antagonists of conforming and nonconforming delinquent behavior. The implication is that when conformity is achieved, delinquency ceases to be a problem. It is suggested by this author that theories of control need to go beyond the parameters of conforming and nonconforming delinquent behavior. Some other considerations might include: conforming behavior in different sociocultural settings which may lead to either delinquency or nondelinquency; theoretical ramifications of control theory with respect to adult crime; the application of control theory to the various forms of nondelinquent behavior; addressing the conflict between the legal definitions of delinquent behavior; considerations of control within various interac-

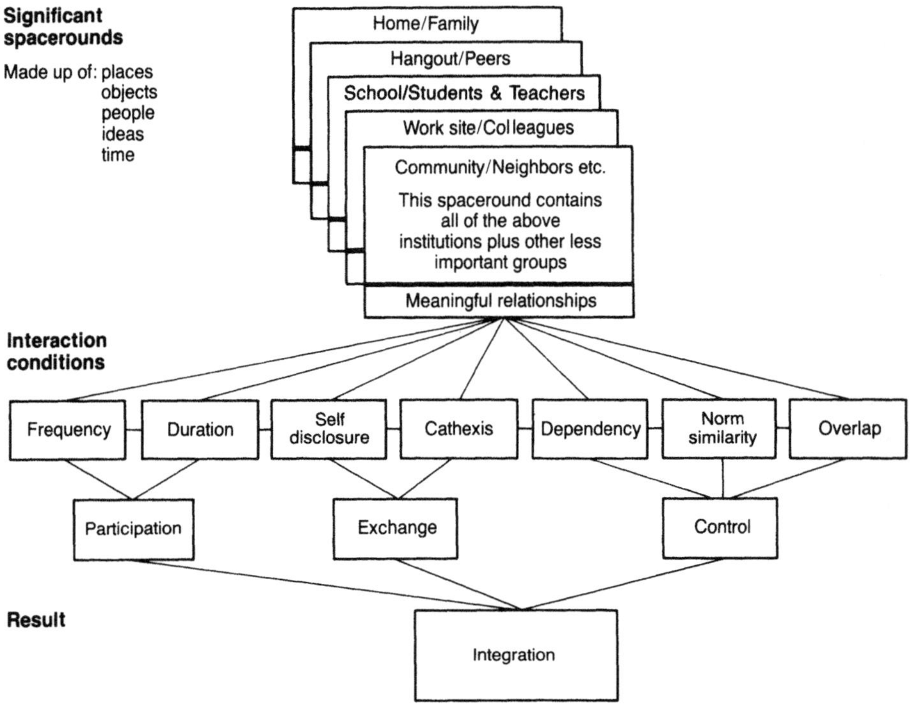

FIGURE 5.1. The theory of spaceround integration

tive settings; and finally, the relevance of individual cognitive functions in the total scheme of explaining juvenile delinquency.

In an attempt to further develop control theory, especially with regard to the above-mentioned considerations, this author and Jacobsen (1982) proposed a theoretical concept which we referred to as "spaceround integration." This proposal is an attempt at recognizing behavior in a more phenomenological way. It takes into account the macroprocesses and microprocesses of social psychic structures and how they influence behavior through significant spacerounds. [This concept was derived from a somewhat similar concept, "placerounds", originally developed by John Lofland (1969) in his book, *Deviance and Identity.*]

Significant spacerounds refers to patterned behavioral phenomena which have special importance to individuals and which are affected by such macrostructural artifacts as political systems, cultures, and governments, and such microstructural artifacts as groups, individuals, feelings, and ideas. These spacerounds may be traditional or nontraditional social-psychic situations. All spacerounds have five main components: people, places, ideas, objects, and time. An important character of these dimensions, and hence of spacerounds generally, is that they are mutable. Examples of some of the more common significant spacerounds are: home/family, schools/education, churches/religion, work sites/job, offices/officials, communities/neighbors, and hangouts/peers.

The term "spaceround" represents an attempt to bring together conceptually the multifaceted quality of a social-psychic happening with given people at a special place with unique ideas, with particular objects and only at an express time. Spacerounds refer to situations where and when the above-mentioned five dimensions interact with a degree of regularity in an identifiable pattern. By adding the adjective "significant" we limited spacerounds to those situational settings which were important to individuals and which were, in part, similar to social institutions. Within these significant spacerounds there exist "meaningful relationships".

Meaningful relationships represent the bond between an actor and other persons. An actor's different behaviors result from differential bonding to components (usually people) within different spacerounds. In the context of this theoretical model, objects also play an important role (hardware, a similar concept also identified by Lofland, refers to physical objects used in interactions which impute a particular identity to the persons associated with them). We contended that objects can and do function as interaction partners and that a range of interactive potential exists for objects. However, for purposes of this discussion, we focused primarily on person to person interactions, which we proposed were conditioned or affected primarily by seven *interaction conditions*: frequency of contact, duration of contacts, self disclosure, cathexis, dependency, norm similarity, and overlap.

Frequency refers to the number of contacts a person has with a person or object.

Duration refers to the length of time a given relationship has lasted.

Self disclosure refers to the degree of intimacy which interacting persons permit between each other. It is that character of mutual openness one allows with other persons which results in the sharing of intimate information.

Cathexis refers to the affective energizing force between a person and another person or an object. It is the investment or value of emotional or mental energy expended between interacting partners.

Dependency refers to the degree of control another person or object has over the outcome of an interaction. This may also be referred to as the power element in a relationship. It is characterized by the controllability of access to resources.

Norm similarity refers to the degree to which there is norm consensus between interacting persons. Norms are herein defined as behavioral expectations for which sanctions exist. Their influence on most people is usually stronger than that of formal sanctions.

Overlap refers to the degree of interaction between different spacerounds. To the extent that overlap is high (where many people from different spacerounds interact), the extent of meaningfulness in the corresponding relationships increases.

These conditions logically occur in the sequence presented above, and thus can be grouped into three categories. Frequency and duration are *participation* conditions; that is, they provide the opportunity for people to become acquainted with one another and are necessary for the onset of relationships. Self-disclosure and cathexis are *exchange* conditions and involve the give and take elements of relationships. Dependency, norm similarity, and overlap fall under the rubric of *control* and represent conditions that exert a managing influence over relationships. Each of these conditions ultimately plays a critical role in the extent to which a person is integrated in a given spaceround.

In traditional terms, *integration* refers to a social/physical process which brings together differing behavioral elements (Fairchild, 1968, p. 159). However, in this model spaceround integration refers to the process that brings together the five mutable components of place, objects, people, ideas, and time, and moves toward the synchronization and coordination of these elements to minimize conflict and maximize harmony.

Spaceround integration is a condition of the spaceround itself. The logical opposite of this term is *spaceround dysintegration*, which describes a condition whereby the interaction components are not "working together" towards common ends and where there is high conflict. The final consideration applies to spacerounds which are separate from the larger societal activities and is referred to as *spaceround isolation*. The spaceround itself is not participating in the community, nor does it directly contribute to the community's goals.

When speaking of an *individual's integration* in a given spaceround, we are speaking of the process whereby a person learns to deal with the elements of that spaceround and, if successful, becomes synchronized with its other interactive components. Thus, when a person is well integrated into a particular spaceround, he or she "fits in."

The opposite phenomenon to individual integration is *individual isolation*. Isolation implies estrangement from interaction within the spaceround in which one is a member. It is characterized by interactive separation from most of the usual spaceround activities. The most extreme form of isolation would imply: minimal contacts, low duration, no self-disclosure, no cathexis, a difference in norms, a lack of dependency, and no overlap with the persons (and objects) in that spaceround. *Individual dysintegration* represents the status of a person whose presence causes problems, one who cannot or will not adapt, and one who does not "fit in." This person would have a moderate number of contacts with variable duration, limited self-disclosure and cathexis, a difference in norms, variable dependency, and overlap. When considering the two variables of individual integration and spaceround integration, the paradigm in Figure 5.3. explains the probable outcome of these variables.

Using the concepts of individual integration and spaceround integration, this theory suggests that delinquency results when a youth is poorly integrated into a well (or legally) integrated spaceround (such as a community or a family) or when an individual is well integrated into a poorly (or illegally) integrated spaceround (like some peer groups). Conversely, law-abiding behavior is expected when a youth is well integrated into a well integrated spaceround or when a youth is isolated or does not "fit in" to an illegal or poorly integrated spaceround. [This position resembles the perspective taken by Elliott et al. (1985, p. 38) where they state that "delinquency is the result of a differential bonding to conventional and delinquent groups."]

The Study

As a by-product of a larger study (see Dussich, 1985), parts of the spaceround integration model were tested for a preparatory study. The two spacerounds "community" and "hangout" were selected because they represent extremes in *spaceround integration*. The spaceround "community" is herein described as a loosely built aggregation of different types and sizes of smaller spacerounds. In a typical community the degree of integration is determined by how well people in homes, worksites, schools, hangouts, etc. function together toward common goals. A community spaceround's norms are both formal and informal, and are relatively stable. This is the largest spaceround among those which affect people directly. The specific spaceround used in this study was the town of Hannover, Germany.

The spaceround "hangout" is herein described as a place where groups of persons of similar ages, interests, and backgrounds interact at specific times. Typical of this spaceround is a pub, street corner, or clubhouse where specific teenagers who know each other meet as often as every evening or at least once per week. Integration results when there is a relative absence of conflict and a high degree of gratification derived by members when together in this spaceround. This spaceround's norms are usually informal and subject to frequent changes.

The specific spacerounds used in this study were those which belonged to two German youth samples mentioned below.

To measure *individual integration*, two youth groups were selected: a delinquent group of parolees and a law-abiding group from the same town. Each group was given exploratory interviews which focused on their typical problems. All problems were then organized into spacerounds and prioritized as to the extent of severity.

Findings

The results of the interviews are shown in Fig. 5.2. The most problematic spacerounds are shown at the top; the least problematic are shown at the bottom.

Percentages were derived by using the frequency a spaceround was mentioned for each group. For purposes of this study, many problems operationally identified low individual integration and conversely few problems meant high individual spaceround integration. The results indicate that within a well

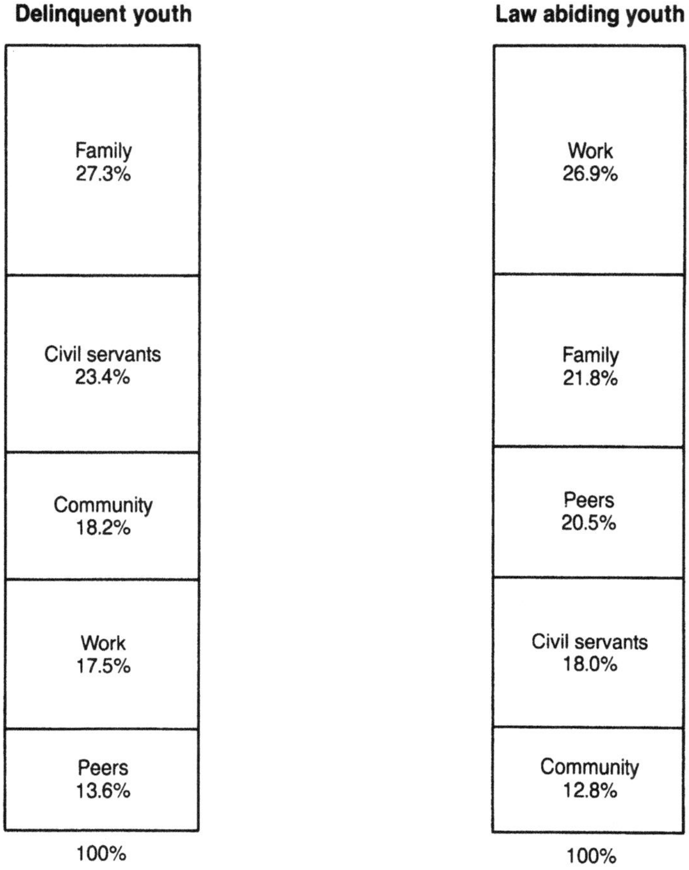

Chi-squared	Tau	Contingency coefficient	Degrees of freedom	Probability
5.969	0	0.158	4	0.20

FIGURE 5.2. Problematic spaceround comparisons

		Extent of spaceround integration	
		High	Low
Extent of individual integration	High	Low delinquency	High delinquency
	Low	High delinquency	Low delinquency

FIGURE 5.3. The spaceround – individual paradigm

integrated spaceround (community), a well integrated person usually has few problems and usually behaves in a law-abiding manner. A poorly integrated individual in this same spaceround with many problems usually behaves in a delinquent manner. Within the isolated spaceround (hangout) a well integrated person usually has few problems, yet usually behaves in a delinquent manner. Conversely, a poorly integrated person in this same spaceround can behave in a law-abiding manner.

Conclusions

Using these data, the paradigm shown in Fig. 5.3, is useful in explaining the interaction between spaceround integration and individual integration. These data support the theoretical basis of the paradigm such that understanding the behavioral dynamics of this model is helpful in explaining and predicting delinquency and other behaviors within other spacerounds.

It is my contention that this work lends support not only to the control theory tradition, but to the value of integrating other theoretical traditions shown in the earlier work by myself and Jacobsen (1982) and the more recent work by Elliot et al. (1985).

References

Cavan, R.S., & Ferdinand, T.N. (1975). *Juvenile delinquency.* Philadelphia: Lippincott.

Conger, R.D. (1976). Social control and social learning models of delinquent behavior. *Social Problems, 20,* 4.

Department of Health, Education and Welfare (DHEW). (1972). *Juvenile court statistics 1971* (Publication No. (SRS) 73: 03452). Washington, DC: Author

Dussich, J.P.J. (1985). *Perspectives in control theory: social coping of youth under supervision.* Cologne: Heymanns.

Dussich, J.P.J., & Jacobsen, H.-F. (1982). Social coping: eine Theorie zur Erklärung problemlösenden Verhaltens (social coping: a theory to clarify problem-solving behavior In H. Kury (Ed.), *Prävention abweichenden Verhaltens: Maßnahmen der Vorbeugung und Nachbetreuung (KFN).* Cologne: Heymanns.

Elliot, D.S., Huizinga, D. & Ageton, S.S. (1985). *Explaining delinquency and drug use.* Beverly Hills, CA: Sage.

Fairchild, H.P. (1968). *Dictionary of sociology.* Totowa,NJ: Littlefield, Adams.

Friday, P.C., & Hage, G. (1976) Youth crime in postindustrial societies: an integrated perspective. *Criminology, 14,* 347–368

Hindelang, M.J. (1973). Causes of delinquency: a partial replication and extension. *Social Problems, 20,* 4.

Hirschi, T. (1969). *Causes of delinquency.* Berkeley: University of California Press.

Kobrin, S., Hellum, F.F., & Peterson, J.W. (1980). Offense patterns of status offenders. In D. Shichon, H. Kelly (Eds.), *Critical issues in juvenile delinquency.* Lexington, MA: Lexington Books.

Lofland, J. (1969). *Deviance and identity.* Englewood Cliffs, NJ: Prentice-Hall.

Lyerly, R.R., & Skipper, J.K. (1981) Differential rates of rural-urban delinquency: a social control approach. *Criminology, 19,* 3.

Merton, R.K. (1957). *Social theory and social structure.* New York: Free Press.

Poole, E.D., & Regdi, R.M. (1979). Parental support, delinquent friends, and delinquency: a test of interaction effects. *Journal of Criminal Law and Criminology, 70,* 2.

Sari, R.C., & Vinter, R.D. (1975). Juvenile justice and injustice. *Resolution, 1,* 45.

Smith, C.P. & Alexander, P.S. (1980). *A National assessment of serious juvenile justice system: the need for a rational response. Reports of the National Juvenile Justice Assessment Centers:* Vol. 1 [Summary]. Washington, DC: U.S. Department of Justice, LEAA, OJJDP.

Snyder, H.N. & Hutzler, J.L. (1981). *The serious juvenile offender: the scope of the problem and the response of juvenile courts.* Washington, DC: National Center for Juvenile Justice.

Sutherland, E.H., & Cressey, D.R. (1966). *Principles of criminology* (7th ed.). Philadelphia: Lippincott.

Task Force Report of Juvenile Justice and Delinquency Prevention (1977). Washington, DC: LEAA, U.S. Department of Justice, Government Printing Office.

6
Situational Effects on the Decisions of Adolescent Offenders to Carry Out Delinquent Acts. Relations to Moral Reasoning, Moral Goals, and Personal Constructs

ROBERT W. GOLDSMITH, GUNILLA THROFAST, and PÄR-ERIC NILSSON

Introduction

Society has an obvious interest in understanding the individual and situational factors which contribute to delinquent behavior in adolescents. The present study, of largely cognitive and social psychological orientation, investigates a variety of such factors in two groups of adolescent boys – the one consisting of boys with overt problems of delinquency, and the other of boys not known to possess such problems. The aspects of behavior examined include moral reasoning and moral development level, goal priorities and values, the manner of evaluating the wrongness of various delinquent acts, the personal constructs used in assessing significant others, the readiness to carry out delinquent acts of various types, and the dependence of this on situational factors. The study's point of theoretical departure is the question of the applicability to delinquent behavior of Kohlberg's theory of moral development (Kohlberg, 1969, 1976, 1981, 1984; Kohlberg & Freundlich, 1973; Kohlberg, Levine & Hewer, 1983). Various of the factors other than moral development level considered here are ones, of seeming relevance to delinquent behavior, about which Kohlberg's theory has relatively little to say or which work within the framework of his theory has tended to neglect.

Moral Development Level and Delinquency

Kohlberg has done much to establish the investigation of moral reasoning as an important area of psychological research. At the same time, there has been considerable controversy regarding both his theory and his empirical approach (cf. Gibbs & Schnell, 1985; Kohlberg, Levine & Hewer, 1983; Kurtines & Gewirtz, 1984; Peltzer, 1986). In Kohlberg's view (Jennings, Kilkenny & Kohlberg, 1983), higher levels of moral reasoning have an "insulating" effect in making an adolescent better able to withstand incentives for behaving delinquently. Kohlberg's theory, closely related to that of Piaget's (1932), conceives of moral development passing through an invariant sequence of stages (up to the final stage an individual attains), each new stage involving a higher level of moral reasoning than the previous one. Any given stage is seen as integrating and transforming the moral reasoning of all previous stages, and as constituting an unified whole through the overall moral view it represents. Kohlberg's theory is a structural one in that the form rather than the content of moral reasoning is emphasized. Thus, Kohlberg does not consider moral reasoning to be reducible to the mere expression of specific moral values, norms, or attitudes (cf. Colby, Kohlberg & Kauffman, in press; Gibbs & Widaman, 1982).

For measuring moral development level, Kohlberg has made extensive use of an interview technique in which the subject is presented with various *moral dilemmas* (see Colby & Kohlberg, in press; Colby, Kohlberg, Candee, Gibbs, Hewer & Speicher-Dubin, in press); these are hypothetical situations involving conflict between different moral principles. In a wide variety of studies using Kohlberg's and related measures, juvenile delinquents have been shown to be, on the average, low in moral development level for their age (cf. Blasi, 1980; Gibbs & Widaman, 1982). Blasi (1980) indicates, however, that the relationships found have not been sufficiently strong for moral reasoning level alone to appear to provide an adequate explanation of delinquency.

Values, Goal Priorities, and Delinquency

In focusing on the form rather than the content of moral reasoning, Kohlberg does little to illuminate the role of specific values and goal priorities in delinquent and nondelinquent behavior. Rest (1984) has taken a step in this direction, emphasizing the interplay of competing values, and of moral versus nonmoral goals, in the cognitive and decisional processes leading to moral behavior. Similarly, Damon (1984) considers conduct to be strongly influenced by the degree of centrality of moral goals to self-identity and by the individual's readiness to interpret situations in moral terms. Delinquency proneness in adolescents has also been found to relate negatively to degree of "moral belief" (Sheley & Bailey, 1985) and to the degree of possessing a "conventional value orientation" (Cernovich, 1978).

The question of the extent to which the values of delinquent and nondelinquent adolescents differ has been considered within the framework of various sociological theories. According to *subcultural theories* (Cohen, 1955; Miller, 1958), delinquency is readily engendered in certain subcultural groups by the values its members hold. In contrast, three other sociological theories, closely related to one another – Sykes' and Matza's (1957) *neutralization theory*, Matza's and Sykes' (1961) *theory of subterranean values*, and Matza's (1964) *theory of drift* – propose that delinquents and nondelinquents have essentially similar values but, for reasons specified by the theory in question, fail at times to act in accordance with these values.

Delinquency and the Cognition of Others

The values and goals adolescents possess can be assumed to be strongly influenced by their cognitions of significant others. One manner of conceiving of such cognitions is in terms of *personal construct theory* (Kelly, 1955; see also Bannister & Mair, 1968). According to this theory, persons tend to structure their world – in the present context that part of their world significant others and the self represent, all of whom can be referred to as *elements* – using a finite set of *constructs*, or bipolar dimensions. Such constructs are assumed to be specific both for the person who uses them (hence the term *personal*) and for the set of elements to which they apply. For studying personal constructs a *repertory grid technique* (Kelly, 1955; see also Fransella & Bannister, 1977) is frequently employed (see below). Data obtained with this technique can also be used to assess *cognitive complexity*. Cognitive complexity has been assumed to increase as moral development (Selman, 1980), or development generally (Schroder, Driver & Streufert, 1966), progresses.

Delinquency and Situational Factors

Within recent years there has been a strong interest in the effects of situational factors on decisions to commit delinquent or criminal acts (e.g., Brantingham & Brantingham, 1981; Byrne & Sampson, 1986; Carroll, 1978). From a "rational choice" perspective (Cornish & Clarke, 1986), the decision to carry out a juvenile delinquent act can be considered as involving the adolescent's attempt to weigh, partly in terms of his or her goal priorities and value system and partly in terms of the perceived characteristics of the situation, the positive and negative consequences the act can have. Research on moral behavior has likewise been increasingly concerned with situational factors. According to Staub (1984), both internal and external aspects of the environment can activate the goals relevant to moral conduct. Kurtines (1984) sees moral choices as being the conjoint result of situational factors and the individual's characteristic manner of applying moral rules and principles.

Method

Subjects

Two groups of 12 male subjects each, matched for age (mean age 17.2 years, age range 15–20 years, 7 subjects in each group being in the age range 17–18), participated in the investigation. The one group consisted of delinquent youths from a reform school in southern Sweden. They had been assigned to the school – initially for a period of 6 months, extendable for additional 6-month periods – after other societal measures had been deemed unsuccessful. The other group, serving as controls and also of interest in their own right, consisted of youths who had terminated their education after 9 years of public school. Participation was voluntary. A small remuneration was paid, somewhat higher in the control group, though neither group had knowledge of the other and the reform school boys, told what those who took part would earn, seemed satisfied with the amount.

Contact with the boys at the reform school regarding the possibility of participating was established by the second author, who had been working at the school for several years. She emphasized the extracurricular nature of participation, the complete confidentiality of individual results, and the use of these only for purposes of the study. This, together with the fact that decisions regarding possible extensions of the boys' stay at the reform school were made, as the boys generally knew, not by the school but by the courts and by the authorities in the communities from which they came, can be seen as mitigating strongly against any danger of the delinquent subjects misunderstanding the test situation as being one that could affect the length of their stay at the school. Participation of the control subjects was solicited by phone, using a list which a school psychologist provided of boys who had dropped out of public school after ninth grade and who, to the best of his knowledge, had no history of serious delinquent problems.

Due to the small size of the samples, caution is in order in connection with the interpretations presented of the results, the investigation being of largely exploratory character.

Procedure

The second and third authors tested the delinquent subjects, two other persons testing the control subjects. To facilitate testing of the delinquent subjects, instructions and test questions were presented to both groups orally, answers being obtained orally and recorded by hand. The following five test procedures were employed.

Delinquent Behavior Interview

The Delinquent Behavior Interview aimed at studying the subject's readiness to engage in delinquent acts of various types and the role he perceived situational factors to have. A list of 24 delinquent acts was read to the subject (see Table 6.1). In response to each, the subject was to indicate whether he felt he might, under some conditions at least, carry out the act in question. If his response was affirmative, he was to specify under what conditions this could occur.

Note that two of the acts, 5 and 10, dealing with use or threat of violence, might be considered as delinquent or not, depending on the circumstances. Act 1, crossing the street against a red light, is one for which pedestrians in Sweden could until recently be fined.

Act Evaluation Task

In order to compare how wrong the subject considered various delinquent acts to be and explore the basis for judgments of wrongness, six of the acts appearing in the task just described – acts 7, 14, 15, 19, 23, and 24 (Tables 6.1, 6.2) – were employed again. On each of eight successive trials, a different set (triad) of three of the six acts was shown, each act appearing on a separate card. The subject was to indicate on any given trial which act he considered to be most wrong to carry out. He was also to specify why he felt the act to be the most wrong of the three. The procedure as a whole represents basically an abbreviated form of repertory grid test (see below) yielding a set of constructs applying to the six acts or to various of these.

Sociomoral Reflection Measure

The Sociomoral Reflection Measure is a questionnaire developed by Gibbs and Widaman (1982) designed to measure moral development level. It consists of both multiple-choice and open-ended questions, answers to questions of the latter sort being decisive to scoring. The questionnaire is based directly on the Kohlberg technique and makes use of the same moral dilemmas. In most respects, the scoring system also agrees with the one currently employed in the Kohlberg procedure (Colby, Kohlberg, Candee, Gibbs, Hewer & Speicher-Dubin, in press), though it differs in assuming four stages of moral development rather than the five which Kohlberg (1982; Kohlberg, Levine & Hewer, 1983) has recently advocated. It yields as an overall measure of moral development level the *Sociomoral Reflection Maturity Score (SRMS),* the possible values of which range from 100 to 400, with each whole stage number being represented as a multiple of 100 on the scale. This score is based on ratings the subject receives on each of eight different *Norms*, or separate areas of moral reasoning. Two of these, *Norm Conscience* and *Norm Family Affiliation*, are mentioned below. The questionnaire, translated into Swedish, was administered orally (see above) rather than in its pencil-and-paper form. Although no empircial answer can be given to the question of the validity of the test in this version for measuring what the original test aims to assess, one can note that investigations using translated and sometimes locally adapted versions of Kohlberg's testing procedure have been reported to yield basically similar results in a wide variety of countries and cultures (cf. Snarey, 1985), though critics have claimed there to be definite cultural biases nevertheless, both in the test and in the underlying theory (see, e.g., Kaminsky, 1984; Peltzer, 1986; Snarey, 1985).

Goal Ranking Task

To gain insight into the subject's value orientation and goal priorities, use was made of a set of 38 cards on each of which a brief designation of some goal appeared (see Table 6.3). Initially the subject was to sort the cards into two piles: those with goals he considered worth aiming at and those he did not. He then was to sort the cards with goals he viewed as worthwhile into three categories: goals of greatest importance, of lesser importance, and of least importance. If the number of cards in any of the three categories appeared so large as to impede the task that was to follow, the subject was asked to sort through the cards in that category again and place them into two subcategories: goals of somewhat greater importance and of somewhat less. Finally, the subject was to rank order the cards in each category or subcategory in terms of importance. This yielded a rank ordering of all the goals the subject considered desirable.

Repertory Grid Test

In the Repertory Grid Test the subject was first asked to think of five persons who played or had played an important role in his life, or toward whom his attitude was particularly positive or negative – significant others, therefore – and was to write the name or some other designation of each of these persons and himself on a set of six cards, one person on each card. On each of eight trials then the procedure was as follows: A triad of cards was shown and the subject was to indicate which two persons in the triad appeared most alike. He was also to specify in what way they were alike or differed from the third person, the likeness or difference the subject named being taken to represent a construct. All six cards were then shown to the subject, who was to rank order them in terms of the construct, from the person who was highest on the construct to the person who was lowest.

Results and Discussion

Readiness to Engage in Delinquent Acts

Table 6.1 indicates, for each of the acts presented in the Delinquent Behavior Interview, how many subjects in each group responded to the act *affirmatively*, that is, considered it possible they might carry it out. Note the division of the table into four blocks of delinquent acts, based upon the absolute and relative frequencies of affirmative response by subjects of the two groups. As can be seen, there is no act for which the frequency of affirmative response is greater in the control than in the delinquent group and there are eight of the acts for which the tendency for a greater number of delinquent than control subjects to respond affirmatively is statistically significant (Fischer test).

TABLE 6.1. Numbers of delinquent (D) and control (C) subjects who responded affirmatively (n_{affirm}) to the various delinquent acts presented in the Delinquent Behavior Interview ($n = 12$ for both groups)

Item no.	Order of presentation	n_{affirm}		
		D	C	
1	(1)	11	11	Cross the *street* against a red light
2	(22)	12	9	Skip *classes* in school
3	(2)	9	7	Ride on a *train* without paying
4	(13)	7	7	Take a *magazine* from a waiting room
5	(14)	5	4	Resort to *violence*
6	(18)	4	3	*Smash* a street lamp
7	(24)	3	2	Take money or things of value from *home*
8	(11)	11	5***	Enter a *building* where you're not allowed to be
9	(6)	11	4**	Keep a *wallet* that you find
10	(5)	10	5	*Threaten* someone with violence
11	(4)	9	5	Say nothing to the *cashier* when you get too much change back
12	(3)	9	3***	Take an unlocked *bike*
13	(8)	7	4	Buy something you know is *stolen*
14	(15)	7	3	Take something in a *store* without paying
15	(12)	3	1	*Destroy* someone's things on purpose
16	(17)	10	0*	Break into a *car*
17	(19)	10	0*	*Break in* somewhere to steal
18	(20)	6	0**	Not bother paying after eating in a *restaurant*
19	(10)	5	0***	Carry out a *practical joke* with the risk of someone being injured
20	(23)	5	0***	Take money from outer garments hanging in a *cloakroom*
21	(7)	0	0	Damage a public *phone*
22	(9)	0	0	Steal money from a *friend's parents*
23	(16)	0	0	Loan money from a *good friend* without paying it back
24	(21)	0	0	Steal money from a *buddy*

Note. For rough descriptive purposes, items are arranged (top to bottom) in 4 blocks, depending on whether n_{affirm} (1) differs little if at all for the two groups (items 1–7), (2) differs more markedly (items 8–15), (3) is 0 for C but not D (items 16–20), (4) is 0 for both groups (items 21–24). Group differences at a-levels 0.01, 0.02, and 0.05 (Fischer) are shown by *, **, and ***. Italicized item nos. designate items appearing again in the Act Evaluation Task. Italicized words in the act descriptions represent brief act designations used in the Appendix.

The number of acts responded to affirmatively, which in the following serves as the *Delinquency Proneness* measure, ranged between 6 and 18 (of the 20 selected at all) for the delinquents (mean 12.83), and between 1 and 12 for the controls (mean 6.08), a difference which was statistically significant ($P < 0.002$, Mann-Whitney U-test; note that all P-values to be reported are two-tailed).

Perceived Situational Effects on the Readiness to Engage in Delinquent Acts

In the Appendix a brief summary is presented of the basic content of subjects' statements when asked in the Delinquent Behavior Interview under what conditions they could imagine carrying out those acts to which they responded affirmatively. Subjects' statements appear to reflect both similarities and differences in the value orientations of the two groups. A lesser willingness of the delinquents to accept societal norms seems evident. Eight of the delinquents claimed, for one or more of the acts, that they would carry out the act regardless of the circumstances, whereas only one control subject expressed himself in this way. Five of the delinquent but none of the control subjects declared, for one or more of the acts, that they would not carry out the act if the victim, or potential victim, was someone they knew. Such a statement seems indicative of a stage 2 orientation in Kohlberg's terminology, one of morality being seen as based not on principles external to the self but on perspectives arising through interactions with others. This is a stage of moral development Kohlberg (Kohlberg, Kauffman, Scharf & Hickey, 1975) considers to be typical of adolescent offenders. On the other hand, as results presented below indicate, the differences between the two groups in moral development level appear to be less than one might expect.

Evaluation of Delinquent Acts

Table 6.2 shows means of *selection frequency* – that is, selection as the act most wrong of those in a triad – for each of the six acts included in the Act Evaluation Task. Significant group differences in this measure were obtained

TABLE 6.2. Means of selection frequencies shown by the delinquent (D) and the control (C) group on the Act Evaluation Task (n = 12 in each group)

Item no.		Subject groups D	Subject groups C	
5	Resort to violence	2.75	1.08	$P<0.01$
7	Take money or things of value from home	2.33	1.58	
14	Take something in a store without paying	0.00	0.33	
17	Break in somewhere to steal	0.16	2.50	$P<0.0001$
20	Take money from outer garments hanging in a cloakroom	0.42	1.00	
21	Damage a public phone	2.33	1.50	

Note. Items are numbered as in Table 1. The P-values shown are for the Mann-Whitney U-test. The highest selection frequency possible was 4.0.

for acts 5 and 17 ($P<0.01$ and $P<0.0001$, respectively, Mann-Whitney U-test); for the same two acts, the within-group differences in selection frequency were likewise significant ($P<0.01$ for each group, Wilcoxon test). The results suggest that delinquent subjects tend to view the use of violence as considerably more wrong than breaking in to steal, whereas for control subjects the opposite is the case. For the delinquents there are three of the acts for which the mean selection frequencies are very low (acts 14, 17, and 20), implying these acts, which all involve theft, to be viewed as relatively harmless (though theft from members of the family, act 7, seems to be regarded quite differently). For the control subjects only act 14, taking something in a store without paying, has a comparably low selection frequency.

The term "violence" in item 5 is obviously open to differing interpretations. The delinquents' apparent readiness to consider resorting to violence as the worst act of all may partly reflect their conceiving of a more extreme and dangerous form of violence than the control subjects did. It may also reflect a tendency on their part of limit the frame of reference for their negative judgments of violence, condemning serious violence within the immediate peer group but failing to do so in various other contexts (cf. discussion of group loyalty goals below).

To compare the moral reasoning of the two groups, a ten-category system based in large part on Kohlberg's analysis of moral reasoning was developed for classifying the motivations subjects gave for their selections. The categories employed were the following:

1. *Generalized Empathy* (emphasizing that some person could be hurt in a direct way by the act, without referring to any specific person)
2. *Abstract Moral Principles* (all such principles except any that might otherwise be placed in categories 1, 4, or 10)
3. *Conscience* (emphasizing that one would have a bad conscience)
4. *Golden Rule* (any statements which could be seen as expressing this rule)
5. *Badness* (emphasizing how bad a particular act is or what a serious offense it represents)
6. *Practical Considerations* (mentioning aspects of practical but not moral character)
7. *Life and Safety* (emphasizing that either life or safety of others may be threatened in an indirect way by the act in question)
8. *Personal Contact* (indicating that one's knowing the victim makes the act particularly bad)
9. *Punishment* (indicating possible negative consequences for oneself, other than dealt with in category 3)
10. *Family Principles* (citing principles applying to family interactions)

Nine of the categories were seen as falling into two major classes, one class involving categories that seemed more characteristic of a higher level of moral reasoning – these were the categories 1–5 – the other involving categories that seemed characteristic of a lower level – the categories 6–9. Judging a category to belong to the one class or the other followed in our estimation, with two exceptions, quite directly from characteristics of the moral development stages Kohlberg describes (Colby, Kohlberg & Kauffman, in press; Gibbs & Widaman, 1982). Including category 5 in the higher class took account of Burton's (1984) view that many moral responses of a mature character occur in a largely automatic fashion, without the need for conscious reasoning. Category 6 was included in the lower class since needs of life and safety were seen as being so basic to human experience that a high degree of internalization of social norms did not seem implied by reference to them. Category 10 was excluded altogether since it was felt that motivations of this category might well reflect quite differing levels of moral reasoning.

A difference score, representing the number of motivations given which belonged to categories 1–5 (the higher class) minus the number belonging to categories 6–9, was obtained for each subject, a score referred to as the *Wrongness Evaluation* score. This score was found to be significantly higher for the control than for the delinquent group ($P<0.02$, Mann-Whitney U-test). The same score was found to correlate positively, in the delinquent though not in the control group, with the SRMS score (see below) of the Sociomoral Reflection Measure ($r_s = +0.63$, $P<0.05$, for the delinquents; $r_s = -0.05$ for the controls, cf. Table 6.4). The significant positive correlation here suggests it to be possible, on the basis of a Kohlberg or closely related type of moral development level score, to predict how delinquents will reason about the wrongness of specific types of delinquent act. The failure to obtain a correlation of this sort for the control group may possibly be attributable to the variance of the Wrongness Evaluation scores being much less in the control group, Bartlett's test for the homogeneity of variance in the two groups yielding $P = 0.003$.

Level of Moral Development

According to their SRMS scores on the Sociomoral Reflection Measure the moral development level of the controls was on the average somewhat higher than that of the delinquents, though the difference was not statistically significant, the respective means being 284 (range 206–338) and 273 (range 206–319). A significant group difference was obtained, however, on Norm Conscience of the same test ($P<0.05$, Kolmogorov-Smirnov), the median of that score (as well as the mode) being at the transition 3/4 level for the controls (i.e., between stages 3 and 4) and at the transition 2/3 level for the delinquents. The latter result is contrary to what one would expect on the basis of Kohlberg's theory, with its assumption of moral development stages representing structural wholes, though it quite fits an alternative model which Rest (1979) has proposed, according to which stage unity need not be found and moral reasoning level can differ for various areas of moral reasoning. Caution is in order in regard to the result just mentioned, however, since a Friedman one-way analysis of variance carried out for each group separately failed to show for either group a significant within-group difference in the scores assigned the various Norms.

On the basis of Kohlberg's theory one could hypothesize that a negative relationship would be found between SRMS and Delinquency Proneness scores. However, the correlation between the two variables was close to zero in both groups (see Table 6.4).

The issue of possible cultural differences arose in connection with two of the multiple-choice questions on the test, concerning the importance of children helping their parents "even when their parents have broken a promise" and "even when it means that the children won't get to do something they want" (questions 4 and 6, respectively, of problem 2). The alternative "not important" (as opposed to "important" or "very important") was selected by at least half the subjects in each group in the former case and by several of the delinquent subjects in the latter. Such answers are not specifically foreseen in the scoring examples of the Gibbs and Widaman (1982) manual. In a personal communication (11 January 1987), Gibbs suggested that the answers to the former question may reflect a current and partly culturally dependent trend in parent-child relationships.

Goal Priorities

Table 6.3 shows, for each of the goals included in the Goal Ranking Task, the mean of the ranks the subjects in each group assigned it, its rank on the basis of this mean, and the number of subjects in each group who selected it. In these and other computations, goals which a subject failed to select were assigned the mean of the unused ranks remaining in the set of 38. Since data were not available for two of the subjects due to an error in test administration, results for that group were based on 10 rather than 12 subjects.

It was hypothesized that giving a high priority to moral goals and goals of self-esteem (both of which will be referred to as *law-abiding goals*) would be associated with a tendency to abstain from delinquent acts, and that giving a high priority to goals of a hedonistic character, of group loyalty, and of freedom from adult control (all of which will be termed *non-law-abiding goals*) would be associated with a tendency to carry out delinquent acts. Considering goals of self-esteem as law-abiding assumed that recognition as being law-abiding tends to enhance self-esteem, even if self-esteem may perhaps, in delinquents in particular (cf. Kaplan, 1978), be temporarily increased by the carrying out of a delinquent act. Viewing goals of group loyalty as non-law-abiding focused on possible group pressures to behave delinquently. Similarly, regarding goals of freedom from adult control as non-law-abiding emphasized the potential use of such freedom to delinquent ends.

To obtain measures of goal priorities, 20 goals judged to be of the one sort or the other and selected as worthwhile by the majority of subjects in both

TABLE 6.3. Means of the ranks the delinquent (D) and control (C) subjects ($n = 10$ and $n = 12$, respectively) assigned the various goals in the Goal Ranking Task, ranks of these means, and numbers of subjects selecting the goals as being of interest (selection frequencies)

Item no.	Means of ranks		Ranks of rank means		Selection frequencies		
	D	C	D	C	D	C	
1	8.2	4.2	2	1	10	12	Be truthful and honest
2	11.2	8.1	7.5	2.5	9	12	Be a good person
3	11.2	8.1	7.5	2.5	9	12	Help others
4	7.0	8.9	1	4	10	12	Be considered reliable
5	17.5	9.0	19	5	7	12	Have a good conscience
6	8.7	10.2	3	6	9	12	Be fair toward others
7	8.9	10.6	4	7	10	12	Have a good reputation
8	12.6	11.3	9	8	9	11	Have others' trust
9	9.6	11.8	5	9	9	12	Be loyal toward others
10	10.4	12.9	6	10	10	12	Share with those in need
11	15.7	13.6	13	11	9	11	Be liked by others
12	15.0	15.0	11	12	8	11	Be respected by others
13	20.7	16.0	23	13	7	11	Have good judgment
14	16.6	16.1	17.5	14	6	9	Not be selfish
15	15.6	16.2	12	15	8	12	Have lots of fantasy
16	19.3	16.8	20	16	8	12	Know a lot
17	16.6	17.7	17.5	17	8	9	Be able to do whatever you want
18	16.0	17.9	15	18	9	9	Always have a good time
19	15.9	18.5	14	19	8	11	Really be appreciated
20	16.2	19.5	16	20	8	9	Be able to get by on your own
21	14.8	19.8	10	21	9	10	Have plenty of money
22	23.6	20.4	26	22	4	9	Succeed in everything you undertake
23	22.9	21.0	25	23	6	10	Be strong
24	25.7	21.1	28	24	5	11	Be good looking
25	23.8	22.5	27	25	6	10	Be considered important
26	19.9	23.9	22	26	6	6	Have a lot of responsibility
27	27.0	26.9	29	27	3	6	Have a chance to get revenge
28	29.7	26.9	32	28	2	4	Get to be well known
29	21.0	27.4	24	29	7	5	Be able to buy all you want
30	29.1	27.5	31	30	2	7	Always be right
31	29.8	27.9	33	31	1	4	Be felt sorry for by others
32	19.8	28.6	21	32	6	2	Not be lonely
33	30.3	29.2	35	33	1	3	Have a lot of power
34	29.9	29.9	34	34	2	3	Be the one who decides
35	31.2	31.2	37.5	35	0	2	Be in the center of attention
36	30.6	31.3	36	36	1	2	Be considered a hero
37	27.7	31.5	30	37	2	1	Be tough
38	31.2	32.3	37.5	38	0	1	Have control over others

Note. Goals were presented to the subject in random order. Goals are numbered in the table in accordance with the control group's ranking of them.

TABLE 6.4. Correlations (r_s) within the delinquent (D) and control (C) groups between composite goal evaluation measures – Moral/Group; Moral/Pleasure; Moral, Esteem; and Moral, Esteem/Pleasure, Group – and the Delinquency Proneness, Wrongness Evaluation and SRMS (moral development level) measures

	D			C		
	Delinquency Proneness	SRMS (moral development level)	Wrongness Evaluation	Delinquency Proneness	SRMS (moral development level)	Wrongness Evaluation
Moral/Group	*−0.65*[d]	+0.58	*+0.81*[b]	−0.49	−0.44	+0.08
Moral/Pleasure	−0.47	*+0.63*[d]	+0.62	−0.42	*−0.60*[d]	+0.20
Moral, Esteem	−0.60	+0.52	*+0.76*[c]	*−0.84*[a]	−0.13	−0.06
Moral, Esteem/ Pleasure, Group	−0.61	*+0.63*[d]	*+0.78*[b]	*−0.62*[d]	−0.33	+0.03
Delinquency Proneness		−0.15	−0.42		−0.07	−0.04
SRMS			*+0.63*[d]			−0.05

Note. For correlations involving the composite goal evaluation measures, $n = 10$ for D and $n = 12$ for C; for other correlations, $n = 12$ for both groups. Achievement of significance levels 0.001, 0.01, 0.02, and 0.05 is indicated by [a], [b], [c], and [d] respectively.

groups were classified into four different categories: (1) *Morality* (abbreviated *M*: goals 1, 2, 3, 5, 14); (2) *Self-esteem* (*E*: goals 8, 11, 12, 19, 25); (3) *Group Loyalty* (*G*: goals 4, 6, 7, 9, 10); (4) *Pleasure and Freedom* (*P*: goals 17, 18, 20, 21, 29). The assignment of some of the goals to their respective categories may appear somewhat arbitrary. In all cases of doubt, assignments were based on empirical considerations involving partly the question of whether it was the delinquent or the control group which assigned the goal a higher average rank, and partly results of a brief study in which five psychologists were each shown the 20 goals and were asked to sort them into the four categories, placing five goals in each.

The sum of the ranks a subject assigned the goals of a given category was taken as a measure of the subjective importance of the category for him. The measures thus obtained will be designated as m, e, g, and p, respectively. In order to examine the relative importance to the subject of goals of the one category as compared with one or more of the others, four *composite goal measures* were formed: *Moral/Group* (the relative importance of moral goals as compared with goals of group loyalty, computed as $g-m$), *Moral/Pleasure* (the relative importance of moral goals as compared with goals of pleasure and freedom, computed as $p-m$), *Moral, Esteem* (the combined importance of moral goals and goals of self-esteem, computed as $m+e$), and *Moral, Esteem/*

Pleasure, Group [the relative importance of the law-abiding as compared with the non-law-abiding goals, computed as $(g+p)-(m+e)$].

On each of the composite goal measures the scores of the control subjects tended to be higher than those of the delinquents ($P<0.05$ for Moral/Group and for Moral/Pleasure; $0.05<P<0.10$ for Moral, Esteem and for Moral, Esteem/Pleasure, Group, Mann-Whitney U-test), suggesting the control subjects to give greater weight to moral goals.

Table 6.4 shows within-group correlations (r_s) of the four composite goal measures with Delinquency Proneness, SRMS, and Wrongness Evaluation, as well as of the latter three measures with one another. The results imply that giving greater weight to moral goals or to these and goals of self esteem is associated in both groups with a lesser tendency to engage in delinquent acts and, for the delinquent group, with a higher level of moral reasoning (Wrongness Evaluation) and moral development (SRMS). At the same time, for the control group a greater emphasis on moral goals appears to be associated not with a higher but with a lower level of moral development.

The latter finding seems to run counter to what Kohlberg's theory would lead one to expect, though the theory makes no specific prediction in this regard. If the finding is indeed a valid one, that and the more expected result obtained for the delinquent group could be interpreted in the following way:

1. Normal adolescents (controls) may tend, as moral development progresses and the perspective of moral reasoning broadens, to broaden their goal interests as well. This could yield an increase in the emphasis on goals outside the moral sphere and a net reduction in the importance attached to moral goals.
2. Since controls tend to live under more socially integrated conditions, goals of pleasure, group loyalty and freedom from adult control should be less incompatible with moral goals and goals of self-esteem for them than they are for delinquents – whose closest peer group contacts are often with others of delinquent bent, and for whom goals of group loyalty, pleasure, and freedom from adult control are more likely to be of delinquent character. This should mean that for controls moderate decreases in the weight attached to moral goals should be less likely to produce appreciable increases in delinquent behavior. This in turn should facilitate the occurrence of that which is described under point 1.
3. Delinquents, due to the strong goal incompatibility with which they are faced, should tend to be exposed to what in terms of *cognitive dissonance theory* (Festinger, 1957) would be a high degree of cognitive dissonance. Since an incompatibility should also exist between non-law-abiding goals and the "general moral view" (Colby, Kohlberg & Kauffman, in press) which any of the higher levels of moral development represent, delinquents should tend to be exposed as well to marked increases in cognitive dissonance as moral development level becomes higher. Such increases could be avoided if, concomitant with attainment of a higher level of moral

development, greater weight than before was given to law-abiding goals. In this view, avoidance of cognitive dissonance leads delinquents to a greater extent than controls to change their goal priorities in the direction of greater emphasis on law-abiding goals as moral development level increases. Although this interpretation is speculative, it suggests particular resources for improvement in their adjustment to society which delinquents may possess.

The correlations in Table 6.4 indicate no direct relationship between moral development level and delinquency proneness. The pattern of correlations as a whole, though not permitting definite conclusions regarding causal relations to be drawn, suggests nevertheless for the delinquents the possible existence of two causal chains, such that in the one chain moral development level affects goal priorities and these in turn affect delinquency proneness, and in the other moral development level affects the manner of evaluating the wrongness of various delinquent acts and this in turn affects the readiness to carry out such acts. Signs indicative of the final link in the latter chain are weak. At the same time, the protocol results of the Delinquent Behavior Interview do appear to illustrate for both groups various ways in which the readiness to carry out particular delinquent acts can be affected by the manner of evaluating the subjective rightness or wrongness of them in specific situational contexts.

Comparing in Table 6.3 for the various goals the overall ranks the respective group assigned them reveals a particularly large group difference for goal 5, "Have a good conscience," which the control group ranked much higher ($P < 0.05$, Mann-Whitney U-test). This seems to parallel the finding reported above of delinquents scoring low on Norm Conscience of the Sociomoral Reflection Measure. Taken together, the two results suggest that a weakly developed conscience may be a factor in the occurrence of serious delinquent problems.

One can note, in Table 6.3 again, that for the delinquents four of the five top ranked goals belong to category G (Group Loyalty) and only one to category M (Morality), whereas for the controls the opposite is the case. This suggests that delinquents strongly orient their goal priorities to the expectations and desires of the immediate peer group. Such a tendency can be considered instrumental in their gaining and retaining membership in delinquent gangs.

Although group differences in the overall ranks assigned many of the goals may appear rather small (cf. Table 6.3), the results suggest that even subtle differences in goal priorities – and thus presumably in values generally – can have an important bearing on delinquency and law abidingness.

Personal Constructs

Repertory grid test results were complete for all but two of the subjects, one of the delinquents appearing unable to carry out the task and another (whose data were nevertheless included) supplying only six rather than eight constructs. Analysis of the constructs themselves suggested these to cast light on subjects' sense of security or insecurity both in their relations with significant others and in their life situation generally, as well as on their possible preoccupation with matters of the lawfulness or lawlessness of the behavior they themselves or significant others displayed. For comparing the two groups in this respect, the following set of categories, into which each of the constructs could be classified, was formed:

1. *Social Interaction* (constructs reflecting the subject's view of how the person acts toward him or how he experiences interacting with the person)
2. *Reliability and Support* (constructs expressing the degree to which the subject experiences the other person's support or feels he can rely on him or her)
3. *Depth of Personal Contact* (constructs concerning the subject's more intimate relations with or his feelings toward the person)
4. *Abstract Assessments* (constructs involving characteristics the person is seen to possess, without apparent reference to matters of self-interest)
5. *Retrospection* (constructs concerning what occurred or was the case earlier, including those constructs of this type which might otherwise be placed in other categories)
6. *Realization of Interests* (constructs concerning the satisfaction of special or common interests through contact with the person)
7. *Lawbreaking or Lawfulness* (constructs referring to a person's tendency to break the law or to be law-abiding).

Constructs of categories 1, 2, and 3, dealing with having close, satisfying, and secure relations with significant others, were selected more frequently by the delinquents than the controls ($P<0.02$, Mann-Whitney U-test). When the analysis was widened, however, to include those constructs, otherwise of the same character, which because of their retrospective nature were classified in category 5, no significant group difference was found ($P>0.10$). Thus, the delinquents seem to place greater emphasis on qualitative aspects of their relations with significant others in a here-and-now perspective. This can be interpreted as reflecting greater insecurity on their part, insecurity which could well contribute to the formation of delinquent gangs.

There were nine of the delinquent subjects who included one or both of their parents among the five significant others selected for the grid test. For each of these subjects a measure was obtained of how close on the average to the negative end of the scale on the various constructs the one or the other of the two parents was placed; if both parents were included in the grid, the measure applied to that parent whose rating on the construct was more negative. Those delinquent subjects whose parent ratings of this sort were more negative tended to show a greater number of constructs of the Social Interaction category ($r_s = 0.82$, $n = 9$, $P<0.01$). This suggests that parental rejection or parental inadequacy can contribute heavily to delinquents' insecurity.

Constructs of category 7 (Lawbreaking and Lawfulness) were selected by seven of the delinquents ($n = 11$) but none of the controls ($P<0.01$, Fischer), scarcely surprising in view of the differing circumstances of the two groups. Seven of the 11 constructs of this category were of the *lawful* type. One of the constructs of the *unlawful* variety, "good at stealing," a construct suggestive of subcultural values conducive to the carrying out of delinquent acts, was named by two of the subjects.

Constructs of the three remaining categories, 4, 5, and 6, were chosen more frequently by the controls than the delinquents ($P<0.002$, Mann-Whitney U-test). These are categories which, for reasons that follow, were taken to reflect a sense of security on a personal or social level: (a) constructs of category 4 involve assessments of others made without apparent reference to self-interest; (b) constructs of category 5 refer to the past in an emotionally neutral or positive way; (c) constructs of category 6 concern primarily, not the relation to the other person as such, but the person's instrumentality in allowing one to enjoy certain pleasurable activities. In addition, constructs of category 4 seem to reflect what Selman (1980) terms a "third person perspective," which Kohlberg (Colby, Kohlberg & Kauffman, in press) deems a prerequisite to stage 3 of moral development. Altogether, the controls ($n = 12$) chose some 34 constructs of this category, the delinquents ($n = 11$) only 11.

Meaningful comparisons of the subjects regarding how they rated themselves in relation to others could not be obtained since direct or implicit references to the self (e.g., "listens to me") were contained in many of the constructs themselves, making self-ratings ambiguous.

To assess cognitive complexity, data concerning the ranks subjects assigned the five significant others and themselves on the various constructs were analyzed with the help of an Apple II-Plus computer, using the Focus program of the Planet package (Shaw, 1980, 1982). That program performs a two-way hierarchical cluster analysis of the individual subject's data, yielding clusters of elements and clusters of constructs, and also percentage measures of the degree to which the elements, constructs, or component clusters in any given cluster match. A *Cognitive Complexity* score was obtained by computing the mean of the subject's matching scores for the element clusters and construct clusters separately, determining the within-group rank of each and averaging the two ranks. This measure, which showed a close to zero correlation with moral development level (SRMS) in both groups, was found to correlate negatively with Delinquency Proneness in the delinquent group ($r_s = -0.65$, $n = 11$, $P<0.05$), indicating the less cognitively complex subjects to be more delinquent prone. In light of Bieri's (1955) finding of a positive relationship between cognitive complexity and accuracy in predicting the behavior of others, as well as the general assumption mentioned above that behavior tends to become more cognitively complex as development progresses, the result suggests delinquent youths with more serious problems of delinquency to possess a lower degree of sociocognitive development.

Final Comments

This result and others obtained for the delinquent group imply that even adolescents with serious delinquent problems may differ markedly in the degree and pattern of the difficulties they encounter in adjusting to society. This highlights the importance of individualizing efforts to help.

The results as a whole suggest a variety of factors – specifically, goal priorities, wrongness evaluation tendencies, cognitive complexity, moral development level, feelings of insecurity, parental rejection or inadequacy, and situational factors of various types – to be related, directly or indirectly, to the readiness to engage in delinquent acts. Moral development level appeared to be related to delinquency proneness in only an indirect way, via goal priorities and possibly wrongness evaluation tendencies in what could be viewed as parallel causal chains having moral development level as their point of origin.

Such causal chains, if present, would suggest the role of moral development level in connection with delinquency proneness to be a broad and general one. At the same time, since delinquent actions tend to reflect practical moral decisions, moral reasoning could be thought also to be related to delinquent behavior in a more direct and specific way. A distinction might be drawn between Kohlberg's approach to reasoning behavior, which focuses on the high degree of consistency of the individual's reasoning about moral questions, and that of research on individual decision-making (see Slovic, Fischhoff & Lichtenstein, 1977; Hogarth, 1980; for reviews), which has emphasized the decision-maker's inconsistencies in reasoning about decision alternatives. Kohlberg's empirical findings are based on measures he and his colleagues have developed through a process of gradual refinement (cf. Colby & Kohlberg, 1984) conducted within a theoretical framework parallel to that of Piaget's (1932). Kohlberg's system, though highly general, may be too far removed from the contradictions which decisions are likely to contain to illuminate adequately the reasoning processes by which specific delinquent acts come about. Procedures and measures better adapted to such a task seem called for. The use of the Delinquent Behavior Interview, the Act Evaluation Task, and the Goal Ranking Task, and of measures based on these, represents a modest attempt in this direction. Further work along such lines is needed.

Acknowledgment. The investigation was supported by a research grant to the first author by the National Council for Crime Prevention, Sweden.

References

Bannister, D., & Mair, J.M.M. (1968). *The evaluation of personal constructs.* New York: Academic.

Bieri, J. (1955). Cognitive complexity-simplicity and predictive behavior. *Journal of Abnormal and Social Psychology, 51*, 263–275.

Blasi, A. (1980). Bridging moral cognition and moral action: a critical review of the literature. *Psychological Bulletin, 88*, 1–45.

Brantingham, P. J., & Brantingham, P. L. (1981). *Environmental criminology*. London: Sage.

Burton, R. V. (1984). A paradox in theories and research in moral development. In W. M. Kurtines & J. L. Gewirtz (Eds.), *Morality, moral behavior, and moral development* (pp. 193–207). New York: Wiley.

Byrne, J. M., & Sampson, R. J. (Eds.). (1986). *The social ecology of crime*. New York: Springer-Verlag.

Carroll, J. S. (1978). A psychological approach to deterrence: the evaluation of crime opportunities. *Journal of Personality and Social Psychology, 36*, 1512–1520.

Cernovich, S. A. (1978). Value orientations and delinquency involvement. *Criminology: An Interdisciplinary Journal, 15*, 443–458.

Cohen, A. (1955). *Delinquent boys, the culture of the gang*. Chicago: The Free Press of Glencoe.

Colby, A., & Kohlberg, L. (1984). Invariant sequence and internal consistency in moral development stages. In W. M. Kurtines & J. L. Gewirtz (Eds.), *Morality, moral behavior, and moral development* (pp. 41–51). New York: Wiley.

Colby, A., & Kohlberg, L. (in press). *The measurement of moral judgment. Volume I. Theoretical foundations and research validation*. New York: Cambridge University Press.

Colby, A., Kohlberg, L., Candee, D., Gibbs, J., Hewer, A., & Speicher-Dubin, B. (in press a). *The measurement of moral judgment, Volume II. Standard issue scoring manuals*. New York: Cambridge University Press.

Colby, A., Kohlberg, L., & Kauffman, K. (in press b). Theoretical introduction to the measurement of moral judgment. In A. Colby, & L. Kohlberg (Eds.) *The measurement of moral judgment. Volume I. Theoretical foundations and research validation*. New York: Cambridge University Press.

Cornish, D. B., & Clarke, R. V. (Eds.). (1986). *The reasoning criminal. Rational choice perspectives on offending*. New York: Springer-Verlag.

Damon, W. (1984). Self understanding and moral development from childhood to adolescence. In W. M. Kurtines & J. L. Gewirtz (Eds.), *Morality, moral behavior, and moral development* (pp. 109–127). New York: Wiley.

Fransella, F., & Bannister, D. (1977). *A manual for repertory grid technique*. New York: Academic.

Gibbs, J. C., & Schnell, S. V. (1985). Moral development "versus" socialization. A critique. *American Psychologist, 40*, 1071–1080.

Gibbs, J. C., & Widaman, K. F. (1982). *Social intelligence. Measuring the development of sociomoral reflection*. Englewood Cliffs, NJ: Prentice Hall.

Hogarth, R. (1980). *Judgement and choice. The psychology of decision*. New York: Wiley.

Jennings, W. S., Kilkenny, R., & Kohlberg, L. (1983). Moral-development theory and practice for youthful and adult offenders. In W. S. Laufer, & J. M. Day (Eds.), *Personality theory, moral development & criminal behavior* (pp. 281–355).

Kaminski, H. (1984). Moral development in a historical perspective. In W. M. Kurtines, & J. L. Gewirtz (Eds.), *Morality, moral behavior, and moral development* (pp. 400–413).

Kaplan, H. B. (1978). Deviant behavior and self-enhancement in adolescence. *Journal of Youth and Adolescence, 7*, 253–277.

Kelly, G. A. (1955). *The psychology of personal constructs*. New York: Norton.

Kohlberg, L. (1969). Stage and sequence: the cognitive-developmental approach to socialization. In D.A. Goslin (Ed.), *Handbook of socialization theory and research* (pp. 347–480). Chicago: Rand McNally.
Kohlberg, L. (1976). Moral stages and moralization. In T. Lickona (Ed.), *Moral development and behavior: theory, research and social issues.* (pp. 31–53).
Kohlberg, L. (1981). *Essays on moral development. Volume 1. The philosophy of moral development.* San Francisco: Harper & Row.
Kohlberg, L. (1982). Foreword. In J.C. Gibbs & K.F. Widaman, *Social intelligence. Measuring the development of sociomoral reflection* (pp. ix-x). Englewood Cliffs, NJ: Prentice Hall.
Kohlberg, L. (1984). *Essays on moral development. Volume 2. The psychology of moral development.* San Francisco: Harper & Row.
Kohlberg, L., & Freundlich, D. (1973). Moral judgment in youthful offenders. In L. Kohlberg, & E. Turiel (Eds.), *Moralization, the cognitive developmental approach.* New York: Holt, Rinehart & Winston.
Kohlberg, L., Kauffman, K., Scharf, P., & Hickey, J. (1975). The just community approach to corrections: a theory. *Journal of Moral Education, 4*, 243–260.
Kohlberg, L., Levine, C., & Hewer, A. (1983). *Moral stages: a current formulation and a response to critics.* Basel: S. Karger.
Kurtines, W.M. (1984). Moral behavior as rule-governed behavior: a psychosocial role-theoretical approach to moral behavior and development. In W.M. Kurtines & J.L. Gewirtz (Eds.), *Morality, moral behavior, and moral development* (pp. 303–324). New York: Wiley.
Kurtines, W.M., & Gewirtz, J.L. (Eds.). (1984). *Morality, moral behavior, and moral development.* New York: Wiley.
Matza, D. (1964). *Delinquency and drift.* New York: Wiley.
Matza, D., & Sykes, G.M. (1961). Juvenile delinquency and subterranean values. *American Sociological Review, 22*, 664–670.
Miller, W. (1958). Lower class culture as a generating milieu of gang delinquency. *Journal of Social Issues, 14*, 5–19.
Peltzer, U. (1986). *Lawrence Kohlbergs Theorie des moralischen Urteilens. Eine wissenschaftstheoretische und forschungspraktische Analyse.* Opladen: Westdeutscher Verlag.
Piaget, J. (1932). *The moral judgment of the child.* London: Routledge & Kegan Paul.
Rest, J. (1979). *Development in judging moral issues.* Minneapolis: University of Minnesota Press.
Rest, J.R. (1984). The major components of morality. In W.M. Kurtines & J.L. Gewirtz (Eds.), *Morality, moral behavior, and moral development* (pp. 24–38). New York: Wiley.
Schroder, H.M., Driver, M.J., & Streufert, S. (1967). *Human information processing.* New York: Holt, Rinehart & Winston.
Selman, R.L. (1980). *The growth of interpersonal understanding.* New York: Academic.
Shaw, M.L.G. (1980). *On becoming a personal scientist. Interactive computer elicitation of personal models of the world.* New York: Academic.
Shaw, M.L.G. (1982). *Planet. Personal learning, analysis, negotiation & elicitation techniques.* Concord, Ontario, Canada: Centre for Person-Computer Studies.
Sheley, J.F., & Bailey, K.D. (1985). New directions in anti-theft policy: reductions in stolen goods buyers. *Journal of Criminal Justice, 13*, 399–415.
Slovic, P., Fischhoff, B., & Lichtenstein, S. (1977). Behavioral decision theory. *Annual Review of Psychology, 28*, 1–39.
Snarey, J.R. (1985). Cross-cultural universality of social-moral development. A critical review of Kohlbergian research. *Psychological Bulletin, 97*, 202–232, 411.

Staub, E. (1984). Steps toward a comprehensive theory of moral conduct: goal orientation, social behavior, kindness, and cruelty. In W. M. Kurtines & J. L. Gewirtz (Eds.), *Morality, moral behavior, and moral development* (pp. 241–260).
Sykes, G. A., & Matza, D. (1975). Techniques of neutralization: a theory of delinquency. *American Sociological Review, 16*, 664–670.
Thrasher, F. (1927). *The gang.* Chicago: University of Chicago Press, 1927.

Appendix

Brief summary of remarks of the delinquent (D) and control (C) subjects in the Delinquent Behavior Interview when asked under what conditions they could imagine carrying out the acts to which they responded affirmatively. Note that the acts are numbered as in Table 1 (complete texts of the items are presented there). Various statements or types of statement, as well as the numbers of subjects in the respective groups ($n = 12$ for each group) who made such statements, are italicized. Details concerning statements some of the categories include are shown in parentheses; *d* and *c* denote the group membership of certain of the subjects.

1. Street: *practical reasons: 7 D, 11 C* (in a hurry; no cars; not much traffic; not dangerous; no police; no one looking); *under all conditions: 4 D.*
2. Classes: *lack of interest: 9 D, 9 C* (dull classes; don't feel like going to school; tired; tired of school; school is dull; depends on how I feel; prefer being elsewhere; want to do something I've decided on myself: *c*; if others can, so can I: *c*); *under all conditions: 3 D.*
3. Train: *practical reasons: 6 D, 7 C* (lack of money; necessary; forced to; no alternative; no one checking; important; escaped from reform school: *d*; only a short stretch: *c*); *under all conditions: 3 D.*
4. Magazine: *desire to have it: 6 D, 6 C* (want it; need something to read; hadn't read it before; didn't finish reading it there; interesting; avoid buying it: *d*; even if I had the money: *d*; "I figure it's such a small thing and taking it doesn't do much harm, even if I'm against it in principle": *c*); *under all conditions: 1 D*; *(no specification): 1 C.*
5. Violence: *personal conflicts: 5 D, 4 C* (objectionable or aggressive behavior of the other; "if I'm in the right, e.g. ... so he'd take back things I could be jailed for": *d*; to get my possessions back: *c*; when someone tries to get ahead in line: *c*).
6. Smash: *being drunk: 3 D, 1 C; nothing better to do: 1 D, 1 C; angry: 1 C.*
7. Home: *really need money: 1 D, 1 C; parents broke their promise: 1 D; "all of them – Dad, Mother and her boyfriend – should be punished": 1 D; just a small amount: 1 C.*
8. Building: *theft 8 D* (need money; to steal; something there I want; couldn't get money from welfare); *place to sleep: 2 D; under all conditions: 1D; "if there's something there that I can use that no one wants": 1 C; enter a sports stadium: 1 C; fun: 1 C, 1 d; (no specification or unclear): 2 C.*

9. Wallet: *under all conditions: 5 D, 1 C; not if I know the person: 4 D; monetary considerations: 2 D, 3 C* (needing money: 2 *d*; only money, not documents: *c*; if there's a lot of money in it: *c*; "if it's a grown-up's wallet with a lot of money in it... not if it's the wallet of a boy": *c*).
10. Threaten: *threats or aggressive or objectionable behavior by the other: 5 D, 4 C; anger or desire for revenge: 4 D; getting someone to respect you: 1 D; more for fun: 1 C.*
11. Cashier: *not if I know the person: 6 D; under all conditions: 2 D, 1 C; "I'd never say no – they're the ones to blame": 1 D; "it's the cashier's responsibility; stores do well anyway and make big profits": 1 C; "if I need the money and the amount is small: 1 C; (no specification): 2 C.*
12. Bike: *emergency, real need: 2 C; other needs or situational pressures: 7 D, 1 C* (in a hurry; need to get somewhere; a long way to walk; bad conditions; tired; no bus; no telephone; lack of money; for ease of getting places); *under all conditions: 2 D.*
13. Stolen: *if it's not of great value: 1 C; other cost and value aspects: 4 D* (valuable and cheap, cheap, depends on what it is); *under all conditions: 1 D; if the person selling it needs money: 1 D; not if I know the victim: 1 D; if the seller didn't steal it: 1 C; if no one can check that it's stolen: 1 C; (no specification): 1 C.*
14. Store: *needing or wanting something, lack of money to pay: 4 D, 1 C; under all conditions: 3 D* ("when I see something I want, even if I have the money"); *craving for food or sweets: 2 C.*
15 Destroy: *anger, revenge: 2 D, 1 C; for example, a car or something of that sort: 1 D.*
16. Car: *needs, desires, enjoyment: 9 D* ("in a hurry – one car more or less makes no difference"; "if it's tremendously important and I'm in a tremendous hurry"; "so as to steal something"; fun; excitement; escaped from reform school; needing to get somewhere or to get around in; needing money); *under all conditions: 1 D.*
17. Break in: *needing or wanting money or things: 9 D* ("alcohol or drugs there or things I want"; "no money and no help from social welfare"); *under all conditions: 1 D.*
18. Restaurant: *hungry, no money: 4 D; if I feel like it: 1 D; "even if I had the money I'd do it – save the money": 1 D.*
19. Practical joke: *revenge, not liking someone: 1 D; failed to see the dangers: 1 D; "if the joke is tremendously funny": 1 D; "take the risk – if I wanted to have fun I'd do it": 1 D; under all conditions: 1 D.*
20. Cloakroom: *monetary considerations: 5 D* (needing money; escaped from reform school; any money that I found; if it's a large amount).

7
Crime Specialisation, Crime Displacement and Rational Choice Theory

DEREK B. CORNISH and RONALD V. CLARKE

Introduction

Criminological explanation has an important, if not always well recognised, role to play in the construction of effective crime control policies. In this context, the assumption behind many traditional accounts, that crime is the expression of the offender's personality and attitudes, has been particularly influential. Indeed, it reflects a bias towards dispositional thinking which appears as endemic to theorising about crime as it is to theorising about human behavior in general (Ross, 1977). Just as such dispositional assumptions once fuelled the rehabilitative ideal, now in consequence of its apparent failure they underpin the increasing advocacy of "social" crime prevention – that is, those measures which attempt to ameliorate the social, educational, economic and community disadvantages thought to be responsible for the creation of criminal attitudes and values (Clarke & Cornish, 1983).

Dispositional assumptions also continue to provide a ready source of opposition to "situational" preventive measures which seek to increase the risks and difficulty of offending (Clarke, 1983). This opposition to situational prevention takes the form of two related theoretical criticisms. The first concerns the supposed inevitability of crime displacement – the idea that, where barriers are raised to the commission of a particular criminal act, crime will be displaced to some other place, time, target or type of offence (Reppetto, 1976). The second objection, from the same "dispositional" stable, relates to the fact that the offender is usually seen as a generalist, ready to engage more or less indiscriminately in a variety of criminal acts. The concept of the offender as generalist thus reinforces that of crime displacement, and together these undermine the attractiveness of situational approaches to the explanation and control of crime. After all, there would be little point in going to the trouble and expense of introducing situational measures if all they succeeded in doing was to shift crime around.

We have suggested elsewhere that such objections to situational crime prevention lose much of their force where the offender is seen not as driven by internal forces over which he or she has little control, but as choosing to commit crimes in order to meet commonplace needs for such things as money, sex and excitement (Cornish & Clarke, 1986a). Within such a "rational choice" perspective (cf. Clarke & Cornish, 1985; Cornish & Clarke, 1986b), the decision-making processes in question will not necessarily be sophisticated, or be based upon adequate or accurate information: the offender characteristically displays limited rather than normative rationality. The nature of the decision task (for example, whether to become involved in, continue, or desist from a particular form of criminal activity or, once the decision to commit has been made, the problems of target selection) will also have an important bearing upon these processes. Moreover, a further crucial conceptual distinction is drawn between these decision tasks: decisions concerning involvement and cessation are differentiated from "criminal event" decisions – those concerned with the tactics of carrying out particular criminal acts. This distinction is held to have important implications for crime control, since it both helps to identify potentially fruitful points for intervention and offers a clear rationale for the development of situational as well as "social" crime prevention measures. Lastly, the rational choice perspective is crime-specific in its orientation; hence, involvement and event models of criminal decision-making are always developed in relation to particular types of crime. This stems from the belief that crimes differ in the needs they serve and in the demands they make of the potential offender. It follows from this view that only where crimes serve the same needs at similar cost will displacement and generalisation of offending be likely outcomes.

The justification for this crime-specific form of analysis is developed further in the present chapter by making use of the concept of the "choice-structuring properties" of offences – that is, the particular constellation of opportunities, costs and benefits offered by specific crimes. The potential usefulness of this concept will be illustrated with reference to the analysis of different forms of gambling and suicide, both of which behaviors, like crime, are often treated as undifferentiated phenomena. First, however, since the strength of the case against situational crime prevention and, more generally, the rational choice perspective depends upon the quality of the empirical data concerning displacement and generalisation, it is necessary to review this evidence briefly.

Displacement and Generalisation: The Empirical Evidence

In general, the empirical evidence relating to displacement appears consistent with the rational choice perspective. Displacement is by no means inevitable. Instead, it seems only to occur in certain circumstances, especially those in which an alternative offence apparently serving the same need can be committed without too much additional risk or effort. A number of examples supporting this proposition have been discussed elsewhere (Cornish & Clarke,

1986a). Perhaps the clearest example, however, concerns the introduction of steering-column locks in Great Britain and West Germany. When these were introduced to all new cars in Great Britain in 1971, "joy-riders" turned their attentions instead to older, unprotected cars, and there was no overall decline in vehicle theft. In West Germany, however, steering-column locks were simultaneously introduced in 1966 to new and old cars alike. This resulted in a massive decline in all car thefts, presumably because joy-riders would have had to have gone to much greater lengths to remove a car (Mayhew, Clarke, Sturman, & Hough, 1976).

As for the controversy over whether offenders are specialists or generalists, the available evidence seems at first sight somewhat less supportive of the rational choice perspective. Indeed, it might be argued that the rational choice perspective itself predicts too much specialisation. The emphasis upon the crime-specific nature not only of the decisions surrounding the particular criminal event (an elaboration, after all, of the situational approach) but also of those surrounding initial involvement, continuing involvement and desistance, is often misleadingly seen to entail some degree of crime specialisation on the part of the offender. This, however, is to mistake the function of such decision models: to say that the models are offence-specific is *not* to say that the offenders in question commit only these offences. Nor does it suggest that their involvement is necessarily always prolonged, since the involvement models can account equally well for intermittent or "one-off" offending. The fact that tactical decision-making will be crime-specific hardly needs labouring. But the rational choice perspective also claims that the study of involvement decisions is best approached from a crime-specific standpoint. This is because the patterns of opportunities, rewards and costs offered by different crimes are themselves so various that to ignore these differences is to reduce severely the ability of crime prevention policy to target its efforts accurately[1].

The emphasis upon the rationality of offending implicit in this perspective does, however, suggest that so long as stability exists in the opportunities, costs and benefits available to the offender, these will tend to support specialisation in particular forms of crime. The alternative view – that, since criminal histories frequently show evidence of generalisation, offenders are prone, presumably because of their "criminal dispositions", to engage indiscriminately (and effectively, " irrationally") in a variety of criminal acts – is therefore at odds with the rational choice approach. Evidence that offenders are generalists can then be used to predict or explain the occurrence of crime displacement, and the two notions together provide critics of the situational approach with apparently powerful arguments against its proposals.

---

[1] Even involvement in a range of crimes, commonly regarded as evidence of a criminal disposition, would on this analysis occur as the result of separable learning histories and motivations, although in practice it may be difficult – because of the context within which the crimes occur (community, school, peer group or family) – to trace and isolate their origins.

Leaving aside for the moment the soundness of the conclusions so drawn, the empirical evidence as to whether offenders are generalists or specialists is itself far from clear-cut. The conventional view, recently stated by Klein (1984) on the basis of his survey of existing studies, is that offenders, particularly juveniles, are crime-generalists who choose their offences "cafeteria-style" from a wide menu of options[2]. However, existing studies of the generalisation-specialisation issue are plagued by inadequacies in the data bases and statistical analyses used, defects which Klein readily acknowledges. Reliance upon official data may fail to uncover the true frequency or nature of offending, such as the extent of specialisation in less readily detected though common property offences. Lack of satisfactory information about the actual date of the offence (Lab, 1984) may conceal short-run episodes of specialisation. Defects in the design of self-report studies – the use of overlong recall time-scales, the related failure to date offences accurately (if at all) within these time-scales, or the use of response sets which truncate the true frequency distribution for offences (cf. Elliott & Ageton, 1980) – can often hinder efforts to secure reliable information about sequences or clusters of offences. More generally, the overloading of studies with first or infrequent offenders, students or juveniles (and the failure to explore the possibility of crime specialisation within population subgroups, cf. Elliott & Ageton, 1980; Klein, 1984) can by definition be expected to reduce the likelihood of finding evidence of specialisation.

Turning to methods of statistical analysis, correlational techniques fail properly to utilise what data on offence sequencing there is, while factor-analytic methods have the additional drawback of encouraging dispositional explanations of whatever patterns or lack of patterns they uncover. By contrast, research which employs stochastic techniques to examine offence-to-offence transitions – whether between an offence and its immediate predecessor or, less restrictively, predecessors (Lab, 1984) – seems a more promising approach. Although early studies using these methods found evidence of considerable crime switching by offenders (cf. Kempf, 1986), Kempf's own work, based on an analysis of the 1958 Philadelphia cohort, has found rather more evidence of specialisation than hitherto.

The foregoing discussion implies that so-called evidence of generalisation may often be an artifact of the methodological inadequacies of existing studies. This is not, however, to suggest that specialisation as traditionally understood is the norm in criminal activity. It is true that ethnographic studies have on occasion supplied relevant evidence of specialisation for both adult and juvenile populations. The very titles of some of the better known of these (*The Fence; The Booster and the Snitch; The Jack-Roller*) suggest considerable specialisation, but clearly the notion that offenders make their "careers" in particular forms of crime is a questionable one. Instead, a more general

[2] Klein's review also takes in studies of escalation in crime seriousness. Since the latter do not directly address the issue of offence specialisation, however, their inclusion somewhat exaggerates the weight of evidence favouring generalisation.

message of such studies is that it is only possible to explain the particular forms of crime committed by the offenders under study through an analysis of their everyday lives and needs. This view suggests, as does a rational choice perspective, that it might be more fruitful to view specialisation or generalisation in terms of the offender's responsiveness to stability and change in the opportunities, costs and benefits associated with particular forms of offending.

If this is the case, such specialisation as there is will probably be of limited duration, and may be concealed within a matrix of disparate offences. Such short sequences – in the form of "parallel specialisation" (where specialisation in one type of offence is occurring at the same time as other offences or offence sequences are being committed) or the form of "serial specialisation" (where short sequences of one type of offending are followed by sequences of another) – may well remain concealed until adequate data sets are properly analysed. Lastly, it seems unduly restricting to limit the notion of specialisation to crimes of identical nature. Tremblay (1986) points out that credit card bank frauds are functionally related to a range of prior offences such as wallet theft and false bank account opening. In real life, the satisfactory execution of certain offences may involve the commission of different, intermediate ones (commercial robbery may involve the theft of vehicles and the offer or use of violence, for example), although these may appear in the offender's record as isolated crimes. Similarly, the hunt for specialised patterns of offending should also be extended to investigating the restricted offence repertoires claimed to be characteristic of particular subgroups of offenders (cf. Chaiken & Chaiken, 1984).

The idea that more detailed analyses might reveal sporadic patterns of specialisation in one or a limited number of offences over comparatively brief periods of time is not offered as a way of either saving the concept of specialisation or subverting it. Neither specialisation nor its opposites (generalisation, cafeteria-style offending or versatility) seem to the present authors to be theoretically fruitful ways in which to conceptualise consistency and variability in criminal behavior: they carry with them too many misleading connotations. The debate concerning stability and change in patterns of offending has often been ill-served by the language in which it has been conducted. Specialisation and generalisation are terms which both paradoxically tend to appeal to dispositional thinking, the former to specific and the latter to general criminal dispositions. Where such assumptions are being made, and especially when they go unrecognised, they draw attention away from the rationality of offending and its responsiveness to costs, benefits and opportunities.

The Concept of Choice-Structuring Properties

The discussion so far has suggested that explanations of phenomena such as displacement, specialisation and generalisation are best pursued by recasting the problem as the search to identify the circumstances under which consistency or variability of offending occurs. On this analysis, patterns of offending are functions of the opportunities, rewards and costs perceived by the offender during the course of criminal decision-making to be operating in relation to particular types of crime.

In the remainder of this chapter we wish to develop this analysis further by making use of the concept of "choice-structuring properties" – those single or multiple features of particular criminal activities which make them differentially available and attractive to certain individuals at certain times. Our argument will proceed by analogy. We will seek to show that it is the unique combination of choice-structuring properties exhibited by different forms of gambling (off-course betting, roulette and lotteries, for example) and different methods of suicide (hanging, gassing and shooting, etc.) which lead to their selection by particular subgroups. Closer attention to these properties, it will be argued, can help to establish the likely limits of displacement in relation to both groups of activities traditionally regarded as pathologically motivated (such as suicide), and those (such as gambling and crime) looked on as more commonplace.

Gambling

Moral censure of gambling, concern about its social and economic consequences, and clinical data on "compulsive" gamblers have all served to enhance the attractiveness of explanations which, on the one hand, blur distinctions amongst the different forms of gambling and, on the other, ascribe involvement to pathological motivation. As with criminal behavior, a preoccupation with the allegedly deviant nature of the activity has tended to lead to the neglect of important situational determinants, and this tendency is enhanced where, as in the case of heavy gambling, the activity is perceived as minority behavior within a low socio-economic group.

In a review of the research on gambling, one of the present authors (Cornish, 1978) concluded that there was in fact little or no evidence favouring pathological explanations of gambling, even at "excessive" levels of involvement. Instead, study of gambling motivation suggested that, while the behavior did not conform to normative models of economic rationality, much gambling could be explained as financially motivated once due attention was given to the individual's financial requirements, the necessarily bounded rationality of the gambler's information-processing and decision-making processes, and the limited nature of the available information. Incorrect understandings of probability theory, the inappropriate use of other simplifying judgmental heuristics, and overestimation of the role of skills could all be expected to make gambling behavior deviate from a rational economic model, especially since such perceptions and cognitions were also actively manipulated by gambling operators. A more careful consideration of the varieties of gambling behavior – especially as portrayed by ethnographic accounts – also suggested that a range of non-financial motives were important reasons for gambling.

As a result of this review of the research, a reinterpretation of the data on gambling behavior was attempted which, like the rational choice perspective on crime discussed above, it was hoped would give due credence to what was known about the activity and, in particular, about its situational determinants. First, it was asserted that gambling was "reasonable", that is, not pathological behaviour. Second, it was considered unhelpful to view gambling as a homogeneous activity. Given the manifold motivations to which its various forms appealed and the ways in which these activities were structured in order to induce participation, it was felt that explanations of gambling behavior should always be couched in relation to particular forms of gambling. Thirdly, as in the case of crime, it seemed that the role of situational factors in determining gambling behavior would be best elucidated were distinctions between involvement and event decisions to be made.

For the purposes of this discussion the original distinction between the "ecologic opportunities" provided for the various forms of gambling and their inherent features (or "structural characteristics") has not been retained. Instead, these are merged, in Table 7.1, to form a list of the main "choice-structuring properties" of gambling – those characteristics which jointly determine the unique amalgam of opportunities, costs and benefits offered by particular gambling activities.

Choice-structuring properties are often related to each other (for example, 3 and 4), and particular forms of gambling may combine numbers of these properties in mutually enhancing ways. The majority of choice-structuring properties in the list are cast in the form of bipolar dimensions. A shorter list,

TABLE 7.1. Choice structuring properties of forms of gambling

1. Availability (number and location of betting shops, gaming clubs, bingo halls, etc.).
2. Awareness of type of gambling activity (e.g. open vs. restricted access; advertising)
3. Frequency of events for staking (high – fruit-machines; low – lotteries)
4. Elapsed time before payment (short – roulette; long – lotteries)
5. Amount staked per play (high – some gaming; low – fruit-machines)
6. Range of odds and stakes (wide – e.g. betting)
7. Probability of winning an individual bet (high – "odds on" bets; low – lotteries)
8. Payout ratio (high – lotteries)
9. Disruption of financial value-system ("chips" in gaming clubs; provision of credit)
10. Degree of personal participation (high – craps, poker; low – lotteries)
11. Skills needed or perceived (handicapping; memory for cards or numbers)
12. Role of luck (e.g. dreambooks in "numbers")
13. Courage or nerves required (bankers' games; cards)
14. Related to other attractions or activities (football; horses; fast living; food and drink)
15. Masculine/feminine (e.g. poker versus bingo)
16. Social cachet (gaming club versus betting shop)

based on the suggestions of Weinstein and Deitch (1974), was originally drawn up as a way of conceptualising the relationship between form of gambling and likelihood of excessive involvement. Forms which promoted continuous gambling ("high" on 1, 2, 3, 4), offered a wide range of odds and stakes (6) and provided "action" (e.g. "high" on 10, 11, 13, 14) were thought particularly likely to encourage the punter to over-extend himself or herself and hence to require careful regulation. Moreover, forms of gambling with very similar dimensional "profiles" seemed likely to have similar appeal, and it was thought that generalisation or displacement would be more likely to occur in relation to these.

The emphasis on gambling as rational behavior, on the importance of choice-structuring properties of different forms of gambling, and on the need to draw distinctions between involvement and event decisions was considered to have important implications for the regulation of gambling. Given the many reasons for initial involvement in gambling and, hence, the difficulty of designing cost-effective social prevention policies, the situational approach implied by this analysis seemed likely to be the most fruitful one. Knowledge of the choice-structuring properties of different forms of gambling and how these relate to people's perceptions of these activities as satisfying certain of their needs for excitement, money etc., suggests a means of controlling excessive gambling through regulation of the opportunities, rewards and costs involved.

It also has the merit of conforming to many existing conceptions about the important situational determinants of gambling. Regulatory bodies such as the British Gaming Board, and gambling operators, appear to have a considerable understanding of the choice-structuring properties inherent in various forms of gambling and of their likely relationship to intensity of involvement. Much attention is therefore paid by both sides to the manipulation of opportunities, costs and benefits, whether in the hopes of increasing or decreasing rates of participation in relation to particular forms of gambling or for the purposes of encouraging or discouraging generalisation and displacement between similar forms.

Suicide

Beginning with Durkheim (1897/1952), typologies of suicide have paid far more attention to the presumed motivational states of the individuals concerned than to the nature of the act itself. In particular, theorists have paid scant attention to methods of death, on the assumption that a genuinely suicidal individual will always find a method and, hence, that different methods are interchangeable. Local or national variations in preferred methods are seen merely to reflect differential availability or different traditions in relation to their use. Thus, for example, Durkheim explained the comparative infrequency of suicides by hanging in England on the grounds that this was regarded as a dishonourable form of death associated with the execution of traitors and criminals. More recently, the high rate of gun suicides in the United States (particularly in the South) has been linked to the widespread ownership of firearms and the associated development of "gun cultures" (Farmer & Rohde, 1980; Lester, 1984).

Given the lack of importance attached to method, it might be expected that the concept of "choice-structuring properties" would be of less explanatory value for suicide than for gambling, where it seems much clearer that these properties play a role in causation. However, some recent evidence of the important part played by method in the aetiology of suicide has been provided by the unexpected 35% decline of suicides in England and Wales between 1963 and 1975 (Clarke & Mayhew, 1988; Kreitman, 1976; Kreitman & Platt, 1984). Though the reasons for this fall have been much disputed, it is now widely thought to have been the result of the removal of carbon monoxide from the public gas supply. This came about, first, through the adoption of new manufacturing processes for so-called town gas and, later, through the wholesale replacement (between 1968 and 1977) of town gas by natural gas from the North Sea. People were therefore no longer able to use a method of suicide which had once accounted for about half of all such deaths in the country.

The fact that, deprived of gas, few potential suicides killed themselves in some other way is perhaps explained by the very real advantages of domestic gas as a means of death: it was not only highly lethal but also painless, clean, easy and required relatively little courage or preparation. Unable to identify an equally acceptable alternative, most of the affected individuals seem to have abandoned the idea or, perhaps, tried but failed to kill themselves with some less lethal method. More generally, this suggests that the translation into effective action of what are frequently ambivalent or transitory suicidal feelings will importantly depend on the nature of the opportunities for suicide available to the individual concerned. Some people may simply be unable to contemplate killing themselves in one way while being quite prepared to use another. For example, women seem to prefer "non-violent" methods that do not disfigure and do not involve loss of blood (Marks, 1977).

Rather than ignoring method, therefore, it may be more profitable to treat suicide as a collection of separate but related behaviors distinguished by the methods and subgroups involved. The degree of "displacement" between different methods may be much less than is commonly thought. There may even be "specialists" in less lethal methods such as wrist-slashing or overdosing. Moreover, national and local variations in methods resulting from differential opportunities for suicide may just as much reflect differences in the *incidence* of the behavior as in its forms. In these respects, therefore, suicide may have much in common with gambling and with crime. It may also be the case that research into the choice-structuring properties of different methods of suicide and people's attitudes to these may have important preventive implications.

There is little relevant research to draw upon, but speculation suggests a list of possible choice-structuring properties of different methods of suicide (such as poisoning, cutting, suffocation and hanging, drowning, electrocution,

TABLE 7.2. Choice structuring properties of methods of suicide

1. Availability of method (own a car?)
2. Awareness of the method (e.g. knowledge about car exhaust gases)
3. Technical skills needed (hanging; gassing)
4. Planning necessary (buy a gun; save-up drugs)
5. Likely pain (cutting wrists)
6. "Courage" needed (high building; train)
7. Consequences of failure (permanent disability; publicity)
8. Disfigurement after death (hanging vs. overdose)
9. Danger/inconvenience to others (car crash; subway leap)
10. Messy/bloody (wrist-cutting)
11. Discovery of body (by loved ones or strangers)
12. "Contamination of nest" (i.e. avoid home)
13. Concealed death – through shame; for insurance (autocrash; drowning; overdose)
14. Certainty of death (perceived/actual)
15. Time taken to die when conscious (poisons, wrist-cutting)
16. Scope for second thoughts (swim back to shore; turn off gas)
17. Chances of intervention ("fate"; estranged lover)
18. Symbolism (cleansing by fire; harakiri; hanging dishonourable)
19. Masculine/feminine (e.g. guns)
20. Dramatic impact (lovers leap vs. overdose)

shooting and jumping). In Table 7.2 an illustrative list of 20 such properties is given. The relative importance of these is unknown and there may be others more significant that have been omitted. Some of the properties are related either in practice or conceptually: in practice, for example, most bloody methods may need courage; and conceptually, the properties might be grouped in terms of the "opportunities" (1–4 in the list), "costs" (5–13) and "benefits" (14–20) associated with the various methods. Some of the costs and benefits have both positive and negative valences depending upon the motivation of the individual concerned. Thus, one individual may wish to spare relatives the shock of discovering the body, whereas another may deliberately inflict this upon them. Again, those half hoping to be saved might avoid methods chosen by those more determined to die[3].

However provisional, the list should help to clarify the important role which may be played by the choice-structuring properties of different forms of suicide. Moreover, any theory of suicide which includes the choice-structuring properties of different methods will necessarily have to give a central position to the mental processes that may underlie and sustain each act of suicide.

[3] The risks, or potential costs, associated with a particular form of gambling are also intimately linked to its benefits and, indeed, form part of its characteristic attraction. This would make the clustering of such properties in terms of opportunities, costs and benefits a rather more tentative exercise.

These include the ways in which an individual predicament comes to be defined as intolerable, the accompanying feelings of depression and hopelessness, the manner in which solutions are sought and evaluated, how the idea of suicide first comes to be entertained, and how plans are made and put into effect. The definition of life as no longer worth living, the decision to end it, and the choice of a method may be interactive rather than sequential. It is not unlikely, for example, that those who feel suicide is prohibited to them for reasons of family or religion may soon put it out of their minds and may redefine their situation or find other solutions. Those with no such prohibitions may reinforce the idea of suicide with thoughts about others who have killed themselves and may only abandon the idea when unable to identify a practicable or acceptable method. Those who do identify such a method may go on to develop realistic plans, including a detailed scenario of the place and the time of their deaths. This mental preparation may also reinforce feelings of hoplessness and the belief that there is "no way out".

While elements of such a theory are to be found scattered in the literature, they might usefully be integrated under the same kind of rational choice or decision perspective that the present authors have developed in respect of crime. Though the main focus of theoretical analysis would be the feelings and thought processes underlying the suicide decision, other important components of the theory would concern the motivational and situational contexts of suicide. The former may not be especially problematic since almost any of the misfortunes and miseries of the human condition seem capable of providing the motivation. The latter will include features of daily life that might impede or facilitate suicide – such as the availability of an acceptable means of death.

Such a view of suicide has profound implications for prevention. Some of these relate to crisis intervention programmes insofar as these are able to reach individuals in temporary though lethal despair, rather than less profoundly unhappy young women (Lester, 1986). More important, perhaps, are the implications for what Seiden (1977) calls the "public health/public policy" approach to prevention. This involves the reduction of opportunities for suicide through stiffer gun control laws, elimination of carbon monoxide from public gas supplies and from car exhausts, barriers or reduced public access at notorious jump-sites, restrictions on the sale of poisonous substances, and a range of measures designed to prevent overdosing, including tighter prescribing rules and the development of safer alternative drugs.

Implications for Crime Control

Different as the choice-structuring properties are for forms of gambling and methods of suicide, both lists reflect the detailed operation in practice of the three broad classes of situational variables – opportunities, costs and benefits

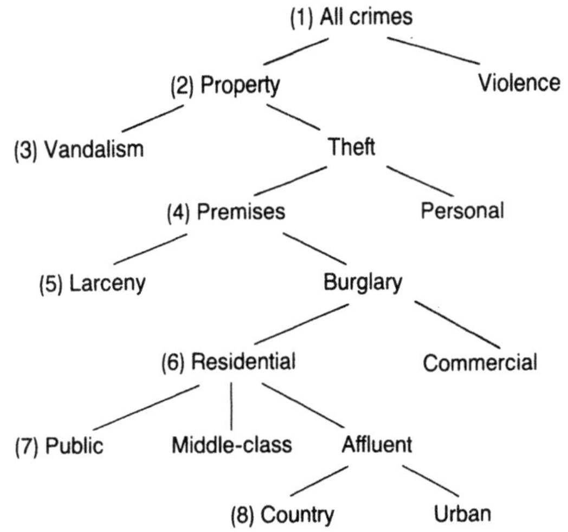

FIGURE 7.1. Levels of specificity

– to which the rational choice perspective draws attention. In the cases of gambling and suicide, the development of such lists of choice-structuring properties seems likely both to enhance the explanatory power of rational choice analyses and to assist the development of more adequate prevention and control policies. It is therefore likely that for crimes, too, the further step of translating the opportunities, costs and benefits associated with particular offences into the relevant choice-structuring properties will enable situational crime prevention objectives to be more fully realised. As in the cases of suicide and gambling, for example, the establishment of choice-structuring properties in respect of particular offences would clarify the uniqueness of their appeals and, hence, enable estimations about the likelihood of displacement to be made with more certainty[4].

Before this can be done, however, a number of practical and theoretical problems will have to be solved. For a start, unlike the case for suicide and gambling, it will be unhelpful to construct a list of choice-structuring properties for crime in general. "Crime", after all, subsumes a much more heterogenous collection of behaviors serving a wider variety of needs. (This, indeed, is why gambling and suicide were chosen to illustrate our discussion.) Instead, it may be necessary to construct such lists for subcategories of crime, and the problem then becomes one of selecting an appropriate level of specificity. The nature of this difficulty may be clarified by reference of Figure 7.1.

A useful rule-of-thumb might be to pursue the making of distinctions between types of crime only as far as practical crime prevention considerations require. Determining the appropriate level, then, is always likely to be a

[4] Lists of choice-structuring properties in respect of theft involving cash and of illegal substance abuse have recently been developed by the present authors (Cornish & Clarke, 1987).

pragmatic business, influenced primarily by considerations of public concern, harm and cost. Detailed empirical studies of particular offences will also help, by suggesting the circumstances under which finer distinctions (for example, between types of residential burglary: cf. Clarke & Cornish, 1985; or between forms of child abuse) might have implications for crime prevention policy. Distinctions are particularly likely to be useful where it becomes clear that such subcategories appeal to different motivations, or where the offences appear to be the work of different offender subgroups.

Apart from these problems, the main barrier at present to the drawing-up of lists of choice-structuring properties in relation to particular crimes is the lack of empirical data: more information is required about why offenders select particular offences to commit. Future research will need to pay attention to two related aspects of this question. On the one hand, in order to find out more about opportunity dimensions, ecological studies of the distribution of crimes are required. On the other hand, it is also vital to find out more about offenders' perceptions of opportunities and of costs and benefits (the motivational dimensions), and for this purpose more ethnographic and interview research is needed. Such studies will help to determine how these perceptions develop, the circumstances under which incorrect perceptions may occur, and the extent to which initial perceptions about opportunities, costs and benefits may alter as the result of experience or peer-group influences.

Tremblay's (1986) study of credit card bank frauds in Canada illuminates these and other issues raised in this chapter. His findings suggest, for example:

1. That different forms of crime may be functionally related through the strategic part they play in a larger criminal enterprise (wallet theft, false bank account opening and credit card bank fraud)
2. That offender subgroups (such as "checkmen") may specialise in broad, though related, categories of offences (quantity credit and cheque frauds)
3. That where the choice-structuring properties of familiar and novel forms of crime are similar (credit card bank fraud and previous cheque and credit card frauds), identification of novel criminal opportunities will be swift, and displacement more likely
4. That participation by offenders in criminal knowledge networks will enhance perceptions of such opportunities, costs and benefits
5. That diffusion of such knowledge about opportunities via the media may recruit a wider public of potential offenders (although this was not the case in Tremblay's study)
6. That the outcome may be the development of specialised crime waves of limited duration
7. That the time span of these episodes will be regulated by the constantly changing choice-structuring properties of a particular form of crime (opportunities and rewards for credit card bank fraud expanded as the result of changes in commercial practice; opportunities contracted and risks and effort increased as a function of subsequent criminal activity)

8. That the blooming and fading of such temporary specialisations may be a characteristic feature of involvement within certain broad categories of crime
9. Lastly, that even where everything (knowledge; familiarity; functional equivalence between novel and existing offences) apparently favours displacement, it is not thereby rendered inevitable (only 10% of "checkmen" apparently switched crimes).

Knowledge of the actual and perceived choice-structuring properties of different forms of crime – an elaboration of the rational choice perspective's emphasis upon opportunities, costs and benefits associated with particular types of offence – will help to provide a better understanding of the circumstances under which stability or change in offending occurs. In particular, such an approach offers crime prevention policy, and especially situational approaches, a way of predicting when phenomena such as crime switching (or "displacement") are likely to become serious obstacles. More generally, it provides a way of conceptualising the dynamic interplay which exists amongst situational factors, criminal perceptions, offender decision-making and criminal behavior.

References

Chaiken, M.R., & Chaiken, J.M. (1984). Offender types and public policy. *Crime and Delinquency, 30,* 195–226.

Clarke, R.V. (1983). Situational crime prevention: its theoretical basis and practical scope. In M. Tonry, N. Morris (Eds.), *Crime and justice: an annual review of research:* Vol. 4 (pp. 225–256). Chicago: University of Chicago Press.

Clarke, R.V., Cornish, D.B. (Eds). (1983). *Crime control in Britain.* New York: State University of New York Press.

Clarke, R.V., & Cornish, D.B. (1985). Modeling offenders' decisions: a framework for research and policy. In M. Tonry & N. Morris (Eds.), *Crime and justice: An annual review of research:* Vol. 6 (pp. 147–185). Chicago: University of Chicago Press.

Clarke, R.V., & Mayhew, P. (1988). The British gas suicide story and its criminological implications. In M. Tonry & N. Morris (Eds.), *Crime and justice: an annual review of research:* Vol. 10 (pp.79–116). Chicago: University of Chicago Press.

Cornish, D.B. (1978) *Gambling: a review of the literature and its implications for policy and research* (Home Office Research Study No. 42). London: H.M.S.O.

Cornish, D.B., & Clarke, R.V. (1986a). Thinking about displacement. In K. Heal, G. Laycock (Eds.), *Situational crime prevention: from theory into practice* (pp. 1–24). London: H.M.S.O.

Cornish, D.B., & Clarke, R.V. (Eds.). (1986b). *The reasoning criminal: rational choice perspectives on offending.* New York: Springer.

Cornish, D.B., & Clarke, R.V. (1987). Understanding crime displacement: an application of rational choice theory. *Criminology, 25,* 933–947.

Durkheim, E. (1897/1952). *Suicide.* London: Routledge and Kegan Paul.

Elliott, D.S., & Ageton, S.S. (1980). Reconciling race and class differences in self-reported and official estimates of delinquency. *American Sociological Review, 45,* 95–110.

Farmer, R. D. T., & Rohde, J. R. (1980). Effect of availability and acceptability of lethal instruments on suicide mortality. *Acta Psychiatrica Scandinavica, 62*, 436–446.

Kempf, K. (1986). Offense specialization: does it exist? In D. B. Cornish & R. V. Clarke (Eds.), *The reasoning criminal: rational choice perspectives on offending* (pp. 186–201). New York: Springer.

Klein, M. W. (1984). Offence specialisation and versatility among juveniles. *British Journal of Criminology, 24*, 185–194.

Kreitman, N. (1976). The coal gas story. United Kingdom suicide rates, 1960–1971. *British Journal of Preventive and Social Medicine, 30*, 86–93.

Kreitman, N., & Platt, S. (1984). Suicide, unemployment, and domestic gas detoxification in Britain. *Journal of Epidemiology and Community Health, 11*, 359–368.

Lab, S. (1984). Patterns in juvenile misbehavior. *Crime and Delinquency, 30*, 293–308.

Lester, D. (1984). *Gun control: issues and answers.* Springfield, IL: Thomas.

Lester, D. (1986). Preventing suicide: past failures and future hopes. Paper to Conference on Suicide, King's College, London, Ontario, Canada, May 27–30.

Marks, A. (1977). Sex differences and their effect upon cultural evaluations of methods of self-destruction. *Omega, 8*, 65–70.

Mayhew, P., Clarke, R. V., Sturman, A., & Hough, M. (1976). *Crime as Opportunity* (Home Office Research Study, No. 34). London: H. M. S. O.

Reppetto, T. A. (1976). Crime prevention and the displacement phenomenon. *Crime and Delinquency, 22*, 166–177.

Ross, L. (1977). The intuitive psychologist and his shortcomings: distortions in the attribution process. In L. Berkowitz (Ed.), *Advances in experimental social psychology:* Vol. 10 (pp. 173–220). New York: Academic.

Seiden, R. H. (1977). Suicide prevention: a public health/public policy approach. *Omega, 8*, 267–276.

Tremblay, P. (1986). Designing crime. *British Journal of Criminology, 26*, 234–253.

Weinstein, D., & Deitch, L. (1974). *The impact of legalized gambling: the socioeconomic consequences of lotteries and off-track betting.* New York: Praeger.

8 Questioning Convicted Burglars: A Contribution to Crime Prevention

INGRID M. DEUSINGER

Problem

To prevent crime, police may be called upon to assess, for various sections of cities and towns, the risk that crimes of breaking and entering will occur. The level of risk is in part a function of the location of buildings and streets and of the construction of parts of buildings, such as windows and doors. How can such a complex problem as this best be dealt with?

Police can be thought to combine general criminological considerations with specific experience from past cases, and to assume that their view of how burglars judge the attractiveness of objects and the attendant risks and costs is basically correct. Adequate scientific investigation of these matters is largely lacking, however. Instead, the individual policeman or detective is usually forced to rely on information he has been able to acquire through personal experience or by word of mouth. Knowledge of how the majority of offenders plan their misdeeds and reckon their risks and their chances of success is very limited, as is insight into what induces them to carry out such acts under specific conditions.

Although it will never be possible to predict the planning of a particular crime by an individual perpetrator by means of a differential psychological assessment, reasonable predictions of how the majority of potential offenders tend to think and to act can perhaps be made. Such predictions can contribute to preventing future crimes and to solving past ones. Bennett and Wright (1983) assume that offenders have at their disposal important information regarding how crimes tend to be planned and carried out, information which could be useful in the fight against crime.

The study reported here (see also Deusinger, 1985) is of pilot character and the first of its kind in the Federal Republic of Germany (FRG); it attempts (as does the study by Bennett and Wright, 1983) to glean knowledge useful in crime prevention from the experience of criminals. Specifically, the investigation examines the topography of burglaries in detached houses and other single-family dwellings, in flats, and in shops from the offender's point of view. To this end, persons sentenced for burglaries were questioned during their imprisonment regarding the planning and carrying out of crimes, for which they could be considered experts. The apparent insights into crime topography thus obtained were compared with those obtained from two other groups of subjects, one consisting of policemen and the other of ordinary noncriminal adults without specific experience in this topic.

Major Questions and Rationale

There were five questions of major interest:

1. Whether buildings differ markedly in their degree of attractiveness to experienced burglars. In terms of the present investigation, this is the question of whether the houses subjects were shown differed notably in the frequency with which the subjects judged them to be an inducement to an experienced burglar to break in.
2. Whether buildings already broken into tend to be more attractive to experienced burglars than those which have not.
3. Whether convicted offenders are ready to share at least some of their experience in an investigation such as the present one. Partial correspondence of the information obtained from the policemen who were tested could suggest such a readiness. It would also lend support to the assumption held by police that their assessment of how criminals view the risk of detection and the attractiveness of what can be stolen basically agrees with the assessments of criminals – an assumption which is relevant to police counseling on crime prevention and to the efforts of police to solve crimes.
4. Whether knowledge obtained from convicted offenders supplements present knowledge and thus contributes to the prevention and solving of crimes.
5. Whether "criminal know-how" consists in part of ideas of logical origin and independent of concrete experience with burglary. Partial correspondence of the information obtained from the criminal group with that obtained from those without specific experience would suggest this.

Method

Test Materials

On the basis of results of a preliminary investigation involving presentation of 297 slides and 297 colour prints of some 25 buildings to 10 subjects of differing education drawn from the normal population (none of whom took part in the main investigation), a series of 183 slides and 183 colour prints showing 18 of the buildings and their surroundings from different angles were assembled for use in the main investigation. Of these buildings 11 were single-family detached houses, one a single-family terraced house, 5 multifamily houses and one a shop. The houses differed in type (e.g. mansion, bungalow and prefabricated house) and price category. The pictures were taken by a professional photographer. For reasons of security, buildings were chosen which, insofar as could be ascertained, did not fall within the areas of operation of the criminals who were tested. We asked the photographer, with police help, to find houses that had already been broken into as well as others, similar in type and standard in analogous residentials areas, that, insofar as police knew, had not been burgled.

We tried to match the houses which had been broken into with those which had not in terms of type of residential area, type of house, and price category. However, we do not consider the houses to be "matched pairs" in any strict sense. The purpose in including pictures both of houses which had been broken into and of those which had not was to study whether houses which had been broken into would be judged as encouraging burglary more frequently than would houses of a similar type and standard.

Each building was represented by a series of pictures (slides and prints) accompanied by an explanatory text, the text being read out orally to the subject while the slides were shown.

In addition, on the basis of talks with police experts, a standardized interview involving the following 25 questions was developed:

1. What characteristics of this building might encourage burglary to be committed?
2. Which characteristics of the building make breaking and entering easy?
3. What is there about the building that at first glance would tend to encourage or discourage someone from breaking in?
4. When does a burglar decide to commit a burglary?
5. How does a burglar set about choosing the buildings he will break into?
6. How does an experienced burglar equip himself? What tools does he take along? Are there certain tools he only takes with him on breaking particular types of buildings?
7. How does he go about the job? Does he first use a well tried method to open doors (front doors, backdoors, doors of flats), windows, locked cupboards, etc.? Does he keep to this method or does he vary it according to conditions?
8. Once he has decided to break in and enter, what does he expect to find inside?
9. Where does he look for gold and jewelry?
10. What types of buildings are especially attractive to a burglar? Why? Which types are of average attractiveness? Why? Which ones are just barely attractive? Why?
11. What do burglars want most?

12. What conditions must be present for a burglar to desist from carrying out a burglary he has planned?
13. What conditions must be present for a burglar to break off a job once he has started it?
14. Do most burglars just up and go off to a job? What sets things off?
15. Or is it the case that a burglary is usually planned carefully beforehand? How does this come about?
16. Do most burglars consider it best to work alone, to do a job together with a partner he can trust, or to do it together with several persons he can trust? Why?
17. Does a burglar know already before breaking in what it is he is looking for and what he will take?
18. Are there things a burglar takes for himself or persons close to him which he doesn't pass on to others?
19. Does a burglar already know beforehand roughly where he can convert things from the burglary into cash?
20. With what prices can a burglar reckon, with what fraction of the actual value?
21. Does the burglar think of the risk of being detected and/or of the severity of the possible sentence?
22. What does a burglar think about the persons whose things he takes? Does he feel pity for the victim?
23. What are the personal conditions that need to be met for a person to decide to commit a burglary?
24. With what sum of money does a burglar reckon on the average for a job: in a single-family house? in a flat? in a restaurant? in a shop? (a jewelry shop? a fur shop? a shop with electrical or electronics equipment? a leather store?)
25. Before breaking and entering, does a burglar try and gain legal entry to a building that appears interesting in order to obtain an impression of what is worth taking?

Carrying Out the Study

Subjects were tested individually, being presented with projected slide pictures, shown in a predetermined order, of a given building and a text accompanying each picture. In addition, subjects could view the same pictures as colour prints in an album in which the order of the pictures was the same. The order of presentation of the different buildings was varied systematically. The central question regarding each building, addressed to each person in all three groups, was "Does this building induce an experienced burglar to break and enter? Is it inviting? Why?"

The statements of subjects in all three groups were written down without noting names. Subjects were also allowed to see all notes that were made during testing. No tape recordings were made since it was felt that this could have an adverse effect on testing. Testing of the 32 inexperienced subjects was divided up between three different testers, none of whom knew which of the buildings had been broken into earlier.

The criminals tested were not asked about the planning of their own crimes, but were consulted, so to speak, as "experts"; they were asked to evaluate the buildings just as they felt an experienced burglar would evaluate them, and to answer the questions in the same way as an experienced burglar would. We thus asked the imprisoned criminals to evaluate the buildings and answer the questions either as they would if they were free, or as they would have while they were still free, formulations which we judged as being ethically acceptable. Some of the criminals made very personal statements. When this occurred, they were always asked whether these could be written down. It was expressly pointed out to them that they did not have to impart their deeply personal thoughts.

The pictures and the testing procedure appeared to set off dynamic processes in subjects in all three groups, much as one could expect in use of a projective technique. We thus felt bound to point out repeatedly to a number of the criminal subjects that, although they could use personal material to answer the questions, they were not required to do so. The 25 questions of the standardized interview were put to the subjects after they had been presented with pictures of the first building. After they had answered all of the 25 questions, the first three of which pertained to the building at hand, they were to go on to evaluate the remaining 17 buildings in the same way, questions 1–3 being used each time to elicit their views.

Subjects

Three groups of persons, each representing a convenience sample, served as subjects: (1) 20 male criminals, 16–23 years of age, experienced in burglary; regarding the vocational training they were engaged in at the time of testing, 11 were receiving training as craftsmen (bakers, painters, etc.), three had broken off their training as craftsmen, one was working for his high school diploma (*Abitur*) and five were in other training; (2) 10 police officers, 30–45 years old, involved with crimes of burglary for 3–16 years; of these, three specialized in burglaries of flats, two in serious gang crimes involving burglary, one in burglaries of shops and business premises, two in burglaries of restaurants and kiosks, one in criminal investigation at the site of crimes, and one in advice on preventing burglary; (3) 32 persons form the general population, 20–39 years of age, without specific experience regarding crime; this group comprised 15 males who were 24–39 years old (seven students and eight persons who had completed vocational training) and 17 females who were 20–35 years of age (14 of them students, of whom two had also completed vocational training and three nonstudents who had completed vocational training).

Prison authorities selected those in the criminal group as "experienced burglars of single-family homes" on the basis of information in their files. A relatively homogeneous group in terms of age was aimed at. All of the particularly young offenders we examined proved to be "experts" with a multitude of burglaries behind them, in some cases well over 100. The 16-year-old burglar, for example, had already begun gaining experience at about the age of eight and was an expert on antiques.

Evaluation of Data

Content analysis was made of the more than 2600 free comments the 62 subjects provided in response to the 18 buildings with the 25 questions each in the standardized interview. Subjects' comments regarding whether a particular building would induce a burglar to break in were classified into three categories: definitely "yes" (inducement), definitely "no" (non-inducement), and both "yes" and "no" (partial inducement). These results are presented below. In addition, content analysis is underway of those characteristics of buildings which subjects of the three different categories felt were an inducement to a burglar to break in or desist from breaking in. The results of this analysis, which considers both word frequencies and meaning, will be presented elsewhere.

The approach of having subjects provide free comments to questions regarding inducements to break in or desist from doing so appeared better adapted to determining whether convicted criminals were ready to impart their "expert" experience than would questions yielding more terse and clearcut answers or requiring simply that a selection be made among predetermined alternatives. At the same time, such an approach does have the disadvantage of the scoring not being entirely objective.

The degree of objectivity in scoring was investigated by having each of three psychologists evaluate the free comments of the 32 subjects in the group who had no special experience with crime. Two of the psychologists had each interviewed 10 of the subjects in that group. The concordance between classifications in the assignment of answers to the three categories was found to be $W = 0.60$ ($p < 0.001$, where minimum $r_s = 0.58$ and maximum $r_s = 0.90$), results which were considered to be satisfactory.

Results and Discussion

Table 8.1 indicates, for each of the buildings within the five different categories, the number of subjects in each group who felt that for a burglar the building represented an inducement, a partial inducement, and a non-inducement to break in, respectively. For the offenders and the other groups of

TABLE 8.1. Numbers of subjects in each group who were classified as having judged the respective building as providing an *inducement* (I; frequency at the left in each column), a *partial inducement* (P; frequency in the middle) or a non-inducement (N; frequency at the right) to break in

Building type	Item number	Groups											
		Offenders ($n = 20$)			Police ($n = 10$)			Normal male ($n = 15$)			Normal female ($n = 17$)		
		I	P	N	I	P	N	I	P	N	I	P	N
Single-family houses broken into	8	16	4	0**	10	0	0**	12	3	0**	12	5	0**
	1	11	8	1**	7	3	0**	4	8	3	5	9	3
	3	10	5	5	4	5	1	7	6	2	6	3	8
	13	15	1	4**	10	0	0**	8	3	4	4	7	6
	11	12	3	5	7	1	2	9	4	2*	6	5	6
	2	9	6	5	8	1	1*	1	7	7*	3	7	7
Single-family houses not broken into	22	12	4	4*	9	1	0**	10	4	1**	11	3	3*
	21	3	0	17**	2	3	5	0	4	11**	2	4	11*
	16	10	3	7	5	3	2	5	8	2	5	9	3
	25	6	8	6	4	3	3	6	4	5	4	5	8
	24	16	2	2**	7	1	2	2	7	6	3	5	9
	18	8	3	9	6	4	0*	4	8	3	5	9	3
Multifamily houses broken into	5	6	4	10	7	3	0**	6	4	5	5	4	8
	6	5	7	8	7	3	0**	6	8	1	7	6	4
	9	6	3	11	9	0	1**	6	6	3	10	6	1**
Multifamily houses not broken into	17	2	3	15**	1	3	6	1	4	10**	3	6	8
	19	2	1	17**	3	7	0	0	5	10**	0	5	12**
Shop broken into		1	1	18**	5	1	4	0	3	12**	1	3	13**

Note: Null hypothesis that probability of inducement answer equals probability of non-inducement answer tested with binominal test for the first four types of buildings and with χ^2 for the last. * $p<0.05$, ** $p<0.01$

subjects alike, the buildings obviously differ in the degree they are seen to elicit a readiness of burglars to break in. In contrast to what Bennett and Wright (1983) found, none of the offenders considered each and every building to induce breaking and entering. However, for each building there was at least one offender who did view the building as clearly encouraging a break-in.

There often appeared to be a connection between the type of burglary an offender had specialized in and his manner of assessing a building's characteristics. There was a general tendency for offenders to indicate that a burglar would look for cash as well as for such goods as jewellery, electronics equipment and antiques for which receivers were to be had and a market existed. Burglary by contract was reported frequently.

TABLE 8.2. Classification of subjects' comments regarding houses of different types in terms of whether these were seen to clearly induce ("yes" response) or clearly not induce ("no" response) burglars to break in

Group	*n*	Single-family houses				Multifamily houses			
		6 houses broken into		6 houses not broken into		3 houses broken into		2 houses not broken into	
		Yes	No	Yes	No	Yes	No	Yes	No
Offenders	20	73	21	55	45	17	29	4	32
Police	10	46	4	33	12	23	1	4	6
Normal	15	41	18	27	28	18	9	1	20
Normal	17	36	30	30	37	22	13	3	20

Table 8.2 compares the buildings that had been broken into with those that had not, regarding the frequencies of subjects judging the buildings to clearly induce versus clearly not induce burglars to break in. Generally speaking, the houses that had been broken into were more frequently seen to encourage break-ins.

As can be seen in Table 8.1, the assessments the offenders made of the houses appear to tally in part with those of the other groups. It thus appears that convicted offenders are indeed willing to pass on at least a portion of their know-how (cf. Deusinger, 1985). Servay and Rehm (1986), studying offenders other than burglars, obtained comparable results, though they found that offenders were somewhat reticent about revealing their more specialized knowledge and tended instead to provide more common-sense accounts of how criminals act. Our own impression is that there are considerable individual differences in this respect. Also, common-sense accounts may be indeed of considerable value in understanding crime.

It is not possible to adequately measure a person's readiness to communicate. Attempting insofar as possible to comprehend the offenders point of view can be important for crime prevention. Insight into how the offender thinks can best be obtained in a relatively neutral situation (cf. Cook, 1986; Lösel, 1987).

As can be seen in Table 8.2, the police more frequently judged both the single- and the multifamily houses to be a clear inducement to a burglar to break in than did the offenders. This suggests that learning more of how burglars assess buildings in terms of whether or not to break in could aid police in crime prevention.

The fact, as evident in Table 8.1, that the relative frequencies of answers of the different types obtained for the noncriminal group are similar in many respects to those obtained for the other two groups suggests that common-sense ideas of largely logical origin are an important element in criminal know-how.

In summary, the results of this study, though of tentative character, imply that buildings differ markedly in the extent to which they incourage burglars to break in and enter, and that the experience regarding such matters which offenders can provide can supplement the knowledge of police and contribute to the prevention and solution of crimes.

Acknowledgment. The investigation was supported by the Federal Crime Office (Bundeskriminalamt) of the Federal Republic of Germany.

References

Bennett, T., Wright, R. (1983). Home office. *Research Bulletin, 15,* 18–20.

Cook, P. J. (1986). Criminal incapacitation effects considered in an adaptive choice framework. In D. B. Cornish & R. V. Clarke (Eds.), *The reasoning criminal. Rational choice perspectives of offending.* New York: Springer.

Deusinger, I. M. (1985). Auch „auffallend gesicherte" Objekte laden zum Einbruch ein. Eine Bewertung des Untersuchungsverfahrens „Täterbefragung" mit Hilfe empirischer Befunde. *Kriminalistik, 8,* 391–392.

Deusinger, I. M. (1986). Die Nutzung des Täterwissens aus der Sicht des Psychologen. Erfahrungen aus einer wissenschaftlichen Untersuchung zum Wohnungseinbruch. In *Symposium: Nutzung der Sicht des Täters und des Täterwissens auf die Verbrechensbekämpfung, Sonderband der BKA-Forschungsreihe* (pp. 61–71). Wiesbaden: Bundeskriminalamt.

Lösel, F. (1987). Psychological crime prevention: Concepts, evaluations and perspectives. In K. Hurrelmann, F.-X. Kaufmann, & F. Lösel (Eds.), *Social intervention: Potential and constraints* (pp. 289–313). Berlin: de Gruyter.

Servay, W., Rehm, J. (1986). Bankraub aus der Sicht der Täter. Wiesbaden: Bundeskriminalamt.

Part Two Legal Thought, Attribution, and Sentencing

Introduction

JOCHEN HAISCH

The following section contains papers on legal psychology which address two main themes: (a) the psychological analysis of judicial decision-making processes, and (b) the utilization of attribution theory within the context of courtroom proceedings. These two focal points reflect a development which has taken place within legal psychology in recent times (Carroll & Payne, 1977; Konečni & Ebbesen, 1982).

In the early 1970s, as the analysis of courtroom procedures became popular in Germany, the influence of psychology was negligible. The field of research was dominated by sociology (Lautmann, 1972), which to some extent was able to heighten public awareness of critical aspects of the judicial system through a number of studies, some of which were quite spectacular (Opp & Peuckert, 1971). However, this was only one aspect of the findings of legal sociology; another aspect was the reaction of the judiciary, which, being decisively negative, served to greatly impede applied empirical research in this field. Consequently, for many years simulation proved to be the only method of carrying out research into the legal and the judicial system. This is a result of recent research in legal psychology not only in Europe (Chapman, Müller, & Blackman, 1984), but seems to be true elsewhere (Kassin & Wrightsman, 1985; Monahan & Walker, 1985). However, the simulated events were so varied and diverse that using the term "simulation" to describe them all tends to be misleading. This is demonstrated in Figure 1.

Figure 1 shows that the term "simulation" is applied to a very broad area of research within a legal framework. It is apparent that the simulation can apply to various real events, that is, to the person involved, to the case in question, and to the decision-making process. Especially those simulations in which all three dimensions apply are regarded critically, that is, those situations in which student subjects deal with fictitious cases in a laboratory situation. However, criticism of simulated events should include all of the possible variations of simulated criminal cases.

In the following section a great variety of simulations are examined, from "pure simulations" (students, fictitious cases, laboratory experiments) to

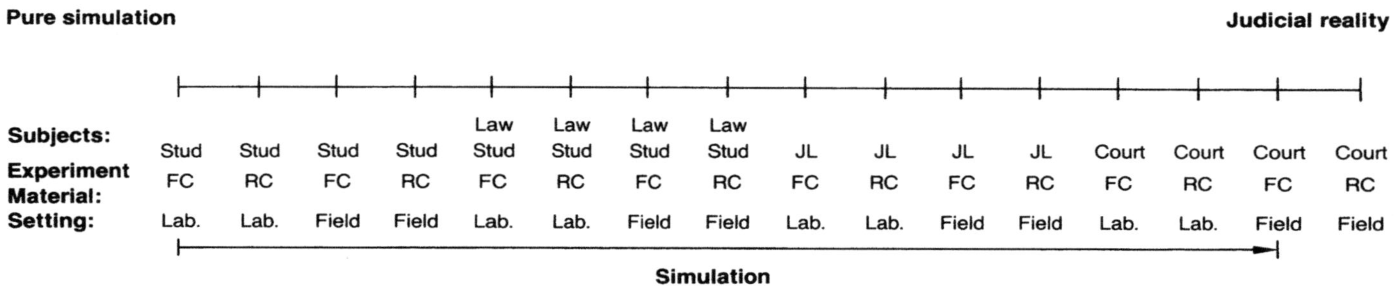

FIGURE 1. Empirical studies in the field of jurisprudence: from studies involving "pure simulation" to studies in the "judicial reality". RC, real cases; FC, fictitious cases; Stud., students (excluding law students); Law Stud., law students; JL, Junior Lawyers; Court, judicial decision-makers; Lab., laboratory experiment; Field, field study within the courtroom

simulations approximating real events (judicial authorities, real cases, field studies). For the following reasons, all of these simulations are important for psychological research pertaining to jurisprudence.

1. Historical Factors. Due to the above-mentioned reaction of the judicial authorities to the empirical studies carried out by judicial sociology in the early 1970s, it became virtually impossible to undertake an empirical investigation of judicial decision-making processes in a natural setting. An alternative solution was the use of student subjects, fictitious cases, and laboratory experiments. An instrumentarium of this kind can be applied to a wide variety of psychological research into judicial matters, such as the assessment of the degree of justice in court cases, the validity of criminal verdicts, and the prediction of courtroom decisions and sentences.

2. Methodological Factors. (a) An examination of reform measures within a natural setting can only be carried out after they have been decided upon and executed. In contrast, the situation in a simulation is such that, depending on the area which is to be reformed, the various aspects of the simulation enable us to assess the likelihood of achieving the desired results of any reform. (b) Field studies in a natural setting (in this case within the "judicial reality") are burdened with a variety of well-documented methodological problems which essentially revolve around the lack of control in such studies. However, these difficulties can be compensated by examining the consistency of results from correlative field studies in the judicial reality and from studies of simulations in laboratory experiments.

3. Intradisciplinary Factors. For a long time, research into judicial matters suffered from being a domaine of relatively few fields of study, being neglected by other important disciplines. Experimental psychologists, for example, as such have shown little interest in this field. On the other hand, the development of legal psychology was to some extent based upon the fact that through the use of simulations, experimental methods were introduced to research.

Aside from the importance which simulation has had for judicial aspects of psychological research into legal procedures, it has also been of great importance for legal psychology as such.

1. Historical Factors. With the aid of simulation, experimental research is able to test current psychological theories. Such research has for a long time been given priority, and the development of a research paradigm which corresponds to simulation proved to be a prerequisite for a broader examination of psychological theories within the context of jurisprudence.

2. Methodological Factors. Ideally, rigourous testing of theories and their eventual modification should – circumstances permitting – be based on cause and effect relationships. However, this can only be achieved in simulated laboratory experiments. The value of simulations within the framework of judicial proceedings, therefore, is that a theory can be tried and tested in a new area to which it is applicable. If the results of investigations which are more or less accurate approximations of reality prove to be inconsistent, a successful theory must be able to account for such inconsistencies; otherwise such results should serve as an indication that the theory needs to be modified or replaced.

3. Intradisciplinary Factors. The development of legal psychology was greatly influenced by a development within social psychology which was based on an increasing orientation towards applications within this discipline. Consequently, the application of social psychology to legal problems made a major contribution to the development of applied social psychology as well as to the development of legal psychology (Kaplan, 1986) which extended beyond the bounds of the traditional fields of forensic and criminal psychology. In approaching this field on a broader basis, social psychology was, of course, initially assisted by the application of traditional, above all, experimental research methods.

However, the apparent value of simulation studies in the area of legal proceedings for jurisprudence and for psychology can only be brought to bear when each field recognizes the authority of the other. The following contributions by psychologists and legal experts have been written in the spirit of such mutual acceptance.

The Contributions

The Contributions to Psychological Decision-Making Processes

At the extreme end of our diagram ("pure simulation") we find the study by *Hommers* and *Anderson.* In this study, student subjects were confronted with fictitious cases in a laboratory situation. From this starting point, the authors developed an extensive research program on judicial decision-making, with the aim of combining phenomenological and experimental methods with the greatest possible proximity to real situations. The basis of this program is, in the aforementioned sense, a pure simulation which is directed towards the applicability of the authors' information-integration theory and corresponding methodology. The pure simulation experiment demonstrates the usefulness of this approach inasmuch as it shows which cognitive processes are relevant in deciding upon delinquents who are responsible for damages, given varying degrees of restitution. The algebraic decision scheme used by the subjects in the course of the experiment is based on cognitive processes which to some extent deviate considerably from legal considerations. One would expect that the application of the authors' theory and methods to a situation approximating reality should lead to interesting results when examining the process of judicial decision-making.

The contribution by *Maya Bar-Hillel*, not being based on empirical research, cannot be regarded within the framework of the above diagram. Nevertheless, she offers clear and concrete suggestions as to the possibility of analyzing and improving decisions in criminal and civil court cases. It should be clear therefore. that empirical research based on *Bar-Hillel*'s model of analysis would be allocated to the extreme end of the diagram of judicial reality. However, it seems reasonable to assume that the requirements demanded by such empirical research would necessitate the inclusion of simulation.

Bar-Hillel's analysis begins with an original argument, which claims that many errors in judgment can be recognized with the aid of a so-called decision-assisting grid. For the analyses of courtroom decisions, the relevant grid is the psychological theory of decision-making under uncertainty. This decision-making grid is applied to judicial decisions regarding rules of accepting or rejecting evidence in civil and criminal proceedings and regarding commitment to pretrial custody, and to the examination of sources of judicial uncertainty during the process of reaching a decision.

The results of the analysis in no way advocate the unrestrained use of the decision-assisting grid in all possible problems pertaining to legal decisions. On the other hand, *Bar-Hillel* refers to additional problem constellations within the area of jurisprudence which could be analyzed with the grid. The application of such analyses should prove to be exciting and, at the same time, of great value for empirical research.

Sealy gives an account of further studies into decision-making processes. His summary of empirical results is based on simulations which range from one extreme of the diagram to the other. Whereas the so-called shadow juries consist of members of a panel of jury members who attend an actual court case and then discuss it while being observed, the so-called mock juries usually consist of students who assume the role of jury members and who judge fictitious cases under laboratory conditions. *Sealy* gives a detailed explanation as to why the simulation (which can, of course, incorporate varying degrees of "realness") is obligatory in analyzing the decision-making processes of jury members. It is interesting to note that the results of the Anglo-American studies reported in this chapter, although varying in their degree of approximation to reality, nevertheless show concordant results – a concordance which seems to demonstrate the importance of the simulation findings for judicial "reality."

The studies by *Schünemann* and *Bandilla* on judicial decision-making processes are close approximations of courtroom reality. Nevertheless, these studies are classified as simulations according to the diagram. Although courtroom judges and junior lawyers are examined in their capacity as decision-makers, the studies are not undertaken within the framework of real courtroom proceedings, and the cases, although based on real events, are nevertheless fictitious. *Schünemann* and *Bandilla* direct their interest towards two themes: (a) the quality of courtroom decisions that follow the inquisitorial and the adversary models of procedures, and (b) the perseverance effect in such decisions. As a consequence, these authors refer on the one hand to Thibaut and Walker's (1975) studies and attempt to replicate these authors' findings within the framework of the inquisitorial court procedures, while at the same time orientating themselves towards the studies on perseverance by Nisbett and Ross (1980). In comparing the models of procedures, it is interesting to note that neither the inquisitorial nor the adversary procedures are clearly supported by *Schünemann* and *Bandilla*'s findings, but that these findings tend to favor a mixed model. In addition, *Schünemann* and *Bandilla*'s perseverance effect shows a relationship to *Bar-Hillel*'s analysis. The examination of the phenomenon of perseverance in simulated courtroom procedures in which pretrial evidence is manipulated and verdicts are observed fails to take the judge's information processing into account – a method which is viewed critically by *Bar-Hillel*. It can therefore be expected that a combined examination of the contributions by *Bar-Hillel* and *Schünemann* and *Bandilla* will prove stimulating for the further development of psychological research into jurisprudence.

The final contribution in the following section is by *Bierhoff, Buck* and *Klein* and represents an attribution-theory approach. In addition, it again deals with pure simulation. The value of simulation in the area of psychological research into judicial verdicts is discussed in detail by the authors. As a consequence of their discussions, the authors include law and nonlaw students in their studies in an attempt to gather information on the importance of the variable "expertise."

In addition to examining impression formation, the authors base their work on attribution processes and propose a two-step model in which stimuli, such as the respectability of the accused, are seen to affect the attribution process of the judge. These attributions, in turn, have an effect on the overall assessment of the accused and on the severity of sentence. The empirical results, which seem to support the two-step model, are interesting inasmuch as sentences passed by law students are more extreme than those passed by nonlaw students. These findings are discussed in the context of Shaver's (1985) sequence model of blame attributions.

Assessment and Future Prospects

In what way do the papers presented in this section contribute towards psychological research into jurisprudence? This question can be approached within the framework of exemplary psychological training programs which can be applied to judicial decision-making (Haisch, 1983). At present, a comprehensive psychological theory of judicial decision-making does not exist, either for the special case of legal problem-solving or in terms of a general psychological theory of decision-making. As long as such a theory is lacking, definitions regarding the skills needed by judicial decision-makers, the regulation of suitable training techniques and the stipulation of procedures which contribute to consistency in decision-making skills must remain arbitrary (see Bernstein, 1982). Nevertheless, a preliminary theoretical basis of the kind presently available provides a platform on which preliminary training programs for judicial decision-makers can be developed. However, this does not mean that the (psychological) skills needed by these decision-makers are fully recognized, that the relevant problems have been completely established, or that conditions which support the stability of the required skills are completely known. In other words, the optimum training techniques can only be of provisional validity. If, however, the simulations contained in this chapter should contribute towards the further development of a psychological theory of jurisprudence – which is doubtless the case – then this contribution (which, after all, allows for partial experimental testing of theoretical positions) will also be directed towards answering the following questions: Which legal problems of a psychological nature are to be regarded as relevant? Which skills must judicial decision-makers possess, and how can the stability of these skills be established?

In approaching these questions, the contribution of simulations would therefore be towards the establishment of a basis on which psychological training programs for judicial decision-makers could be developed and carried out.

References

Bernstein, G.S. (1982). Training behavior change agents: A conceptual review. *Behavior Therapy, 13*, 1–23.

Carroll, J.S., & Payne, J.W. (1977). Crime seriousness, recidivism risk, and causal attributions in judgments of prison term by students and experts. *Journal of Applied Psychology, 62*, 595–602.

Chapman, A.J., Müller, D.J., & Blackman, D.E. (1984). Some applications of psychology to law (Special Issue). *International Review of Applied Psychology, 33* (1).

Haisch, J. (1983). Trainingsprogramme für Richter. Zur Reduktion von Urteilsverzerrungen in Strafverfahren. In J. Haisch (Ed.), *Angewandte Sozialpsychologie*. Bern: Huber.

Kaplan, M.F. (Ed). (1986). *The impact of social psychology on procedural justice*. Springfield, IL: Thomas.

Kassin, S.M., & Wrightsman, L.S. (Eds). (1985). *The psychology of evidence and trial procedure*. Beverly Hills, CA: Sage.

Konečni, V.J., & Ebbesen, E.B. (Eds.). (1982). *The criminal justice system. A social-psychological analysis*. San Francisco: Freeman.

Lautmann, R. (1972). *Justiz – Die stille Gewalt*. Frankfurt: Athenäum.

Monahan, J., & Walker, L. (1985). *Social science in law: Cases and materials*. Mineola, NY: Foundation press.

Nisbett, R., & Ross, L. (1980). *Human inference: Strategies and shortcomings of social judgment*. Englewood Cliffs: Prentice Hall.

Opp, K.-D., Peuckert, R. (1971). *Ideologie und Fakten in der Rechtssprechung*. Munich: Goldmann.

Shaver, K.G. (1985). *The attribution of blame*. New York: Springer.

Thibaut, J., & Walker, L. (1975). *Procedural justice: A psychological analysis*. Hillsdale, NJ: Erlbaum.

9
Algebraic Schemes in Legal Thought and in Everyday Morality

WILFRIED HOMMERS and NORMAN H. ANDERSON

Legal thought may have unique value for cognitive science. A primary characteristic of legal thought is its focus on valuation and integration of evidence. Even simple cases typically involve multiple pieces of evidence, each of which has to be evaluated for its implications with respect to the judgment to be made, and all of which have to be integrated to arrive at an overall judgment. In this respect, legal thought is similar to psychological decision theory, which is also concerned with valuation and integration of information.

What is distinctive about legal thought is that it has been in the process of development for centuries, as illustrated in the historical survey of the concept of recompense (Hommers, 1983a, 1986). The legal thought of today embodies the thinking of generations of legal scholars. Legal thought thus represents a highly developed, albeit complex system of knowledge that has an active role in the operation of society. Lawyers and judges must become experts in the understanding and use of this system of knowledge. Their own cognitive processes are thus highly structured and so are of direct interest to psychological science.

It is the theme of this chapter that legal thought and cognitive theory have much to offer each other. They have natural commonality in their mutual concern with valuation and integration of evidence, as already noted, as well as commonality in relation to morality, which is as important in everyday life as in the law. Because of its long sociocultural development, legal thought may be considered an expert cognitive system, interesting in its own right, and also as a heuristic for the understanding of everyday morality. It should be fruitful, as Hommers (1981, 1985) has argued, to develop genuine two-way interaction between legal thought and cognitive theory.

Algebraic schemes of evidence integration are considered in this chapter to illustrate one area for developing mutual interaction between legal thought and cognitive theory. Algebraic schemes have been suggested by many writers on legal thought, perhaps as a natural consequence of the primary problem of quantifying judgment to fit the offense and the offender. Independently, algebraic schemes have been considered in many areas of cognitive decision theory, including moral judgment. These algebraic schemes provide an interesting area for the two-way interaction with mutual benefit to both fields. One moral issue is considered here to illustrate some possibilities for such two-way interaction.

The Case of Recompense

The case of recompense provides a good example for the study of algebraic schemes. Legal thought has long been concerned with recompense, as illustrated in the prescription of the Judaic code that four sheep shall be repaid for one stolen sheep (Exodus, 22, 1). Other examples are given in the historical survey by Hommers (1983a, 1986). Recently, psychologists have also begun to study recompense in everyday morality (Piaget, 1932; Berscheid & Walster, 1967).

The case of recompense emphasizes the problem of integration, for recompense does not stand alone but in relation to some harmful act. Hence it is necessary to integrate the damage from the act together with the recompense to arrive at a judgment of deserved punishment. But this is not enough, for legal thought and everyday morality both agree that the *culpa*, including intent and responsibility (Hommers, 1983b), behind the harmful act must also be taken into account. Thus, all three variables have to be integrated to arrive at a judgment of deserved punishment.

One specific hypothesis, suggested by both legal thought and everyday morality, is that the integration obeys the simple algebraic scheme

$$\text{Deserved Punishment} = \text{Culpa} + \text{Damage} - \text{Recompense}.$$

This may be called scheme S, since recompense reduces deserved punishment by subtraction. This algebraic scheme parallels the blame schema studied in everyday morality (Anderson, 1983; Hommers & Anderson, 1985; Leon, 1980; Surber, 1982) and also seems in line with § 46 of the Penal Code from 1975 of the Federal Republic of Germany. According to Maurach, Gössel, and Zipf (1978), two components of sentencing are distinguished: harmdoer and act, which correspond to culpa and damage in the cited scheme. Recompense is considered to affect both components: it diminishes the damage caused by the act; and it raises the moral character of the harmdoer, thereby diminishing culpa which depends on both purpose and negligence. A related legal scheme appears in the concept of mitigating circumstances of the British Court of Appeal Criminal Division (Thomas, 1970).

However, a different legal scheme for recompense has also been proposed. This appears in the sentencing theory of the German legal scholar Von Linstow (1974), who proposed a formula with 15 variables for calculating punishment of traffic violations. Recompense was incorporated as a multiplicative factor with values between 0.8 and 1.0:

Deserved Punishment = (Culpa + Damage) × Recompenes.

By this formula, values of recompense less than 1 would reduce the deserved punishment. This may be called scheme M, since recompense reduces deserved punishment by multiplication.

The existence of two different algebraic schemes raises two questions. First, which scheme ought the judge follow? This is the prescriptive question. Second, which (if either) scheme is actually followed in intuitive judgment, by laypersons or by experts? This is the descriptive or cognitive question. Both questions are interesting and important. As a prescription Von Linstow's calculation rule has been criticized by legal scholars (e.g., Bruns, 1974, 1980; Zipf, 1977). The present discussion, however, is primarily concerned with the cognitive question, which, nevertheless, is relevant to the actual operation of legal systems. Despite their focus on the prescriptive question, legal schemes must make some allowance for nonprescriptive facts: human processing capabilities and human values. Accordingly, it is desirable to find some empirical test of schemes S and M.

A fundamental difficulty arises in any attempt to test such algebraic schemes. This concerns measurement of values and is relevant even in a prescriptive context. To use either of the two schemes as prescriptions for judges' decision making, as Thomas (1970) and Von Linstow (1974) suggest, would require prior measurement of the values of culpa, damage, and recompense. But values are to some degree intuitive, not prescriptive, and are left in greater or lesser degree to the discretion of individual judges. This is clearly necessary for culpa, which is not objectively measurable but rather an attribution made by the judge. Even damage may involve nonmaterial components, loss of reputation, for example, that must be evaluated by the individual judge's intuition. Although the same algebraic scheme may be prescribed for all judges, some nonprescriptive element of value must still be allowed for. Thus, even to apply schemes S and M as prescriptive rules is not generally possible without a means of measuring values.

This measurement problem appears even more strongly in the descriptive cognitive approach, for different individuals clearly have different values irrespective of which of the two schemes is employed. Cognitive theory cannot prescribe what values a person ought to have, but instead must take cognizance of what they are. Two persons may both use scheme S to judge deserved punishment, but they will arrive at different judgments because they have different values, especially for the nonmaterial variable of culpa. To test whether they do indeed use scheme S, therefore, it seems necessary to know their personal values of culpa, damage, and recompense, for the values of one person will not add up to yield the judgments of the other person.

A solution to this problem of measuring individuals' values at the same time as testing the scheme's validity has been developed as part of the functional measurement methodology of the theory of information integration (Anderson, 1981, 1982). The essential idea of functional measurement is to use the algebraic structure of the scheme as the base and frame for measurement. If the algebraic scheme holds empirically, the data from a suitably designed experiment will exhibit a corresponding pattern. The pattern of the data is diagnostic of the operative scheme. The values themselves, moreover, may be derived from this data pattern. Functional measurement can thus transform the schemes from qualitative verbalisms to exact quantitative laws of cognition in combination with a solution of the measurement of the values.

The following experiment illustrates how functional measurement methodology may be applied to test schemes S and M in an exact way. The subjects in this experiment were laypersons. That was appropriate due to the demonstrational purposes of the experimental analysis, i.e., the testing of laypersons was not designed for drawing conclusions about actual expert decision-making. Since the very same method may be used to study judgments of legal experts, the extension of this approach to legal thinking is discussed in the second half of this chapter.

Experimental Analysis

Legal thought, as already indicated, has suggested two algebraic schemes for the effect of recompense. One claims that recompense is subtractive; the other claims that recompense is multiplicative. The experiment reported in this section illustrates how functional measurement methodology can be used to distinguish between these two schemes – while still allowing for personal values of each individual judge.

Previous work in this research program has found that recompense is nonadditive in its effects (e.g., Hommers & Anderson, 1985). The pattern of the data thus disagreed with the subtractive scheme and was, indeed, consistent with a multiplying scheme. These results were not definitive with respect to the two schemes, however, because the same data pattern could be produced by an averaging rule with differential weighting for recompense. The averaging rule, however, has a cognitive structure similar to that of the subtracting scheme. The purpose of this experiment was to test between multiplying and averaging processes of recompense integration.

Using the stamp scenario of Hommers and Anderson (1985), subjects were told stories about two stamp collectors, one of whom ruined some stamps belonging to the other. They were told to imagine that they were the victim and to say how much the offender should be punished. The stories presented culpa, damage, and recompense information. The three levels of culpa described accidental, careless, and intentional acts. The two levels of damage stated that two or ten stamps were ruined. The three levels of recompense stated that none, half, or all of the ruined stamps were replaced by the offender. Subjects received information about just two of the three specified variables on each trial.

This information was presented according to the two-factor designs shown in the three panels of Figure 9.1. In addition, judgments were obtained based on each single piece of information to provide scale-free, crossover tests that discriminate between the averaging and multiplying rules.

Subjects made their punishment judgments on a graphic rating scale. General procedure was similar to that used in previous experiments (Hommers & Anderson, 1985) employing the methodology of functional measurement. Subjects were students from introductory psychology courses at the University of California, San Diego.

Three main results were obtained. First, the culpa-damage integration was additive, whereas the recompense-damage and recompense-culpa integrations were nonadditive. Second, the scale-free tests supported the averaging rule and disagreed with the simple subtracting and multiplying rules. Third, the paradoxically large effect of recompense observed in previous work was confirmed.

Integration Rules

The data are summarized in Figure 9.1, in which each panel represents the integration rule for one pair of information variables. In the left panel, the two solid curves portray the damage-culpa integration. The number by each curve represents the number of damaged stamps, so the difference between the two solid curves shows how the damage variable affects the judgement of punishment. The upward trend of these curves represents the effect of culpa, with more punishment being assigned for greater culpa.

The main characteristics of these two solid curves is that they are parallel. By virtue of the parallelism theorem (Anderson, 1981), this implies that damage and culpa are integrated by an adding-type rule. This replicates previous work that has studied these two variables (Hommers & Anderson, 1985; Leon, 1980; Surber, 1982).

The three solid curves in the center panel portray the integration rule for recompense and culpa. These curves, however, appear to be quite nonparallel. Nonparallelism implies that the integration does not obey an adding rule. Similarly, the two solid curves in the right panel portray the integration rule for recompense and damage. Here again, the nonparallelism points to a nonadditive integration. Recompense is thus nonadditively processed.

Evidence for Averaging

Closer analysis of the data shows that the integration rule is actually one of averaging for all three pairs of variables. The averaging rule has some fundamental consequences for cognitive theory so the data analysis needs detailed consideration. The key to the analysis lies in the relation between the dashed curve and the solid curves in each panel. Each dashed curve represents judg-

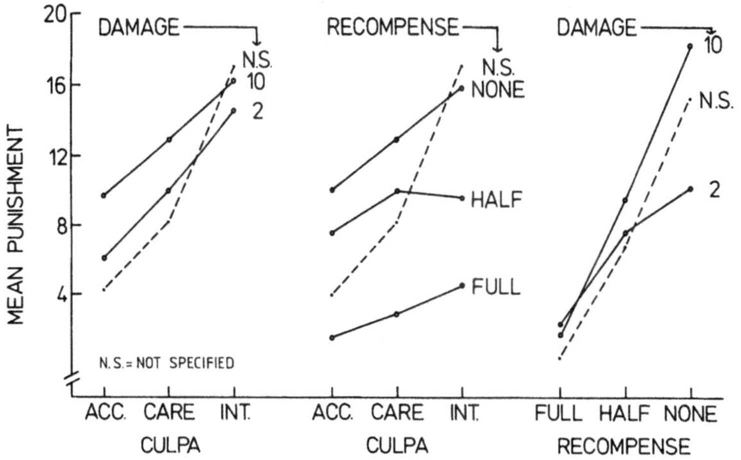

FIGURE 9.1. Assigned punishment as a function of culpa, damage, and recompense. Each panel gives factorial graph for one two-factor design, with the two moral variables listed as curve parameter and on horizontal axis. *Dashed curves* denote response to single moral variable listed on horizontal axis (*ACC.*, accidental; *CARE.*, careless; *INT.*, intentional)

ments based on just one variable. In the left panel, for example, the label N.S. means that damage was not specified so the judgment was made only on the basis of culpa. The fact that the dashed curve crosses over one or more of the solid curves provides the critical support for averaging.

The logic of this crossover test (Anderson, 1981) applies as follows to the present task. In the left panel, both the additive and the averaging rules can account for the parallelism of the solid curves, but only the averaging rule can account for the crossover. To see this, note that the dashed curve represents judgments based on culpa information alone. Comparison of the dashed curve with the solid curve labeled 2 shows what happens when the information is added that two stamps were damaged. If this information had an additive effect, then the solid curve would have to lie entirely on one side of the dashed curve. This prediction does not require that the additive effects be mathematically exact, only that the direction of effect be the same at each point. The crossover thus is not consistent with any form of summation model.

Under the averaging hypothesis, the added information about two damaged stamps is averaged in with the culpa information. This is the milder level of damage and may be assumed to have a value around the midpoint of the scale. Since this value is greater than the leftmost point on the dashed curve, averaging it in will raise the response; and since this value is lower than the rightmost point on the dashed curve, averaging it in will lower the response. In this way, the averaging model accounts for the crossover in the left panel of Figure 9.1.

In the other two panels of Figure 9.1, the theoretical issue is to test between the averaging and the multiplying rules. Here again the issue rests on a comparison of the dashed and solid curves. The averaging rule provides a straightforward account of the crossover, in accord with the logic already discussed.

In contrast, the multiplying rule cannot account for these data patterns. This rule requires that the dashed and solid curves form a linear fan with a common point of intersection. But in the center panel, the dashed curve intersects the two solid curves at different elevations, and the solid curves would only intersect if extrapolated to the left. Similarly, in the right panel, the dashed curve intersects the lower solid curve around half recompense, whereas the two solid curves intersect around full recompense. These data pattern are therefore sharply inconsistent with the multiplying rule. In short, these empirical analyses support a revised scheme S and infirm scheme M.

Paradoxical Effect of Recompense

Recompense had a much larger effect than the damage for which recompense was given. This, may be seen in Figure 9.1 by comparing the left and center panels. The effect of damage is given by the vertical separation between the two damage curves labeled 2 and 10 in the left panel. Similarly, the effect of recompense is given by the vertical separation among the curves in the center panel. As can be seen, the effect of recompense is three or four times larger than the effect of damage. This is paradoxical because the objective value of recompense is necessarily restricted by the damage.

This paradoxically large effect of recompense has been observed previously (Hommers & Anderson, 1985, in preparation). The theoretical interpretation is that recompense has two components. One component refers to the actual damage, and constitutes material restitution. The second component refers to the moral character of the harmdoer; recompense decreases the culpa of the harmdoer and thereby decreases the assigned punishment according to the foregoing blame schema. This second component makes it possible for the effect of recompense to be greater than the actual damage.

This large effect of recompense may seem to differ from legal thought. Von Linstow's (1974) formula represented recompense as a multiplicative factor between 0.8 and 1.0. Since this multiplies (culpa+damage), the reduction in punishment could mathematically exceed the damage term, but only if culpa were much larger than damage. But scheme M cannot account for the three-to-fourfold effect observed in Figure 9.1. On the other hand, the report of Thomas (1970, p. 197) on the sentencing policy of the British Court of Appeal Criminal Division indicates that small amounts of recompense are ineffective: only "quite obviously quite substantial restitution" is an important factor. Although the present experiment did not test small amounts of recompense, the foregoing two-component interpretation implies that even apology or remorse, without any material restitution, could have sizeable effects in contrast to the British Court of Appeal. Of course, this contrast between legal thought and everyday morality may reflect the severity of the offenses. Whereas the culpa component may be large relative to a few ruined stamps among friends, it may be small relative to the offenses that reach the courts.

Functional Measurement Methodology

A detailed exposition of functional measurement cannot be given here, but a few comments are needed to indicate how it may be useful for further study of legal schemes. For illustration, consider the hypothesis that culpa and damage are integrated by an adding-type scheme:

$$\text{Punishment} = \text{Culpa} + \text{Damage}.$$

The natural way to test this scheme is to measure punishment, culpa, and damage, and check whether they do indeed add up. But this imposes stringent measurement conditions. If the three variables are measured on rank-order scales, for example, they will surely not add up. In general, they will only add up if the three variables are measured on true psychological scales, in this case on scales with equal intervals and a known zero point.

How to obtain true psychological scales has been controversial in psychology since Fechner's study of psychophysical laws. Only recently has a method been developed with reasonably general capability for such psychological measurement. One part of this method is the *parallelism theorem*, which was applied to test the hypothesis that the culpa-damage integration obeyed an adding-type rule. By virtue of the parallelism theorem, an observed pattern of parallel data curves implies an adding-type rule of integration. Prior measurement of culpa and damage is not needed to test this integration rule. No more is necessary than that the response of judged punishment be on a scale with equal intervals – but this itself follows from observed parallelism. The parallelism theorem is thus a powerful tool because it can simultaneously validate the response measure and the integration rule.

The information about the values of the stimulus variables, in this case culpa and damage, is contained in the distances among the points in the graphs. For example, the closeness of the two solid curves in the left panel of Figure 9.1 implies that ten damaged stamps is not considered much worse than two damaged stamps. Recompense had far larger effects, as already noted in the discussion of the vertical separation of the solid curves in the middle panel. These considerations may be put into quantitative form to obtain true psychological scales of the stimulus variables.

Of special importance is that the parallelism theorem can be applied to the data of individual subjects. The graph in the left panel of Figure 9.1 is an average over the group of subjects. Thus, it rests on the uniformity assumption that all subjects are similar with respect to the scheme. But similar graphs can be constructed for each individual using several trials per stimulus to control for measurement error. The basic aspect of this topic is taken up later in the discussion of personal design.

Functional measurement methodology is not a routine recipe. Success depends on the use of certain experimental techniques (see Anderson, 1982, Chap. 1). Success also depends heavily on the actual operativeness of algebraic schemes of integration. Fortunately, experimental studies in many different areas of psychology have found extensive evidence for a general cognitive algebra (see Anderson, 1981, Chap. 1). The present experiment may illustrate something of the potential of this approach to test the cognitive validity of schemes of legal thought.

Legal Schemes as Heuristics for Cognitive Science

The foregoing experimental results have illustrated how legal thought can serve as a heuristic for cognitive science. This approach goes beyond mere comparison of prescriptive schemes with moral cognition to use those schemes as part of substantive inquiry. Two or three aspects of this approach deserve comment.

Structure of Recompense

The functional measurement analysis yielded an unexpected empirical answer to the two conflicting legal schemes for recompense: Both were partly correct, as represented in the averaging rule. The scale-free tests ruled out the hypothesis of scheme S that recompense operates by simple subtraction. These tests also ruled out the hypothesis of scheme M that recompense operates by simple multiplication. Instead, the operative rule was found to be averaging with differential weighting. The integration process itself is thus one of subtraction. At the same time, however, the differential weights act multiplicatively as a level-specific modifier on the values of recompense. This differentially weighted averaging produces the fan pattern seen in the middle and right panels of Figure 9.1. At the surface level this fan pattern would seem to support the prescriptive multiplying rule of Von Linstow (1974). The deeper cognitive analysis revealed a rather different and more complex structure of recompense.

The problem of structure also appears in the paradoxical effect of recompense. Although nominally bounded by the actual damage, recompense actually had far larger effects. This result, together with the averaging rule, suggests that recompense may not be a distinct moral category. Thus, the simple prescriptive theory of recompense, where recompense is a mitigating factor only in the case of a "quite obviously quite substantial restitution" (Thomas, 1970, p. 197), is not valid in layperson's judgments in two respects. First, even half recompense reduced punishment considerably. Second, recompense had a more complex structure than culpa and damage, as shown by the differential weighting of recompense instead of constant weighting for culpa and damage. These comments suggest that recompense effects may be mediated by more basic moral categories. Legal thought, as indicated by § 46 of the German Penal code (1975), suggests a two-component structure of recompense (Bruns, 1974, 1980; Maurach, Gössel, & Zipf, 1978; Zipf, 1977). The act component refers to the actual decrease of damage, and the harmdoer component refers to moral virtue demonstrated by the act itself.

Two directions of further work deserve consideration: (a) the structure of recompense, and (b) the generality and universality of the findings on harm and recompense. With respect to the structure of recompense, further empirical work is needed to explore the two-component theory from § 46 more carefully. For example, the nonadditivity of recompense may be associated with one of the two components inherent in voluntary recompense by the harmdoer: remorse and compensation. This might be studied with a duplex response procedure in which subjects make two separate judgments, one for punishment and one for recompense. These two judgments correspond to the foregoing act and harmdoer components, reflecting the dual structure of civil and criminal law.

With respect to generality, experimental tests are needed with other scenarios than the damaged stamps, which may differ in content, in severeness of the harm, and in complexity of the circumstances. With respect to universality, the validity for different populations, especially for experts such as lawyers and judges, may be examined. Finally, further work may meaningfully extend the general strategy by using other legal schemes as heuristic tools for cognitive science (Hommers, 1981, 1988; Hommers & Anderson, in preparation).

Process and Value

The prescriptive schemes of legal thought included a distinction between process and value. Processes should obey general rules, whereas values may be personal. Valuation, of course, is a matter of expert judgment, and is also sensitive to particulars of the actual situation. In legal thought, however, values are not totally personal; much valuation is constrained by the sentencing frames of the Penal codes or by the guidelines ("Taxes") of Court Benches. Nevertheless, the law leaves some room for personal valuation that is not explicitly prescribed and not regarded as error or deviance.

A parallel distinction between general processes and personal values appears in the theory of information integration. Integration theory allows and indeed insists that values are sensitive to individual and situation. The rules for integrating these values, however, are considered to have substantial invariance. This rule generality provides a theoretical foundation for value analysis by means of functional measurement methodology.

Value analysis, of course, has a different emphasis in legal thought than in the theory of information integration. Integration theory is descriptive and makes no attempt to constrain values to any prescriptive norm. Rather it aims at cognitive analysis, beginning with the problem of measuring personal values. Legal thought, in contrast, tries to standardize and reduce personal values in order to make the sentences of judges more uniform. Despite this prescriptive emphasis, there is a need for cognitive analysis of value in legal judgments. This may be seen in divided court decisions, which presumably result because different judges put different values and weights on the same evidence. Some allowance for personal values is inherent in the operation of legal systems, represented in the discretion of individual judges. Some cases, moreover, are so complicated that experts as well as laypersons may use simplified schemes to integrate the evidence in place of the prescriptive scheme. To determine this, however, requires analysis in terms of personal values. Hence it is desirable, even necessary, to analyze legal judgment within a cognitive framework. This problem is taken up in the following section.

Analysis of Algebraic Schemes in Legal Psychology

Linear Models for Correlational Analysis

In legal psychology the statistical approach of linear regression models for correlations is widely used as illustrated in the seminal field studies of bail setting and sentencing reported by Konečni and Ebbesen (1982). This statistical approach depends on aggregating many cases, each coded in terms of pertinent variables. Criminal sentences, for example, could be coded in terms of severity of sentence, together with such predictor variables as kind and severity of offense, extenuating circumstances, prior offenses, and so forth. Thus coded, the data could be subjected to ordinary multiple regression analysis or to log-linear analysis (e.g., Haberman, 1978), which performs similar functions for qualitative, categorical data.

Such statistical analysis has many uses. Foremost is that it provides an overview of the operation of legal systems that is essential for evaluating how and how well they function. Unexpected benefits may also be obtained. For example, a nuisance finding that complicated the statistical analysis of bail setting by Ebbesen and Konečni (1975) was that one or another important piece of information was absent in about 35% of the cases. This missing information reflects the exigencies and distractions of the courtroom situation. As noted by Anderson (1976, 1981), much might be done for justice by the simple device of instituting a standard information schedule for each case.

Nevertheless, this correlational approach has well-known limitations, especially as concerns causal interpretation from the correlational data base. In their study of sentencing, for example, Konečni and Ebbesen (1982) were unable to distinguish two simple and quite different causal models. Another example comes from the present experiment, in which the scale-free tests were able to distinguish between the multiplying model and the differential weighted averaging model. The linear regression approach generally cannot distinguish between these two models, although they represent quite different cognitive processes. For cognitive theory, therefore, the statistical approach has limited relevance. The valuation and integration operations in the statistical model are unlikely to bear any clear or definite relation to the valuation and integration processes of individual judges.

As regards valuation, the statistical approach depends on selection and coding of variables, which must then be applied uniformly across a heterogeneous mass of cases. The judge, in contrast, evaluates the evidence by reference to a background of expert knowledge, involving legal, sociological, cultural, and moral variables that have no representation in the statistical model.

As regards integration, the statistical models have repeatedly been shown to misrepresent cognitive process. This has been found in clinical psychology, personnel selection, and Bayesian decision theory, where statistical methods outperformed clinical psychologists in predicting outcome of therapy, but were insensitive and misleading about cognitive process (see Anderson, 1981, pp. 22–23, 91; Wright, 1984, Chap. 6). Some signs indicate the same for legal judgment (Anderson, 1982, pp. 304, 306; Konečni & Ebbesen, 1975). Moreover, Ebbesen and Konečni (1982, p. 291ff.) found that severity ratings of judges and probation officers contributed most to the sentencing variance. However, no attempt was made to explain the processes that determine the severity ratings. Thus, for analysis of cognitive process, it seems essential to use stronger methods than linear regression.

Observational Analysis

A natural approach for the study of algebraic schemes in cognitive processes in legal thought and practice is through analysis of actual cases. This may be done phenomenologically, with a focus on single cases, following the case tradition of Anglo-Saxon law. Indeed, judges' opinions constitute a phenomenological data base, for they reflect judges' valuation and integration processes. This is the natural place to begin the study of judicial judgment. Such phenomenological reports can provide priceless information about cognitive processes. Of special interest are background knowledge and cognitive operators developed through extended legal experience.

Judges' opinions are self-report data, of course, and so must be expected to suffer the same limitations and pitfalls that have been found with self-report data throughout psychology. An example appears in Bauer's (1984) study of sentencing by German judges in traffic cases. Although length of sentence had a high correlation with the facts of the case, the written justifications were largely stereotypic commonplaces that had little relation to length of sentence.

For both legal analysis and cognitive analysis, therefore, in-depth interviews of the judges would be desirable to reduce ambiguity and incompleteness of the written record. In the present approach, however, these phenomenological data are not ends in themselves, but rather a beginning for experimental analysis. The problem is to find some way to embed experimental analysis of cognitive process within realistic legal settings. This problem is considered next.

Embedding Method and Personal Design

A primary goal of the present theory is to unite phenomenological and experimental analysis for the study of judgment and decision in natural settings. Phenomenological analysis can provide invaluable clues about cognition, but these clues are notoriously fallible. In the meaning constancy studies of person cognition, for example, it seemed phenomenological clear and apparent that trait adjectives strongly affected each others' meanings in a person description. Cognitive analysis showed this to be untrue (Anderson, 1981, Chap. 3). The methods of information integration theory were able to distinguish cognitive reality from phenomenologically illusion. This unified phenomenological-experimental approach may be obtainable with use of embedding method and personal design.

The embedding method, as the name suggests, involves embedding an integration task within a relevant social context. The purpose of the embedding is to allow experimental manipulation of some stimulus information within the chosen social context. Personal design carries this to the limit by constructing the integration task within the knowledge system of a selected individual.

Embedding within a legal setting could begin with a base case from some actual jurisdiction, selected to allow realistic manipulation of relevant variables. Multiple variants would then be constructed, each differing in realistic specifics from the base case. Such variables could include purposiveness of the offense, extenuating circumstances, motivation and personal character of the harmdoer, and so forth. By using factorial-type design, as in the present experiment, the patterning in the data can allow straightforward diagnosis of certain integration rules, as illustrated in Figure 9.1. Although group data were analyzed here, the same procedures can be applied to individual data.

Personal design carries the embedding method further by using the individual for selection both of the base case and of the stimulus information variables. Since task and design are both personalized, the assumption of uniformity across subjects would no longer be necessary. Moreover, phenomenological and prior observational analyses could be incorporated within a rigorous experimental design and extended through experimental analysis. Personal design can allow for knowledge that does not ascend to the level of consciousness and phenomenological report. Many cognitive factors will never reach the phenomenological level. These include unconscious or unverbalizable motivations, as well as cultural and judicial assumptions so taken for granted that the judge is unaware of making them. This application of the functional measurement methodology may provide a validational framework for phenomenology and observation in case studies that enables separation of cognitive reality from phenomenological illusion.

Some loss of realism is inevitable even with the embedding method. A personal design would ordinarily be presented in the quiet of a judge's chambers, not in the hubbub of the courtroom. Missing, therefore, would be multifarious aspects of courtroom atmosphere, including informational cues not in the personal design, together with lapses of attention and flashes of humor and irritation that distinguish an actual court. But what is being studied is the cognitive system of the judge, which is assumed to be the same in chambers as on the bench. The integration rules may thus be expected to have reasonable generality, even though the specific information being integrated may differ markedly across cases. The valuation processes, similarly, may be expected to be reasonably general, even though the specific information being evaluated is variable across cases. Although loss of courtroom realism could be serious for sociological studies of actual outcomes, many process questions can be studied outside of the actual courtroom.

Personal design would be expected to elucidate the judge's ideal of justice, which may differ from courtroom practice for various reasons already indicated. If this is a limitation, it is also an advantage, and it may even be instructive for judges to face their actual mode of operation dissected in this manner (Anderson, 1976).

The case method of instruction in law has an important similarity to the embedding method. Study of past cases in lawbooks may actually have less realism than cases in a personal design, yet it is a preferred mode of instruction. The case method could, moreover, be coupled with the embedding method. Law students would thus consider not just the single case, but a number of variant cases designed to have legal interest and to satisfy conditions for functional measurement. In this way, it would be possible to embed the study of legal cognition within legal curricula.

Acknowledgment. This work was supported by a grant from the Stiftung Volkswagenwerk, Hannover, Federal Republic of Germany, by Grant Ho 920/2-1 from the Deutsche Forschungsgemeinschaft, and by Grant BNS82-12461 from the National Science Foundation.

References

Anderson, N. H. (1976). *Social perception and cognition* (Tech. Rep. CHIP 62). San Diego: La Jolla: Center for Human Information Processing, University of California.

Anderson, N. H. (1981). *Foundations of information integration theory.* New York: Academic.

Anderson, N. H. (1982). *Methods of information integration theory.* New York: Academic.

Anderson, N. H. (1983). *Psychodynamics of everyday life: blaming and avoiding blame* (Tech. Rep. CHIP 120). San Diego: La Jolla: Center for Human Information Processing. University of California.

Bauer, G. (1984). Der Strafzumessungsvorgang als stufenweise Konkretisierung des gesetzlichen Strafrahmens. Mannheim: Jur. Diss.

Berscheid, E., & Walster, E. (1967). When does a harmdoer compensate a victim? *Journal of Personality and Social Psychology, 6*, 435–441.

Bruns, H.J. (1974). *Strafzumessungsrecht. Gesamtdarstellung* (2nd. ed.). Cologne: Heymanns.

Bruns, H.J. (1980). *Leitfaden des Strafzumessungsrechts.* Cologne: Heymanns.

Ebbesen, E.B., & Konečni, V.J. (1975). Decision making and information integration in the courts. The setting of bail. *Journal of Personality and Social Psychology, 32*, 805–821.

Haberman, S.J. (1978). *Analysis of qualitative data*: Vol. 1. New York: Academic.

Hommers, W. (1981). Recht und Psychologie: ein wechselseitiges Verhältnis. In W. Michaelis (Ed.), *Bericht über den 32. Kongreß der Deutschen Gesellschaft für Psychologie in Zürich 1980* (pp. 699–704). Göttingen: Hogrefe.

Hommers, W. (1983a). Zur quantitativen Theorie von Wiedergutmachungskognitionen unter Gewinnung ihrer Grundmerkmale aus der Jurisprudenz. In G. Lüer (Ed.), *Bericht über den 33. Kongreß der Deutschen Gesellschaft für Psychologie in Mainz* 1982 (pp. 588–595). Göttingen: Hogrefe.

Hommers, W. (1983b). *Die Entwicklungspsychologie der Delikts- und Geschäftsfähigkeit.* Göttingen: Hogrefe.

Hommers, W. (1985). Recht und Psychologie: ein wechselseitiges Verhältnis – zur Gegenstandsbestimmung der Rechtspsychologie. *Universitas, 39*, 1323–1332.

Hommers, W. (1986). Ist „Voller Ersatz" immer „Adäquater Ersatz?" Zu einer Diskrepanz zwischen Regelungen des Gesetzbuches im EXODUS und der Adäquatheits-These der Equity-Theorie. *Psychologische Beiträge, 28*, 164–179.

Hommers, W. (1988). Implizite Willenstheorien des rechtlichen Denkens aus empirisch-psychologischer Perspektive. In H. Heckhausen, F. Weinert, & F.E. Gollwitzer (Eds.), *Wollen und Handeln.* Berlin Heidelberg New York: Springer.

Hommers, W. (in press). Implicit phsychological theories of legal thought on sentence and liability. In P.J. Van Koppen, & D.J. Hessing (Eds.), *Lawyers on psychology and psychologists on law.* Amsterdam: Swets & Zeitlinger.

Hommers, W., & Anderson, N.H. (1985). Recompense as a factor in assigned punishment. *British Journal of Developmental Psychology, 3*, 75–86.

Hommers, W., & Anderson, N.H. (in preparation). Moral algebra of harm and recompense.

Konečni, V.J., & Ebbesen, E.B. (Eds.). (1982). *The criminal justice system: a social-psychological analysis.* San Francisco: Freeman.

Leon, M. (1980). Integration of intent and consequence information in children's moral judgments. In F. Wilkening, J. Becker, & R. Trabasso (Eds.), *Information integration by children.* Hillsdale, NJ: Erlbaum.

Maurach, R., Gössel, K.H., & Zipf, H. (1978). *Strafrecht. Allgemeiner Teil*: Part 2 (5th ed.). Heidelberg: Müller.

Piaget, J. (1932). *The moral judgment of the child.* London: Kegan Paul.

Surber, C.F. (1982). Separable effects of motives, consequences, and presentation order on children's moral judgments. *Developmental Psychology, 18*, 257–266.

Thomas, D.A. (1970). *Principles of sentencing. The sentencing policy of the court of appeal criminal division.* London: Heinemann.

Von Linstow, B. (1974). *Berechenbares Strafmaß.* Berlin: Schweitzer.

Wright, G. (1984). *Behavioral decision theory.* Beverly Hills, CA: Sage.

Zipf, H. (1977). *Die Strafzumessung.* München: Beck.

10
Decision-Making and the Law: A View from the Grid *

MAYA BAR-HILLEL

The theme of this talk is an exploration of the relationship between decision-making and law, perceived as that existing between an observation point and an observation. This places it somewhere in the domain of philosophy of science. The presentation will rely on the metaphor of a *grid*. The idea is borrowed from Tversky and Kahneman (1986).

Grid Arguments

Students of perception are familiar with the Müller-Lyer visual illusion, perhaps the most famous of all visual illusions. In this illusion, two straight and parallel line segments of equal length are embedded in a "context" that makes one of them appear longer than the other (Figure 10.1 a). There are several ways to become convinced that the two lines are in fact of equal length. One is to measure them. We shall call this the *analytical* way. Another is to impose an appropriate grid upon the figure (Figure 10.1 b). Note that this does not alter our perception of the two line segments when the grid is removed again (neither does the measurement), yet it provides an *argument* for why the two lines "must" be of equal length, and the argument retains its force even when the grid is removed.

A third method is to remove the interfering "context" (Figure 10.1 c). This method has some properties in common with the second one (e.g., it does not alter the original perception; it provides an overriding argument, but – like the illusion itself – it is visual rather than analytical). For present purposes, the second one is the purest example of what I have in mind, because it leaves the original figure untouched and affects our perceptions merely by showing

---

* This chapter comprises the lecture notes for a talk delivered at a conference on Psychology and Law in Braunschweig, West Germany, in October 1985.

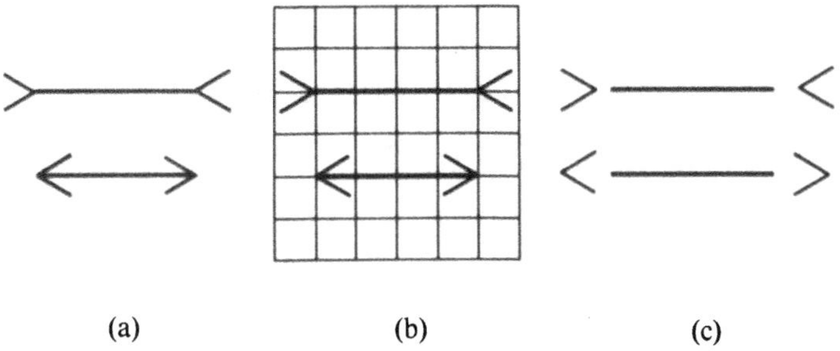

FIGURE 10.1. The Müller-Lyer illusion, as seen with (b) and without (a) a grid, and with (a) and without (c) the distractors

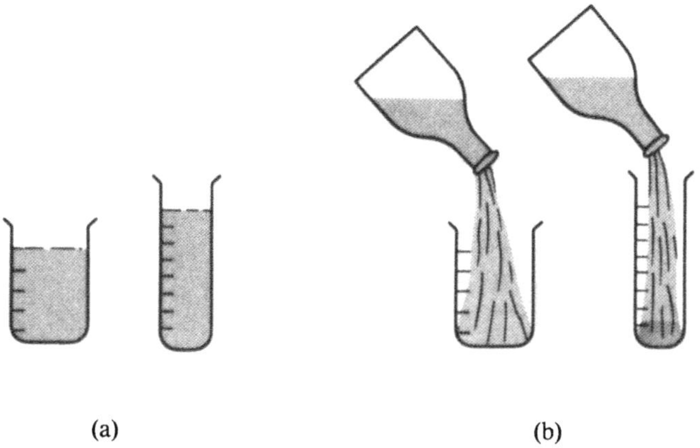

FIGURE 10.2. Piaget's judge-a-volume test, with (a) and without (b) the original water source

it to us through a grid. In any case, I am content to call both these methods *grid arguments.*

Grid arguments are used in many contexts, with greater or lesser success. Consider, for example, the famous Piagetean question regarding which of two containers has more water in it (Figure 10.2a). For most adults, the fact that both containers were filled from identical containers constitutes a grid argument that the two containers contain the same amount of water (Figure 10.2b). Although the argument is not analytical (the volumes have not been measured), and although it does not alter the original perception, adults find it overriding. Not so children.

In the final example, the grid argument does not even convince most adults. I refer to the famous choice problem first devised by Allais, and simplified to its bare essence by Tversky and Kahneman (1981), whose version I will use here. Suppose you are given a choice between 500 DM outright, and the toss of a coin that will give you 1000 DM on heads and nothing on tails (or, if you prefer, vice versa) (Figure 10.3a). Most people firmly prefer the former. Sup-

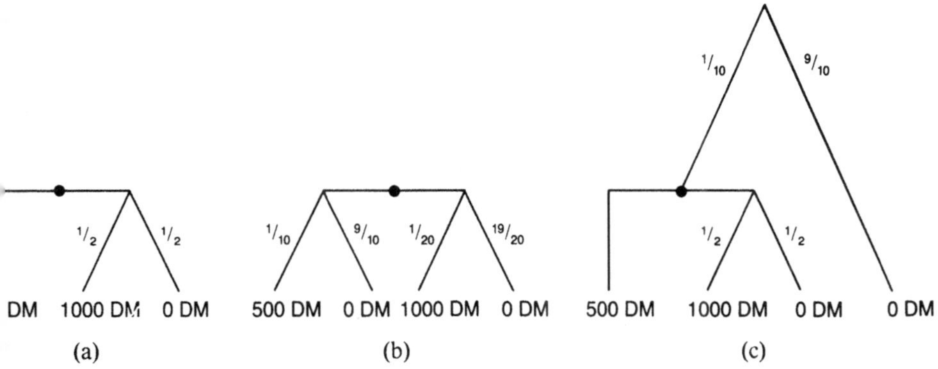

FIGURE 10.3. Tversky and Kahneman's pseudo-certainty effect. The two-stage gamble (c) is equivalent to (b), but judged psychologically like (a)

pose now that you are presented with a different choice. This time, you can either obtain 500 DM with a probability of 1/10, or 1000 DM with a probability of 1/20 (Figure 10.3 b). Here most people prefer the second possibility. The grid argument is provided by the third choice problem: the choice is again as it was in the first case (Figure 10.3 a), but you will only get an opportunity to choose if you manage to pull a red chip out of a bag containing 10% red chips and 90% black ones. You must indicate *now* what choice you will make if successful on the chip drawing (Figure 10.3 c). Formally, the third choice is identical to the second one (i.e., both yield the same outcomes with the same probabilities); intuitively, however, it seems identical to the first one (i.e., the part of it "that matters" is identical to the first). Hence, the first choice and the third choice must be identical, *up to "what matters"* (which, according to Expected Utility Theory, is the *ratio* of the probabilities of winning in the compared gambles).

Many people do not find this argument overriding. Among other reasons, note that in this example there is no analytical method to bolster the grid argument, as there was in the previous two examples, so if you are not convinced by the grid argument, you are not convinced. The question of what people find what arguments with respect to what phenomena to be appealing, convincing, compelling, or overriding is a fascinating topic for research – but it is not the topic of the present talk. I have only provided these examples to acquaint the reader with the metaphor of grid arguments.

Grids can be applied on a much greater scale than in the previous examples. Sometimes an entire discipline provides a grid through which a very wide panoply of phenomena can be observed. Two notable examples are Economics and Sociobiology. To put it very crudely and simplistically, the grid that Economics provides is the presupposition that all human behavior, including social behavior and social institutions, is rational and motivated towards maxi-

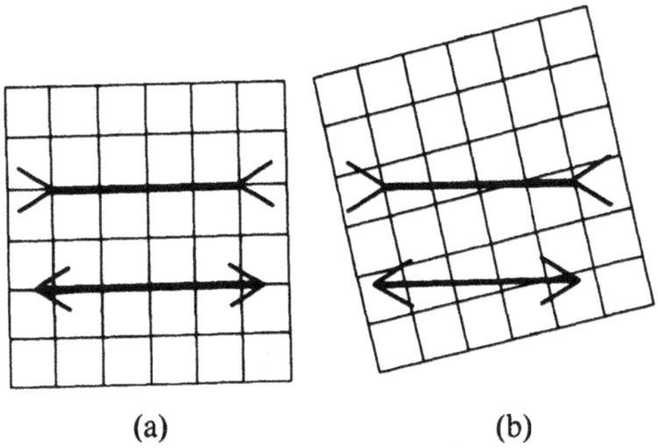

FIGURE 10.4. The Müller-Lyer illusion, as seen with a helpful (a) vs. unhelpful (b) grid

mization of one's utility. The grid that Sociobiology provides is the presupposition that all human behavior, including social behavior and social institutions, is ultimately genetically determined, being the evolutionary outcome of certain genetic units acting in pure self-interest, to preserve and maximally reproduce themselves. Thus, the economic point of view might explain philanthropy by, say, the tax advantages it confers, and sociobiology might explain individual altruistic behavior by showing how it increases the survival chances of certain genes. These perspectives are extremely powerful, but involve a considerable amount of debate around the correct identification of their basic elements (e.g., just *what* are rational people trying to maximize, or just *what* genetic units are the relevant ones for a theory of evolution).

What these perspectives share is the belief that there is something consistent and regular that imparts sense and coherence to what might seem to the casual observer to be a noisy set of complex unrelated phenomena. Indeed, some people regard these grids not merely as grids through which human behavior can be observed, but as the underlying grids (in the sense of structures, skeletons) which actually hold it all together.

Of course, when viewed in the correct manner through a grid, it becomes very apparent that lines that are *not* of equal length are not of equal length. The grid provides as compelling an argument for determining that two lines are not of equal length as for determining that they are (Figure 10.4a). But a grid sometimes provides no conclusive argument at all. In other words, some things when viewed from a grid just do not look much more orderly than they looked before. In the case of the arrows, this might happen, for example, if the grid is misaligned (Figure 10.4b).

We could go on and on this way, cataloguing ways in which "data" and "models" might fail to match, and suggesting how such mismatches might be interpreted, but this introduction is probably sufficient here, and we can turn to the application of the metaphor to the subject at hand.

The Set Up

"The Law" is a very broad domain. In the present discussion, we shall consider only courtroom trials involving legal fact-finding, and particularly the Law of Evidence that governs them. Excluded are such areas of the law as legislation, although no doubt a great deal of decision-making gets done there as well. The grid shall be provided by the Theory of Decision-Making under Uncertainty (e.g., Luce & Raiffa, 1957).

The theory of decision-making under uncertainty begins with a set of actions (also called "alternatives" or "options") among which the decision-maker chooses. The outcomes of the choice, among which the decision-maker is assumed to have well-ordered preferences, depend jointly on the chosen action and on which of a set of mutually exclusive and exhaustive "states of the world" (will) obtain. These states of the world are taken to be exogenous contingencies. The theory is an embodiment of a certain notion of *rationality*, in the form of certain *axioms* or *consistency requirements*, which identify the best action(s) for the decision-maker.

Several scholars have sought to apply this particular grid (though they did not employ the metaphor) to this particular area of the law (e.g., Alan Cullison, Richard Eggleston, John Kaplan, and Stuart Nagel). The idea is both attractive and natural. The function of judges and juries is quite naturally referred to as "decision-making," and the trial situation provides natural candidates to fill the various roles in the decision-making theory.

In a trial, the "actions" are the verdicts (e.g., in a criminal case – "guilty" vs. "innocent"; in a civil case – "for the plaintiff" vs. "for the defendant"). These can be further refined in terms of the sentencing, which, when not uniquely determined by the verdict, is at least constrained by it, but might require a separate decision. The "states of the world" are the unknown true facts of the matter at issue (e.g., whether the defendant is or is not guilty as charged). The outcomes are the contingencies attendant upon the court decision. Their evaluation in terms of preferability (technically referred to as "utility") is normatively taken to be from the point of view of the "society" on behalf of which the court is acting, rather than from the personal perspective of judge or juror.

Table 10.1 is a typical representation of a criminal trial decision as a decision matrix, as it appears, for example, in Nagel, Lamm, and Neef (1981). The

TABLE 10.1. Criminal trial decision as a decision matrix: rows = decision options; columns = possible states of the world

	Guilty p	Innocent $1 - p$
Acquit	a	b
Convict	c	d

rows represent the decision options: to acquit or to convict. The columns represent the two possible states of the world: the defendant's guilt or innocence. The cell entries represent the desirabilities (or undesirabilities) of the possible outcomes. Their value determines the threshold value for conviction. In other words, for every probability-of-guilt p it is possible to determine which of the two options – acquittal or conviction – has the greater utility. Since the (expected) utility of acquittal is equal to $a \cdot p + b(1-p)$, and the (expected) utility of conviction equals $c \cdot p + d(1-p)$, it is – according to expected utility theory – "rational" to convict if and only if $p/(1-p) > (d-b)/(a-c)$. Thus, the p value resulting at the end of a trial, after integration of all the evidence presented, the arguments, the impressions, etc. determines which verdict should be brought in. (Note that this representation makes no assumption that in point of empirical fact this is how jurors explicitly or implicitly reason).

What Legal Decision-Making Is Not

A didactic note is in order here. It is important to distinguish between decision variables (e.g., "to acquit" vs. "to convict") and between state variables (e.g., "defendant is guilty" vs. "defendant is innocent"). In everyday parlance the verb " decide" is often used with respect to the latter, although its (technical) use should be restricted to the former alone. Cullison, for example, says: "deciding what happened in a case is at heart a matter of evaluating probabilities" (1969, p. 538). But jurors do not decide what happened in a case, any more than a doctor decides what the patient is suffering from, or an archeologist decides what period an artifact dates from, or a metereologist decides the weather. These matters are altogether outside the power of the decision-maker to decide. They are what they are. To be sure, they are unknown to the decision-maker – that is the sense in which the decision-making is done under uncertainty. To guide the choice, some assessment of the likelihood of these events is in order. Sometimes – though not always – "to decide that X," where X is a state variable, is tantamount to deciding to act *as if* X. But strictly speaking, one does not "decide that X" if X is a state variable, but rather one might decide to act on X, or come to believe that X, or assign some probability to X, etc. – or one "judges that X".

The distinction is not merely semantic. One of its implications is that from the perspective of decision theory, decisions are not rendered erroneous by a mismatch between the action chosen and the state of the world. Thus, a decision to acquit a guilty defendant is not a *wrong* decision. A wrong decision is one whose utility is lower than that of an alternative. On the other hand, a belief that a guilty defendant is innocent *is* a wrong belief. Does one "decide" whether to believe something or not? That is a philosophical question way beyond the scope of this paper. But some variables can sometimes be conceptualized as either state or decision variables. For example, the social value of some outcome can be conceived of either as an ontologically real entity out there to be assessed, or as a value that the society is free to set as it will. But even under the latter conceptualization, this social decision is not the one we are interested in here. We are interested only in deciding on the verdict as a function of the established probability of guilt and the evaluation of the outcomes.

Another implication of this distinction is that legal fact-finding differs from legal decision-making, though the latter depends on the former. The following anecdote clarifies the distinction. Some years ago I was asked to give a series of talks on decision-making to the participants of a course held by the Israeli Social Security Institute. The participants were being trained, my caller explained, to *decide* whether or not a certain worker filing for worker compensation benefits was entitled to them, and how much compensation should be awarded. Most of the course involved lectures on worker compensation laws, but someone thought it would be fitting to have lectures on decision-making as well. With an intent to make my lectures as relevant as possible, and to see what areas of decision theory I should cover within the short time span proposed, I asked my caller to give me some examples of the kind of decision problems these trainees would later face on the job. The prototypical problem, it seemed, was more or less as follows:

A person comes to the Social Security office with a broken arm. According to his story, he fell on his way home from work and broke his arm. This contingency entitles him to compensation. The Social Security representative suspects, however, that the arm was actually broken over the weekend, in a recreational accident, in which case no compensation is due. The representative, I was told, now has to *decide* where the accident occurred. I was then regaled with several anecdotes of how in the past clever clerks had discovered the truth, saving the Institute much money, or how naive clerks had been duped into paying undeserved benefits, etc. My lectures were intended to teach the listeners how to be more effective decision-makers.

Listening to these stories, the realization dawned upon me that the problems faced by these clerks had little to do with what I knew as decision-making. Indeed, they were not really "deciding" anything at all; they were *fact-finding*! What circumstances entitle a worker to compensation (e.g., an accident on the way home from work) had already been decided upon by the legislators; the amount of compensation to which a worker was entitled was predetermined as a function of several variables (e.g., income, severity of the injury, etc.) which could be looked up in a table. The clerks were not deciding whether compensation was due, or how much – all this was decided upon in advance. The clerks only needed to "decide" what the facts of the matter were – and these, of course, were not theirs to be decided! My supposed expertise in decision-making had nothing to do with how to find out whether a person is telling the truth, or how to get people to be truthful, and this seemed to be the major problem faced by the trainees. I never gave my series of lectures there.... .

In summary, it can be said that Decision-Making can provide the law with a framework for setting policies, rather than with an aid in reaching verdicts in specific cases. The judicial task in a particular trial consists of ascertaining the facts of the matter and judging the applicability and relevance of various precendents, rules, and policies, from which the actual decision then follows.

"A View from the Grid"

Standards of Proof

There exist several standards of proof that are required in different types of trial. Criminal trials are governed by the standard of "beyond a reasonable doubt," while civil cases are usually governed by the "preponderance of evidence" (or "balance of probabilities") standard, and sometimes by the "clear and convincing evidence" standard. While these standards are not stated quantitatively, the criminal standard is usually taken to mean that for conviction, the probability with which guilt must be established must be very high (some writers in the judicial literature focus on the *nature* of the doubt that still permits conviction, rather than on its magnitude, calling, for instance, for "moral certitude," but none question that the probability of guilt must at least be large). The civil standard is usually taken to mean that the decision goes with whichever side presented the more likely version, although some civil cases call for higher probabilities of guilt, intermediate between the first two standards.

Notice that the criminal standard entails that we might acquit a defendant even if the case for the prosecution is stronger than the case for the defense; even if – had the truth been ascertainable – we would have, at even odds, bet on "guilt" rather than "innocence"; indeed, even if we tend to believe the accused to be guilty. So this standard does not try to maximize *the probability of being right* (i.e., predicting accurately), but rather to maximize *the utility of the decision*. When it is relative utility, rather than relative probability, that is being maximized, decision theory often recommends courses of actions that are more likely, in retrospect, to be unsuited to the facts of the matter than suited to them (I use this cumbersome language to avoid using the expression that I earlier advocated against: "more likely to be right than wrong"). On the other hand, the preponderance of evidence standard is purely and simply comparative. It goes solely with the probabilities. Why this difference?

A common interpretation is that the difference in the standards reflects the difference in the cost structure of the two types of trial. In a criminal trial, the costs are perceived to be highly asymmetrical. The withdrawing of a person's liberty and the attachment of a criminal stigma are considered so severe that the undesirability of inflicting them on an innocent person is upheld as heavily outweighing the undesirability of setting a guilty person free, even if that person is probably guilty. For example, Justice William Blackwell is often quoted as having stated that "it is better for ten guilty persons to go free than to convict one innocent person." In the typical civil case, however, the issue at stake is money – namely, in whose hands a disputed amount will ultimately come to rest, the plaintiff's or the defendant's; and, more specifically, whether the defendant will be forced to transfer funds to the plaintiff, either because they were his to begin with or by way of compensation. For example, A claims that his contract with B does not obligate him to provide B with a certain commodity, whereas B claims that it does, and that A's failure to supply the commodity caused B monetary loss. Will A have to compensate B, or not? In either kind of possible judicial error, one side will be out of pocket to the same tune, namely, by the amount at issue, thus rendering them symmetrical.

Sometimes, however, even a civil case has an asymmetrical cost structure, as when one side is charged with fraud, and would suffer more than monetary loss (i.e., severe reputational damage) if it lost the case. These seem to be the cases in which a higher standard of proof – the "clear and convincing evidence" standard – is brought to bear. Indeed, Eggleston (1983) offers the following quote from Lord Denning via Lord Pearce:

> In criminal cases the charge must be proved beyond reasonable doubt, *but there may be degrees of proof within that standard...* So also in civil cases, the case may be proved by a preponderance of probability, *but there may be degree of probability within that standard...* (depending) on the subject matter. A civil court, when considering a charge of fraud will naturally require... a higher degree of probability than... (when considering)... negligence... (N)ot... so high a degree as (in) a criminal court, ... but still it does require a degree of probability which is commensurate with the occasion. (p. 131, italics mine)

It is an interesting empirical program to check whether there is a correlation between probability-of-guilt and cost of erroneous conviction (i.e., severity of the offence) in practice. According to a hypothetical questionnaire administered to judges, jurors, and students by Simon and Mahan (1971), there would seem to be.

Inadmissible Evidence

In many judicial systems, most notably the Anglo-Saxon, and especially American, law, some types of evidence are ruled "inadmissible," i.e., they cannot be presented to the court. Inadmissible evidence can be divided into two rough classes: evidence that is deemed irrelevant, and so would just consume the court's time and add noise, and evidence that is denied although it is unquestionably relevant. It is the second category that is interesting from a decision theory point of view. Some examples of inadmissible categories of evidence are hearsay, prior convictions, illegally obtained evidence, opinion of nonexperts, and – an item that has been much debated in recent years – polygraph test results.

Ben-Shakhar, Lieblich, and Bar-Hillel (1982) recently did a decision theory (or cost-benefit) analysis of polygraph test results as evidence in criminal cases. Given their estimates of the validity of such results (e.g., the expected percent of correct identification of both innocent and guilty suspects), and of the societal cost of convicting an innocent defendant versus acquitting a guilty one, they were able to establish that basing a verdict on a polygraph test results in less "utility" than ignoring the test. In a later paper, Ben-Shakhar, Bar-Hillel, and Lieblich (1986) argued even against considering polygraph test results as just one additional evidential item among many, on grounds similar to those underlying the decision to disallow evidence as to an accused's prior convictions (except under special circumstances), namely, that their prejudicial impact outweighs their probative impact.

Preventive Detention

People who have been charged with some crime, and occasionally even people who are only being investigated for some crime, are often detained prior to trial and conviction. The reason for such pretrial incarceration is generally either to prevent the suspect from tampering somehow with the investigation or the evidence, or fear that he might commit additional crimes before the trial. In the latter cases, the decision to imprison a person prior to trial is based on a prediction of dangerousness. Such predictions, however, are notoriously unreliable, in no small part for the simple reason that criminal behavior, even by past criminals, is such a low base-rate (i.e., rare) event (e.g., Dershowitz, 1969; also Monahan, this volume). Clearly, this decision is also rendered under uncertainty. The detainee, if released, either would or would not commit another crime. If he would, this would no doubt be a severe outcome. If, on the other hand, he would not, his imprisonment would have been in vain. According to the logic that seems to underlie the standard of criminal conviction, this, too, is a severe outcome, and – under the circumstances – a far likelier one.

The same is true, of course, with respect to all potentially dangerous people, but it is completely out of the question to detain an ordinary citizen, who is not under suspicion of having committed any crime, merely because he is judged to be dangerous.

Compare now the requisite standards for incarcerating these three types of people: a person on trial for having committed a crime, a person suspected of a past crime and considered likely to commit a future one, and a person who is simply considered dangerous (i.e., likely to commit a crime in the future). Legally speaking, all are presumed innocent until proven guilty. The first would be imprisoned only if his past criminal behavior had been established with a very high probability; the second would be imprisoned on the (unreliable) prediction of future criminal behavior, which typically has a low probability of being borne out; the third cannot be imprisoned at all, irrespective of the probability with which it can be established that he or she might commit a future crime. These three cases, considered jointly from a decision theory perspective which takes into account only the probabilities of the possible states of the worlds and the societal costs of the various outcomes, would seem to be inconsistent. The decision theory grid, therefore, has either failed to capture the essence of these three decisions or has shown an inconsistency in the social policy underlying them.

Sources of Judicial Uncertainty

The previous example showed how two types of uncertainty (whether a person has committed a crime, or whether he might commit a crime) can result in different decisions even if the costs of the possible outcomes and the magnitude of the uncertainty are held constant. There are other legal examples that show that the same amount of uncertainty, when it derives from different sources, might result in a different legal decision. Consider, for example, a civil case in which a plaintiff claims that a defendant is to blame for certain damages caused the plaintiff. In some jurisdictions, if the court is satisfied that the damage is worth $X, the plaintiff will be awarded the full sum even if the court is, say, only 70% sure that the damages were the defendant's fault. Suppose, however, that the defendant's blame has been established with certainty, but that there is only a 70% chance that the damage will amount to $X. In the latter case, courts operating within the Anglo-Saxon system will only award the defendant 70% of $X. Why, asks Eggleston (1983), "should a plaintiff who only persuades the court that it is 51% probable that he has suffered damages in the past get the full amount, while a similar plaintiff whose proof relates to the future may only get 51%?" (p. 222).

From the perspective of the decision theory grid, this question has "no clear logical answer" (ibid., p. 222). Indeed, in some legal systems damages are divided proportionately to the assignation of blame, even with respect to past events (e.g., "comparative negligence" in American courts). Recently in the United States, a youth won an immense settlement from the New York City Subway Authority. This youth had thrown himself under an oncoming train in a failed suicide attempt. He survived, but with very severe bodily damage. The court ruled that though most of the blame for the accident was clearly the youth's, the Subway Authority was also partly to blame (e.g., for failing to put up effective rails preventing such attempts), and awarded the youth some small fraction of the huge amount he sued for (Time Magazine, Summer, 1984).

Other Issues That Could Be Grist for the Grid

I have concluded the examples I wanted to present in this talk: two that make sense when reconstructed from the decision theory perspective, and two that seem paradoxical when viewed through it. Many other legal phenomena could be viewed from this grid, while others do not lend themselves so readily to such a reconstruction. Further examples of the former are other categories of inadmissible evidence, the notion of reasonable man, legal presumptions, optimal jury size, and the optimal voting rule for combining jurors' opinions (see, e.g., Gelfand & Solomon, 1975; Nitzan & Paroush, 1985), compromise verdicts, and sentencing. A possible example of the latter are comparisons of different legal systems (e.g., Anglo-Saxon vs. Continental, trial by jury or without, pros and cons of the adversary system).

References

Ben-Shakhar, G., Lieblich, I., & Bar-Hillel, M. (1982). An evaluation of polygraphers' judgments: a review from a decision theoretic perspective. *Journal of Applied Psychology, 67*, 701–713.

Ben-Shakhar, G., Bar-Hillel, M., & Lieblich, I. (1986). Trial by polygraph: scientific and juridical issues in lie detection. *Behavioral Science and the Law, 4*, 459–479.

Cullison, A. D. (1969). Probability analysis of judicial fact-finding: a preliminary analysis of the subjective approach. *Toledo Law Review, 3*, 538–598.

Dershowitz, A. M. (1969). The law of dangerousness: some fictions about predictions. *Journal of Legal Education, 23*, 24–47.

Eggleston, R. (1983). *Evidence, proof and probability* (2nd ed.) London: Weidenfeld and Nicholson.

Gelfand, A. E., & Solomon, H. (1975). Modeling jury verdicts in the American legal system. *Journal of the American Statistical Association, 69*, 32–37.

Kaplan, J. (1968). Decision theory and the factfinding process. *Stanford Law Review, 20*, 1065–1092.

Luce, R. D., & Raiffa, H. (1957). *Games and decisions.* New York: Wiley.

Nagel, S., Lamm, D., & Neef, M. (1981). Decision theory and juror decision making. In L. C. Solev (Ed.), *The trial process* (pp. 353–386). New York: Plenum.

Nitzan, S., & Paroush, J. (1985). *Collective decision making: an economic outlook.* Cambridge, MA: Cambridge University Press.

Simon, R. J., & Mahan, L. (1971). Quantifying burdens of proof. *Law and Society Review, 5*, 319–330.

Tversky, A., & Kahneman, D. (1981). The framing of decisions and the psychology of choice. *Science, 211*, 453–458.

Tversky, A., & Kahneman, D. (1986). Rational choice and the framing of decisions. *Journal of Business, 59*, 251–278.

11
Decision Processes in the Jury Room

A. PHILIP SEALY

Introduction

The Anglo-American adversary process in the criminal justice system and, to a lesser extent in the civil justice system, is marked by a clear distinction, in theory, between matters of fact and matters of law, decisions in the former case being for the lay-person, the "fact-finder", and in the latter, for the judge. As Devlin (1956) remarks, the judge makes two formal warnings at the outset of the trial addressed to members of the jury:

1. "The facts are for you, the law is for me" (Devlin, 1956)
2. "Throughout this trial it is for the Crown to prove its case, not for the defendant to prove his innocence" (Glanville Williams, 1968).

Thus, at the outset of a trial, the rules are defined and the roles prescribed. The rules are set out in the instructions on burden of proof (Cornish, 1969; Cross & Wilkins, 1979; Glanville Williams, 1968). These rules of instruction and exclusion control the evidence admissible in court and attempt to control the interpretations placed on such evidence. The rules can produce fine, perhaps even pedantic, distinctions, such as that quoted by Underwood (1977) where two interpretations of proof were contrasted: proof "beyond reasonable doubt" and proof with "clear and convincing evidence". These are assumed to be two distinguishable criteria of "proof". There are many other rules of evidence that constrain and control the evidence reaching the court (LSE Jury Project, 1978). Similarly, the roles of fact-finders and sentencer are explicitly separated: the role of the judge in dealing with the substantive evidence is strictly that of arbiter of admissibility and summarizer of the case as a whole; a sentencing role for the jury is frequently specifically proscribed (e.g. the instruction to try the facts, regardless of potential sentence if guilt is determined). Thus the jury stands at the focal point of contested trials, where facts and law are separated. Hence, then, the importance of attempting to understand the likely processes involved in jury decision-making.

Several problems arise in considering this issue, the first being those associated with the secrecy and anonymity of the jury. Secrecy, amongst other things, means that the jury deliberation cannot be directly observed, or, indeed, reconstructed after the decision. Anonymity implies that neither individually nor collectively may jurors be asked to justify or explain their decision. Although direct observation is impossible because of the constraints surrounding the jury, such observation of jury processes would be difficult to interpret since there are unique and idiosyncratic features to each trial and to each manner of conducting a trial. A second problem arises from the nature of research into trial by jury, namely the choice of critical independent variables. There are two sources of theory for making such a choice of research objectives: the body of knowledge contained in jurisprudence and the varieties of theory found interesting by psychologists. This distinction leads to incompatible choices. For example, of the 72 citations of research on juries – almost all American (Bray & Kerr, 1982) – exactly 50% required the "jurors" to make a judgment on a continuous scale, usually a 7-point one from "1 = definitely guilty" to "7 = definitely innocent", or the reverse. This is a fairly usual practice in psychological experiments, but is impossible to interpret from a legal point of view where dichotomous decisions are required – guilty or not guilty. Likewise, some researchers (cf. Landy & Aronson, 1969) use the formula "1 = definitely sure of guilty vs. 7 = definitely sure of innocence". Here two variables are confounded, decision and certainty. It is not difficult to show that these are independent of each other. Rules that have little or no influence on decisions (e.g. majority vs. unanimous instruction) have a statistically significant effect on confidence. Similarly, discussion may not alter jurors' decisions but have significant effects on their confidence (Sealy, 1978). Again, a number of experiments using jury-like material have manipulated the variable of interpersonal attractiveness (Izzett & Leginsky, 1974; Landy & Aronson, 1969; Ostrom, Werner, & Saks, 1978). Now, in the real world of the courtroom, no one can control "attractiveness", nor can it be used in the arguments presented, regardless of the putative influence it might have. There is, therefore, a possibility that whilst psychologists pursue their own – legitimate – concerns, they will contribute little to the understanding of the courtroom situation as it exists in reality.

In all of the research quoted here, there has been a vast amount of observed material, whether in the form of completed questionnaires or reviewed audiotapes of discussion. The material – empirical data – has been collected because of the richness of the field, not through the urgency of theory: Darwin did not visit South America because it represented a test-tube for his theory of natural selection. Whilst not elevating the present research beyond its merits, inductive approaches to social research are by no means devoid of validity. Hence, no "theories" led to the selection of what was observed in the cases of research to be quoted in the following pages and, likewise, no "theories" were refuted by observations quoted.

By the same token lawyers use such terms as "*mens rea*" to denote the well-researched area of the psychology of intentionality, which is diverse and complicated (cf. Weiner, Russell, & Lerman, 1978). This incompatibility of law and psychology can create substantial methodological problems in studying the jury. There are three basic methods by which the jury can be examined: first, general surveys of jury decisions of which the study of Kalven and Zeisel (1966) is the most famous, although those of Zander (1974) and Baldwin and McConville (1980) are important in the analysis of the English jury system. However, this research, crucial as it is, only shows what juries do, not how they do it. The two major types of research into this latter problem involve the use of "shadow" juries or simulated or "mock" juries. The shadow jury is one that sits in court, observes the case in full and then makes a decision in conditions under which it can be observed. The Oxford studies (McCabe & Purves, 1974) and the later Chicago studies (Zeisel & Diamond, 1978) exemplify this approach. There are several advantages to this approach, chief amongst them being that, by avoiding the use of audio or video tapes and allowing "jurors" to see the real court proceedings as they unfold, it provides high external validity (Campbell & Stanley, 1963). Problems arise partly from the vagaries of cases, such as their length and the possibility of a change of plea at any stage of the trial. They also arise from the difficulties of sampling shadow jurors. The Oxford method was somewhat ad hoc – searching for volunteers – whereas the Chicago studies were much more ingenious, although requiring a high level of co-operation from the courts, namely recruiting two shadow juries, one from the empanelled jurors not called for a trial and one from those rejected from serving as a result of challenges. A final problem arises from the types of comparison that can be made in jury processes between uniquely different types of case.

The simulated jury has higher internal validity (Campbell & Stanley, 1963) by dint of allowing many juries to listen to the same case, sometimes with systematic variations, but is short on external validity. With these considerations in mind the remainder of this paper will be devoted to a consideration of the processes of deliberation within a jury. This is not to say that other issues are not important: problems of jury size (cf. Davis, Kerr, Atkin, Holt, & Meek, 1975), juror bias (Sealy, 1982) or the effects of rules of instruction (cf. Sealy & Cornish, 1973) are of equal if not greater relevance to the overall analysis of the jury. Of the many researches undertaken in this area, particular attention will be paid to those carried out in Chicago, Oxford, Yale and London.

The Chicago Studies

In the first instance Kalven and Zeisel (1966) were concerned with the extent to which judges agreed with juries in their decisions over cases that were recent and vivid in their (the judges') memories. Each judge reported on one case selected as "typical". Table 11.1 shows the results of 3576 such cases, although

TABLE 11.1. Kalven and Zeisel's findings regarding judge-jury agreement (3576 cases)[a]

Judge and jury convict	62%
Judge and jury acquit	13.4%
Judge wishes to convict; jury acquit	16.9%
Judge wishes to acquit; jury convict	2.2%
Overall judge-jury agreement	75.4%

[a] Note that there were some "hung" decisions

TABLE 11.2. Judges' views on jury acquittals (Birmingham) (Baldwin & McConville, 1979)

No strong view about the justification of acquittal	62%
Some doubts about acquittal	6%
Serious doubts about acquittal	31%
Total $n = 114$	
Total number of cases 500, of which 45% were acquitted by jury (23% on instructions from judge or because no jury was empanelled, with the case withdrawn)	

TABLE 11.3. Reasons for disagreements between judges and juries (Kalven & Zeisel, 1966)

Disagreement (as seen by judge) about the interpretation of evidence	49%
Feelings about the law	30%
Disparity in the performance of opposing counsel	4%
Facts the judge alone knew	2%
(No reply or no opinion)	13%

as Bottoms and Walker (1972) point out, only 19% of judges replied to their postal questionnaires. The important part of Table 11.1 lies in the 19.1% of disagreements, of which a majority represented the jury's wish to acquit whilst the judge, alone, would have wished to convict. It is important, first, to describe their findings, which indicate that, over a wide area of the United States, judges and juries agreed in their verdicts. Rather similar results have been presented with regard to the English[1] system of administering criminal justice (cf. Baldwin & McConville, 1979; Zander, 1978), as shown in Table 11.2.

Table 11.3, reconstructed from the original research report, shows the character of the reasons judges give for the rare disagreement in decisions. Several things are worth noting. First, disagreements about the interpretation of

[1] It is important to note that the Scottish system differs significantly from the English. Uncertain ("not proven") verdicts are permitted, jury size is variable (up to 13) and finally the decision to prosecute is in the hands of the Procurator Fiscal – a lawyer, but not a policeman – a person whose powers extend beyond that of the English Director of Public Prosecutions (DPP) in the sense that he can demand additional inquiry.

evidence represent the largest single reason for verdict disagreements. Secondly, two obvious features of the trial seem *not* to be particularly important features in judges' disagreements with juries. In only 4% of cases of disagreement was the disparity of performance of the contesting adversary lawyers thought by judges to be a significant feature of the reason for disagreement. In only 2% of cases was the reason given for disagreement as "facts known only to the judge". This usually meant the judge's recognition of a persistent offender. Of the rest of the reasons given, 30% concerned "feelings about the law". It is important to make clear that out of 3576 cases, judges and juries agreed in 75.1%. These "feelings" – attitudes might be a better term – concerned the following five features of the trial:

1. Gravity of outcome of the case, with the jury tending to acquit, despite the evidence, where little objective harm was done
2. Triviality of the charge, such as theft of property of little value
3. Disapproval of the law
4. Apparent desire by the accused to effect restitution
5. Victim provocation.

Thus, in general, judges and juries agree about verdict. Where they disagree it seem to be largely as a result of differing interpretations of the facts, but there does seem to be an area in which juries apparently allow themselves to express, by their judgments, attitudes to the law.

In pursuing their researches further, the Chicago group analyzed the discussions of a number of simulated juries. This was undertaken largely from the viewpoint of Bales's (1950) interaction process analysis, which attempts to obtain a view of the nature of the group decision by means of studying individual contributions to it. In a series of articles (Strodtbeck, 1962; Strodtbeck & Mann, 1956; Strodtbeck, James, & Hawkins, 1957) a number of issues were addressed such as the role of gender and status in degree of participation in deliberation, as well as the frequency of certain general classes of argument used as a function of the majority or minority status of jurors at a given point in the trial. Their results can briefly be summarized as follows:

a) Status and Gender. Working on the assumption that each juror should contribute 1/12 (8.3%) to the discussion, the proportions of contributions to deliberation were found to be as shown in Table 11.4.

The line drawn on the table indicates where the contribution is less than expected by chance (below the line). The table shows that females contributed less to the deliberation than males (the average difference being 3.4%). This, of course, is in part or largely because females were in a minority on the jury. Where the reverse obtains, as in some recent studies at the LSE (cf. Johannesen, 1986; Lee, 1984), the disproportion in contribution is reversed – males contribute less – *and* the disproportion is much greater.

b) Valued Contributions. Where jurors were invited to state whose contributions were most useful in discussion, average votes received out of 12 as a maxi-

TABLE 11.4. Proportions of contributions of jurors to discussion according to sex and class

	Males	Females
Upper middle class	12.9	9.1
Lower middle class	10.8	7.8
Skilled manual	7.9	4.8
Unskilled	7.5	4.6

TABLE 11.5. Average votes received by jurors as an assessment of their contributions, according to sex and class

	Males	Females
Upper middle class	6.8 (0.53)	3.2 (0.35)
Lower middle class	4.2 (0.39)	2.7 (0.35)
Skilled manual	3.9 (0.49)	2.0 (0.42)
Unskilled manual	2.7 (0.36)	1.0 (0.22)

mum were as shown in Table 11.5. In parentheses is the proportion of "helpful" remarks to participation rate, implying, for instance, that upper middle class males contributed most, and more of their contributions were seen as helpful as compared with unskilled manual class women, who participated least and whose contributions were viewed by fellow jurors as least helpful. This, of course, may represent prejudice as much as reality.

c) Use of Arguments. The use of different arguments is, as one might expect, always greater for the majority than the minority jurors, although this effect seems only to apply in the first quarter and last quarter of the deliberations, especially in hung juries. In the middle half of the deliberations each side produces an approximately equal number of different arguments, although it is unclear whether this varies as a function of the preferred verdict of the majority. Overall, these results show some, perhaps not expected, structural features of jury deliberation and in so doing have implications for the practical problems of how juries might equitably be composed. They lack any searching statistical analysis, but this, as will be seen later, often lies in the difficulty of finding an appropriate metric for analysing discussion. One final point is worth commenting on: the extent to which the nature of a case requires varied jury composition. As Strodtbeck et al. state: "If status differences are present in the jury room it is almost certain that they arise in part because the varied requirements of deliberation ... (require) the differential experiences associated with status" (p. 714). This is a point too complex to discuss here, but it has implications regarding the possibility of specialized juries for particular cases (e.g. fraud).

The Oxford Studies

Using the shadow jury technique, of the 30 cases they (McCabe & Purves, 1974) studied, the comparison between the verdicts of the real and the shadow jury were as follows:

Both shadow and real jury wished to convict 30%. Both shadow and real jury wished to acquit 30%.

Shadow juries wished to convict and real juries to acquit 13%. Shadow juries wished to acquit and real juries to convict 7%.

The remaining juries were "hung". This means that in terms of verdicts the shadow juries were, surprisingly perhaps, very similar to real juries, which lends some validity to conclusions drawn from analysing their deliberations. The following were the major characteristics of the shadow jury in relation to the case:

1. It tended towards *leniency* in two ways. First, even with substantive evidence (e.g. the possession by the accused of fairly obviously stolen goods and his suspicion that they were stolen), a juror could still remark: "That still doesn't make him guilty." Secondly, when the jury concurred that some important evidence or witness was not produced in court.
2. The jury was very concerned with *rules of instruction*. For example, in one case (handling stolen goods), the discussion *started* with the Foreman saying „We have to go back to the remarks of the judge on corroboration *before* we can get very far" (p. 45). In other words, discussing rules of court procedure can frequently take priority over organising the evidence. This point will arise again in discussion of the extent to which rules are understood and constrain argument.
3. The jury sometimes felt exasperated at not having apparently *specious defences* properly commented on by the prosecution. Possessing a stolen bicycle, with the implication that he stole it, the defence was that he bought if from an unknown person who preferred to sell the bicycle and use the proceeds to take a taxi. The jury found this "surprising", especially as the police made no attempt to trace the taxi firm that might be concerned.

In all of these juries, there seemed to be a strong sense of equity and avoidance of spurious consensus, but it has to be said that the themes that emerge from this research are subjective and selective.

The Yale Studies

Saks (1977), in his study of effects of group size and decision rule, produced some interesting findings about the effects of these variables on the types of argument used. Fifty-eight juries were empanelled from the jury lists in an Ohio county district. Six-person juries differed from 12-person juries in the following ways:

1. Deliberation was shorter
2. Participation was less (per juror)
3. Recall of testimony was poorer
4. Arguments about conviction were better recalled.

However, the two sizes of jury did *not* differ in terms of:

1. Number of arguments produced
2. Number of arguments about acquittal recalled
3. Satisfaction with, and feelings or reasonableness of, the deliberation.

The variation of decision rule (majority vs. unanimity) also affected deliberation. If the rule was to reach unanimity:

1. Fewer arguments for acquittal were recalled
2. More arguments for acquittal occurred.

However, there were no differences in:

1. Arguments generated
2. Amount of communication
3. Conviction arguments recalled.

Now these are, of course, very general statements about the occurrence of arguments under different conditions, not about the content of those arguments.

The Studies at the London School of Economics

Amongst other things in this series of studies an attempt was made to trace specific substantive themes through deliberation on two cases, one of theft and one of rape, through, respectively, 34 and 22 mock juries recruited on a representative basis from the general population. The questions to be asked concerned specific elements of the trial and how they were used by different factions in the discussion. The following tables give some indication of just why analysis of the deliberation is so critical.

Table 11.6 indicates that the experimental variables had little effect on the *private* verdicts jurors arrived at after hearing the full trial[2] and before deliberation, but that significant effects did emerge after deliberation.

[2] An audio tape produced from the court transcript lasting respectively 1 1/4 hours (theft) and 1 1/2 hours (rape).

TABLE 11.6. The effects of various rules of evidence and exclusionary rules on verdicts (LSE Jury Project, 1978)

Experimental variable	Case	*n*	Pre-deliberation	Post-deliberation
Burden of proof	Theft	312	No effect	No effect
Burden of proof	Rape	257	No effect	Significant effects
Majority verdict	Theft	48	No effect	No effect
Corroboration	Rape	257	No effect	Significant effects
Recent complaint	Rape	257	No effect	Significant effects
Inclusion of similar previous record	Theft	312	No effect	Significant effects
Inclusion of similar previous record	Rape	257	No effect	Significant effects
Inclusion of dissimilar previous record	Theft	312	No effect	Significant effects
Inclusion of dissimilar previous record	Rape	257	No effect	Significant effects

Taking each of the research findings in turn, it is useful to ask whether different arguments occurred in the different experimental conditions. There were immense methodological problems in analysing lengthy discussions (lasting between 30 min and 2 h) by groups of 12 people who sometimes seemed all to be talking at once (up to 10% of discussion was uninterpretable for this reason). The methods used in this part of the research can be summarised as follows:

Stage 1: All discussions recorded on audio-tapes.

Stage 2: Teams of raters listened to each tape five times, having been given prior instructions about the experiment.

Stage 3: The first hearing of the discussion was for the purpose of familiarisation; no ratings were made.

Stage 4: The teams listened to the tapes a second time and rated each 5-min period for the following main characteristics:

a) Its task relevance
b) Whether it represented monologue, dyadic discussion or several simultaneous discussions
c) Its rateability as mentioned above
d) If irrelevant, the extent to which it involved discussion of the purpose of the experiment per se
e) Procedural matters, such as electing a foreman or taking notes.

Stage 5: The teams listened to the tapes again and made general ratings of the contributions in terms of whether they involved:

a) Asking questions and seeking information
b) Making suggestions
c) Providing information
d) Providing interpretations

e) Suggesting solutions and/or decisions
f) Providing compromise suggestions to resolve deadlocks
g) Relieving tension, for example, by joking or agreeing with others' suggestions;

Stage 6: On the fourth listening to the tapes raters tried to assess the proportion of time spent discussing particular salient substantive features of the trial for each 5-minute period. Raters also tried to assess whether the material was discussed as suggesting the guilt of the defendant, his/their innocence or neutrally.

Stage 7: The final listening to the tape attempted to isolate which individual jurors talked most, and in what way, about which particular features of the trial.

Stage 8: The ratings were pooled, leaving out any raters who failed to complete the entire sequence, and these pooled ratings were then analysed in terms of:
a) Location within the trial (early, middle, late)
b) The experimental variables (instructions on proof and previous convictions)
c) The ultimate decision of the jury (guilty, not guilty or hung).

The task of sorting and analysing ratings was a formidable one and the results to be presented here are derived mainly from stages 4 and 6. The raters were compared for dependability, which varied from stage to stage, but the average inter-rater reliability across all trials was $r = 0.62$ for stage 4, 0.56 for stage 5, 0.52 for stage 6 and 0.29 for stage 7. However, since these figures involved summing across many different groups of raters and 56 discussions in all, they must be treated with extreme caution, providing as they do only an estimate of the general order of reliabilities.

Summarising the results, the following trends emerged:

1. Percentage of time spent on relevant discussions in the case of theft:

(Across 34 juries)	86% (±3%)
Unrateable	8% (±1.5%)
Other matters (procedural, personal etc.)	5% (–)
Discussing the experiment	<1% (–)

2. Percentage of time spent on discussions in the rape case mainly concerned with:

Defendant Harrison	56% (±4%)
Defendant Bryce	14% (±1.5%)
The victim	13% (± <1%)
Unrateable	13% (± <1%)
The experiment	1% (–)
Procedural/personal matters etc.	2% (–)

Thus in both trials the discussion was largely relevant and there was little variation between discussion by different juries in the time spent on relevant, task-orientated discussion. That is to say, most juries spent most of their time in relevant discussion, the parenthetical figures referring to one standard error of the distributions across discussions. It is noteworthy that in the case of rape the most substantial proportion of the discussion concerned the defendant Harrison. It is about him that the judge said in his summing up: "You may think that, by his own admission, Harrison largely convicts himself." Despite this, much discussion concerned this defendant and in particular, if guilty, whether he was guilty of rape or attempt. For the other defendant there was greater doubt; the judge's summing up again: "It is largely a matter of his word against hers since there is no independent corroboration of her account."

In the rape discussions a good deal of time was devoted to the victim, Mary. Most discussion was concerned with three features of her behavior: her possible "provocativeness", her likely consent and the possibility that she invented the "tale" to cover her embarrassment. Finally, procedural matters were often difficult for jurors to cope with: electing a foreman usually devolved into self-selection (e.g. the first person to speak or to admit prior experience of jury service). Taking votes was an unpredictable affair but occurred several times in each deliberation, more frequently, as might be expected, in the latter part of discussion. One jury, which by private ballot was unanimous at the outset of deliberation, took 25 minutes of heated discussion before a vote revealed their unanimity.

The second of these analyses concerned looking at specific features of evidence as they emerged in discussion. It should be pointed out here that the pattern of argument was seldom coherent: in any 5-min period several different issues might arise, combining sometimes two or even three different themes in one comment. In the theft case four major issues arose in argument: the bulkiness of the allegedly stolen meat, the likelihood of a collusion to entrap the defendant, the relevance of his previous criminal record and the importance of burden of proof. Of the experimental variables used in this case, it was the admission of a similar previous record for the defendant that significantly influenced post-deliberation verdicts. The most striking effects are set out in Table 11.7, from which two things emerge: first, the introduction of the previous record for dissimilar offences reduced the overall use of this argument in discussion (see line y in the table), and, secondly, whatever the condition the same set of information was used equally to support an overall view of the defendant's guilt or his innocence. In other words, the same facts were used in opposite ways in argument.

When considering the possibility that the defendant was a victim of collusion, the results set out in Table 11.8 emerged. In contrast to the previous table, it would appear that where a *dissimilar* record was mentioned (line y), there was *more* discussion of likely collusion on the part of the defendant's employers, either in his favour, against or in an uncertain manner. Since the experimental variation of the defendant's previous criminal record apparently affected the use of these arguments, it is worth spelling out how much time was spent discussing this topic. Table 11.9 shows the average time spent as a

TABLE 11.7. The use of arguments for the defendant, against him or neutral, in respect of the weight of meat, as a function of the experimental variables (average rated no. of minutes per 5-min period)

Experimental variable		Arguments used		
		For the defendant	Against	Uncertain
x	Similar previous record	1.1	1.4	1.7
y	Dissimilar record allowed	0.8	0.6	1.4
z	Similar record disallowed	1.4	1.3	1.7
Co	No record mentioned	1.6	1.2	1.5

TABLE 11.8. Arguments about collusion

	In favour	Against	Uncertain
x	0.8	0.9	0.5
y	1.2	1.0	0.9
z	0.7	0.6	0.4
Co	0.8	0.6	0.5

TABLE 11.9. Average time in minutes spent discussing previous criminal record per 5-min period

	In favour	Against	Neutral
x	0.2	0.9	<0.1
y	0.8	0.1	<0.1
z	0.8	0.6	<0.1
Co	0.5	0.6	<0.1

function of the experimental variables. Given that the average length of discussion was just over 2 h, this can be seen as indicating that between 20 and 25 min spread throughout the deliberation was spent discussing the defendant's criminal record, *even where none was presented* (control condition) and for at least two conditions (y and z) substantially using the record as favouring an *acquittal.*

A certain amount of time was spent discussing the concept of proof and reasonable doubt. This topic was discussed equally amongst all experimental conditions, the average time per 5-min period being about 0.5 min, i.e. about 12–15 min total time. As will be seen below, discussion of the topic tended to occur later in the deliberation. One important feature here, though, is the extent to which the instruction was correctly portrayed in the discussion: where the instruction was the orthodox one ("reasonable doubt") it was correctly described and used in 54% of the discussions of this topic; where alternative instructions were given (i.e. "sure and certain" or "balance of probabilities") they were correctly defined in 22% and 19% of the discussions respectively. For the rest of the discussion "proof" was talked about, but without any juror stating clearly what the given criterion was.

Finally, from our analyses of the theft case the use of specific arguments can be discussed in the light of the attempt to support or refute a general tendency in the discussion to defend or attack minority opinion, or in the light of position within the discussion. The following summarises this aspect of the research:

1. In *supporting* a tendency towards a *guilty* verdict, there was a tendency to stick to *concrete facts*, and argument consisted mainly of reiterating them.
2. In *supporting* a tendency towards *acquittal*, there was a search for alternative explanations for the events.
3. In *refuting* a tendency towards a *guilty* verdict, there was a greater use of procedural issues within the group.
4. In *refuting* a tendency towards acquittal, there was greater use of arguments about "unreasonable doubt".

Arguments may be used for or against the defendant or merely be mentioned in a neutral manner. For the 28 juries in the main experimental design the overall proportions were as shown in Table 11.10. The surprising observation here is that even with juries that eventually convict, the arguments are used evenly for or against the defendant. No variations were found between specific arguments.

Turning to the discussions in the rape case, two general overall impressions must be noted: first, that the discussions were very animated and, as indicated before, relevant, and, secondly, across all experimental conditions the effects of instructional variation was markedly mediated by discussion. However, the analyses of the discussions of the rape case revealed many uncompromisingly negative features:

TABLE 11.10. Proportion of time spent using arguments favourably, unfavourably or indifferently as a function of eventual verdict

Eventual verdict	Proportion of time spent		
	In favour	Neutral	Against
Guilty (3)	0.17	0.13	0.16
Hung (17)	0.18	0.12	0.10
Acquit (8)	0.29	0.17	0.10

1. There were no differences in topics of argument between different experimental conditions.
2. Although effectively altering the verdict, there was very little discussion of the significance of introducing the second defendant's previous criminal record.
3. There was little or no variation in types of argument used by majority or minority status jurors.
4. There was no variation in the types of argument used at various stages of the discussion, with the exception that the majority of the discussion related to the second defendant occurred within the last 10 min or so of the discussion, which averaged just over 2 h in length.

The major findings from the analyses concerned the topics most frequently discussed and their uses, in terms of the decisions ultimately reached. Thus the results in this case must be summarised in a slightly different way from those in the previous one, presenting the arguments used in terms of the frequency of presentation and their usage to justify or support verdicts of guilty or not guilty for each defendant in turn. The first defendant (Harrison) admitted having, or attempting, sexual intercourse, admitted that the victim did not consent and admitted "pulling", if not "dragging", her to the scene of the alleged crime. Table 11.11 sets out the arguments used with regard to him. This table can be read as follows. Of the time spent discussing the defendant Harrison, 7.1% was spent discussing the fact that he had or attempted to have intercourse with the victim and this pointed to his being not guilty as charged. This aspect of the results is particularly disturbing since it means that for a substantial proportion of the discussion, the jury can agree to certain "facts" – the occurrence of intercourse, the use of some physical force, the distress and injury to the victim and her failure to consent – and yet still argue for an acquittal.

With regard to the second defendant, it has already been noted that much less time was spent discussing his likely guilt and that discussion tended to occur towards the end of deliberations. What time was spent on him was in-

TABLE 11.11. Arguments related to decisions with regard to defendant Harrison

Topic of argument	Time spent proportionately arguing for decision of		
	Not guilty	Guilty of attempt	Guilty of rape
He had/attempted intercourse	7.1	9.0	9.5
He held the victim by arm/ pushed her/struck her etc.	5.5	7.4	8.7
Victim was distressed/nose bleeding etc.	5.2	7.3	8.2
Victim did *not* consent	0.3	0.8	2.7

TABLE 11.12. The time spent solely discussing the victim's reactions and behavior, subdivided by use of argument (% of time)

Reaction/behavior	With a view to:		
	Acquittal	Conviction	Uncertain
Her inconsistency in accounts	29	3	2
Her encouragement	12	–	–
Her failure to resist	13	–	–
Other (e.g. her distress)	2	13	6
Unrateable	Approximately 20		

conclusive and virtually no discussion arose of his previous criminal record. The burden of the argument seemed very much a fall-out effect – a decision to convict the other defendant implied accepting the victim's account and thus tended to incriminate this defendant. However, no jurors (out of 257) wished to acquit the first defendant and convict the second, whereas 34% wished to acquit the second defendant whilst convicting the first.

A good deal of time in deliberation was spent discussing the behavior of the victim, and here three themes received prominence, all pointing juries in the direction of acquittal. First, her evidence was frequently cited as "inconsistent" because her accounts at the magistrate's court and the crown court (over 8 months later) showed some discrepancies. Secondly, she was viewed as encouraging and, *therefore*, consenting to intercourse by allowing the first defendant to kiss her prior to the offence. Thirdly, she did not resist as strongly as she might have done. On average, over the 22 juries 13% of the discussion (about 15.5 min out of 2 h) was spent solely discussing the victim's reactions. Of course, the discussions occurred at various points in the deliberation but usually clustered in the middle part. Averaging the raters' allocation of time spent on these topics the results shown in Table 11.12 were obtained. Two things should be noted here. The inconsistency in her evidence was slight, solely concerning whether "she kissed the defendant" prior to the assault or was "kissed by him". The latter was her evidence at the crown court. The kissing was not mentioned in the earlier statement. Her "inconsistency" emerged on cross-examination by the defence. Secondly, it must be stressed that this does not show how much these arguments weighed, compared with all other evidence, towards the final verdict.

Discussion

Research on juries dispels several cherished myths about them and provokes consideration of alternative ways of administering justice. Juries of the sort analysed here ("shadow", simulated or quasi juries) do tend to be task orientated, to be involved in the decision to be made and to be serious. With the cases described in the experiments cited, few decisions seemed perverse in the sense that essential features of the case were ignored or distorted in deliberation or the decision was arrived at by eccentric and irrelevant arguments. However, the jury does not seem to act on the injunction "The law is for me, the facts are for you" (see p. 163). Rather, it discusses the facts in the light of the decision and within the constraints imposed by the court.

As far as orientation towards a decision is concerned, juries act differently, as far as one can tell, in different situations. Different arguments are used to support a majority tendency towards acquittal than those used to support the opposite tendency; minority factions in a jury will use different arguments to resist an acquittal from those used to resist a conviction. Similarly, different arguments predominate as a conviction decision becomes imminent, as compared with an acquittal, whilst yet other arguments predominate in attempts to resolve the "hung jury" situation. These effects do not seem to be the result of a particular individual's penchant for particular arguments, but rather a function of the group process. Likewise, jurors' personal characteristics (e.g. age, education level, social status, etc.) may be related to the amount of participation, or likely leadership, but do not, as far as can be seen, relate to particular styles of argument or bias in interpretation.

With regard to the fact-finding role of the jury, three things stand out. First, the facts are clearly established and agreed but are interpreted in discussion in opposite ways. Thus, in the LSE research, the weight of the allegedly stolen meat was agreed – factually – but used by some to argue that it was too heavy to move surreptitiously (hence he was not guilty) or that it was easy for a man of his work experience to dislodge it without being seen (hence, guilty). In the rape case, the condition of the victim was agreed (crying, dishevelled and bleeding from the nose), but the facts were used by some to indicate the use of force (guilty verdicts) and by others to indicate attempts to claim, falsely, that she had not consented (not guilty). In these cases the facts were established, but they did not "speak for themselves" as far as a verdict was concerned. A second aspect of this dominance of interpretation over mere establishment concerns the need for elaboration beyond the stated facts in order to justify or rationalise an interpretation. This elaboration – which occupies a considerable part of deliberation – can become so complicated as to be untenable, but the jury certainly tries in discussion to fill in the narrative gaps with what they consider to be reasonable assumptions. The third feature of the fact-finding or rather the fact-interpreting process lies in jurors' commentary on deficiencies in the case. Thus in the Oxford case of possessing a stolen bicycle, the jury was inclined to accept a flimsy defence because no attempt had been made to rebut it, and in the LSE theft case, the introduction and acceptance in court of a previous criminal record could be used to indicate either that the defendant had felonious tendencies or that the case was weak and any information seemed to be used, even if fundamentally irrelevant, to secure a conviction. This commentary is seldom direct – see the small amount of time *specifically* discussing the conduct of the case in the LSE juries – rather it is indirect and concerns putting different argumentative weight on particular established facts as a function of their perceived role in the court's construction of the case.

The rules constraining jury deliberation (rules of instruction and rules of inclusion) have complex effects that are scarcely susceptible to more than the most general interpretation. Rules may be understood but be of apparently little relevance to decisions in some types of case but significantly relevant in others; rules of instruction may be varied but still in discussion be supplemented or modified by jurors' own expectations. Rules may be incomprehensible and may provoke virtually no direct discussion but still significantly influence verdicts. Some rules may be ignored (e.g. no consideration to be given to previous criminal record), others may be invented (frequent discussion of the non-existent rules about "circumstantial" evidence). But, in all, jurors do not seem to heed to admonition to act merely as fact-finders; rather they argue as interpreters of the evidence, as interpreters of the way evidence is presented and, on occasion, as critics of the conduct of the case. In so doing perhaps they perform as Hastings (1950) wrote, a task "which no lawyer could have done".

References

Baldwin, J., & McConville, J. (1979). *Jury trials.* Oxford: Clarendon.

Bales, R.F. (1950). *Interaction process analysis. A method for the study of small groups.* Reading, MA: Addison-Wesley.

Bottoms, A.E., & Walker, M. (1972). The American jury: a critique. *Journal of the American Statistical Association, 67,* 773–779.

Bray, R.M., & Kerr, N. (1982). Methodological considerations in the study of the psychology of the courtroom. In N. Kerr & R.M. Bray (Eds.), *The psychology of the courtroom.* New York: Academic.

Campbell, D.T., & Stanley, J.C. (1963). *Experimental and quasi experimental designs for research.* Chicago: Rand McNally.

Cornish, W.R. (1968). *The jury.* London: Lane.

Cross, R., & Wilkins, R. (1979). *Evidence.* London: Sweet and Maxwell.

Davis, J.H., Kerr, N.L., Atkins, R.S., Holt, R., & Meek, D. (1975). The decision processes of 6 and 12 person mock juries assigned unanimous and 2/3 majority rules. *Journal of Personality and Social Psychology, 32,* 1–14.

Devlin, Lord P. (1956). *Trial by jury.* London: Stevens.

Glanville Williams. (1968). *The proof of guilt.* London: Stevens.

Hastings, P. (1950). *Cases in court.* London: Heinemann.

Izzett, R., & Leginsky, W. (1974). Group discussion and the influence of defendant characteristics in a simulated jury setting. *Journal of Social Psychology, 93,* 271–279.

Johannesen, N. (1986). *A study of the way in which impressions of the victim and judge's instructions to ignore such impressions affect the discussion and verdict of the jury.* Unpublished master's thesis, London School of Economics, University of London.

Kalven, H., & Zeisel, H. (1966). *The American jury.* Boston: Little Brown.

Landy, D., & Aronson, E. (1969). The influence of the character of the criminal and his victim on the decisions of simulated juries. *Journal of Experimental and Social Psychology, 5*, 141–152.

Lee, W. (1984). Rules of instruction on evidence admissible in a trial of rape. Unpublished B. Sc. thesis, London School of Economics.

LSE Jury Project. (1978). *Group functioning and jury deliberation.* Final report to SSRC, London School of Economics.

McCabe, S., & Purves, R. (1971). *The jury at work.* Oxford: Blackwell.

McCabe, S., & Purves, R. (1974). *The shadow jury at work.* Oxford: Blackwell.

Ostrom, T. M., Werner, C., & Saks, M. (1978). An integration theory analysis of jurors' presumptions of guilt or innocence. *Journal of Personality and Social Psychology, 36*, 436–450.

Saks, M. (1977). *Jury verdicts.* Lexington, MA: Lexington Books.

Sealy, A. P. (1975). The jury. Decision making in a small group. In H. Brown & R. Stevens (Eds.), *Social behaviour and experience.* London: Hodder and Stoughton.

Sealy, A. P. (1978). Group functioning and jury deliberation. Report to SSRC. London.

Sealy, A. P. (1982). Another look at social psychology aspects of juror bias. *Law and Human Behavior,* 5, 187–200.

Sealy, A. P., & Cornish, W. R. (1973). Juries and the rules of evidence. *Criminal Law Review,* April, 208–223.

Strodtbeck, F. (1962). Social process, the law and the jury. In W. M. Evan (Ed.), *The law and sociology.* New York: Free Press.

Strodtbeck, F., & Mann, R. D. (1956). Sex role differentiation in jury deliberations. *Sociometry, 19*, 3–11.

Strodtbeck, F., James, R. S., & Hawkins, C. (1957). Social status in jury deliberations. *American Sociological Review, 22*, 713–719.

Underwood, B. (1977). The thumb on the scales of justice: burdens of persuasion in criminal cases. *Yale Law Journal, 86*, 1299–1348.

Weiner, B., Russell, D., & Lerman, D. (1978). Affective consequences of causal attributions. In J. H. Harvey, W. J. Ickes, & R. F. Kidd (Eds.), New directions in attribution research: Vol. 2. Hillsdale, NJ: Erlbaum.

Zander, M. (1974). Are too many professional criminals avoiding conviction? *Modern Law Review, 37*, 28.

Zeisel, H., & Diamond, S. (1978). The effect of peremptory challenges on jury and verdict. *Stanford Law Review, 30*, 491–531.

12
Perseverance in Courtroom Decisions *

BERND SCHÜNEMANN and WOLFGANG BANDILLA

Perseverance can be assumed to often have an appreciable effect on the thought processes involved in judicial decision making. The phenomenon reflects the everyday experience that "people often do not believe evidence that opposes some theory they hold" (Nisbett & Ross, 1980, p. 169). Perseverance can be described (cf. Ross et al., 1975) as the tendency for information the decision maker initially considered crucial to a decision to retain its influence even when shown to be useless or irrelevant. Obviously, such a tendency runs counter to the basic aim in the judicial process, that of searching for truth (cf. Herrmann, 1971; note that no distinction is made here between material and formal truth). It is often assumed, nevertheless, that a judge's or jury's processing of the information relevant to a case is done objectively and that "extra-legal variables" play no appreciable role.

On the other hand, empirical results suggest judicial judgment may indeed be influenced by a number of extra-legal variables. In a somewhat pragmatic classification of these, Haisch (1983) differentiates between the influence of the object of judgment, the influence of the judgmental situation, and the influence of those who judge. Although perseverance can be thought to relate to all three of these, particular emphasis will be placed in the present paper upon the influence of the judgmental situation on the judge's tendency to perseverate.

Situational Effects on Judicial Judgmental Processes

It can be assumed that judicial systems differ in the extent to which they tend to elicit perseverance tendencies on the part of judges or jury members. In this connection one can note that the courts of most countries employ the one or

* The research described in this contribution was supported by the *Deutsche Forschungsgemeinschaft.*

the other of two fundamentally differing procedural systems, the adversary and the inquisitorial systems. The former tends to characterize the U.S. judicial system, and the latter the judicial systems of various European countries. However, one should note that ideal embodiments of these two types of systems are present neither in the U.S. nor in Europe (cf. Blumberg, 1967; Goldstein & Marcus, 1977). Also, some countries such as Japan possess a mixture of the two systems (cf. Saito, 1984).

The adversary system is essentially characterized by the records of pretrial investigation not being known to judges or jury members prior to trial and by the presentation or eliciting of evidence during trial being largely in the hands of the public prosecutor or the defence attorney in a criminal trial, and of the competing parties in a civil case. Thus, the judge has a relatively passive role here, being faced with the task of considering carefully the arguments presented him in court by the opposing parties, without his being familiar in advance with the pretrial records. In contrast, the inquisitory system is characterized by the judge having a thorough knowledge of results of the pretrial investigation, and thus of material incriminating the accused in the case of a criminal trial, prior to trial. Conduct of the proceedings lies in the hands of the court, meaning that the judge is in a privileged position during the trial as compared with the parties involved. The judge's manner of conducting the trial determines to a great extent the search for truth and thus the final result.

The two types of proceedings in their ideal form differ, therefore, in two major respects:

1. In the judge's role in the trial, and
2. In his knowledge, or ignorance, of the facts of the case prior to trial.

Empirical Support for Perseverance Effects

As psychological findings generally suggest, perseverance effects on the processing of information could be expected in both types of trial, insofar as the veracity and implications of the evidence are less than certain. Results of experiments on judgment formation and opinion change provide excellent examples of this, as in studies of sequence effects (e.g., Anderson & Barrios, 1961; Thibaut & Walker, 1975), of concept- or schema-directed information-processing (e.g., Schank & Abelson, 1977; Wyer, 1980; Wyer & Srull, 1981; Taylor & Crocker, 1981), of systematic distortion of information by use of judgmental heuristics (e.g., Nisbett & Ross, 1980; Tversky & Kahneman, 1983), and of the distortion of information through dissonance reduction (e.g., Festinger, 1957; Frey, 1981).

On the basis of such results, one would expect that, in the judicial decision-making situation, knowledge by the judge of results of the pretrial investigation in a criminal trial could easily tend to produce an one-sided evaluation of the evidence in the direction of incriminating the defendant. Thus, information processing in a criminal trial could easily become oriented primarily to that version of reality presented in the pretrial investigation.

Consequently, a tendency can be assumed to exist on the part of the court to undervalue the diagnostic worth of information which questions this reality, and to overvalue information which supports the guilt of the accused. An initially high expectation of the defendant's guilt should tend to easily be reinforced during the course of a trial and to lead to an increase in the adjudged probability of guilt, even if the evidence as a whole might in fact point in the opposite direction. Such an effect could be expected to be greater under the inquisitory system, where the conduct of the trial is largely in the judge's hands and the search for truth is mainly determined by the judge – and not, as in the adversary system, by the exchange of arguments between the contending parties. Both the judge's dominant position within the framework of the inquisitory system and his knowledge there of the pretrial investigative results should tend, in the inquisitory system, to produce a more one-sided use of incriminatory evidence. In a critical comment on Thibaut and Walker's (1978) views regarding the two types of trial systems, Schünemann (1985) has referred to an "unholy alliance" between the judge's control of the hearing of evidence and his prior knowledge of the results of earlier investigation.

In contrast, Thibaut and Walker assume that in inquisitory trials there are generally fewer mistakes in the reconstruction of reality than there are in adversary trials. They base this assumption on the concept of control and on the consideration of two major trial objectives, that of truth and that of justice. In those authors' view, placing control of proceedings in the hands of the contending parties, as it occurs in the adversary system, enables a trial to achieve a fairer result, whereas the more firm control of the trial and of decisions by the judge in the inquisitory system better satisfies demands for "truth" (see also Hayden & Anderson, 1979). Thibaut and Walker thus feel that the judge's monopoly of control favors optimal information-processing in the inquisitory trial.

A number of studies (e.g., La Tour, 1978; Lind & Lissak, 1985) do provide empirical support for Thibaut and Walker's assumption that adversary trials are perceived as being fairer. Without wishing to impugn the value of such studies per se or to question the importance that assessments of justice be positive, such assessments nevertheless seem of secondary importance as compared with correctness in the reconstruction of reality. It would seem of dubious value, therefore, that certain trial conditions be regarded as fair if they tend to create wrong judgments.

Studies of Information Processing and Judgment in Judicial Situations Involving Equivocal Evidence

Only relatively few empirical studies within the judicial decision-making area concern directly the cognitive processes involved in deciding whether or not the defendant is guilty. Such findings would be of particular relevance to cases where the defendant protests his or her innocence despite evidence supposedly to the contrary.

One can ask, for example, how an incriminating statement by a witness is evaluated if in later cross-examination his or her statement proves to be wrong or useless. Hatvany and Strack (1980) dealt with this question in a simulation experiment based on the adversary model. They assumed there to be three possible effects such a statement might have: (1) that the contents of the statement are not taken into consideration in the final judgment (logical approach); (2) that the discredited statement is taken into consideration in the final judgment – but in a manner contrary to its originally incriminating content, the jury trying so to speak, to compensate for the wrongful incrimination of the accused ("overcorrection"); (3) that the jury takes the statement of the witness into consideration despite its being useless (perseverance effect).

To examine these possibilities empirically, Hatvany and Strack carried out an investigation involving two civil law cases presented to subjects on video. The results appeared to be quite clear; with the single exception of an occurrence of the overcorrection phenomenon, subjects (students) proceeded in a logical way, not taking the discredited statement into consideration in the final judgment. In no case was a perseverance effect discernible. This result suggests that in the adversary system potentially wrong judgments can be corrected by the contending parties being able to intervene. The even distribution between the two parties of control of the trial can thus be seen, according to these results, as tending to lead to the attainment of "truth" in an undistorted way under adversary conditions. As it would appear to the present authors, however, this is only the case if the information presented at trial is the only basis for judgment. If, on the other hand, extensive information incriminating the accused is available to the judge in advance, then perseverance effects should emerge. Such should be the case at an inquisitory trial, where the proceedings are mainly determined by the judge.

Support for these assumptions is provided by various empirical studies of the German trial system, concerning the manner in which previous knowledge of a case influences the processing of information. One should note in this connection that in terms of German criminal trial procedure the results of the public prosecutor's investigations are pre-assessed by the judge. Before trial proceedings are initiated, a judge must check whether the investigative results contain sufficient clues for a subsequent conviction. Only if the judge believes the probability of such a conviction to be higher than 50% may he decide in favor of a trial. If such is the case, the judge's subsequent processing of the evidence and conduct of the trial can be seen as strongly influenced by the anticipation of a later conviction.

Such an assumption of distorted information-processing was examined in an experimental study by Haisch (1977). Participants (judicial service trainees serving as experts on legal questions, and students serving as laymen) were to evaluate brief descriptions of fictitious criminal cases. All cases were of an ambivalent character, in that the evidence spoke partly for and partly against the guilt of the accused. Before presentation of a case, 50% of the subjects were informed and 50% not informed of the evidence incriminating the accused. The subjects' task was to estimate the probability that the accused was guilty. The results suggested that the experts on legal questions tended to give greater weight to the incriminating evidence than to the exonerating evidence, and that their initial expectations regarding the evidence thus tended to persevere. This apparent distortion of evidence, however, was not based on previous knowledge of the records, since it occurred only under the circumstances of subjects having no previous knowledge of them. Under such circumstances, the hint of a forthcoming trial was apparently sufficient for the legal experts to presume there to be a high probability that the accused was guilty.

Further light was cast on the influence of previous knowledge of investigative records on perseverance effects in a study by Schünemann (1983). This study involved a simulation experiment in which the material of a real case was employed so as to increase external validity. The facts of the case were such that the question of guilt could not be decided definitely. The material consisted of records of the prosecutor's investigation and of the trial proceedings before a German court. The basic question was whether perseverance effects were more pronounced when the information contained in records of the pretrial investigation more clearly incriminated the accused. To check this two alternative versions of the pretrial investigative information were employed. For one group of subjects (group A) the pretrial records contained mainly information pointing clearly to the guilt of the accused, whereas for a second group (group B) it was less definitely incriminating. The task for both groups was to read the records first of the pretrial investigation and then of the trial proceedings. The record of the trial proceedings was identical for both groups. Subjects were to decide, after considering all of the information, whether the accused should be found guilty or not. Note that perseverance effects on information processing were inferred indirectly from judgments of guilty or innocent made at the end of the trial; as discussed by Bandilla (1986), the external validity of direct measures of over- or underevaluation of the information presented at trial, for example on the basis of assessments subjects have made of witness testimonies, is questionable.

In contrast to frequent studies involving student participants, the subjects here were without exception German professional judges, which was obviously desirable in terms of external validity.

Of the 37 judges who participated, 22 were allotted to test group A, the group which could more readily be expected to find the accused guilty due to the more incriminating nature of the information which they received concerning results of the pretrial investigation. For the 15 judges in group B it was expected, in contrast, that greater doubts regarding the guilt of the accused would be evident. In line with this, it was hypothesized that in group A perseverance effects would occur to a greater extent than in group B. The results confirm this hypothesis: In group A 82% ($n = 18$) decided on a verdict of guilty and only 18% ($n = 4$) on acquittal. In contrast, in group B the respective percentages were 53% ($n = 8$, guilty) and 47% ($n = 7$, acquittal).

In interpreting this result, one should bear in mind that during the experiment participants perceived the presented information as passive observers, quite unlike the manner in which judges evaluate evidence in criminal trials in Germany, where an inquisitorial type approach is employed. Thus, it is possible that the findings just reported are partly a function of the passive-observer role the subjects were given and that perseverance effects could be even greater if subjects had an inquisitorial type role while evaluating evidence. The latter possibility appears to be at variance with Thibaut and Walker's (1978) assumption that in an inquisitorial type system comparably fewer judgmental errors occur. A study by the present authors relevant to the question thus raised will be reported on below.

Before taking up that study, the results of another investigation by the present authors in which perseverance effects were of focal interest will be examined. A question this investigation considered, in addition to that of the effect of previous knowledge of the evidence upon the processing of information during the trial, was how the final judgment would be affected by the appearance at the end of the trial of a witness whose testimony tended to exonerate the accused. The results of a study by Thibaut and Walker (1975) are relevant in this connection. In a simulation experiment, these authors systematically varied both the sequence of appearance of the two reporting parties (prosecutor and defense attorney) and the sequence of incriminating versus exonerating evidence being presented by the respective parties. The results indicated that the statements of the party who reported last had a greater influence on the final judgment, and also that the factual content of these statements affected the judgment arrived at.

In the study by the present authors, employing material and tasks almost identical to those of the Schünemann (1983) investigation, a "recency effect" was hypothesized, in that it was assumed that a witness for the defence whose testimony appeared at the end of a trial would tend to increase the probability of a judgment of "not guilty" being made. In contrast to the Schünemann study, the participants were not professional judges but postgraduate judicial service trainees. They thus possessed the judicial knowledge necessary for assessing the case but had no practical experience in presiding over a trial. Altogether, 63 postgraduate judicial trainees took part, each being assigned to one of four different test conditions on the basis of whether or not pretrial investigative results which tended to incriminate the accused were known to subjects prior to the trial and of whether or not the testimony of a witness whose statements tended to exonerate the accused appeared at the end of the trial. In addition to carrying out tasks of the same sort as in the Schünemann (1983) study, subjects were to evaluate retrospectively the plausibility and thus the relevance of the various witnesses' testimonies.

The results again indicated a perseverance effect based on prior knowledge of the pretrial investigative material but only to a clear extent when no supposedly exonerating witness appeared at the end of the trial. The participants familiar with pretrial investigative information decided for conviction more frequently (68%) than did those without such information (47%). Although this was true to a much lesser extent for those subjects who were presented with the testimony of an exonerating witness at the end, a highly unexpected result was that, both with prior knowledge of the pretrial investigation and without, most of those subjects presented with the seemingly exonerating witness at the end decided for conviction (80% and 67% respectively).

This result thus represented the opposite of the recency effect found by Thibaut and Walker (1975). One possible explanation of this surprising result might be that, because of their inexperience, participants were overwhelmed in attempting to evaluate the material. Another might be that the testimony presented at the end was not evaluated in isolation but in the context of the other testimonies. In analyzing these results, Bandilla (1986) hints at the latter interpretation, suggesting that, because of its timing, the exonerating testimony was evaluated in line with the participants' reigning expectations of the accused's guilt and that it may also have produced a reinterpretation and reevaluation of the earlier evidence in accordance with prior expectations.

In another study by the authors, referred to briefly above, in which the effect of the judge's conducting and active search for the truth versus being a passive observer was investigated, trial situations were simulated largely corresponding to the German or the Anglo-American trial system. Either results of the pretrial investigations were known to the participants and they had the chance of controlling to a considerable extent the search for truth through asking their own questions during the trial, as is usual in the German trial system – or they had no knowledge of the pretrial investigation records, which meant that the evidence presented at trial was the only basis for judgment, as in the Anglo-American system. In addition, for completeness of design, two further combinations of test conditions not actually found in any existing judicial system were included, the subjects presented with those conditions either actively conducting the trial without knowledge of the pretrial investigative records, or being familiar with those and having a passive observer role during the trial. (Note that, as Bandilla, 1986, indicates in a critical commentary, the results of a somewhat similar study, by Weissmann, 1982, are uninterpretable since the latter two sets of conditions were not included.) Presentation of information was controlled by a microcomputer. This allowed the amounts of information presented to be identical under all four test conditions.

The dependent variables were 1) the judgments subjects arrived at and 2) how well subjects could remember the testimonies presented during the trial.

Memory performance was measured by a questionnaire which the subject filled out after deciding on the question of guilt. The questionnaire concerned eleven of the testimonies presented at the trial. For each such testimony, one or two similar but false alternatives were presented alongside the correct one, the participants' task being to identify the correct testimony. A similar method was used in a study by Greene (1981), who found that testimonies consistent with the judgment made are better remembered. The material of the experiment was based on the same case as employed in the earlier studies. The participants were 35 professional German judges with extensive experience at their jobs. (The results for 23 prosecutors, who were tested at the same time, are not of interest in the present context.) Each of the judges was assigned to one of the four sets of conditions.

The following questions were of particular interest: How are information processing and decision-making influenced by the judge's role at the trial (passive observation or active search for truth)? What effect does knowledge of the pretrial investigative records have in this context? Are perseverance effects furthered by the judge's having a monopoly on control? Does an expectation of a later conviction existing already before the trial begins lead to one-sided use of information? Although the results do provide answers to these questions, of considerable interest in their implications, it is suggested that conclusions be drawn cautiously in view of the small numbers of participants.

Clear differences in the judgments given emerged between the various sets of test conditions. Knowledge of the pretrial investigative records appeared to only have a marked effect on judgment under condition of the judges being able to conduct the trial through the questioning of witnesses; being familiar with the pretrial investigative records, 100% of the judges ($n = 8$) decided on conviction, whereas without previous knowledge of the case only 27% ($n = 3$) did so. In contrast, under conditions in which the judges were in a passive observer role, differences attributable to the presence or lack of previous knowledge of the case were much less, the rates of conviction with knowledge of the pretrial investigation and without being 100% and 71%, respectively. The results as just presented are shown in Fig. 12.1.

The conditions under which judges had no knowledge of the pretrial records and conducted the trial actively (category III in the figure) were also those in which the testimonies presented at trial were best remembered. On the average, some 9.3 of the 11 testimonies were recalled without mistake by the judges in this group, the rate of errors being particularly low for those judges in this group who decided that the accused should be acquitted. For these judges, only minor distortion of recall were apparent. Memory performance was markedly worse for judges in the three other categories, with the average number of testimonies that could be properly recalled ranging between 6.2 and 6.9.

The results as a whole suggest that active conduct of a trial by a judge who is without previous knowledge of a case offers the best solution to the task of processing information in an objective-neutral way. This is a "mixed form" of

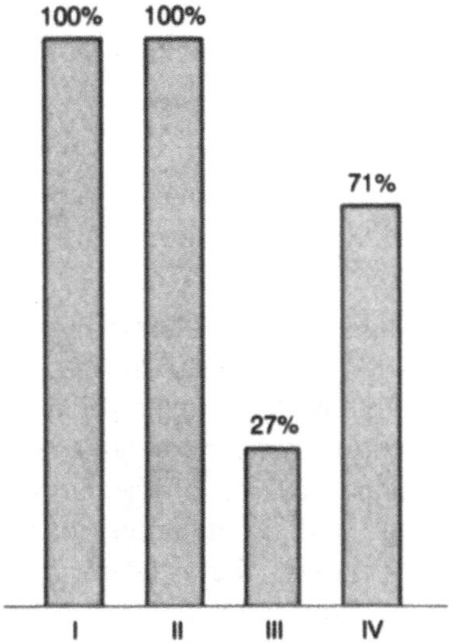

FIGURE 12.1. Rates of conviction under four different conditions: *I*, Knowledge of the pretrial records, active participation; *II*, Knowledge of the pretrial records, passive participation; *III*, No knowledge of the pretrial records, active participation; *IV*, No knowledge of the pretrial records, passive participation

trial which corresponds to neither the German nor the American system. In this connection, one can note a peculiarity of the German criminal trial system that has thus far not been discussed and which may likewise be conducive to the occurrence of perseverance effects, namely the fact that both the prosecutor and the judge are obligated to the same trial objective, that of the "material search for truth." Thus, if the prosecutor has made an indictment, the judge knows already prior to the trial that another decision-making authority – bound to the same trial objective – assumes there to be a high probability that the accused is guilty. Because of having this prior knowledge, the judge may possibly adopt the prosecutor's pre-evaluation of the evidence in a somewhat uncritical way. This phenomenon of the orientation of one role player to a prior evaluation made by another can be referred to as a "shoulder check" between the judge and the prosecutor.

This phenomenon was examined more closely in a further study of ours using the same investigative material, which both prosecutors and judges evaluated. The prosecutors' task was to decide whether to press charges on the basis of the information given them. The judges received the same information together with the additional knowledge that the prosecutor had made an indictment. The judges had to decide, on the basis of the pretrial records, whether they would decide to conduct a criminal trial. Results were clear: only few of the prosecutors decided to press charges (24%) whereas, in contrast, the majority of the judges saw enough incriminating features in pretrial records to decide to conduct a trial (56%). It thus appeared that in their decision making the judges orientated themselves primarily to the prosecutor's pre-evaluation of the evidence.

Concluding Remarks

The question arises of whether conclusions pertaining to legal policy can be drawn from such simulation experiments as these and of what conclusions these are. First Thibaut and Walker's assumption that the "discovery of the truth" aspect of the inquisitory system is advantageous appears to have received no support. The extreme position of the judge in the inquisitorial type system found in Germany, in which the judge not only has knowledge of the pretrial records but also conducts the investigation during trial himself, has been found in the latest German studies to produce strong perseverance effects. In our own studies (Schünemann, 1983; Bandilla, 1986) it has been argued that Weissmann's (1982) recommendation for counterbalancing judgmental perseverance are inadequate. These suggestions for reform, similar to those of Baumann (1980), involve assigning the judge a passive role, making use of an adversary system in cross-examination, and the judge's being familiar with the pretrial records prior to the trial. The latter aspect, combined with the judge having a passive role, can be assumed to increase rather than reduce perseverance. The results of our studies as cited here suggest that judgmental perseverance can best be reduced if the judge lacks knowledge of the pretrial investigation and possesses an active role in investigation carried out during the trial. This applies to conditions under which a professional judge makes all decisions concerning the case himself. The purely adversary model of the American trial, in terms of which judgmental perseverance caused by shoulder-check effects between the prosecutor and the judge is avoided by a transfer of decisions regarding conviction to a jury consisting of lay judges only, is an alternative.

Whether better results in terms of the discovery of truth can be expected through lay judges making decisions after taking part in proceedings in a passive way or through professional judges making decisions after actively conducting investigation during trial without knowledge of the pretrial records, cannot yet be stated on the basis of the empirical results available. It is worthy of note, however, that the rather ponderous approach of jury trial is only employed in about 2% of all trials in the USA (Schumann, 1977). Thus, it can be deemed to be excluded as a standard procedure in criminal trials there. The mixture of trial procedure types described above, consisting of elements of both the adversary and inquisitory models and characterized by a judge conducting the investigations actively and deciding the case himself, without knowledge of the prosecutor's investigation, therefore appears worthy of further research.

References

Anderson, N. H., & Barrios, A. A. (1961). Primacy effects in personality impression formation. Journal of Abnormal and Social Psychology, *63*, 346–350.

Bandilla, W. (1986). Kontextabhängige Informationsverarbeitung im bundesdeutschen Strafverfahren. Dissertation thesis, University Mannheim.

Baumann, J. (1980). Novelle zur Strafprozeßordnung – Alternativentwurf, Tübingen: Mohr.

Blumberg, A. (1967). The practice of law as confidence game. Law and Society Review, *1*, 15–39.

Festinger, L. (1957). A theory of cognitive dissonance. Evanston: Row, Peterson.

Frey, D. (1981). Informationssuche und Informationsbewertung bei Entscheidungen. Bern: Huber.

Goldstein, A., & Marcus, M. (1977). The myth of judical supervision in three "inquisitorial" systems: France, Italy and Germany. Yale Law Journal, *87*, 240–283.

Greene, E. (1981). Whodunit? Memory for evidence in text. American Journal of Psychology, *94*, 479–496.

Haisch, J. (1977). Die Verarbeitung strafrechtlich relevanter Informationen durch Juristen und Laien in simulierten Gerichtsverfahren. Archiv für Psychologie, *129*, 110–119.

Haisch, J. (1983). Richterliche Urteilsbildung. In W. Seitz (Ed.), Kriminal- und Rechtspsychologie. Ein Handbuch in Schlüsselbegriffen. Munich: Urban and Schwarzenberg.

Hatvany, N., & Strack, F. (1980). The impact of a discredited key witness. Journal of Applied Social Psychology, *10*, 490–509.

Hayden, R. M., & Anderson, J. K. (1979). On the evaluation of procedural systems in laboratory experiments – a critique of Thibaut and Walker. Law and Human Behavior, *3*, 21–38.

Herrmann, J. (1971). Die Reform der deutschen Hauptverhandlung nach dem Vorbild des anglo-amerikanischen Strafverfahrens. Bonn: Roehrscheid.

La Tour, S. (1978). Determinants of participants and observer statisfaction with adversary and inquisitional modes of adjudication. Journal of Personality and Social Psychology, *36*, 1531–1545.

Lind, E. A., & Lissak, R. I. (1985). Apparent impropriety and procedural fairness judgments. Journal of Experimental Social Psychology, *21*, 19–29.

Nisbett, R. E., & Ross, L. (1980). Human inference: strategies and shortcomings of social judgement. Englewood Cliffs: Prentice Hall.

Ross, L., Lepper, M. R., Hubbard, M. (1975). Perseverance in self-perception and social perception: biased attributional processes in the debriefing paradigm. Journal of Personality and Social Psychology, *32*, 880–892.

Saito, S. (1984). Der japanische Strafprozeß als Kompromiß zwischen anglo-amerikanischem und deutschem Strafprozeßmodell. In M. Irle (Ed.), Sozialwissenschaftliche Entscheidungsforschung. University Mannheim.

Schank, R., & Abelson, R. (1977). Scripts, plans, goals and understanding: an inquiry into human knowledge structures. Hillsdale: Lawrence Erlbaum.

Schumann, K. J. (1977). Der Handel mit Gerechtigkeit. Frankfurt/M.: Suhrkamp.

Schünemann, B. (1983). Experimentelle Untersuchungen zur Reform der Hauptverhandlung in Strafsachen. In H. J. Kerner, H. Kury, K. Sessar (Eds.), Deutsche Forschungen zur Kriminalitätsentstehung und Kriminalitätskontrolle, 1109–1152. Köln: Heymanns.

Schünemann, B. (1985). Kognition, Einstellung und Vorurteil bei der Rechtsfindung. In E.-J. Lampe (Ed.), Beiträge zur Rechtsanthropologie, 68–84.

Taylor, S. E., & Crocker, J. (1981). Schematic basis of social information processing. In E. T. Higgins, P. Herman, M. Zanna (Eds.), Social cognition: the Ontario symposium (Vol. 1). Hillsdale: Erlbaum.

Thibaut, J., & Walker, L. (1975). Procedural justice: a psychological analysis. New York: Free Press.

Thibaut, J., & Walker, L. (1978). A theory of procedure. California Law Review, *66*, 541–566.

Tversky, A., & Kahneman, D. (1983). Extensional versus intuitive reasoning: the conjunction fallacy in probability judgment. Psychological Review, *90*, 293–315.

Weissmann, U. (1982). Die Stellung des Vorsitzenden in der Hauptverhandlung. Die Entwicklung einer Verfahrensordnung zum Wechselverhör mit einer empirischen Studie über den „Passivrichter". Göttingen: Hogrefe.

Wyer, R. S. (1980). The acquisition and use of social knowledge. Basic postulates and representative research. Personality and Social Psychology Bulletin, *6*, 558–573.

Wyer, R. S., Srull, T. K. (1981). Category accessibility: some theoretical and empirical issues concerning the processing of social information. In E. T. Higgins, C. P. Herman, M. P. Zanna (Eds.), Social cognition: the Ontario symposium (Vol. 1) (1980), Hillsdale: Erlbaum.

13
Attractiveness and Respectability of the Offender as Factors in the Evaluation of Criminal Cases

HANS WERNER BIERHOFF, ERNST BUCK, and RENATE KLEIN

Introduction

Although rules of law and administrative guidelines were developed during past centuries, a complete understanding of the criminal justice system must take into account the actual options available to the judge (Ebbesen & Konečni, 1982; Krahé, 1985). Most of the rules of law contain only general guidelines for decisions which have to be applied according to the principle of discretion and thus leave enough room for extralegal factors.

The German criminal justice system specifies procedural rules which are relevant in this regard. The guidelines for judicial sentencing emphasize that the court should consider carefully the pros and cons. The motives and goals of the offender, the consequences of the crime, the general background of the offender, his/her former life, and his/her personal and economic situation should be taken into account (§ 46 StGB).

These guidelines describe a judgmental task which is closely related to processes of impression formation and person perception (Bierhoff, in press). For example, the court is obliged to integrate the assumed motives of the offender with social cues (e.g., social respectability as an indicator of personal/economic situation), social history, and prior record. Therefore, the sentencing decision as an integration task should include information which is frequently termed "extralegal" factors (e.g., the personal and economic situation of the offender). Clearly, the empirical investigation of the influence exerted by these extralegal factors upon the sentencing decision is important for legal psychology.

In most legal systems with a jury (e.g., in the U.S.), jurors have to decide about a defendant's guilt. In addition, to the extent that they find the defendant guilty they, or the presiding trial judge, have to decide upon an appropriate punishment by choosing a sentence out of the range of sentencing options.

The criminal justice system and the sentencing process seem to be affected by several judgmental processes. First, the nature of the offense must be clarified by investigating how the critical events took place and who caused them. This investigation is closely related to causal attributions. Second, judges or jurors, depending on the legal system concerned[1], have to decide whether or not the offender is responsible for the offense and whether he/she is guilty (Shaver, 1985). In addition, factors like social history, prior record, status, and first impressions may influence the decisions about the nature of the offense and the sentencing process.

Several social psychological approaches can be utilized for an understanding of the sentencing process. The impression formation paradigm offers a convenient tool for the analysis of social cues in criminal cases (Carroll & Wiener, 1982). Essentially, the analysis focuses on variables of the offender (and the victim) which have been proved to be relevant for the impression formation process. For example, the attractiveness and social respectability of a target person exert a strong influence on first impressions (Dion, 1986; McArthur, 1982). Therefore, it is reasonable to investigate whether these variables have an influence on the attributions and evaluations of an offender in the legal setting.

In addition, attribution research points to a possible relationship between causal explanations in terms of dispositional inferences and situational attributions on the one hand and harshness of sentences on the other. Situational attributions offer excuses or justifications for the behavior of the offender. While excuses mitigate the personal blameworthiness of the actor, justifications refer to special circumstances and norms which reduce the accountability of the target person (Felson & Ribner, 1981). From theory and research the hypothesis is derived that dispositional inferences vis-à-vis the offender elicit more severe sentences from judges/jurors (Carroll & Wiener, 1982).

A combination of the impression formation paradigm with attribution research leads to a two-stage model of the sentencing process which is elaborated more fully later in the chapter. On the basis of identifiable cues (e.g., social attractiveness of the offender), the balance of internal (dispositional) and external (situational) attributions is affected. In the second step, attributions exert an influence on the evaluation of the offender as good or bad and on the assignment of punishment by jurors/judges.

In the second section we will present evidence on the influence of extralegal factors on attributions and sentences. We will focus primarily on attractiveness and social respectability as social cues. In the third section we will extend this analysis by considering additional variables (e.g., sex of the subject and sex of the target person) which exert a moderating influence on the impression formation process. In addition, we will present empirical evidence from our own research which indicates that social cues are important determinants of causal attributions in a hypothetical case of a traffic offense. Finally, we will discuss

[1] Although the authors are well aware of the differences in the roles of judge and jurors in different legal systems, both will hence be used interchangeably because the underlying judgmental processes can be considered similar.

evidence for the assumed relationship between causal attributions and harshness of sentences.

Most of the relevant research has been conducted with students or law graduates (for notable exceptions, see Carroll, 1978; Konečni & Ebbesen, 1982). What are the consequences of this restriction of the subject population? Sporer (1982) extensively discussed issues of population validity, i.e., the relationship between studies based on student samples and the applicability of the results to judicial sentencing. Nonexpert decision-makers differ in a number of characteristics (e.g., legal training, educational level, and age) from real judges. Therefore, inferences from experimental results to the criminal justice system should be drawn with caution.

A number of considerations must be taken into account. Generalizations are more justified when the data come from advanced law students than from unsophisticated college students. Law students have considerable expertise although they lack the vocational experience of real judges. In addition, in most of the studies certain hypotheses on the impression formation process are tested which are derived from social-psychological theories. Theory testing is much less dependent on representative samples than is parameter estimation, i.e., the assessment of absolute values. Most of the researchers are not so much interested in the absolute level of responses (e.g., punishment recommendations) as in the pattern of responses between experimental conditions. The analysis of the patterns of the dependent variables is less likely to be biased by sample restrictions than are parameter estimates (Hendrick & Jones, 1972). Such an analysis of the pattern of responses is crucial for theory testing, which is considered as the primary goal of studies on legal decision-making (Sporer, 1982). Finally, the logical alternative to the selection of students as subjects in sentencing studies is confronted with serious drawbacks (Sporer, 1982). Real judges as participants in a social-psychological study on extralegal factors in judicial decision-making are likely to respond defensively in many situations because their personal ability to find appropriate answers is under study. As a consequence, their responses may reflect the social desirability of the alternatives (cf. Konečni & Ebbesen, 1979). As experts, real judges are aware of the problems of judicial sentencing. They might be motivated to present a fair and rational image of the criminal justice system. Therefore, judges are not necessarily the better subjects in studies on legal decision-making.

This discussion urges us to be especially careful when it comes to the question of the generalizability of the results of social-psychological studies to the criminal justice system. Precautionary measures are necessary. First, special emphasis must be placed on studies which are based on law students and law graduates because these samples are intermediate between college students and real judges (Sporer, 1982). Second, comparisons with studies of members of the criminal justice system (e.g., Carroll, 1978; Konečni & Ebbesen, 1982) should be encouraged. Third, the independent and dependent variables should be selected carefully to make sure that they represent the decision-making process of judicial sentencing. Since economic and personal characteristics of the offender are mentioned explicitly as relevant input factors for the sentencing process by the German law (see above), the employment of such input variables for the investigation of the judicial decision process is fully justified.

A related point which is discussed by Sporer (1982) is the paper-defendant problem. Subjects are asked to consider hypothetical cases while judges are occupied with real cases. The main issue with regard to this problem is the similarity between hypothetical cases and real cases. In addition, the involvement of the subjects should be high. Since it is necessary to conduct experimental studies in addition to correlational studies, it is not feasible to abandon the experimental approach which is closely related to hypothetical scenarios. If appropriate precautions are taken, the experimental approach to judicial decision-making can shed light on the causal determinants of the decision process.

Respectability and Attractiveness as Extralegal Factors

Jurors and judges form impressions of defendants which are influenced by extralegal factors like the physical appearance and social respectability of the target person. As a general rule, the influence of these extralegal factors is likely to decrease as legal rules and policies become more and more unequivocal. On the other hand, the influence of extralegal factors on the verdict is likely to increase as the ambiguity of rules and procedural guidelines increases [cf. Sporer's (1982) analogy of the defendant and his/her offense as an "ambiguous stimulus" in the Sherif tradition].

Two contradictory hypotheses about the effect of social respectability and physical attractiveness are found in the literature. First, high physical attractiveness/social respectability is assumed to promote sympathy with the defendant. This halo effect should lead to more lenient verdicts.

Landy and Aronson (1969) described the defendant as a respectable person (having a respectable job and a positive social image) or as an unattractive person (having a job with low reputation and a mean social image). Results indicated that judges sentenced the unattractive defendant more severely than the respectable defendant. This pattern of results was replicated by Sigall and Landy (1972), where an attractive, warm, and friendly defendant elicited a more lenient sentence than an unattractive cold, and unapproachable defendant.

In a similar vein, Nemeth and Sosis (1973) found that an attractive defendant who held a distinguished job in a firm, led a happy family life, and was described as friendly, received a more lenient sentence than an unattractive, divorced defendant, who worked as a janitor and had little contact with his colleagues. The defendant was described as a drunken offender who had caused an accident in which a pedestrian died. Being drunk was attributed more to internal factors with the unattractive target person than with the attractive target person. The unattractive person was more likely to be seen as somebody who regularly drinks alcohol than the attractive target person. This can be taken as an indication that the person with low respectability was blamed more for the accident than the respectable person. Therefore, one may assume that subjects tend more easily to infer dispositional causes for a person with low respectability than for a respectable person.

The importance of social respectability was further elaborated by Miller, Chino, Harney, Haines, and Saavedra (1986) on the basis of a distinction between conformity status and power status. While the target person's conformity status (low: the defendant is a troublemaker; high: the defendant is a good citizen and a loyal taxpayer) influenced recommended punishment in the expected direction (cf. Konečni & Ebbesen, 1982), the power status – defined by the prestige of the occupation of the defendant – did not influence assigned punishment.

Reynolds and Sanders (1975) varied salience of attractiveness in a partial replication of the Landy and Aronson (1969) study. They concluded that attractiveness influenced juror judgments only if it was described in a salient and distinct manner. When attractiveness was salient the attractive defendant received only a less severe sentence. Reynolds and Sanders argued that judgments are influenced by the most salient cues. In Izzett and Leginski's (1974) study the unattractive defendant was sentenced more harshly than the attractive defendant. Yet this effect reached significance only before group discussion. After group discussion judgments about attractive and unattractive defendants did not differ significantly, although there was a nonsignificant tendency to discharge the attractive defendant.

Finally, Efran (1974) pointed out that high physical attractiveness had a positive influence on juror decisions. Attractive persons were guilty less often and received less severe sentences.

The second hypothesis on the effects of defendant attractiveness on juror decision-making holds that attractive persons are likely to be sentenced very harshly if the defendant is perceived to have used his/her social or physical attractiveness to carry out his/her criminal plans. This responsibility hypothesis assumes that high social attractiveness implies high status, and above-average knowledge, power, and competence, which make a person responsible for his/her conduct. Empirical evidence consistent with the responsibility hypothesis was presented by Sigall and Ostrove (1975) with regard to physical attractiveness and by Bray, Struckman-Johnson, Osborne, McFarlane, and Scott (1978) with regard to social attractiveness.

To sum up, a defendant's attractiveness will lessen severe punishment if it did not promote the crime. On the other hand, jurors will recommend more severe sentences if they think the defendant took advantage of his or her attractiveness when committing the crime.

Social attractiveness or respectability depends not only on the target person's status but also on the person's conduct. Finney, Merrifield, and Helm (1976) varied both aspects of attractiveness. They also tested the effect of juror perspective: subjects made their decisions as observers or took the defendant's perspective. Subjects read the description of a stimulus person who had an automobile accident (cf. Walster, 1966). He parked a rented car at the top of a steep hill. Apparently, the hand-brake was not on, so the car rolled down the hill, smashed against a telephone booth, and was severely damaged. The stimulus person's role respectability was varied with his job as a bank president, bank teller, or bank janitor. Next, behavioral respectability was independently varied. With low behavioral respectability the person was described as incompetent and unsuccessful in his job. In the condition with high behavioral respectability, the person performed his job very well and was successful. Subjects were asked to estimate the responsibility for the accident on 15-point rating scales. The scales measured dispositional (internal) and situational (external) attributions. Ratings were made from the actor's (stimulus person) and the observer's viewpoint. Observer subjects attributed less situational responsibility and more internal responsibility (cf. Jones & Nisbett, 1971). Observer subjects were not influenced by role respectability in their internal attributions. Role respectability, however, did influence situational attributions: ratings for the teller were significantly higher than for the janitor, with the president somewhere in between. Moreover, for the teller the accident was seen as less serious than for either the president or the janitor. Subjects indicated that the teller had less ability to prevent the accident then either the president or the janitor.

The results supported the authors' hypothesis that subjects as observers base responsibility attributions on role information. However, their prediction that high role respectability would foster internal attributions was not supported. Internal attributions were lowest with medium role respectability. Subjects as actors were hypothesized to base their responsibility attributions on behavioral information. The results indicate that behavioral respectability influenced situational as well as internal attributions. For subjects as observers, behavioral information did not influence the responsibility attributions. Subjects as actors with high behavioral respectability made less situational attributions for the accident than subjects as actors with low behavioral respectability. Actors of high behavioral respectability were assigned less punishment than were actors of low behavioral respectability. Behavioral respectability information did not influence seriousness ratings of the accident.

To sum up, the subjects' perspective influenced their judgments in several ways. Observer subjects relied more heavily on role information, while actor subjects used behavioral information. High behavioral respectability fostered lenient sentences for all levels of role respectability. Role respectability exerted an influence on sentences only when behavioral respectability was low. The hypothesis that high role respectability in general leads to high internal responsibility attributions was not supported. Least responsibility was attributed to the teller. The authors suggested a defensive attribution explanation. Subjects might have considered the teller's role as most similar to their own position or expectations for future jobs. With regard to the teller, they could have imagined themselves getting involved in a similar problem. In an exploratory study, student subjects assigned greater likelihood to being a teller themselves than to being a president.

In one of our own experiments (Bierhoff, Buck, Demski, Hildebrand-Hetz, & Klein, unpublished data) we also varied the behavioral respectability of a stimulus person by a written instruction (cf. Finney et al., 1976). The offender was described as respectable (friendly and generous) or not respectable (troublemaker). She was involved in an automobile accident. The description of the accident allowed for internal causal attributions as well as for external causal attributions. Male and female law students ($n = 60$) and psychology students ($n = 59$) rated several plausible causes for the accident and then assigned the appropriate level of punishment for the offender.

Two independent variables were varied in a factorial design: sex of target person and behavioral respectability of target person (high/low). Sex of subjects and branch of study were included in the statistical analyses.

Dependent variables included seven explanations which were judged plausible (1) or implausible (7) on 7-point rating scales. There were four situational explanations ("insufficient street lighting," "pedestrian in dark clothes," "careless pedestrian," "wet street"). Low scores indicated agreement and therefore situational attributions. There were also three personal explanations, with low scores indicating internal attribution ("driver didn't care," "driver was drunk," and "driver didn't pay attention").

Intercorrelations of situational and personal explanations were inspected. We found significant positive correlations among situational and among personal factors, while correlations between situational and personal explanations were negative.

TABLE 13.1. Factor loadings of the causal attributions on the first general factor

Explanation	Factor loading
Internal causes	
Driver didn't care	−0.53
Driver was drunk	−0.51
Driver didn't pay attention	−0.53
External causes	
Insufficient street lighting	0.82
Pedestrian in dark clothes	0.61
Careless pedestrian	0.45
Wet street	0.23

Note. A principal axis factor analysis was computed with communality estimates in the main diagonal. The loadings were extracted in 9 iterations. The eigenvalue of the first factor was 2.114. The first factor explains 30.2% of the variance. The second eigenvalue was 0.649.

A factor analysis of these intercorrelations suggested a one-factor solution, with opposite signs of the loadings for internal and external explanations (Table 13.1). A two-factor solution proved unsatisfactory because internal and external explanations were not separated by the two rotated factors. In addition, the second eigenvalue was smaller than 1. The general factor which is represented in Table 13.1 reflects the tendency to prefer external attributions over internal attributions.

We therefore decided to compute a univariate analysis of variance with a combined index of causal explanations as well as a multivariate analysis of variance with all causal explanations as dependent measures. Sex and respectability of the target person and sex of subjects and branch of study entered the analysis as independent variables. All results reported below were significant in both types of analyses.

To calculate the combined index of responsibility attributions, internal ratings were reversed and the ratings of all explanations were averaged. High means on this index indicated internal responsibility attributions whereas low means indicated external attributions.

Subjects also indicated whether they considered punishment necessary. They were asked to select an option from a range of sentencing decisions which varied from no punishment to imprisonment.

On the basis of the empirical evidence reviewed, we concluded that a person with high social attractiveness will be more easily discharged and receive more lenient punishment than a person with low social attractiveness (as long as the crime is perceived to be independent of the attractiveness). Therefore, we expected a main effect of the stimulus person's respectability on responsibility attributions and sentencing. A highly respected person should evoke a tendency for situational attributions and mild punishment, whereas a less respected person should evoke a tendency for internal attributions and severe punishment.

Responsibility attributions depended on the target person's respectability [$F\,(1, 102) = 6.89$, $P = 0.01$]. Subjects assigned less personal responsibility to a respectable target ($M = 3.17$) than to a target with low respectability ($M = 3.69$). This effect was also significant in the multivariate analysis of variance [$mF\,(7, 96) = 4.62$, $P < 0.001$]. At the univariate level the influence of target respectability was especially pronounced for the explanation "insufficient street lighting" [$F\,(1, 102) = 26.37$, $P < 0.001$], which had the highest loading on the internal-external attribution factor (cf. Table 13.1).

Extralegal Factors: Additional Considerations

Research on gender stereotypes suggests a hypothesis concerning the effect of the stimulus person's sex (cf. Bierhoff, in press). As the female stereotype includes caring, warmth, and social awareness, one may expect subjects to rate a female stimulus person who behaves in correspondence with the female stereotype more positively. In contrast, the female stimulus person whose behavior is inconsistent with the female stereotype is expected to be rated more negatively.

We can only speculate on how male and female subjects are influenced by the female stereotype. But it seems not too far-fetched to suppose that male subjects rely more heavily on schematic conceptions about women than female subjects because male persons may have less access to information about women's behavior.

Empirical evidence concerning the effect of subject sex on sentencing is contradictory. Some studies have reported that men tend to assign harsher sentences than do women (see Nemeth, 1981, p. 322). On the other hand, in some studies women assigned more severe sentences than men when they had to judge about rape (Davis, Kerr, Atkin, Holt, & Meek, 1975; Davis, Kerr, Stasser, Meek, & Holt, 1977). Moreover, the decisions of male and female subjects depend on whether they are made before or after group discussion (cf. Kaplan, 1985; Sporer, 1986). In a study by Bray et al. (1978), men assigned harsher sentences than women only before a group discussion. After group discussion, the sentences of men and women did not differ significantly from each other.

Another variable concerns conservative/liberal attitudes. Nemeth and Sosis (1973) found that students who lived in a conservative college recommended harsher punishments than students who attended a liberal college. Moreover, conservative students were more influenced by the target person's attractiveness than liberal students. They assigned more severe punishment to an unattractive as opposed to an attractive target person. Haisch (1981) found that law students recommended more severe punishments than other students. On the assumption that psychology students report more liberal attitudes than law students, law students should recommend harsher sentences than psychology students. On the other hand, Sporer (1979) reported less severe punishment by law students (who apparently had a more sophisticated knowledge about the effects of long-term imprisonment than students from a liberal arts college).

Our own study contains relevant information on the stimulus person's respectability and gender as well as on subjects' sex and branch of study. Results in Table 13.2 indicate that respectability of the stimulus person exerted a particularly strong influence when male subjects rated a female target person. This tendency, which was evident for both psychology students and law students, was especially pronounced for law students. These results make clear that the general influence of the target person's respectability is emphasized in some groups of observers depending on the sex of the target person and reduced in other groups. Although respectability is a powerful factor in responsibility attributions, modifying factors must be taken into account.

Looking at the conditions in which the respectability effect is especially strong, we note that the factors which were discussed above as potential in-

TABLE 13.2. Attributions as a function of respectability, sex of target, and attitude and sex of subjects

Group of judges	Target person			
	Respectable		Not respectable	
	Male	Female	Male	Female
Psychology students				
Male	3.29 (9)	2.57 (5)	3.71 (4)	3.52 (8)
Female	3.46 (5)	3.16 (10)	3.26 (11)	3.74 (6)
Law students				
Male	3.51 (9)	2.73 (9)	3.67 (9)	4.71 (5)
Female	2.88 (6)	3.69 (6)	4.36 (6)	3.34 (10)

Note. Higher numbers indicate more internal attribution. Cell number is in parentheses. The four-way interaction was significant [univariate F (1, 102) = 5.67, $P<0.05$; multivariate F (7, 96) = 3.73, $P<0.001$].

dependent influences on the attribution ratings exerted the expected effects. Males who read the scenario of a female target person were strongly influenced by the target person's respectability. In addition, females who read the scenario of a male target person showed the same pattern of results. This was especially true for law students. This is not surprising because results of earlier studies had indicated that conservative students were more influenced by the target person's respectability than liberal students. Presumably, in our study law students were more conservative than psychology students. Depending on facilitative or inhibiting factors, the respectability effect was emphasized or vanished completely as a function of students' sex and presumed attitude.

Relationship Between Causal Attributions and Sentencing

Until now we have primarily looked at the relationship between extralegal factors (i.e., respectability/attractiveness) and internal/external attributions. Next we discuss the relationship between causal attributions and sentencing and present additional data from our own study.

The results of Haisch (1980, 1981) point to a significant correlation between attributions and sentencing. This relationship – internal attributions foster more severe sentencing – can be accounted for by the following reasoning. When a person manifests deviant behavior in spite of inhibiting circumstances (conformity with normative pressures from his/her reference group), dispositional inferences are encouraged (Jones & Davis, 1965). Inhibiting circumstances should elicit internal attributions (i.e., the target person is assumed to be a person who is disposed to act in a deviant manner), while socially approved deviant behavior should elicit more situational attributions. Therefore, dispositional inferences on the basis of a deviant behavior pattern of the target person are likely to foster more severe sentences. This should be especially true if supporting information about former deviant behavior is available.

In Carroll and Payne's (1977) study, too, students and parole board members (justiciary "experts") assigned harsher punishments when the crime was supposed to be caused by internal factors. For experts, this result was limited to cases in which the causes for the crime were described to be stable over time. Carroll (1978) noted a tendency for parole board members to prefer internal and stable explanations for crimes. In summary, internal attributions for a crime seem to foster harsher sentences than external attributions (see also Calhoun, Peirce, Walters & Dawes, 1974).

In our study, subjects tended to assign lenient sentences. Only a minority of 10.1% recommended a "severe" punishment. Type of punishment was used to compute a recommended punishment index with high values indicating severe sentences. Our expectation that subjects assign more severe sentences the more internal their causal attributions are, was supported by a significant correlation between causal attributions and recommended punishments ($r = -0.33$, $P < 0.001$). Subjects who preferred dispositional explanations tended to favor severe punishment. Only the linear component of this relationship was significant. The correlation was especially pronounced for law students ($r = 0.40$, $P < 0.001$) but still significant for psychology students ($r = 0.24$, $P < 0.05$).

Because we were interested in whether sentencing interacted with target respectability and sex of target, we dichotomized the recommended punishment index and used the new variable as an independent factor in the analysis of variance of the attribution index. The new factor assumed two values: 0 = subjects who recommended no punishment at all or monetary punishment ($n = 81$) and 1 = judges who recommended prison ($n = 38$).

Recommended punishment entered analysis of variance of attributions together with respectability and sex of the target person. Besides the respectability main effect (see above), a significant punishment main effect emerged [$F(1, 110) = 17.50$, $P < 0.001$]. Causal attributions appeared to be more situational in cases given mild punishment ($M = 3.15$) than in cases given severe punishment ($M = 3.97$).

Main effects were modified by a two-way interaction of respectability and punishment [$F(1, 110) = 13.75$, $P < 0.001$]. Table 13.3 contains the corresponding means. Subjects who recommended mild or no punishment were hardly influenced by target respectability. In contrast, respectability influenced subjects who recommended severe punishment to quite an extent. Rigorous subjects held a low respectability target more responsible for the accident than a highly respectable target. The interaction effect also emerged in a multivariate analysis of variance [$mF(7, 104) = 5.76$, $P < 0.001$].

TABLE 13.3. Causal attributions as a function of target respectability and punishment

Punishment	Target respectability	
	High	Low
Low	3.12 (41)	3.18 (39)
High	3.18 (17)	4.61 (21)

Note. Higher numbers indicate more internal attributions. In parentheses, number of cases per cell.

To sum up, results support the notion of a two-stage model of punishment recommendation as was advocated by Carroll and Payne (1976, 1977) and Haisch (1980, 1981). In a first step, according to this model, a subjective interpretation of the target event determines whether the event is situationally or personally explained. In a second step, causal attribution influences recommended punishment: as situational attribution increases, sentences become more lenient.

This analysis is based on a heuristic approach which is derived from a more comprehensive model of the processes which underlie the attribution of blame (Shaver, 1985). In his sequential model of the attribution of blame, Shaver (1985, p. 166) depicted the necessary elements for the determination of blameworthiness. This analysis presumes an "ideal" observer who follows a prescriptive standard. The necessary elements for the attribution of blame for an offense comprise personal causation, foreseeability, intentionality, free will, ability to distinguish right from wrong, and a failure to justify or excuse the action (Shaver, 1985, p. 173). We have looked at personal causation as a relevant factor for the attribution of blame. Obviously, studies are needed which allow for a variation of the other factors (e.g., free will vs. coercion). Note that we described a scenario which rendered these necessary elements highly likely. Further studies should be devoted to the more complex theory of the attribution of blame.

On the basis of our simplified version of the more comprehensive model we found that causal attributions and punishment recommendations were significantly correlated. Nevertheless, responsibility attributions and punishment recommendations differ in their direct antecedents. Complex interactions of our independent variables influenced subjects' attributions, whereas assigned sentences seemed to be quite independent of these factors. Respectability of the target person, in particular, influenced causal attributions but did not affect sentences.

An analysis of variance with four between-subject factors (sex and respectability of the target person, sex and branch of study of subjects) and one within-subject factor (index of responsibility attributions and index of recommended punishment) led to a significant two-way interaction of responsibility and the repeated measures factor [$F(1, 101) = 6.68$, $P < 0.02$], which indicated that respectability affected causal attributions to a greater extent than it affected assigned punishment. Moreover, the five-way interaction approached significance [$F(1, 101) = 3.72$, $P < 0.06$], indicating that the four-way interaction (see Table 13.2) primarily determined attributions.

How do these results affect the two-stage model of punishment recommendation? First, one must point to the fact that factors determining attributions only partially influenced sentences as well. Punishment recommendation was related to attributional patterns, which depended on the target person's sex and respectability and subjects' sex and branch of study. Second, the relation between responsibility attributions and sentences tended to be closer for law students, although the correlation for psychology students also reached significance.

Target person's respectability exerted most influence on the attributions of subjects who recommended severe punishments. In addition, one should take into account that noticeable cross-sex effects characterized responsibility attributions of the law students: Male law students attended to target respectability when evaluating a female target. Female law students were likewise influenced by the target's respectability when they rated a male target (see Table 13.2).

Consistent with the two-stage model of recommended punishment, a significant linear relationship between causal attributions and sentencing emerged. External attributions were associated with mild sentences. Students took causal attributions into account when deciding on punishment. Following the two-stage model of sentencing one may propose a judgmental process during which subjects first draw more or less correspondent inferences to the target person and then decide on adequate punishment.

Acknowledgments. The authors would like to thank Siegfried Sporer and Jochen Haisch for their helpful suggestions.

References

Bierhoff, H.W. (in press). *Person perception and attribution.* New York: Springer.

Bray, R.M., Struckman-Johnson, C., Osborne, M.D., McFarlane, J.B., & Scott, J. (1978). The effects of defendant status on the decisions of student and community juries. *Social Psychology, 41,* 256–260.

Calhoun, L.G., Peirce, J.R., Walters, S., & Dawes, A.S. (1974). Determinants of social rejection for help seeking: locus of causal attribution, help source, and the "mental illness" label. *Journal of Consulting and Clinical Psychology, 42,* 618.

Carroll, J.S. (1978). Causal attributions in expert parole decisions. *Journal of Personality and Social Psychology, 36,* 1501–1511.

Carroll, J.S., & Payne, J.W. (1976). The psychology of the parole decision process: a joint application of attribution theory and information-processing psychology. In J.S. Carroll, & J. W. Payne (Eds.), *Cognition and social behavior* (pp. 13–32). Hillsdale, NJ: Erlbaum.

Carroll, J. S., & Payne, J. W. (1977). Crime seriousness, recidivism risk, and causal attributions in judgments of prison term by students and experts. *Journal of Applied Psychology, 62,* 595–602.

Carroll, J. S., & Wiener, R. L. (1982). Cognitive social psychology in court and beyond. In A. H. Hastorf, & A. M. Isen (Eds.), *Cognitive social psychology* (pp. 213–253). New York: Elsevier/North-Holland.

Davis, J. H., Kerr, N. L., Atkin, R. S., Holt, R., & Meek, D. (1975). The decision processes of 6- and 12-person mock juries assigned unanimous and two-thirds majority rules. *Journal of Personality and Social Psychology, 32,* 1–14.

Davis, J. H., Kerr, N. L., Stasser, G., Meek, D., & Holt, R. (1977). Victim consequences, sentence severity, and decision processes in mock juries. *Organizational Behavior and Human Performance, 18,* 346–365.

Dion, K. K. (1986). Stereotyping based on physical attractiveness: issues and conceptual perspectives. In C. P. Herman, M. P. Zanna, & E. T. Higgins (Eds.), *Physical appearance, stigma, and social behavior: The Ontario symposium:* Vol. 3 (pp. 7–21). Hillsdale, NJ: Erlbaum.

Ebbesen, E. E., & Konečni, V. J. (1982). Social psychology and the law: a decision-making approach to the criminal justice system. In V. J. Konečni, & E. E. Ebbesen (Eds.), *The criminal justice system* (pp. 3–23). San Francisco: Freeman.

Efran, M. G. (1974). The effect of physical appearance on the judgment of guilt, interpersonal attraction, and severity of recommended punishment in a simulated jury task. *Journal of Research in Personality, 8,* 45–54.

Felson, R. B., & Ribner, S. A. (1981). An attributional approach to accounts and sanctions for criminal violence. *Social Psychology Quarterly, 44,* 137–142.

Finney, P., Merrifield, C., & Helm, B. (1976). The actor's behavioral history, his current role, and the divergence between actor and observer responsibility attributions. *Journal of Research in Personality, 10,* 358–368.

Haisch, J. (1980). Zur Anwendung der Attributionstheorie auf die Strafzumessung in simulierten Strafverfahren: spezialpräventive und generalpräventive Bestrafungsziele bei der Strafzumessung. *Psychologie und Praxis, 24,* 13–20.

Haisch, J. (1981). Vollständigkeit der Attributionsanalyse und Ursachen delinquenten Verhaltens: zur Vorhersage der Strafzumessung durch Juristen und Laien. *Psychologie und Praxis, 25,* 1–9.

Hendrick, C., & Jones, R. A. (1972). *The nature of theory and research in social psychology.* New York: Academic.

Izzett, R. R., & Leginski, W. (1974). Group discussion and the influence of defendant characteristics in a simulated jury setting. *Journal of Social Psychology, 93,* 271–279.

Jones, E. E., & Davis, K. E. (1965). From acts to dispositions. In L. Berkowitz (Ed.), *Advances in experimental social psychology:* Vol. 2 (pp. 219–266). New York: Academic.

Jones, E. E., & Nisbett, R. E. (1971). *The actor and the observer: divergent perceptions of the causes of behavior.* Morristown, NJ: General Learning.

Kaplan, M. F. (1985). Effect of issue and decision rule on normative and informational influence in jury deliberation. Paper presented at the Fourth International Conference on Justice and Law, Nags Head, NC.

Konečni, V. J., & Ebbesen, E. E. (1979). External validity of research in legal psychology. *Law and Human Behavior, 3,* 39–70.

Konečni, V.J., & Ebbesen, E.E. (1982). An analysis of the sentencing system. In V.J. Konečni, & E.E. Ebbesen (Eds.), *The criminal justice system* (pp. 293–332). San Francisco: Freeman.

Krahé, B. (1985). Die Zuschreibung von Verantwortlichkeit nach Vergewaltigungen: Opfer und Täter im Dickicht der attributionstheoretischen Forschung. *Psychologische Rundschau, 36*, 67–82.

Landy, D., & Aronson, E. (1969). The influence of the character of the criminal and his victim on the decisions of simulated jurors. *Journal of Experimental Social Psychology, 5*, 141–152.

McArthur, L.Z. (1982). Judging a book by its cover: a cognitive analysis of the relationship between physical appearance and stereotyping. In A.H. Hastorf, & A.M. Isen (Eds.), *Cognitive social psychology*, (pp. 149–211). New York: Elsevier/North Holland.

Miller, R.J. Chino, A.F., Harney, M.K., Haines, D.A., & Saavedra, R.L. (1986). Assignment of punishment as a function of the severity and consequences of the crime and the status of the defendant. *Journal of Applied Social Psychology, 16*, 77–91.

Nemeth, C.J. (1981). Jury trials: psychology and law. In L. Berkowitz (Ed.), *Advances in experimental social psychology:* Vol. 14 (pp. 309–367). New York: Academic.

Nemeth, C., & Sosis, R.H. (1973). A simulated jury study: characteristics of the defendant and the jurors. *Journal of Social Psychology, 90*, 221–229.

Reynolds, D.E., & Sanders, M.S. (1975). Effect of defendant attractiveness, age, and injury on severity of sentence given by simulated jurors. *Journal of Social Psychology, 96*, 149–150.

Shaver, K.G. (1985). *The attribution of blame.* New York: Springer.

Sigall, H., & Landy, D. (1972). Effects of the defendant's character and suffering on juridic judgment: a replication and clarification. *Journal of Social Psychology, 88*, 149–150.

Sigall, H., & Ostrove, N. (1975). Beautiful but dangerous: effects of offender attractiveness and nature of the crime on juridic judgment. *Journal of Personality and Social Psychology, 31*, 410–414.

Sporer, S.L. (1979). Legal and extra-legal factors in judicial sentencing. Paper presented at the meeting of the Eastern Psychological Association. Philadelphia, PA.

Sporer, S.L. (1982). *Reducing disparity in judicial sentencing: a social-psychological approach.* Frankfurt: Lang.

Sporer, S.L. (1986). Justice as fair and equal treatment before the law: the role of individual vs. group decision making. In H.W. Bierhoff, R.L. Cohen, & J. Greenberg (Eds.), *Justice in social relations* (pp. 283–298). New York: Plenum.

Walster, E. (1966). Assignment of responsibility for an accident. *Journal of Personality and Social Psychology, 3*, 73–79.

Part Three Eyewitness Testimony

Introduction

HERMANN WEGENER

Statement analysis deals with the psychological processes which are of importance when making testimonies of self-experienced events and actions, especially within the framework of eye witness testimonies. Here, situational circumstances and individual characteristics during the encoding, the retention, and the reproduction phases often play an important part as possible sources of error. Cognitive, emotional, and motivational variables determine the validity of a statement.

Psychological research has been concerned with this phenomenon since the turn of the century. As a result, statement psychology has been cautiously developed into an extensive, practical branch of applied psychology, with various stages of different research activities and multiple paradigm changes.

The first studies by W. Stern (1902) and O. Lipmann (1904) in Germany and H. Münsterberg (1908) in the United States placed the main emphasis upon experimentally investigating witness testimonies. These laboratory experiments, however, indicated that only a small number of details were correctly replicated (e.g., from previously presented pictures). It is, therefore, not astonishing that severe criticisms were raised against these inadequate and undifferentiated methods (A. Moll, 1908; O. Mönkemöller, 1930). This first disappointing start was followed by a period in which the psychologists, who were occasionally consulted by the courts, used their own case material as the basis for assessing witness testimonies, instead of general experimental results (W. Stern, 1926).

After World War II, there was renewed interest in statement psychology; for example, in the Federal Republic of Germany there was a rapid increase in the number of appointments of psychological expert witnesses by courts (Undeutsch, 1954). The disadvantageous findings during the early experimental phase were now corrected by the observation that in most of the cases, the witnesses gave correct statements in court.

Psychological experts in the two german States and in Scandinavia (Arntzen, 1970; Szewczyk, 1973; Trankell, 1971; Undeutsch, 1967) established criteria catalogs based on their experiences in order to differentiate true from false reproductions. Here, emphasis was placed on characteristics of statement behavior and statement content. The confession of the accused often served as an external control criterion to test the validity of the criteria. An experimental examination of the criteria was specifically rejected as being useless due to an alleged lack of ecological validity (Arntzen, 1970; Trankell, 1971; Undeutsch, 1967). Essentially, O. Lipmann (1925; *Grundriß der Psychologie für Juristen*, quoted in Undeutsch, 1967, p. 177) emphasized a differentiation between "competence to testify" and the motivationally determined "credibility," or "trustworthiness."

In the 1970s a new paradigm change followed which led back to an experimental approach to statement psychology. In Great Britain and the United States there was a rapid increase in the number of experimental studies dealing with perception, memory, and reproduction processes and person recognition performances in testimonies (cf. e.g., Clifford & Scott, 1978; Gudjonsson & MacKeith, 1982; Loftus, 1979; Wells, 1978; however, questions dealing with the intention to tell the truth were experimentally examined only by those psychologists (Raskin, 1982; Steller, 1987) who dealt with the polygraph technique. Shortly thereafter, experimental research followed which dealt with linguistic and paraverbal indicators of a witness's intention to tell the truth and provided methodological criticisms of the existing criteria (Köhnken & Wegener, 1982, 1985; Wegener, 1981), with the goal of scientifically supporting individual statement analysis through court experts. In the German-speaking countries, the conflict concerning the merits and demerits of experiments within statement psychology is still not over. However, it is to be expected in the future that within statement psychology, as in other areas of applied psychology, experimental research will gain in importance in the exploration of indicators of intention to tell the truth.

The following section first contains two reports which stem from general and social psychology. They are concerned with processes of perception and memory, which both play an important role in statement psychology.

Within the framework of new perception-cognition research, *Lilli* discusses the determination of witness testimony by processes of categorization, expectation, person, role, and event schemata, and cognitive rules. The reported findings offer a series of valuable approaches to witness psychology. Lilli's research, which bears a close connection to the subsequent chapters, points to many sources of error and causes of distortion in the later reproduction of, and during the perception and interpretation of, an object, event, or action.

Wippich first describes on the basis of his own experimental work in the field of cognitive psychology, the processes of encoding, storing, and retrieval of information in human memory. The selecting and organizing processes in respect of information are heavily influenced by attitudes, intentions, and prior knowledge. The script concept supposes that typical, frequently experienced events stored as schemata support the memory function. Here, nonperceived or nonexistent (unreal) aspects can be added due to the "script knowledge." On the other hand, memory is more accurate as regards atypical, deviating elements of events or actions. Besides the scripts, Wippich assumes nonschematic subsystems in the human memory, in which specific, relevant information is permanently stored. Favorable for reproduction is the reinstatement of the same or a similar context during reproduction and encoding.

Both papers offer many implications for the applied field of witness psychology, which future studies on perception and memory should take into account.

Loftus reports experiments on the effects of false or suggestive information which is applied between the time of experiencing and reproduction, and which misleads the witness. This postevent information distorts previously stored memories. The degree of recollection change depends on several variables. The most important is the subject's detection of the discrepancy between original memory and misleading information. There are several theoretical approaches to this phenomenon. Loftus discusses these on the basis of her own experiments. Important for the distortion of memory is whether the new information is added before or after the conscious act of retrieval, since from this moment on, the memories can hardly be altered by "free radicals" of new information. The possibility of a blending of memories should also be observed; recall would then be a combination of parts of the original and parts of the additional information. Therefore, the question is important as to how the two sources of information interact with each other. The importance of Loftus' research for the psychology of eyewitness testimony is obvious.

Stephenson et al. report experiments that test the correspondence of collaborative testimony and individual testimonies. This problem is of importance especially for joint (mutual) testimonies of police officers. Group remembering is a neglected topic in both social and cognitive psychology. The authors have collected reports of interviews of police officers and students (two to four subjects), individually or in connection with questionnaires and free recall computed according to ratings of confidence, accuracy, completeness, implicational errors (not contradicting the original), and confusing errors (contradicting the original). Overall the results showed that in collaborative testimonies, potentially useful information is excluded by conventionalization. Group memory enhances the danger of collective bias by selective processes and by defining ideas of what is relevant. If one member of the group represents the group testimony, the written report is not used to refresh the memory but as a substitute for the memory. Therefore, individuals should be required to take personal responsibility for their testimony. In addition, there is no doubt that statements by several witnesses would lead to a greater completeness of the joint testimony.

The collaboration of police officers as witnesses cannot be prevented. The results of this contribution deserve to be attributed great importance in the praxis of and research into the adversarial as well as the inquisitorial system.

Köhnken, who has published elsewhere a series of experimental studies on this topic, gives an overview of basic concepts, theoretical approaches, research paradigms, and empirical results of statement credibility. His concern is to discover overt indicators relevant to the assessment of credibility of a statement (defined by the intention or motivation to tell the truth). Empirical results have proved that content analysis and extralinguistic behavior are important sources of information for the judgment of credibility.

Suggestions for future research include a taxonomy of relevant dimensions of witness statements, potentially relevant variables for the classification with regard to credibility, intraindividual comparisons between true and deceptive statements, processes of generating a statement, and, last but not least, analysis of the judgment process. These and other suggestions for research, as well as the experimental designs proposed by Köhnken, seem suitable for improving the theoretical basis of forensic statement analysis.

Raskin and Steller treat the problem of assessment of credibility in cases of child sexual abuse, which has increased very markedly during recent years. At present, there are two approaches to credibility assessment: polygraph examination of accused persons and statement analysis of the child's allegations. The polygraph results, combined with a statement analysis, usually lead to rapid solution of a case. In the years 1983–1985, 56% of all accused persons who were examined at the University of Utah by the polygraph technique were diagnosed as truthful in their denials (the accuracy of a polygraph examination is reported as 85%–95%). Since 1954, statement analysis has been the major method used by experts in the Federal Republic of Germany. The basic hypothesis is a difference in quality and content between truthful and false testimonies. The procedure uses a system of reality criteria which has been developed by several European authors. The relative importance of these criteria has been modified by new empirical findings. To sum up, the combined utilization of the polygraph technique and statement analysis can improve the effectiveness of the investigation process and minimize a possible negative impact on the examined child. The nonverbal indicators mentioned in Köhnken's contribution could, after further testing of their usefulness in forensic practice, supplement statement analysis.

Sporer describes experimental studies on person identification by a witness. Verbal and visual processes within the encoding, retention, and retrieval phases are discussed. It seems that persons who are labeled as criminals are more likely to be identified in a (perpetrator-present) lineup than others. The facilitative effect of an enriched verbal encoding context can be shown. There is little experience about the retention phase in this respect, but we can assume that misleading post-event information induces false visual choices. Further research is needed with regard to improving the recognition performance through the help of verbal mnemonics. The correlation between giving a description and recognition is very low, except in the case of conspicuous characteristics.

To summarize, the findings in this field are inconsistent. Nevertheless, Sporer concludes the chapter with some interesting and important remarks which are addressed to the researcher as well as to the forensic practitioner.

References

Arntzen, F. (1970). *Psychologie der Zeugenaussage. Einführung in die forensische Aussagepsychologie.* Göttingen: Hogrefe.

Clifford, B., & Scott, J. (1978). Individual and situational factors in eyewitness testimony. *Journal of Applied Psychology, 63*, 352–359.

Gudjonsson, G.H., & MacKeith, J.A. (1982). False confessions. Psychological effects of interrogation. A discussion paper. In A. Trankell (Ed.), *Reconstructing the past.* Stockholm: Norstedt.

Köhnken, G., & Wegener, H. (1982). Zur Glaubwürdigkeit von Zeugenaussagen. Experimentelle Überprüfung ausgewählter Glaubwürdigkeitskriterien. *Zeitschrift für Experimentelle und Angewandte Psychologie, 29*, 92–111.

Köhnken, G., & Wegener, H. (1985). Zum Stellenwert des Experiments in der forensischen Aussagepsychologie. *Zeitschrift für Experimentelle und Angewandte Psychologie, 32*, 104–109.

Lipmann, O. (1904). Neuere Arbeiten zur Psychologie der Aussage. Sammelbericht. *Journal für Psychologie und Neurologie, 3*, 245–249.

Loftus, E.F. (1979). *Eyewitness testimony.* Cambridge, MA: Harvard University Press.

Moll, A. (1908). Die forensische Bedeutung der modernen Forschung über die Aussagepsychologie. *Ärztliche Sachverständigen-Zeitung,* 85–89, 108–113.

Mönkemöller, O. (1930). *Psychologie und Psychopathologie der Aussage.* Bibliothek der Kriminalistik. Heidelberg: Winters.

Münsterberg, H. (1908). *On the witness stand. Essays on psychology and crime.* New York: Clark & Booardman.

Raskin, D.C. (1982). The scientific basis of polygraph techniques and their uses in the judicial process. In A. Trankell (Ed.), *Reconstructing the past* (pp. 317–371) Stockholm: Norstedt.

Steller, M. (1987). *Psychophysiologische Aussagebeurteilung – wissenschaftliche Grundlagen und Anwendungen der Lügendetektion.* Göttingen: Hogrefe.

Stern, W. (1902). Zur Psychologie der Aussage. *Zeitschrift für die gesamte Strafrechtswissenschaft, 22*, 315–370.

Stern, W. (1926). *Jugendliche Zeugen in Sittlichkeitsprozessen.* Leipzig: Quelle and Meyer.

Szewczyk, H. (1973). Kriterien der Beurteilung kindlicher Zeugenaussagen. *Probleme und Ergebnisse der Psychologie, 46*, 47–66.

Trankell, A. (1971). *Der Realitätsgehalt von Zeugenaussagen.* Göttingen: Hogrefe.

Undeutsch, U. (1954). Die Entwicklung der gerichtspsychologischen Gutachtertätigkeit. *Bericht über den 19. Kongreß der Deutschen Gesellschaft für Psychologie.* Göttingen: Hogrefe.

Undeutsch, U. (1967). Beurteilung der Glaubhaftigkeit von Aussagen. In U. Undeutsch (Ed.), *Forensische Psychologie. Handbuch der Psychologie* (Vol. 11). Göttingen: Hogrefe.

Wegener, H. (1981). *Einführung in die Forensische Psychologie.* Darmstadt: Wissenschaftliche Buchgesellschaft.

Wells, G.L. (1978). Applied eyewitness testimony research: System variables and estimated variables. *Journal of Personality and Social Psychology, 12*, 54–57.

14
The Perception of Social Events and Behavior Sequences

WALDEMAR LILLI

Introduction

Social perception is one of the central themes of social psychology, and within this area of the discipline some quite decisive changes have been observable during recent decades.

The very original question pursued especially by the so-called "new look in perception" has been the perceptual changes that take place under the influence of motives and needs. Among other reasons, an adequate answer to this question has not been provided because it proved impossible to separate out a "pure" perceptual effect. Although some attempts were made during the 1960s and 1970s to find statistically independent measures of perceptual and judgmental responses (e.g., by signal detection methods, see Svets, Tanner, & Birdsall, 1966; Upmeyer, 1971), and these attempts appeared successful, effects of cognitive elements could not really be isolated by these procedures.

Even at the beginning of social perception research, Bruner and Postman (1951) recognized perceiving, thinking, drawing inferences, and judging to be only parts of a whole cognitive construction enabling the person to make sense of his social world. With their theory of (social) perception, they tried to expand upon these considerations: The perceptual process, according to their line of reasoning, is governed by expectational hypotheses, or cognitive predispositions, which enable the person to solve and interpret forthcoming perceptual situations. It is astonishing that in modern cognitive social psychology we find very few references to this integrative concept, though its basic ideas can be found quite often as elements of more recent cognitive concepts (e.g., Neisser, 1976; Snyder & Cantor, 1979).

In forensic psychology, we usually find a partition of the whole process into a perceptual, an interval, and a reproduction phase (Loftus, 1979; Undeutsch, 1967; Wegener, 1981). The accuracy of witness account is seen as strongly influenced by perceptual conditions.

Today, the field of social perception/cognition is dominated by a series of concepts of limited scope which treat the individual more or less as an active information processor. The primary point is no longer the pure perceptual process with all its unresolved problems, but rather the levels of information processing, the organization of the cognitive system, and its structural and functional pecularities. (The term perception could therefore be substituted by the term cognition within this chapter.)

What Does the Person Perceive?

One of the ideas which is most often cited in modern literature on social perception/cognition is that, as Bruner (1957) has put it, *perception involves a process of categorization.* This has at least three implications:

1. Categories or schemata must already be available before the person comes into contact with a stimulus situation.
2. Categorization of incoming information always means loss of information as to the stimulus.
3. Social perception/cognition is therefore a process of active (re)construction of social reality by the perceiver. At the least it is a slightly simplified and at the most an erroneous reconstruction. Considerations of this kind have a long tradition in philosophy, perhaps since Aristotle, who acknowledged that humans were not at all prepared for any kind of "correct" perception. Particularly in modern cognition research, one of the dominant questions concerns the mechanisms of these shortcomings (e.g., Nisbett & Ross, 1980).

If the process of social perception starts before an event occurs, as we have argued above, the question arises as to *what the perceiver does with incoming information.* There are several answers to this question though sometimes they do not really differ very much.

A first answer refers to a rather seldom explicitly named basic characteristic of human information processing: the necessity of selective information extraction in view of spatial, temporal, and cognitive capacity limitations on the part of the perceiver. These limitations will be compensated to a certain extent by supplementary tendencies of the cognitive organization. It is primarily this basic characteristic which enables the person to cope with stimulus complexity and simplicity as well. In other words: *During the ongoing perceptual process, some information is neglected while other information is added.*

A second answer refers to the kind of information which enters the perceptual system and also the way in which the perceiver starts in construing an observed social event. It should be mentioned here that recent concepts are almost exclusively concerned with the perceiver and much less with the stimulus to be observed. This may be seen as a deficit, and indeed only a few researchers (e.g., Gibson, 1970) have developed concepts pertaining to the stimulus side. Nevertheless, the problem is addressed by several authors, for example by Kahneman, Slovic, and Tversky (1982) and by Nisbett and Ross (1980), when they point to the distinction between theory- and data-driven aspects of information processing.

Some principles, however, can be ascertained which provide hints to the way in which ongoing information processes are released or even directed by primary contacts with stimulus situations. First, the question arises as to which parts of the stimulus immediately receive the attention of an observer and what dissolves the figure from the ground. The well-known primacy effect means that a first item of information may determine the whole impression of a stimulus, particularly if this first item allows subsequent information to be integrated.

The vividness criterion, usually mentioned in connection with the availability heuristic, refers to situatively striking information if it is (1) emotionally interesting, (2) concrete and imagery provoking, and (3) proximate in a sensory, temporal, or spatial way (Nisbett & Ross, 1980). According to the availability heuristic, information which is more available also has a higher probability of determining the perception of an event; if may serve as an anchor in the interpretation of a stimulus (Fischhoff & McGregor, 1980).

If we now turn to the observer and try to establish how incoming information is handled, we have to consider the preconditions of stimulus analysis, namely cognitive representations. While up to now the human being has been viewed as an active information processor, some important changes of emphasis must be mentioned: The "new look in perception" and its subsequent analyses mainly attended to "hot" cognitions; needs, drives, and motives were seen as the criteria of information selection. But causal relationships of those "hot" cognitions could never be explained so that the assumed dynamics of the perceptual process remain unclear (Markus & Zajonc, 1985). Together with the development of attribution research, a tendency arose to look for the "cold" cognitions only, e.g., the selection mechanisms, the biases, and the errors in human information processing, in order to find more parsimonious models of explanation.

Cognitive representations are the inner individual realizations of objects and events of the perceptual world. A one-to-one relationship between stimulus object and its representations is no longer assumed. Cognitive representations of objects and events are the only route of access of the individual to reality. Thus, information can only be treated by the individual on the basis of given perceptual, cognitive, or knowledge structures. These structures refer to the organization of related representations of events, objects, and persons.

Cognitive representations as bases of human information processing imply a frame of reference for a whole series of concepts: Bruner (1951) spoke of "hypotheses", and this was echoed in a nearly identical manner 30 years later by Snyder (1981), without referring to Bruner. It was Neisser (1976) who popularized the term "schema" within social perception/cognition research. A great number of models and concepts have since emerged which all try to clarify the nature of cognitive representations. Bruner and Tagiuri (1958) used the term "implicit theories" in person perception (more general: Epstein, 1973); Jones and Thibaut (1958) referred to "inferential sets"; Rosch (1973) initiated a concept of "categories," Tajfel (1969, 1982) that of social categories and stereotypes (also: Hamilton, 1981; Lilli, 1982); Cantor and Mischel (1977, 1979) presented the idea of the "prototype," while Stotland and Canon (1972) reformulated the whole of cognitive social psychology in terms of schemata. Tesser and Cowan (1975, 1977) made an attempt also to classify attitudes as cognitive representations. Abelson (1976; Schank & Abelson, 1977) formulated his "script" concept, and Forgas (1981) had the idea of "social episodes." (This catalogue is not a complete one.)

The more or less obvious basic unifying idea seems to be that information process is a categorical and schematic. Recent years have witnessed a tendency toward convergence between different views in this area (Markus & Zajonc, 1985). A few survey articles (Hastie, 1981; Taylor & Crocker, 1981) tried to establish some order; for our purposes it seems convenient to accept the proposal by Taylor and Crocker to view most of the social cognition concepts in terms of schemata. These authors distinguished between these classes of schemata: (1) person schemata, including self-schemata, (2) role and group schemata, and (3) event schemata, behavioral schemata, or scripts. In the following sections these three distinctions are employed in considering the perceptions of eyewitnesses.

Person and Person-in-Situation Schemata

In the person perception process, two kinds of schemata can be distinguished: on the one hand, trait schemata are involved if persons per se represent the stimulus in question: on the other hand, person-in-situation schemata are at work if the actions and behavior of persons in social situations are observed. It is primarily the latter case which is of interest within the context of this chapter.

Housebreakers or robbers can be seen as examples of situationally determined schemata; the latter consist of goal-directed actions which can be assumed in a given situation and of appropriate persons who usually are observed in such situations. Schemata like that of robbers and housebreakers are cognitively available quite easily (Cantor, 1980), because they include very particular kinds of behavior. Therefore, if an observer is called into the witness box, it is entirely possible that parts of his evidence may not be based on his observations but on his well-developed robber schema.

Obviously, some principles of object schemata are also effective in complex schemata of this kind. The principle of category similarity (Cantor & Mischel, 1977; Cantor, Mischel, & Schwartz, 1982) may cause the observer to attribute traits and actions to all housebreakers in an identical manner so that the direct experience of a single housebreak – particularly in extreme cases – could have a schema-activating function only. Otherwise, the housebreaker schema is, according to Rosch, Mervis, Gray, Johnson, and Boyes-Braem (1976), on a level of very concrete categories with lots of details. The higher the level of abstraction, the less the amount of detailed information included in that schema, and the higher its pregnancy the less it overlaps with other categories. Concrete schemata of this kind help the observer to recall schema-consistent information in cases where inconsistent and irrelevant information is also available.

It may be an interesting question at which stage of the information process such schemata effects occur: Is it already at the input stage, or is it at the output stage only? Results of research permit a really Solomonic answer: there is evidence for both stages of the process (Howard & Rothbart, 1980; Wyer, Srull, Gordon, & Hartwick, 1980). But the observer is also capable of interpreting information in the light of an actually appearing schema. A schema seems to be most effective if it is available and used at both stages of the information process.

Role Schemata

Since role schemata include the observer's knowledge of certain norm-directed modes of behavior, they are important for our concerns. If an observer has once identified a person as a foreigner or a homosexual, as a banker or as a police spy, very often no possibility is given to this person to escape from this stereotype. All those traits become affixed which are enclosed in the category concerned, and the perceiver does not care to what degree – if at all – these traits really characterize that person.

With his stereotypic schemata the observer is able to reduce the variability within the group to which a perceived person is seen as belonging, and possible alternative views of that person are thus excluded (Lilli, 1982; Park & Rothbart, 1982; Tajfel, 1982; Wilder, 1981). But the observer himself is also subject to field forces of this kind. What can be concluded from current research is that members of outgroups will be perceived on the basis of rather simple and rigid schemata compared to the perception of ingroup members. At this point, it may be interesting to note that particularly research into stereotyping in a certain way goes beyond the actual perspective of "cold" cognitions, including affect and behavior: To recognize a person as a member of a gang indeed means much more than only identifying him on the basis of visible gestures and behaviors. At the same time, it means that feelings of fear and defense will arise and could induce the observer not to go out at night and to lock his house securely.

Now, to which research results should attention be drawn?

It seems obvious that stereotypic role schemata fix the observer upon his very first contact with a stimulus situation (Klatzki, Martin, & Kane, 1982), mainly in an affective sense. Role and group memberships can also be recalled very easily, while detailed information often vanishes almost totally. At the same time, detailed information which fits the group stereotype is easily available (Rothbart, Evans, & Fulero, 1979). And in the light of recently received information, for example, that the person is a parson or that he has been imprisoned, a reinterpretation of the whole situation is conceivable via the activation of quite another schema (Snyder & Uranowitz, 1978).

Event Schemata

It seems plausible and appropriate to real situations (Johansson, von Hofsten, & Jansson, 1980) to include the perception of events and their cognitive representation within the focus of research interest. Cognitive concepts and structures which refer to event sequences occurring in well-known social situations are called event schemata or scripts (Abelson, 1981). The most often cited example is the restaurant script, that is the usually expected sequence of events when a person goes into a restaurant. Scripts include (1) single aspects – so-called props – in the observation of a traffic accident, for instance, the damaged car, (2) roles, for example, of the driver of that car or of another person involved in the accident, and (3) sequential rules, i.e., to call the police before the damaged car is removed. Scripts also include certain norms of correct successive event sequences (even sequences of time, cf. Bellezza & Bower, 1982) and conceptions of the parts (actions and scenes) of an event, its hierarchical and sequential order.

Event schemata are abstractions of everyday experiences, and they serve for the understanding of future experiences. *In addition, it is because schemata of this kind are available to the observer that he or she is capable of telling complete stories of events.*

Perhaps two results should be especially mentioned here: the "ghost effect" (Bower, Black & Turner, 1979) and the effect of information inconsistent with a certain schema. The ghost effect refers to the fact that memory gaps which appear when observing different events with the same script are filled in according to the general case. This can lead to curious changes in the recall of single events. For instance, if a person has watched three successive soccer games on television (perhaps during the world championship in Mexico), the general case of soccer games may be evoked so often that the probability of erroneous recall of single events increases.

It may be due to the number of elements and the hierarchical and sequential order of a script that the appearance of differences from it can interrupt the script processing. In this case, inconsistent information receives great attention. There are some studies showing that information inconsistent with the script is recalled more easily, while this is true for consistent information in studies with quite different schemata (Graesser, Woll, Kowalski, & Smith 1980; Smith & Graesser, 1981).

Cognitive Rules

Fairly independent of shapes and contents of cognitive structures, one might ask whether the observer may not even use certain more or less simple strategies and rules instead of schemata, scripts, or episodes to manage the great variety of situations he is concerned with. Some of the cited concepts do indeed point to cognitive rules. Markus and Zajonc (1985) see a hopeful tendency in social cognition research not to increase further the number of structural concepts but to identify underlying principly similar rules.

If we take a brief look at the history of perception/cognition research, it can be seen that this is not really a new development:

1. Early trends in the psychology of perception were characterized by an abandonment of elementarism and an acceptance of gestaltism which was thought to govern the formation of perceptions. Up to now, the consistency principle is perhaps the most influential example of gestalt tradition, which, for instance, was used by Heider (1958) in his model of balance, a structure of relationships with three elements, an observer (P), another person (0), and an object of judgment (X). We know from research that balanced information is easier learned and better recalled than unbalanced information (De Soto, Henley, & London, 1968; Picek, Sherman, & Shiffrin, 1975; Sentis & Burnstein, 1979).
2. Perhaps the most general and simple principle of rules may be that of linearity on the basis of which hierarchical and transitive relationships can be organized (Tsujimoto, Wilde, & Robertson, 1978). In studies with correspondingly ordered stimuli, for instance persons, it was found that in the absence of other information, particularly spatial proximity was interpreted in terms of positive feelings (Kuethe & Stricker, 1963; Little, 1968).
3. From the very beginning of impression formation research by Asch (1946), the question was addressed as to the way in which a perceiver puts together pieces of information to form an overall impression of a person. Asch himself formulated the change-of-meaning hypothesis, an assumption that information is grouped around certain central items; with some modifications, this thesis still holds. Later, Norman H. Anderson (1974) brought his "cognitive algebra" into play, which means that the combination of information follows certain mathematical rules. The psychological foundation of this concept, however, has not yet been elucidated.
4. The view of the human being as an active information processor received a fresh impetus from the notion of causal explanations which Kelley (e.g., Kelley & Michela, 1980) introduced into attribution research: Information is combined in a way that corresponds to a covariation of causes and effects.
5. According to Tversky and Kahneman (e.g., 1974), the perceiver, besides having certain knowledge structures at his disposal, uses heuristics, rather simple rules of thumb, in solving judgmental tasks. Two of the most important

heuristics are the availability heuristic and the representativity heuristic. The availability heuristic is used if issues of frequency, probability, and causality are to be judged. The representativity heuristic allows the observer in many cases to reduce inferential tasks to simple similarity judgments. The basic idea of this rather new research perspective is to point to the judgmental shortcomings and errors which occur if criteria of frequency, probability, and representativity are not taken into account adequately.

Two examples of some importance may be addressed here:

1. Jones and Nisbett (1972) studied the divergence of causal interpretations by an actor and an observer, where the observer inferred dispositive causes for the behavior but the actor made situative causes responsible: When the actor handed one dollar to a beggar in the street because he looked so sad, the observer interpreted this behavior as generosity.
2. Taylor and Fiske (1978; see also McArthur & Solomon, 1978) depicted the relationship between causal evaluation and availability: If a person is somehow salient – by skin color, for instance, or by virtue of being a single woman within a group of men – he or she will become a causal agent in the eyes of an observer. A similar phenomenon described by Chapman (1967) is the illusory correlation effect; if subjects are asked to estimate the number of stimuli randomly presented previously, the less often presented stimuli are regularly the most overestimated ones (Lilli & Rehm, 1983, 1984).

Concluding Remarks

In this chapter I have briefly considered the main aspects of perception/cognition that may affect an observer. Overall, what should be said about the value of this basic research for the practical field of perception and eyewitness testimony? There are at least four points of some importance.

1. Under normal circumstances an observer tries to avoid errors and biases in his perceptions and judgments.
2. Eyewitness testimonies, however, are communicated perceptions under extraordinary conditions. To be sure, the performance of an observer as an eyewitness could not be seen as worse than usual. If a person knows beforehand that he or she may be called as a witness, his or her performance may even be better than usual.
3. One cannot point out often enough that – psychologically seen – asking a witness is equivalent to an experimental treatment situation. As we know, this has certain consequences for the recall and report of what was perceived. Even if a witness were able to communicate his observations extensively, it is the *kind of questions* he will be asked which substantially deter-

mine his answers. As we know from research, a further influence on perceptual responding stems from personal involvement of the observer: his interest and the strength of his personal involvement in a situation.

4. The need for caution in the application of basic research should be stressed. In many cases the *heuristic* value of one or the other basic study or theory will be immediately visible. But this should not at all be the only view in the transfer of knowledge from basic to applied issues. A second step should consist of a more precise inspection of basic theories and research concepts. It will then be necessary to evaluate the research paradigms with the help of which results have been gained.

Some social perception concepts have indeed been utilized by forensic psychology (see the chapters by Köhnken, by Steller & Raskin, and by Loftus, this volume).

All in all, social perception/cognition research not only offers a series of valuable approaches to the field of the witness testimony, but is also useful in other fields of psychology and law.

References

Abelson, R.P. (1976). Script processing in attitude formation and decision making. In J.S. Caroll & J. Payne (Eds.), *Cognition and social behavior.* Hillsdale, NJ: Erlbaum.

Abelson, R.P. (1981). The psychological status of the script concept. *American Psychologist, 36,* 715–729.

Anderson, N.H. (1974). Cognitive algebra. In E.C. Carterette & M.P. Friedman (Eds.), *Handbook of perception*: Vol. II. New York: Academic.

Asch, S.R. (1946). Forming impressions of personality. *Journal of Abnormal and Social Psychology, 41,* 258–290.

Bellezza, F.S., & Bower, G.H. (1982). Remembering script-based text. *Poetics, 11,* 1–23.

Bower, G.H., Black, J.B., & Turner, T.J. (1979). Scripts in memory for text. *Cognitive Psychology, 11,* 177–220.

Bruner, J.S. (1957). Going beyond the information given. In H. Gulber, G. Terrell, & M. Wertheimer (Eds.), *Contemporary approaches to cognition.* Cambridge, MA: Harvard University Press.

Bruner, J.S., & Postman, L. (1951). An approach to social perception. In W. Dennis, R. Lippit, & K.T. Behanan (Eds.), *Current trends in social psychology.* Pittsburgh: University of Pittsburgh Press.

Bruner, J.S., & Tagiuri, R. (1958). The perception of people. In G. Lindzey (Ed.), *Handbook of social psychology:* Vol. II. Reading, MA: Addison-Wesley.

Cantor, N. (1980). Perceptions of siuations: Situation prototypes and personsituation prototypes. In D. Magnusson (Ed.), *The situation: An interactional perspective.* Hillsdale, NJ: Erlbaum.

Cantor, N., & Mischel, W. (1977). Traits as prototypes: Effects on recognition memory. *Journal of Personality and Social Psychology, 35,* 38–48.

Cantor, N., & Mischel, W. (1979). Prototypes in person perception. In L. Berkowitz (Ed.), *Advances in experimental social psychology:* Vol. 12. New York: Academic.

Cantor, N., Mischel, W., & Schwartz, J. (1982). Social knowledge: Structure, content, use and abuse. In A. Hastorf & A. Isen (Eds.), *Cognitive social psychology.* New York: Elsevier North-Holland.

Chapman, L. J. (1967). Illusory correlation in observational report. *Journal of Verbal Learning and Verbal Behavior, 6,* 151–155.

DeSoto, C. B., Henley, N. M., & London, M. (1968). Balance and the grouping schema. *Journal of Personality and Social Psychology, 8,* 1–7.

Epstein, S. (1973). The self-concept revisited: or a theory of a theory. *American Psychologist, 28,* 404–416.

Fischhoff, B., & MacGregor, B. (1980). *Judged lethality* (Decision Research Report 80-4). Eugene, Oregon: Decision Research Unit.

Forgas, J. P. (1981). Affective and emotional influences on episode representations. In J. P. Forgas (Ed.), *Social cognition.* London: Academic.

Gibson, J. J. (1970). *The perception of the visual world.* Boston: Houghton Mifflin.

Graesser, A. C., Woll, S. B., Kowalski, D. J., & Smith, D. A. (1980). Memory for typical and atypical actions in scripted activities. *Journal of Experimental Psychology, 6,* 503–515.

Hamilton, D. L. (1981). *Cognitive processes in stereotyping and intergroup behavior.* Hillsdale, NJ: Erlbaum.

Hastie, R. (1981). Schematic principles in human memory. In E. T. Higgins, C. P. Herman, & M. P. Zanna (Eds.), *Social cognition: The Ontario symposium:* Vol. I. Hillsdale, NJ: Erlbaum.

Heider, F. (1958). *The psychology of interpersonal relations.* New York: Wiley.

Howard, J. W., & Rothbart, M. (1980). Social categorization and memory for ingroup and outgroup behavior. *Journal of Personality and Social Psychology, 38,* 301–310.

Johansson, G., von Hofsten, C., & Jansson, G. (1980). Event perception. *Annual Review of Psychology, 31,* 27–63.

Jones, E. E., & Nisbett, R. E. (1972). The actor and the observer: Divergent perceptions of the causes of behavior. In E. E. Jones, D. E. Kanouse, H. H. Kelley, R. E. Nisbett, S. Valins, & B. Weiner (Eds.), *Attribution: Perceiving the causes of behavior.* Morristown, NJ: General Learning.

Jones, E. E., & Thibaut, J. W. (1958). Interaction goals as bases of inference in interpersonal perception. In R. Tagiuri & L. Petrullo (Eds.), *Person perception and interpersonal behavior.* Stanford, CA: Stanford University Press.

Kahneman, D., Slovic, P., & Tversky, A. (Eds.). (1982). *Judgment under uncertainty: Heuristics and biases.* Cambridge: Cambridge University Press.

Kelley, H. H., & Michela, J. L. (1980). Attribution theory and research. *Annual Review of Psychology, 31,* 457–501.

Klatzky, R. L., Martin, G. L., & Kane, R. A. (1982). Influence of social category activation on processing of visual information. *Social Cognition, 1,* 95–109.

Kuethe, J. L., & Stricker, G. (1963). Man and woman: Social schemata for males and females. *Psychological Reports, 13,* 655–661.

Lilli, W. (1982). *Grundlagen der Stereotypisierung.* Göttingen: Hogrefe.

Lilli, W. (1984). Die Hypothesentheorie der sozialen Wahrnehmung. In D. Frey & M. Irle (Eds.), *Theorien der Sozialpsychologie: Vol. I. Kognitive Theorien.* Bern: Huber.

Lilli, W., & Rehm, J. (1983). Theoretische und empirische Untersuchungen zum Phänomen der „illusorischen Korrelation“. I. Ableitung von Randbedingungen für das Auftreten von Effekten der illusorischen Korrelation aus dem Konzept der Verfügbarkeitsheuristik. *Zeitschrift für Sozialpsychologie, 14,* 251–261.

Lilli, W., & Rehm, J. (1984). Theoretische und empirische Untersuchungen zum Phänomen der Zusammenhangstäuschung, II: Entwicklung eines Modells zum quantitativen Urteil und Diskussion seiner Implikationen für die soziale Urteilsbildung. *Zeitschrift für Sozialpsychologie, 15,* 60–73.

Little, K.B. (1968). Cultural variations in social schemata. *Journal of Personality and Social Psychology, 10,* 1–7.

Loftus, E.F. (1979). *Eyewitness testimony.* Cambridge, MA: Harvard University Press.

Markus, H., & Zajonc, R.B. (1985). The cognitive perspective in social psychology. In G. Lindzey & G.E. Aronson (Eds.), *The handbook of social psychology*: Vol. I (3rd ed., pp. 137–230). New York: Random House.

McArthur, L.Z., & Solomon, L.K. (1978). Perceptions of an aggressive encounter as a function of the victim's salience and the perceiver's arousal. *Journal of Personality and Social Psychology, 36,* 1278–1290.

Neisser, U. (1976). *Cognition and reality.* San Francisco: Freeman.

Nisbett, R., & Ross, L. (1980). *Human inferences: Strategies and shortcomings of social judgment.* Englewood Cliffs, NJ: Prentice Hall.

Park, P., & Rothbart, M. (1982). Perception of outgroup homogeneity and levels of social categorization: Memory for the subordinate attributes of ingroup and outgroup members. *Journal of Personality and Social Psychology, 42,* 1051–1068.

Picek, J.S., Sherman, S.J., & Shiffrin, R.M. (1975). Cognitive organization and coding of social structures. *Journal of Personality and Social Psychology, 31,* 758–768.

Rosch, E., Mervis, C.B., Gray, W., Johnson, D., & Boyes-Braem, P. (1976). Basic objects in natural categories. *Cognitive Psychology, 8,* 382–439.

Rosch, E.H. (1973). Natural categories. *Cognitive Psychology, 4,* 328–350.

Rothbar, M., Evans, M., & Fulero, S. (1979). Recall for confirming events: Memory processes and the maintenance of social stereotyping. *Journal of Social Psychology, 15,* 343–355.

Schank, R.C., & Abelson, R.P. (1977). *Scripts, plans, goals, and understanding: An inquiry into human knowledge structures.* Hillsdale, NJ: Erlbaum.

Sentis, K.P., & Burnstein, E. (1979). Remembering schema consistent information: Effects of a balance schema on recognition memory. *Journal of Personality and Social Psychology, 37,* 2200–2211.

Smith, D.A., & Graesser, A.C. (1981). Memory for actions in scripted activities as a function of typicality, retention interval, and retrieval task. *Memory and Cognition, 9,* 550–559.

Snyder, M. (1981). Seek and ye shall find: Testing hypotheses about other people. In E.T. Higgins, C.P. Herman, M.P. Zanna (Eds.), *Social cognition: The Ontario symposium:* Vol. 1. Hillsdale, NJ: Erlbaum.

Snyder, M., & Cantor, N. (1979). Testing hypotheses about other people: The use of historical knowledge. *Journal of Experimental and Social Psychology, 15,* 330–342.

Snyder, M., & Gangestad, S. (1981). Hypothesis-testing processes. In J.H. Harvey, W. Ickes, & R.F. Kidd (Eds.), *New directions in attribution research:* Vol. 3. Hillsdale, NJ: Erlbaum.

Snyder, M., & Uranowitz, S.W. (1978). Reconstructing the past: Some cognitive consequences of person perception. *Journal of Personality and Social Psychology, 36,* 941–950.

Stotland, E., & Canon, L. (1972). *Social psychology: A cognitive approach.* Philadelphia: Saunders.

Swets, J.A., Tanner, W.P., & Birdsall, T.G. (1966). Decision processes in perception. *Psychological Review, 68,* 301–340.

Tajfel, H. (1969). Social and cultural factors in perception. In G. Lindzey & E. Aronson (Eds.), *The handbook of social psychology:* Vol. 3. Reading, MA: Addison-Wesley.

Tajfel, H. (1982). *Gruppenkonflikt und Vorurteil.* Bern: Huber.

Taylor, S.E., & Crocker, J. (1981). Schematic bases of social information processing. In E.T. Higgins, C.P. Herman, M.P. Zanna (Eds.), *Social cognition: The Ontario symposium:* Vol. 1. Hillsdale, NJ: Erlbaum.

Taylor, S.E., & Fiske, S.T. (1978). Salience, attention, and attribution: Top of the head phenomena. In L. Berkowitz (Ed.), *Advances in experimental social psychology:* Vol. 11. New York: Academic.

Tesser, A., & Cowan, C.L. (1975). Some effects of thought and number of cognitions on attitude change. *Social Behavior and Personality, 3,* 165–173.

Tesser, A., & Cowan, C.L. (1977). Some attitudinal and cognitive consequences of thought. *Journal of Research in Personality, 11,* 216–226.

Tsujimoto, R.N., Wilde, J., & Robertson, D.R. (1978). Distorted memory for exemplars of a social structure: Evidence for schematic memory processes. *Journal of Personality and Social Psychology, 36,* 1402–1414.

Tversky, A., & Kahneman, D. (1974). Judgment under uncertainty: heuristics and biases. *Science, 185,* 1124–1131.

Undeutsch, U. (1967). Beurteilung der Glaubhaftigkeit von Zeugenaussagen. In U. Undeutsch (Ed.), *Handbuch der Psychologie:* Vol. 11. *Forensische Psychologie.* Göttingen: Verlag für Psychologie.

Upmeyer, A. (1971). Social perception and signal detectability theory: Group influence on discrimination and usage of scale. *Psychologische Forschung, 34,* 285–294.

Wegener, H. (1981). *Einführung in die forensische Psychologie.* Darmstadt: Wissenschaftliche Buchgesellschaft.

Wilder, D.A. (1981). Perceiving persons as a group: Categorization and intergroup relations. In D.L. Hamilton (Ed.), *Cognitive processes in stereotyping and intergroup behavior.* Hillsdale, NJ: Erlbaum.

Wyer, Jr. R.S., Srull, T.K., Gordon, S.E., & Hartwick, J. (1982). Effects of processing objectives on the recall of prose material. *Journal of Personality and Social Psychology, 43,* 674–688.

15
Remembering Social Events and Activities

WERNER WIPPICH

Overview and Introduction

From an applied perspective one of the most interesting questions about human memory may be the remembering (or forgetting) of social events and activities. In everyday life the human memory system may be seen as predominately occupied with the encoding, storing, and retrieval of social information. Mostly, however, this concern does not stand out as the focus of our own conscious mental life. We have learned to handle myriads of information packages in social interactions rather automatically. Interruptions of ongoing activities, surprising events and actions, or entering new and less known settings, for example, may change this "mindless" form of social information processing and capture our conscious attention. Witnessing an accident or crime, for example, will certainly trigger our attention to the ongoing event and may shortly afterwards become a "memory problem." Learning retrospectively (from detectives or from newspapers) that one may have participated in a critical incident will surely give rise to attempts at remembering social events and actions. Thus, at least the applied aspect of witness research within the broader field of legal psychology should and does involve an interest in the more basic problem of what to expect of human beings in remembering social events. How are we to estimate the possibilities and limitations of potential rememberers? Are there ways of facilitating and improving the retrieval of social events? These are some of the questions which will be discussed in this chapter with an eye to possible applications for witness research.

Despite at least 100 years of experimentation, it may be surprising that until recently human memory research was not well prepared to answer questions of this sort. Research had been preoccupied with seemingly more simple problems (such as the remembering of word lists). Since the revival of cognitive psychology, we are better equipped to attempt some answers concerning the remembering of social events. Optimism in this regard seems appropriate, the more so as research is beginning to enter everyday life situations (Bruce, 1985; Neisser, 1982; Wippich, 1984, 1985; for reviews). But optimism does not mean that we should expect simple answers. Social events and actions are to be viewed as mnemonically multifarious, complex, and dynamically changing information. Imagine listening to this paper being delivered at a conference. What might be memorable about this little "social event"? The gestures, voice, and appearance of the lecturer, perhaps; temporal and spatial context information; style and content of arguments; visible and inferred reactions of the public; your own reactions to the person or to his arguments; inferences you have drawn on the basis of the lecture, and much more. What you will encode of this huge information complex does not depend solely on the social event itself, as it may be represented "objectively" on a videotape. Your attitudes, intentions, and preknowledge influence how you will register the lecture, how you will organize the information, and what you will select for further processing and elaboration. What you may remember in the end is furthermore dependent on your retrieval environment and on what you will accept as a memory. It is well-known that much more information may be available to human memory than is currently accessible at a given retrieval attempt. The access to previously stored complex social information may be blocked due to missing or inadequate retrieval cues, emotional arousal, or motivational factors, for example.

This brief sketch should have made it clear that only some basic evidence concerning what it takes to remember social events can be discussed. I shall tend to emphasize those aspects which may be interesting to witness research. At the outset I shall introduce some concepts and constructs from social cognition research. The so-called script construct is described more precisely since it is well suited to provide some answers to my questions. The answers will then be illustrated by two research examples. Scripts are one class of schemata, and social cognition research is dominated by schema constructs. In my view, memory for social events implies more than schema theories are ready to concede. As a correction or supplement to schematic views, at the end of this article I shall describe the concept and phenomenon of so-called reality monitoring, which will be illustrated by a further research example.

Social Cognition Research

Models and methods of memory research have become an important part of social psychology. A considerable amount of research activity has been devoted to the processing, representation, and utilization of social information within a special branch of social psychology, called social cognition (see Wyer & Srull, 1984). Standard investigations usually confront subjects with verbal descriptions of persons or groups, their traits, and/or their behaviors. This restriction on verbal information is not without its critics (Forgas, 1983; Taylor, 1981), but it has advantages, too (Black, Galambos, & Read, 1984). Sometimes, subjects are told to expect later memory testing. Mostly, however, they are given other objectives such as to form an impression of a described person. This is an incidental learning situation, if memory for the descriptions is tested later without a prior warning. All of these general types of experimentation are devoted to so-called episodic memory problems. That is, one wants to know what a person can remember about specific social information having been presented at a particular place and time.

What people do remember about social episodes is not solely determined by the given information, however. Episodic memories are heavily influenced by the structure, organization, and contents of the preknowledge of the information processor at encoding as well as at retrieval. Therefore, a further central issue for social cognition research is the modeling of representations for permanent social beliefs and knowledge structures (Cantor & Mischel, 1979; Lingle, Altom, & Medin, 1984). Social knowledge is seen as part of a semantic memory system. At present it seems to be heuristically useful to separate this permanent knowledge store from an episodic memory system (Tulving, 1983).

The representation of social knowledge is a controversial topic, however. On the one hand, one is discussing the format of information representations (abstract-propositional and/or spatial-analogue formats, for example). On the other hand, the subdivision of social knowledge domains has not been clearly settled. According to Wyer and Gordon (1984), one may distinguish between representations of person types, of groups and roles, of selves, of beliefs and opinions, and of event and behavioral sequences. Some of these domains may be represented like categories (knowledge of persons, for example). Others may be represented like schemata (knowledge of events). Furthermore, knowledge domains must be interconnected. Categorical person knowledge may be part of schematic social event knowledge, for example. This interlocking of various knowledge structures is an important proposition (and problem): If prior world knowledge does influence the processing of a concrete social event, then episodic representations of this event are contingent on what knowledge types are active at the various processing stages. Identical events may be remembered quite differently if one observer or actor is primed for person knowledge and another one pays special regard to the actions and action sequence, for example.

To simplify the matter, the following discussion will take it for granted that social events and actions are predominately encoded and stored within an event knowledge framework. This type of knowledge is also called "scripts," which are one class of schemata. Before discussing the script construct, an attempt should be made to outline the general meaning of schemata (see Brewer & Nakamura, 1984; Rumelhart, 1980). In general, a schema can be conceptualized as an abstract generic knowledge structure that contains interrelationships among its typical components (variables) and the typical attributes of the components. Schemata are thus viewed as organized, holistic knowledge packages composed of variables. The organization of variables is seen as a consequence of meaningful experiences within one knowledge domain and entails temporal, spatial, and/or causal connections among aspects of experiences. A schema functions by guiding the interpretations, inferences, expectations, attention, and later retrieval of various inputs. Schemata may function in this regard like an abstract framework of which empty slots or variables will be filled by concrete evidence, whereas irrelevant or inconsistent episodic information may be disregarded or filtered out. That is, if aspects of the information one receives instantiate variables in a frame of a schema, this schema may be activated for use in interpreting and binding the specific evidence. In this process, other schema-related features may be inferred to exist in the evidence.

Scripts

First, I shall introduce some general aspects of the script concept. Later, relations to witness research are discussed and clarified by means of two research examples.

The Psychological Status of the Script Construct

Many everyday life activities and events (such as going shopping) take the same form and nearly the same sequence. It is resonable to suppose that human beings acquire extensive knowledge packages about such routine actions and events in their daily lives from the time of early childhood (Nelson & Gruendel, 1981). The script construct has been introduced by Schank and Abelson (1977) to describe generalized knowledge structures about sequences of actions and events in well defined situations. A script title, such as eating at a restaurant, can be conceptualized as an address in semantic memory, representing subordinated scences (entering, ordering, eating, paying). For each scene one knows typical actions (Bellezza & Bower, 1982). Furthermore, the script contains roles (e.g., hostess, waiter, customer, and cashier), and props (e.g., tables, chairs, and menus). The temporal and causal sequence of various scenes may be more or less predetermined in the knowledge representation (Abelson, 1981). Script-based knowledge structures should influence the planning and execution of activated intentions. Scripts should also be utilized in the process of encoding, interpreting, drawing inferences, and guiding the retrieval of social events occurring in the real world. That is, new episodes can be processed in a top-down fashion or knowledge-determined mode if prior script knowledge is available for interpretation. The components or variables of the script have slots that can be filled by specific input that is encountered in an episode. Alternatively, the variable slots of a script may be filled inferentially with typical values during comprehension. When a script's variable slots have been filled, the script is said to be instantiated. And an instantiated script corresponds to an episodic memory trace that has been encoded as having occurred at a specific time and place.

Is there any empirical evidence for the psychological reality of the script construct? Semantic memory research has shown that we can expect a high degree of agreement among different people if they are asked to enumerate from memory events and actions typically occurring in a given situation (Bower, Black, & Turner, 1979). High agreement is also found in sequences of enumerations of actions and events and in ratings of the importance of various parts of hypothetical scripts (Galambos & Rips, 1982). Such results are to be expected if scripts are based on experiences shared by most members of a given culture. Episodic memory research has shown that events are remembered much better if their presentation corresponds to the canonical script order (Bower & Clark-Meyers, 1980). Organizing information according to script structures may even be more favorable to memory performance than other organizational devices, such as clustering according to taxonomic categories (Rabinowitz & Mandler, 1983). Furthermore, errors in episodic remembering are predictable within the framework of the script construct. Typical or to be expected actions and events of a script that may be missing in a concrete experience may be "remembered" because they have been thought of and added to the episodic representation at encoding or at retrieval (Graesser, 1981).

Relations to Witness Research

Despite an explosion of witness research in the last decade, there are seemingly few references to script models in this context. This is surprising since there are many relations of which I shall mention only three, being relevant to two experiments reported later in this chapter. First, it should be self-evident that a testimony will often be concerned with social events and actions. If the processing of such information is heavily influenced by script-based knowledge, we must be concerned with the possibility that "memories" will often include events and actions that are part of a script structure and "happened" only in the knowledge store of the witness (and not in reality).

In the witness stand, one may be concerned most typically with events and actions that may be denoted as deviations from normal scripts, interruptions in the normal course of event sequences, or atypical actions. What is the memorial fate of such information? This is an interesting point since global schematic positions usually suppose that such information is filtered out and not encoded (Alba & Hasher, 1983). Models of script processing take another and more specific view. For example, Graesser (1981) has developed a "script-pointer-plus-tag" model according to which information that is interpretable in terms of a script is retained via "pointers" to the generic script, along with an indication of the values of the information that instantiate the script variables. It follows that this "pointed to" episodic representation is apt to contain instantiations of script-related variables that were not actually specified in the original episode. In other words, it may contain intrusions of script-relevant events and actions. On the other hand, if features of the actual information do not match attributes of the generic script (e.g., atypical events and actions), they are appended to the episodic representation as "tags." It follows that one should expect more accurate memories for atypical information, at least over shorter retention intervals. The two experiments will examine this proposal.

Looking at witness research over the last few years, a "new look" seems to be emerging. Whereas former research repeatedly demonstrated the unreliability, incorrectness, and suggestibility of witnesses (for review see Loftus, 1979), the new look movement is trying to correct these extremely negativistic evaluations (Yuille, 1980, 1984). At this new stage of research, theoretically well founded measures that may contribute to better witness evidence are being tried out. The two experiments discussed below may be seen as a contribution to this research endeavor within the context of social information processing.

Remembering Scripts in Various Contexts

Episodic remembering has been shown to be context dependent (Tulving & Thomson, 1973; Wippich, 1985). For example, it has been demonstrated that memory performance is better when the learning and testing environments, or when the mood states at learning and at recall, are the same than when they differ (Bower, 1981; Wippich, 1981). In our first investigation the environmental context was varied in a 2×2 design at encoding as well as at retrieval (for further details, see Wippich, Mecklenbräuker, & Hoffmann, 1985). Script-based texts were studied by 48 students either in a familiar (at home) or in a foreign environment (at the institute). One day later subjects were asked for incidental recall and recognition in the same (congruence) or in the different environment. We wanted to find out whether even meaningful social events are remembered better under congruent environmental conditions. If so, this would be an important clue for witness research. As was mentioned in the introduction, information may be available to memory but currently inaccessible at the retrieval stage. Congruent environmental conditions at retrieval may be useful in providing access to stored but blocked social information.

Another goal of this experiment has already been described in the preceding section, i.e., to ascertain whether there are any differences in the memory for typical and atypical social events and actions. In order to investigate this question, we constructed a script-based text according to German norms. The text described a normal day in the life of a fictitious person and contained propositions which were based on four scripts (getting up in the morning, buying a pair of trousers, visiting a lecture, and going to a movie). For each script we formulated six critical statements of which two were very typical according to the norms ("washing in the morning," for example), two were moderately typical ("boiling water"), and two were atypical (mishaps or interruptions such as "knocking over the alarm clock"). Subjects studied the text in order to form an impression of the described person. At recognition

TABLE 15.1. Mean recall and recognition (in percentages) for typical, moderately typical, and atypical script-based statements (experiment 1)

	Typical	Moderately typical	Atypical
Recall	18.3	23.8	55.3
Recognition:			
Hits	73.2	59.6	81.8
False positives	50	21	1

testing, subjects had to distinguish between old and new typical, less typical, and atypical script propositions.

The following results are relevant (and significant at least at the 0.05 level) for our purposes: As can be seen from Table 15.1, memory performance was heavily influenced by the typicality variable. With respect to recognition, one must consider both the hits ("old" information is identified as old) and the false positives ("new" information is falsely recognized). Conspicuously high is the false-alarm rate for typical script information (50%): Subjects very often "remember" events and actions that are only part of their knowledge store and have not really happened. Combining hits and false positives into the so-called sensitivity index of signal-detection theory (d′), both the recognition and the recall results demonstrated a strong advantage for atypical events and actions, thus corroborating the script-pointer-plus-tag model (Graesser, 1981).

Perhaps even more important is a further result of this study, not shown in the table: Congruent environmental contexts (studying at the institute and retrieving at the institute, for example) clearly improved the recall of social information (see below for further discussion).

Our next experiment was, with one exception, a replication of the first one. This time we did not vary the environmental context but changed in a similar 2×2 design an "internal context" variable, the so-called state of self-awareness. Research in the personality and social psychology domain has shown that the attention of persons may be directed more at the outer world or at the person him- or herself. We were interested in the state of private self-awareness where people may register their own inner life more intensely and more precisely. Self-awareness research has demonstrated that minimal situational cues (such as hearing one's name or seeing one's face in a small mirror) may evoke private self-awareness (Buss, 1980; Carver & Scheier, 1981). So, before studying the script-based text, half of our subjects had to look in a small mirror while the other half did not see a mirror. One day later at retrieval, this mirror manipulation was again introduced, thus leading to a 2×2 design. Some results of this study are shown in Table 15.2. Again, we did find rather strong typicality effects, replicating the results of our first study. Somewhat surprisingly, however, there was one discrepancy from the results of the first experiment: We did not find a similar "congruency effect" for the internal context variable. Whereas

TABLE 15.2. Mean recall and recognition (in percentages) for typical, moderately typical, and atypical script-based statements (experiment 2)

	Typical	Moderately typical	Atypical
Recall	30.8	31.8	48.1
Recognition:			
Hits	69	60.6	81
False positives	46.9	13.3	0.03

in the first experiment the overlap of environmental contexts at encoding and at retrieval was decisive (and nothing else), we did not find a similar interaction in the second study. Inducing self-awareness at encoding had a positive effect on later remembering of social information, but self-awareness at testing as well as the critical interaction remained insignificant.

Discussion and Some Implications

First, it should be conceded that our research was not directly inspired by concerns with testimonies. Nevertheless, the results have some implications for this applied field. If a witness has to remember social events and actions, it is to be expected that some of his or her "memories" will be based solely on scripts in semantic memory, and not on facts or happenings. Furthermore, and this is perhaps a more surprising result, atypical or distinct events and actions have a quite good chance of "surviving" in memory, in comparison to typical or stereotypically to-be-expected events and actions. These results have been found in both experiments, but they are based on text information. To what degree can our results be generalized to more naturalistic information and to various everyday life situations? Although there is a need for further research on this topic, the existing evidence is not at variance with our conclusions. Experiments with subjects who had to remember real-life activities have reported similar results (Brewer & Dupree, 1983; Nakamura, Graesser, Zimmerman, & Riha, 1985). In our research, subjects were studying under an impression set. Should we expect other results with other sets or perspectives? This is an interesting question for which we have no ready answer. Nevertheless, it should be emphasized that our subjects had no memory expectations. This seems to be a realistic condition if one considers the usual "recruitment" of a witness. Subjects were not actively involved in the events but only read about them. Should similar results be expected if persons are participating in a social interaction? This is an interesting question, too. Engelkamp and his collaborators have repeatedly shown that doing something leads to better memory performance than only seeing that something or hearing about it (Zimmer & Engelkamp, 1984). On the other hand, if subjects are heavily and personally involved in the processing of social events, this may introduce some biases in their recall (see Greenwald, 1980). Our script-based materials were rather "neutral" and not emotionally laden. Should we expect similar results if witnesses of social events are facing violence and are confronted with threatening conditions? Performing experimental research into such interesting topics is not only difficult but also poses ethical problems. As far as we know, emotionally stressful scenes may be especially memorable, but they can make witnesses amnestic for preceding events and actions (see Loftus & Burns, 1982).

One can enumerate a host of further variables that may be implicated and important in the encoding of social events and actions. From the standpoint of witness research, however, variables that affect (or may affect) the encoding of social information have the status of "estimator variables" (Wells, 1978). The juridical system has no control over these variables since they have occurred in the distant past. Members of the juridical system may reflect on those variables and may estimate their influence on the accuracy and reliability of witness evidence. The estimation process can be facilitated and supported, however, by taking into account psychological research results (such as ours).

Within the context of witness research, so-called system variables are under the control of the juridical system (Wells, 1978). How and when to ask a witness, for example, are controllable and changeable events. In this regard, our research is informative, too. According to the results of the first study, memory performance is better when the testing and critical event environments are the same that when they differ. In the real world, however, it will not always be possible to place a witness stand in the environment where the event took place. Fortunately, there are other ways of taking into account the context dependency of human memory in testimonies. S. M. Smith (1979), for example, has shown that remembering in a new environment can be improved substantially if subjects are trying mentally to imagine and reinstate the environmental context of the to-be-reported event. The mental reinstatement method has just been successfully employed within witness research (Krafka & Penrod, 1985). Geiselman, Fisher, Firstenberg, Hutton, Sullivan, Avetissian, and Prosk (1984) and Geiselman, Fisher, Mackinnon, and Holland (1985) are developing successful cognitive interview techniques, including mental reinstatements of contextual information at the time of remembering. Before witnesses begin to answer questions regarding an incident, they are instructed in the use of four general memory retrieval techniques to aid their recall: First, they are asked to try to reinstate in their minds the context surrounding the incident ("think about what the room looked like ... think about what you were feeling at the time and think about your reactions to the incident"). In addition, they are obliged to write down everything, to recall the events in different orders, and to adopt the perspective of others who were present during the incident.

The results of these studies are encouraging. They are especially remarkable since improvements in recall by mental reinstatements seem to have no negative side effects. This is in sharp contrast to more controversial techniques, such as hypnosis (for a review, see M.C. Smith, 1983), for which improvements in recall are mostly accompanied by intrusions of false information.

According to the results of our second study, inducing the state of self-awareness at the time of recall will be a less powerful measure. Self-awareness may improve the encoding of personal and social information, but this effect is beyond the reach of the juridical system and may be used for estimation purposes only. Retrospectively, it may come as no surprise that inducing private self-awareness at retrieval does not influence memory performance. Remembering concrete events may be an act that invokes and involves private self-awareness automatically (Buss, 1980). Further research on this topic is needed, however. It may be, for example, that so-called public self-awareness (being concerned with aspects of one's self that are observable to the public) can have negative effects on the testimony of a witness (Kassin, 1984).

Reality Monitoring

So far I have stressed schema positions in this review, and models of schemata are currently dominating research in the cognitive as well as the social cognitive domain (Taylor & Crocker, 1981). In this last section, I shall try to correct and complement this picture. The human memory system may be operating "schematically" but this is not the whole story. Experimental research has shown, for example, that people can remember without prior warning seeming trivialities, such as jokes in a lecture, with extreme accuracy even after extended retention intervals (Kintsch & Bates, 1977). Others have reported that persons may not only remember important social events of contemporary history, such as the murdering of President Kennedy, but also quite detailed information about their personal circumstances and reactions to those events as they experienced them 10–15 years ago (Brown & Kulik, 1977). These and other astonishing memory feats, which are difficult to verify, of course, may be interpreted as examples of nonschematic potentialities of human storage systems. Newer models of memory (e.g., Johnson, 1983) postulate "sensory" and "perceptual" subsystems functioning as permanent storage devices for aspects of event information. In any case, one should not disregard seemingly "superficial" event information as totally irrelevant for the remembering of social events. Human memory may be composed of various subsystems or levels of storage, and not all of these systems may function "schematically." In this final section, I shall exploit this idea on the basis of research concerning an important topic, so-called reality monitoring.

Usually one thinks of a social event as involving at least two persons interacting with each other. And in this respect, testimonies are often concerned with "who has done or said it" questions. Critical events and the persons involved in them may be known, but it may be unclear to the juridical system whether person x or person y was responsible for certain actions, for example.

To what extent and by which mechanisms is the memory system capable of such discriminations? Johnson and Raye (1981) have published a nonschematic model of reality monitoring devoted to such problems. According to the authors, people remember information from two basic sources: that derived from external sources (obtained through perceptual processes) and that generated by internal processes (such as thought or imagination). Of particular interest are the processes people use in deciding whether information had an external or an internal source, a process they call "reality monitoring." They propose that, as a class, internally generated memories may differ from the class of externally derived memories along specific dimensions, being available permanently (thus, this model goes far beyond the framework of schema positions). Specifically, externally derived memories may have more spatial and temporal contextual attributes coded in the representation of the event than do internally generated memories. Furthermore, they should also have more sensory attributes. And finally, they may be more semantically detailed. On the other hand, internally generated memories may typically have more operational attributes coded in the trace. If the two classes of representations generally differ in these ways, these dimensions could be used to decide the origin of a trace regardless of the particular content of the memory involved. One implication of the model should be emphasized: discriminations between instances from within a class (two externally derived memories, for example) should be more difficult than discriminations between instances drawn from separate classes (one externally and one internally generated memory), since the former should be based on more overlapping attributes.

I would like to report briefly on some aspects of a third investigation, thus concretizing some statements of the model. In the course of an alleged opinion poll study, students received some pro- and contra-arguments concerning an actual problem about educational grants. In one condition ("external-external"), given arguments were attributed to two different external sources (persons). In the other condition ("external-internal"), some arguments were attributed to an external source and others had to be generated by the subjects themselves. By matching the arguments across the two conditions, both groups were processing identical contents. One week later subjects were surprised with a memory test. In a recognition test composed of all arguments from the first phase ("old") plus an equal number of new ones, they had to decide about the old-new status of statements and, for recognized items only, about the source of origin.

Responses on the test were first scored for simple recognition (hits), without regard to identification of origin, and for the number of new items incorrectly called old (false alarms). As can be seen from Table 15.3, memory for occurrence (hits) was quite good (the rate of false alarms was very low and comparable for the two conditions). Subjects in the "internal-external" condition, however, had higher scores than subjects in the "external-external" condition. Tests for simple main effects clearly showed that this group difference is attributable solely to the nearly perfect performance on self-generated

TABLE 15.3. Mean recognition (hits) and discrimination scores (in percentages) for (a) "internal-external" and (b) "external-external" source conditions (experiment 3)

Recognition	(a)	"Internal" arguments y		"External" arguments x
		97.1	>	89.6
	(b)	"External" arguments y		"External" arguments x
		90.2	=	88.6
Discrimination	(a)	94.8		
	(b)	59.7		

arguments. The latter result is typical for memory research: self-generated information is remembered extremely well (see, for example, the so-called generation effect, Slamecka & Graf, 1978).

Reality monitoring performance was scored by computing a proportion (multiplied by 100, see Table 15.3): The number of arguments correctly attributed to the source of origin was divided by the total number of arguments correctly recognized as old. As can be seen from the table, there is a clear advantage for the "internal-external" condition, a result to be expected from the model.

Finally, let us dare again to jump from here to the applied field of witness research. There are good reasons to expect problems of discrimination if witnesses have to attribute remembered actions or events to two or more foreign persons. Witnesses who were involved in the actions, however, may have an easier task discriminating between their own actions and those of others. Such results (and the underlying model) may be used in estimating potential capabilities of witnesses. Currently, we are doing research which may be useful within the context of system variables (Wells, 1978): Are there any measures that may improve the process of reality monitoring at the time of the testimony?

This article should have made it clear that there are many open (and practically useful) research questions for the field of legal psychology and witness research which are of interest to more basic research endeavors within general psychology, too. As this volume shows (see contributions of Loftus, of Raskin and Steller, or of Köhnken), many of the theories and results that have been discussed here are currently "in use" within witness research. Furthermore, modern research has well founded bases of its own that are not incompatible with the models and results as discussed by us (see Undeutsch, 1967).

References

Abelson, R.P. (1981). Psychological status of the script concept. *American Psychologist, 36*, 715–729.

Alba, J.W., & Hasher, L. (1983). Is memory schematic? *Psychological Bulletin, 93*, 203–231.

Bellezza, F.S., & Bower, G.H. (1982). Remembering script-based text. *Poetics, 11*, 1–23.

Black, J.B., Galambos, J.A., & Read, S.J. (1984). Comprehending stories and social situations. In R.S. Wyer & T.K. Srull (Eds.), *Handbook of social cognition:* Vol. 3 (pp. 45–86). Hillsdale, NJ: Erlbaum.

Bower, G.H. (1981). Mood and memory. *American Psychologist, 36*, 129–148.

Bower, G.H., & Clark-Meyers, G. (1980). Memory for scripts with organized vs. randomized presentations. *British Journal of Psychology, 71*, 369–377.

Bower, G.H., Black, J.B., & Turner, T.J. (1979). Scripts in memory for texts. *Cognitive Psychology, 11*, 177–220.

Brewer, W.F., & Dupree, D.A. (1983). Use of plan schemata in the recall and recognition of goal-directed actions. *Journal of Experimental Psychology. Learning, Memory and Cognition, 9*, 117–129.

Brewer, W.F., & Nakamura, G.V. (1984). The nature and functions of schemas. In R.S. Wyer & T.K. Srull (Eds.), *Handbook of social cognition:* Vol. 1 (pp. 119–160) Hillsdale, NJ: Erlbaum.

Brown, R., & Kulik, J. (1977). Flashbulb memories. *Cognition, 5*, 73–99.

Bruce, D. (1985). The how and why of ecological memory. *Journal of Experimental Psychology: General, 114*, 78–90.

Buss, A.H. (1980). *Self-consciousness and social anxiety.* San Francisco: Freeman.

Cantor, N., & Mischel, W. (1979). Prototypes in person perception. In L. Berkowitz (Ed.), *Advances in experimental social psychology*: Vol. 12 (pp. 4–53). New York: Academic.

Carver, C.S., & Scheier, M.F. (1981). *Attention and self-regulation.* New York: Springer.

Forgas, J.P. (1983). What is social about social cognition? British Journal of Social Psychology, 22, 129–144.

Galambos, J.A., & Rips, L.J. (1982). Memory for routines. *Journal of Verbal Learning and Verbal Behavior, 21*, 260–281.

Geiselman, R.E., Fisher, R.P., Firstenberg, I., Hutton, L.A., Sullivan, S., Avetissian, I., & Prosk, A. (1984). Enhancement of eyewitness memory: an empirical evaluation of the cognitive interview. *Journal of Police Science and Administration, 12*, 74–80.

Geiselman, R.E., Fisher, R.P., Mackinnon, D.P., & Holland, H.L. (1985). Eyewitness memory enhancement in the police interview: cognitive retrieval mnemonics versus hypnosis. *Journal of Applied Psychology, 70*, 401–412.

Graesser, A.C. (1981). *Prose comprehension beyond the word.* New York: Springer.

Greenwald, A.G. (1980). The totalitarian ego. *American Psychologist, 35*, 603–618.

Johnson, M.K. (1983). A multiple-entry, modular memory system. In G.H. Bower (Ed.), *The psychology of learning and motivation*: Vol. 17. New York: Academic.

Johnson, M.K., & Raye, C.L. (1981). Reality monitoring. *Psychological Review, 88*, 67–85.

Kassin, S.M. (1984). TV cameras, public self-consciousness, and mock juror performance. *Journal of Experimental and Social Psychology, 20*, 336–349.

Kintsch, W., & Bates, E. (1977). Recognition memory for statements from a classroom lecture. *Journal of Experimental Psychology: Human Learning and Memory, 3*, 150–168.

Krafka, C., & Penrod, S. (1985). Reinstatement of context in a field experiment of eyewitness identification. *Journal of Personality and Social Psychology, 48*, 58–69.

Lingle, J.H., Altom, M.W., & Medin, D.L. (1984). Of cabbages and kings. In R.S. Wyer & T.K. Srull (Eds.), *Handbook of social cognition:* Vol. 1 (pp. 71–117). Hillsdale, NJ: Erlbaum.

Loftus, E.F. (1979). *Eyewitness testimony.* Cambridge: Harvard University Press.

Loftus, E.F., & Burns, T.E. (1982). Mental shock can produce retrograde amnesia. *Memory and Cognition, 10*, 318–323.

Nakamura, G.V., Graesser, A.C., Zimmerman, J.A., & Riha, J. (1985). Script processing in a natural situation. *Memory and Cognition, 13*, 140–144.

Neisser, U. (Ed.). (1982). *Memory observed.* San Francisco: Freeman.

Nelson, K. & Gruendel, J. (1981). Generalized event representations. In M.E. Lamb & A.L. Brown (Eds.), *Advances in developmental psychology:* Vol. 1. Hillsdale, NJ: Erlbaum.

Rabinowitz, M., & Mandler, J.M. (1983). Organization and information retrieval. *Journal of Experimental Psychology: Learning, Memory and Cognition, 9*, 430–439.

Rumelhart, D.E. (1980). Schemata: the building blocks of cognition. In R.J. Spiro, B.C. Bruce & W.F. Brewer (Eds.), *Theoretical issues in reading comprehension* (pp. 33–58). Hillsdale, NJ: Erlbaum.

Schank, R., & Abelson, R. (1977). *Scripts, plans, goals and understanding.* Hillsdale, NJ: Erlbaum.

Slamecka, N.J., Graf, P. (1978). The generation effect. *Journal of Experimental Psychology: Human Learning and Memory, 4*, 592–604.

Smith, M.C. (1983). Hypnotic memory enhancement of witnesses: Does it work? *Psychological Bulletin, 94*, 387–407.

Smith, S.M. (1979). Remembering in and out of context. *Journal of Experimental Psychology: Human Learning and Memory, 5*, 460–471.

Taylor, S.E. (1981). The interface of cognitive and social psychology. In J.H. Harvey (Ed.), *Cognition, social behavior, and the environment* (pp. 189–211).

Taylor, S.E., & Crocker, J. (1981). Schematic bases of social information processing. In E.T. Higgins, C.P. Herman, M.P. Zanna (Eds.), *Social cognition* (pp. 89–134). Hillsdale, NJ: Erlbaum.

Tulving, E. (1983), *Elements of episodic memory.* New York: Oxford University Press.

Tulving, E., & Thomson, D. (1973). Encoding specificity and retrieval processes in memory. *Psychological Review, 80*, 352–373.

Undeutsch, U. (1967), Beurteilung der Glaubhaftigkeit von Aussagen. In U. Undeutsch (Ed.), *Handbuch der Psychologie:* Vol. 11. *Forensische Psychologie* (pp. 26–181). Göttingen: Hogrefe.

Wells, G.L. (1978). Applied eyewitness – testimony research: system variables and estimator variables. *Journal of Personality and Social Psychology, 36*, 1546–1557.

Wippich, W. (1981). Lernen in vertrauter oder fremder Umgebung: Kontexteffekte beim Behalten. *Schweizerische Zeitschrift für Psychologie, 40*, 40–54.

Wippich, W. (1984). *Lehrbuch der angewandten Gedächtnispsychologie:* Vol. 1. Stuttgart: Kohlhammer.

Wippich, W. (1985). *Lehrbuch der angewandten Gedächtnispsychologie:* Vol. 2. Stuttgart: Kohlhammer.

Wippich, W., Mecklenbräuker, S., & Hoffmann, I. (1985). Skripte in fremder oder vertrauter Umgebung: Kontexteffekte beim Behalten. *Schweizerische Zeitschrift für Psychologie, 44*, 43–55.

Wyer, R.S., & Gordon, S.E. (1984). The cognitive representation of social information. In R.S. Wyer & T.K. Srull (Eds.), *Handbook of social cognition*: Vol. 2 (pp. 73–150). Hillsdale, NJ: Erlbaum.

Wyer, R.S., & Srull, T.K. (Eds.). (1984). *Handbook of social cognition*: Vols. 1–3. Hillsdale, NJ: Erlbaum.

Yuille, J.C. (1980). A critical examination of the psychological and practical implications of eyewitness research. *Law and Human Behavior, 4*, 335–345.

Yuille, J.C. (1984). Research and teaching with police: a Canadian example. *International Review of Applied Psychology, 33*, 5–23.

Zimmer, H.D., & Engelkamp, J. (1984). Planungs- und Ausführungsanteile motorischer Gedächtniskomponenten und ihre Wirkung auf das Behalten ihrer verbalen Bezeichnungen. *Zeitschrift für Psychologie mit Zeitschrift für Angewandte Pyschologie, 192*, 379–401.

16
Distortions in Eyewitness Memory from Postevent Information*

ELIZABETH F. LOFTUS

A British Lord who wants to confuse a hunting dog that is wandering in the English countryside might draw a piece of smelly fish across the trail. When used this way, such pieces of fish are referred to as red herrings. A lawyer who wants to divert interest from a weakness in his or her case might use a strategy such as assigning blame to some mysterious other suspect. Such a strategy is called a red herring. And Agatha Christie, when she wants to mislead the readers of her latest mystery novel, has been known to plant a bogus clue. Such clues are called red herrings. British Lords, lawyers, and Agatha Christie have red herrings in common, but they are not the sole devotees of such diversionary tactics (Sautter, 1982). Some researchers of human memory also are fond of red herrings. In the study of human memory, a red herring is a piece of false or suggestive information that misleads the rememberer.

Over the past decade, I have been studying a type of red herring, and the impact it has on recollection. I have been studying postevent contamination, which is new information that people unwittingly incorporate into their previously stored memories.

The basic procedure used in this research is quite simple. Subjects witness a complex event, like a film of a crime or accident. Subsequently some receive new, often misleading, information (red herrings) about the event. Control subjects do not. Finally, all subjects attempt to recall the original event.

When exposed to misleading, postevent information, subjects have misrecalled the color of a car that was green as being blue, a yield sign as a stop sign, broken glass or tape recorders that never existed, and even something as large and conspicuous as a barn when no barn was ever seen (see Loftus, 1979, 1983; and Hall, Loftus, & Tousignant, 1984; for reviews of this work).

In this article, I briefly review the past work. Then I discuss some new experiments and some theoretical issues that are stimulated by the work.

* This research was supported by a grant from the National Institute of Mental Health.

Past Work

In a typical experiment, subjects sel a complex event and are then asked a series of questions that expose them to postevent information. Typically, some of the questions are designed to present misleading information, i.e., to suggest the existence of an object or detail that did not in fact exist. Thus, in one study subjects first watched a film of a car accident. Misled subjects were asked "How fast was the white sports car going when it passed the barn while travelling along the country road?" There was no barn in the film. Control subjects answered a question at did not mention a barn. A week later, all subjects were asked whether they had seen a barn in the film. Misled subjects were more likely to later "recall" having seen the nonexistent barn than were subjects who had not been asked the misleading questions. Why does this occur? One hypothesis is that the questions are effective because they contain information -- in this case false information – that becomes integrated into the person's recollection of the event, thereby supplementing that memory.

In other studies, we have shown that new information can do more than simply supplement a recollection: it can occasionally alter, or transform, a recollection. Thus, in one study, subjects saw a series of slides depicting successive stages in an accident involving a car and a pedestrian. During the slide series, the car, a red Datsun, was seen travelling along a side street toward an intersection at which there was a stop sign for half of the subjects and a yield sign for the others. Some subjects then received a question containing a piece of misinformation: for example, the question "Did another car pass the red Datsun while it was stopped at the stop sign?"contains a piece of misinformation when asked of subjects who actually saw the yield sign. Finally, subjects were tested for their recollection of the sign with a forced choice recognition test. Depending upon the time intervals that occurred between the slides, the intervening questions, and the final recollection, as many as 80% of subjects indicated that their recollections were consistent with the misinformation.

The alteration of recollection appears to be a fact of life. It is of theoretical and practical interest to know something about the conditions under which people accept suggestive information and the conditions under which they resist such information. Put another way, which conditions encourage distortion in recollection and which seem to minimize it. As it happens, there are a number of separate lines of research, each of which helps to delimit the boundary conditions for the recollection change phenomenon. These superficially unrelated lines of research have been tied together within the umbrella of a single common principle: the principle of "discrepancy detection."

Detection of Discrepancies

To see the role of discrepancy detection at work, consider some empirical findings concerning recollection change:

1. Time Intervals. The intervals of delay between viewing an initial event, encountering a subsequent misleading message, and engaging in a final test have been found to be major determinants of changes in memory for an event. The number of subjects whose recollection is distorted increases with longer intervals between an event and subsequent misinformation. Put another way, recollection change appears to be enhanced by the fading of the original memory.

2. Form of Postevent Information. The syntax of a postevent message influences the likelihood of its acceptance. When the misinformation is embedded in a minor clause of a sentence or question, it has more influence than when it is the focus of the sentence or question. One explanation for this result is that less attention is given to misinformation when embedded in a minor clause. In this case, misinformation is casually or unintentionally assimilated. When placed at the focus of the question, misinformation receives more critical and direct attention and likelihood of its rejection is enhanced.

3. Event Factors. A variable that causes event details to be poorly stored creates a situation that is ripe for the acceptance of postevent information. So, for example, events that are briefly presented, peripherically presented, or presented under conditions of high stress lead to greater acceptance of subsequent postevent information.

4. Warnings. When people are warned about the possibility that they might receive misinformation, they are better able to resist it. Apparently this occurs because the warning causes them to scrutinize the misinformation and such scrutiny leads to a greater likelihood that the misinformation will detected. One result that is related to the beneficial impact of a warning is the finding that when misinformation is too blatantly incorrect, people reject it. Red herrings can be misused or overused. Even hunting dogs are confused only temporarily, and after too many false starts, the dogs learn to overlook the foul smell.

In sum, these are a few of the independent variables that influence the degree of recollection change. At first glance they seem to be only superficially related to one another. However, in all of these cases, the subject's detection of discrepancies between the original memory and the postevent information (or failure to detect discrepancies) appears to be a crucial factor. With a long interval between event and misinformation, with misinformation that is subtly embedded, with information acquired in the course of viewing a violent event, the ability to detect discrepancies is minimized. Conversely, when subjects are warned about the likelihood of incorrect information, they scrutinize the postevent information and the likelihood of detecting a discrepancy is enhanced. Thus, the detection of discrepancies appears to be an important mediating variable, i.e., a common underlying factor in the operation of a number of other variables. This leads naturally to the proposal of a basic principle of recollection change: change in memory for an event is more likely to occur if discrepancies between the original event and postevent information are not detected while the postevent information is being processed.

New Evidence for Discrepancy Detection

By discrepancy detection, we are referring to the detection of a conflict between original memory and postevent information that occurs at the time the postevent information is processed. If we are correct about the important role that discrepancy detection plays in the acceptance of postevent information, we might predict that subjects who – on their own accord – read the postevent information slowly would be more resistant to that information than subjects who read it quickly.

Data bearing on this hypothesis can be found in Tousignant, Hall, and Loftus (1986). The first experiment in this series involved three major phases. First, subjects viewed a set of slides depicting a wallet snatching. One slide showed a woman walking by a tavern, for example. After viewing the slides, subjects were exposed to some new information, and finally they were tested. In the last two phases all presentation and responding was done via an Apple II microcomputer.

The postevent information was presented via a narrative. Two versions of the narrative were created, each 15 sentences long. Ninety "misled" subjects received seven critical pieces in the narrative. Ninety control subjects received neutral information. As an example of misinformation, subjects read that the victim walked under an overhanging restaurant sign when the actual sign was for a tavern. Misled subjects read that the victim's friend had short curly black hair, when the hair was actually red. Subjects read the sentences one at a time, indicating by pressing a button when they wished the next sentence to appear. Their reading times were recorded.

Finally subjects were tested. We found first of all that misled subjects made more errors, which is to be expected. But of major interest to the present discussion is the analysis comparing misled subjects who resisted the misinformation with misled subjects who accepted the misinformation. We found that subjects who read the postevent narrative more slowly tended to be more resistant to the postevent misinformation. So, for example, the "highly suggestible" subjects took an average of 7.6 s per sentence to read the narrative, while the "accurate" subjects took an average of 10.1 s per sentence.

Later experiments in this series revealed that subjects who naturally read more slowly were more likely to detect a discrepancy between what they were reading and what they had stored in their memory. Moreover, subjects who were instructed to read slowly were more likely to detect a discrepancy than those who were instructed to read quickly. Taken together, these results suggest that the longer reading times are associated with a greater scrutiny of postevent information. This leads to an increased likelihood that discrepancies will be detected and that the misinformation will be resisted.

Exposure to postevent information does have one unexpected benefit, however. It can enhance memory for details about the critical item, at least in some subjects. This was shown recently in a study by Willem Wagenaar and Hans Boer (1987), who showed subjects a series of pictures depicting an auto accident. In one of the pictures, a car was seen at a stop light (the light was red, yellow, or green). Afterwards, some subjects received misinformation referring to a stop sign, and others did not. When asked whether it was a stop light or stop sign, control subjects were correct 78% of the time, whereas misled subjects were correct 62% of the time. This is the usual misinformation effect.

What is slightly more interesting is that all subjects were then asked to report on the color of the traffic light. Of the control subjects who had been correct about the stop light, 47% were correct about its color. On the other hand, of "misled" subjects who were still correct about the stop light, 66% were correct about its color.

There are two ways to think about this finding. One is uninteresting, and ascribes the effect to mere subject selection. Consider a situation in which 60% of the control subjects remember the light and 40% do not. The subjects who remember the light should all choose the correct response on the test. The subjects who do not remember the light, will guess, and they should be correct 50% of the time. Thus, the total percent correct for the control group should be 60% (all who really remember) plus 20% (half of the subjects who do not), or 80%. When these subjects then give the color of the light, the subjects who "guessed" should have a low probability of being accurate, and they drag down performance. Now consider the misled subjects. Assume that as in the control group, 60% of the misled subjects remember the light, and 40% do not. Assume, for simplicity, that all who do not remember the light are biased by the postevent information to choose the stop sign. Many more subjects will wrongly choose the stop sign. Of those relatively fewer individuals who stick with the correct stop light because of their strong memory for it, they would naturally have better memory for the color of the light.

A second, and more interesting, way of thinking about the finding that subjects who receive misinformation but are still correct about the stop light have better memory for its color is to presume that the misinformation affected the postevent rehearsal of the critical object. It is possible that the misinformation caused some subjects to review their memory for the object, and in doing so caused some to extract additional information about that object, namely information about its color. In fact there is some evidence for this notion that misinformation can aid memory when one examines overall performance on the color of the light. Of those who were misinformed, 55% were correct about the color; of control subjects only 45% were correct about the color.

The discussion thus far constitutes a brief review of past work. I now want to turn to a number of recent published attacks on this work. In order for you to appreciate these attacks, I must raise the important issue of the fate of the underlying memory traces.

Fate of Memory

Suppose a person sees a yield sign, then receives misinformation about a stop sign, and now recalls seeing a stop sign. What happened to the original yield sign in memory? Did the misinformation simply cover up the original information with a layer of garbage that could be peeled away revealing the original information? This is the "coexistence" hypothesis, which assumes that the original information exists in memory along with the postevent information. The introduction of postevent information, under this position, is thought to make the original memories simply less accessible but still potentially recoverable at some future time.

Alternatively, did the misinformation alter the trace of the yield sign in such a way that the original trace could not be recovered in the future? This is the "alteration" hypothesis, and it suggests that the original memory representations are altered when postevent information is processed.

This distinction has enormous practical importance since it bears on attempts one might make to correct a memory after it has been biased. Under the coexistence view, but perhaps not the alteration view, it makes sense to vigorously pursue retrieval techniques (such as hypnosis or context reinstatement) that might access the original information. Under the alteration view, one's efforts might be placed elsewhere, for example in the realteration of memory.

The coexistence versus alteration distinction also has theoretical importance. The coexistence view is consistent with the idea that all information, once stored, remains in memory more or less permanently. The alteration view implies a true loss due to updating, substitution, or blending of new inputs.

Coexistence frameworks derive their support from studies that show successful recovery of original memories (see for example, Morton, Hammersley & Bekerian, 1985). One demonstration of recovery is that of Bekerian and Bowers (1983). Bekerian and Bowers followed a procedure similar to that used before with one modification. The original procedure had three essential phases. In phase 1, subjects were presented with a slide sequence depicting an auto-pedestrian accident. Assume that it included a car passing a yield sign. In phase 2, misled subjects were given some postevent information, for example, that the traffic sign was a stop sign. (Control subjects got consistent information.) In phase 3, all subjects were given pairs of slides, and from each pair they had to choose the slide they saw before. The critical slide pair asked subjects to indicate whether they saw a stop sign or a yield sign.

The original test procedure presented the test pairs in random order with respect to the original sequence. That is, a large number of test pairs were presented prior to the critical pair, and the order of these test pairs bore no relationship to the chronological order of the event.

But Bekerian and Bowers also used a modified test procedure, one that they believed would have a better chance of reinstating the original context and enabling subjects to extract original information. The modified procedure involved presenting test pairs in sequential order, or an order that matched the order seen during the initial slides. In both cases, the critical stop/yield pair occurred in the ninth position.

When Bekerian and Bowers used the random test procedure, they found the typical result, namely misled subjects performed worse than controls (60% correct vs. 94% correct). However, with the sequential test procedure misled subjects performed as well as controls (87% correct vs. 85% correct).

Based upon these results, Bekerian and Bowers concluded that the effects of misleading information are dependent on the type of retrieval conditions existing at the time of testing. They claimed that loss of original memory is not inevitable once new information is given. They suggested that their results support the "headed-records" theory of Morton et al., and that once new information is received, subjects construct a new memory, as a result of which the original memory may be rendered less accessible but remains "undisturbed" (p. 143).

Another view on the matter came from McCloskey and Zaragoza (1985). Like Bekerian and Bowers, McCloskey and Zaragoza used a three-phase paradigm, with one modification. Subjects saw a sequence of slides depicting an office burglary. The sequence contained a number of critical items, one of which shows a man holding a hammer. Then subjects read a narrative describing the events shown in the slides. In the control condition, the narrative gave no specific information about the critical item – it was referred to simply as a tool. In the misled condition, the narrative referred to the critical item as a screwdriver. After reading the narrative, the subjects were tested on what they saw. The original test procedure required subjects to choose between the hammer, the originally seen item, and the screwdriver, the item presented to the misled subjects as misleading postevent information.

McCloskey and Zaragoza felt that this test was not adequate for telling whether the original memory has been modified since the postevent information could simply bias some subjects towards choosing the other object. So they created a modified procedure in which such bias presumably could not operate. In the modified procedure, the misleading information – the screwdriver – was not included as an option on the test. Instead the subjects were asked to choose between the original item – the hammer – and a new item: a wrench. If misleading information impairs subjects' memory (by erasing the original or making it less accessible), then misled subjects should show poorer test performance than control subjects, even in the modified procedure. However, if misleading information does not influence memory for the original information, then control and misled conditions should not differ.

McCloskey and Zaragoza carried out six experiments, involving approximately 800 subjects, with the modified test procedure. Experiments were similar to each other except for variations in minor details. Subjects saw series of 79 slides showing a man stealing a calculator from an office. Subjects then read a narrative describing the theft, and finally took a test. Collapsed across the six experiments, the results showed the usual misinformation effect when the suggested item was an option on the test (37% correct for misled subjects and 72% correct for control subjects). However, with the modified test in which the subjects could not choose the suggested item, misled subjects performed as well as controls (72% correct vs. 75% correct).

Based upon these findings, McCloskey and Zaragoza concluded that misleading postevent information does not impair subjects' ability to remember what they originally saw. Moreover, they argue firmly that misleading information neither erases the original information nor makes it inaccessible.

In sum, two lines of investigation have led researchers to the conclusion that the original memory is either made less accessible by postevent information (Bekerian & Bowers) or, even more strongly, it has no effect on memory at all (McCloskey & Zaragoza). Are they right? I think not. With the aid of two ideas – the "free radical" and the "conscious act of retrieval" – borrowed from Tulving (1983), we may be able to distinguish between those situations where it is possible to recover the original information and those situations where it may not be possible. What appears crucial is whether the critical manipulation occurs prior to conscious recollection or afterward.

Why might conscious recollection be important? Suppose the postevent information leaves a "free radical" or "free fragment" in memory, that is a bit of episodic information detached from the rest of the memory for the episode. Like the free radicals of the chemical world, Tulving believes these bits of memory are highly reactive and unstable. It may be that at the time of the final test, these fragments become laminated, via the act of conscious retrieval, to the memory of the episode. Accordingly, prior to conscious retrieval it is still possible to separate these bits from the original engram whereas afterwards it may be exceedingly difficult, if not impossible to do so. We have now conducted several experiments that provide support for our proposition that once subjects consciously retrieve a piece of misinformation, they are not readily induced to recover the original engram. Prior to conscious retrieval, they are. In short, we propose that bits of misleading postevent information may exist as free fragments until a subsequent act of retrieval completes the recoding process. In both the Bekerian and Bowers work and the McCloskey and Zaragoza work, the manipulations occurred prior to or concurrently with the conscious act of retrieval of the episode.

This line of thinking has led us to propose a second principle of memory change, called the Recollection Principle: "Change in memory for an event is completed by the act of recollection." (This principle might have been called the Principle of Memory Sclerosis, after Arteriosclerosis, to convey the idea that the act of recollection causes a hardening of the memory.)

The McCloskey and Zaragoza work presents an additional problem for assessing whether the original trace has been altered by the postevent information. The test between hammer and wrench allows no avenue for compromise between memory traces, or for the expression of subtle or minor changes that could have occurred in memory traces. People might choose hammer over wrench simply because it is closer to their stored representation. To put this another way, the test between hammer and wrench may force subjects to discriminate between two objects neither of which matches their stored memory representation. This would occur if subjects, before being tested, were entertaining a recollection that embodied a bit of both objects. Given the opportunity, subjects might be willing to show that they had blended information from the two sources into a compromise memory.

Consider a subject who saw a hammer and received misinformation about a screwdriver. Suppose that the misinformation produced a slight alteration in memory, resulting in a memory representation that contained features of hammer and screwdriver. The test between hammer and wrench does not permit the expression of subtle or minor changes that could have occurred in the memory traces. That is, the McCloskey and Zaragoza test may be forcing subjects to discriminate between two objects neither of which matches what they have in memory. Given the opportunity, subjects may be quite willing to show that they had blended information from the two sources. If a "hammer-screwdriver" existed in the real world, and were an option on the test, perhaps subjects would choose it. In order to determine whether subjects truly have intact the original pristine memory representation, it is necessary to provide subjects with the opportunity to indicate the existence of blend memories and observe that they reject the blend in favor of the original.

The Blending of Memories

A study of Weinberg, Wadsworth, and Baron (1983) bears on this issue. Weinberg et al. used a testing procedure similar to McCloskey and Zaragoza but obtained a different result. Subjects in Weinberg et al. viewed a sequence of slides, including a car at a yellow yield sign. Next some subjects received misleading information about a stop sign. Finally subjects were tested in one of two ways. The original testing procedure involved a choice between a yellow yield sign and a stop sign. The modified testing procedure involved a choice between a yellow yield sign and a red yield sign. Contrary to the findings of McCloskey and Zaragoza, subjects in the Weinberg et al. study performed more poorly in the misled condition than in the control condition, even when the suggested item was not an option on the test. McCloskey and Zaragoza attribute the discrepancy in results to an unfortunate choice of items coupled with a failure to counterbalance. They argue that faced with a yellow and red yield sign, many subjects will choose the alternative most similar to a stop sign, namely the red yield sign. In short, the misleading "stop sign" information creates a bias toward the selection of the incorrect alternative on the test.

Another way to look at the Weinberg et al. experiment is that their selection of a critical item was absolutely fortunate. The red yield sign, in one sense, contains features of both the original information (the shape of the yield sign) and the misleading postevent information (the color of the stop sign). Thus, it embodies a compromise between the two sources of information. Its inclusion as a test alternative permits some subjects to show that their memory reflects features of both the original and the postevent information.

In other research we have demonstrated that postevent suggestions can produce altered memories that represent a compromise between the original and the postevent sources. For example, in several studies, subjects have received misleading information about the color of certain key objects. In one set of studies (Loftus, 1977), subjects saw a series of color slides depicting an autoaccident with a pedestrian. In the series, a green car drives past the accident but does not stop. Some time after viewing the slides of the accident, some subjects were exposed to the information that the car that had passed the accident was blue. Finally subjects looked at a color wheel containing color strips and were given a list of objects that had appeared in the slides. Among other colors, the wheel contained some green strips, some blue ones, and some that were an intermediate bluish-green. The task was to pick the color that best represented the subjects' recollection of each of the objects.

These studies showed that subjects given the "blue" information tended to pick a blue or bluish-green as the color that represented their recollection of the car that passed the accident. Some of these subjects picked a solid blue while others picked a bluish-green, indicating greater or lesser influence of the misleading information. The choice of bluish-green and simultaneous rejection of the true green indicates that subjects have some elements of the original information in memory but have been shifted toward a bluer color by the postevent suggestion.

In other work, we have produced compromise memories by allowing subjects the freedom to describe in detail the objects they have seen. For example, in one set of studies, subjects saw a set of color slides of a wallet-snatching incident. In the last few slides there is a brown pickup truck. Misled subjects received the suggestion that the vehicle was a car. Control subjects did not. Later all subjects were asked whether they saw the vehicle, and if so to describe it. What is a blend between a pickup truck and a car? Perhaps a station wagon. Would misled subjects actually describe a station wagon? No control subject described a station wagon. However, several misled subjects explicitly did. One female subject wrote: "The car was a dark-colored station wagon. I think." A male subject wrote: "metallic light green station wagon."

While these idiosyncratic descriptions are sometimes difficult to analyze, our preliminary analyses suggest that they may be an excellent tool for assessing whether modifications in memory have occurred as a result of postevent inputs.

Studies such as these suggest that the way a subject is tested will influence what the subject chooses. If the opportunity exists to describe a memory or to choose an alternative that contains features of both the original and the postevent inputs, some subjects will take advantage of that opportunity. If McCloskey and Zaragoza had permitted their subjects to choose a blend between a hammer (the original object) and a screwdriver (the suggested object), perhaps they would have done so. The test they used may simply not have been sensitive enough to show that the alteration of memory had occurred. More attention should be given to designing studies in which compromise memories are investigated. For this, we need special types of items. We need, for example, to show people an event in which they see a goat, and later tell them it is a sheep. Goat and sheep? How is that going to work? Until recently this would not have been the kind of item we needed, but modern physiology has come a long way, and may indirectly be able to contribute something to the study of memory distortions. Scientists at the Institute of Animal Physiology in Cambridge, England, mingled new embryos from both sheep and goats ... producing a creature that looks like a zookeeper's prank – a geep: the perfect object for testing whether memory for a goat has been modified. If someone has seen a goat and later receives a suggestion about a sheep, when, theoretically, should a "geep" memory occur? (1) If a discrepancy is not detected while the "sheep" information is being processed. (2) If the response alternatives permit the choice of a blended memory, or a geep. (3) If the person is induced to recall a geep. The act of recall should solidify the memory.

On the question of the fate of memory, it is probably fruitless to search for exclusively original or suggested memories, since it appears that our memories may be complex blends of both. Old questions such as: "Is there total destructive updating?" or "Can we find a completely untampered and pristine original memory?" seem extreme. New questions such as "How do the two sources of information interact and evolve with one another?" are more appropriate. The issue of destructive updating versus pristine original memories is too simplistic. Memories are not neat photos containing only the original or only the suggested information. Instead they may be more like montages containing original and suggested features blended into a holistic representation.

References

Bekerian, D.A., & Bowers, J.M. (1983). Eyewitness testimony: Were we misled? *Journal of Experimental Psychology. Learning, Memory, and Cognition*, *9*, 139–145.

Hall, D.H., Loftus, E.F., & Tousignant, J.P. (1984). Postevent information and changes in recollection for a natural event. In G.L. Wells & E.F. Loftus (Eds.), *Eyewitness testimony: psychological perspectives.* Cambridge: Cambridge University Press.

Loftus, E.F. (1977). Shifting human color memory. *Memory and Cognition, 6,* 696–699.

Loftus, E.F. (1979). *Eyewitness testimony.* Cambridge: Harvard University Press.

Loftus, E.F. (1983). Misfortunes of memory. *Philosophical Transactions of the Royal Society of London, 302,* 413–421.

McCloskey, M., & Zaragoza, M. (1985). Misleading post-event information and memory for events: arguments and evidence against memory impairment hypothesis. *Journal of Experimental Psychology: General, 114*, 3–18.

Morton, J., Hammersley, R.H., & Bekerian, D.A. (1985). Headed records: a model for memory and its failures. *Cognition, 20*, 1–23.

Sautter, C. (1982, December). How to win with diversionary tactics. *Savvy*, pp. 26–27.

Tousignant, J.P., Hall, D., & Loftus, E.F. (1986). Discrepancy detection and vulnerability to misleading post-event information. *Memory and Cognition, 14*, 329–338.

Tulving, E. (1983). *Elements of episodic memory.* Cambridge: Cambridge University Press.

Wagenaar, W., & Boer, H. (1987). Misleading post-event information: testing parameterized models of integration in memory. *Acta Psychologica, 66*, 291–306.

Weinberg, H.I., Wadsworth, J., & Baron, R.S. (1983). Demand and the impact of leading questions on eyewitness testimony. *Memory and Cognition 11*, 101–104.

17
Collaborative Testimony by Police Officers: A Psycho-legal Issue

GEOFFREY M. STEPHENSON, NOEL K. CLARK
and BROMLEY H. KNIVETON

One of the reasons why four men on trial at the Old Bailey in London were acquitted of serious conspiracy and petrol bomb charges some years back in 1983 was, according to the Sunday Times report, that "Eight policemen had compiled their prosecution notes together in a police canteen, in apparent ignorance of rules which forbid joint preparation." (Shirley, 1983). Although the judge may have thought that the police canteen was an inappropriate venue for the meeting (in fact, the canteen was almost certainly the only room in the Station capable of accommodating eight policemen in any degree of comfort), the main point at issue, of course, was not the venue for their meeting, but the collaboration, especially of such a seemingly large number of collaborators. In this chapter we would like to describe a series of experiments that have systematically explored the effects on the quality of testimony of having two or more witnesses, including police officers, testify to what they have heard.

Background to the Studies

There are no legal rules forbidding collaboration by police officers or anyone else. As one of the officers involved in the case referred to, said after the acquittal of the men, "I've never heard of that regulation. In eight years of service I have always made notes up with other officers." The only rule is that if you do collaborate, you should say so. It still happens that a skillful lawyer may sometimes trap an inexperienced officer into denying that he or she collaborated, and then point to the more or less identical notes of two or more officers as evidence of collaboration, thereby discrediting the testimony. Collaborative testimony itself is admissible, and indeed, one officer may give evidence on behalf of a group of officers, the other officers not being called to give evidence because their notes are literally identical with those of the chosen representative or they have all signed one account in the same notebook.

The official authorisation of this practice in England goes back to 1953 to the case of R. v. Bass, before the Court of Criminal Appeal. The trial judge had not permitted the jury to see the notebooks of two officers, who denied collaborating. In the course of their judgment their Lordships had this to say:

This court has observed that police officers nearly always deny that they have collaborated in the making of notes, and we cannot help wondering why they are the only class of society who do not collaborate in such a matter. It seems to us that nothing could be more natural or proper, when two persons have been present at an interview with a third person, than that they should afterwards make sure that they have a correct version of what was said. Collaboration would appear to be a better explanation of almost identical notes than the possession of a superhuman memory. (p. 1067)

Note that the judges seem to have no doubt that collaboration can be anything other than beneficial. By collaboration two officers can "make sure" they have a correct version of what happened. Later cases established that more than two could collaborate, presumably making even more sure they have a correct version! And if more than two, why not eight?

There are important legal issues raised by this practice. Briefly, if there is disagreement between the officers, how do they resolve the conflict? If one officer agrees to something he believes to be false because *others* assert it, the jury is surely deprived of its right to decide on the facts and that officer in effect commits perjury. Moreover, if an officer assents to a statement he does not know to be true from the evidence of his *own* senses, that evidence is strictly speaking hearsay evidence only. Furthermore, if an officer gives evidence some of which originates from the perception of others in a group, he can hardly, as a representative, be reliably cross-examined as to its truth.

This last problem in group testimony is illustrated in a quite different context by Jan Vansina (1973) in his book *Oral Tradition: A Study in Historical Methodology.* Oral traditions are said to derive from a chain of testimonies, and the "group testimony" has a character of its own, according to Vansina. A spokesman is appointed and the testimony rehearsed in secret, to ensure full agreement before the public rehearsal. He states, of group testimony amongst the Kuba peoples:

The fact that such a testimony is the concern of a group gives it a special character of its own. All those present must be in agreement about all the facts related, and nothing can be related that has not been agreed to unanimously. The testimony then acquires the character of an official statement, and at the same time it is a "minimum" statement, for some of the members of the group may know fuller details about some of the facts which are not included in the account. (p. 28)

It is certainly true, as with the Kuba peoples, that the "group testimony" by police officers has the character of an "official statement" and that not everything is said that *could* be said. The experiments to be described have something to say about this.

Collaborative testimony in formal settings, like a Court of Law, or the "group testimony" in public meetings as described by Vansina, is but one example of "group remembering". Group remembering is a neglected topic in both social and cognitive psychology, the importance of which is gaining recognition in isolated studies, for example, of juries (Hartwick, Sheppard, & Davis, 1982), eyewitness testimony (Hollin & Clifford, 1983), interpersonal relationships (Wegner, Giuliano, & Hertel, 1985) and everyday discourse (Edwards & Middleton, in press). There can be no doubting its prevalence or its importance. The skill of remembering itself develops socially, when for example, parents correct what they see to be the misperceptions or misrepresentations in the accounts of past events offered by their young children. Within a family, or any group, events will be socially recalled, and traditions thereby established, that play an important role in maintaining the cohesiveness of the group concerned (Martin, 1982). Committees of all sorts rely on one another's remembering skills. For example, tired members of an Appointing Committee face a difficult job of group remembering at the end of a day's interviewing, and when the first member sums up comments on the performance of a candidate whose very existence some members of the Committee have probably forgotten, all may nod gratefully in agreement. Members of a jury may have to agree, in their final deliberations, on what was said some weeks, even months ago.

Sir Frederick Bartlett in his pioneering and still-influential 1932 study of Remembering, got close to doing some experiments on group remembering. As he stated in the Preface:

> To begin with, I was interested mainly in the conditions of individual perceiving, imagining and remembering; but it soon appeared that, in numerous cases, social factors were playing a large part. Hence I also used some experiments which would help to show what occurs when material is dealt with in succession by a number of persons all belonging to the same social grouping. (p. vi)

He refers, of course, to that well-known psychology practical standby, the method of serial reproduction, in which a story is passed on from one person to another, in writing. Bartlett's experimental studies of social recall stopped with this method of serial reproduction, and it was not until 1953 with Perlmutter's isolated study that collaborative recall was studied using Bartlettian materials. What Bartlett might have called the "method of social reproduction" was not, apparently, employed again until 1982, in the first study of the present series by Stephenson, Brandstätter and Wagner. We shall briefly describe that study, as its provocative results led directly to the formulation of the subsequent work.

Dyadic Confidence and the Role of Implicational Errors

Bartlett's "reconstructive" theory of remembering relied in part on an analysis of the errors introduced by subjects into accounts they gave of stories they had heard recounted. In particular Bartlett used a strange and confusing North American Indian folk-tale called "The War of the Ghosts." Using a German translation of that story (*Der Geisterkrieg*), Stephenson, Brandstätter, and Wagner (1982) used as subjects in their experiment adults resident in the City of Linz in Austria who were recruited by telephone. *Der Geisterkrieg* was recorded on tape, 61 subjects recruited, and run within a 2×2 factorial design in which "social performance" (dyadic vs. individual) and delay (immediate vs. 1 week) were the two factors. Subjects simultaneously read and listened to the tape over headphones, and were then required in the Immediate condition, after being distracted briefly for a few minutes, to produce a single version of the story either by themselves or in pairs ("dyads"). The story was to be as complete as possible, and the dyads were encouraged to discuss the story between themselves and to agree on a single version. Various ratings of their confidence in the accuracy and completeness of the story were obtained. Subsequently, the individuals and dyads were asked to compete a 14-item questionnaire concerning details of the story, e.g. "How many men were in the canoe?", and to assess their degree of confidence in each of their 14 answers on a 4-point verbally anchored scale from "guessing" through to "certain".

As expected, dyads produced more correct answers than individuals, both immediately and following 1 week's delay. It is the data for confidence and accuracy, however, that we wish to discuss at this point, and which became the main preoccupation of that study. Both individuals and dyads gave *subjectively* valid ratings of their answers to the questionnaire. That is, confidence for correct was higher than confidence for incorrect answers. *Objectively*, however, groups were distinctly less valid than were individuals with respect to their incorrect answers. Whereas individuals tended to be "doubtful" about wrong answers, dyads were at least "fairly confident" about the truth of their errors. And whereas individuals would be at least "fairly confident" about correct answers, dyads would be "certain". On the assumption that a correct answer has an ideal rating of "certain", and an incorrect answer an ideal rating of "guessing", a testimonial invalidity score was determined, being the discrepancy between the actual and ideal confidence rating for each answer. Dyads were highly valid on correct answers with an invalidity score approaching "0": they were very nearly "certain" about correct answers. But for incorrect answers they were too confident – well-nigh "fairly certain" on average with a testimonial invalidity score approaching "2" – indicating them to be nearly 2 scale points adrift on the 4-point scale of confidence. As for errors in the *stories* produced by dyads and individuals, one clear effect emerged: the tendency of dyads to produce more *implicational* errors than individuals. Implicational errors are those statements that go beyond the original, but do not contradict it; dyads produced nearly twice as many such errors as did individuals. There was no such difference for "confusional" errors – those errors which actually contradicted a statement in the original story. This distinction between the two types of error is an important one, indicated by the correlations between errors (confusional and implicational) and various measures of competent performance. Those for implicational errors were positive and substantial, whereas those for confusional errors approximated to zero. It was as though making implicational errors facilitated the reconstruction of the story.

Remembering in Dyads and Groups: Social Direction and Control

The War of the Ghosts, though more naturalistic material than nonsense syllables, as Bartlett did not fail to point out, is a weird story, and for the next experiment (Clark, Stephenson, & Rutter, 1986; Stephenson, Clark, & Wade, 1986) in England, using the more conventional arrangement of student subjects in the context of a 1st-year Practical, we wrote a script of a fictional interrogation by two police officers, one male and one female, of a woman who alleged she had been raped. The script was duly rehearsed and recorded on audio tape, with amateur actors – the departmental secretary, a postgraduate student and a research fellow – taking the three roles. The reading lasted about $4\frac{3}{4}$ min. In addition, in this experiment we included a four person group condition, eliminated the delay condition, and inserted a distractor task between the subjects hearing the dramatised version of the interrogation and writing it up. This time subjects were told to imagine they had been asked in Court to give an account of what had happened in the interrogation they had just heard. There is no doubt that the interrogation was of compelling interest to the student subjects. The script had an abrasive character, being based roughly on the authors' recollections of a real-life interrogation whose showing in the BBC Thames Valley "Police" series resulted in much criticism of the police handling of the case. A questionnaire was also devised and again subjects were asked to state their level of confidence in the answers they gave. The members of each dyad, as before, and the members of each four-person group, produced only one story between them, one set of answers and one set of ratings.

Figure 17.1 presents the interaction between group size and correctness of answers with respect to testimonial invalidity. As in the previous experiment, dyads were more valid than individuals on correct answers, less valid on incorrect answers. Observe, however, the steep rise in invalidity of incorrect answers in the four-person groups. These groups were virtually certain of the correctness of their wrong answers. This effect brings to mind Janis's characterisation of "invulnerability" as a feature of what he termed "groupthink" (Janis, 1972). It also brings to mind the evidence that individuals in groups tend to

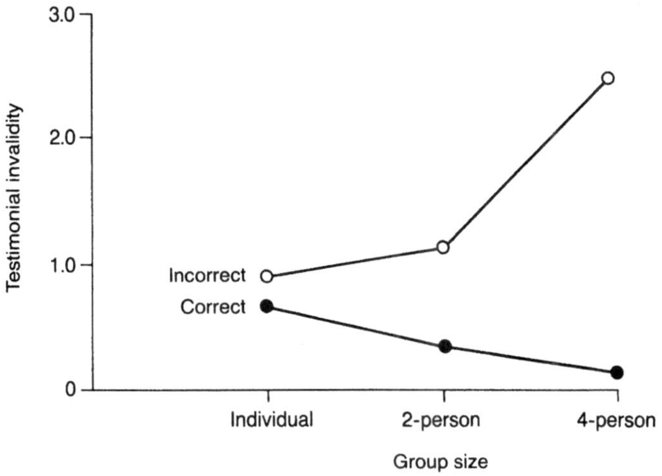

FIGURE 17.1. Interaction of group size and correctness on the testimonial invalidity of questionnaire answers

come to more extreme judgments than do individuals when acting alone. If the extreme confidence we have observed in groups is regarded as an instance of "group polarisation" (e.g. Myers, 1983) we may assume that the individual desire to express confidence is very general and becomes virtually an imperative within the larger group.

The nature of group remembering was further explored in this experiment by dividing the original interrogation and each account of the interrogation produced by individuals, dyads and four-person groups into its constituent propositions. Each proposition in each protocol was then examined and scored as Correct if it corresponded to a proposition in the original. Incorrect propositions were subdivided into implicational errors (termed "reconstructions" on this occasion), confusional errors and metastatements. Metastatements were statements about the characters, their motives and attitudes, and statements about the content or organisation of the text: e.g. statements refering to the lack of sympathy of the officers or to their "exhaustive" questioning would be classified as metastatements.

It should first be stated that there were no significant differences in the total number of coded propositions between the three conditions, i.e. the *amount* written did not differ in terms of the number of propositions generated. Their distribution amongst the different categories of correct and incorrect propositions did vary considerably, however, as Figure 17.2 indicates. Group size was clearly associated with the number of correct propositions, four-person groups having about twice as many correct as individuals. There were few confusional errors in any of the conditions, and as before, no significant differences, but contrary to the previous finding, there were also no significant differences in the number of reconstructions. The new category of meta-

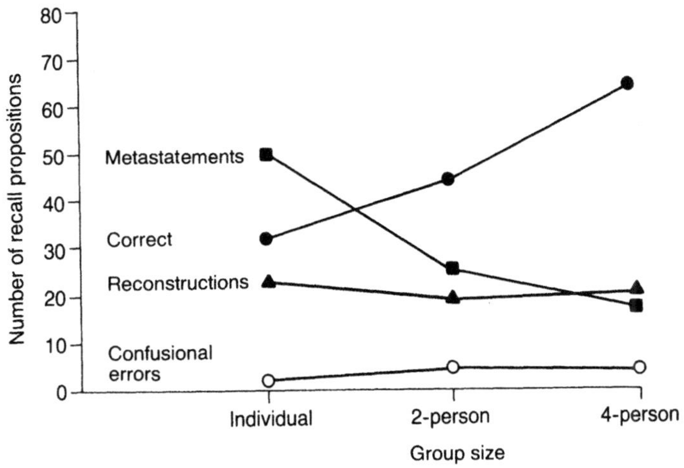

FIGURE 17.2. Distribution of proposition types in free recall protocols

statement, however, can be seen to have counterbalanced the group effect on correct propositions, individuals making up in metastatement what they lacked in correctness. Something approaching 50% of individuals' propositions were metastatements.

There is no doubt that when two or more persons together recall the interrogation they suppress the expression of evaluative, descriptive comment. Their feelings, the feelings of the woman, and the manner and behavioral style of the police are subordinated to the attempt to reconstruct the events of the night in question, as provided by the testimony given by the woman. Given the apparently increased single-mindedness of group recall, it came as no surprise that an analysis of the propositions recalled by individuals, dyads and four-person groups indicated enhanced overlap within the group conditions compared with the individual conditions. This was demonstrated in two ways. Firstly, the probability that a proposition will recur was estimated. For example, the individuals recalled in total 145 propositions between them, the dyads 147. Whereas the individual propositions had only a 17.7% chance of occurring in any one protocol, the probability was 27% in the dyadic condition. Individuals, in other words, were more idiosyncratic. Secondly, the Spearman-Brown reliability coefficient was significantly higher in the dyadic and group conditions than in the individual condition, demonstrating again the greater consistency of group remembering.

Groups, the Police and Conventional Recall

The same experimental design was employed in a third experiment which compared police and student performance, again using the text of the interrogation

(Clark, 1987). We thought, correctly as it turned out, that policemen would find the text quite convincing in itself, but we were not at all convinced that they would find the acting sufficiently credible for our purposes. In this experiment we therefore decided to present the interrogation visually, on photographic slides. The text was subdivided and presented in sequence on 12 slides to successive groups of at least seven policemen or seven students, the members of each group then being randomly allocated to the individual, dyad or four-person conditions. "Excess" subjects above the seven were used to boost mainly the individual, then the dyadic conditions. The police subjects were all uniformed police officers, mainly constables, attending training courses; all had at least 3 years' experience in the Force.

Police in England are no strangers to the task of summarising an interrogation, either as individuals or in groups, and we expected, firstly, that the police would recall more of the interrogation, and, secondly, would be more similar in what they recalled than their student counterparts. The second expectation derived from our belief that police officers, by virtue of their shared social identity and common experience of interrogation itself and the requirements of successful prosecution of suspects, would have acquired similar notions of what is desirable and appropriate to remember from an interrogation.

On the questionnaire, there was no doubting the police superiority. Individual policemen and police dyads and four-person groups answered more questions correctly than did students. When recalling freely, however, individual policemen did not fare well; they were consistently worse than individual students. On the other hand, policemen in dyads and four-person groups did better than students on the free recall task. For example, Figure 17.3 portrays the results for the number of correctly recalled propositions. Individual policemen were not as productive in recall as were individual students. It can be seen that police dyads were nearly twice as productive as were individual policemen (90.4 vs. 53.2). There was little difference, however, between the three student conditions. The different effect of the conditions on police and students was statistically significant, as was the main effect of group size. Maybe the individual policemen were handicapped in some way in the free recall task, as their cued recall on the questionnaire was not comparatively impaired. Certainly, individual policemen were not as productive overall as were individual students. The police were far more productive than were students in the two group conditions, but less productive in the individual condition, the interaction again being highly significant statistically. This greater productivity nonetheless took its toll in the number of errors, both confusional and especially reconstructive. Police produced many more reconstructive errors than did students, especially in the dyadic and four-person group conditions. For confusional errors, the pattern was less clear-cut but the overall police/student difference was apparent. Common to both reconstructions *and* confusional errors was a significant interaction between group size and subject group, with individual students producing more errors than student groups. The most startling difference in propositional content appeared, however, in

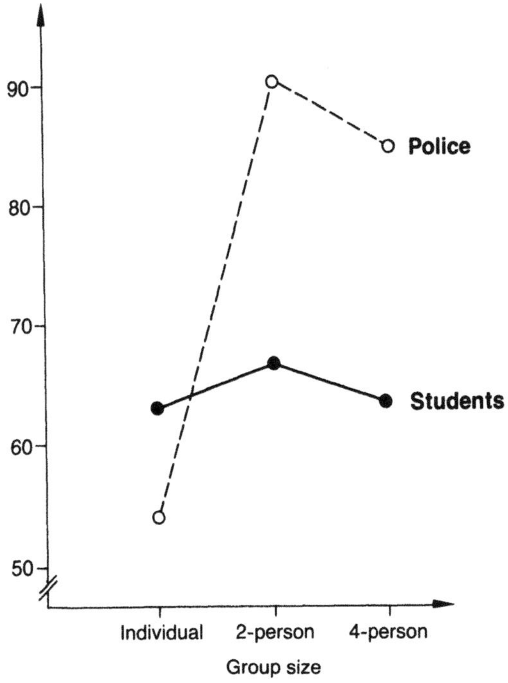

FIGURE 17.3. Number of correctly recalled propositions in free recall protocols

the case of metastatement. Metastatement was, on average, a negligible factor in the police dyads and four-person groups, and students produced far more metastatement overall. Police are certainly less likely to comment in an evaluative way on the behavior of the participants in the interaction, on their own feelings, or in a general way on the interrogation.

Some of these findings suggest that the police respond more to the stimulus of the group, making the differences between police and students especially salient in the group conditions; more correct propositions, but less metastatement and more errors. Whilst there is probably some truth in this, the assertion must be strongly qualified. Some part of these effects is undoubtedly a by-product of the narrative strategies employed by students and police (Clark, Stephenson, & Kniveton, 1986). In the dyadic and four-person group conditions especially, police tended to employ a *script* strategy rather than a *story* strategy. That is, they reconstructed the dramatic form of the original in direct speech attributed to specified participants, rather than writing a story-like description using indirect speech. In a script there is, of course, little room for evaluative comment, whereas reconstructive errors are perhaps encouraged by the demands of rationalising questions and replies in script form. Every "answer," for example, must be given a question. Script writers predominated in the police condition, whereas students were predominantly story writers. However, there were approximately equal numbers of script and story writers amongst *individual* policemen, enabling a reliable comparison to be made between the two kinds of free recall. There were no differences between script and story writers on the questionnaire, indicating no difference at least in cued recall. However, there were considerable differences in free recall, in particular with respect to reproductive free recall (correctly recalled propositions), metastatements, reconstructive errors and confusional errors. All these differences were in the same direction as the differences between groups of policemen and groups of students, script writers producing more correct propositions, more of both kinds of error, but less metastatement. Because police groups mainly adopted a script strategy, whereas student groups were predominantly story writers, we cannot rule out the possibility that this difference in narrative strategy was the principal determinant of the student/police differences.

The second general expectation in the police experiment was that police would be more similar in what they recalled than students. We have seen that groups were more similar than individuals, as if reflecting a common expectation about the nature of the task, and needing to agree about that in order to proceed in an efficient way. Police, of course, are likely to be in greater agreement still about how to proceed. An effective way to explore this possibility is to analyse the *gists* produced by students and police in the three conditions.

In this, as in the previous experiments, groups, in both student and police conditions, failed to maximise individual potential. On the basis of how much *individuals* recalled, predictions can be made regarding how much could in principle be recalled by two persons or four persons working collaboratively. In practice, actual performance was considerably less than could be expected. Whereas, for example, on the basis of individual performance, we could have expected four policemen to produce 177 correct items, in practice, only 84 correct propositions appeared in their free recalls. Now, such "group process loss", as Steiner (1972) characterised it, is a feature of group performance, arising from the difficulties of co-ordinating the contributions of members. A more important reason for the loss, however, in this case, is that groups agree more on what is the *gist* of the interrogation, its essential elements, and policemen especially so. This is evident in an analysis of the percentages of propositions recalled by over 50% of individuals and groups within each recall condition (Figure 17.4). Groups, it is apparent, have a much larger "gist" than do individuals in both police and student conditions. In the case of four-person police groups, for example, about 18% of the original was recalled correctly by 50% of the groups, whereas only 8% was recalled by 50% of the individual policemen. Groups are *selecting*, and selecting *conventionally* from what is available in the recollections of individuals. Similarly, police subjects are more conventional in this respect than are students, thereby confirming our general expectation about the *consistency* to be expected in the police subjects. Groups select, and they select consistently, and police select more consistently than do students.

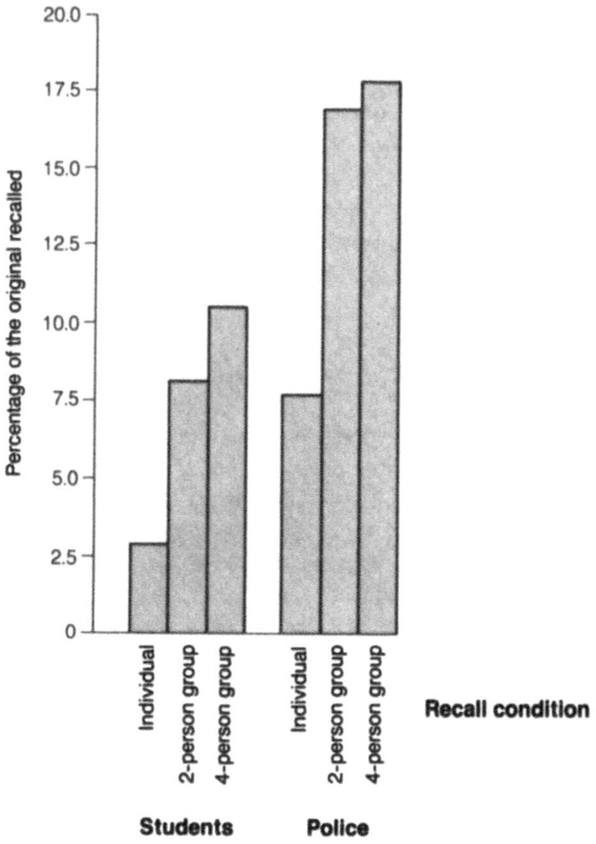

FIGURE 17.4. Gist analysis: percentages of the original "interrogation" propositions recalled by over 50% of individuals/groups within each recall condition

Group Over-confidence Examined

In all the experiments described so far, dyads, and especially four-person groups, are more confident overall than are individuals about the truth of their answers to the questionnaire items, inappropriately so for wrong answers. Whilst still discriminating between right and wrong answers, the tendency is for groups to move up the scale of confidence, no doubt because, in the words of the Appeal Court, by collaborating they believe that are "making sure" they have a correct answer. In all these experiments individuals were compared directly with groups in order to examine the effect of collaboration on individuals who had not previously rehearsed or recalled the events in question. However, a fourth experiment, using students from the University of Bristol, examined the possibility that this group effect might be modified by having individuals first perform the tasks alone before meeting their partner for purposes of collaboration (Stephenson, Abrams, Wagner, & Wade, 1986). In this experiment, a video-recorded extract from a real-life interrogation was used. Again, the interrogation was of a woman alleging she had been raped, and was of the same length as the simulated interrogation. So instead of listening to an audio-recording, or reading a script, subjects watched the video-taped extract.

Two experimental conditions were established. In one, the subjects, after watching the interrogation and performing the distracter task, immediately formed dyads, who recalled freely and wrote down the interrogation and answered a questionnaire as in the previous experiments. They were then split, and again performed the two tasks as individuals. Let us call that the DI condition (dyadic-individual). In the second condition, ID, the order in which the tasks were undertaken was reversed, individual followed by dyad. The experimental design enabled us to examine the basis on which individuals in groups, when in conflict about which is the correct answer, actually decide what answer to record. The results showed clearly that "truth" does not always win. A "truth-wins" model significantly overestimated group performance. On the other hand, a "confidence-wins" model accurately predicted group performance. It appears that group remembering is confidence-led. When there is disagreement between individuals, the more confident member of the dyad normally gets his or her way.

The results for confidence (Table 17.1) demonstrated an overall difference between the DI and ID conditions, and a significant second-order interaction showed that this difference was located largely in the results for incorrect answers. Note especially the increase from 1.64 to 2.29 in confidence for wrong answers, as the less confident individuals moved into the group situation. That 2.29 dyadic figure was nonetheless below both the dyadic and individual figures for incorrect answers in the DI condition, 2.54 and 2.40. This suggests that there may be some merit in individuals attempting the recall tasks prior to group discussion and decision.

The effect of the group upon confidence, and upon confidence for incorrect answers especially, using this time a video-recording of a real life interrogation, is nevertheless strongly evident in these as in the previous results.

TABLE 17.1. Confidence for correct and incorrect questionnaire answers in dyadic individual (DI) and individual-dyadic (ID) conditions

	Correct answers		Incorrect answers	
	DI	ID	DI	ID
1st measurement	2.89	2.64	2.54	1.64
2nd measurement	2.82	2.76	2.40	2.29

Questionnaire condition Free recall preparation	Individual (I)	Dyadic (D)
Individual (I)	II (9 pairs)	ID (9 pairs)
Dyadic (D)	DI (9 pairs)	DD (9 pairs)

FIGURE 17.5. Experimental design used by Stephenson & Wagner (1988)

What really gives rise to this? One problem of interpretation follows from the fact that before making their ratings of confidence, dyads have decided not only on the answers to specific questions, as in an interrogation, but have also freely discussed the events together. To which of these "group factors" can we attribute the excessive confidence? Either or both of these may be the decisive factor in determining the misplaced confidence in incorrect answers.

To examine this question a fifth experiment was carried out at Kent (Stephenson & Wagner, 1988), in which dyadic/individual free recall and dyadic/individual questionnaire recall were *independently* manipulated in 2×2 factorial design. Subjects viewed the video-tape of the interrogation and were then, after the distracter task, allocated to a dyadic or to an individual condition to undertake *only* the free recall task. They were then reassigned to an individual or dyadic condition for the questionnaire task (Figure 17.5). This design makes it possible to examine separately the effect of prior group discussion and of dyadic questionnaire performance on the quality of response to the questionnaire.

The results clearly showed that prior discussion in the free recall task had a beneficial effect on the number of correctly answered questionnaire items, especially in the individual questionnaire condition. Individuals coming from the dyadic free recall condition when answering the questionnaire do about as well on the questionnaire as do dyads, whereas individuals answering the questionnaire having come from the individual free recall do considerably less well than the equivalent dyads.

Figure 17.6 demonstrates a beneficial effect of dyadic free recall on questionnaire performance, with respect to confidence. The results portrayed are for confidence in *correct* and *incorrect* answers. The solid lines are for those dyads with prior discussion (dyadic free recall), and the broken lines for those without (i.e. individual free recall). Correct answers again receive a higher confidence rating, but the effect of prior discussion is evident only in the confidence ratings for *incorrect* answers. For correct answers, the lines are indistinguishable. Prior discussion, firstly, *reduces* confidence for wrong answers. Secondly, this reduction is especially in dyadic performance on the questionnaire. Prior discussion had the effect of *lowering* the confidence in incorrect answers, whilst having no effect on confidence for correct answers. Individuals who freely recalled alone, were *especially* vulnerable when they entered a dyad for the first time to answer the questionnaire, their average con-

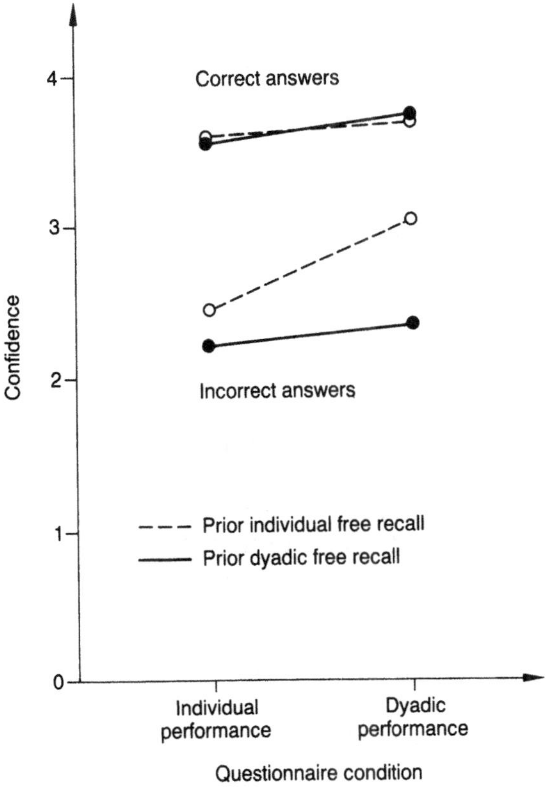

FIGURE 17.6. Confidence for correct and for incorrect answers to questionnaire items

fidence in incorrect answers being misleadingly high, at the "fairly confident" level.

We have additional data which throw light on why those in the ID condition should have felt so confident about all their answers, including those that were incorrect. An analysis of the free recall protocols indicated that the individual protocols contained substantially less information indicating knowledge of the answers to the questionnaire than did the protocols of the dyads. The ID subjects were therefore subject to the greatest contrast in knowledge when they answered the questionnaire, for their dyadic performance on the questionnaire showed the customary superiority. A questionnaire administered after the experiment to all subjects showed that those in the ID condition judged the task to be easier, their partner's contribution to be greater and their partner to be more dominant, than those in the DD condition. In addition, they were less likely to discuss what confidence level they should employ in any particular case. The picture emerges of a substantial diffusion of responsibility in this condition, answers being assumed correct by virtue of the partner having agreed to them.

Conclusions: The Propriety of Collaborative Testimony

Collaborative testimony, at least by police officers, is thoroughly established in English legal proceedings. Is this appropriate? In this concluding section we wish to consider what implications our results have for this question.

It is clearly better that collaborative testimony, when it occurs, should be openly acknowledged, partly to avoid the time-wasting wrangles about the admissibility of evidence, and also to permit the jury to draw their own conclusions about the quality of such evidence. Having said that, it seems to us that there are three main dangers in the practice of collaborative testimony:

1. Potentially useful information is excluded by groups. Bartlett emphasised the importance of what he termed "conventionalisation" in all recall. Groups especially, do adopt a conventional strategy, being more consistent than individuals, and they exclude the more idiosyncratic information characteristic of individual recall.
2. Group remembering encourages collective bias. In the case of police, there is a natural bias arising from their role in our adversarial system of justice. Even under the new Police and Criminal Evidence Act (1984), they and they alone are responsible for the gathering and presentation of evidence. The experiments we have described show clearly that groups have a more definite idea of what is relevant than do individuals, and police officers much more so than students. Group remembering is *selective* remembering, and the police, in the interests of successful prosecution, have every reason to be selective.
3. The practice of permitting one officer to *represent* a group is one which these experiments alone would suggest is of dubious propriety. Undoubtedly, the confidence expressed in that testimony will reflect the objectively undiscriminating confidence of the group. Group remembering inherently embodies conviction.

The final point is perhaps the most important, and raises the more general question of the status of written accounts by police officers as they are employed in legal proceedings. Written police statements, whether or not made collaboratively, are introduced in Court under the "refreshing memory" rule, a rule which Archbold states as follows: "a witness may refresh his memory by reference to any writing made or verified by himself concerning and contemporaneously with the facts of which he testifies." The interpretation of "contemporaneously" is problematic, but it is generally accepted that, to qualify, the events in question must have been "fresh in the mind" when the note was made or verified. The problem is that frequently the document used by police officers to "refresh the memory" is effectively employed as a *substitute* for the memory. Under cross-examination, police frequently refuse to go beyond the written statement they use to "refresh the memory," claiming often that what is written is both an accurate and, moreover, a *complete* account of what occurred or what was said, thereby ruling out effective cross-examination. Moreover, this unshakeable front is reinforced when the written account bears the imprimatur of the group. The account is then an unchangeable text from which no departures can reasonably be made by any one individual member of the group. There is, so far as we are aware, no precedent for the cross-examination of a group.

Individuals should be required to take personal responsibility for testifying to the truth of facts as stated in a written document, and should not be in the position merely of communicating an unalterable group decision to the Court. This view gains yet more point given the clear evidence coming from all the experiments, that objectively the testimony of a group is less valid than the testimony of individuals. All of what a group decides – rightly or wrongly – is given virtually "certain" status. Individuals are more likely to express doubt at appropriate places.

We are, of course, not saying that collaboration between police officers should be excluded in the recording of evidence. Indeed, our evidence suggests that the subsequent testimony of individuals may actually benefit from joint discussion and free recall in writing of the events that had been observed. Together, two individuals produce a more complete account than either does alone, and it is a more clearly focussed account reflecting an agreed estimate of its purpose. This makes a jointly produced document of some value in its own right, and it no doubt has a strategic value in the prosecution process. It may serve to focus the mind on material that is relevant to the prosecution decision, and the joint product may benefit, in the case of officers who have worked together in the past, from the teamwork, or "transactive" memory processes, as described by Wegner (1986). However, the subsequent evidence of the two individuals, as individuals, can (a) reveal more than is contained in the collaborative statement and (b) be more testimonially valid than their future combined performance, or performance by just one officer as a "representative" merely testifying to the truth of the joint statement. By permitting collaborative testimony in Court, we simultaneously suppress facts known only to individuals, and squander the potential benefits of earlier collaboration.

References

Bartlett, F. C. (1932). *Remembering: a study in experimental and social psychology.* Cambridge: Cambridge University Press.

Bass v., R. (1953). *All England Law Reports, 1,* 1064–1068.

Clark, N. K. (1987). *The analysis and prediction of individual and group remembering.* Ph. D. thesis, University of Kent.

Clark, N. K., Stephenson, G. M., & Kniveton, B. K. (1986). Script-writers or story-tellers? The consequences of divergent recall strategies for police officers. Paper presented at B.P.S. Annual Conference, April, Sheffield.

Clark, N. K., Stephenson, G. M., & Rutter, D. R. (1986). Memory for a complex social discourse: the analysis and prediction of individual and group recall. *Journal of Memory and Language, 25,* 295–313.

Edwards, D., & Middleton, D. (in press). Joint remembering: constructing an account of shared experience. *Discourse Processes, 19*, 423–459.

Hartwick, J., Sheppard, B.H., & Davis, J.H. (1982). Group remembering: research and implications. In R.A. Guzzo (Ed.), *Improving group decision making in organisations* (pp. 41–72). London: Academic.

Hollin, C.R., & Clifford, B.R. (1983). Eyewitness testimony: the effects of discussion on recall accuracy and agreement. *Journal of Applied Social Psychology, 13*, 234–244.

Janis, I.L. (1972). *Victims of groupthink.* Boston: Houghton Mifflin.

Martin, J. (1982). Stories and scripts in organizational settings. In A.H. Hastorf & A.M. Isen (Eds.), *Cognitive social psychology.* Oxford: Elsevier.

Myers, D.G. (1983). Polarising effects of social interaction. In J.H. Davis & G. Stocker-Kreichgauer (Eds.), *Group decision processes.* London: Academic.

Perlmutter, H.V. (1953). Group memory of meaningful material. *Journal of Psychology, 35*, 361–370.

Shirley, J. (1983, August 14). How the police beat the police. *Sunday Times,* p. 4.

Steiner, I.D. (1972). *Group process and productivity.* London: Academic.

Stephenson, G.M., & Wagner, W. (1988). Origins of the misplaced confidence effect in collaborative recall. *Applied Cognitive Psychology* (forthcoming)

Stephenson, G.M., Brandstätter, H., & Wagner, W. (1982). An experimental study of social performance and delay on the testimonial validity of story telling. *European Journal of Social Psychology, 13,* 175–191.

Stephenson, G.M., Abrams, D., Wagner, W., & Wade, G. (1986). Partners in recall: collaborative order in the recall of a police interrogation. *British Journal of Social Psychology, 25*, 341–343.

Vansina, J. (1973). *Oral tradition: a study in historical methodology.* Harmondsworth: Penguin Books.

Wegner, D.M. (1986). Transactive Memory. In B. Mullen & G.R. Goethals (Eds.), *General theories of group behaviour.* New York: Springer.

Wegner, D.M., Guiliano, T., & Hertel, P.T. (1985). Cognitive interdependence in close relationships. In W. Ickes (Ed.), *Compatible and incompatible relationships* (pp. 253–276). New York: Springer

18 Behavioral Correlates of Statement Credibility: Theories, Paradigms, and Results

GÜNTER KÖHNKEN

Basic Concepts and Research Approaches to Witness Psychology

A central goal of each trial process is the reconstruction of past events. The available information, whether it be factual evidence or verbal statements of the accused or of eyewitnesses, has to be evaluated in the light of this basic task. In the case of factual evidence, the evaluation task is basically a question of interpretation of facts while the facts themselves are only seldom in question. Things are quite different, however, if the evaluation has to be based on witness statements. Witness statements cannot be taken at face value. There are, in fact, numerous factors which might lead to discrepancies between the actual course of past events and details of a statement. The degree of congruence between a statement and the original stimuli will be referred to as the *reliability* of that statement. The various reasons for unreliable witness accounts can be classified into two basically different groups of factors:

First, witnesses, although trying to give a correct and complete report of an event or a precise description of a person, may be subject to unconscious and unintended errors, caused for example by simple forgetting, suboptimal perception conditions, misleading postevent information, or biased instructions (see, e.g., Clifford & Bull, 1978; Davies, Ellis, & Shepherd, 1981; Lloyd-Bostock & Clifford, 1983; Loftus, 1979; Shepherd, Ellis, & Davies, 1982; Wegener, Köhnken, & Steller, in press; Wells & Loftus, 1984, for reviews of this line of research). These factors affect an aspect of the reliability of a statement which will be referred to as the *accuracy*.

Alternatively, a witness may try to deceive the court, i.e., withhold, falsify, or substitute information with the deliberate intent of fostering in another person a belief or understanding which the deceiving witness knows to be false or invalid (an operationalization of deception that is shared by most researchers in the field, see, e.g., Krauss, Geller, & Olson, 1976; Miller, Bauchner, Hocking, Fontes, Kaminski, & Brandt, 1981; Zuckerman, DePaulo, & Rosenthal, 1981). The intention or motivation to tell the truth or to lie will be referred to as the *credibility* of a statement.

These two perspectives of unreliability of witness statements correspond with two distinct approaches of experimental research. Almost all experiments in the realm of witness *accuracy* have been designed to examine the effects of particular factors on the accuracy of witness accounts. This type of research may therefore be designated as *factorial.* The knowledge which is based on factorial research allows an estimation of the likelihood that a given factor has affected the accuracy of a statement or, if the factor is under the control of the criminal justice system, avoidance of particular impairments caused by that factor. For example, if we know that biased instructions increase the likelihood of false positive identifications, then the police can be instructed to use neutral or unbiased lineup instructions in order to avoid identification errors (Köhnken, 1984; Malpass & Devine, 1984). While this type of knowledge has considerably increased during the past two or three decades, our instruments for evaluating the accuracy of a given testimony by applying certain evaluative criteria are still very limited. One of the few consistent results that we currently have is the fact that subjective confidence is obviously *not* a valid indicator of accuracy (Deffenbacher, 1980; Stephenson, 1984; Wells & Murray, 1984). Only very recently attempts have been made to investigate whether the accuracy of witness statements can be assessed on the basis of certain characteristics of the verbal behavior (Schooler, Gerhard, & Loftus, 1986).

On the other hand, the research on the *credibility* of witness statements has almost exclusively been evaluative, i.e., the investigations have primarily been designed to analyze the potential of certain behavioral criteria to discriminate reliably between true and deceptive statements. As a consequence of this research emphasis, there are still considerable deficits in our empirical knowledge concerning the factors which might increase or decrease the likelihood of deceptive witness statements.

In this chapter, the theoretical backgrounds and the basic research paradigms of evaluative research on statement credibility will be reviewed. The methodological procedures which have been used in previous research will be discussed with regard to the particular conditions of witness statements (as opposed, for example, to other fields of communication and interaction in social psychology). Modifications and extensions of the previous research strategies and procedures will be proposed which are assumed to be more representative and ecologically valid for the situation of witness statement analysis.

Theoretical Approaches to Credibility Assessment

The basic prerequisite of any reliable assessment of credibility is the assumption that truth or deception can be inferred from some kind of overt indicators which are consistently related to credibility. Two fundamentally different strategies for the search for such indicators of credibility have been discussed in the literature. In early approaches, a personality construct of "general trustworthiness" was assumed, and it was suggested that this trait determines whether a witness tells the truth in a particular statement. Credibility thus was ascribed to the *witnesses* rather than to their *evidence* (Stone, 1984). Therefore, the general reputation of the witness, his or her life style, personal history, and especially whether he or she had ever lied before would be the crucial pieces of information for the evaluation of the veracity of a particular statement. If this retrospective analysis led to the assumption of a generally unreliable character, it would be concluded in a kind of extrapolation that the current statement was not truthful.

This approach of general trustworthiness has been seriously questioned, particularly by Undeutsch (1967, 1982, 1984). It is, in fact, a trivial and everyday experience that a generally honest person may have particular motives for lying under certain circumstances and that a person of bad reputation may tell the truth concerning a particular issue (Stone, 1984). This experience has also received scientific support from modern approaches to personality theory, i.e., interactionistic views (Magnusson & Endler, 1977). According to Undeutsch (1967, 1984), not the general honesty of the witness but the truthfulness of the present statement has to be determined.

This view of credibility assessment has important implications for the investigation of overt indicators of truth and deception. If lying or truth-telling is primarily a situation-specific behavior (a view which is now widely accepted by psychologists though not consistently by jurists), then overt and diagnostically relevant clues to deception could only be found in behaviors closely related to the critical statement itself. Based on this view, behavioral correlates of truth and deception could possibly be found in four behavioral areas:

1. The content of the statement under consideration (e.g., the amount of detail, the logical consistency, the account of unusual details; see Arntzen, 1983; Köhnken & Steller, 1988; Littmann & Szewczyk, 1983; Steller & Köhnken, 1988; Undeutsch, 1984);
2. The way the statement is verbally presented, i.e., the speech or extralinguistic behavior (e.g., speech rate, filled pauses, speech disturbances, richness of vocabulary; see DePaulo, Rosenthal, Rosenkrantz, & Green, 1982; DePaulo, Stone, & Lassiter, 1985a; Köhnken, 1985);
3. The accompanying nonverbal behavior of the witness (e.g., gaze, smiling, gestures, shrugs, adaptors, foot and leg movements; see DePaulo et al., 1985a; Köhnken, 1986; Zuckerman & Driver, 1985; Zuckerman et al., 1981);
4. Psychophysiological phenomena (e.g., electrodermal responses, blood pressure, heart rate, respiratory rate; see Horvarth, 1984; Steller, 1987; Waid & Orne, 1981).

In the context of witness statement analysis, the psychophysiological phenomena are of only limited value, since the traditional approaches to physiological detection of deception, particularly the guilty knowledge technique (cf. Podlesny & Raskin, 1977; Steller, 1987), require detailed and reliable information about the event in question. This information, however, is not available, otherwise the evaluation of witness statements would not be necessary. Hence, diagnostically relevant indicators of the veracity of a statement could only be found in three behavioral systems: (1) the content of the statement, (2) the accompanying extralinguistic behavior, and (3) the nonverbal behavior.

Are there theoretically anchored reasons for expecting consistent behavioral correlates of truth and deception within these behavioral systems? According to Zuckerman et al. (1981), deception is no basic affect and it is, therefore, unlikely that it will be directly associated with specific verbal or nonverbal expressions. Thus, no particular "lie-symptom" can be expected (DePaulo et al., 1985a; Köhnken, 1982, 1985; Stone, 1984; Zuckerman et al., 1981). Deceiving or truth-telling does, however, involve various fundamental processes which in turn may be expected to influence overt behavior (Ekman, 1981, 1985; Ekman & Friesen, 1969; Kraut 1980; Zuckerman et al., 1981). Four such processes have been discussed in relation to credibility assessment: attempted control, arousal, felt emotion, and cognitive processes.

1. Attempted control. According to Zuckerman et al. (1981), people try to conceal their deceptions by means of a controlled restraint of behavior. However, in their attempt to avoid possible clues to deception they may exhibit a behavioral pattern that appears planned, trained, not spontaneous, or unnatural. Furthermore, since not all behavioral channels can be controlled equally well, discrepancies between various behaviors may occur, i.e., inconsistent or even contradicting messages from different communication channels (e.g. Zuckerman, Driver, & Koestner, 1982). According to Ekman (1981, 1985), the verbal channel, for example, can be more effectively controlled than the various nonverbal channels, because it has a greater sending capacity and senders are more practiced in its use and control. This view implies that a deception may not best be detected by the analysis of a single behavior, but rather by a holistic approach involving the simultaneous evaluation and comparison of different behavioral systems.

2. Arousal. Research on physiological detection of deception has shown that truthful and deceptive answers to particular questions are accompanied by different intensities of physiological processes (Podlesny & Raskin, 1977; Raskin, 1982; Steller, 1987; Waid & Orne, 1981). According to the conditioned response hypothesis, lies are accompanied by autonomic responses because the critical questions are by themselves associated with traumatic experiences. From a conflict theoretical point of view, the psychophysiological responses are the result of conflicting tendencies to lie and to tell the truth. The punishment hypothesis states that the mental anticipation of a punishment which would be contingent on an uncovering of the lie produces an increased physiological reactivity. These processes may also influence the nonverbal and extralinguistic behavior of a deceiver (DeTurck & Miller, 1985; Hemsley, 1977; Scherer, 1984;

Scherer & Bergmann, 1984). According to Hemsley (1977), this state of increased arousal should cause an increase in frequency and intensity of nonverbal behaviors.

3. The affect theory assumes that lies are closely related to certain affective states, particularly guilt about engaging in deception and anxiety about being discovered. In addition to these negative emotions, positive affects may also appear. Ekman (1985) has suggested that the deceiver may feel proud or joyful as a consequence of an apparently successful deception and called this affect "duping delight." The involved emotions may result in negative or nonimmediate behaviors. According to Ekman and Friesen (1972) anxiety may cause increases in the occurrence of adaptors and illustrators.

4. Cognitive approaches to deception seem to be particularly important in the context of statement credibility assessment. They are based on the central assumption that the creation of a deceptive statement is a more difficult task than telling the truth about a certain event (Köhnken, 1982). Usually, the police or the court already has some information concerning the critical event. In addition, the witness is usually required to give repeated statements to the police, the court, and perhaps a psychological expert. Records or even transcripts of these statements are kept in the case file and are available to the court. Thus, the deceiver has to take care that he does not produce any inconsistencies or even contradictions to these known facts and his own previous statements. This should cause a higher load of working memory and increased cognitive efforts for the necessary control and comparison processes. Since the overall amount of processing resources is limited, the performance of other, less important tasks should be impaired (Köhnken, 1982, 1985). The impairment of speech production as a consequence of information overload has, for example, been demonstrated by Goldman-Eisler (1968) and, in the context of the analysis of statement credibility, by Köhnken (1985).

These information processing approaches have primarily been discussed with regard to nonverbal and extralinguistic behavior. Things are less clear, however, as far as content-related criteria of credibility are concerned. While Arntzen (1983) does not explicitly discuss any theoretical model at all, Undeutsch (1967, 1984) states a working hypothesis according to which "truthful accounts of self-experienced real events differ in certain characteristics from entirely or partially invented stories" (1984, p. 57). This hypothesis is primarily based on the assumption that a witness will generally not be able to create an invented statement with content qualities comparable to those contained in a report on an observed real event. However, the hypothesis is rather global and makes no specified predictions as to which particular content characteristics will be different in true and deceptive statements.

There are, however, some general theories which can be applied to the explanation of content-related correlates of statement credibility. Script and schema theories (Brewer & Nakamura, 1984; Graesser & Nakamura, 1982;

Lilli, this volume; Schank & Abelson, 1977; Wippich, this volume) predict, for example, that fabricated statements would primarily be constructed from the person's general knowledge contained in scripts or schemas. Thus, we would not expect unusual accounts from a deceiving witness or phenomenal accounts of details which were not understood. These details are, by definition, not part of the schema-based knowledge and can, therefore, not be constructed from schema knowledge alone. Furthermore, a systematic application of general theories of memory and social cognition (e.g., Pryor & Day, 1985; Wyer & Srull, 1984, 1986) to statement content analysis would probably allow a more precise definition with higher discriminating power of certain criteria. If, for example, the statement could be divided into schema-related and non-schema-related parts, we would expect more pronounced differences between true and deceptive reports in those aspects which are not elements of a schema. The finding that reality-based statements contain more details than invented stories (Köhnken & Wegener, 1982) may primarily be due to the non-schema-related parts of the statements.

The predictions from these theories are, at least as far as nonverbal and extralinguistic behaviors are concerned, not mutually exclusive. Pupil dilation, for example, may be expected as a correlate of deception on the basis of an arousal approach as well as from the assumption that deceptions produce a greater cognitive load (cf. Kahneman, 1973). A clear decision in favor of one of these models is, therefore, impossible. The observed behavioral correlates of truth and deception are probably the result of an interaction of several basic processes, including the automatic occurrence of arousal- or emotion-related behaviors, the attempt to control these behavioral changes, and the cognitive capacity for the performance of various control processes (Köhnken, 1986).

Research Paradigms and Procedures

Research on the analysis of truth and deception has been conducted from two different perspectives. One approach has focused around the *encoding* or *expression* side of credibility and has attempted to determine objectively measurable behavioral correlates of truth and deception. Another approach is primarily concerned with the *decoder's* perspective or the *impression* side of credibility. From this point of view it has been investigated whether judges are able to detect deceptive messages and which behaviors are associated with judgments of deception. These two perspectives can be combined to form a more general model of nonverbal communication which was originally proposed by Scherer (1978, 1982) and is modified here to illustrate the process of credibility assessment (see Figure 18.1).

The model is based on the assumption that traits or transient states are externalized in the form of distal cues in a person's appearance and behavior. In the theoretical discussion it has been argued that the intention to deceive or

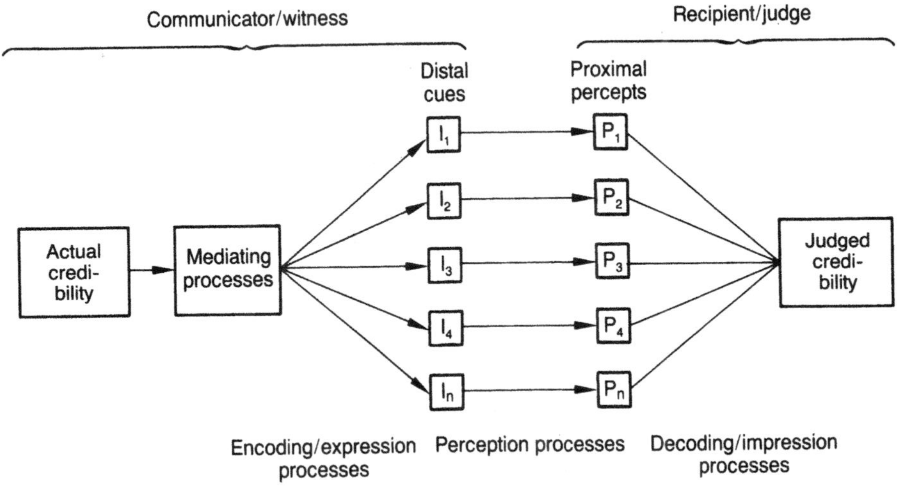

FIGURE 18.1. Modified Brunswickian lens model

to tell the truth is *not directly* externalized in distal cues but only mediated by basic psychological processes like arousal and cognitive effort. Thus, although usually designated as "behavioral correlates of credibility," these behaviors are actually correlates of the mediating processes. An additional inferential step is necessary to draw any conclusion regarding the credibility of a statement.

The distal cues are the input to the perceptual process of the judge, whose attribution of credibility is assumed to be based on his proximal percepts of the distal cues and the processing of this input according to certain inferential decision-making strategies. Behavioral cues to deception are, however, not the only input for the judgment of statement credibility, as we shall see later.

In the basic paradigm for the study of behavioral correlates of credibility, subjects are instructed to give either true or deceptive reports on certain issues. Their verbal, extralinguistic, and/or nonverbal behavior is then analyzed with particular coding systems and the average occurrence frequencies or intensities of various behaviors during true and deceptive messages are compared. In a typical experiment, subjects are asked to take 1 min to describe someone they like, dislike, dominate, and submit to (or feel indifferent or ambivalent about). Each of these target persons is described in two modes – truth and deception. In the truthful mode, subjects are instructed to describe their true feelings towards the target. In the deceptive mode, they are asked to convince the interviewer that their feelings are opposite to what they actually feel (e.g., DePaulo & Rosenthal, 1979; DePaulo, Rosenthal, Rosenkrantz & Green, 1982; Zuckerman, Amidon, Bishop, & Pomerantz, 1982; Zuckerman, Kernis, Driver, & Koestner, 1984; Zuckerman, Koestner, & Alton, 1984). Usually, only the middle 20 s of the videotaped messages are used for the coding and comparison of behaviors. In some experiments, other deception tasks have been used, including, for example, interviews with a critical question concerning the subject's grade point average (Cody & O'Hair, 1983), descriptions of film contents (Köhnken, 1985; Köhnken & Wegener, 1982) or pictures (Riggio & Friedman, 1983), description of own feelings while viewing pleasant or highly distressing film sequences (Ekman & Friesen, 1974; Ekman, Friesen, & Scherer, 1976), and positive feedback from teachers for good or poor performance of their students (Feldman, 1976; Feldman, Devin-Sheehan, & Allen, 1978).

The same variety of deception tasks has been used for the investigation of the impression side or decoder's perspective of the lens model, i.e., the judgment of truth and deception. Usually, the senders are audio- or videotaped during message production and a sample of these tape recordings with true and deceptive statements is then presented to the decoders with the instruction to judge each message according to its credibility. In almost all experiments, untrained and unexperienced subjects have been used as judges. The only basis for their judgments is the sender's verbal or nonverbal behavior, i.e., they usually have no additional information concerning the sender, the content of their messages, possible motivational factors, the background of their judgment task, etc.

The basic question underlying this line of research concerns the accuracy of judges in discriminating between true and deceptive statements. This differentiation between truth and deceit is usually referred to as *deception accuracy* (cf. DePaulo et al., 1985a; Ekman & Friesen, 1969). To assess whether certain channels of communication are more revealing than others, judges are provided with particularly edited stimulus material. In many experiments, for example, videorecordings of the sender's face or body, audiorecordings of the voice, and written transcripts of the statements are prepared and presented to the judges in isolation or in various combinations with the other sources (e.g., DePaulo, Lanier, & Davies, 1983; DePaulo, Lassiter, & Stone, 1982; DePaulo, Rosenthal, Green, & Rosenkrantz, 1982). Some recent studies have examined whether the ability to discriminate between true and deceptive statements can be improved by experience or training (Köhnken, 1987; Zuckerman, Koestner, & Colella, 1985; Zuckerman, Koestner, & Alton, 1984) or whether professionals with some amount of experience in detecting deception are more successful than subjects without such experience (DePaulo & Pfeifer, 1986; Köhnken, 1987; Kraut & Poe, 1980).

Correlates of Credibility: Empirical Results

Several recent meta-analyses on more than 40 experimental studies on behavioral correlates of deception (DePaulo et al., 1985a; Zuckerman & Driver, 1985; Zuckerman et al., 1981) provide empirical evidence that there are in fact substantial associations between the credibility of a message and overt behaviors. DePaulo et al. (1985a), for example, demonstrated that of 24 different verbal, nonverbal, and extralinguistic behaviors, 14 were significantly related to credibility. In the area of extralinguistic behavior, liars, on the average, engage in more and/or longer speech hesitations, produce more speech errors such as stutter, repetition, and grammatical errors, and show longer response latencies. Another stable finding shows an increase in voice pitch during deceptive communication. The nonverbal behavior of deceivers is characterized by increased frequencies of eyeblinks and dilated pupils. In addition, they show self-manipulating gestures like scratching, hair-pulling, manipulation of objects, etc. (adaptors). The content of deceptive messages includes more irrelevant information than true reports, and more negative and overgeneralized statements which are also less immediate. Comparisons of different communication channels provide evidence for the hypothesis that liars will show more interchannel discrepancies. Their reports appear more rehearsed and less spontaneous than do true statements.

This pattern of behavioral correlates of credibility is the result of purely quantitative meta-analyses and as such represents average group differences across various studies. The group differences in the single experimental studies are themselves averages across subjects. Hence, the finding of significant associations between credibility and various behaviors does not mean that all studies have revealed the same results or that all subjects exhibit identical and consistent clues to deception. While response patterns of single subjects are almost never published, there is some evidence of contradictory results on the level of single experimental studies. To give but one example, Cutrow, Parks, Lucas, and Thomas (1972) and Hocking and Leathers (1980) reported decreases in eyeblink frequencies during deception, while Hemsley and Doob (1979) observed substantial increases in eyeblinks. Inspection of the tables in the Zuckerman et al. (1981) review reveals that this is not the only example of contradictory results. Contradictory change patterns like these may lead to the final result that existing differences between truth and deception cancel each other out.

Quantitative meta-analyses are powerful tools for theoretical analyses and the estimation of the reliability and stability of research results on a certain issue. However, the knowledge of *average* differences between groups is not a sufficient basis for the evaluation of *particular* statements. For this task, more detailed information is needed concerning the conditions under which certain behavioral changes are to be expected. One approach to this problem has been the examination of certain personality constructs in relation to correlates of credibility such as machiavellianism (Christie & Geis, 1970; Exline, Thibaut, Hickey, & Gumpert 1970), gender (Cody & O'Hair, 1983; DePaulo, Rosenthal, Rosenkrantz, & Green, 1982; Feldman & White, 1980; Mehrabian, 1971), age (DePaulo & Jordan, 1982; DePaulo, Jordan, Irvine, & Laser, 1982; Feldman, Jenkins, & Popoola, 1979; Morency & Krauss, 1982), and self-monitoring (Miller et al., 1983; Riggio & Friedman, 1983). The results of this line of research are at present not sufficient for individual decisions on credibility, too, but they may explain to some extent the inconsistencies obtained across studies.

Another promising attempt is the examination of situational factors which might moderate observable clues to deception. Particularly the degree of motivation for successful lying has been considered an important variable with regard to witness statements (e.g., Miller & Burgoon, 1981). Zuckerman et al. (1981) and Zuckerman and Driver (1985) have therefore performed separate meta-analyses on studies with high and low motivation conditions. Contrary to what might be expected, the general result of these analyses demonstrates that highly motivated senders exhibit more clues to deception than their less motivated counterparts. In addition, liars with high and low motivation to succeed with their lies show different behavioral changes during deception. Highly motivated subjects, for example, seem to increase their eyeblink frequency while senders with low motivation blink less (Köhnken, 1986). Other situational factors which have been examined are unprepared vs. planned and rehearsed deceptive statements (Cody & O'Hair, 1983; Miller et al., 1983), and the publicness of interaction between the deceiver and the interviewer (Feldman et al., 1979; Krauss et al., 1976).

To summarize this line of research, several meta-analyses have convincingly demonstrated that there are in fact behavioral correlates of credibility. These results, however, reflect a high degree of abstraction and therefore are not easily applicable to the evaluation of the credibility of particular statements. Some of the observed inconsistencies on the level of single studies may be resolved by differential analyses with regard to various personality and situational variables.

Judgments of Credibility: Empirical Results

Research on judgments of credibility has primarily examined to what extent people are able to discriminate between true and deceptive messages, on which behavioral cues of the sender they base their judgments, and how different sources of information (i.e., access to different communication channels) and their various combinations influence the judgments.

Apparently, people are somewhat sensitive to the credibility of messages. In most studies, the overall accuracy rate of lie detection typically falls in a range of 45% – 60% when 50% accuracy is expected by chance alone (DePaulo et al., 1985a; Kraut, 1980; Zuckerman et al., 1981). Although not impressive, deception accuracy exceeds chance in almost all published studies. If accuracy at detecting lies is computed separately from accuracy at detecting the truth, results usually show a truthfulness bias, i.e., truthful messages are identified with more accuracy then deceptive ones (Zuckerman et al., 1981).

Theoretically, accuracy in detecting deceptions should be low if only highly controllable communication channels like the face or the message content are available to the judge. The combined results of more than 30 studies support this expectation for the face, but not for the verbal channel. If judges only have access to facial cues, their accuracy scores do not exceed chance level. Furthermore, judges performed even worse when facial cues were available in combination with other channels, compared with the same channel or multichannel combinations not including the face. Obviously, facial cues provide misleading information to the judges, resulting in a decrease of deception accuracy. Contrary to expectation, however, the words of the message, i.e., the verbal content, play an important role in the successful detection of deception. Deception accuracy increases significantly when words are added to content-filtered voice cues and even a transcript alone enables judges to reach considerable accuracy rates. "The assumption that nonverbal channels are more important in the communication of deception than the verbal cues is simply not true" (Zuckerman et al., 1981, p. 27). However, another picture may emerge if judgment accuracy for highly and weakly motivated senders is computed separately. A study by DePaulo et al. (1983) shows that only if the senders were not highly motivated to lie successfully were their lies most easily detected from verbal cues. Under conditions of high motivation, however, the verbal content did not contribute any relevant information for the judgment of credibility.

Which behaviors are interpreted by judges as indicative of deception? An answer to this question may be important for attempts to improve deception accuracy. If, for example, judges overestimate the informativeness of faking channels like the face or underutilize highly discriminative cues, they should achieve only poor accuracy scores. Research on perceived cues to deception shows that this is, at least in part, the case. Judges generally rate messages as more deceptive if senders smile less, gaze less, and show fewer postural shifts. In the field of extralinguistic behavior, statements are perceived as more deceptive if senders speak more hesitantly and slowly, with higher voice pitch, and with various speech errors (see DePaulo, Rosenthal, Rosenkrantz, & Green, 1982; DePaulo et al., 1985a). While cues like smiling, gaze, response latency, or speech rate are actually not significantly related to credibility and therefore should mislead the judges, they underestimate the power of pupil dilation and adaptors.

Recently, attempts have been made to improve the accuracy of detecting deception. DePaulo, Lassiter, and Stone (1982) found that simply directing subject's attention to the more revealing communication channels increased their ability to discriminate truth from deceit significantly. In two studies, Zuckerman et al. (1984) and Zuckerman et al. (1985) investigated the effects of feedback on learning to detect deception. The results of these experiments show that feedback had some positive effects on deception accuracy for lies enacted by the same sender but no or only small benefits for the judgments of other senders' messages. In a study with police officers as judges and deception tasks with a higher similarity to witness statements, Köhnken (1987) found no training effects of special instructions for the observation and evaluation of verbal and nonverbal behavior in relation to credibility. Furthermore, DePaulo and Pfeifer (1986) did not find any beneficial effects of on-the-job training in detecting deception.

To summarize, the empirical evidence suggests that judges are able to discriminate between truthful and deceptive messages slightly but significantly above chance. Deception accuracy for highly motivated liars is generally better than for senders with low motivation, particularly if judges have access to nonverbal and extralinguistic behaviors as opposed to the verbal content of messages and facial cues. Attempts to improve deception accuracy by training showed some beneficial effects within senders, but not across different senders.

Suggestions for Procedural Modifications in Future Research

The majority of research on behavioral correlates and judgments of deception has been conducted in the area of everyday communication and interaction. These settings and not the evaluation of witness statements have been considered as "more important for more of the people more of the time" (DePaulo et al., 1985a, p. 334). This perspective of research on deception has of course had consequences for the construction and selection of experimental procedures and particularly of deception tasks. If we are primarily interested in "everyday, interpersonal context in which people might lie to make a good impression, to ingratiate themselves, or to keep the social machinery running smoothly" (DePaulo et al., 1985a, p. 334), then deception tasks in which, for example, senders conceal their negative attitudes towards other people may be appropriate. If, however, the evaluation of witness statement credibility is the focus of our interest, then different experimental procedures and deception tasks are required which are more similar to the typical characteristics of witness situations. In the following section, some suggestions for procedural modifications will be outlined and discussed.

The most important modifications in studies on behavioral correlates of credibility as well as on judgments of credibility concern the characteristics of the deception tasks. Several authors have emphasized that behavioral correlates of deception may vary with context, particularly with the characteristics of the deception task (e.g., DePaulo et al., 1985a; Kraut, 1980; Zuckerman et al., 1981). A taxonomy of relevant dimensions of witness statements may, therefore, be helpful in determining the generalizability of research findings obtained with certain procedures. Table 18.1 lists some of the potentially relevant variables for the classification of witness statements with regard to credibility assessment.

Only a small segment of this broad spectrum of possible deception tasks has been examined in previous research. In addition, Stone's (1984) extensive discussion of circumstances under which the issue of credibility arises in court practice demonstrates that this segment is probably not very characteristic of witness statements. It is rather unlikely that witnesses will be required to give statements on their feelings and attitudes towards other people (Miller &

TABLE 18.1. Some potentially relevant dimensions of witness statements with regard to credibility assessment

Length of the statement (short vs. long)
Verifiability of the content (verifiable vs. not verifiable)
Availability of other pieces of evidence
Complexity of the reported event (complex vs. simple)
Amount of schematic knowledge of the witness on the event in question
Duration of the reported event (short/singular vs. long/repeated)
Emotionality of the reported event (emotionally arousing vs. neutral)
Type of possible lie (concealment, exaggeration, creation of new details)
Direction of the statement (allegation vs. exoneration)
Scope of possible deception (single details vs. whole statement)
Personal involvement (uninvolved bystander vs. participant or victim)
Sequence of statements (first report vs. repeated report)

Burgoon, 1981). Instead, they are asked about social situations and events, physical environments, personal appearances, clothing, etc. This constitutes a tremendous difference from the standard deception tasks used in many previous experiments. Feelings and attitudes are private "events," not verifiable for the experimenter or the subject-judges. By contrast, factual statements on social events have to be fitted into physical and social environments, time schedules, etc. Usually there are other pieces of evidence or other witness accounts which would allow the police or the jury to check and countercheck the statements of a witness. It is obvious that under these conditions considerably more sophisticated and complex control procedures have to be performed by the deceiving witness than for the confabulation of private feelings. Furthermore, witness statements in critical cases are usually longer than 1 min. The longer the interrogation takes, the more difficult it becomes for the witness to keep track of his story and to avoid logical inconsistencies between various parts of his statement and external facts. People who might get away with a 1-minute lie may have considerable problems in successfully deceiving law enforcement professionals with 1-hour lies. The deceiver's task becomes even more complicated with repeated interrogations. Usually, witness accounts are transcribed or at least summarized and entered in the file. This material is therefore available in later interrogations to the police but not to the witness. Thus, the deceiver has not only to take care of possible contradictions and inconsistencies with external facts like social situations, time schedules, physical environments, and other details of his present statement, but also with his own previous reports. As a result, the construction of a false statement should be a much more difficult and cognitively demanding task for the deceiver than the construction of the typical lies on private feelings in previous experimental studies.

Another critical issue concerns the procedures of data analysis. Almost all our knowledge on behavioral correlates of credibility is based on average group differences of occurrence frequencies which are themselves averaged across each single statement as a whole. This double averaging may, however, cover potential individual and/or time-dependent clues to deception. If, for example, different individuals show varying or even contradictory behavior changes during deception (depending, perhaps, on the initial or "normal" behavioral patterns), these changes will cancel each other out when they are averaged across subjects. In the case of extended statements, the occurrence of deception cues may also be limited to certain parts of the statement. Averaging across the whole statement may then also cover actually existing cues. *Intraindividual* comparisons between true and deceptive statements of the *same senders* and the analysis of the *process* of generating the statement may, therefore, provide more precise and diagnostically relevant information for the assessment of statement credibility (Köhnken, 1986).

The suggested modifications of the deception tasks are also important from the lie detector's perspective, since the detection of deceptive statements may become easier as the task difficulty for the deceiver increases. The overall accuracy scores reported in previous experiments may, therefore, underestimate the actual accuracy at detecting deception in contexts which are more similar to witness situations. This may particularly be the case if law enforcement professionals instead of undergraduate psychology students are used as subject-judges. The few studies which have involved police officers or customs inspectors as judges (DePaulo & Pfeifer, 1986; Köhnken, 1987; Kraut & Poe, 1980) did not show any superiority in comparison to inexperienced students, but this may be due to the relatively artificial deception tasks which were used as stimulus material.

Another important procedural aspect concerns the structure of the judgment task. The typical judgment context which has been used in previous experiments was relatively unstructured, compared with the highly structured interrogation procedure in physiological detection of deception. This has led to ambiguities in the interpretation of behavioral cues, i.e., it is sometimes unclear whether certain behavioral cues have to be perceived as indicative of deception or of deception-unrelated arousal.

Finally, a more detailed analysis of the judgmental process seems to be necessary. The judgment of statement credibility must be conceived as an impression formation and decision-making process. The nonverbal, extralinguistic, and content-related cues are probably only one source of input to this process. Another source is the judge's general knowledge or beliefs regarding contextual factors which might motivate witnesses to lie or to tell the truth and his stereotypes of behavioral clues to deception. Research on communicator credibility in the context of attitude change and persuasion has demonstrated that subjectively ascribed motivational factors might influence the evaluation of messages *independent* of accompanying behaviors (Hass, 1981; Petty & Caccioppo, 1981). The interpretation of particular behavioral cues may vary according to these background variables and lead to different final decisions. In addition to this general background knowledge, the judge usually has some information concerning the details of the particular case. This information may come from other witness statements, from other pieces of evidence, or from his basic world knowledge. The analysis of the judgmental process may be incomplete without taking into consideration this general and case-specific background knowledge. Furthermore, among other factors, cognitive heuristics (Sherman & Corty, 1984), the relationships between memory and judgment (Hastie & Park, 1986) and between judgment and decision (Pitz & Sachs, 1984), and the learning from experience in decision making (Einhorn, 1980) obviously play an important role in the judgment of statement credibility. Future research should, therefore, conceive the judgment of statement credibility as a social judgment and decision-making task with more input variables than only the witnesses' behavior and include these factors in the experimental designs.

References

Arntzen, F. (1983). *Psychologie der Zeugenaussage. Systematik der Glaubwürdigkeitsmerkmale.* München: Beck.

Brewer, W. F., & Nakamura, G. V. (1984). The nature and functions of schemas. In R. S. Wyer & T. K. Srull (Eds.), *Handbook of social cognition:* Vol. 1 (pp. 119–160). Hillsdale, NJ: Erlbaum.

Christie, R., & Geis, F. L. (Eds.). (1970). Studies in machiavellianism. New York: Academic.

Clifford, B., & Bull, R. (1978). *The psychology of person identification.* London: Routledge and Kegan Paul.

Cody, M. J., & O'Hair, H. D., (1983). Nonverbal communication and deception: differences in deception cues due to gender and communicator dominance. *Communication Monographs, 50,* 175–192.

Cutrow, R. J., Parks, A., Lucas, N., & Thomas, K. (1972). The objective use of multiple physiological indices in the detection of deception. *Psychophysiology, 9,* 578–588.

Davies, G. M., Ellis, H. D., Shepherd, J. W. (Eds.). (1981). Perceiving and remembering faces. London: Academic.

Deffenbacher, K. A. (1980). Eyewitness accuracy and confidence: Can we infer anything about their relationship? *Law and Human Behavior, 4,* 243–260.

DePaulo, B. M., & Jordan, A. (1982). Age changes in deceiving and detecting deceit. In R. S. Feldman (Ed.), *Development of nonverbal behavior in children* (pp. 151–180). New York: Springer.

DePaulo, B. M., & Pfeifer, R. L. (1986). On-the-job experience and skill at detecting deception. *Journal of Applied Social Psychology, 16,* 249–267.

DePaulo, B. M., & Rosenthal, R. (1979). Ambivalence, discrepancy, and deception in nonverbal communication. In R. Rosenthal (Ed.), *Skill in nonverbal communication* (pp. 204–248). Cambridge, MA: Oelgeschlager.

DePaulo, B. M., Jordan, A., Irvine, A., & Laser, P. S. (1982). Age changes in the detection of deception. *Child Development, 53,* 701–709.

DePaulo, B. M., Lassiter, G. D., & Stone, J. I. (1982). Attentional determinants of success at detecting deception and truth. *Personality and Social Psychology Bulletin, 8,* 273–279.

DePaulo, B. M., Rosenthal, R., Green, C. R., & Rosenkrantz, J. (1982). Diagnosing deceptive and mixed messages from verbal and nonverbal cues. *Journal of Experimental and Social Psychology, 18*, 433–446.

DePaulo, B. M., Rosenthal, R., Rosenkrantz, J., & Green, C. R. (1982). Actual and perceived cues to deception: a closer look at speech. *Basic and Applied Social Psychology, 3*, 291–312.

DePaulo, B. M., Lanier, K., & Davis, T. (1983). Detecting the deceit of the motivated liar. *Journal of Personality and Social Psychology, 45*, 1096–1103.

DePaulo, B. M., Stone, J. I., & Lassiter, G. D. (1985a). Deceiving and detecting deceit. In B. R. Schlenker (Ed.), *The self and social life* (pp. 323–370). New York: McGraw-Hill.

DePaulo, B. M., Stone, J. I., & Lassiter, G. D. (1985b). Telling ingratiating lies: effects of target sex and target attractiveness on verbal and nonverbal deceptive success. *Journal of Personality and Social Psychology, 48*, 191–203.

DeTurck, M. A., & Miller, G. R. (1985). Deception and arousal: isolating the behavioral correlates of deception. *Human Communication Research, 12*, 181–201.

Einhorn, H. J. (1980). Learning from experience and suboptimal rules in decision making. In T. S. Wallsten (Ed.), *Cognitive processes in choice and decision behavior* (pp. 1–20). Hillsdale, NJ: Erlbaum.

Ekman, P. (1981). Mistakes when deceiving. *Annals of the New York Academy of Sciences, 364*, 269–278.

Ekman, P. (1985). *Telling lies.* New York: Norton.

Ekman, P., & Friesen, W. V. (1969). Nonverbal leakage and clues to deception. *Psychiatry, 32*, 88–105.

Ekman, P., & Friesen, W. V. (1972). Hand movements. *Journal of Communication, 22*, 353–374.

Ekman, P., & Friesen, W. V. (1974). Detecting deception from the body or face. *Journal of Personality and Social Psychology, 29*, 288–298.

Ekman, P., Friesen, W. V., & Scherer, K. R. (1976). Body movement and voice pitch in deceptive interaction. *Semiotica*, 16, 23–27.

Exline, R. V., Thibaut, J., Hickey, C. B., & Gumpert, P. (1970). Visual interaction in relation to machiavellianism and an unethical act. In R. Christie & F. L. Geis (Eds.), *Studies in machiavellianism* (pp. 53–75). New York: Academic.

Feldman, R. S. (1976). Nonverbal disclosure of teacher deception and interpersonal affect. *Journal of Educational Psychology, 68*, 807–816.

Feldman, R. S., & White, J. B. (1980). Detecting deception in children. *Journal of Communication, 30*, 121–128.

Feldman, R. S., Devin-Sheehan, L., & Allen, V. L. (1978). Nonverbal cues as indicators of verbal dissembling. *American Educational Research Journal, 15*, 217–231.

Feldman R. S., Jenkins, L., & Popoola, O. (1979). Detection of deception in adults and children via facial expressions. *Child Development, 50*, 350–355.

Goldman-Eisler, F. (1968). *Psycholinguistics: experiments in spontaneous speech.* New York: Academic.

Graesser, A. C., & Nakamura, G. V. (1982). The impact of a schema on comprehension and memory. In G. H. Bower (Ed.), *The psychology of learning and motivation*: Vol. 16 (pp. 60–109). New York: Academic.

Hass, R. G. (1981). Effects of source characteristics on cognitive responses and persuasion. In R. E. Petty, T. M. Ostrom, & T. C. Brock (Eds.), *Cognitive responses in persuasion* (pp. 141–172). Hillsdale, NJ: Erlbaum.

Hastie, R., & Park, B. (1986). The relationship between memory and judgment depends on whether the judgment task is memory-based or on-line. *Psychological Review, 93,* 258–268.

Hemsley, G. D. (1977). Experimental studies in the behavioral indicants of deception. Thesis, University of Toronto.

Hemsley, G. D., & Doob, A. N. (1979). The detection of deception from nonverbal behaviors. Paper presented at the meeting of the Canadian Psychological Association, Quebec.

Hocking, J. E., & Leathers, D. G. (1980). Nonverbal indicators of deception: a new theoretical perspective. *Communication Monographs, 47,* 119–131.

Horvarth, F. (1984). Detecting deception in eyewitness cases: problems and prospects in the use of the polygraph. In G. L. Wells & E. F. Loftus (Eds.), *Eyewitness testimony: Psychological perspectives* (pp. 214–255). Cambridge: Cambridge University Press.

Kahneman, D. (1973). *Attention and effort.* Englewood-Cliffs: Prentice Hall.

Köhnken, G. (1982). Sprechverhalten und Glaubwürdigkeit: eine experimentelle Studie zur extralinguistischen und textstilistischen Aussageanalyse. Thesis, University of Kiel, FRG.

Köhnken, G. (1984). Zum Beweiswert von Identifizierungen durch Augenzeugen: eine methodologische Analyse. *Forensia, 5,* 1–21.

Köhnken, G. (1985). Speech and deception of eyewitnesses: an information processing approach. *Proceedings of the XXIII International Congress of Psychology:* Vol. 7 (pp. 117–139). Acapulco, 1984. Amsterdam: North-Holland.

Köhnken, G. (1986). Verhaltenskorrelate von Täuschung und Wahrheit – neue Perspektiven in der Glaubwürdigkeitsdiagnostik. *Psychologische Rundschau 37,* 177–194.

Köhnken, G. (1987). Training police officers to detect deceptive eyewitness statements. Does it work? *Social Behavior, 1,* 1–17.

Köhnken, G., & Steller, M. (1988). The evaluation of the credibility of child witness statements in the German procedural system. In G. Davies (Ed.), The child witness: Do the courts abuse children? Leicester, British Psychological Society.

Köhnken, G., & Wegener, H. (1982). Zur Glaubwürdigkeit von Zeugenaussagen. Experimentelle Überprüfung ausgewählter Glaubwürdigkeitskriterien. *Zeitschrift für Experimentelle und Angewandte Psychologie, 29,* 92–111.

Krauss, R. M., Geller, V., & Olson, C. (1976). Modalities and cues in the detection of deception. Paper presented at the meeting of the American Psychological Association, Washington.

Kraut, R. E. (1978). Verbal and nonverbal cues in the perception of lying. *Journal of Personality and Social Psychology, 36,* 380–391.

Kraut, R. E. (1980). Humans as lie detectors: some second thoughts. *Journal of Communication, 30,* 209–216.

Kraut, R. E., & Poe, D. (1980). On the line: the deception judgements of customs inspectors and laymen. *Journal of Personality and Social Psychology, 39,* 784–798.

Littlepage, G. E., & Pineault, M. A. (1981). Detection of truthful and deceptive interpersonal communications across information transmission modes. *Journal of Social Psychology, 114,* 57–68.

Littlepage, G. E., McKinnie, R., & Pineault, M. A. (1983). Relationship between nonverbal sensitivities and detection of deception. *Perceptual and Motor Skills, 57,* 651–657.

Littmann, E., & Szewczyk, H. (1983). Zu einigen Kriterien und Ergebnissen forensisch-psychologischer Glaubwürdigkeitsbegutachtung von sexuell mißbrauchten Kindern und Jugendlichen. *Forensia, 4,* 55–72.

Lloyd-Bostock, S. M. A., & Clifford, B. R. (1983). *Evaluating witness evidence: recent psychological research and new perspectives.* Chichester: Wiley.

Loftus, E.F. (1979). *Eyewitness testimony.* Cambridge: Harvard University Press.

Magnusson, D., & Endler, N.S. (Eds.). (1977). *Personality at the crossroads: current issues in interactional psychology.* Hillsdale, NJ: Erlbaum.

Malpass, R.S., & Devine, P.G. (1984). Research on suggestion in lineups and photospreads. In G.L. Wells & E.F. Loftus (Eds.), *Eyewitness testimony: psychological perspectives* (pp. 64–91). Cambridge: Cambridge University Press.

Mehrabian, R. (1971). Nonverbal betrayal of feeling. *Journal of Experimental Research on Personality 5,* 64–73.

Miller, G.R., & Burgoon, J.K. (1981). Factors affecting assessments of witness credibility. In R. Bray & N. Kerr (Eds.), *The psychology of the courtroom.* New York: Academic.

Miller, G.R., Bauchner, J.E., Hocking, J.E., Fontes, N.E., Kaminski, E.P., & Brandt, D.R. (1981) "... And nothing but the truth": How well can observers detect deceptive testimony? In B.D. Sales (Ed.) *Perspectives in law and psychology*: Vol. II. *The trial process* (pp. 145–179). New York: Plenum.

Miller, G.R., DeTurck, M.A., & Kalbfleisch, P.J. (1983). Self-monitoring, rehearsal, and deceptive communication. *Human Communication Research, 10,* 97–117.

Morency, N.L., & Krauss, R.M. (1982). The nonverbal encoding and decoding of affect in first and fifth graders. In R.S. Feldman (Ed.), *Development of nonverbal behavioral skill* (pp. 181–199). New York: Springer.

Petty, R.E., & Cacioppo, J.T. (1981). *Attitudes and persuasion.* Dubuque: Brown.

Pitz, G.F., & Sachs, N.J. (1984). Judgment and decision: theory and application. *Annual Review of Psychology, 35,* 139–163.

Podlesny, J.A., & Raskin, D.C. (1977). Psychological measures in the detection of deception. *Psychological Bulletin, 84,* 782–799.

Pryor, J.B., & Day, J.D. (Eds.). (1985). *The development of social cognition.* New York: Springer.

Raskin, D.C. (1982). The scientific basis of polygraph techniques and their use in the judicial process. In A. Trankell (Ed.), *Reconstructing the past: the role of psychologists in criminal trial* (pp. 317–371). Stockholm: Norstedt.

Riggio, R.E., & Friedman, H.S. (1983). Individual differences and cues to deception. *Journal of Personality and Social Psychology, 45,* 899–915.

Schank, R.C., & Abelson, R.P. (1977). *Scripts, plans, goals and understanding.* Hillsdale, NJ: Erlbaum.

Scherer, K.R. (1978). Personality inference from voice quality: the loud voice of extroversion. *European Journal of Social Psychology, 8,* 467–487.

Scherer, K.R. (1982). Methods of research on vocal communication: paradigms and parameters. In K.R. Scherer & P. Ekman (Eds.), *Handbook of methods in nonverbal behavior research* (pp. 136–198). Cambridge: Cambridge University Press.

Scherer, K.R. (1984). The nonverbal dimension: a fad, a field, or a behavioural modality? In H. Tajfel (Ed.), *The social dimension: European developments in social psychology* (pp. 160–183). Cambridge: Cambridge University Press.

Scherer, K.R., & Bergmann, G. (1984). Vocal communication. *German Journal of Psychology, 8,* 57–90.

Schooler, J.W., Gerhard, D., & Loftus, E.F. (1986). Qualities of the unreal. *Journal of Experimental Psychology: Learning, Memory, and Cognition, 12,* 171–181.

Shepherd, J.W., Ellis, H.D., & Davies, G.M. (1982). *Identification evidence: a psychological examination.* Aberdeen: Aberdeen University Press.

Sherman, S.J., & Corty, E. (1984). Cognitive heuristics. In R.S. Wyer & T.K. Srull (Eds.), *Handbook of social cognition:* Vol. I (pp. 189–286). Hillsdale, NJ: Erlbaum.

Steller, M. (1987). *Psychophysiologische Aussagebeurteilung – wissenschaftliche Grundlagen und Anwendungen der Lügendetektion.* Göttingen: Hogrefe.

Steller, M., & Köhnken, G. (1988). Statement analysis: credibility assessment of children's testimonies in sexual abuse cases. In D.C. Raskin (Ed.), *Psychological techniques in law enforcement.* (in press).

Stephenson, G.M. (1984). Accuracy and confidence in testimony: a critical review and some fresh evidence. In D.J. Müller, D.E. Blackman, & A.T. Chapman (Eds.), *Topics in psychology and the law* (pp. 229–248). Chichester: Wiley.

Stone, M. (1984). *Proof of fact in criminal trials.* Edinburgh: Green and Son.

Undeutsch, U. (1967). Beurteilung der Glaubhaftigkeit von Aussagen. In U. Undeutsch (Ed.), *Handbuch der Psychologie*: Vol 11. *Forensische Psychologie* (pp. 26–181). Göttingen: Hogrefe.

Undeutsch, U. (1982). Statement reality analysis. In A. Trankell (Ed.), *Reconstructing the past* (pp. 27–56). Stockholm: Norstedt.

Undeutsch, U. (1984). Courtroom evaluation of eyewitness testimony. *International Review of Applied Psychology, 33,* 51–67.

Waid, W.M., & Orne, M.T. (1981). Cognitive, social and personality processes in the physiological detection of deception. In L. Berkowitz (Ed.), *Advances in experimental social psychology:* Vol. 14 (pp. 61–106). New York: Academic.

Wegener, H., Köhnken, G., & Steller, M. (in press). *Forensische Aussagepsychologie.* Berlin Heidelberg New York: Springer.

Wells, G.L., & Loftus, E.F. (Eds.). (1984). *Eyewitness testimony: psychological perspectives.* Cambridge: Cambridge University Press.

Wells, G.L., & Murray, D.M. (1984). Eyewitness confidence. In G.L. Wells & E.F. Loftus (Eds.), *Eyewitness testimony: Psychological perspectives* (pp. 155–170). Cambridge: Cambridge University Press.

Wyer, R.S., & Srull, T.K. (1984). *Handbook of social cognition.* Hillsdale, NJ: Erlbaum.

Wyer, R.S., & Srull, T.K. (1986). Human cognition in its social context. *Psychological Review, 93,* 322–359.

Zuckerman, M., & Driver, R.E. (1985). Telling lies: verbal and nonverbal correlates of deception. In A.W. Siegman & S. Feldstein (Eds.), *Multichannel integrations of nonverbal behavior* (pp. 129–147). Hillsdale, NJ: Erlbaum.

Zuckerman, M., DePaulo, B.M., & Rosenthal, R. (1981). Verbal and nonverbal communication of deception. In L. Berkowitz (Ed.), *Advances in experimental social psychology:* Vol. 14 (pp. 1–59). New York: Academic.

Zuckerman, M., Amidon, M.D., Bishop, S.E., & Pomerantz, S.D. (1982). Face and tone of voice in the communication of deception. *Journal of Personality and Social Psychology, 43,* 347–357.

Zuckerman, M., Driver, R., & Koestner, R. (1982). Discrepancy as a cue to actual and perceived deception. *Journal of Nonverbal Behavior, 7,* 95–100.

Zuckerman, M., Kernis, M.R., Driver, R., & Koestner, R. (1984). Segmentation of behavior: effects of actual deception and expected deception. *Journal of Personality and Social Psychology, 46,* 1173–1182.

Zuckerman, M., Koestner, R., & Alton, A.O. (1984). Learning to detect deception. *Journal of Personality and Social Psychology, 46,* 519–528.

Zuckerman, M., Koestner, R., & Colella, M.J. (1985). Learning to detect deception from three communication channels. *Journal of Nonverbal Behavior, 9,* 188–194.

19 Assessing Credibility of Allegations of Child Sexual Abuse: Polygraph Examinations and Statement Analysis

David C. Raskin and Max Steller

Introduction

Sexual abuse of children has been recognized as a serious social and legal problem for more than 30 years. In the United States it was estimated in 1955 that the incidence of sexual abuse was 1.9 per million (Weinberg, 1955), and by 1969 the estimates had risen to 40 per million (DeFrancis, 1969). In 1981 there were 1.3 million reports of child abuse and neglect, of which approximately 7% were sexual in nature (National Center on Child Abuse and Neglect, 1981), indicating a rate of approximately 385 per million population. However, on the basis of surveys, many professionals have argued that child sexual abuse is significantly underreported. National studies have estimated annual rates of sexual abuse to be as high as 5% of all children, amounting to 150000–200000 new incidents per year (Finkelhor & Hotaling, 1984). Obviously, this problem merits a great deal of scientific and legal attention.

In order to remedy the problem of underreporting in the United States, governmental and law enforcement agencies, civic groups, schools, and the mass media have undertaken programs designed to educate adults and children about the nature and the extent of child sexual abuse and to encourage children, parents, teachers, physicians, and others to report suspected instances of sexual abuse. As a result, reports have increased approximately 300% in the last 3 years (Utah Division of Family Services, 1985), but this has been accompanied by a dramatic increase in the proportion of "unfounded" reports. As many as 65% of all reports of maltreatment of children may be "unfounded" (Besharov, 1985). According to Jones and McGraw (1987), fictitious accounts of sexual abuse may exceed 8% of the cases which are processed far enough to result in a formal evaluation by a psychiatrist or psychological expert on the assessment of children.

Referrals to the University of Utah for polygraph examinations of persons accused of sexual abuse increased approximately 400% in the period from 1983 to 1985. However, during the same period the proportion of accused persons who were diagnosed as truthful in their denials of the accusations increased by 56%. Interestingly, cases in which the polygraph results indicated the presence of fictitious allegations have certain characteristics in common with cases where Jones and others have found fictitious allegations. The most common factors associated with false allegations include domestic relations disputes, contested or acrimonious divorces, and battles over child custody or visitation rights. Often they are accompanied by evidence of psychiatric diagnosis of one or more parties (Jones & McGraw, 1987).

A major problem in the investigation and adjudication of sexual abuse cases is the assessment of the credibility of reports of child sexual abuse. Frequent lack of physical evidence, parental reluctance or denials, the child's psychosocial or cognitive immaturity, the possible effects of suggestions and pressure from parents and authority figures, occasional motives for making false reports, and general problems related to the accuracy and credibility of child witnesses all contribute to the substantial difficulties in determining the facts and achieving appropriate resolutions of large numbers of cases. It is critical that accurate assessments of the credibility of accusations be made in the early stages of investigations of such cases. However, in the United States current procedures for interviewing and assessing the credibility of victims, complaining witnesses, and alleged perpetrators are grossly inadequate.

Investigations of cases of child sexual abuse in the United States frequently suffer from inadequate interview methods employed by poorly trained interviewers. Interviews are typically conducted by law enforcement personnel with little training in psychological techniques of interviewing, or by persons trained in social work, psychiatry, or clinical psychology with emphasis on helping the victim. The interviews often fail to yield detailed information which could assist in resolving the case. Furthermore, interviewers frequently assume that the accusations are true and that the only purpose of the interview is to help the child state more clearly the nature of the sexual acts. As a result, many interviews are excessively supportive, suggestive, and leading. Such interviews conflict with the legitimate investigative purpose of assisting in the determination of facts. When such approaches are used, it is not surprising that the interviewer obtains a statement from the child which is consistent with a predetermined end point. Poorly conducted interviews raise questions about the results and unnecessarily complicate the investigative and judicial process.

A comprehensive methodology is needed for evaluating the credibility of allegations of sexual abuse of children in order to avoid many of the problems inherent in present practices. The quality of investigations and prosecutions will be enhanced by providing definite criteria and outcomes on which to base decisions for actions to be taken after the initial report. Polygraph examinations may be effective for direct assessment of the credibility of denials made by the accused (Raskin, 1982), and statement analysis is designed to assess the credibility of a child's testimony (Undeutsch, 1967). Statement analysis is not appropriate for the accused who denies the allegations, nor are polygraph examinations effective with preadolescent children (Lieblich, 1971; Voronin, Konovalov & Serikov, 1970). The appropriate use of polygraph examinations and statement analysis can provide a solid basis for determining whether or not to proceed with a criminal case or what formal actions to take in other settings.

Polygraph Techniques

Polygraph techniques are used extensively in criminal investigations in the United States, Canada, Israel, and Japan, although they are unused in Europe. Properly conducted polygraph examinations provide direct assessments of the credibility of accused persons in almost all types of cases, and frequently they can be used with complainants and other witnesses. The procedure requires 2 h or longer and must be conducted by a trained and experienced professional. A psychologist with special training in polygraph techniques is preferred, but many federal and law enforcement polygraph examiners in the United States are well trained and highly skilled.

The most frequently employed polygraph technique is the control question examination (Raskin, 1982, 1986). It begins with a pretest interview which includes obtaining the subject's consent to be examined, a general explanation of the purpose of the examination to be conducted, a description of the polygraph procedures and the instrumentation to be employed, a detailed discussion of the allegations and an opportunity for the subject to explain his position on the matter, and a review and discussion of the specific wording of each question to be asked on the test.

The polygraph question sequence usually consists of 10 or 11 questions which are repeated at least three times while palmar skin resistance, relative blood pressure, and respiration are recorded on the polygraph instrument. The question sequence includes three or four relevant questions concerning the allegations and two or three control questions. The relevant questions are very specific and deal directly with the most important aspects of the allegations. The control questions cover subject matter of similar nature during a period of time prior to the alleged incident. However, control questions are vague and general. They are designed and explained in such a manner that all subjects will agree to answer them "No" but will be untruthful in that denial or will be unsure that their denial is completely truthful. For example, a relevant question in a sexual abuse case might be "Did you ever place your penis in Susan's genital area?" An accompanying control question might be "Other than what you told me, prior to 1985 did you ever engage in a sexual act of which you should be ashamed?" The subject would answer "No" to each of the relevant and control questions.

During the polygraph test, guilty subjects are most concerned about being detected on the relevant questions, and they produce relatively strong physiological reactions to them as compared with the control questions. That result is interpreted by the examiner as indicative of deception to the relevant questions. However, innocent subjects are certain that their answers to the relevant questions are truthful. They are most concerned that they might appear to be deceptive on the test because of their concern about their lack of truthfulness on the control questions. Therefore, their relatively stronger reactions to the control questions are interpreted by the examiner as indicative of truthfulness to the relevant questions.

After the polygraph recordings have been obtained, the diagnosis of truth or deception is made solely on the basis of a numerical scoring of the physiological responses (Raskin, 1979). Using a standard set of response criteria, the relative strength of reactions to each presentation of relevant and control questions is observed and assigned a score on a 7-point scale which ranges from -3 to $+3$ for each physiological parameter. If the reaction to the relevant question is dramatically stronger than to the corresponding control question, a score of -3 is assigned to that comparison. If the control question produced a dramatically stronger reaction, a score of $+3$ is assigned. Strong differences are assigned scores of 2 with the appropriate sign, noticeable differences are assigned scores of 1, and no difference is assigned a 0.

Each relevant question presented during the three or more repetitions of the question sequence is evaluated for each of the physiological measures, and the scores are summed for the entire test. Total scores of -6 or lower provide a diagnosis of deception, scores of $+6$ or higher indicate truthfulness, and scores smaller than 6 in either direction are inconclusive. Approximately 90% of such results are conclusive and provide a definite diagnosis of truth or deception on the relevant issues. Numerous studies have demonstrated high interrater reliability for numerical scoring, usually in excess of 0.90 (Raskin, 1982).

Polygraph techniques have proven very effective in criminal investigations and the resolution of specific issues in other contexts (Raskin, 1986). The scientific literature demonstrates that competently performed polygraph examinations have accuracies in the order of 90% (Raskin, 1982). The extensive literature on laboratory mock-crime simulations demonstrates accuracies which often exceed 90%, and the available field data indicate that accuracies in the range of 80%–90% may be achieved (see Table 19.1).

It should be noted that the majority of errors tend to be false positives (innocent persons who produce deceptive test results) rather than false negatives (guilty persons who produce truthful results). The predominance of false positive errors is probably due to a combination of the unavoidably provocative nature of the questions concerning accusations against innocent subjects, the contexts in which such examinations are administered, and polygraph examiners' frequent lack of adequate psychological sophistication needed to counteract those problems.

Extensive field experience with polygraph techniques indicates that a high rate of confessions can be obtained following deceptive outcomes of tests performed on accused persons, especially if the polygraph result is combined with a statement analysis which supports the credibility of the child victim. Such

TABLE 19.1. Percent accuracy of polygraph tests

	Laboratory studies[a]		Field studies[b]	
	Guilty	Innocent	Guilty	Innocent
Correct	88	86	86	76
Wrong	3	7	10	19
Inconclusive	9	7	4	5
Decisions correct	97	92	90	80

[a] Data summarized from Raskin, 1986, p. 43
[b] Data derived from Office of Technology Assessment, 1983, p. 52

outcomes usually lead to rapid resolution of cases, including many guilty pleas which obviate the necessity for a trial in which the child victim would be required to testify. On the other hand, the increasing controversy over false accusations, especially in cases which involve domestic relations disputes, underscores the need to discover such problems early in the process.

The use of polygraph techniques in the resolution of sexual abuse allegations is illustrated by a case referred to the University of Utah in 1984. Two girls aged 8 and 9 had accused their stepfather of sexually molesting them. The husband and wife had recently separated, and the mother and her girls were living at the home of a friend. They related the allegations, which included attempted sexual intercourse, to a sympathetic police officer during taped interviews. The accused was arrested and jailed, but he adamantly denied the allegations. The prosecutor and defense attorney agreed to attempt to resolve the case on the basis of a polygraph examination of the accused by the first author.

The polygraph test on the stepfather included the three relevant questions: "Did Susan ever touch your penis with her hand?", "Did you ever put your penis in Susan's genital area?", "Did you ever rub or press your penis against Barbara?" The results indicated that he was truthful in his denials. The mother was then tested concerning possible coaching of the girls, but her results were also definitely truthful. However, a careful analysis of the recorded interviews using the principles and criteria of statement analysis revealed a number of problems with the allegations by the girls, including the releasing situation which occurred during an explicit sexual discussion between the girls and the teenage girl with whom they were temporarily residing. When a reinterview of the two girls produced substantial changes in major aspects of the allegations, they finally admitted to the prosecutor that the teenage girl had coached them to make the allegations against their stepfather. He was exonerated, and the family was reunited.

Statement Analysis

The described case illustrates that polygraph techniques and statement analysis can be combined to resolve difficult cases since they provide independent information to assess the veracity of disputed allegations.

In 1954, the Supreme Court of the Federal Republic of Germany ruled that expert witnesses (specialized psychologists or psychiatrists) must be brought into the case to assess the truthfulness of children's or juveniles' testimonies if these constitute the only or main evidence, not corroborated by other evidence. Since that time, statement analysis has been the major method employed by experts. Arntzen (1982) stated that psychiatrists are no longer active in this field and statement analysis has become a domain of forensic psychologists. He estimated that during the past 30 years experts have been appointed to assess witness testimonies in 30000–50000 cases in Germany. According to Undeutsch (1982), statement analysis has yielded statements which have been evaluated as credible in approximately 90% of cases, and expert testimony has been very helpful in obtaining convictions. The remaining 10% of statement analyses revealed results which cast doubt on the credibility of the accusation and raised questions about the advisability of proceeding with prosecution. The data demonstrate that in many instances statement analysis uncovers new information which strengthens the case against the alleged perpetrator. In some cases, information can be obtained which clearly demonstrates that the accusation is not true.

Extensive descriptions of statement analysis have been published in Germany by several authors (e.g., Arntzen 1970, 1983; Szewczyk, 1973; Undeutsch, 1967), but this method is not well known in the United States. Recently, Undeutsch (1982, 1984), who laid the foundation for the broad acceptance of statement analysis by German courts, has published in English.

The basic hypothesis of statement analysis is that descriptions of self-experienced events differ significantly in quality of the content from descriptions which are not based on direct observations or experience but are products of imagination. The "reality criteria" or "content criteria" (terms which are used interchangeably) reflect specific features which differentiate truthful from invented testimonies.

The procedure for assessing a statement by means of content analysis is known as criteria-based statement analysis. It must be related to the verbal and intellectual abilities of the witness, as well as the nature of the reported event. As the cognitive abilities of a witness increase and the complexity of the event diminishes, the application of statement analysis produces less definitive results. The veracity of a high quality statement is less convincing if the intellectual and verbal abilities of the witness are well developed. However, a negative outcome of statement analysis concerning an alleged event which lacks complexity does not necessarily indicate deception by the reporting person.

The interview technique used to elicit the statement is another important factor which may influence the quality of a testimony, especially when given by a child or juvenile witness. The quality of a statement, as measured by the number of reality criteria which are fulfilled, is to a great extent determined by its length. The length and therefore the quality of the statement is also dependent on the interview technique used by the investigator and the context of the interview. An assessment by means of statement analysis requires lengthy narratives, but leading or suggestive questions during the interview can produce a statement which cannot be properly analyzed by means of reality criteria. Courtroom testimony by a child normally does not provide sufficient material to conduct a statement analysis. An extensive interview by a trained professional in a less formal atmosphere is necessary to produce statements which can be adequately analyzed according to the reality (content) criteria described below.

Experimental research has shown that leading questions decrease the accuracy of the testimony of children and adults who are motivated to tell the truth (Dent, 1982; Lipton, 1977; Loftus & Davies, 1984). Therefore, free narratives by child witnesses are important in order to assess the veracity of the statement, as well as to ensure the accuracy of truthful statements. Psychologists usually have less difficulty in avoiding leading, suggestive, or reproachful questions than do police investigators who have different training, background, and professional goals. Many psychologists are trained in nondirective interview techniques which assist the interviewee to give rather long (unguided) statements. However, a "helping" attitude tends to produce interview mistakes which interfere with the purposes of fact finding.

Some countries (e.g., Israel) require that specially trained psychologists (or similar professionals) interview child witnesses in sexual abuse cases (Goodman, 1984, p. 18). The statement analysis technique may be applied in the analysis of the content of a (transcribed) statement, and it also includes interview guidelines for obtaining adequate materials to be analyzed. Due to space limitations, the interview technique which is used in conjunction with statement analysis cannot be discussed here in detail (for a practically oriented description, see Steller, Raskin, Yuille, & Esplin, in preparation). What follows is confined to the presentation of statement analysis as an evaluation method.

Table 19.2 presents a system of content criteria. This system constitutes an integration of criteria listed by Undeutsch (1967), Arntzen (1970, 1983), and Szewczyk (1973) (cf. also Dettenborn, Fröhlich, & Szewczyk, 1984). This integrated system was developed because the original approaches are substantially lacking in systematic organization, precise definitions, and distinctions among criteria (Steller & Koehnken, in press). The goal was to organize the different approaches which had been presented in the German literature.

The categorization in Table 19.2 is based on a logical structure which can be examined easily. Therefore, the system can be used directly in practice and research, and assessment of the quality of statements can be conducted by employing the sequence of categories in the system. One first considers the statement as a whole, then attention is focused on details of the statement which become progressively more specific. The integrated system also has

TABLE 19.2. Content criteria for statement analysis (adapted from Steller & Koehnken, in press)

General characteristics	
1.	Logical structure
2.	Unstructured production
3.	Quantity of details
Specific contents	
4.	Contextual embedding
5.	Descriptions of interactions
6.	Reproduction of conversation
7.	Unexpected complications during the incident
Peculiarities of the content	
8.	Unusual details
9.	Superfluous details
10.	Accurately reported details misunderstood
11.	Related external associations
12.	Accounts of subjective mental state
13.	Attribution of Perpetrator's mental state
Motivation-related contents	
14.	Spontaneous corrections
15.	Admitting lack of memory
16.	Raising doubts about one's own testimony
17.	Self-Deprecation
18.	Pardoning the perpetrator
Offense-specific elements	
19.	Details characteristic of the offense

heuristic value, and the criteria listed within one category may be supplemented on the basis of future research.

In addition to organizing the content criteria reported by different authors, clear descriptions and distinctions of the criteria were developed, and a brief overview of the different content criteria and related scientific and practical problems is presented in order to evaluate the use of criteria-based statement analysis for assessing the validity of child witnesses in cases of sexual abuse.

The first major category of reality content criteria includes those which refer to the statement as a whole. Such criteria can be assessed without reference to the details of the contents of the statement. "Logical structure" is equivalent to the "homogeneity criterion" described by Trankell (1971, p. 126). It is fulfilled when different details in a testimony independently describe the same course of events. Neither the accounts of unusual details (criterion 8) nor the appearance of unexpected complications in the event (criterion 7) necessarily interfere with logical consistency.

The second criterion, "unstructured production," is based on the assumption that false testimonies are generally characterized by a continuous, structured, chronological manner of representation. A reproduction style showing lack of constraint is characterized by an unorganized manner of presentation. If the fragments of the statement are capable of being joined together into a unified whole, that is consistent with credibility of the statement.

A relatively large number of details in a statement fulfills the third criterion when, for example, the exact place is described, persons are described in detail from different aspects, or the succession of events is described step by step. However, repetition of details should not be counted. Only new facts or details should be taken into consideration.

The second major category of content criteria includes those with specific contents. In this step of the statement analysis, individual parts of the statement are the focus of assessment in terms of the presence or extent of certain types of descriptions. "Contextual embedding" as a content criterion means that the report about the event under investigation contains specific facts or events of peripheral interest which show the anchoring of the event within the totality of the situation. "Descriptions of interactions" refers to reports which contain a chain of mutual actions and reactions. These mutually dependent actions can take the form of conversations. If the content of conversations is combined with a dialogue which distinguishes the roles of the speakers by providing a virtual replication of a verbal interaction, that is considered a separate content criterion. An important aspect of this criterion is whether a witness reexperiences the original verbal context of the situation while providing the statement. Accounts of unexpected complications during the incident (e.g., unforeseen interruptions) constitute another structural content criterion.

A third category of content criteria includes those features of a statement which reflect the concreteness and vividness of the statement. Criteria consisting of peculiarities of the content can be obtained from very different parts of a statement. Accounts of unusual and superfluous details or accounts which refer to the witness's or the perpetrator's mental state clearly are criteria of reality, but the criterion of accurately reported details misunderstood requires some explanation. Arntzen (1983, p.31) and Szewczyk (1973, p. 57) described it as details which lie "beyond the horizon of the witness's comprehension," following the lead of Undeutsch (1967, p. 141). This criterion occurs in a statement if a child witness incorrectly interprets a (correctly described) observation. Phenomenal accounts of actions or details not understood occur in a statement when the reporting (child) witness does not understand them, but they are understood by the (adult) interviewer. "Related external associations" addresses a more specific interrelationship. For example, in describing an incestuous relationship, a related external association would occur if the witness (the daughter) reports about conversations with the alleged perpetrator (the father) in which they discussed the sexual experience of the daughter with other partners.

The fourth group of content criteria includes those which refer indirectly to the content of a statement. At this point one considers details concerning specific contents of the statement (for example, spontaneous corrections of one's own testimony, anticipated objections to the veracity of one's own testimony). These points define the relationship between the witness and his/her testimony and provide an opportunity to draw conclusions about the motivation of the witness for false accusations. At the same time, they are content criteria because they can be inferred solely by the content of a statement (e.g., a typed transcript) without considering other information regarding the motivation of the witness for false accusations.

In the second and third categories the *cognitive* aspect is the main aspect under investigation. The question is whether a witness would be able to fabricate contents which have qualities such as those described by the criteria. In the fourth category of criteria, the *motivational* aspect is dominant. One must assess the probability that a witness who gives false testimony would be likely to make spontaneous corrections, admit lack of memory, or raise doubts about his/her own statement by pointing out possible objections to its correctness. If such details occur in a statement, this is considered a sign of its veracity. Additionally the mentioning of unfavorable, self-incriminating details and of details which tend to favor the accused (e.g., explanations or exonerations of his behavior) are counted as reality criteria.

Elements of the testimony which do not relate to the general vividness of the statement but which relate to the crime in a typical way are assessed separately. This extraordinary status is based on the fact that reality criteria of the fifth category may not be present in many credible testimonies. On the other hand, the expert must have specific competence in order to deal with this category of reality criteria. He/she must have knowledge and experience concerning the typical ways in which sexual crimes are perpetrated. Special value is placed on those descriptions in a statement which contradict everyday knowledge but provide correct offense-specific elements, i.e., descriptions contrary to commonly held beliefs concerning sexual assaults of children by strange, unknown persons who use violence. In cases of incest, for example, a long period of the incestuous relationship consists of relatively "harmless" sexual behavior. There is a progressive development as well as a change in the attitude of the victim towards the perpetrator of the crime. These elements can be considered as offense-specific (as shown by empirical research) and at the same time contradict the beliefs held by most nonprofessionals.

The content criteria described above can be judged as "present vs. nonpresent" or can be rated in terms of the extent to which they are fulfilled in a certain statement. This leads to an assessment of the quality of the statement and the probable degree of its reality. Referring to the basic assumption of statement analysis by content criteria, the quality assessment gives information about the probability that the witness has actually experienced the alleged event. At present, this probabilistic evaluation of the veracity of a statement cannot be made quantitatively by means of a statistical error of estimate. The rules for combining data and drawing conclusions are not yet explicitly defined or even quantified, and we must resist the temptation to establish quasi-objective measures or cut-off scores about which we do not yet have sufficient knowledge. The clinical assessment of the veracity of statements by use of statement analysis appears to be very useful. As in other fields of applied psychology, clinical judgment can yield valid diagnoses even in the absence of systematic methods for quantifying the diagnostic process.

Undeutsch (1982, 1984) and Arntzen (1982) presented very optimistic pictures of the infallibility of statement analysis by pointing out an error rate of "zero" in their case files by using court decisions and confessions as their criteria. At the same time, they explicitly ruled out the possibility of experimental research on statement analysis because of significant differences between the laboratory and field situation. They claimed that the context of a sexual crime with its accompanying emotions cannot be simulated in the laboratory. However, "ecological validity" does not necessarily mean "realism." Therefore it was pointed out at the beginning that there exists a *hypothesis* which underlies statement analysis. This hypothesis can be adequately tested by experiments. The results of experimental studies on statement analysis (e.g., Koehnken & Wegener, 1982) must then be critically scrutinized to determine whether they can be generalized to the field.

Steller and Koehnken (in press) evaluated the present state of research on statement analysis. On the basis of the lack of adequate research they recommended systematic future research which would include studies of interrater reliability of the individual reality criteria as well as multivariate analyses to determine the weights which should be applied to the various criteria in order to differentiate truthful and invented statements. Considering the amount of experience with the use of statement analysis in the judicial process in Germany, statement analysis seems to merit substantial effort in terms of systematic research and continuous improvement.

Concluding Remarks

The availability and utilization of polygraph and statement analysis techniques for assessing credibility in sexual abuse cases can increase the speed and effectiveness of criminal proceedings in meritorious cases, minimize the negative impact on children produced by the investigative and judicial processes, and prevent unnecessary and costly investigations and trials.

It is critical that the described techniques for assessing credibility are employed in the early stages of investigations of sexual abuse cases. Reifen (1975) has described the Israeli procedure. Whenever a complaint is lodged with the police concerning a sexual assault in which a child was involved, a specially trained "youth interrogator" is called by the police to investigate the case. This is done not only to preserve the first statement of the child for judicial decisions concerning the further prosecution of the case, but also to avoid possible traumatic effects of repeated interviews on child witnesses (Whitcomb, Shapiro, & Stellwagen, 1985, p. 60). Audiovisual recordings of the interview may even be used instead of a court appearance of the victim in certain cases (Bernstein & Claman, 1986). Another method to avoid or minimize a possible secondary victimization of the child witness by courtroom hearings could be to project video and audio information from a "testimonial room" to the courtroom by closed circuit television (Whitcomb et al., 1985, p. 129). However, any procedures which do not require the child to testify in court may infringe upon the constitutional rights of the accused (Goodman, 1984; Melton, 1984).

The anticipated reduction in investigative efforts required to evaluate sexual abuse allegations, increased rates of convictions and guilty pleas in substantial cases, and the early exoneration of the falsely accused should demonstrate the effectiveness of the interview and polygraph approaches described in this presentation. A combination of statement analysis interviews and evaluation techniques of the alleged child victims and polygraph examination of the accused persons provides powerful methods for investigating and rapidly resolving a large proportion of allegations of sexual abuse of children. Both techniques must be conducted by specially qualified professionals trained in different fields of psychology. Optimal gain for the judicial process can be achieved when each method is applied in the same case by separate experts who work independently.

References

Arntzen, F. (1970). *Psychologie der Zeugenaussage. Einführung in die forensische Aussagepsychologie.* Göttingen: Hogrefe.

Arntzen, F. (1982). Die Situation der forensischen Aussagepsychologie in der Bundesrepublik Deutschland. In A. Trankell (Ed.), *Reconstructing the past: the role of psychologists in criminal trials* (pp. 107–120). Stockholm: Norstedt and Soners.

Arntzen, F. (1983). *Psychologie der Zeugenaussage. Systematik der Glaubwürdigkeitsmerkmale.* München: Beck.

Bernstein, B.E., & Claman, L. (1986). Modern technology and the child witness. *Child Welfare, 65*, 155–163.

Besharov, D.J. (1985). "Doing something" about child abuse: the need to narrow the grounds for state intervention. *Harvard Journal of Law and Public Policy, 8*, 539–589.

DeFrancis, V. (1969). *Protecting the child victim of sex crimes.* Denver, CO: American Humane Association.

Dent, H.R. (1982). The effects of interviewing strategies on the results of interviews with child witnesses. In A. Trankell (Ed.), *Reconstructing the past: the role of psychologists in criminal trials* (pp. 279–297). Stockholm: Norstedt and Soners.

Dettenborn, H., Fröhlich, H., & Szewczyk, H. (1984). *Forensische Psychologie.* Berlin: Deutscher Verlag der Wissenschaften.

Finkelhor, D., & Hotaling, G.T. (1984). Sexual abuse in the national incidence study of child abuse and neglect: an appraisal. *Child Abuse and Neglect, 8*, 23–33.

Goodman, G.S. (1984). Children's testimony in historical perspective. *Journal of Social Issues, 40*, 9–31.

Jones, D., & McGraw, J.M. (1987). Reliable and fictitious accounts of sexual abuse to children. *Journal of Interpersonal Violence, 2*, 27–45.

Köhnken, G., & Wegener, H. (1982). Zur Glaubwürdigkeit von Zeugenaussagen. Experimentelle Überprüfung ausgewählter Glaubwürdigkeitskriterien. *Zeitschrift für Experimentelle und Angewandte Psychologie, 29*, 92–111.

Lieblich, I. (1971). Manipulation of contrast between differential GSRs in very young children. *Psychophysiology, 7*, 436–441.

Lipton, J.P. (1977). On the psychology of eyewitness testimony. *Journal of Applied Psychology, 62*, 90–93.

Loftus, E.F., & Davies, G.M. (1984). Distortions in the memory of children. *Journal of Social Issues, 40*, 51–67.

Melton, G.B. (1984). Child witnesses and the first amendment: Psychological dilemma. *Journal of Social Issues, 40*, 109–123.

National Center of Child Abuse and Neglect (1981). *Study findings: national study of the incidence and severity of child abuse and neglect.* Washington, DC: Department of Health and Human Services.

Office of Technology Assessment (1983). *Scientific validity of polygraph testing: a research review and evaluation.* Washington, DC: U.S. Government Printing Office.

Raskin, D.C. (1979). Orienting and defensive reflexes in the detection of deception. In H.D. Kimmel, E.H. van Olst, & J.F. Orlebecke (Eds.), *The orienting reflex in humans* (pp. 587–605). Hillsdale, NJ: Erlbaum.

Raskin, D.C. (1982). The scientific basis of polygraph techniques and their uses in the judicial process. In A. Trankell (Ed.), *Reconstructing the past: the role of psychologists in criminal trials* (pp. 317–371). Stockholm: Norstedt and Soners.

Raskin, D.C. (1986). The polygraph in 1986: scientific, professional and legal issues surrounding application and acceptance of polygraph evidence. *Utah Law Review, 1986*, 29–74.

Reifen, D. (1975). Court procedures in Israel to protect child-victims of sexual assaults. In I. Drapkin, & E. Viano (Eds.), *Victimology: a new focus:* Vol. 3. *Crimes, victims, and justice* (pp. 67–72). Lexington: Lexington Books.

Steller, M., & Köhnken, G. (in press). Criteria-based statement analysis: credibility assessment of children's testimonies in sexual abuse cases. In D.C. Raskin (Ed.), *Psychological methods for investigation and evidence.* New York: Springer.

Steller, M., Raskin, D.C., Yuille, J., & Esplin, P. (in preparation). *Sexually abused children: interview and assessment techniques.* New York: Springer.

Szewczyk, H. (1973). Kriterien der Beurteilung kindlicher Zeugenaussagen. *Probleme und Ergebnisse der Psychologie, 46*, 47–66.

Trankell, A. (1971). *Der Realitätsgehalt von Zeugenaussagen.* Göttingen: Hogrefe. (English edition 1972: Reliability of evidence, Beckmans, Stockholm).

Undeutsch, U. (1967). Beurteilung der Glaubhaftigkeit von Aussagen. In U. Undeutsch (Ed.), *Handbuch der Psychologie: Vol. 11. Forensische Psychologie* (pp. 26–181). Göttingen: Hogrefe.

Undeutsch, U. (1982). Statement reality analysis. In A. Trankell (Ed.), *Reconstructing the past: the role of psychologists in criminal trials* (pp. 27–56). Stockholm: Norstedt and Soners.

Undeutsch, U. (1984). Courtroom evaluation of eyewitness testimony. *International Review of Applied Psychology, 33*, 51–67.

Utah Division of Family Services. (1986). *Central register for child abuse and neglect.* Salt Lake City, UT: Utah Department of Social Services.

Voronin, L.G., Konovalov, V.F., & Serikov, I.S. (1970). K voprosu o vzaimodeistvii osoznannykh sledovykh protsessov v nernoi sisteme [Interaction of conscious and unconscious trace processes in the nervous system]. *Doklady Academi Nauk SSSR, 195*, 1237–1239.

Weinberg, S. (1955). Incest behavior. New York: Citadel.

Whitcomb, D., Shapiro, E.R., & Stellwagen, L.D. (1985). *When the victim is a child: issues for judges and prosecutors.* Washington, DC: National Institute of Justice.

20
Verbal and Visual Processes in Person Identification

SIEGFRIED LUDWIG SPORER

Introduction

Among the numerous topics that have recently been investigated in the psychology of eyewitness testimony (cf. Lilli, this volume; Loftus, 1979; Wippich, this volume; Yarmey, 1979), the question of person identification has received particular attention (for reviews, see Clifford & Bull, 1978; Ellis, 1984; Penrod, Loftus, & Winkler, 1982; Shapiro & Penrod, 1986; Shepherd, Ellis, & Davies, 1982; Sporer, 1983a, 1983b, 1984b). In person identification, a witness (either victim or bystander) of a crime is asked by the police to identify "the one who did it" in a live lineup or in a photospread of mugshots. Motivated by the repeated occurrence of cases of mistaken identification, researchers have attempted to explore the conditions that are likely to influence the accuracy of an identification as well as ways to reduce the possibility of error (so-called estimator and system variables, respectively: Wells, 1978).

There are a number of unresolved questions but one particularly intriguing issue from both a theoretical and a practical point of view has been the question of the role that verbal and visual processes may play in an identification decision. A frequently cited case may illustrate some of the issues involved (Doob & Kirshenbaum, 1973):

The case of Shatford. Shatford had been suspected of having been one of two men who had robbed 7000 dollars from a department store in Canada. Shortly thereafter, the cashier was barely able to give a description of the two robbers. Only three elements emerged from her testimony: (1) both perpetrators looked sufficiently similar to each other to have been brothers; (2) they were well-dressed; (3) they were "rather good-looking." Three days later, the witness was supposed to help the police in constructing a photofit picture of the criminals. She was reported to have said that she had nothing to contribute because she could not recall their features at all. Nonetheless, the witness later "identified" the suspect in a lineup amidst 11 foils.

How could this woman point to the suspect without being able to remember what he looked like? Several alternative "explanations" may account for this. For one thing – and we will review evidence relevant to this point in the last section of this chapter – it could have been possible that the impression of the crime left a memory trace that was not sufficiently strong to make possible a *verbal* description of the perpetrator but nonetheless sufficed to allow a *visual* recognition, i.e., a decision based on the visual comparison of a stored image with the members in the lineup.

Doob and Kirshenbaum focused their attention on a different possibility. The cashier created a verbal label "rather good-looking" at encoding (or soon thereafter), and stored this label (with or without the image of the perpetrator) in memory. Confronted with the lineup and under the pressure of the police to come up with a positive decision (cf. Köhnken & Maass, 1985) she "recognized" the most attractive person in the lineup, i.e., the suspect, given that he was the most attractive in the queue. Doob and Kirshenbaum sought to test this alternative hypothesis by presenting the lineup photographs to 20 nonwitnesses (students) who were asked to rate them according to their attractiveness. Twenty-one additional students were asked to pick somebody if all they knew about him was that he was "rather good-looking." For both questions the suspect emerged as the most attractive person in the lineup, which led the authors to conclude that this rival hypothesis could not be ruled out, thus casting doubt on whether or not the witness's identification was based on true recognition.

Clifford and Bull (1978) view this case as well as additional studies as evidence that verbal labels may strengthen (but possibly also transform) the encoding of a person and hence may be used as retrieval cues for recognition. On the other hand, these labels might also misguide witnesses into false identifications. Clearly, the issue of verbal and visual processes in person identification could be crucial although we should caution against overinterpretation of the anecdotal evidence from a single case study.

Verbal and Visual Processes Within an Integrative Framework of Eyewitness Testimony

Consideration of the role of verbal and visual processes in person identification should not be posed as an either-or question, nor is a discussion of the relative contributions of either form of mental process meaningful at an encompassing level. Rather, we first need to break down this general issue into several, only partially related phenomena that can be discussed in the light of recent empirical findings.

Both psychological researchers (e.g., Loftus, 1979; Penrod et al., 1982; Sporer, 1983a, 1984b) and legal scholars (e.g., Peters, 1972) have divided the

Environmental input	Perception phase	Retention phase	Retrieval phase
EXTERNAL: "outer world"	*action of perpetrator:* face, body + movements, voice + situational context	*postevent information:* *verbal:* conversations, interrogations, press reports *visual:* photofit exposure, mugshot exposure	*lineup:* expectations pressure to decide reinstatement of context: *verbal* retrieval cues *visual* retrieval cues
INTERNAL: reaction of witness, "inner world"	expectations, interpretation, focusing of attention encoding strategies • stereotypes • labeling • elaboration integration	• *verbal* rehearsal • *visual* rehearsal person description photofit construction integration of information	• person description • person identification metamemory: judgment of confidence reasons for identification

FIGURE 20.1. Typical cognitive, verbal, and visual processes in the perception, retention, and retrieval phases. The terms marked with an *asterisk* will be exemplified by data from empirical studies being conducted by the author

temporal sequence of an eyewitness account/identification into three stages: a perceptual or encoding phase, a retention phase, and a retrieval phase. The present framework (cf. Figure 20.1), which is derived from an integrative model of the psychology of testimony proposed by Sporer (1983b, 1984a), further distinguishes between *external* inputs the witness is confronted with by the environment, and the (internal and external) *subjective* responses by the individual witness. Within this framework, the role of typical verbal and visual processes (and other cognitive) processes at each of the three stages will be discussed.

Verbal and Visual Processes at the Perceptual Phase

If we limit our considerations firstly to the perceptual phase, the primary question we have to deal with is the role of verbal and visual processes at the encoding of the crime situation, particularly the appearance of the perpetrator and his actions. By virtue of his actions, the criminal is likely to become the focal point of attention; to use a time-honored analogy from Gestalt psychology: he becomes a figure against the ground, the latter being the environmental and situational context of the criminal act. I shall return to this analogy in the last section on the retrieval phase.

Eyewitness testimony concerning details of an event has long been known to be subject to various sources of error that cannot be discussed here in any detail (for reviews, see Clifford & Bull, 1978; Loftus, 1979; Wegener, 1981; Yarmey, 1979). *Verbal descriptions* of the perpetrator's facial characteristics and physical appearance (e.g., body, clothes) are frequently scanty, superficial, and imprecise, and deteriorate rapidly over time (Ellis, Shepherd, & Davies, 1980; cf. Sporer, 1988b, for a review). Our apparent difficulties in describing other people effectively are probably due to our inability to find appropriate verbal descriptors for our visual impressions of a person. Although our language appears to be rich in providing character attributes as a means of describing others, appropriate descriptors to denote physical appearance in a well-differentiated manner are relatively scarce. This linguistic deficiency hampers verbal encoding, and thus later verbal recall.

Hence, both researchers and practitioners have moved toward pictorial modes of reproduction such as the identikit or the photofit system as a more effective means of reconstructing a perpetrator's appearance (cf. Davies, 1983). This trend is also indicative of a more generally observable shift in focus toward visual processes in facial processing research.

Depending on the nature of the crime, there are a large number of external factors that may influence perception and encoding of the perpetrator and his actions. Most of these factors are visual in nature, although factors impinging upon other sense modalities, above all the criminal's voice, should not be neglected (see Hammersley & Read, 1988, for a review of this research). Surprisingly, many researchers (e.g., Buckhout, 1974) have regarded it as a truism that certain physical parameters are important determinants of later identification, such as the distance of the witness from the criminal or the level of illumination, although to my knowledge they have never been investigated systematically. Other visual factors, such as the criminal's disguise or weapon visibility, have been of more interest to psychologists (cf. Loftus, 1979), presumably because they trigger theoretically more intriguing psychological processes (e.g., arousal) which in turn may influence encoding and thus later identification attempts.

Internal factors at encoding, i.e., the witness's subjective reactions, are also numerous (e.g., prior expectations, familiarity with the situation, attention, arousal). Therefore, I shall restrict the discussion to those variables that specifically address my underlying theme of verbal and visual processes. In particular, I shall focus on two selected topics: (1) the role of criminal stereotypes in the perception and recognition of others, and (2) the effects of verbal and/or visual encoding upon later recognition/identification.

Criminal Stereotypes and Person Identification

The existence of social stereotypes and their influence upon our perceptions of people has been a traditional topic of research in social psychology (cf. Bierhoff, 1986; Lilli, 1982, this volume). Lilli (this volume) has summarized the general implications of the literature on the social psychology of stereotypes for our understanding of the psychology of eyewitness testimony. In this section, we will focus upon particular issues of stereotypes and their influence upon eyewitness identifications. Stereotypes exist about, among other things, the relationship between body builds, physiognomy and other physical appearance characteristics (including ethnicity), and certain personality characteristics. For example, Dannenmeier and Thumin (1964) found that nursery students overestimated the height of persons in accordance with differences in status and authority (cf. Clifford & Bull, 1978; Yarmey, 1979).

Buckhout (1974) describes a classic experiment by Allport, in which subjects were tachistoscopically exposed to a scene in a subway station in which a white man with a razor in his hand was standing next to a black man. According to a stereotype supposedly prevalent at that time, 50% of the subjects attributed possession of the razor to this black man.

If stereotypes can influence our perceptions of people and events in such a way, they may also have an important influence upon our recollection of them (Snyder & Uranowitz, 1978). Are there also certain criminal stereotypes that may distort our perceptions and thus tint our memory in person descriptions and identifications?

One of the problems with the literature on the relationship between social stereotypes and criminality is that most authors do not clearly keep apart two distinct though not necessarily separate empirical issues (cf. Bull, 1979, for a laudable exception): (1) Is there empirical evidence that persons with particular bodily characteristics or with certain physiognomic features are more likely to *commit* (certain) crimes than persons not displaying these characteristics? And: (2) Does the general populace, or certain subgroups thereof (e.g., women, police officers, judges), *believe* that persons who display such characteristics are more likely to be inclined to commit, or to have actually committed, certain crimes. The latter issue may further be clouded by the fact that people may not, for reasons of social desirability, readily admit to holding such overt beliefs but nonetheless may be (perhaps unconsciously) influenced by such covert implicit assumptions in their perception and hence recognition.

While supportive evidence for the first issue may be a contributing factor in the formation of the beliefs addressed in the second issue, beliefs in the existence of a relationship between physical characteristics and proneness to criminality could nonetheless be prevalent without having a basis in reality. An interesting twist in this argument has been suggested by Bull (1979), who has provided some evidence that the underlying chain of causation may in fact be reversed: Stereotypic beliefs may act as self-fulfilling prophecies in the sense that they may lead to social rejection of certain types of people who in turn are "driven into criminality" as a response to the experienced deprivation (cf. already Straith & DeKleine, 1938, cited in Bull, 1979).

While "beauty and the beast" may remain a common fairy tale-like topic in belletristic literature and films, in hard reality we have to reckon with the possibility that physical, and particularly facial, disfigurement may lead to social rejection. For example, in two elegant field experiments Bull and his associates tested the social rejection hypothesis as a function of facial disfigurement (port-wine stain or scar). Operationalizing negative attitude as unobtrusively measured physical distance, Rumsey, Bull, and Gahagan (1982) could show that, when crossing a busy London street, pedestrians would keep a larger distance from a person thus stigmatized with make-up than from the same person with her normal face. Bull and Stevens (1981) demonstrated that facial stigma also influenced the frequency and amount of donations made during a door-to-door charity collection.

These field studies nicely mesh with evidence from laboratory studies that facial abnormalities lead not only to judgments of low attractiveness but also to attributions of dishonesty (Bull, 1979). There is also evidence from earlier studies that stereotypic notions in the eye of the beholder are shared in that certain facial characteristics may be associated with certain types of crime in an above-chance fashion (Bull & Green, 1980; Goldstein, Chance, & Gilbert, 1982; Secord, 1958; Shoemaker, South, & Lowe, 1973; Thornton, 1939). And as Bull (1979, referring to Liggett, 1974) noted for person identification, it is the belief that matters and not necessarily the validity of the underlying stereotypes.

Given suboptimal encoding situations as they are frequently found in criminal encounters, later attempts at identification of suspects may be biased by the witness's notion of who in the present lineup may look most like the criminal "who did it". After all, most witnesses will not take instructions that caution them against perpetrator-lineups too seriously when the police have gone to the trouble of constructing a lineup and presenting it to them.

It is also important to note that for such a stereotypic bias to operate in a lineup choice a common sharing of stereotypes for certain appearance-crime associations is not a necessary prerequisite for a particular witness as long as he/she encounters someone who fits his/her *individual* subjective conception of what a "mugger," "robber", or "rapist" looks like. In the following, results from one of my own experiments will be presented that support this latter point.

Method for Experiment 1

Subjects and Materials. Stimulus faces were eight photographs taken from a criminological journal of men who were known to have murdered police officers in post-war Germany. During presentation, only the head and neck were visible to rule out any cues from clothing, while during the test phase both head and shoulders with the respective clothing were shown to ensure that the task was one of person recognition rather than mere stimulus recognition (cf. Bruce, 1982), and to make recognition more difficult (cf. Engelhardt, 1986; Sporer & Engelhardt, 1985). Forty subjects – mostly students in the early twenties but also some older schoolteachers – participated in the study; 24 were tested after 1 day, the other 16 after 2 weeks.

Procedure. Subjects were introduced to an experiment on "person perception" in which they were to rate four faces assembled in a booklet either on 27 physical characteristics (e.g., round, elongated, bony) or on 27 bipolar character traits (e.g., pleasant-unpleasant, violent-gentle, honest-dishonest). Subjects saw each face only for 5 s, after which they were to fill out the rating scales for about 3 min (off-time). After all four faces had been rated, subjects were told that the persons shown had been participants in a murder case: two of them burglars who had shot a policeman, and the other two uninvolved witnesses. Subjects ranked the four persons along a dimension from "1: looks most likely to be one of the murderers" to "4: looks least likely to be one of the murderers" (i.e., "most likely to be one of the witnesses"). Of the eight faces, four were assembled in each booklet in a completely counterbalanced Latin-square fashion to rule out any effects of particular idiosyncracies of the individual faces. The following day ($n = 24$) or after a fortnight ($n = 16$), subjects' recognition memory was tested with a YES-NO procedure with four "old" faces randomly mixed with four "new" faces.

Results and Discussion of Experiment 1

Space limitations preclude a detailed report of all findings of this study. Hence we will focus only on those data relevant to the stereotype issue. Recognition rates deteriorated rapidly from the 1-day (hits: 66.7%) to the 2-week delay condition (hits: 53.1%; $z = 1.723$, $p < 0.043$, one-tailed). As the latter performances were basically at chance level, the evaluation of stereotypic beliefs on recognizing targets can only be meaningfully analyzed for the 1-day condition ($n = 24$).

Although great care was taken to counterbalance faces during presentation and test, certain target persons were much more frequently rank ordered to "look most (or more) like one of the murderers," or to "look most (or more) like one of the witnesses," indicating that people do regard certain physiognomies as more likely to belong to criminals. However, more pertinent to our present discussion is the finding that the likelihood of a target being recognized the following day was strongly related to whether or not subjects had subjectively judged a target person to look more like one of the murderers or more like one of the witnesses (cf. Figure 20.2).

Figure 20.2 shows the hit rates (averaged across stimulus faces for particular simulus sets) as a function of subjects' rankings. Persons who were perceived to look most like one of the murderers were recognized 87.5% of the time (i.e., by 21 of 24 subjects), followed by the "second murderer" (79.2%),

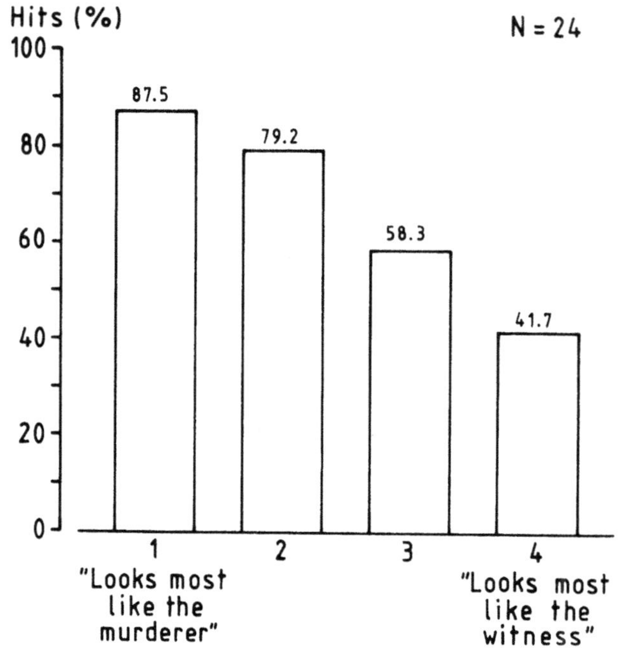

FIGURE 20.2. Hit rates as a function of subjects' rankings in experiment 1

"second witness" (58.3%), and the person who "looked most like the witness" [41.7%; tests for trends, Pflanzagl, 1962, p. 172: $T(3) = 3.66$, $p < 0.001$]. It seems that the categorization required from the subjects' led to a more durable memory trace (and hence recognition) for faces classified into the emotionally laden category "murderer" than for a "witness."

What do these results imply for our understanding of the operation of criminal stereotypes in making lineup choices? The data indicate that at the perceptual phase – or immediately thereafter – observers may attach criminal labels to certain faces more readily than to others in an above-chance fashion. Secondly, this labeling process does seem to lead to more durable encoding and consequently to differential forgetting in the sense that targets labeled as criminals in the context of a crime situation would be more likely to be identified later than persons not categorized in this way.

However, we should not overgeneralize from this small number of subjects and this small sample of faces. Also, these data only address positive identifications ("hits") in perpetrator-*present* lineups. They do not address the forensically perhaps more important issue of whether or not criminal stereotypes will trigger false identifications in a perpetrator-*absent* lineup. In correspondence with research by Bull and others presented above, this possibility should always be reckoned with at a criminal lineup.

Verbal Elaboration and Labeling

Stereotypes are but one means by which observers may categorize person information. There are other ways of linking the incoming visual information from a face (or from a person in a given situation) to our semantic memory about people. In the following, we are particularly interested in the question of how verbally elaborating on or labeling a face affects recognition.

There is some interesting basic research on the role of verbal information for the encoding of visual stimuli, in particular faces. Before we review this research, several distinctions have to be stressed that may serve as important mediating variables and may also help us to reconcile partially contradictory findings. First, we need to distinguish whether or not the verbal information that is supposed to lead to a more elaborated memory trace for a particular face is provided by the experimenter or has to be self-generated by the subject. In our discussion, we will refer to the first possibility as *verbal contextual elaboration* whereas the term *labeling* will be reserved for cases in which subjects actively – be it implicitly, or explicitly by instruction – generate verbal labels for the persons shown (that may help them to recognize the faces later). Second, we have to take into consideration whether or not subjects perceive the verbal information presented in the case of contextual elaboration to be congruent with the person depicted. Third, we need to distinguish whether or not the verbal information (externally provided or internally self-generated) is also (made) available to the subject as a retrieval cue in the sense of a *reinstatement of context.*

One of the first studies to systematically investigate the role of verbal and visual processes for the recognition of faces and other "complex configurations" such as ink blots and snow crystals was presented by Goldstein and Chance (1970). Their experiment 1 showed a clear advantage of faces (71% hits) over ink blots (46%) and snow crystals (33%), which the authors attributed to the greater subjective familiarty of faces over the other two classes of stimuli. Of course, this explanation cannot account for the significant difference between ink blots and snow crystals.

In experiment 2, Goldstein and Chance sought to determine whether or not the obtained face superiority effect might have been brought about by the greater associative value. To the question to "... write a word or phrase that each picture reminds you of or looks like," responses to faces were most frequent (205), followed by ink blots (179) and snow crystals (132). Yet nonsignificant (and even negative) rank order correlations between the recognizability of a stimulus and the frequency of associative responses to a face (−0.24 for immediate, −0.18 for delayed testing) did not suggest verbal mediation as a determinant of facial recognition. However, the authors also noted that mere associative responses may not be an optimal verbal coding technique for facilitating recognition. In another experiment more fully described in Goldstein and Chance (1976), they found superior recognition when subjects were instructed to write "some one thing about the face which you believe will help you recognize it when you see it again" (82% hits) than when instructed to associate (71%). Although these findings were paralleled by recall data (35% vs. 23% correct recall of verbal labels), the authors were struck by the undifferentiated nature of the verbal descriptors provided (e.g., "dark hair," "looks mean," "looks intelligent"). Similarly undifferentiated labels have also been observed in several experiments conducted by the present author (cf. experiment 2 below).

Other authors also failed to find a facilitative effect of verbal encoding on later recognition. In two experiments designed to investigate whether accompanying descriptive labels (e.g., information on the target's height, occupation, habits, frequented environments, etc.) would produce more elaborated encoding and hence increased recognition, no significant effects were observed (Baddeley & Woodhead, 1982, exps. 1 and 2). In a different vein, Malpass, Lavigueur, and Weldon (1973), who sought to improve facial recognition by verbal and visual training, found an improvement on several verbal usage variables but no concomitant improvement in visual recognition. Moreover, a canonical correlation analysis rendered no interpretable pattern of relationship between verbal measures and the visual recognition parameters.

To my knowledge, the only set of studies to have demonstrated a facilitative effect of an enriched verbal encoding context was reported by Kerr and Winograd (1982). In four experiments, Kerr and Winograd (1982) provided strong evidence that an elaborated verbal encoding context led to consistently higher recognition of faces than when the faces were unaccompanied by these elaborations. The elaborations consisted of short phrases describing personality characteristics, hobbies, professions, etc. (e.g., "he is an alcoholic," "he's a vegetarian," "he smokes cigars," "he's a psychiatrist"); these phrases were identical or similar to those used in the Watkins, Ho, and Tulving (1976) study. Adding more than one phrase further improved recognition in one but not the other three experiments, which the authors attributed either to the constraints of the experimental situation – the short presentation interval of 8 s for both facial display and aural presentation of the accompanying phrases – or the lack of integration of the unrelated phrases. It is also interesting to note that recognition was facilitated irrespective of the ability to actually *recall* the appropriate phrases (which turned out to be extremely low; cf. also Goldstein & Chance, 1970).

Finally, Kerr and Winograd's experiment 4 also showed that recognition is even higher when the elaborating phrases are reinstated at test but that the elaboration at encoding nonetheless has a facilitative effect independent of the reinstatement of context effect. In this experiment, Kerr and Winograd used a two-alternative forced-choice test [visual presentation of two faces and reading aloud the phrase(s) appropriate for one of the two faces] which may be particularly sensitive for demonstrating the facilitative effect of verbal reinstatement cues. However, if we want to apply these results to criminal lineups, the nature of this design without an old label-new faces control group does not rule out the possibility that the *reinstatement of context* in a target-absent lineup might lead to a shift in response criterion rather than truly better discrimination. Of course, if such a bias were to operate in criminal identifications where we do not know whether or not the true perpetrator is present, it could have fatal consequences in terms of false identifications.

Although this issue should more appropriately be discussed in the section on the retrieval phase (cf. Figure 20.1), I cannot review here the host of studies that have recently emerged to investigate the usefulness of reinstatement of context as a means of improving eyewitness identifications (cf. Davies, 1986; Malpass 1988, for reviews). I would point out only that the techniques employed may also be classified as verbal (such as the guided interview technique of Malpass & Devine, 1981) or visual [such as Krafka & Penrod's (1986) showing of physical objects from the scene of the crime before conducting a lineup; cf. Sporer, 1985, for a similar suggestion].

Verbal and Visual Processes at the Retention Phase

Compared with both the encoding and the retrieval phase, relatively little research has dealt with verbal and visual processes at the retention phase. Nevertheless, two issues may be singled out that are also at the heart of our discussion on verbal and visual memory for persons.

The first concerns the duration of the retention interval although it appears philosophically naïve to speak about delay as such as a cause of forgetting. Rather, we should think of the influence of intervening events as the causal factors operative during the retention interval. Relatively little is known about these underlying causal factors, and we can only briefly review the available evidence from studies that have systematically varied the length of the retention interval (cf. Ellis, 1984; Shapiro & Penrod, 1986; Shepherd et al., 1982, for reviews).

From basic research on memory we would expect the typical logarithmic decay function so often found in the Ebbinghaus tradition with verbal materials (e.g., Zechmeister & Nyberg, 1982). However, recognition memory for visual stimuli has normally been found to be much superior, even after exposure to a large number of stimuli and substantial delay periods (cf. Clifford & Bull, 1978; Shepherd et al., 1982, for reviews). But does this also hold for recognition memory for people, particularly their faces?

Unfortunately, most laboratory studies on facial recognition, which usually have used extremely short retention intervals between presentation of study items and test (e.g., 2 min or approximately 15 min filled with some activity to avoid extreme recency effects), do not tell us anything about the effect of delay. Also, ecologically more valid staged event studies on person recognition are also of little value with regard to this particular question, because they differ from each other on so many points that direct comparisons between them are difficult to make.

In laboratory studies on facial recognition that have manipulated the delay interval (e.g., the study by Goldstein & Chance, 1970, cited above), recognition rates have not necessarily deteriorated over moderate time periods (e.g., 2 days, 2 weeks; cf. Ellis, 1984). However, some decline may be observed when the recognition task is made more difficult (e.g., by changing the pose between study and test as done by Krouse, 1981; by adding clothes as a context not present during the encoding phase, as done in experiment 1 presented above; or by using a large number of faces in a continuous recognition paradigm, which increased the rate of false alarms in a study by Kolers, Duchnicky, & Sundstroem, 1985).

The most relevant studies for person identification under more natural conditions have been conducted by Egan, Pittner, and Goldstein (1977) and by Shepherd et al. (1982). While the former found an increase in false alarms after an 8-week delay interval (without a decrease in hits), Shepherd et al. found no change in false alarms even after 11 months. Correct identifications did decline, however, in the 11-month condition compared with the 1-week, 1-month, and 3-month conditions.

Based on these studies we may follow Ellis's (1984) conclusion that delay itself (i.e., the simple interference by faces in everyday life) does not necessarily imply a deterioration in facial recognition as is typically found with verbal materials. However, the relatively poor performances found in some studies, particularly in those using live events or films, suggest that the typical picture-superiority effect observed in facial recognition paradigms may not be so potent when encoding conditions are poor (e.g., lack of attention, arousal, etc.). Future research should systematically address such interactions between encoding variables and various delay intervals.

The second issue is whether, and how, specific crime-related events and the witness' processing of these events during the retention interval may affect later identification decisions. These factors may exert a positive influence, or they may hamper identifications. For example, Sporer (1988a) has recently suggested that facial recognition of a small set of target faces may be increased by various forms of verbal and/or visual rehearsal over a 1-week retention period. More practically, we would like to know how repeated descriptions of a criminal event and/or a suspect (e.g., at multiple police or court interrogations) may affect identification (cf. the issue of labeling discussed above).

Some of the most fascinating research on eyewitness testimony has dealt with the issue of misleading *postevent information*; such research was pioneered by Loftus and her colleagues (cf. Loftus, 1979, this volume). While we cannot review here the theoretical, and practical intricacies of these studies, we will point out their relevance for the verbal-visual issue. For example, Loftus and Green (1980) showed that subjects shown the face of a man and later exposed to a misleading description (e.g., suggesting that his hair was curly when in fact it was straight) would somehow incorporate – or even supplant or assimilate (?) – this new information into their memory and consequently offer falsified descriptions (i.e., *verbal* reproductions), make false lineup selections (i.e., *visual* recognitions), or construct erroneous facial composites (i.e., visual reproductions). Jenkins and Davies (1985) and Davies and Jenkins (1985) extended these findings by demonstrating that postevent *visual* information in the form of a misleading facial composite could also distort memory and result in both erroneous facial descriptions and in false identifications. Relatedly, both legal scholars and researchers have warned against the exposure to mugshots before a lineup as this may lead to unconscious transference, i.e., falsely identifying a person depicted on the mugshots (Brown, Deffenbacher, & Sturgill, 1977; Gorenstein & Ellsworth, 1980).

While much may remain to be learned about the intricacies of the underlying processes and some mediating variables (e.g., exposure time, salience of misleading details, etc.), these results do demonstrate that the verbal and visual memory systems (Tulving, 1985) seem to interact at some level, at least as far as person descriptions and identifications are concerned.

Verbal and Visual Processes at the Retrieval Phase

Many of the phenomena discussed in the section on the perceptual/encoding phase could also be discussed as retrieval phenomena and vice versa. Encoding and retrieval are closely linked in modern theorizing on human memory and, as a consequence, much of the research we have summarized in that section could also have been discussed here. For example, the reinstatement of verbal and visual context as a practical application of the encoding specificity principle (Tulving & Thomson, 1973) is by its very nature both an encoding and a retrieval phenomenon.

Verbal Labels as Retrieval Cues

One particular issue is whether or not the verbal labels an observer may generate to commit a face to memory may serve as an effective retrieval cue for later recognition. In the following, an experiment is reported in which subjects were asked to write down any thoughts that would help them memorize the presented faces. Later, in one condition of the experiment, before the recognition test they were allowed to study their *verbal* descriptions as retrieval cues. In another condition, subjects were asked to *visualize* as many of the faces as possible which they had seen at study. While some authors would clearly predict an advantage for the verbal labeling group, particularly since the labels were self-generated (e.g., Clifford & Bull, 1978), one might also expect, on the contrary, that the focus on visual processing in the visual rehearsal group—as a more stimulus-adequate way of processing faces—would lead to superior recognition performance.

Method for Experiment 2

Subjects and Materials. Subjects were 23 (8 male, 15 female) psychology majors at the University of Heidelberg. Materials were 36 black-and-white 35-mm slides of unfamiliar faces of men between 18 and 52 years of age. To ensure that the study involved person recognition rather than mere stimulus recognition (cf. Bruce, 1982), there were two versions of each face, one in three-quarter view and one in frontal view.

Procedure. During the presentation phase, subjects were exposed to 18 faces (nine frontal, nine three-quarter view) for 5 s each. They were instructed to commit the faces to memory to be able to recognize them later. After the presentation of each face there followed a 15-s interstimulus interval during which subjects were supposed to write down the thoughts that were supposedly helping them to memorize the faces (e.g., distinctive features, character traits, whether the person reminded them of somebody, etc.).

After a 15-min lecture period on key issues of the psychology of eyewitness testimony, subjects were given a YES-NO recognition test involving the 18 "old" faces from the presentation phase (but now in alternative pose) randomly mixed with 18 new faces.

Results and Discussion of Experiment 2

Data on hits and false alarms as well as common signal detection measures on sensitivity and bias were subjected to a 2×2 sex of subject by retrieval conditions ANOVA. Table 20.1 shows the means of these measures for the two retrieval conditions, collapsed over the sex of subjects factor, which did not approach significance for any of them. The only significant effect was on the number of hits, which were higher in the *visual* retrieval than in the verbal condition. The means of false alarms, d' and A', differed in the corresponding direction but did not reach significance, probably due to the sample size, which is relatively small when compared with other facial recognition studies.

The results are remarkable insofar as subjects in the verbal cue condition who tried to visualize the target faces on the basis of their verbal descriptions

TABLE 20.1. Means of hits (%), false alarms (%), d', logbeta, A' and beta" for verbal and visual retrieval conditions of experiment 2 ($n = 23$)

Retrieval conditions	Hits	False alarms	d'	logbeta	A'	beta"	n
Verbal cues	57.9	21.8	1.19	0.31	0.77	0.26	12
Visual rehearsal	67.2	19.2	1.51	0.27	0.82	0.21	11
F (1,19)	6.12	<1	<1	<1	2.01	<1	
$p<$	0.023	NS	NS	NS	0.18	NS	

and could use their own notes on the target faces as a retrieval cue recognized *fewer* old faces than subjects who were simply trying to visualize them before the recognition test.

In line with other facial recognition studies presented above (e.g., Goldstein & Chance, 1970), these findings also point to an advantage of visual over verbal processing of faces which again might be due to the lack of distinctiveness of the verbal descriptions used by our subjects. This argument is supported by an inspection of subjects' protocols at the encoding phase which typically contain rather general, nonunique descriptions (e.g., "long hair," "looks like a priest," "looks old," etc.).

Still, the results seem to be at odds with findings by Kerr and Winograd (1982, exp. 4), presented above, that short phrases read to the subjects by the experimenter would function as effective context reinstatement cues at the test phase. The important differences between Kerr and Winograd's study and our study, however, are that in our study subjects had to generate labels themselves – which apparently they did not do very well – and that they themselves had to find the label appropriate for a given face in their list rather than being presented with them as in a typical retrieval-cue paradigm. Future research should clarify whether subjects could profit from their self-generated labels when they are provided as retrieval cues along with the faces. Such a study should also include an old label paired with new faces control group to rule out shifts in response bias as an alternative explanation.

It is also an open question to what extent observers "automatically" attach verbal labels to other people's faces, and how these will affect later recognition. Of course, any "automatic" process is difficult to manipulate experimentally, and the present study that allowed subjects to jot down their ideas freely probably comes fairly close to assessing these processes. Perhaps a more rigorous method for measuring the frequency and content of this labeling process would be to have subjects "think aloud" when presented with individual faces and then content-analyze the transcribed verbal protocols. In this way we might also learn more about *what type of labels* might be useful for *differential* recognition of particular faces (cf. the later section on person description). But again, considering the difficulties subjects seem to have in generating verbal labels both in the present and in other studies, this line of research would not seem very promising owing to its overreliance on verbal instead of visual processes.

In practical terms, we would like to know whether or not witnesses, when prompted with their descriptions of the perpetrator given earlier to the police, would be more likely to make a correct decision at a lineup or photospread than witnesses not prompted with their descriptions. This question brings us to another important theme in our discussion of verbal and visual processes, i.e., the relationship between person descriptions and person identifications, to which we will return in the last section.

Person Identification and Memory for Details

In the section on verbal and visual processes at the perceptual phase we described the criminal and his actions as the "figure," and the surrounding circumstances, the scene of the crime, as the "ground." If we take this *Gestalt* analogy seriously, we would predict that memory for central details of a crime should be unrelated, or even inversely related, to memory for peripheral details of the situation. A corollary of this proposition with respect to person identification would be that a witness's likelihood of correctly identifying the culprit in a lineup should be inversely related to the amount of detail he/she can recall regarding peripheral details of the crime situation. In fact, there is some experimental evidence from a staged-incident study by Wells and Leippe (1981) of either zero correlations or even some negative correlations between certain peripheral details and the probability of a correct identification ($r = -0.41$, $p < 0.05$, for all 11 items).

However, the evidence presented by Wells and Leippe should be considered with caution: for one thing, they do not distinguish between central and peripheral details in their study, and secondly, some of the details they asked subjects to recall were of such minor importance (e.g., "where was the light switch in the room?") that knowledge of them may be more indicative of diversion of attention than of individual differences in memory capabilities. Of course, a witness who does not fully attend to the perpetrator is also less likely to encode his physiognomy and hence to identify him later. Another difficulty with this type of research is that in a real crime situation, a distinction between central and peripheral details will always be difficult to make post hoc.

Nonetheless, the importance of the nature of the relationship between a person identification and details of the eyewitness account is also stressed by some anecdotal evidence indicating that – from a metamemorial perspective (cf. Sporer, 1983b, 1984b) – jurors or judges may be more likely to believe a witness's identification if he/she seems to have a "good memory" in general, i.e., if he/she is able to impress the court with a rich recollection of all kinds of details regarding the circumstances of the crime.

But this metamemorial assumption is exactly at the heart of one of the key questions of this paper, namely whether and how this form of verbal memory (verbal reproduction of both verbal and visual details of the crime) is related to visual memory (person identification), and whether we may have to differentiate these two kinds of performance as being the result of two distinct memory systems (cf. Tulving, 1985, for a lucid discussion of the relationship between these two memory systems).

Person Description and Person Identification

One particular form of verbal memory that may or may not be related to the correctness of a later identification is the verbal description of the perpetrator given to the police soon after the incident. While witnesses' descriptions of criminals have long been known to be notoriously bad (cf. Münsterberg, 1908; Stern, 1903–1906), the nature of their *relationship* – expressed as a (point-biserial) correlation – with an identification has only very recently received increased attention.

The primary motive for this new research was a decision by the U.S. Supreme Court in Neil vs. Biggers (1972) which listed the "accuracy of a prior description" as one of the criteria to be used in judging identification evidence. Wells and Murray (1983) have reviewed the psychological evidence available to evaluate the Court's intuition-based opinion. Particularly, they have criticized the use of the prior description criterion on both logical and empirical grounds.

The logical arguments put forth by Wells and Murray remain pertinent: e.g., focusing upon the *similarity* between the criminal's description and the defendant's appearance (the so-called congruence) rather than upon the "accuracy" of the description, which would presume knowledge of the true perpetrator. However, more recent empirical studies (e.g., Pigott & Brigham, 1985; Pigott et al., 1985; Sporer, 1986; Wells, 1985) as well as an older German study by Wegener (1966) allow for somewhat more differentiated conclusions. Although space limitations preclude a more thorough discussion (see Sporer, 1988b, for a detailed review), some of the major findings may be summarized as follows:

Both laboratory studies on facial recognition (e.g., Malpass et al., 1973; Sporer, 1986, exp. 1; Wells, 1985) and ecologically more valid studies employing staged incidents (e.g., Pigott & Brigham, 1985; Pigott et al., 1985; Sporer, 1986, exp. 2; Wegener, 1966) show in general either zero or only slightly positive correlations between description accuracy (or the number of descriptors provided) and identification accuracy. However, under certain circumstances this correlation may increase. Sporer (1986, exp. 1), for example, found that rehearsal of the targets during the delay interval boosted the canonical correlation between the number of physical and trait descriptors on the one hand and hits and false alarms on the other (without rehearsal: canonical $r = 0.22$, *NS*; with rehearsal: $r = 0.75$, $p < 0.007$). Wells (1985), using individual target pictures (rather than subjects) as the unit of analysis, found a significant positive correlation of $r = 0.25$ between description and recognition accuracy, indicating that certain faces may lend themselves better to description than others, possibly due to their greater distinctiveness. Finally, Sporer (1986, exp. 2), in a staged incident study, observed that subjects who made an identification attempt (be it a correct *or* a false identification) recalled less physical descriptors of the target than subjects who refused to make a lineup choice.

Taken together, these studies seem to indicate that we ought to caution against the use of person descriptions as a means of judging the likelihood of an identification attempt being correct or not. Witnesses unable to provide detailed descriptions of a criminal (perhaps due to linguistic deficiencies in describing other people) may nonetheless be able to pick the true culprit from the lineup. On the other hand, witnesses who provide a fairly detailed description (we have no way of knowing whether this description will be accurate) may nonetheless choose the wrong person in a target-absent lineup. However, there may be important mediating variables such as the describability of individual targets or the amount of rehearsal during the retention interval that could increase the correlation between person descriptions and identifications, and hence the postdictive value of the former. For example, a witness who notes a distinctive feature of the perpetrator (e.g., a birthmark above the right eyebrow) and/or rehearses this feature over an extended period may use this information effectively at a later lineup.

Conclusions

The different types of phenomena at the perceptual, retention, and retrieval phases that we have considered relevant for our discussion on verbal and visual processes in person identification do not easily lend themselves to an encompassing integration. We have presented some evidence that verbal coding, be it in the form of contextual verbal elaboration or implicit labeling, may influence later identification decisions. But we have also reviewed evidence showing that reliance on more purely visual processing of facial information may be superior.

How can we integrate these partially contradictory findings? One explanation that would reconcile these seemingly inconsistent results could proceed as follows: While verbal labels – either provided by the environment (experimenter) or self-generated by the observer – may at times lead to an increased recognition performance over other encoding strategies, verbal or partial verbal encoding may still be *suboptional* when compared with purely visual processing both at encoding and retrieval. For example, one could speculate that verbal descriptions or labels may be effective retrieval cues for particular subsamples of faces that contain certain distinct (if not unusual) features (e.g., a hooked nose, off-standing ears) but less so for more "typical," "average-looking" faces. This notion could also account for the typically low correlations between description and recognition measures that are usually obtained by *averaging* recall and recognition scores over a large number of presumably typical and atypical faces. For typical faces, where verbal labels may be more difficult to come by or to associate with the faces concerned, more purely visual processing may be more effective.

We need to focus to a greater extent on theoretical models of face processing that also allow us to take individual differences among faces into account. But even if we did arrive at a deeper understanding of these issues through laboratory studies on facial recognition, we would still have to check whether the findings would hold under ecologically more valid settings relevant for person identifications of criminals. We hope that the integrative framework outlined here will serve as an organizational schema in which we can relate previously unrelated findings and thus contribute to the cross-fertilization of different research traditions.

Acknowledgments. This research was supported by a grant from the Deutsche Forschungsgemeinschaft to the author (Sp 262/1–2). The author would like to thank Dr. Hans Werner Bierhoff for commenting on an earlier version of this manuscript, Ms. Sabine Küchler for her help in collecting the data for experiment 1, and Drs. Stefan Hormuth and Norbert Schwarz for their invitation to a seminar in which the data for experiment 2 were collected.

References

Baddeley, A., & Woodhead, M. (1982). Depth of processing, context, and face recognition. *Canadian Journal of Psychology, 36*, 148–164.

Bierhoff, H.W. (1986). *Personenwahrnehmung.* Heidelberg: Springer.

Brown, E., Deffenbacher, K., & Sturgill, W. (1977). Memory for faces and the circumstances of encounter. *Journal of Applied Psychology, 62*, 311–318.

Bruce, V. (1982). Changing faces: visual and non-visual coding processes in face recognition. *British Journal of Psychology, 73*, 105–116.

Buckhout, R. (1974). Eyewitness testimony. *Scientific American, 231*, 23–31.

Bull, R. (1979). The influence of stereotypes on person identification. In D.P. Farrington, K. Hawkins, & S. Lloyd-Bostock (Eds.), *Psychology, law and legal processes* (pp. 184–194). Oxford: MacMillan.

Bull, R., & Green, J. (1980). The relationship between physical appearance and criminality. *Medicine, Science and the Law, 20*, 79–83.

Bull, R., & Stevens, J. (1981). The effects of facial deformity on helping behaviour. *Italian Journal of Psychology, 8*, 25–33.

Clifford, B., & Bull, R. (1978). *The psychology of person identification.* London: Routledge and Kegan Paul.

Dannenmeier, W., & Thumin, F. (1964). Authority status as a factor in perceptual distortion of size. *Journal of Social Psychology, 63*, 361–365.

Davies, G. (1983). Forensic face recall: the role of visual and verbal information. In S. Lloyd-Bostock & B.R. Clifford (Eds.), *Evaluating witness evidence: recent psychological evidence and new perspectives* (pp. 103–123). Chichester: Wiley.

Davies, G. (1986). Context effects in episodic memory: a review. *Cahiers de Psychologie Cognitive, 6*, 157–174.

Davies, G., & Jenkins, F. (1985). Witnesses can be misled by police composite pictures: How and when. In F.L. Denmark (Ed.), *Social/ecological psychology and the psychology of women* (pp. 103–115). Amsterdam: Elsevier.

Doob, A.N., & Kirshenbaum, H.M. (1973). Bias in police lineups–partial remembering. *Journal of Police Science and Administration, 1*, 287–293.

Egan, D., Pittner, M., & Goldstein, A.G. (1977). Eyewitness identification: photographs vs. live models. *Law and Human Behavior, 1*, 199–206.

Ellis, H.D. (1984). Practical aspects of face memory. In G.L. Wells & E.F. Loftus (Eds.), *Eyewitness testimony: psychological perspectives* (pp. 12–37). New York: Cambridge University Press.

Ellis, H. D., Shepherd, J. W., & Davies, G. M. (1980). The deterioration of verbal descriptions of faces over different delay intervals. *Journal of Police Science and Administration, 8*, 101–106.

Engelhardt, H. (1986). Zum Einfluß von Kontext auf das Wiedererkennen von Personen. Eine experimentelle Untersuchung über Kleidung als Hinweisreiz. Unveröffentlichte Diplomarbeit, University of Erlangen-Nürnberg, FRG.

Goldstein, A. G., & Chance, J. E. (1970). Visual recognition memory for complex configurations. *Perception and Psychophysics, 9*, 237–241.

Goldstein, A. G., & Chance, J. E. (1976). Recognition of faces and verbal labels. *Bulletin of the Psychonomic Society, 7*, 384–386.

Goldstein, A. G., Chance, J. E., & Gilbert, B. J. (1982). Facial stereotypes of good and bad guys: a replication and extension. Paper presented at the Annual Meeting of the Psychological Association in Minneapolis, Minnesota.

Gorenstein, G. W., & Ellsworth, P. C. (1980). Effect of choosing an incorrect photograph on a later identification by an eyewitness. *Journal of Applied Psychology, 65*, 616–622.

Hammersley, R., & Read, D. S. (1988). Stimmidentifizierung. In G. Köhnken & S. L. Sporer (Eds.), *Zeugenidentifizierung: Psychologisches Wissen, Probleme und Perspektiven.* Göttingen: Hogrefe.

Jenkins, F., & Davies, G. (1985). Contamination of facial memory through exposure to misleading composite pictures. *Journal of Applied Psychology, 70*, 164–176.

Kerr, N. H., & Winograd, E. (1982). Effects of contextual elaboration on face recognition. *Memory and Cognition, 10*, 603–609.

Köhnken, G., Maass, A. (1985). Realism, reactance, and instructional bias in eyewitness identification. In F. L. Denmark (Ed.), *Social/ecological psychology and the psychology of women* (pp. 141–163). Amsterdam: Elsevier.

Kolers, P. A., Duchnicky, R. L., & Sundstroem, G. (1985). Size in the visual processing of faces and words. Unpublished manuscript, University of Toronto.

Krafka, C., & Penrod, S. (1985). Reinstatement of context in a field experiment on eyewitness identification. *Journal of Personality and Social Psychology, 49*, 58–69.

Krouse, F. L. (1981). Effects of pose, pose change, and delay on face recognition performance. *Journal of Applied Psychology, 66*, 651–654.

Ligett, J. (1974). *The human face.* London: Constable.

Lilli, W. (1982). *Grundlagen der Stereotypisierung.* Göttingen: Verlag für Psychologie.

Loftus, E. F. (1979). *Eyewitness testimony.* Cambridge, MA: Harvard University Press.

Loftus, E. F., & Greene, E. (1980). Warning: even memory for faces may be contagious. *Law and Human Behavior, 4*, 323–334.

Malpass, R. S., & Devine, P. G. (1981). Guided memory in eyewitness identification. *Journal of Applied Psychology, 66*, 343–350.

Malpass, R. S., & Devine, P. G. (1987). Improving identification evidence. In G. Köhnken & S. L. Sporer (Eds.), *Zeugenidentifizierungen: Psychologisches Wissen, Probleme und Perspektiven.* Göttingen: Hogrefe.

Malpass, R. S., Lavigueur, H., & Weldon, D. (1973). Verbal and visual training in face recognition. *Perception and Psychophysics, 14*, 285–292.

Münsterberg, H. (1908). *On the witness stand. Essays on psychology and crime.* New York: Doubleday, Page.

Neil vs. Biggers (1972). 409 U.S. 188, 93 S. Ct. 375; 34 L. Ed. 2d 401.

Penrod, S., Loftus, E., & Winkler, J. (1982). The reliability of eyewitness testimony: a psychological perspective. In N. L. Kerr & R. M. Bray (Eds.), *The psychology of the courtroom* (pp. 119–168). New York: Academic.

Peters, K. (1972). *Fehlerquellen im Strafprozeß*: Vol. 2. Karlsruhe: Müller.

Pflanzagl, J. (1962). *Allgemeine Methodenlehre der Statistik*: Vol. 2. *Höhere Methoden unter besonderer Berücksichtigung der Anwendung*. Berlin: de Gruyter.

Pigott, M.A., & Brigham, J.C. (1985). Relationship between accuracy of prior description and facial recognition. *Journal of Applied Psychology, 70*, 547–555.

Pigott, M.A., Brigham, J.C., & Bothwell, R.K. (1985). A field study of the relationship between description accuracy and identification accuracy. Unpublished manuscript, Florida State University.

Rumsey, N., Bull, R., & Gahagan, D. (1982). The effect of facial disfigurement on the proxemic behavior of the general public. *Journal of Applied Social Psychology, 12*, 137–150.

Secord, P. (1958). Facial features and inference processes in interpersonal perception. In R. Tagiuri & L. Petrullo (Eds.), *Person perception* (pp. 300–315). Stanford: Stanford University Press.

Shapiro, P.N., & Penrod, S. (1986). Meta-analysis of facial identification studies. *Psychological Bulletin, 100*, 139–156.

Shepherd, J.W., Ellis, H.D., & Davies, G.D. (1982). *Identification evidence*. Aberdeen: Aberdeen University Press.

Shoemaker, D., South, D., & Lowe, J. (1973). Facial stereotypes of deviants and judgments of guilt or innocence. *Social Forces, 51*, 427–433.

Snyder, M., & Uranowitz, S.W. (1978). Reconstructing the past: some cognitive consequences of person perception. *Journal of Personality and Social Psychology, 36*, 941–950.

Sporer, S.L. (1983a). Allgemeinwissen zur Psychologie der Zeugenaussage. In H.J. Kerner, H. Kury, & K. Sessar (Eds.), *Deutsche Forschungen zur Kriminalitätsentstehung und Kriminalitätskontrolle* (pp. 1191–1245). Cologne: Heymanns.

Sporer, S.L. (1983b). Kernprobleme der Psychologie der Personenidentifizierung: ein multimethodaler Ansatz zur Überprüfung juristischer Alltagspsychologien. Proposal to the Deutsche Forschungsgemeinschaft.

Sporer, S.L. (1984a). Ein integratives Modell zur Psychologie der Zeugenaussage. Paper given at the 34th congress of the Deutsche Gesellschaft für Psychologie, Vienna.

Sporer, S.L. (1984b). Forschungsparadigmen für das Wiedererkennen von Personen. Paper given at the 26th conference of experimental psychologists, Nürnberg.

Sporer, S.L. (1985). Lineup procedures in the Federal Republic of Germany: an exploratory archival analysis. In F.L. Denmark (Ed.), *Social/ecological psychology and the psychology of women* (pp. 69–90). Amsterdam: Elsevier.

Sporer, S.L. (1986). Person description and person identification: a critical review and some fresh evidence. Paper presented at the Biennial Meeting of the American Psychology-Law Society in Tucson, Arizona.

Sporer, S.L. (1988a). Long-term improvement of facial recognition through visual rehearsal. In M.M. Gruneberg, P.E. Morris, & R.N. Sykes (Eds.), *Practical aspects of memory: current research and issues* (Vol. 1, pp. 182–188). Chichester: Wiley.

Sporer, S.L. (1988b). Psychologische Aspekte der Personenbeschreibung. In G. Köhnken & S.L. Sporer (Eds.), *Zeugenidentifizierungen: psychologisches Wissen, Probleme und Perspektiven*. Göttingen: Hogrefe.

Sporer, S.L., & Engelhardt, H. (1985). Soziale Determinanten des Gedächtnisses für Personen. Vortrag gehalten auf der 27. Tagung experimentell arbeitender Psychologen in Wuppertal, FRG.

Stern, W. L. (1903–1906). Beiträge zur Psychologie der Aussage. (2 Vols.). Leipzig: Barth.

Thornton, G. R. (1939). The ability to judge crime from photographs of criminals: a contribution to technique. *Journal of Abnormal and Social Psychology, 34*, 378–383.

Tulving, E. (1985). How many memory systems are there? *American Psychologist, 40*, 385–398.

Tulving, E., & Thomson, D. M. (1973). Encoding specificity and retrieval processes in episodic memory. *Psychological Review, 80*, 352–373.

Watkins, M. J., Ho, E., & Tulving, E. (1976). Context effects in recognition memory for faces. *Journal of Verbal Learning and Verbal Behavior, 15*, 505–517.

Wegener, H. (1966). Experimentelle Untersuchungen über die Personenbeschreibung und -identifizierung durch 10–12jährige Kinder. In J. Gerchow (Ed.), *An den Grenzen von Medizin und Recht* (pp. 115–125). Stuttgart: Enke.

Wegener, H. (1981). *Einführung in die Forensische Psychologie*. Darmstadt: Wissenschaftliche Buchgesellschaft.

Wells, G. L. (1978). Applied eyewitness-testimony research: system variables and estimator variables. *Journal of Personality and Social Psychology, 36*, 1546–1557.

Wells, G. L. (1985). Verbal descriptions of faces from memory: Are they diagnostic of identification accuracy? *Journal of Applied Psychology, 70*, 619–626.

Wells, G. L., & Leippe, M. R. (1981). How do triers of fact infer the accuracy of eyewitness identification? Using memory for peripheral details can be misleading. *Journal of Applied Psychology, 66*, 682–687.

Wells, G. L., & Murray, D. M. (1983). What can psychology say about the Neil vs. Biggers criteria for judging eyewitness accuracy? *Journal of Applied Psychology, 68*, 347–362.

Yarmey, A. D. (1979). The effects of attractiveness, feature saliency and liking on memory for faces. In M. Cook & G. Wilson (Eds.), *Love and attraction* (pp. 51–53). Oxford: Pergamon.

Zechmeister, E. B., & Nyberg, S. E. (1982). *Human memory. An introduction to research and theory.* Monterey, CA: Brooks/Cole.

Part Four Correctional Treatment: Clinical and Organizational Aspects

Introduction

FRIEDRICH LÖSEL

This part of the volume is dedicated to the area of correction within the criminal justice system. The contributions mainly refer to the area of imprisonment. It was necessary to set such a priority for reasons of space, even though in the area of juvenile delinquency and petty offences the numerous approaches of nonintervention, of deinstitutionalization, of diversion, of community services, and of mediation between offenders and victims are also of great interest in psychology (see Albrecht & Schädler, 1986; Decker, 1985; Farrington, 1985; Heinz, 1987; Klein, 1979; Kury & Lerchenmüller, 1981; Lösel, 1987; Schur, 1973). On the other hand it is especially the reaction to relatively persistent and serious criminality that remains a central problem for the criminal justice system, as the majority of offenders are convicted only once or twice, whereas a small group of repeatedly convicted are responsible for a high percentage of the (registered) delicts (cf. Farrington, 1983; Steffen, 1984; Wolfgang, Figlio, & Sellin, 1972; see also Blumstein, Cohen, & Farrington, 1988 vs. Gottfredson & Hirschi, 1986). Albee's (1987) argument that even through effective corrective measures a decrease in prevalence cannot be achieved is therefore questionable with regard to the criminality. However, as research on the "hidden figure" shows, correction (and even selective incapacitation) of official offenders can only have a very limited influence on the number of crimes (e.g., Elliott, Dunford, & Huizinga, 1987).

As with all reactions of society to its offenders, there are substantial cultural and historical differences in the field of imprisonment. For example, in the Netherlands and a few other West European countries the number of prisoners per 100000 capita is far below that in the United States or some of the Eastern Bloc countries (Kaiser, Kerner, & Schöch, 1983). In a country like Germany, the proportion of enforced prison sentences when compared to the total number of criminal sanctions has decreased during the past 100 years from 76% (German Empire) to about 6% (Federal Republic of Germany) in favor of fines. On the other hand, imprisonment rates have been remarkably stable (Moitra, 1987). Differences or changes depend on the rates of (severe) crime but probably also on economic conditions as well as the values and interests held by the elites which influence the society's crime policies. Whether the developments in crime are actually influenced by changes in the practice of criminal sanctions is something that can hardly be proved conclusively. This is because of the numerous uncontrolled third variables, the problems of official statistics, and often insufficient long-term data. Available longitudinal analyses give strong support neither to the idea of criminogenic effects nor to that of deterrence effects (Moitra, 1987).

Besides long-term tendencies – e.g., the relative decrease in prison sentences and the change to more informal sociotherapeutic and pedagogic measures – there are also some quite rapidly changing trends. Examples are the rise and descent of the concept of treatment and the revival of the idea of punishment and deterrence. Even though some of these concepts govern the discussion of crime policies from time to time, the developments in practice are, as a rule, more continuous and by no means one-dimensional. Heterogeneous concepts, such as that of institutional treatment, of decarceration, or of selective incapacitation, do certainly coexist. This is an expression of the different objectives which influence crime policies, such as, for example, the compensation of guilt, the protection of the general public, general prevention, special prevention, aspects of humaneness, and financial savings. That is why one should be sceptical of too general, short-term diagnoses of "changes" in crime policy. Under a more continuous perspective the following points, among others, become important for psychological research into correction:

Empirical Evaluation. Although normally the effects of criminological research do not bear heavily on the practice of crime policies (see Quensel, 1984; Wilkins, 1987), the tendency to substantiate corrective measures with empirical findings has clearly increased. Despite numerous methodological problems and only partially encouraging results, it is the area of institutionalized and community treatment where the most comprehensive attempts have been made to substantiate measures of special prevention in an empirical way (Lösel, Köferl, & Weber, 1987). It is necessary to continue practice and research in this field since, due to demographic developments, relief of the criminal justice system is beginning to become apparent (cf. Blumstein, 1983; Dünkel, 1987). This offers better opportunities for scientifically guided experiments. Renowned evaluation reports, such as those by Lipton, Martinson, and Wilks (1975) or Sechrest, White, and Brown (1979), should be considered not so much as instruments on which to base direct policies, but as contributions that improve the understanding of a complex social problem in the long run (see Leviton & Hughes, 1981). For example, in the Federal Republic of Germany it was the evaluation of experiments in treatment that instigated the search for more valid figures regarding recidivism within the normal penal system. National statistics of recidivism, important for comprehensive evaluations, have been compiled for only 2 years (see Uhlig, 1987).

Greater Sensitivity to Small Changes. In the criminal justice system, reforms and concrete measures are not seldom subjected to exaggerated expectations.

Persistent criminality, however, seems to be one of the areas in which behavioral changes are particularly difficult to achieve (Kazdin, 1987). Institutions of correction and treatment produce not only their own negative side-effects (see Ortmann, 1987) but are also embedded in complex societal systems and counteractive influences which do not promise "decisive" effects (see Opp, 1979). For example, young offenders released from prison fare particularly badly in German statistics of recidivism (Uhlig, 1987). However, even from radical changes in the imprisonment of juveniles only moderate repercussions in crime statistics could be expected. Because juvenile prisoners mostly represent a negative selection after several unsuccessful community measures and because of the distribution of age in crime, it is precisely in this group of offenders that a high likelihood of recidivism can be expected (see Hirschi & Gottfredson, 1983). As is the case in concomitant time series, true or quasi-experiments are often too insensitively laid out for the detection of "real" effects (Boruch & Gomez, 1977). A more realistic assessment is needed. Rosenthal (1983), for example, shows in his Binomial Effect Size Display that the correlation of $r = 0.20$, usually considered to be low, corresponds to an increase in the success rate due to treatment of 40%–60%. This is an effect which, in the area of medical surgery, for example, would be considered practically significant.

Differentiation of Measures. The criminal justice system is based on equal treatment and thus also on uniform types of reaction to correction. But if interactions of persons and situations are seen from a psychological standpoint, one can hardly expect certain measures of intervention to have similar effects on all persons affected. Without ignoring the criticisms concerning problems of "delegalization" or informal decisions, which are difficult to control (see Lerman, 1975), it seems clear that essential sources of increased efficiency of correction and treatment measures probably lie in further differentiation. In the course of this, for example, the negative side-effects of decarceration (see Scull, 1977) can be put down to, among other things, the fact that some experiments were initiated without the necessary differentiation of target groups and alternative measures. Another example is treatment. Different groups of offenders, measures, and contexts are being "lumped together" in discussion without clarifying whether essential functional features of a treatment have actually been realized, whether the measures are combined adequately, and what constellations are necessary in order to be able to expect fairly consistent effects. Romig (1978), for instance, showed that only those pedagogic-psychological measures for juvenile delinquents promise relative success which are based on differentiated diagnoses of the problem, which include the immediate environment and improve concrete abilities to interact, which display careful implementation and supervision, and which might also supply qualifications applicable in school or professional life.

The Perspective of Organization. A large part of correction and treatment research is aimed exclusively at criminals. The respective institutions or their staff are regarded as homogeneous factors. In many areas of evaluation, however, it has become evident that there are problems of implementation and monitoring that may lead to the failure of a program (Rossi & Freeman, 1982). In contrast to this, for example, Moos (1974) was able to show that characteristics of the correctional climate clearly vary and that they are connected with the effectiveness of the institutions. The amount of influence which the aims of certain legal measures have on "the actual functioning of the criminal justice system" can be put into concrete terms only at the level of the attitudes and behavioral patterns of those directly involved (cf. Ebbesen & Konečni, 1982). Increased research on staff in the area of correction is, however, not only relevant with regard to the effects on the criminal but also with regard to occupational stress in this profession, all in all lending organizational research a significance of its own (see Long, Shouksmith, Voges, & Roache, 1986).

The psychological aspects briefly mentioned and other aspects of correction and treatment research are discussed in the following studies in an exemplary way. Some of the chapters simultaneously offer an insight into the German penal system, which differs from the US situation in many respects.

The contribution by *Friedrich Lösel* and *Peter Köferl* includes an appraisal of the evaluation research of social therapy with adult prisoners being carried out in the Federal Republic of Germany. Not only traditional methods of secondary analysis are employed, but also the more recent method of statistical meta-analysis (cf. Bangert-Drowns, 1986; Glass, McGaw, & Smith, 1981). The meta-analysis shows by different models that there is a main effect of sociotherapeutic institutions, which is relatively independent of the characteristics of the primary studies. Beside the specific results, the study is also interesting because of this methodological approach. We consider a similar study based on the much more extensive empirical US material with its greater potential for differentiation worthwhile, and we understand that such a study is presently being carried out by the Russell Sage Foundation (T. Cook, personal communication; for first results see Lipsey, 1988).

The contribution by *Helmut Kury* deals with a detailed empirical evaluation study on the psychological treatment of young remand prisoners. The situation of pretrial detention is a special problem of imprisonment, a problem which focuses less on rehabilitation than on the avoidance of prisonization effects. Programs and evaluations are very scarce in this field. Helmut Kury's study compares different measures on the basis of behavior therapy and client-centered counseling. The multi-method approach and the careful recording of implementation and monitoring problems should be particularly emphasized. This approach enables Kury to draw concrete conclusions for relevant situations despite the only moderate consistency of the reported effects.

In his contribution, *Albert Hauber* presents alternative sanctions for juvenile offenders in community settings, as applied in the Netherlands. Similar programs are being carried out in the Federal Republic of Germany, among other countries (for a summary, see Heinz, 1987). What is particularly remarkable about Hauber's reported program is the fact that it uses a differentiation of the target population according to the intensity and type of the delinquent behavior. According to this approach, certain measures should not be applied to the wrong groups. Different mottos, such as "always catch and strongly punish" vs. "big problems need individual coaching" turn out to be quite relevant. In the present paper there is an emphasis on the presentation of the theoretical basis and the practical layout of the program. The evaluation is made on a qualitative basis; one may look forward to further comparative data.

The chapter by *Willi Seitz* reports on an empirical study on correctional officers. It deals with the connections between personality traits, general attitudes, and special attitudes towards prisoners. On the one hand the study follows the tradition of personality-related psychological concepts concerning the role of prison officers, as developed by Niederhoffer (1967) or Poole and Regoli (1980), with the example of cynicism. On the other hand concepts of attitude theories are applied. A series of correlations emerge, e.g., between dispositions of egocentric isolation or the sense of duty and the belief in the therapeutic effects of work or the intolerance toward the personal needs of prisoners. Even if one keeps in mind the special problems of correlative data, the findings still suggest that prison officers are not just a passive object of institutional influences, but that they also take a more or less active part in the shaping of the institution's environment.

The final contribution by *Friedrich Lösel* and *Thomas Bliesener* is devoted to the psychologists in the penal system, who play an important role as mediators for the organizational development. The structure of role perceptions, the structure of activities, and their dependence on situational conditions are investigated in an empirical study carried out in the Federal Republic of Germany. In path models, the personnel-prisoner ratio, the governing party of the state, and the type of prison are particularly connected with the dimensions of the activities and not so much with role perceptions. It becomes evident that the penal system should not only be seen from the special standpoint of the "total institution" (Goffman, 1962); rather, general theoretical organization models may also be applied successfully.

Perhaps more general correlations are expressed in such findings, which lead – although in a very speculative manner – to the following question: Does not the degree to which society stereotypes and stigmatizes institutions of the criminal justice system correspond to the degree to which these institutions stereotype and stigmatize the criminal offenders (and vice versa)?

References

Albee, G. W. (1987). Powerlessness, politics, and prevention. The community mental health approach. In K. Hurrelmann, F. Kaufmann, & F. Lösel (Eds.), *Social intervention: Potential and constraints* (pp. 37–52). Berlin: de Gruyter.

Albrecht, H. J., & Schädler, W. (Eds.). (1986). *Community service.* Freiburg i. Br., FRG: Max-Planck-Institut für ausländisches und internationales Strafrecht.

Bangert-Drowns, R. (1986). Review of developments in meta-analytic method. *Psychological Bulletin, 99*, 388–399.

Blumstein, A. (1983). Prisons: Population, capacity, and alternatives. In J. Q. Wilson (Ed.), *Crime and public policy* (pp. 229–250). San Francisco: ICS.

Blumstein, A., Cohen, J., & Farrington, D. P. (1988). Criminal career research: Its value for criminology. *Criminology, 26*, 1–35.

Boruch, R. F., & Gomez, H. (1977). Sensitivity, bias and theory in impact evaluations. *Professional Psychology, 8*, 411–434.

Decker, S. H. (1985). A systematic analysis of diversion. *Journal of Criminal Justice, 13*, 207–216.

Dünkel, F. (1987). *Die Herausforderung der geburtenschwachen Jahrgänge. Aspekte der Kosten-Nutzen-Analyse in der Kriminalpolitik.* Freiburg i. Br., FRG: Max-Planck-Institut für ausländisches und internationales Strafrecht.

Ebbesen, E. B., & Konečni, V. J. (1982). Social psychology and the law: A decision making approach to the criminal justice system. In V. J. Konečni & E. B. Ebbesen (Eds.), *The criminal justice system: A social-psychological analysis* (pp. 3–23). San Francisco: Freeman.

Elliott, D. S., Dunford, F. W., & Huizinga, D. (1987). The identification and prediction of career offenders utilizing self-reported and official data. In J. D. Burchard & S. N. Burchard (Eds.), *Prevention of delinquent behavior* (pp. 90–121). Newbury Park, CA: Sage.

Farrington, D. P. (1983). Offending from 10 to 25 years of age. In K. T. van Dusen & S. A. Mednick (Eds.), *Prospective studies in crime and delinquency* (pp. 17–37). Boston: Kluwer-Nijhoff.

Farrington, D. P. (1985). Delinquency prevention in the 1980's. *Journal of Adolescence, 8*, 3–16.

Glass, G. V., McGaw B., & Smith, M. L. (1981). *Meta-analysis in social research.* Beverly Hills, CA: Sage.

Goffman, E. (1962). *Asylums: Essays on the social situations of mental patients and other inmates.* Chicago: Aldine.

Gottfredson, M., & Hirschi, T. (1986). The true value of lambda would appear to be zero: An essay on career criminals, criminal careers, selective incapacitation, cohort studies, and related topics. *Criminology, 24*, 213–233.

Heinz, W. (1987). Neue ambulante Maßnahmen nach dem Jugendgerichtsgesetz – Empirische Bestandsaufnahme und kriminalpolitische Perspektiven. *Monatsschrift für Kriminologie und Strafrechtsreform, 70*, 129–154.

Hirschi, T., & Gottfredson, M. (1983). Age and the explanation of crime. *American Journal of Sociology, 89*, 552–584.

Kaiser, G., Kerner, H.-J., & Schöch, H. (1983). *Strafvollzug* (3rd ed.). Heidelberg: Müller.

Kazdin, A. E. (1987). *Conduct disorders in childhood and adolescence.* Beverly Hills, CA: Sage.

Klein, M. W. (1979). Deinstitutionalization and diversion of juvenile offenders: A litany of impediments. In N. Morris & M. Tonry (Eds.), *Crime and justice: An annual review of research* (Vol. 1, pp. 145–201). Chicago: University of Chicago Press.

Kury, H., & Lerchenmüller, H. (Eds.). (1981). *Diversion – Alternativen zu klassischen Sanktionsformen* (Vols. 1–2). Bochum: Brockmeyer.

Lerman, P. (1975). *Community treatment and social control.* Chicago: University of Chicago Press.

Leviton, L.C., & Hughes, E.F. (1981). Research on the utilization of evaluations. A review and synthesis. *Evaluation Review, 5*, 525–548.

Lipsey, M. (1988). Juvenile delinquency intervention. In H.S. Bloom, D.S. Cordray, & R.J. Light (Eds.), *Lessons from selected program and policy areas* (pp. 63–83). San Francisco: Jossey-Bass.

Lipton, D.S., Martinson, R., & Wilks, J. (1975). *The effectiveness of correctional treatment. A survey of treatment evaluation studies.* New York: Praeger.

Lösel, F. (1987). Psychological crime prevention: Concepts, evaluations and perspectives. In K. Hurrelmann, F. Kaufmann, & F. Lösel (Eds.), *Social intervention: Potential and constraints* (pp. 289–313). Berlin: de Gruyter.

Lösel, F., Köferl, P., & Weber, F. (1987). *Meta-Evaluation der Sozialtherapie.* Stuttgart: Enke.

Long, N., Shouksmith, G., Voges, K., & Roache, S. (1986). Stress in prison staff: An occupational study. *Criminology, 24*, 331–345.

Moitra, S.D. (1987). *Crimes and punishment. A comparative study of temporal variations.* Freiburg i. Br., FRG: Max-Planck-Institut für ausländisches und internationales Strafrecht.

Moos, R.H. (1974). *Evaluating treatment environments: A social ecological approach.* New York: Wiley.

Niederhoffer, A. (1967). *Behind the shield.* Garden City, NY: Doubleday.

Opp, K.D. (1979). *Strafvollzug und Resozialisierung.* Munich: Fink.

Ortmann, R. (1987). *Resozialisierung im Strafvollzug.* Freiburg i. Br., FRG: Max-Planck-Institut für ausländisches und internationales Strafrecht.

Poole, E.D., & Regoli, R.M. (1980). Work relations and cynicism among prison guards. *Criminal Justice and Behavior, 7*, 303–314.

Quensel, S. (1984). Kriminologische Forschung: Für wen? Oder: Grenzen einer rationalen Kriminalpolitik. *Kriminologisches Journal, 16*, 201–217.

Romig, D.A. (1978). *Justice for our children.* Lexington: Lexington Books.

Rosenthal, R. (1983). Assessing the statistical and social importance of the effects of psychotherapy. *Journal of Consulting and Clinical Psychology, 51*, 4–13.

Rossi, P.H., & Freeman, H.E. (1982). *Evaluation. A systematic approach.* Beverly Hills, CA: Sage.

Schur, E.M. (1973). *Radical non-intervention: Rethinking the delinquency problem.* Englewood Cliffs, NJ: Prentice Hall.

Scull, A.T. (1977). *Decarceration: Community treatment and the deviant. A radical view.* Englewood Cliffs, NJ: Prentice Hall.

Sechrest, L., White, S.O., & Brown, E.D. (Eds.). (1979). *The rehabilitation of criminal offenders: Problems and prospects.* Washington, DC: National Academy of Sciences.

Steffen, W. (1984). Untersuchung der Möglichkeiten des datenmäßigen Abgleichs von Täterbegehungsmerkmalen zur Fallzusammenführung. In Bundeskriminalamt (Ed.), *Symposium: Perseveranz und Kriminalpolizeilicher Meldedienst* (pp. 17–48). Wiesbaden: Bundeskriminalamt.

Uhlig, S. (1987). Rückfall und Hilfe zur Resozialisierung. *Bewährungshilfe, 34*, 293–305.

Wilkins, L.T. (1987). Making criminology policy relevant? In M.R. Gottfredson & T. Hirschi (Eds.), *Positive criminology* (pp. 154–172). Beverly Hills, CA: Sage.

Wolfgang, M.E., Figlio, R.M., & Sellin, T. (1972). *Delinquency in a birth cohort.* Chicago: University of Chicago Press.

21
Evaluation Research on Correctional Treatment in West Germany: A Meta-analysis

FRIEDRICH LÖSEL and PETER KÖFERL

Compared with the United States and several West European countries, the institutionalization of treatment for criminals is only a relatively recent development in the Federal Republic of Germany (FRG). In 1969 § 65 StGB (Strafgesetzbuch; Penal Law) on placement in a sociotherapeutic prison was introduced as a major legal basis and one of the major advances in penal reform. The goal of this legislation was that the courts would order placement in a sociotherapeutic prison for the following groups of prisoners:

1. Recidivists with serious personality disorders
2. Dangerous sexual offenders
3. Young adult criminals who have been assessed as especially crime-prone
4. Criminally nonresponsible or reduced responsibility offenders, if placement in a sociotherapeutic prison would appear to provide a better opportunity for resocialization than treatment in a psychiatric clinic

As there was a lack of clarity regarding both the assignment criteria and treatment methods, and, in addition, a lack of resources, the implementation of § 65 StGB has been postponed. However, in nearly all West German states, model prisons were set up to gather experience and develop generalizable concepts. The placement of prisoners was not part of the court's judgments as proposed in § 65 StGB, but was arranged as a "prison solution": On demand prisoners could be transferred from "normal" prisons under § 9 StVollzG (Strafvollzugsgesetz; Prison Law).

It can hardly be denied that the original formulation of § 65 StGB was difficult to implement. This was due to the need for a rapid expansion of social therapy and precise diagnosis of different groups of offenders, the low flexibility in placement, and so forth. For this reason, many considered an "extended prison solution" desirable, in which every prisoner whose previous behavior indicated that he or she would commit further crimes if not given social therapy should be placed in sociotherapeutic prisons (cf. Kaiser, Dünkel, & Ortmann, 1982). After almost 20 years of controversy surrounding the legal basis for sociotherapeutic prisons, § 65 StGB was finally withdrawn toward the end of

1984, and – through limited amendments to § 9 StVollzG – the procedures applied up to that time were consolidated in the following manner:

§ 9 – Placement in a sociotherapeutic prison
(1) A prisoner can, if he or she agrees, be transferred to a sociotherapeutic prison, if the particular therapeutic resources and social assistance in the prison are indicated for his or her resocialization. He or she can be returned to a normal prison if it becomes apparent that these resources and assistance are not successful.
(2) Transfer to a sociotherapeutic prison requires the consent of the governor of the sociotherapeutic prison.[1]

This established the sociotherapeutic prison as a separate department of the prison service that should serve its further differentiation (cf. Dolde, 1982, p. 47). In contrast to § 65 StGB or the "extended prison solution," this was only a granting of permission. Because of this, supporters of social therapy feared that this legal settlement would not encourage expansion. On the basis of the amendment to § 123 StVollzG, a sociotherapeutic institution may also be restricted to only single departments within a normal prison. This does not exclude the possibility that these can be described as being "sociotherapeutic" without providing any fundamental differentiation to the normal prison (cf. Dünkel, Nemec, & Rosner, 1985).

As the quantitative expansion, with a present count of ca. 1.5% of all West German prison places, also remained below expectations, disappointment among the supporters of sociotherapeutic prison policy is not surprising (cf. Schüler-Springorum, 1986). Up to now, there are 11 sociotherapeutic prisons or prison departments within the FRG and West Berlin, with ca. 650 prison places for adults (for a description of these prisons cf. Lösel, Köferl, & Weber, 1987; Schmitt, 1981). With one exception, places are only available for male prisoners. Most of the prisons are physically and organizationally autonomous. They normally contain between ca. 26 and 60 places; only the West Berlin prison is significantly larger, with 230 places. Personnel-prisoner ratios are more favorable than in normal prisons: The prisoner-total personnel ratio is approximately 2:1, and the prisoner-therapeutic personnel ratio lies between 6:1 and 16:1. The length of treatment varies from 1 to 3 years. The selection of prisoners is not restricted to the offender groups designated in § 65 StGB, which was obviously intended for a norm deviation on the borderline to psychiatric illness. Most cases, however, involve recidivists with serious criminal records who particularly meet the provisions of the above-mentioned groups 1 and 3.

There is no unified concept of treatment design. What is shared is that, in accordance with the concept of social therapy, the measures are not just applied to the individual and specific symptoms, but include living conditions, group processes, and organizational and institutional factors (cf. Egg, 1984).

[1] This is not an official translation of West German law. Serious legal readers are requested to refer to the original literature.

None of the prisons are committed to only a single therapeutic direction or school (for the main forms of treatment for antisocial behavior, cf. Lösel, 1983). In general, psychotherapeutic concepts in the traditional sense have been reduced in favor of social training models and the reduction of deficits in competence for everday life. The encouragement of contacts with the outside world, work places in the community, intensive use of the potential of day trips and holidays, and preparation for release belong to the central planning measures of almost all sociotherapeutic prisons.

Particularly in the latter fields, social therapy has served and continues to serve as a model for developments in normal prisons (for proposed models for the future, cf. Driebold, Egg, Nellessen, Quensel, & Schmitt, 1984). Even though the legal regulation and the quantitative expansion of sociotherapeutic prisons has fallen short of many expectations, the institution has also been strengthened. For example, through a reformulation at § 7 StGB, the current design of prison policy is that each prisoner should be assessed to see whether he or she can be placed in a sociotherapeutic prison. Despite the already foreseeable abolition of § 65 StGB, new prisons or departments were still being established in recent times. The older prisons have overcome their original conceptual problems, crises, and the high external pressure for success and have achieved a relative stabilization without stagnation. This has improved the preconditions for an empirically based program development (cf. Posavac & Carey, 1980, pp. 299 ff.). In line with the experiences in many fields, such a long-term, conceptual use of evaluation research appears to be more frequent than the direct, instrumental use within the framework of political decision processes (Leviton & Hughes, 1981).

The description of developments in the FRG broadly corresponds to the course of the international discussion. On the one hand, the perspective that treatment was *the* concept for prison policy was much too optimistic; on the other hand, from the very beginning a great number of objections were expressed from a wide variety of directions in criminal policy. For example, it was claimed that treatment in prisons did not provide a sufficient deterrent, did not involve adequate punishment of guilt, generated excessive costs, neglected security, "individualized" and "pathologized" crime problems, led to an involuntary personality adaptation, contained decisions of insufficient legal transparency, would be compensated by opposing prisonization effects, and was unable to provide a preparation for the situation of freedom because of the nature of imprisonment (cf., e.g., Egg, 1984, pp. 49–65; Kury, 1986, pp. 38–52).

The majority of these arguments have neither been exposed to empirical investigation nor conclusively studied methodically. The frequent and pronounced confusion of questions of values with questions of fact has possibly hindered the achievement of the stage of "rational analysis," as presented in the four-stage model of the rationality of political reform by Cronbach, Ambron, Dornbusch, Hess, Hornik, Phillips, Walker, and Weiner (1980, p. 92). In the course of time, and especially in the course of evaluation research in the

United States, the discussion on the treatment of offenders has, however, generally become more sober. "Treatment euphoria" – insofar as it ever existed – has abated, without, however, as is frequently maintained, generally turning away from the treatment approach. Treatment is now considered to be just *one* of many concepts of criminal policy, for which the basic questions of its effectiveness and which forms are effective for which offenders are insufficiently answered (cf. Kaiser, 1986; Sechrest, White, & Brown, 1979).

Since the secondary evaluations that were performed on earlier research by Bailey (1966), Logan (1972), and, in particular, Lipton, Martinson, and Wilks (1975), there has been more pessimistic judgment of the effects of treatment of offenders. However, even Martinson himself did not interpret his own findings as supporting his superficial, widespread "nothing works" formulation (cf. "Interview," 1978), and later reviews arrived at a more optimistic point of view (e.g., Corrado, 1981; Farrington, 1983; Gendreau & Ross, 1980; Romig, 1978). Nevertheless, nearly all authors point to methodological failings that seriously limit the power of the available findings. What influence the mostly not completely avoidable methodological deficits have on the direction of the findings is, however, unclear according to the meta-analyses of general psychotherapeutic research (e.g., Smith, Glass, & Miller, 1980; Wittmann & Matt, 1986). Furthermore, the treatment of offenders is defined so broadly that single, relatively successful approaches are often "overwhelmed" by the breadth of programs. To summarize according to types of treatment is often problematic, since it is uncertain whether the concepts concerned have actually been implemented (cf. Quay, 1977; Sechrest, White, & Brown, 1979, pp. 37 ff.). A more precise stipulation of effect size is required when "weak" effects are discussed (cf. Sechrest & Yeaton, 1982). For example, Rosenthal (1983) demonstrated that the practical significance of even so-called weak treatment effects is underestimated in evaluation research.

A further problem concerns the application of research findings from the United States to other countries. Despite wide-ranging international differences in prisons, comparative empirical research has scarcely begun (cf., e.g., Akers, Gruninger, & Hayner, 1976). For example, treatment measures in the United States have often been linked to an uncertain length of time that depends on the decisions of a parole board. To a greater extent than in Europe, research is oriented toward young offenders and "open" prisons or community-oriented programs. Often only short-term elements of treatment have been included, without designing framing conditions in a sociotherapeutic sense. Models such as the Patuxent Institution in Maryland or the Federal Correctional Institution in Butner, North Carolina appear to provide the closest comparisons with the sociotherapeutic prisons in the FRG (cf., e.g., Lejins, 1982; Morris, 1974; Wilkins, 1978; Witte, Woodbury, Smith, Barreto, & Beaton, 1983).

Even when Holland and the Scandinavian countries are considered, which to some extent provided models for social therapy in the FRG, the generalizability of experiences and findings is unclear. Offender treatment in these countries is, and was, likewise characterized by different legal framing conditions and concepts of pathology. While treatment establishments have been abandoned in Scandinavia because, among other reasons, the design has remained similar to prisons and has been relatively unsuccessful (cf. Christie, 1981, pp. 24 ff.), it must not be forgotten that "normal" prisons in these countries are already comparable to the sociotherapeutic prisons in the FRG. Secondly, despite many years of practical experience in treating prisoners in Western Europe outside of the FRG, very little controlled research has been undertaken (for recent evaluations cf., e.g., Bernhardt, 1984; Emmerik, 1982; Van den Bergh, Van der Plaats, & Niemantsverdriet, 1983).

For these and other reasons, the evaluation of social therapy as a relatively clearly separable institution in the FRG also gains an important function in the international framework. Since the second half of the 1970s, controlled evaluation research has been implemented in the FRG. Up to now, it has only been analyzed in the form of qualitative reviews or summary judgments on its methodological validity (cf., e.g., Blass, 1983; Egg, 1984). There is no systematic appraisal using procedures of meta-analysis (cf. Fricke & Treinies, 1985; Glass, McGaw, & Smith, 1981; Hunter, Schmidt, & Jackson, 1982; Rosenthal, 1984; Wolf, 1986). We have undertaken such an appraisal within the framework of a comprehensive secondary evaluation (cf. Lösel et al., 1987). The present work particularly reports on a differential analysis of the validity and a more precisely defined estimation of effect sizes.

Method

Because of their respective advantages and disadvantages, in the entire study we combined various forms of meta-evaluation (qualitative review of literature, tabular systematizations, and formal, statistical meta-analysis). The present meta-analysis included all systematic outcome evaluations on sociotherapeutic prisons either completely or partially published up to 1985 (including preprints). As we were dealing with a small, relatively well delineated field of research, the problems of biased file drawing are negligible. The basis for the meta-analysis consisted of 16 primary analyses with partially overlapping investigation samples (listed in the appendix). Dependencies between the results of some of the analyses had to be tolerated in order to obtain a sufficient data basis.

We differentiated the studies according to whether either recidivism or personality dispositions were used as criteria of success. Recidivism was operationalized by different criteria (e.g., only recidivistic offences punished by imprisonment, recidivism involving petty offences as well; on the problems involved in criteria of recidivism cf. Lösel et al., 1987, pp. 45–48; Waldo & Griswold, 1979). The follow-up intervals ranged from 3 to 5 years. Personality constructs were mostly operationalized with questionnaires; for example, the

Freiburger Persönlichkeitsinventar (FPI) from Fahrenberg, Selg, and Hampel (1978), the Gießen Test from Beckmann and Richter (1972), attitude scales, or self-ratings. These were administered toward the end of treatment without a follow-up interval.

The following procedures were used in the analysis of the effect studies:

1. Systematization According to Content Categories. A universally applicable analysis scheme was developed to systematize the primary studies. It included features of the prison being evaluated, the participants, the treatment applied, the design, the underlying theory of evaluation or criminality, the gathering and maintenance of samples, data collection, data analysis, and the presentation of results (for a detailed description, cf. Lösel et al., 1987, pp. 102–105).

2. Increase in Information on the Treatment and the Prison Context. In addition to the descriptions available in the primary study, we gathered further information on the treatment and setting conditions. This was advisable because the information given in the single studies varied considerably, and the treatment or evaluation intervals were often located some time in the past. Information was expanded through formative evaluation studies and other publications or restricted publications on the prison in question (cf. Lösel et al., 1987, pp. 198–210).

3. Administration of Feedback Interviews. To gain further information on the primary studies, semistandardized feedback interviews were administered to the original evaluators. This, first of all, solved the problem of indefinite and missing data in primary studies that frequently confronts meta-analyses. As well as increasing the validity, the feedback interview was also intended to recognize the principle that evaluation should not just be conceived as an one-sided activity but as a process of information exchange (cf. Cronbach et al., 1980).

4. Collection of Unpublished Data. Partially within the framework of the feedback interviews and partially using other methods (e.g., referring to a data bank), in some cases statistical data were obtained that had not been reported in the primary studies. This proved to be necessary in order to be able to perform a unified calculation of effect size (see 6).

5. Systematic Coding of Validity Threats. Each evaluation study was investigated and assessed for validity threats by two judges. The procedure we used was based on the system of Cook and Campbell (1979). This system tests for possible validity threats or alternative explanations according to features of statistical validity (7 items), internal validity (13 items), construct validity (10 items), and external validity (3 items). As the system is not "closed," it was specially expanded for our investigation (Lösel & Nowack, 1987): We especially stressed the aspect of the temporal stability of effects with one extra item in the field

TABLE 21.1. The validity judgment scheme

A. Statistical validity
  1. Low statistical power
  2. Violated assumptions of statistical tests
  3. Fishing and the error rate problem
  4. Reliability of measures
  5. Reliability of measurement implementation
  6. Irrelevances in the experimental setting
  7. Random heterogeneity of respondents

B. Internal validity
  1. History
  2. Maturation
  3. Testing
  4. Instrumentation
  5. Statistical regression
  6. Selection
  7. Experimental "mortality"
  8. Interaction with selection
  9. Ambiguity about the direction of causal influence
  10. Diffusion or imitation of treatments
  11. Compensatory equalization of treatments
  12. Compensatory rivalry by respondents receiving less desirable treatments
  13. Resentful demoralization of respondents receiving less desirable treatments

C. Construct validity
  1. Inadequate preoperational explication of constructs
  2. Mono-operation bias
  3. Mono-method bias
  4. Hypothesis guessing within experimental conditions
  5. Evaluation apprehension
  6. Experimenter expectancies
  7. Confounding constructs and level of constructs
  8. Interaction of different treatments
  9. Interaction of testing and treatment
  10. Restricted generalizability across constructs

D. External validity
  1. Interaction of selection and treatment
  2. Interaction of setting and treatment
  3. Interaction of history and treatment
  4. Temporal stability of treatment effects

E. Descriptive validity
  1. Description of treatment concept
  2. Assessment of treatment concept
  3. Assessment of treatment goals
  4. Data on temporal stability of treatment/goals
  5. Data on statistical scores

of external validity and introduced an additional category of validity ("descriptive validity"; 5 items). Although the descriptive validity does not strictly speaking refer to the validity of the results of the primary studies, it has proved to be particularly important within the framework of meta-analysis that certain standards are met regarding the reconstructibility of studies (cf. also Bullock & Svyantek, 1985). Table 21.1 provides a summary of our scheme.

Each of the 39 possible validity threats was judged by two raters on a 4-point scale (no-low-medium-high threat). The interrater agreement was relatively high, especially for the judgment on whether a validity threat was at all present in the corresponding item, with values between 85.7% (statistical validity) and 95.6% (descriptive validity). As is normal with differentiated categorizations, the coefficients were lower if the agreement in the weightings was taken into account (61.9% – 81.0%). In general, the procedure proved to be satisfactory. If the two judges failed to reach agreement, a consensus was reached by discussion.

6. Unified Calculation of Effect Size Indices. A unified calculation of the observed effects was performed for each of the single evaluations. Cohen's (1977) *d*-coefficient (mean difference between treatment and control group divided by the standard deviation of the control group) is most frequently used in treatment research when quantitative effectiveness criteria are applied. In our case, this was used for studies that applied personality variables as success criteria. As, however, qualitative/dichotomous success criteria are present with recidivism, Friedman's (1968) r_m-coefficient was calculated as a universal measure for all the studies. This coefficient can be interpreted in the sense of the binomial effect size display (BESD) from Rosenthal and Rubin (1982) as that percentage by which more participants in the treatment group show changes in the intended direction (e.g., are nonrecidivist) than people without the treatment. The coefficient r_m corresponds approximately to 0.5 d.

As different estimates of effect size were used in the studies on recidivism (e.g., with/without petty recidivism, with/without inclusion of treatment dropouts in the treatment group), and, in any case, several scales served as a criterion in each of the studies using personality variables, we were confronted with the problem of dependent data (cf. Bangert-Drowns, 1986; Glass & Kliegl, 1983). Smith and Glass (1977), Smith, Glass, and Miller (1980), and other authors included each of the single effect sizes in their studies and thus achieved a much higher n than number of the primary studies. For this reason, studies with several indicators of effect size are overweighted in meta-analysis, and the results are not as reliable as the number of effects suggests. Therefore we calculated only one average effect size for each analysis, but we separated studies with both recidivism and personality variables as indicators.

There is no general set procedure for calculating the average effect sizes for each study. We based our calculations on five different models, so that we could estimate the dependence of the results on the methods used (see Table 21.2). The five models can be regarded as a graded estimation of the treatment

TABLE 21.2. Models used in calculation of effect size

Model	Single findings included
1	All r_m scores in a study with $P \leq 0.05$ All further r_m scores treated as zero effects
2	All r_m scores in a study with $P \leq 0.10$ All further r_m scores treated as zero effects
3	All r_m scores in a study without considering significance
4	All r_m scores in a study with $P \leq 0.10$ All further r_m scores ignored
5	All r_m scores in a study with $P \leq 0.05$ All further r_m scores ignored

success in sociotherapeutic prisons. Model 1 represents the most "conservative" and model 5 the most "optimistic" estimation of effects.

Results

Analysis of Validity

The matrix of the validity threats in the single evaluation studies indicated threats in ca. 70% of all entries (cf. Lösel et al., 1987, pp. 212–213). Their distribution was ca. 30% low, 40% medium, and 30% high threat estimations. Each study appeared to be problematic for at least 21 of the 39 possible items. The fact that all the single categories were actually applied – though varying greatly in extent – supported the utility of the judgment grid.

Threat indices were calculated for each single study. This was done by adding together the levels of threat for each single item and calculating a mean threat index for each of the five validity categories (arithmetic mean). In another analysis, we did not weight the single items equally, but performed a more complicated weighting of relevance (cf. Lösel et al., 1987, p. 217). This produced a somewhat greater differentiation of the validity judgments. However, the results were very similar: The rankings of both indices showed correlations of between $\varrho = 0.99$ (statistical validity) and 0.75 (construct validity). The results of the index formation using equal weights are given in Table 21.3.

Table 21.3 shows that all studies indicated a certain degree of threat in all validity categories. However, there was a great variation in the average threat. This applied to both individual studies and the validity aspects. Studies that were comparatively strongly threatened in some validity aspects were relatively highly rated in others. In general, the internal validity in the strictest sense (according to Cook & Campbell, 1979) was less at risk than the statistical validity

TABLE 21.3. Indices of validity threats in the primary studies (mean ratings; scale from 0 = no to 3 = high threat)

Study/ analysis[a]	Statistical validity	Internal validity	Construct validity	External validity	Descriptive validity
a) R Q	1.00	0.92	1.50	1.75	1.80
b) R Q	0.86	0.92	1.50	1.75	1.80
c) R Q	0.86	0.92	1.50	1.75	1.80
d) R Q	0.71	0.62	1.50	1.50	1.80
e) R Q	1.00	0.69	1.50	1.75	2.20
f) R Q	1.14	1.31	1.40	1.75	1.80
g) R Q	1.00	1.23	1.40	1.50	1.60
h) R Q	0.86	1.39	1.40	2.00	1.80
i) R E	1.14	0.54	1.20	1.75	2.20
j) P Q	1.57	1.46	1.60	2.25	1.40
k) P E	1.43	0.54	1.40	2.25	2.20
l) P Q	1.71	1.23	2.00	2.00	2.20
m) P Q	1.71	1.23	1.50	2.25	2.60
n) P Q	1.86	1.23	1.50	2.25	2.80
o) P C	1.43	1.15	1.40	2.50	2.00
p) P Q	1.29	1.46	1.00	1.50	2.00
Mean	1.22	1.05	1.46	1.91	2.00
Mean (R)	0.95	0.95	1.43	1.72	1.87
Mean (P)	1.57	1.19	1.49	2.14	2.17
t-test	7.25	1.53	0.50	3.52	1.81
P ($df = 14$)	0.000	0.149	0.626	0.003	0.091

Abbreviations: C, correlative design; E, experimental design (random assignment); P, personality disposition criterion; Q, quasi-experimental design with nonequivalent control groups; R, recidivism criterion

[a] For sources, see Notes at the end of the chapter

and the construct validity. The highest values could be found in the area of descriptive validity which referred to how well a third person could gain a clear understanding of the treatment concepts, processes, and results.

Regarding the differences between the single studies, Table 21.3 shows the following: The evaluations that used recidivism as a success criterion were significantly more favorably assessed regarding statistical validity and external validity. The differences concerning internal validity and descriptive validity took the same direction but failed to reach significance. With regard to construct validity, both kinds of study appeared to be threatened in a rather similar way.

Analysis of Effect Size

For each evaluation study, the arithmetic mean of the observed effect sizes was calculated according to the five models described above. For the studies using recidivism as a criterion, these mean effects per study were only based on a few r_m scores per study, depending on the operationalization of recidivism. In contrast, in the studies using personality characteristics as criteria, there were sometimes more than 20 single variables, which could, for example, lead to the danger of "fishing for significances." While in the recidivism studies, with the exception of one nonsignificant r_m score, all effects were positive (decrease in recidivism), the studies using personality variables produced the problem of handling results that were contrary to expectations. If one averages the effect-size indicators without taking the negative or positive signs into account, the effects of treatment are overestimated. If, in contrast, one takes the direction of group differences into account, this requires precise hypotheses about how the effects of social therapy should be reflected in the single test scales. However, such hypotheses had only been partially explicated in the studies, and to some extent they were only based on considerations of plausibility. For this reason, two-tailed tests for significance had generally been performed. In addition, in some of the scales not only a positive but also a negative difference between treatment and control group seemed plausible [e.g., for "*Gehemmtheit*" (inhibitedness) or "Offenheit" (openness) in the FPI (Fahrenberg et al., 1978)].

As in our data there were no r_m scores that were both significant *and* clearly contrary to expectations regarding plausibility aspects, we were able to ignore the sign of the r_m scores in models 1, 2, 4, and 5, for in those cases nonsignificant results are set at zero or not included in the model anyway. A maximum of 10% of the nonsignificant effect sizes that were included in model 3 took an unexpected direction according to plausibility aspects. Due to the lack of a clear theoretical foundation, the single r_m scores in these cases were only calculated according to their sums. This means that a tendency to overestimate the effect of treatment has to be assumed in model 3 in the studies using personality variables as a criterion.

The findings on the five estimation models are given in Table 21.4. The effects were generally moderate, but noticeably consistent. The range of the single studies was between $r_m = 0.309$ (study m; models 4 and 5) and 0.000 (several studies; various models) across all estimation models. The mean effect size of the five models varied between 0.075 and 0.136 (column averages), and that of the single studies across all models between 0.017 and 0.255 (row averages). The 95% confidence interval was between 0.077 and 0.181 for the most optimistic effect estimation, and between 0.038 and 0.112 for the most conservative estimation. The most general estimation score for the effect of sociotherapeutic prisons was a score of $r_m = 0.110$. Between the studies using recidivism as a criterion and those with personality variables as criteria there were only low differences in favor of the latter.

TABLE 21.4. Calculation of mean effect sizes (r_m) by the five models

Study/ analysis[a]		Model 1	Model 2	Model 3	Model 4	Model 5	x̄
a)	R Q	0.000	0.050	0.093	0.100	0.000	0.049
b)	R Q	0.186	0.186	0.186	0.186	0.186	0.186
c)	R Q	0.139	0.139	0.139	0.139	0.139	0.139
d)	R Q	0.044	0.073	0.115	0.145	0.174	0.110
e)	R Q	0.141	0.141	0.141	0.141	0.141	0.141
f)	R Q	0.102	0.102	0.102	0.102	0.102	0.102
g)	R Q	0.144	0.144	0.144	0.144	0.144	0.144
h)	R Q	0.000	0.034	0.076	0.136	0.000	0.049
i)	R E	0.000	0.000	0.161	0.000	0.000	0.032
j)	P Q	0.040	0.056	0.110	0.248	0.290	0.149
k)	P E	0.027	0.060	0.133	0.227	0.258	0.141
l)	P Q	0.158	0.158	0.177	0.237	0.237	0.193
m)	P Q	0.206	0.206	0.247	0.309	0.309	0.255
n)	P O	0.000	0.000	0.087	0.000	0.000	0.017
o)	P C	0.000	0.000	0.089	0.000	0.000	0.018
p)	P Q	0.006	0.011	0.027	0.061	0.066	0.034
Mean (R)		0.084	0.097	0.129	0.121	0.098	0.106
Mean (P)		0.062	0.070	0.124	0.155	0.166	0.115
Mean		0.075	0.085	0.127	0.136	0.128	0.110
SD		0.076	0.070	0.052	0.092	0.110	0.071
SE		0.019	0.017	0.013	0.023	0.027	0.018
Confidence interval		$0.038 \leq \mu \leq 0.112$	$0.052 \leq \mu \leq 0.118$	$0.102 \leq \mu \leq 0.152$	$0.091 \leq \mu \leq 0.181$	$0.075 \leq \mu \leq 0.181$	$0.075 \leq \mu \leq 0.145$

Abbreviations: C, correlative design; E, experimental design (random assignment); P, personality disposition criterion; Q, quasi-experimental design with nonequivalent control groups; R, recidivism criterion

[a] For sources, see Notes at the end of the chapter

Relations Between Validity and Effect Size

In the previous effect estimation, all single evaluations or separable substudies were included with equal weighting. This agrees with the procedure and the findings in Smith et al. (1980), in which there was no significant correlation between design quality and effect size. This is contradicted by the fact that methodologically well-controlled studies are more powerful, and also that empirical correlations have been observed between validity and effect size (cf. Glass & Kliegl, 1983; Lösel, 1987; Wittmann & Matt, 1986). The relation between effect sizes and validity for the single studies in our analysis is shown in Table 21.5.

TABLE 21.5. Correlations between the level of the threat to validity and effect size

Validity category	Effect size according to:				
	Model 1	Model 2	Model 3	Model 4	Model 5
Statistical validity	−0.04	−0.11	0.13	0.14	0.25
Internal validity	0.02	−0.02	−0.30	0.08	−0.02
Construct validity	0.45*	0.49*	0.46*	0.52*	0.46*
External validity	−0.16	−0.18	0.12	0.13	0.14
Descriptive validity	0.03	−0.03	0.27	−0.13	−0.07
Multiple correlation	0.58	0.63	0.60	0.56	0.59

* $P \leq 0.05$

The relations were predominantly low or inconsistent across the different models. The construct validity, however, was an exception to this. There was a substantial positive correlation across all models. Studies with a higher construct validity – that means, in particular, studies with a stronger theoretical basis and a better generalizability regarding treatment and effects – accordingly produced lower effects than less valid ones.

Relations Between Treatment Features and Effect Sizes

The relations between content features (type of treatment, clients, institutional context, etc.) and the effect sizes are of particular interest in meta-analyses of treatment research because they provide cues for differential indications and focuses for further treatment development. However, in the present study these problems could not be dealt with conclusively. This was chiefly because the number of studies and prisons was too small. A second problem was that the design of treatment was often not very homogeneous or had not been described clearly enough to provide a valid differentiation of content classes. Nevertheless, we related some treatment features to the effect sizes as a sort of pilot study. These correlations are given in Table 21.6.

Only the variable "size of prison" had a particularly significant correlation to effect size that was consistent across all models. However, when looking at this negative correlation, it should be taken into account that the variance of prison size was essentially determined by the large prison in Berlin, which has been investigated frequently. The conclusion that higher treatment successes could be anticipated in smaller prisons is not sufficiently supported by the research findings available at the present time.

TABLE 21.6. Correlations between treatment characteristics and effect size

Treatment characteristic	Effect size according to:					Average effect size ($\bar{x}$)
	Model 1	Model 2	Model 3	Model 4	Model 5	
Size of prison (number of prisoners)	−0.36	−0.44	−0.56*	−0.49*	−0.40	−0.50*
Ratio: prisoner − total personnel	0.17	0.12	−0.12	−0.07	−0.24	−0.05
Ratio: prisoner − therapeutic personnel	0.41*	0.35	−0.02	−0.09	−0.15	0.09
Average duration of treatment	−0.17	−0.11	−0.42*	−0.12	−0.21	−0.21
Average age of prisoners	0.20	0.26	0.08	−0.09	−0.13	0.03
Proportion of offenders against property	−0.44	−0.51*	−0.06	−0.31	−0.06	−0.34
Proportion of offenders meeting the criteria in §65 StGB	−0.65*	−0.65*	0.06	−0.07	−0.10	−0.38
Dropout rate	−0.21	−0.18	−0.13	−0.04	−0.31	−0.21
Conflict phases in the prison development[a]	−0.08	−0.10	0.24	−0.20	−0.01	0.01
Follow-up interval	0.27	0.30	0.24	−0.44	−0.54*	−0.14

[a] Rank correlations
* $P \leqslant 0.05$

Discussion

The present study differs from "typical" meta-analyses in evaluation research in that it is based only on a small number of studies and a few relevant program implementations (sociotherapeutic prisons). Nevertheless, the method of systematically integrating research findings has proved useful for expanding and providing more precision in evaluation. This particularly applies for the judgment of validity and effectiveness.

As can only be expected with the complicated field conditions of prisons, and as has often been discussed in the literature (e.g., Kury, 1983; Rezmovic, 1979), practical research mostly does not attain the ideal status of the real experiment. Numerous threats to validity or possible alternative explanations for findings are present. In accordance with a flexible multimethod approach, however, we can neither abandon (quasi-)experimental standards, nor can we hope for a hardly feasible experimentum crucis in research into social therapy. Despite the fact that prisoner treatment is relatively new in the FRG compared with other countries, several studies are available that show notable methodological controls. Our findings also show that the problems of validity are not only to be viewed from the perspective of internal validity. With respect to the differences found between the single studies, we cannot sweepingly state that there are evaluations that are more or less "good": they vary according to which category of validity is considered. Internal validity, which traditionally has been a particular focus of attention (e.g., Blass, 1983), is less threatened than external validity with its differentiation by Cook and Campbell (1979) into subcategories of construct validity and a narrowly viewed external validity. The relatively high threat to construct validity in the available studies suggests that it is the theoretical foundation and generalizability of social therapy and its evaluation that particularly leaves much to be desired.

The likewise high level of threat in the descriptive validity that we introduced to complement the construct validity suggests that in future more attention should be paid to a more comprehensible documentation of treatment concepts, content, and results. When we consider this finding, however, it must be taken into account that the extent of the description in, for example, shorter publications or intermediate reports is necessarily less complete, and in some cases the repeated evaluation of one prison may have influenced the form of reporting.

The differences in the level of threat between studies using recidivism and those using personality variables as criteria are in line with expectations. In the former type of study, a "harder" everyday criterion and longer follow-up intervals are present. In the personality variables that are assumed to have an "intervening" function, the theoretical relations require more explanation, multiple measurements are present, and so forth. For these reasons, despite other threats, their construct validity is not decreased.

The correlation between the level of threat to construct validity and the observed effect size suggests that more conservative effect estimations are produced when the theoretical foundation and operationalization of treatment and evaluation are improved. In line with the findings of Smith and Glass (1977), Smith et al. (1980), and others, the internal validity, however, does not correlate with the effect size. This supports the concept of including as much evaluation information as possible in the stocktaking, and not commencing by introducing strict exclusion limitations according to a particular methodological position (cf. Bullock & Svyantek, 1985).

The estimations of the effectiveness of sociotherapeutic prisons are notably consistent. The extent of variation in effect sizes is lower than in general meta-analyses of research in psychotherapy. On the basis of our different models, an r_m of 0.110 can be regarded as a relatively valid estimation of mean effect size (this approximately corresponds to an effect size coefficient d of 0.220). If one takes into account the tendency to overestimate the effects in the personality variables in model 3 (see above), we can conclude the following: the desired effects (e.g., no recidivism) can be anticipated in ca. 10% more prisoners in sociotherapeutic prisons than among offenders in "normal" prisons. This effect estimation contradicts the sweeping judgment that "nothing works." Nevertheless, the average scores found in other meta-analyses of psychotherapeutic evaluation research are between two and four times as high (cf., e.g., Shapiro & Shapiro, 1982; Smith et al., 1980; Wittmann & Matt, 1986). This supports, on the one hand, the practical experience that treatment successes are particularly difficult to obtain in persistent offenders/antisocial personalities (especially under prison conditions). On the other hand, other essential differences must be taken into account when making comparisons with other fields of psychotherapeutic evaluation research: The evaluation of sociotherapeutic prisons is concerned with "real" field studies with multiproblem cases and, at least with recidivism, long follow-up intervals. In contrast, general meta-analyses of research into the effect of therapy contain many analogue studies with university students as clients and "soft" effect criteria without lengthy follow-up assessments (cf., e.g., Shapiro & Shapiro, 1983), which leads to the expectation of higher effect sizes.

As prisoner treatment is often criticized from a cost-utility perspective, it seems valid to discuss our integrative effect estimation from this perspective as well. At first sight, a 10% more favorable success rate compared to normal prisons is not very impressive. For while, in 1986, the cost of a prison place for normal prisons with/without the inclusion of prison-work contributions stood at ca. 101/119 West German marks per day per prisoner (data obtained from the Department of Justice for the state of North Rhine-Westphalia for 1986), the costs for the more personnel-intensive social therapy are estimated as being up to three times as high. However, there is a lack of differentiated financial data (for approaches, cf. Dünkel, 1983, 1987; Neu, 1974) for a detailed and more conclusive cost-utility evaluation (e.g., Barnett, 1985; Glaser, 1983). Alongside exact social therapy costs on the cost side, it is necessary to determine precisely the costs saved on the utility side: the costs to prisons of repeated sentencing, the costs of crime detection, court costs, physical injuries and material damage, social welfare costs for the families of prisoners, the costs of family-related consequences (e.g., developmental disorders among the children), losses in tax revenue, and so forth. This does not even consider, for example, the humanity of prisons or the fears of potential victims. On the basis of our effect estimation, we have carried out very provisional calculations with some of the realistically quantifiable variables. Thereby it is feasible that only if there were a more favorable cost-relation to normal prisons, would our estimated effect size be sufficient to prove that social therapy is also substantially successful from a cost-utility perspective.

More precise research in this direction is indicated: First, because of a demographically based reduction in the population of prisons in the near future (Hesener & Jehle, 1987), the costs of a "normal" prison place will probably also increase (e.g., in North Rhine-Westphalia, with a reduction in prison population of ca. 1200 prisoners, costs of 90/107 West German marks in 1985 have increased by about 12% to the above-mentioned prices in 1986 despite a lower rate of inflation). Secondly, the often very similar effects in primary studies (e.g., Dünkel, 1980; Rehn, 1979) have shown that there are no clear effect differences between different types of social therapy – though their costs can vary greatly regarding prisoner-personnel ratio, length of treatment, and so forth (cf. also Table 21.6). The fact that, up to now, no clear superiority or inferiority has been demonstrated for any particular type of treatment in general psychotherapy research (cf. Glass & Kliegl, 1983; Grawe, 1987; Smith et al., 1980), also supports the inclusion of cost-utility aspects in the further development of sociotherapeutic prisons. For example, the further "opening up" of prisons, increases in outside contacts, and involvement of community social services contained in the model proposals from Driebold et al. (1984) are worthy of investigation from the perspective of both content and costs.

The cost-utility aspect is, however, only one of many that require more attention in the field of evaluation research on prisoner treatment. According to our qualitative and quantitative meta-evaluation, the following appear to be needed (cf. Lösel et al., 1987, pp. 252–260; also Kury, 1986; Ortmann, 1987):

1. A more precise description of the goals and contents of treatment (e.g., selection of participants, treatment concept and its stability, treatment organization and length, framing conditions).
2. A more explicit theoretical foundation for program structures (including the derivation of operationalizable success criteria, separable types of problem behavior, and differential elements of treatment).
3. A greater differentiation of "global" evaluations of the institution in its entirety by using quasi-experimental studies on single elements of treatment.
4. Encouragement of "smaller" flexible evaluation studies of the *process* of treatment instead of too high a concentration on a few "large scale" summative investigations.
5. Empirical analysis and justification of practiced differentiation strategies (e.g., in the choice and reassignment of participants).
6. Differentiation of the criterion of recidivism (e.g., according to seriousness, frequency, length of time, time interval) and development of corresponding conventions for research.
7. Systematic development of multiple success criteria and a stronger integration of recidivism criteria with theory-driven personality constructs and behavior variables (as intermediary criteria).
8. A stronger evaluation orientation in sociotherapeutic prisons making use of those members of staff with competence in psychology and the social sciences.
9. Improved and more unified documentation of the data from evaluation studies in order to simplify integration.

The implementation of such proposals implies that evaluation research that was mostly initiated with reference to § 65 StGB must become less discrete and summative so that evaluation is understood as a continual process of gaining knowledge about a complex social problem (cf. Cronbach et al., 1980).

Notes

The following primary studies or data analyses were included in our meta-analysis of evaluation research into the sociotherapeutic prison (Sozialtherapeutische Anstalt; SthA):

a) Rehn (1979): Release cohort comparison of SthA Hamburg-Bergedorf/SAB and Moritz-Liepmann-Haus/MLH ($n = 189$) with normal prison ($n = 162$)
b) Rehn (1979): Control group comparison of MLH ($n = 90$) with normal prison ($n = 224$)
c) Rehn (1979): Control group comparison of SAB ($n = 49$) with normal prison ($n = 224$)
d) Rehn & Jürgensen (1983): Matched-pairs analysis of SAB ($n = 49$) with normal prison ($n = 106$)
e) Dünkel (1980): Comparison of Department of Social Training in the SthA Berlin ($n = 148$) with normal prison ($n = 889$)
f) Dünkel (1980): Comparison of Department of Education in the SthA Berlin ($n = 64$) with normal prison ($n = 889$)
g) Dünkel (1980): Comparison of Department of Social Therapy in the SthA Berlin ($n = 184$) with normal prison ($n = 889$)
h) Dolde (1981, 1982): Comparison of SthA Ludwigsburg-Hohenasperg ($n = 145$) with normal prison ($n = 107$)
i) Rasch & Kühl (1977, 1978): Comparison of SthA Düren ($n = 30$) with normal prison ($n = 27$)
j) Egg (1979): Comparison of SthA Erlangen ($n = 35$) with normal prison ($n = 60$)
k) Rasch & Kühl (1978): Comparison of SthA Düren ($n = 30$) with normal prison ($n = 27$)
l) Waxweiler (1980): Comparison of Department of Social Therapy in the SthA Berlin ($n = 60$) with normal prison ($n = 30$)
m) Waxweiler (1980): Comparison of Department of Education in the SthA Berlin ($n = 30$) with normal prison ($n = 30$)
n) Waxweiler (1980): Comparison of Department of Social Training in the SthA Berlin ($n = 30$) with normal prison ($n = 30$)
o) Opp (1979): Comparison of SthA Berlin ($n = 97$) with normal prison ($n = 205$)
p) Ortmann (1982, 1984, 1987): Comparison of SthA Berlin ($n = 207$) with normal prison ($n = 192$)

Acknowledgment. The investigation was supported by a grant to the first author by the Department of Research and Technology (BMFT) of the Federal Republic of Germany.

References

Akers, R. L., Gruninger, W., & Hayner, N. (1976). Prison inmate roles: interorganizational and cross-cultural comparisons. *International Journal of Criminology and Penology, 4*, 365–381.

Bailey, W. C. (1966). Correctional outcome: An evaluation of 100 reports. *Journal of Criminal Law, Criminology and Police Science, 57*, 153–160.

Bangert-Drowns, R. L. (1986). Review of developments in meta-analytic method. *Psychological Bulletin, 99*, 388–399.

Barnett, W. S. (1985). *The Perry preschool program and its long-term effects: a benefit-cost analysis.* Ypsilanti, MI: High/Scope Educational Research Foundation.

Beckmann, D., & Richter, H. E. (1972). *Gießen-Test (GT). Handbuch.* Bern: Huber.

Bernhardt, E. (1984). Der dänische Strafvollzug – die weithin unbemerkte Wende. *Zeitschrift für Strafvollzug und Straffälligenhilfe, 33*, 140–144.

Blass, W. (1983). Evaluation im Strafvollzug. Überblick und Kritik vorliegender Studien. In H. Kury (Ed.), *Methodische Probleme der Behandlungsforschung, insbesondere in der Sozialtherapie* (pp. 81–120). Cologne: Heymanns.

Bullock, R. J., & Svyantek, D. J. (1985). Analyzing meta-analysis: potential problems, an unsuccessful replication and evaluation criteria. *Journal of Applied Psychology, 70*, 108–115.

Christie, N. (1981). *Limits to pain.* Oxford: Robertson.

Cohen, J. (1977). *Statistical power analysis for the behavioral sciences* (2nd ed.). New York: Academic.

Cook, T. D., & Campbell, D. T. (1979). *Quasi-experimentation: design and analysis issues for field settings.* Chicago: Rand McNally.

Corrado, R. R. (1981). Using experiments in evaluating delinquency prevention programs. In R. Roesch & R. R. Corrado (Eds.), *Evaluation and criminal justice policy* (pp. 17–28). Beverly Hills: Sage.

Cronbach, L. J., Ambron, S. R., Dornbusch, S. M., Hess, R. D., Hornik, R. C., Phillips, D. C., Walker, D. F., & Weiner, S. S. (1980). *Toward reform of program evaluation.* San Francisco: Jossey-Bass.

Dolde, G. (1982). Effizienzkontrolle sozialtherapeutischer Behandlung im Vollzug. In H. Göppinger & P. H. Bresser (Eds.), *Sozialtherapie. Kriminologische Gegenwartsfragen:* Vol. 15 (pp. 47–64). Stuttgart: Enke.

Driebold, R., Egg, R., Nellessen, L., Quensel, S., & Schmitt, G. (1984). *Die Sozialtherapeutische Anstalt. Modelle für Empfehlungen für den Justizvollzug.* Göttingen: Vandenhoeck and Ruprecht.

Dünkel, F. (1980). *Sozialtherapeutische Behandlung und Rückfälligkeit in Berlin-Tegel.* Berlin: Duncker and Humblot.

Dünkel, F. (1983). Methodische Probleme der Effizienzforschung bei Behandlungsmaßnahmen im Strafvollzug, insbesondere in der Sozialtherapie. In H. Kury (Ed.), *Methodische Probleme der Behandlungsforschung, insbesondere in der Sozialtherapie* (pp. 121–147). Cologne: Heymanns.

Dünkel, F. (1987). Die Herausforderung der geburtenschwachen Jahrgänge. Aspekte der Kosten-Nutzen-Analyse in der Kriminalpolitik. Freiburg i. Br., FRG: Max-Planck-Institut für ausländisches und internationales Strafrecht.

Dünkel, F., Nemec, R., & Rosner, A. (1985). *Organisationsentwicklung und Behandlungsmaßnahmen in einer sozialtherapeutischen Anstalt.* Unveröffentlichtes Manuskript. Freiburg i. Br., FRG: Max-Planck-Institut für ausländisches und internationales Strafrecht.

Egg, R. (1984). *Straffälligkeit und Sozialtherapie.* Cologne: Heymanns.

Emmerik, J.V. (1982). Einige Ergebnisse der Nachuntersuchung von ehemaligen Patienten der Dr. Henri van-der-Hoeven-Kliniek in Utrecht. *Zeitschrift für Strafvollzug und Straffälligenhilfe, 31,* 339–347.

Fahrenberg, J., Selg, H., & Hampel, R. (1978). *Das Freiburger Persönlichkeitsinventar (FPI). Handanweisung* (3rd ed.). Göttingen: Hogrefe.

Farrington, D.P. (1983). Randomized experiments on crime and justice. In M. Tonry & N. Morris (Eds.), *Crime and justice. An annual review of research:* Vol. 4 (pp. 257–308). Chicago: University of Chicago Press.

Fricke, R., & Treinies, G. (1985). *Einführung in die Meta-Analyse.* Bern: Huber.

Friedman, H. (1968). Magnitude of experimental effect and a table for its rapid estimation. *Psychological Bulletin, 70,* 245–251.

Gendreau, P., & Ross, R.R. (1980). Effective correctional treatment: bibliotheraphy for cynics. In R.R. Ross & P. Gendreau (Eds.), *Effective correctional treatment* (pp. 3–36). Toronto: Butterworths.

Glaser, D. (1983). *Towards a cost/benefit assessment of Dutch penal policies.* The Hague: Research and Documentation Center of the Ministry of Justice.

Glass, G.V., & Kliegl, R.M. (1983). An apology for research integration in the study of psychotherapy. *Journal of Consulting and Clinical Psychology, 51,* 28–41.

Glass, G.V., McGaw, B., & Smith, M.L. (1981). *Meta-analysis in social research.* Beverly Hills, CA: Sage.

Grawe, K. (1987). Die Effekte der Psychotherapie. In M. Amelang (Ed.), *Bericht über den 35. Kongreß der Deutschen Gesellschaft für Psychologie in Heidelberg 1986:* Vol. 2 (pp. 515–534). Göttingen: Hogrefe.

Hesener, B., & Jehle, J.M. (1987). *Bevölkerungsbewegung und Strafvollzugsbelegung. Die künftige Entwicklung des Strafvollzugs unter besonderer Berücksichtigung der demographischen Entwicklung.* Wiesbaden, FRG: Kriminologische Zentralstelle.

Hunter, J.E., Schmidt, F.L., & Jackson, G.B. (1982). *Meta-analysis: cumulating research findings across studies.* Beverly Hills, CA: Sage.

Interview with Martinson. (1978, December 9). *Criminal Justice Newsletter, 9,* p. 4.

Kaiser, G. (1986). Aktuelle Ergebnisse kriminologischer Forschung. *Schweizerische Zeitschrift für Strafrecht, 103,* 1–23.

Kaiser, G., Dünkel, F., & Ortmann, R. (1982). Die sozialtherapeutische Anstalt – das Ende einer Reform? *Zeitschrift für Rechtspolitik, 15,* 198–207.

Kury, H. (Ed.). (1983). *Methodische Probleme der Behandlungsforschung, insbesondere der Sozialtherapie.* Cologne: Heymanns.

Kury, H. (1986). *Die Behandlung Straffälliger:* Vol. 1. *Inhaltliche und methodische Probleme der Behandlungsforschung.* Berlin: Duncker and Humblot.

Lejins, P.P. (1982). Maßnahmen zur Behandlung abnormer Täter – Erfahrungsbericht aus den USA. In H. Göppinger & P.H. Bresser (Eds.), *Sozialtherapie. Kriminologische Gegenwartsfragen:* Vol. 15 (pp. 7–31). Stuttgart: Enke.

Leviton, L.C., & Hughes, E.F. (1981). Research on the utilization of evaluations: a review and synthesis. *Evaluation Review, 5,* 525–548.

Lipton, D., Martinson, R., & Wilks, J. (1975). *The effectiveness of correctional treatment.* New York: Praeger.

Logan, C. (1972) Criminology. Evaluation research in crime and delinquency: a reappraisal. *Journal of Criminal Law, Criminology and Police Science, 63,* 378–387

Lösel, F. (Ed.). (1983). *Kriminalpsychologie.* Weinheim, FRG: Beltz.

Lösel, F. (1987). Methodik und Problematik von Meta-Analysen – mit Beispielen der Psychoatherapieforschung. *Gruppendynamik, 18,* 323–343.

Lösel, F., & Nowack, W. (1987). Evaluationsforschung. In J. Schultz-Gambard (Ed.), *Angewandte Sozialpsychologie* (pp. 57–87). Munich: Psychologie-Verlags-Union.

Lösel, F., Köferl, P., & Weber, F. (1987). *Meta-Evaluation der Sozialtherapie.* Stuttgart: Enke.

Morris, N. (1974). *The future of imprisonment.* Chicago: University of Chicago Press.

Neu, A. (1974). Die finanziellen Auswirkungen des Alternativ-Entwurfs. In J. Baumann (Ed.), *Die Reform des Strafvollzugs* (pp. 145–164). Munich: Goldmann.

Ortmann, R. (1987). *Resozialisierung im Strafvollzug.* Freiburg i. Br., FRG: Max-Planck-Institut für ausländisches und internationales Strafrecht.

Posavac, E. J., & Carey, R. G. (1980). *Program evaluation. Methods and case studies.* Englewood Cliffs, NJ: Prentice-Hall.

Quay, H. C. (1977). The three faces of evaluation: What can be expected to work? *Criminal Justice and Behavior, 4,* 341–354.

Rehn, G. (1979). *Behandlung im Strafvollzug.* Weinheim, FRG: Beltz.

Rezmovic, E. L. (1979). Methodological considerations in evaluating correctional effectiveness: issues and chronic problems. In L. B. Sechrest, S. O. White, & E. D. Brown (Eds.), *The rehabilitation of criminal offenders: problems and prospects* (pp. 163–209). Washington, DC: National Academy of Sciences.

Romig, A. D. (1978). *Justice for our children. An examination of juvenile delinquent rehabilitation programs.* Lexington, MA: Lexington Books.

Rosenthal, R. (1983). Assessing the statistical and social importance of the effects of psychotherapy. *Journal of Consulting and Clinical Psychology, 51,* 4–13.

Rosenthal, R. (1984). *Meta-analytic procedures for social research.* Beverly Hills, CA: Sage.

Rosenthal, R., & Rubin, D. B. (1982). A simple, general purpose display of magnitude of experimental effect. *Journal of Educational Psychology, 74,* 166–169.

Schmitt. G. (1981). Sozialtherapie im Überblick. In Bundeszusammenschluß für Straffälligenhilfe (Ed.), *Sozialtherapie als kriminalpolitische Aufgabe* (pp. 123–165). Bonn-Bad Godesberg: Author.

Schüler-Springorum, H. (1986). Die sozialtherapeutischen Anstalten – ein kriminalpolitisches Lehrstück. In H. J. Hirsch, G. Kaiser, & H. Marquardt (Eds.), *Gedächtnisschrift für Hilde Kaufmann* (pp. 167–188). Berlin: de Gruyter.

Sechrest, L. B., & Yeaton, W. H. (1982). Assessing the effectiveness of social programs: methodological and conceptual issues. *Evaluation Studies, 2,* 151–166.

Sechrest, L. B., White, S. O., & Brown, E. D. (Eds.). (1979). *The rehabilitation of criminal offenders: problems and prospects.* Washington, DC: National Academy of Sciences.

Shapiro, D. A., & Shapiro, D. (1982). Meta-analysis of comparative therapy outcome studies: a replication and refinement. *Psychological Bulletin, 92,* 581–604.

Shapiro, D. A., & Shapiro, D. (1983). Comparative therapy outcome research: methodological implications of meta-analysis. *Journal of Consulting and Clinical Psychology, 51,* 42–53.

Smith, M. L., & Glass, G. V. (1977). Meta-analysis of psychotherapy outcome studies. *American Psychologist, 32,* 752–760.

Smith, M. L., Glass, G. V., & Miller, T. I. (1980). *The benefits of psychotherapy.* Baltimore: Johns Hopkins University Press.

Van den Bergh, W., Van der Plaats, L. K., & Niemantsverdriet, J. R. (1983). Die Behandlung psychisch gestörter Straftäter in der van-der-Hoeven-Kliniek in Utrecht. In R. Driebold (Ed.), *Strafvollzug* (pp. 153–166). Göttingen: Vandenhoeck and Ruprecht.

Waldo, G., & Griswold, D. (1979). Issues in the measurement of recidivism. In L. B. Sechrest, S. O. White, & E. D. Brown (Eds.), *The rehabilitation of criminal offenders: problems and prospects* (pp. 225–250). Washington, DC: National Academy of Sciences.

Wilkins, L. (1978). "Treatment" on trial: the case of Patuxent. In N. Johnston & L. Savitz (Eds.), *Justice and corrections* (pp. 670–687). New York: Wiley.

Witte, A. D., Woodbury, D. F., Smith, S. H., Barreto, H., & Beaton, R. (1983). *The effects of a less coercive internal prison environment and gradual re-integration on post-release performance: an evaluation of Morris model of imprisonment as implemented at the Federal Correctional Institution at Butner D.C.* Report for the Bureau of Prisons, July 1983.

Wittmann, W. W., & Matt, G. E. (1986). Meta-Analyse als Integration von Forschungsergebnissen am Beispiel deutschsprachiger Arbeiten zur Effektivität von Psychotherapie. *Psychologische Rundschau, 37*, 20–40.

Wolf, F. M. (1986). Meta-analysis. *Quantitative methods for research synthesis.* Beverly Hills, CA: Sage.

22

Treatment of Young Remand Prisoners: Problems and Results of a Research Project

HELMUT KURY

Methods of treatment evaluation have been increasingly criticized in recent years in view of the frequent lack of convincing success of rehabilitation projects. Recently available findings from relatively comprehensive research in this field have shown that the initial expectations regarding the success of various treatment programs were exaggerated. The results of this research could not confirm with the desired clarity that the intended goal – usually a (significant) reduction in the recidivism rate – had been attained. In part, this contributed to a complete rejection of the treatment concept, especially in penal institutions, and led to a concentration on alternative strategies to deal with the crime problem; for example, diversion programs (cf. Kury & Lerchenmüller, 1981). These results were also partially regarded as proof that traditional prisons were not so bad after all, and that reforms aiming at an "improvement" were therefore unnecessary (cf. Kury, 1986a, 1986b, 1986d; Lösel, Köferl, & Weber, 1987).

Today, the issue of the effects of (psycho)therapeutic treatment in general, and not just for prisoners, requires a much more differentiated consideration than before because of recent findings and methodological improvements (cf. Bastine, 1970; Kury, 1983c, 1986b, 1987; Linster & Wetzel, 1980). Nowadays, the expected effect of a treatment program in prison, and thus its objective, is frequently considered to be the prevention of the harmful effects of prison institutionalization, i.e., prisonization. It can scarcely be denied that the avoidance of further desocialization in prison and the reinforcement of a criminal career is an important task. Lösel et al. (1987) conducted a meta-evaluation that showed that treatment programs could have a rehabilitative effect beyond the above-mentioned avoidance of prisonization effects (for the United States, cf., e.g., Ross & Gendreau, 1980). Despite all the valid criticism of treatment programs in prisons, it is impossible to ignore the fact that they have a considerable significance for the treatment of prisoners, and also that a further development of prison concepts is necessary for ethical reasons.

The Situation in Pretrial Detention

While rehabilitation programs are sporadically administered in correctional institutions, they are rarely to be found in pretrial detention, although the Juvenile Court Act (§ 93, Article 2) requires the inclusion of education in the pretrial detention of young offenders. This requirement is by no means met in practice: Compared to the situation in prisons in the Federal Republic of Germany (FRG), the situation in pretrial detention is considered to be much more unfavorable (cf. Arbeitskreis Strafprozessreform, 1983; Kury, 1986c). A comparison of the detention rates in Western Europe reveals that the FRG, alongside Italy and Austria, has the highest proportion of remand prisoners (cf. Abenhausen, 1983; Kaiser, 1982). In the FRG, pretrial detention is widely ordered despite repeated criticism and the demands of the Juvenile Court Movement for restraint and the replacement of pretrial detention with other measures, especially for young offenders (cf. Kaiser, 1984; Kury, 1986c).

Besides the relatively high proportion of remand prisoners, criticism is also directed at the long duration of pretrial detention in the FRG. Precise data are not available for this, but the average period of detention is estimated at 2–4 months. According to the Work Group on the Reform of Criminal Procedure, the excessive length of pretrial detention is one of the most serious general problems in criminal proceedings.

Particularly as far as young offenders are concerned, the harmful effects of pretrial detention have been pointed out repeatedly. Pretrial detention is indisputably one of the most serious interventions in the life of a citizen (cf. Hauser, 1978).

There is widespread agreement that even if the unfavorable conditions in pretrial detention scarcely permit rehabilitation, attempts should be made to prevent any further desocialization due to the negative effects of incarceration. The legal recommendations for the education of young offenders in pretrial detention are the subject of controversy. Several authors have pointed out the legal problems involved in educating or treating young offenders who have yet to be found guilty by a court of law. However, there is widespread agreement that if the prisoner consents to undergo treatment (voluntary principle), treatment should at least be made available for young offenders. Actual experience with treatment programs in pretrial detention is as yet only available in a few instances in the FRG, and there is a lack of systematic evaluation research into the results of treatment programs.

The Present Study

The Development of the Research Project

One of the most extensive treatment programs for young remand prisoners in the FRG was conducted in Freiburg/Breisgau. Since the early 1970s, Freiburg has attempted to meet the demands of the Juvenile Court Act (JGG) for more education in the pretrial detention of juveniles and young adults to the extent that the difficulties in prisons allow (cf. Wetzstein, 1986). The pretrial detention unit for young prisoners in Freiburg is relatively small and can hold 15–20 inmates. The major objective of the Scientific Institute of the Freiburg Assistance to Youth Association (Wissenschaftliches Institut des Jugendhilfswerks an der Universität Freiburg, WIJHW), founded in the early 1970s, was to improve pretrial detention for young offenders. To attain this goal, the psychologists in the pretrial detention unit for young offenders who were members of this institute initiated a treatment program that essentially consisted of the following elements:

1. The prison officers were trained in nondirective (client-centered) counseling techniques and social-coping strategies.
2. Psychological supervision and psychological consultation were provided in the unit.
3. Leisure-time groups were organized with the participation of a social worker and assistants.
4. Counseling groups (client-centered psychotherapy, Rogers, 1951) and behavior therapy were organized. In the behavior therapy, a modeling program was implemented that was based on Sarason and Ganzer (1969, 1971, 1973). This has produced good results in the United States.

Description of Treatment

In the main investigation, the treatment consisted of counseling therapy (client-centered psychotherapy, Rogers, 1951; Tausch, 1974) and behavior therapy (modeling). This program was complemented by actively supportive measures to create a climate conducive to treatment within the institution. Counseling and leisure-time groups were organized, the officers were offered a weekly consultation and supervision hour, and the staff were trained in nondirective counseling techniques and problem-solving strategies. The therapists made every effort to create a treatment-supportive climate in the pretrial detention unit for young offenders.

As far as the psychotherapeutic treatment is concerned, the procedures used in the nondirective counseling therapy were based on the detailed description of this concept in the literature (cf. Rogers, 1951; Tausch, 1974). However, because of their previous experience with the treatment of young offenders, the therapists were more active than in the description given in the original concept. For instance, they proposed further themes for the single sessions in order to expand the range of problems dealt with. Counseling (client-centered psychotherapy) therapy is particularly indicated for psychological disorders that arise from an incongruence between a person's self-concept and experience. Such incongruences manifest in the form of perception disorders, phobia, a lack of self-assertiveness, and so forth (cf. Biermann-Ratjen, Eckert,

& Schwartz, 1979). In this context, it seems reasonable also to consider social deviance and criminal behavior as an expression of incongruences. "Thus theoretical reasons can be assumed for an indication of counseling therapy in the case of dissocial behavior" (Minsel & Howe, 1983, p. 250, our translation). It can also be assumed that in criminal behavior internal tensions are worked off that are due to the differences between self-concept and actual experience. Moreover, several studies show that criminal behavior is generally accompanied by further psychological problems such as social anxiety and insecurity, a sense of inferiority, aggression, and achievement disorders. An effective psychotherapeutic counseling treatment for these psychological disorders should reduce criminal and abnormal social behavior (cf. Minsel & Howe, 1983, p. 250).

For the behavior therapy, we implemented a modeling program (cf. Sarason & Ganzer, 1969, 1971, 1973). Empirical studies show that it is correct to assume a relation between criminality and deficits in social behavior. In the course of the treatment program, we attempted to remove such behavior deficits (cf. Kury, 1986a; Pielmaier, 1979, 1986). Model learning was combined with role playing. It is shown in the literature that the combination of role playing and model learning is the ideal technique for learning the new and complex behavior patterns that the offenders need (cf. Langlotz & Hommers, 1978; Pielmaier, Pauls, & Blumenberg, 1980, pp. 338–342).

Before the beginning of the treatment program, the therapists developed their own modeling scenes based on the work of Sarason and Ganzer (1969, 1971, 1973) and Ganzer (1974), which would later be applied in the behavior therapy groups. These modeling scenes were revised before the start of evaluation. Additional scenes were worked out and tested in a pilot study. All the modeling scenes, which generally lasted no longer than 5 minutes, were video-recorded to provide a standard format. The 30 best scenes were selected for the behavior therapy treatment program, and one was presented in each therapy session. The sequence of scenes was exactly defined. The 30 scenes and their themes covered five fields of conflict: (1) family, (2) living in an institution, (3) job and occupation, (4) leisure time, and (5) contacts with public authorities (Pielmaier, 1980, 1986; Wetzstein, 1986). Before the modeling scenes were presented in the therapy sessions, the therapists introduced the theme. Then the modeling scene was presented and its contents were discussed. Afterwards the individual group participants acted out the scenes. In a final discussion, they also discussed the most important elements with regard to a generalization of the contents (cf. also Steller, Hommers, & Zienert, 1978).

Usually, between three and five inmates participated in the group sessions. All sessions were tape-recorded, and the role playing of the individual sessions in the behavior therapy was video-recorded. All the therapists took part in the supervision sessions on a regular basis. Each therapist conducted three 75-minute therapy sessions per week. In order to keep the number of participants in each session as low as possible, four comparison groups were formed: two for counseling therapy and two for behavior therapy. Each group was led by a trained therapist who also had experience in the treatment of offenders. The assignment to the two groups was randomized. The average length of treatment per probationer was 26 hours for both counseling and behavior therapy.

Issues of the Study

The goal of the concomitant scientific study was an evaluation of the treatment programs conducted in the pretrial detention unit for young offenders in Freiburg. The following points present the most important issues:

1. Does the psychotherapeutic treatment influence the inmates' personality structure, and if so, in which way?
2. Can prisonization effects be found that could eventually neutralize the effectiveness of treatment?
3. Is the effectiveness of counseling or behavior therapy programs dependent on the participant's personality structure at the start of treatment?
4. Is the effectiveness of counseling or behavior therapy dependent on the subject's offence structure and the length of treatment?
5. Do the two treatments (counseling vs. behavior therapy) show different effects on the inmates?
6. Do the two types of therapy show typical treatment processes?
7. Do treated participants exhibit more law-abiding behavior after release from prison than subjects in comparison groups who do not receive treatment (cf. Kury, 1987)?

Method

Design

There were considerable difficulties in the operationalization of the evaluation design. It was impossible to administer a true experimental design. Since the entire Freiburg pretrial detention institution for young offenders was involved in the rehabilitation program, it was neither reasonable nor ethically acceptable to separate a sample from the offenders as a control group at the beginning of the project. There would also certainly have been legal problems with such a procedure. Furthermore, the 15–20 inmates in the institution would have been too small a group for such a division. So the only possibility was to take as a control group other young male remand prisoners not receiving treatment. The pretrial detention institutions in Rastatt and Mannheim seemed viable because of their proximity, capacity, and the structure of inmates. In order to gain a large enough group of subjects and allow for expected "mortality rates," we took the inmates of both institutions as control groups. The assignment of the subjects in Freiburg to the two treatment groups was randomized.

In order to gain the most differentiated assessment of the treatment effects possible, we selected a pretest-posttest design with an additional process evaluation. In addition, the legal files of all inmates were evaluated. In order to be able to compare the three institutions and also state prisonization effects, we performed a special institution analysis in all three prisons. Finally, we initiated a follow-up study for released subjects and their probation officers to gain data on the prisoners' legal and social behavior after release. The extent of the individual subprojects makes this the most extensive research project of this kind yet to be carried out in the FRG.

The pretests and posttests were administered in the prisons at Freiburg (treatment group), Rastatt, and Mannheim (comparison groups) within 1 week of the subject's arrival in the institution, but before the onset of treatment. The posttests were administered 6 weeks later in order to keep the mortality as low as possible despite the high fluctuation in detention periods.

Since there is still a lack of empirically grounded theories on the personality and treatment of offenders, it was extremely difficult to define the relevant variables and rationally select test procedures for their operationalization. We selected psychological tests with the goal of being able to, on the one hand, state personality variables that can help to classify the inmates with regard to their treatment groups, and, on the other hand, draw conclusions about the effects of treatment. We wanted to use only tests that possess criteria that meet the generally accepted scientific standards. We selected personality tests that dealt with those personality characteristics that are frequently discussed in the literature on criminality, such as extraversion, aggression, risk-taking, self-image, and intelligence, plus the perceived parental child-rearing style. Many studies have shown differences between offenders and nonoffenders on these personality variables (cf. Villmov-Feldkamp, 1976; Villmov-Feldkamp, & Kury, 1983). If a therapy is to have an effect on offenders, it must reduce personality deviances, at least if it is assumed that these deviances are a (concomitant) cause of a further offence (for more detail, cf. Kury, 1987). Most of the personality tests we selected have been shown to be valid in psychotherapeutic research, and they mostly belong to the standard battery of tests used in corresponding evaluation studies. The following tests were applied:

1. The Freiburger Persönlichkeitsinventar (FPI) (Fahrenberg, Selg, & Hampel, 1978), a personality questionnaire
2. The Gießener Fragebogen (GF) (Quensel, 1972; Rieländer & Quensel, 1983), a questionnaire based on the Jesness Inventory (cf. Jesness, 1966, 1971, 1974)
3. A risk questionnaire (RKVF) (Jackson, Hourany, & Vidme, 1972; Schwenkmezger, 1977) and further procedures for assessing risk behavior

4. The LPS intelligence test (Horn, 1962)
5. Questionnaires for the assessment of the subjective risk of delinquency and the negative valence of sanctioning consequences (Lösel, 1975)
6. A questionnaire for the assessment of child-rearing practices (Hermann et al., 1973)
7. The Q-Sort (Helm, 1974) for the assessment of the ideal and the perceived self-image

In addition, each subject was given a comprehensive, standardized interview both pretest and posttest. These interviews collected data on the subjects' personalities and delinquency development, their attitude to psychotherapy, and, in the posttest, the subjective estimation of treatment effects. As data collection was not anonymous, subjects were assured by the research institute that all the data would be used exclusively for the evaluation research and would not be made available to justice officials.

In a pilot test, an assessment was made of the extent to which the subjects considered these instructions to be reliable. This was done to assess whether the project was based on valid test indications. There were no significant differences compared to a random control group who filled in the questionnaires anonymously. We therefore assumed that the subjects did not falsify the test results to any great extent (cf. Kury, 1983a, 1983b, 1987).

In addition to the test data, we also collected information on the offence and the personal background of the offender using a standardized and pretested analysis questionnaire to investigate probation and sentencing files. We also decided to collect additional process data despite the considerable problems that we expected with this. For the process evaluation, all the therapy sessions were recorded on either audio (counseling therapy) or video (modeling within the behavior therapy) tape. Furthermore, both therapists and clients completed a standardized data sheet on the therapy sessions, as is the usual practice in counseling therapy research.

In order to make an ecological comparison, the pretests, posttests, and process evaluations were supplemented with comprehensive information on the three prisons. An experienced psychologist conducted a participant observation study for a period of 1 month in each of the three prisons. In addition, the inmates and staff were given a structured interview on the situation in their respective prisons. They also completed a questionnaire on the social climate of the prison. Finally, we analyzed the extent to which the three prisons differed, and whether these differences could have a specific influence on the personality of the inmates (for more details, cf. Busch, 1986; Kury, 1987). The goal of this additional study was to assess the extent of specific prisonization threats and the level of comparability between the prisons. This information was used to check to what extent the inmates in Mannheim and Rastatt could be compared with the treatment group in Freiburg.

Finally, case histories were studied for up to 2 years after release from prison in order to assess the effect of treatment. Both the probation officers and the remand prisoners were regularly given standardized questionnaires on the situation after release from prison, with special emphasis on social and legal behavior.

Data Analysis

The methodological problems that arise when evaluating the success of therapy treatment are very large and only partially resolved (cf. Bereiter, 1963). Various statistical evaluation strategies which, however, contain specific disadvantages regarding the power of the attained results, have been proposed and discussed (for a "traditional" description of methodological problems, see Harris, 1963; for a more recent summary, see Möbus & Nagel, 1983; Wittmann, 1985). The most frequent design in psychotherapeutic success research is probably the evaluation of simple difference scores between pretests and posttests. This has major disadvantages: For example, natural regression effects and standard correlated measurement errors cannot be taken into account. To allow for these errors, it is sometimes recommended to evaluate regression deviation scores as "corrected" scores (cf., e.g., Cronbach & Furby, 1970; Grawe, 1976, pp. 82–83). In our study, we evaluated simple difference scores as well as regression deviation scores.

Therapy research most frequently uses a two-way analysis of variance for statistical evaluation, in which the different treatment groups define one factor and the various measurement timepoints by repeated measurement function as levels on the second factor. We also used this design for the first step in our evaluation (Dixon, Brown, Engelmann, Frane, Hill, Jennrich, & Toporek, 1981).

The application of the analysis of variance as an evaluation strategy basically points out differences in mean scores, a high variance within the individual cells being considered undesirable. Supporters of a differential psychotherapy research have for many years correctly pointed out that a treatment success or the effects of treatment can only be investigated incompletely by comparing mean scores, because treatment may also affect the variance of posttest scores without simultaneous changes in mean scores (cf. Bergin, 1966; Bergin & Lambert, 1978; Grawe, 1981). In addition to investigating mean score differences, we also tested whether it was possible to determine effects shown by an increase in variance.

In addition to conducting pretest-posttest comparisons with the abovementioned method on the level of individual variables, we also made comparisons on the level of higher dimensions. We chose factor analysis as a methodological strategy for collecting the individual variables on such higher dimensions.

Results

Validity of Test Scores

As nearly all the questionnaires we used had been developed for clinical populations and not specially for prisoners, the interviews in pretrial detention took place in an extreme setting. It was therefore very important to check the validity of our data. We did this with the additional falsification study mentioned above. This indicated that we did not need to expect any or only unimportant falsifying response sets through the use of our test instructions (for more detail, see Kury, 1983a, 1983b, 1987).

Validity was examined with an item analysis of each of the questionnaires and a comparison of our data with that given by the test authors. With only a few exceptions, the consistency coefficients were about alpha = 0.60, which meets generally accepted research standards. The same applies to the item total coefficients. The scores on, for example, the Gießen questionnaire were nonsignificantly higher than the scores on the FPI, developed for the field of clinical psychology. These scores also satisfied the demands discussed in the methodological literature.

The power of the findings on the effects of treatment is possibly restricted by the probationers' drop-out rate during the course of the research project. This is a problem that confronts nearly all longitudinal studies. We had to expect high mortality rates for our test group due to releases, transfers, and refusal to participate by prisoners. Finally, the rate was higher than originally expected. The drop-out rate was nearly the same in all three pretrial detention institutions. From the total of 699 probationers, 164 belonged to the test group in Freiburg, and 535 to the two control groups in Mannheim ($n = 238$) and Rastatt ($n = 297$). While we had 685 interpretable pretest subjects (98%), 6 weeks later there were only 242 (35%) interpretable posttest subjects. Nearly all losses were due to transfers and releases. Only 19 subjects (3%) refused to participate. In order to reduce costs, we evaluated only half of the prison and probation files in the control groups through random selection. We gained access to the files of 388 (88%) from a total of 441 subjects. As each individual interview lasted nearly 1 hour, we randomly selected only half of the subjects from the sample of newly admitted prisoners. From the 313 prisoners for whom a pretest was available, 138 (44%) were also available for the posttest. The outcome of legal proceedings was known for 170 subjects and was obtained from the probation officers during the 2-year-long posttest period. From the total of 164 subjects in the Freiburg test, 107 (65%) participated in the therapy, one-half receiving counseling and the other half behavior therapy. It could be anticipated that overlapping would further reduce the number of subjects through the combination of several data sets. Thus pretests and posttests were available from 60 subjects in the Freiburg test group who participated in therapy.

Since comprehensive pretests were available for nearly all subjects, we were able to test how far the single subgroups differed on their pretest scores, thus providing an indication for any bias in the test results due to selection effects. We compared the single subgroups on a test-scale level and also on the personality dimensions derived by factor analysis (comparison of mean scores). All comparisons showed that significant differences between subgroups were very seldom and random. Thus we conducted a total of 672 significance tests, of which only 48 were statistically significant on the 5% level and 4 on the 1% level. This provides further support for the validity of the data.

Equivalence of Probationer Groups

Since an experimental design with random assignment to treatment and control groups was not possible, the equivalence of the three groups on the criterion variables is a crucial issue. If there were already significant differences before the onset of treatment, we would have to take this into account when interpreting possible differences in the posttests. Therefore we examined the equivalence of the three groups (Freiburg, Mannheim, Rastatt) before the onset of the study. We found considerable differences in the pretests, the first interviews, and in the inmates' offence structures. The Mannheim group deviated clearly from the other two: The subjects in Mannheim showed a more deviant personality structure than the others. There were also differences in the offence structure. There were more offences against property in the Mannheim group and more drug offences, particularly when compared to the Freiburg group. Therefore the equivalence of the three groups is restricted.

Moreover, the institution analysis showed that it was necessary to interpret posttest differences with care. It was shown that the practice of pretrial detention differed significantly across the three institutions: This is also an indication of different prisonization effects on the inmates. It was clear that the degree of deprivation was higher for the Freiburg inmates than for the others despite the treatment program. The daily period of unlocked cells was much shorter in Freiburg (4.24 hs) than in Mannheim (5.13 hs) or Rastatt (5.51 hs). In Freiburg there were no work or sport opportunities. The institutional climate was estimated to be much more unfavorable by the inmates in Freiburg than by the inmates of the other prisons. This may have been an effect of the treatment program, which may have led to a more critical attitude to pretrial detention.

Further individual data from this research stage (especially the participant observation that is reported in Busch, 1986) generally indicated that the conditions in Mannheim were least favorable for rehabilitation while in Rastatt they were considered to be relatively positive. Freiburg seemed to have an intermediate position, and no doubt the treatment program contributed to an improvement in the institutional situation. These unfavorable conditions in Freiburg, especially those concerning the climate, could have led to considerable prisonization harm which could have had a neutralizing effect on the therapeutic treatment. In our opinion, if the treatment program is excluded, pretrial detention in Freiburg was more unfavorable for educational development and the development of personality structure or rehabilitation than in Rastatt. This supports the assumption that the differences between the three groups in the posttests were probably due to the effects of treatment – at least as far as the improvements in the Freiburg inmates are concerned.

Psychological Personality Differences Between Pretrial Detention Prisoners and Nondelinquents and Between Different Offender Groups

Several psychological and criminological studies have reported personality differences between (registered) offenders and nondelinquents (cf. Schuessler & Cressey, 1950; Tennenbaum, 1977; Waldo & Dinitz, 1967; see also Lösel, 1983 a, b; Ortmann, 1987). It is still disputed whether such differences are the cause or (also) the consequences of criminal behavior and punishment: There is widespread agreement that psychological personality deviances in the form of a "more disturbed" personality image among registered offenders can be seen in connection with eventual recidivism. If the psychological treatment of offenders is to be successful, it must have an impact on the client's personality structure that leads to a reduction in the client's psychological stress or deviance and an approach toward the normal population in their test scores.

The issue of treatment success which is reflected in changes in test scores has to be seen in connection with "deviances" on personality dimensions. In this context, we examined the extent to which the deviances in the personality scores in our random sample of pretrial detainels compared to the standard random sample (cf. Kury, 1981).

There were very significant differences between pretrial detainees and the "normal" control group. More than 80% of the mean comparisons were statistically significant, of which 73% (37) reached the 1% level. Generally speaking, the young remand prisoners differed in several personality variables from noncriminal persons and usually in an unfavorable direction. They described themselves as being much more "disturbed" and psychologically impaired. Our subjects had average scores for intelligence and concentration (for details, see Kury, 1987).

The strong deviant profile on nearly all the questionnaires presented by the pretrial detainees in our sample indicated that the tests were sensitive for personality characteristics in these subjects that were of special significance for therapy. Thus these instruments can be seen as valid procedures for the assessment of changes in personality structure: Desirable changes would be approaches to the standard scores that are the means of an indisturbed "normal" population (cf. Grawe, 1976, p. 110).

In order to examine whether there was a connection between offence structure and personality, the remand prisoners were divided into four offence groups: violence, property, drugs, and miscellaneous. The last group contained offenders who could not be assigned to a particular group because they were charged with a variety of offences. These four groups were subjected to analyses of variance for the individual scale means and *t*-tests for independent random samples in order to compare the individual groups.

It was evident that a large proportion of the significant mean differences found in the analyses of variance could be attributed to the deviant scores of the drug offenders. These drug offenders were found to be less aggressive, less easily aroused, more compliant, and more moderate. Their self-descriptions were less typically masculine than in the other groups, who did not differ significantly on any of the 12 FPI scales. The same held for the Gießen questionnaire. The drug offenders had the highest scores on all scales of the intelligence test.

The drug offenders also clearly differed from the other groups in the file analysis. It was apparent that the differences in personality of drug offenders were due to different socialization conditions or a different development of their criminal career. Drug offenders differed from the other offenders on several characteristics. Because of this and the different nature of their crimes, it would seem necessary to assume that they require other measures of rehabilitation, and that rehabilitation programs will show different effects to those in other offenders (cf. Kerner, 1982, pp. 434–437).

Results on the Effects of Treatment

A number of results on the effectiveness of treatment were generated during the course of the research project. Only the most important of these can be reported here (for more details, see Kury, 1986a, 1986b, 1987).

Pretest-Posttest Comparison (Personality Variables). The main comparison of the pretest-posttest data for the single variables (scales) and the comparison of the six dimensions derived by factor analysis for the Freiburg treatment group and control groups in Mannheim and Rastatt only produced a few significant differences, especially in the treatment group. The significant increase in the posttest scores compared to the pretest scores in the subtests of the LPS intelligence test and the total score in the d2 concentration test can be interpreted as repetition effects as the 6-week testing interval was relatively short. A pretest-posttest comparison of the control groups produced a higher number of significant differences and a deterioration in the posttest results in the sense of prisonization effects. The comparison of the two treatment groups (counseling therapy vs. behavior therapy) within the experimental group almost exclusively only showed significant changes in the counseling groups.

A simple pretest-posttest comparison with *t*-tests for independent random samples has the disadvantage, as described above, that factors of offense structure or personality variables (in the following: intelligence and characteristics of the perceived parental child-rearing) that could have influenced the success of treatment are neglected. A multivariate analysis of variance was carried out to consider these variables. In addition, we examined whether the pretest-posttest differences were influenced by duration or the type of treatment (counseling vs. behavior therapy).

The multivariate analysis of variance scarcely revealed any significant differences in development between the pretests and posttests for the treatment group compared to controls. The few significant results could only be regarded as a restricted indication for a treatment effect. We also did not find any clear-cut connection between treatment effects and intelligence test scores, perceived parental child-rearing practices, or offense structure. In addition, we tested whether there was a connection between treatment effect and duration or type of treatment in the Freiburg group.

There were no significant differences in most of the comparisons. However, it can be noted that a relatively large number of single variables took the direction of a favorable development in the pretest-posttest comparisons that related to the increase in therapy duration. This tendency was detected, for example, in eight of the FPI scales.

The calculation of regression-adjusted posttest scores mostly only confirmed the previous findings. The comparison of the factor scores produced two significant differences: factor 1 (bad-tempered, depressive, lacking in confidence, psychologically disturbed) decreased in the treatment group compared to controls, and factor 4 (subjective estimation of delinquency risk) increased significantly. Both results can be interpreted as treatment successes. The increase in variance effect mentioned in psychotherapy research that we anticipated in the treatment group was not found. Table 22.1 summarizes the statistically significant differences found in all the single calculations.

Preinterview-Postinterview Comparison. In addition to the results of the psychological tests, we also examined whether a treatment success was indicated by the responses to the preinterviews and postinterviews. Despite the reservations that some remand prisoners had about talking to psychologists, the problematic trust relationships, and the predominantly unclear preconceptions of such talks, no less than 60% of the subjects indicated in the preinterview that they were willing to discuss themselves and their problems with a psychologist during pretrial detention. In the Freiburg treatment group who were subsequently offered such talks, 55% of the subjects agreed to them. As reasons for their willingness to participate, 37% of the group said they expected to be able to discuss problems together and help each other, 11% expected less help in solving their own problems but more entertainment, or they participated out of curiosity.

As for the subjects' views on the success of treatment, the interviews showed that they did not place much value on the effects of this rehabilitation

TABLE 22.1. Summarized presentation of the statistically significant mean differences (pretest-posttest) for the Freiburg treatment group

Test scales[1]	*t*-test comparison			Multivariate comparison							Regression-corrected scores			
	Freiburg (total group)	CT	BT	Experimental/ control group	Type of therapy		Length of therapy	LPS – total	4 offence groups	MASK	CT + BT (combined)	CT	BT	Group with longer therapy
					CT	BT								
FPI-2	–		–								–		–	–
FPI-6		–	+		–	+	+					–	+	
FPI-8										+				
FPI-9										+				
FPI-M											–		–	
GF-1						+								
GF-2	+		+											
GF-Stig								+						
GF-S2										+				
RKVF-E		+			+	–								
RKVF-F		+												
RKVF-G		+												
SIT-F1	–							+						
SIT-F2		+			+	–								
SIT-F				–										
SIT-G	+	+						+						
Wegewahl			+											
Subj. Del. 6								+						

TABLE 22.1 (continued)

Test scales[1]	*t*-test comparison			Multivariate comparison							Regression-corrected scores			
	Freiburg (total group)	CT	BT	Experimental/ control group	Type of therapy		Length of therapy	LPS – total	4 offence groups	MASK	CT + BT (combined)	CT	BT	Group with longer therapy
					CT	BT								
Neg. Val.														
2									+		+			+
7					–	+								
8													+	+
LPS-1	+	+	+											
LPS-2	+	+	+	+									+	+
LPS-3	+	+	+											
LPS-4	+		+										+	+
LPS-9	+	+	+											
LPS-10	+	+	+											
LPS-12	+	+	+				+							
LPS-G	+	+	+											
d2-GZ	+	+	+										–	–
F-1											–			–
F-3								+						
F-4	–										+	+	+	+
F-5							+							
F-6			+	+										

[1] with at least one significant score

Abbreviations: CT, counseling therapy; BT, behavior therapy; MASK, Marburger Skalen zur Erfassung des elterlichen Erziehungsstiles, a parental upbringing questionnaire; FPI, Freiburger Persönlichkeitsinventar; GF, Gießener Fragebogen; RKVF, Risikofragebogen; SIT, Situationsfragebogen; Subj. Del., subjective assessment of delinquency risk; Neg. Val., negative valence of sanctioning consequences; LPS, Leistungsprüfsystem; d2 – GZ, measure, though some felt that they had profited from the talks. Thirty-one percent of the subjects indicated that their experiences during counseling helped them to cope better with life in prison. The reason they gave for this were that they were able to speak out during these sessions, felt better afterwards, and their attitude toward life and particularly toward offences changed.

The crucial question for the subjective evaluation of treatment effects, namely, whether counseling would help them to cope better with life after release from prison, was answered negatively by nearly three-quarters (73%) of the subjects. The reasons they gave for this unfavorable opinion were that the modeling scenes were not related to their lives and that the counseling talks were too superficial. In contrast, the subjects who gave a positive evaluation said that their attention was drawn to particular points and they now saw some things related to their offence differently.

In all, the results of the interviews indicated subjective estimates of treatment success in between one-quarter and one-third of the subjects.

Process Evaluation. As described above, process data were collected from the start of the evaluation study with data sheets, video-recordings, and tape-recordings of the therapy sessions. This comprehensive material was evaluated in a separate study (cf. Deutschbein, 1986, 1987).

In the data sheets, the subjects gave relatively homogeneous indications that they felt generally good and accepted in the therapy sessions (cf. Table 22.2). However, there were significant differences in the estimation of perceived assistance during pretrial detention and the period following it. While the subjects in the counseling groups estimated that what happened in therapy would help them to cope better with life after release in only 21% of the sessions, those in behavior therapy found 35% of the sessions to be helpful. Counseling clients considered that 22% of the therapy sessions would be helpful for the time after release from prison, and behavior therapy clients expressed this for 42% of the sessions. This estimation difference was also found for other items in the data sheets. The behavior therapy clients indicated that the treatment had made them calmer in 43% of the sessions compared with 30% for the counseling clients. The contents of the sessions were estimated as being meaningful for 76% of the behavior therapy sessions compared to 63% of the counseling sessions.

The differences in the data sheets were relatively low for the therapists. There was a significant discrepancy between the therapists' estimations and those made by the clients. Compared to the clients, who rated only 21% (counseling) or 38% (behavior therapy) of the sessions as being helpful, the therapists felt that the subjects had profited from 83% of the counseling sessions and 75% of the behavior therapy sessions. This tendency for therapists to have a more optimistic and positive attitude toward treatment is known from psychotherapy research.

The clients' evaluation of single sessions changed considerably during the course of therapy, and differences also appeared between the two types of

TABLE 22.2. Average distribution of responses in the therapy data sheets (client questionnaires) split according to counseling therapy (CT) and behavior therapy (BT) groups [number of data sheets (= 100%): CT group 847; BT group 1022; data in percentages; cf. Deutschbein, 1987]

	Is more true		Is less true		Don't know	
	CT	BT	CT	BT	CT	BT
K 1: After today's session, I feel calmer inside	29.5	42.8	66.8	54.8	3.7	2.4
K 2: Today I felt uneasy in the group	7.9	7.6	91.4	91.4	0.7	1.0
K 3: The events in today's group will help me to cope better with my life in the prison	20.8	35.0	75.7	59.8	3.5	5.2
K 4: The events in today's group will help me to cope better with my life after my release from prison	22.2	41.7	74.1	52.6	3.7	5.7
K 5: Today I felt rejected by the group	2.6	3.9	96.1	94.5	1.3	1.6
K 6: I felt that the psychologist doesn't understand me	4.0	5.5	93.5	92.4	2.5	2.2
K 7: Today it was difficult for me to take part in group activities	13.1	16.5	85.2	81.5	1.7	2.0
K 8: I found the contents of today's session meaningful	62.9	75.9	33.2	21.3	3.9	2.7
K 9: Today one of my personal problems was discussed in the group	58.9	50.0	39.1	48.4	2.0	1.6

therapy. Participants in behavior therapy gave increasingly more favorable estimations of the value of treatment for coping better with life during detention and following release after the first third of the treatment period. The counseling clients reported the opposite experience: Their expectations decreased the greater the number of sessions. In contrast to this, personal problems of the clients were discussed more frequently after the tenth session in counseling but not in the behavior therapy groups. This was probably due to the different procedures used in the two types of therapy. We only found the connections between personality dimensions and therapy process scores reported in several previous studies (cf. Sander, 1975; Schwartz, 1975) in isolated instances.

Legal Behavior After Release From Prison. The central criterion of success in treatment evaluation has always been considered to be law-abiding behavior after release from prison. Therefore we examined the differences in recidivism rates for the various groups. Table 22.3 surveys the distribution of subjects with different outcomes of legal proceedings for the three groups. From the 170 subjects in the case history study for the 2-year period after release from prison for whom information on legal proceedings was available, 64 (38%) belonged to the Freiburg treatment group and 106 (62%) to the comparison groups from

TABLE 22.3. Comparison between experimental and control groups on the outcomes of legal proceedings (remission or revocation of probation)

Outcome of legal proceedings	FR		MA/RA		MA		RA		Total (FR+MA+RA)	
	No.	%	No.	%	No.	%	No.	%	No.	%
Remission	39	60.9	57	53.8	19	51.4	38	55.1	96	56.5
Revocation	25	39.1	49	46.2	18	48.6	31	44.9	74	43.5
Total	64	100.0	106	100.0	37	100.0	69	100.0	170	100.0

Abbreviations: FR, Freiburg; MA, Mannheim; RA, Rastatt

Rastatt and Mannheim. While in Freiburg, 61% of the subjects earned a remission and only 39% received revocation, in the comparison group only 54% earned a remission and 46% had their probation revoked. Within the comparison group, the Mannheim subjects had a particularly low success rate, with only 51% earning remission compared to 55% in Rastatt. The revocation rate for the Freiburg treatment group was thus 10% lower than in Mannheim. However, none of these results were statistically significant.

At first sight, these results indicate a treatment success, especially when we remember that the conditions in Freiburg were much worse than in Mannheim or Rastatt and we could therefore anticipate higher revocation and recidivism rates in Freiburg. A comparison of the number of previous convictions in the treatment group and the control groups showed that the subjects in Freiburg had a slightly higher rate of previous convictions (50% compared to 46%), which would also lead to the anticipation of a higher revocation rate in the treatment group. These data also support the assumption of a treatment success.

Judicial decision-making is very important for the size of the revocation rate. We found that sanctioning practices (ordering of pretrial detention, average duration of pretrial detention) differed widely between the three cities. The comparison of the sanctioning pattern based on the proportion of young remand prisoners sentenced to imprisonment showed no intergroup differences. However, there were highly significant differences in probation for young offenders. Judges in Freiburg were found to be considerably more lenient. In Freiburg, 85 (79%) of the remand prisoners were given conditional sentences (probation) or a decision on sentencing was reserved and only 23 (21%) were sentenced to prison. In Mannheim and Rastatt there were twice as many prison sentences (91, 49%), and only 109 (55%) received conditional sentences (probation).

These findings show that judges in Freiburg greatly differed in their sentencing from those in Mannheim and Rastatt. The low recidivism rate in Freiburg suggests that these findings were related to the treatment program, though the present findings do not provide conclusive evidence of this. Nevertheless, it is important to note here that the revocation rate of the probationers in Freiburg was considerably lower than in Rastatt and Mannheim despite more serious criminal records and the greater probability of recidivism, and this suggests a positive effect of the treatment program.

Results of the Interviews with Probation Officers. In order to ascertain the success of treatment, for example, whether treatment had led to improved conflict- and problem-coping behavior, it was important to collect data on social integration (e.g., in the employment and social field) as well as on probation (cf. Kerner, 1985).

The interviews with probation officers revealed that a large proportion of their work consisted in support with release and reintegration, especially in the first weeks and months after release. There are relatively frequent contacts between clients and their probation officers concerning acute problems with accommodation, education, employment, regulation of debts, and other important life questions. It has to be considered that in the standardized interviews in the pretest-posttest study nearly one-fifth of the subjects reported that they had no fixed accommodation after release from prison. More than half of the subjects reported that they would have no job after being released. According to the probation officers, the institutions or courts had only made preparations for the release of about 35% of the remand prisoners; this usually consisted of the provision of accommodation.

If we consider the relation between unemployment at different points in time and the outcome of legal proceedings (proportion of revoked conditional sentences), it becomes evident that the proportion of revocations increased with the duration of unemployment. Obviously, unemployment creates a special stress situation for the probationers, and its financial effects particularly increase the risk of recidivism.

In addition to the persistence of unemployment at the end of the first quarter of probation, we recorded six more indicators of presumed dangers to the process of integration. These related to the 3rd month of probation and were combined to form an "impairment index." This index emphasized aspects of economic stress, social bonds (in the sense of a steady partner relationship), drug use, and the probation officer's assessment of the probationer's social behavior on the dichotomy of "autonomy" versus "dependency" which was used to operationalize the probationer's social competence (cf. Spieß, 1980, 1986).

We found that the proportion of revocations, this means, the extent of the probationer's failure as ascertained by recidivism or the disregarding of probation orders, increased with almost every individual component of the impairment index.

In summary, the results of the interviews with probation officers showed a distinct relation between stress factors and the revocation of probation. Thus the revocation proportion increased if disposable income was low, if debts were high, if there was no regulation of debts, and if there was no steady partner.

Discussion

The findings and experiences with our treatment evaluation show the enormous difficulties involved in such research. There are almost insuperable problems with a meaningful implementation of a treatment program within the highly regulated and regimanted practice of prison or pretrial detention, as well as with the conduct of research itself. The statistical estimation of treatment effects based on multiple measurement is faced with considerable methodological problems which, as yet, are only partially solved. In a longitudinal study on treatment evaluation in pretrial detention, high "mortality rates" are scarcely avoidable, and, as we have shown, they can be very high in pretrial detention. These losses, problems in operationalizing treatment success, and the extreme prison situation – especially in pretrial detention – have uncontrollable effects on test scores, thus making it difficult to obtain valid and generalizable research findings. Therefore, it is not surprising that we can only provide tentative answers to the issues in this study when the complexity of the problems are considered.

The findings on whether psychotherapeutic treatment in pretrial detention has effects on the personality structure are less significant – at least as far as the pretest-posttest comparisons are concerned. To the extent that significant differences arise, they cannot be interpreted homogeneously. Some results suggest that the longer the duration of therapy, the higher the anticipated success of treatment, as indicated by the test-score differences in, for example, the FPI. This may be an indication that the average duration of treatment was too short and thus not intensive enough, which seems plausible when we look at the unfavorable conditions in pretrial detention and the personality structures of the inmates. The ecological comparison of the three institutions reveals that the level of deprivation is much higher in the treatment group than in the control groups. Therefore we have to assume a higher prisonization effect in Freiburg, which has a negative influence on treatment. This finding was confirmed by all experimenters and therapists. Although the treatment procedure has considerably improved the climate in Freiburg, it only supported the rehabilitation measures insignificantly. All the persons involved in the project repeatedly stressed the importance of treatment programs in the avoidance of prisonization harm. This is probably the most important effect of the treatment program.

The less significant results do not permit us to consider how far the effectiveness of counseling or behavior therapy depends on the personality or offence structure of the offender. There are several indications that the behavior therapy program received more approval from the inmates, and its effectiveness for postrelease behavior was estimated to be more favorable. This is probably related to the more stimulative character of the behavior therapy (performance of video scenes). When we look at the offence structure, we see that drug offenders form a special group. This is significantly expressed in their personality structure and socialization background. Pretrial detention is particularly contraindicated for drug offenders, especially probationers suffering from drug addiction. The treatment programs that we offered were probably insufficient and can at best only serve as an impulse to participate in further therapy measures.

We can hardly see any treatment effects, at least for the success criteria we used. However, the courses of the two therapy treatments differed considerably in the individual variables from the data sheets. As the number of sessions increased, participants in behavior therapy more frequently reported that they felt better supported for life in prison or after release than counseling clients. The findings from the interviews indicated that this was because, in the prisoners' view, the practical behavior instructions in the modeling program were easier to realize and were more directly related to their life problems. This was not the case in counseling, in which general problems were discussed more abstractly. However, the counseling clients reported that the problems discussed became increasingly personal. It would appear that the duration of counseling therapy was too short to attain a (significant) treatment effect.

When we look at the estimation of treatment success based on the law-abiding behavior after release from prison, which is the decisive criterion of the success of treatment measures in criminology, the treated remand prisoners show significantly more favorable patterns. Their recidivism rate is about 10% lower than in the most unfavorable group (Mannheim), and still about 6% lower than Rastatt. But we must not forget that the pretrial detention institution in Rastatt is most favorably rated on the level of prisonization. This finding indicates a treatment success, though it has to be taken into account that the difference we found is not inevitably due to the effect of treatment. It also appears plausible that this finding is partially caused by the different sanctioning practices of judges. The findings from the interviews with probation officers highlight the importance of the postrelease period for successful integration into society. In our project, we find that the urgently needed systematic support for former inmates is completely lacking. One-fifth of the probationers had no accommodation when they were released, and more than half of them did not have a job. According to the probation officers, the prisons and courts had only prepared the release of about one-third of the remand prisoners, and this usually only consisted of the provision of accommodation. Despite the high proportion of 46% of young offenders who were unemployed before their incarceration, efforts to obtain work or vocational training were only made for a minute proportion of the 170 subjects. When we consider the relation between unemployment at different points in time and the outcome of legal proceedings (proportion of revoked conditional sentences), it is evident that the proportion of revocations increases with the duration of unemployment. Obviously, unemployment creates a special stress situation for the probationers, and its financial effects pose an increased risk of recidivism.

Our findings underline the limited potential of treatment in prison, especially in pretrial detention. Besides the numerous factors that impede a meaningful realization of a treatment program inside a prison, we have to consider that the inmates will obviously be confronted with serious problems in their living situation after release (cf. Farrington, Ohlin, & Wilson, 1986). Most of them are not given any specific preparation for dealing with these problems. The stress situation that results from, for example, financial problems, high debts, unemployment, the lack of a steady partner, and so forth often reaches such an intensity that we can hardly expect the inmates to be able to cope with these problems on their own on the basis of relatively few treatment sessions in prison. We have to anticipate that particularly in such stress situations the former inmates will relapse into their old, familiar habits, and the risk of new offences will arise. Thus the expectations regarding the success of treatments in prisons do not do justice to the realistic possibilities. It is important that treatment programs are extended to include the postrelease situation and that they offer concrete help and support in solving emerging problems. Rehabilitation treatment should not only concentrate on the time spent in prison but should include the period after release, by, for example, offering concrete assistance from the probation officers after release. The solving of such problems is often beyond the abilities of the offenders. Treatment in prison has to be complemented by concrete support after release. Only then can we anticipate more favorable success rates for treatment programs.

References

Abenhausen, F. (1983). Statistische und empirische Untersuchungen zur Untersuchungshaft. In H. Jung & H. Müller-Dietz (Eds.), *Reform der Untersuchungshaft* (pp. 99–204). Bonn-Bad Godesberg: Bundeszusammenschluß für Straffälligenhilfe.

Arbeitskreis Strafprozeßreform (1983). *Die Untersuchungshaft. Gesetzentwurf mit Begründung.* Heidelberg: Müller.

Bastine, R. (1970). Forschungsmethoden in der klinischen Psychologie. In W. J. Schraml (Ed.), *Klinische Psychologie. Ein Leitfaden für Praxis und Studium.* Bern: Huber.

Bereiter, C. (1963). Some persisting dilemmas in the measurement of change. In C. W. Harris (Ed.), *Problems in measuring change* (pp. 3–20). Madison: Knapp.

Bergin, A. E. (1966). Some implications of psychotherapy for therapeutic practice. *Journal of Abnormal Psychology, 71*, 235–246.

Bergin, A. E., & Lambert, M. J. (1978). The evaluation of therapeutic outcomes. In S. L. Garfield & A. E. Bergin (Eds.), *Handbook of psychotherapy and behavior change: An empirical analysis* (2nd ed, pp. 139–189). New York: Wiley.

Biermann-Ratjen, E., Eckert, J., & Schwartz, H. J. (1979). *Gesprächspsychotherapie: Verändern durch Verstehen.* Stuttgart: Kohlhammer.

Busch, B. (1986). Erhebung institutioneller Variablen. Ökologischer Vergleich der drei U-Haftanstalten Freiburg, Mannheim und Rastatt. In H. Kury (Ed.), *Prognose und*

Behandlung bei jungen Rechtsbrechern. Ergebnisse eines Forschungsprojekts (pp. 237–295). Freiburg i. Br., FRG: Max-Planck-Institut für Strafrecht.

Cronbach, L. J., & Furby, L. (1970). How we should measure 'change' – or should we? *Psychological Bulletin, 74,* 68–80.

Deutschbein, T. (1986). Die prozeßanalytische Untersuchung von Gesprächspsychotherapie und sozialem Training bei Jugendlichen in der Untersuchungshaft. In H. Kury (Ed.), *Prognose und Behandlung bei jungen Rechtsbrechern. Ergebnisse eines Forschungsprojekts* (pp. 393–510). Freiburg i. Br., FRG: Max-Planck-Institut für Strafrecht.

Deutschbein, T. (1987). *Prozeßanalyse bei den Therapien jugendlicher Untersuchungsgefangener.* Rheinfelden: Schäuble.

Dixon, W. J., Brown, M. B., Engelmann, L., Frane, J. W., Hill, M. A., Jennrich, R. I., & Toporek, J. D. (1981). *BMDP statistical software 1981.* Berkeley: University of California Press.

Fahrenberg, J., Selg, H., & Hampel, R. (1978). *Das Freiburger Persönlichkeitsinventar – FPI. Handanweisung* (3rd. ed.). Göttingen: Hogrefe.

Farrington, D. P., Ohlin, L. E., & Wilson, J. Q. (1986). *Understanding and controlling crime. Toward a new research strategy.* (Research in Criminology). New York Berlin Heidelberg Tokyo: Springer-Verlag.

Ganzer, V. J. (1974). The use of modeling techniques in rehabilitation of the juvenile offender. In J. G. Cull & R. Hardy (Eds.), *Behavior modification in rehabilitation setting: Applied principles* (pp. 130–157). Springfield: Thomas.

Grawe, K. (1976). *Differentielle Psychotherapie I. Indikatoren und spezifische Wirkung von Verhaltenstherapie und Gesprächspsychotherapie. Eine Untersuchung an phobischen Patienten.* Bern: Huber.

Grawe, K. (1981). Vergleichende Psychotherapieforschung. In W. R. Minsel & R. Scheller (Eds.), *Psychotherapie* (pp. 149–183). Munich: Kösel.

Harris, C. W. (Ed.). (1963). *Problems in measuring change.* Madison: Knapp.

Hauser, R. (1978). Die Untersuchungshaft im Lichte des Verfassungsrechts und der Menschenrechtskonventionen. *Schweizerische Zeitschrift für Strafrecht, 95,* 225–273.

Helm, J. (1974). Eine vorläufige Kurzform des Persönlichkeits-Q-Sorts (Butler und Haigh). In J. Helm, E. Kasielke, & J. Mehl (Eds.), *Neurosendiagnose. Beiträge zur Entwicklung klinisch-psychologischer Methoden* (pp. 39–56). Berlin: VEB Deutscher Verlag der Wissenschaften.

Herrmann, T. H., Stapf, K. G., & Stäcker, K. H. (1973). Elterliche Bekräftigung in der Erziehung. In G. Reinert (Ed.), *Bericht zum 27. Kongreß der Deutschen Gesellschaft für Psychologie in Kiel* (pp. 475–493). Göttingen: Hogrefe.

Horn, H. (1962). *Leistungsprüfsystem. LPS.* Göttingen: Hogrefe.

Jackson, D. N., Hourany, L., & Vidmar, N. J. (1972). A four dimensional interpretation of risk taking. *Journal of Personality, 40,* 483–501.

Jesness, C. F. (1966). *The Jesness inventory.* Palo Alto, CA: Consulting Psychologists Press.

Jesness, C. F. (1971). *The Jesness behavior checklist.* Palo Alto, CA: Consulting Psychologists Press.

Jesness, C. F. (1974). *Classifying juvenile offenders – the sequential I-level classification manual.* Palo Alto, CA: Consulting Psychologists Press.

Kaiser, G. (1982). Begriff, Ortsbestimmung, Entwicklung und System des Strafvollzugs. In G. Kaiser, H. J. Kerner, & H. Schöch (Eds.), *Strafvollzug. Ein Lehrbuch* (pp. 1–81, 202–255). Heidelberg: Müller.

Kaiser, G. (1984). Die gesetzliche Regelung über den Vollzug der Untersuchungshaft und ihre Reform. In D. Wilke (Ed.), *Festschrift zum 125jährigen Bestehen der Juristischen Gesellschaft zu Berlin* (pp. 299–312). Berlin Heidelberg New York Tokyo: Springer-Verlag.

Kaiser, G. (1985). Kriminalpolitik. In G. Kaiser, H. J. Kerner, F. Sack, & H. Schellhoss (Eds.), *Kleines Kriminologisches Wörterbuch* (pp. 248–253). Heidelberg: Müller.

Kerner, H. J. (1982). Vollzugsstab und Insassen des Strafvollzugs. Strafvollzug als Prozeß. In G. Kaiser, H. J. Kerner, & H. Schöch (Eds.), *Strafvollzug. Ein Lehrbuch* (pp. 255–478). Heidelberg: Müller.

Kerner, H. J. (1985). Ambulante Maßnahmen. In G. Kaiser, H. J. Kerner, F. Sack, & H. Schellhoss (Eds.), *Kleines Kriminologisches Wörterbuch* (pp. 18–21). Heidelberg: Müller.

Kury, H. (1981). Junge Rechtsbrecher und ihre Behandlung. Sozialer Hintergrund, Persönlichkeit und Resozialisierung bei jugendlichen und heranwachsenden Untersuchungshäftlingen. *Zeitschrift für die gesamte Strafrechtswissenschaft, 93*, 319–359.

Kury, H. (1983a). Zur Verfälschbarkeit von Persönlichkeitsfragebogen bei jungen Strafgefangenen. *Zeitschrift für Strafvollzug, 32*, 323–332.

Kury, H. (1983b). Verfälschungstendenzen bei Persönlichkeitsfragebogen im Strafvollzug. *Monatsschrift für Kriminologie und Strafrechtsreform, 66*, 72–74.

Kury, H. (1983c). *Methodische Probleme der Behandlungsforschung – insbesondere in der Sozialtherapie.* Cologne: Heymanns.

Kury, H. (1986a). *Prognose und Behandlung bei jungen Rechtsbrechern. Ergebnisse eines Forschungsprojekts.* Freiburg i. Br., FRG: Max-Planck-Institut für Strafrecht.

Kury, H. (1986b). *Die Behandlung Straffälliger: Sec. 1. Inhaltliche und methodische Probleme der Behandlungsforschung.* Berlin: Duncker & Humblot.

Kury, H. (1986c). Rechtliche und tatsächliche Situation der Untersuchungshaft. In H. Kury (Ed.). *Prognose und Behandlung bei jungen Rechtsbrechern. Ergebnisse eines Forschungsprojekts* (pp. 87–140). Freiburg i. Br., FRG: Max-Planck-Institut für Strafrecht.

Kury, H. (1986d). Problems in the treatment of offenders and in treatment research. *German Journal of Psychology, 10,* 61–80.

Kury, H. (1987). *Die Behandlung Straffälliger: Sec. 2. Ergebnisse einer empirischen Untersuchung zum Behandlungserfolg bei jugendlichen und heranwachsenden Untersuchungshäftlingen.* Berlin: Duncker & Humblot.

Kury, H., & Lerchenmüller, H. (Eds.). (1981). *Diversion – Alternativen zu klassischen Sanktionsformen* (2 vols.). Bochum: Brockmeyer.

Lambert, M. J., Bergin, A. E., & Collins, J. L. (1977). Therapist-induced deterioration in psychotherapy. In A. S. Gurman & A. M. Razin (Eds.), *Effective psychotherapy. A handbook of research* (pp. 452–481). Oxford: Pergamon.

Langlotz, M., & Hommers, W. (1978). Ziele, Aufbau und Durchführung des MURT. In M. Steller, W. Hommers, & H. J. Zienert (Eds.), *Modellunterstütztes Rollentraining (MURT). Verhaltensmodifikation bei Jugenddelinquenz* (pp. 1–32). Berlin Heidelberg New York: Springer-Verlag.

Linster, H. W., & Wetzel, H. (1980). Perspektiven zukünftiger Entwicklung: Aktuelle Trends und Entwicklungslinien psychologischer Therapie. In H. W. Linster, H. Wetzel, B. Arm, V. Chu, U. Doepner, S. O. Hoffman, G. Petersen, & H. Thielen (Eds.), *Veränderungen und Entwicklung der Person. Grenzen und Möglichkeiten psychologischer Therapie* (pp. 327–350). Hamburg: Hoffmann & Campe.

Lösel, F. (1975). *Handlungskontrolle und Jugenddelinquenz. Persönlichkeitspsychologische Erklärungsansätze delinquenten Verhaltens – theoretische Integration und empirische Prüfung.* Stuttgart: Enke.

Lösel, F. (1983a). Empirische Persönlichkeitsforschung und Delinquenzerklärung. In F. Lösel (Ed.). *Kriminalpsychologie* (pp. 29–40). Weinheim: Beltz.

Lösel, F. (1983b). Psychologische Behandlung von Aggressivität und Dissozialität. *Zeitschrift für personenzentrierte Psychologie und Psychotherapie, 2,* 171–185.

Lösel, F., Köferl, P., & Weber, F. (1987). *Meta-Evaluation der Sozialtherapie. Qualitative und quantitative Analysen zur Behandlungsforschung in sozialtherapeutischen Anstalten des Justizvollzugs.* Stuttgart: Enke.

Minsel, W. R., & Howe, J. (1983). Gesprächspsychotherapie bei Delinquenten. In F. Lösel (Ed.), *Kriminalpsychologie* (pp. 248–258). Weinheim: Beltz.

Möbus, C., & Nagel, W. (1983). Messung, Analyse und Prognose von Veränderungen. In J. Bredenkamp & H. Feger (Eds.). *Hypothesenprüfung.* Enzyklopädie der Psychologie: Vol. B/1/5 (pp. 239–470). Göttingen: Hogrefe.

Ortmann, R. (1987). *Resozialisierung im Strafvollzug. Theoretischer Bezugsrahmen und empirische Ergebnisse einer Längsschnittstudie zu den Wirkungen von Strafvollzugsmaßnahmen.* Freiburg i. Br., FRG: Max-Planck-Institut für Strafrecht.

Pielmaier, H. (1979). *Verhaltenstherapie bei delinquenten Jugendlichen.* Stuttgart: Enke.

Pielmaier, H. (Ed.). (1980). *Training sozialer Verhaltensweisen. Ein Programm für die Arbeit mit dissozialen Jugendlichen.* Munich: Kösel.

Pielmaier, H. (1986). Die verhaltenstherapeutischen Gruppen – soziales Training. In H. Kury (Ed.), *Prognose und Behandlung bei jungen Rechtsbrechern. Ergebnisse eines Forschungsprojekts* (pp. 173–185). Freiburg i. Br., FRG: Max-Planck-Institut für Strafrecht.

Pielmaier, H., Pauls, L., & Blumenberg, F. J. (1980). Dissoziale Störungen. In W. Wittling (Ed.), *Handbuch der klinischen Psychologie:* Vol. 5. *Therapie gestörten Verhaltens* (pp. 323–372). Hamburg: Hoffmann & Campe.

Quensel, S. (1972). Soziale Fehlanpassung und Stigmatisierung: ein Test zum Messen der delinquenten Entwicklung. In U. Rehbinder & H. Schelsky (Eds.), Jahrbuch für Rechtssoziologie und Rechtstheorie. Zur Effektivität des Rechts (Vol. 3, pp. 447–490). Opladen: Westdeutscher Verlag.

Rieländer, M., & Quensel, E. (1983). Der Gießener Fragebogen als Instrument in der kriminologischen Forschung und Diagnostik. *Monatsschrift für Kriminologie und Strafrechtsreform, 66,* 84–93.

Rogers, C. R. (1951). *Client-centered therapy.* Boston: Houghton Mifflin Comp.

Ross, R. R., & Gendreau, P. (Eds.). (1980). *Effective correctional treatment.* Toronto: Butterworths.

Rudolph, J. (1975). *Psychische Änderungen durch Gesprächspsychotherapie und deren Bedingungen in der Sicht der Klienten.* Dissertation, University of Hamburg.

Sander, K. (1975). Der Einfluß von Ausgangs-Persönlichkeitsmerkmalen der Klienten auf den Behandlungserfolg in klientenzentrierter Gesprächspsychotherapie. *Zeitschrift für Klinische Psychologie, 2,* 137–147.

Sarason, I. G., & Ganzer, V. J. (1969). Developing appropriate social behavior of juvenile delinquents. In J. D. Krumboltz & C. E. Thoresen (Eds.). *Behavioral counseling: Cases and techniques* (pp. 178–192). New York: Holt, Rinehart & Winston.

Sarason, I. G., & Ganzer, V. J. (1971). *Modeling: An approach to the rehabilitation of juvenile offenders.* Washington: Social and Rehabilitation Service of the Department of Health, Education and Welfare.

Sarason, I. G., & Ganzer, V. J. (1973). Modeling and group discussion in the rehabilitation of juvenile delinquents. *Journal of Counseling Psychology, 20,* 442–449.

Schuessler, K. F., & Cressey, D. R. (1950). Personality characteristics of criminals. *American Journal of Sociology, 55,* 476–484.

Schwartz, H. J. (1975). *Zur Prozeßforschung in klientenzentrierter Gesprächstherapie: Bedingungen des Behandlungseffekts in Anfangsgesprächen.* Dissertation, University of Hamburg.

Schwenkmezger, P. (1977). *Risikoverhalten und Risikobereitschaft. Korrelationsstatistische und differentialdiagnostische Untersuchungen bei Strafgefangenen.* Weinheim: Beltz.

Spiess, G. (1980). Aussetzungspraxis, Bewährungsprognose und Bewährungserfolg bei einer Gruppe jugendlicher Probanden. In: Forschungsgruppe Kriminologie (Eds.), *Empirische Kriminologie* (pp. 425–445). Freiburg i. Br., FRG: Max-Planck-Institut für Strafrecht.

Spiess, G. (1986). *Soziale Integration und Bewährungserfolg. Prozesse strafrechtlicher Statuszuweisung bei jungen Bewährungsprobanden.* Freiburg i. Br., FRG: Max-Planck-Institut für Strafrecht.

Steller, M., Hommers, W., & Zienert H. J. (1978). *Modellunterstütztes Rollentraining.* Berlin Heidelberg New York: Springer-Verlag.

Tausch, R. (1974). Gesprächspsychotherapie (5th–6th ed.). Göttingen: Hogrefe.

Tennenbaum, D. J. (1977). Personality and criminality. *Journal of Criminal Justice, 5,* 225–235.

Villmow-Feldkamp, H. (1976). *Delinquenz und Selbstdarstellung Jugendlicher – eine Persönlichkeitsuntersuchung auf der Basis von Dunkelfeldergebnissen.* Dissertation, University of Konstanz.

Villmow-Feldkamp, H., & Kury, H. (1983). Delinquenz und Persönlichkeit – Zusammenhänge bei Jugendlichen auf der Basis von Dunkelfeldergebnissen. *Monatsschrift für Kriminologie und Strafrechtsreform, 66,* 113–117.

Waldo, G., & Dinitz, S. (1967). Personality attributes of the criminal: An analysis of research studies, 1950–1965. *Journal of Research in Crime and Delinquency, 4,* 185–202.

Wetzstein, H. (1986). Erfahrungen mit den verhaltenstherapeutischen Behandlungsgruppen im Rahmen des Freiburger Behandlungsforschungsprojektes. In H. Kury (Ed.), *Prognose und Behandlung bei jungen Rechtsbrechern. Ergebnisse eines Forschungsprojekts* (pp. 186–202). Freiburg i. Br., FRG: Max-Planck-Institut für Strafrecht.

Wittmann, W. W. (1985). *Evaluationsforschung. Aufgaben, Probleme und Anwendungen.* Berlin Heidelberg New York Tokyo: Springer-Verlag.

23
Influencing Juvenile Offenders by Way of Alternative Sanctions in Community Settings

ALBERT R. HAUBER

Introduction

In this chapter, the background, application, and effects of alternative sanctions for juvenile offenders in the Netherlands are discussed from a psychological viewpoint. Throughout the chapter the need for a differentiated approach is stressed. As regards the research experiences of myself and my colleagues, I shall focus on vandalism and prove that not all vandals require identical treatment.

The Development of Juvenile Delinquency

Like in most West European countries, the last 20 years have witnessed a steep increase in crime in the Netherlands. As Figure 23.1 illustrates, in 1984 2.3 times as many cases were handled by the courts as in 1970. The development of juvenile delinquency shows a similar pattern, a large increase being registered. Although Dutch juvenile law refers to youngsters between the ages of 12 and 18 only and defines delinquency quite strictly, I prefer a broader definition that includes youths up to the age of 25 years. Although it is an exaggeration to regard criminality as synonymous with juvenile delinquency, it is certainly relevant that an estimated two-thirds of all crimes are committed by those under 26 years old. The crimes frequently committed by youths which have increased the most are vandalism, shoplifting, and violence. Table 23.1 shows that over a 15-year period the number of known acts of vandalism in the Netherlands has increased almost tenfold. Moreover, during this period the cost of damages per incident has also increased. As a result of these increases in frequency and the amount of damages per incident, the total is now about 4 million dollars a day. The total damage accruing from small crime in the Netherlands is estimated at 1.5 billion dollars a year (Commissie kleine kriminaliteit, 1986). One further illustration of the rise in juvenile delinquency

TABLE 23.1. Number of incidents of destruction per year known to the police during the period 1970–1985

1970	10334
1975	25322
1980	69779
1983	85206
1984	95612
1985	98799

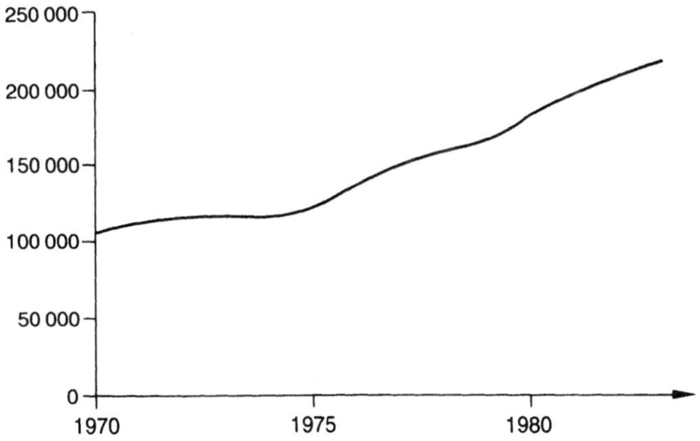

FIGURE 23.1. Number of cases handled by the courts per year in the period 1970–1984 (Source Centraal Bureau voor Statistiek)

can be found in victim studies such as the one carried out with public transport personnel. This shows that there has been an increase in violence against personnel and passengers, and that the average age of the offenders is estimated at around 20 years (Hauber, 1987).

Backgrounds in Juvenile Delinquency

From the results obtained in studies of hidden crime it appears that far more people engage in criminal behavior than is shown by the official records. This is confirmed by the finding that more than 90% of the male students in a Dutch university town admitted having performed illegal activities more than once. Regardless of the general finding that behaving criminally once in a while is normal, this type of behavior is still considered deviant. Particularly the origin of criminal behavior receives much attention.

A number of different ideas have been developed over the years regarding the rise in criminal behavior. Some of these ideas have been systematically articulated in the form of theories and are supported by scientific research. If we look at these theories, it soon becomes clear that it is questionable whether we can call someone a criminal when once in a while they dodge payment on public transportation, damage things, or have a little difficulty in understanding what's theirs and what's not. It is true that some people are quick to label others, but considering there are few people who can swear that they have never erred, the dividing line between criminals and non-criminals is more difficult to draw than some dichotomous thinkers might hope. It would be so much easier if people could be divided into two groups, the good and the bad. Moreover, if you yourself could belong to the good then everything would be in order. But reality is not so simple even if some theories would have us believe that it is. These theories typically state that it is the person's personality structure, also known as character, which decides whether he or she will become a criminal. For example, Eysenck searched for characteristics of the personality structure which lead to crime. After testing subjects in penal institutions, Eysenck (1970) found that unstable extraverted persons have a higher chance of showing criminal behavior than their stable, introverted counterparts. Eysenck sought the explanation of criminal behavior in part in psychological and genetic factors. He failed, however, to consider the effect that living in a closed institution had on the development of the personality structure of his subjects.

Answers to the question why such individuals come to develop a particular personality are found in the works of other authors, e.g., affective neglect (maternal deprivation) during the first years of development (Bowlby & Salter-Ainsworth, 1965), stagnation in an early developmental phase caused by incomplete assimilation of this stage (Herren, 1973), and hereditary components in the gene structure [Christiansen (1977) attemped to show that monozygotic twins, who share the same genetic material, both will be criminals more often than dizygotic twins]. Regardless of how one comes to have a particular personality structure, such theories assume that one's personality is more or less fixed, so that change in behavior is pretty well impossible. This attitude is reflected in the often heard but almost inhuman statements like "once a thief, always a thief" and "a fox may lose his hair but not his nature." In this way, someone who has gone wrong once does not get the chance to learn from his mistake.

A second category of theories lies in complete contrast to the personality theories. According to these theories, man is born as a tabula rasa – a blank slate. There is nothing good or bad about the newborn baby. How the child will develop is completely dependent on the learning effects within the child's environment. In particular Bandura emphasizes the importance of social learning (1977). In the first few years of the child's life, the parents are, of course, of the greatest importance in influencing what the child learns. As the child matures, his friends in the neighborhood begin to play a role as well;

school and still later his work will decide in part how the individual will develop. Particularly Sutherland and Cressey (1974) emphasize in their differential association theory the importance of unconventional friends with a subculture in the neighborhood for the development of criminal behavior among adolescents. In adulthood, the societal structure with its divisions between rich and poor, employed and unemployed, and powerful and powerless will play an essential role. Especially the critical criminologists such as Taylor, Walton, and Young (1975) place extreme importance on the role of the societal structure in the development of deviant behavior.

The third category of theories, I consider to be the most realistic in terms of explaining criminal behavior. Supporters of this theory find both the above-mentioned theories one-sided. Furthermore, as Lösel (1975) rightly reminds us, it is not always possible to separate personality variables and environmental variables. The traditional opposition between these two approaches overlooks the fact that what is learned from the environment – from the parents for example – is internalized and later identified as a personality trait. An illustration in this respect is the trait honesty. If a separation can be made at all between the two groups of variables, then a person's behavior cannot be explained by personality structure or environment alone. It is the interaction between specific personality traits and certain elements in the environment that can lead someone to criminal behavior.

Let us take as an example fare-dodging on public transport. In the Netherlands the public transport situation clearly involves elements which invite fare-dodging: self-service, the small chance of getting caught, and, on trains, the low fine. But however inviting the situation may be, not everyone dodges the payment of fares. Fare-dodging apparently requires a certain type of personality which is characterized by impulsiveness, extraversion, lack of perspective for the future, and need for excitement or revenge. To reverse the situation, a person may want to fare-dodge but if every ride is supervised then there will be no opportunity to cheat. In short, it is an interaction between a certain drive or motivation within the person and the inviting elements in the situation that propel someone in the direction of criminal behavior.

If we apply the aforementioned to juvenile criminality, then we come to the conclusion that a lot of complaints about the behavior of youth indeed appear correct, but to say that youths are the sole cause of such behavior is neither completely fair nor true. Adults play a substantial role as well. Sometimes it is simply a case of youths adopting the model behavior of adults with whom they identify; in other instances the undesirable behavior can be seen as a reaction to adult behavior. In the latter cases, for example, adults may fail to listen to the youngsters' point of view and fail to consider their wants and needs. In this way several forms of juvenile delinquency, such as vandalism, can be seen as a means of getting attention. These youths engage in such behavior because the other choices available to them do not result in the desired attention and further alternatives are just not available to them. Sometimes, such behavior is also an expression of resistance towards decisions in which they were not included.

Reactions to Juvenile Criminality

Reactions to juvenile criminality can be divided into two categories: formal and informal. The informal reactions are those of the public. These are the most spontaneous reactions and typically follow directly upon certain crimes. These reactions are based in feelings of fear. The typical reaction of the public is expressed in the wish to expand the police force and to institute more severe punishment. Similar statements are regularly found in the press, with the effect that a large and important part of the population is no longer willing to maintain its traditional tolerance towards such behavior (Hauber, 1986). This viewpoint was expressed, for example, by Beatrijs Ritsema (1984), who said: "As far as the fight against vandalism is concerned, an increase in the number of patrolling police officers would be more effective. Just like cheaters, smugglers, and tax evaders, the young vandal does not need to be brought to his senses; he knows damn well that what he is doing is wrong. Increasing the chances of being caught would do wonders for the desired changes in mentality."

Such a low level of tolerance is particularly evident among those who themselves have been a victim of vandalism, and perhaps even more so when people fear being a victim in the future. This mentality, which is at odds with the international reputation of the Dutch for being tolerant towards deviance, gives rise to calls for a harsh approach, with more police protection and, where necessary, civilian vigilantes.

Happily, policymakers at both the national and the regional level have not blindly responded to this point of view. Rather they have attempted to arrive at a balanced judgment. Nevertheless, their formal reactions have indeed involved an expansion of the police force even if a smaller one than some of the population would like. Furthermore, this changed policy has resulted in more severe sanctions and a decrease in the percentage of cases dropped among adult offenders and to a lesser extent among juveniles (see Table 23.2). At the same time, according to government reports, experiments are being prepared which are intended to enlarge the social control (Roethof, 1986). Finally, a review of the effectiveness of traditional punishments was carried out. The high percentage of recidivists made it clear that the present sentencing system with reprimands, fines, or restricted freedom does not prevent offenders from continuing their criminal behavior.

TABLE 23.2. Settlements for punishment of adults and juveniles through the years 1981 – 1983

	1981	1982	1983
No. of penal cases for adults	44695	46639	62103
Percentage of cases dropped	81%	79.2%	61.9%
No. of penal cases for juveniles	17854	18242	19889
Percentage of cases dropped	85.3%	82.6%	81.5%

As MacCallum (1973) rightly suggests, the law is not always in the position to force a particular mode of behavior on someone against their will. He states "The law does not and cannot violate a person's conscience by 'forcing' that person to act contrary to his conscience by making it utterly impossible for him to do otherwise." It is motivation that determines the stability of the individual's obedience to the law. In cases where individuals obey the law because of fear of punishment, they will engage in illegal behavior as soon as the source of fear is removed or is absent. Social acceptance determines to an extent the degree to which an individual abides by the law.

Attachment to another individual favors behavior which obtains the other's approval, thereby reinforcing the relationship. The best guarantee of norm-conforming behavior is the internalization of an attitude that a certain form of behavior is appropriate. Then, independent of the threat of punishment or the loss of affection, the individual will behave in accordance with the law. This intrinsic motivation can be the result of a learning process through which, for example, it is seen as appropriate to one's self-image to behave in accordance with the law.

The chance that an attitude will be internalized is quite low among children and adolescents. Adolescents are at a phase in their development where they want to try out all kinds of new behavior and explore the limits of their power and possibilities; this exploration might include criminal behavior. Furthermore, youngsters often complain that their ideas receive insufficient attention. In this regard, juvenile criminality can be understood as a cry for attention. Sometimes this refers to a kind of displaced aggression. Unhappiness as a result of the above, or through an inequality in power whereby the youngster feels powerless, creates a feeling of frustration which can express itself in the anonymous atmosphere of vandalism.

This process is enhanced when the youngster belongs to a group. Identification with the friendship circle is magnified when the youngster has the feeling that he does not count in society, and this feeling is reinforced when his school achievement is also low. If the subcultural norms of the group include criminal behavior and the internalization of legal norm-conforming attitudes has not yet taken place, then the chance that the criminal behavior will be learned is large, as Sutherland and Cressey (1974) have already indicated in their differential association theory.

To facilitate the internalization process, it is desirable that the norm-conforming behavior is rewarded. For this goal there are more possibilities than are presently being utilized. In principle, criminal behavior is currently punished but the low likelihood of being caught and the mild punishment means that such behavior is often rewarded. As a result the environmental polluter can – regardless of a fine – dispose of his waste, the shoplifter can eat free meat, and the fare-dodger can travel for minimum costs.

Animal experiments have shown us (see Crombag, 1983) that behavior, including criminal behavior, is maintained longest when it is intermittently reinforced. This underlines the importance of a consistent reaction. The certainty of sanction teaches the delinquent to realize the consequences of his behavior. This reflection on the way society should react to delinquency gives rise to the question of what further conditions the sanction will have to satisfy in order to increase the chance that not only the attitude but also the behavior of the youth will change:

1. The sanction must be given and carried out as quickly as possible after the act has been committed.
2. There should be an intrinsic relationship between the act and the sanction. This means that the sanction must logically follow from the act.

It is clear that the traditional sanctions typically do not satisfy either of these conditions. Therefore in the late 1970s a commission was set up by the Dutch government to enquire into possible alternative sanctions. Alternative sanctions are simplest to apply to youths because within the juvenile law the possibilities for experiments are obvious, particularly when they include pedagogic elements. At the same time, initiatives developed at the municipal level led to alternative sanctions. The many projects which have arisen during the last few years can be divided into two groups, – learning projects and work projects.

Similar developments have also taken place in neighboring countries that experienced increases in criminality and related problems. Although the initiative was taken in the early 1970s by England with the Intermediate Treatment Project, the development of alternative sanctions received a substantial boost from the "Report on Certain Alternative Penal Measures to Imprisonment" by the Council of Europe (1976). These initiatives were followed not only by the Dutch projects but by West Germany as well. In West Germany, projects such as the Brücke in Munich were extended to other German cities like Cologne and Bremen, and other projects such as the Stop project in Mönchen-Gladbach were introduced. The Skandinavian countries, and especially Denmark, have also done a lot of experiments in this field (Tak & van Kalmthout, 1985).

Viewpoints on Vandalism: The Existing Theories

As vandalism is but one of the many behaviors which fall under the rubric "criminal," theories developed specifically to explain vandalism are exceptional. The existing theories are, nearly without exception, environmentally oriented. They assume that by manipulating the situation, vandalistic behavior can be influenced. The aesthetic theory of vandalism (Allen & Greenberger, 1978) has shown, for example, that when a bus shelter is made of more attractive and costly materials, the barrier to commencement of destruction is substantially higher than for ordinary bus shelters. Support for this theory is found in the research by Van Dullemen and Hauber (1982) among vandals in Rotterdam: after an observation period of 6 months, aesthetically appealing bus shelters showed significantly less damage by vandalism than the traditional ones located in the same city. Nevertheless a similar study also carried out by these researchers in Rotterdam provided no support for the theory. In this study vandalistic behavior was measured in terms of the frequency and severity of damage to two types of streetcar, – streetcars painted by artists and normal (plain) streetcars. A comparison of the results from these two experiments reminds us of the need to refrain from irresponsible generalizations and to pay strict attention to specific circumstances when drawing conclusions.

Proper maintenance has proved very important in preventing destruction, as was illustrated some years ago by Zimbardo (1969). When it is plainly visible that a certain object is damaged, the chance is great that its destruction will be continued by others. From the original object little more will remain than a useless piece of wreckage.

Wise (1982) concludes that only minimal interventions in the environment are necessary in order to avoid destruction. These interventions entail making the environment more attractive in general. As Wise suggests, if you were to place a beautiful vase with flowers in a public toilet and instal a source of music, the chance would be small that someone would disturb the pleasant environment with destructive behavior and graffiti. As mentioned earlier, there is the problem of generalization, which is a big handicap for most of the theories cited above. The lack of differentiation and the absence of specificity regarding the circumstances in which the behavior takes place depletes the reality and usefulness of these theories.

Initiating the Development of a Differentiated Theory of Vandalism

Following the assumption that similar behaviors such as destroying the interior of a bus or train can arise from very different motives and backgrounds, it is important to gather realistic information which can serve as the cornerstone for a theory. A few years ago my colleague and I (Van Dullemen & Hauber, 1982) were approached by the city council of Rotterdam and asked to develop an alternative plan through which vandalism could more effectively be dealt with. In our opinion it would be irresponsible to solve the question without first discussing the subject with vandalistic youngsters. These discussions would have to yield insights into the backgrounds and circumstances which led to the vandalistic behavior. For this purpose the area of study comprised four clusters of socioeconomically deprived neighborhoods. These neighborhoods all had extensive damage due to vandalism.

A sample of 550 youngsters between the ages of 12 and 18 who had been caught by the police for vandalism was used in the study. These youngsters were approached by way of an introductory letter from the university. It was hoped that this would create a neutral and nonthreatening impression on the youths. We contacted more than 500 vandalistic youths as well as several individuals with whom the youngsters were in close contact, such as teachers and social or cultural workers. We located the youths in their natural environment. This could be in their home, at their school, or sometimes even in a pub. The only stipulation was that a trusting relationship had to be built between the youngster and the interviewer. Furthermore, the youths were guaranteed that all the information they gave would remain anonymous; no names would be used in the processing of the data. This was essential for the acquisition of honest information, particularly concerning any criminal behavior.

One of the most important findings of this study was that when looking at vandalistic behavior on the whole, major differences appeared between individuals in terms of the frequency and severity of the acts. Although we could place the entire study group on a descending scale which showed frequency and severity of vandalistic behavior for each subject, I will restrict myself here to the main issue.

Although we are dealing with a continuum rather than a dichotomy, for practical reasons it will suffice to distinguish two groups: the slightly vandalistic (SV) group and the highly vandalistic (HV) group. The division into these two groups was based on answers to questions regarding the extent to which the youths engaged in vandalistic behavior. The various actions were weighted, e.g., placing stones on the streetcar tracks was weighted more heavily than breaking branches of a tree. In this way – after multiplying by frequency – a measure for vandalistic behavior was obtained. The mathematical average of the weighted scores was subsequently used as the dividing line between slightly and highly vandalistic behavior.

From the study it appeared that 76% of the youths were in the SV group and 24% in the HV group. The essential differences between the groups in terms of background and motivation form the first conditions in the development of a differentiated approach to vandalism. The significant differences found between the SV and the HV groups are shown in Table 23.3. From this table we can see that:

1. There were more boys than girls in the HV group
2. In the HV group more negative appraisals regarding school were found
3. The HV group played truant more often than the SV group
4. More members of the HV group preferred being out of the house
5. Members of the HV group frequented social places more often
6. The HV group more often went out with friends and that friendship circle was subject to less changes than in the SV group
7. The parents of the HV group members were less interested in the activities of their children in general and were not interested in where their children went at night
8. The HV group had more frequent and more severe problems than the SV group, particularly concerning family and school

TABLE 23.3. Significant differences between the HV and the SV group

	HV group	SV group	χ^2	*df*	*P*
Negative attitude towards school	41.4%	16.3%	9.6	1	<0.01
Interest in school activities	27.7%	36.8%	4.1	1	<0.05
Truancy	34.3%	29.0%	7.4	1	<0.01
Parents' interest in children	10.4%	41.2%	17.3	1	<0.01
Neighborhood unexciting	32.5%	27.8%	7.7	1	<0.01
Visit other neighborhoods	39.2%	29.7%	12.4	1	<0.001
Prefer being home	14.3%	24.3%	8.1	1	<0.01
Visit risky establishments	37.7%	23.4%	12.8	1	<0.01
Often with friends	27.3%	23.9%	5.8	1	<0.01
Always out with the same friends	22.8%	18.7%	4.0	1	<0.05
Parents know where the youth is	21.0%	38.2%	17.9	1	<0.01
Serious problems	42.4%	12.9%	18.6	1	<0.001
Contact with police	39.9%	14.3%	15.5	1	<0.001

9. Although a majority of the HV group felt that the police should take harsher action; this was still a lower percentage than found for the SV group

It is striking that while the SV group was responsible for a lot of destruction as a group, they differed significantly in background, mentality, and interests from the HV group. Although I agree with Wadsworth (1979) that there exists a significant relation ($\chi^2 = 109.10$; $df = 12$, $p < 0.001$) between parental interest in secondary school education and the frequency of children's juvenile delinquency, I would like to draw attention to the fact that it is often a combination of unfavorable factors which increases the likelihood of vandalistic behavior.

As is shown in Table 23.4, a boy whose parents are not interested in his activities, whose school achievement is poor, and who moreover associates with bad friends has a high chance of engaging in vandalistic behavior. With these background factors, the youth will more likely be a member of the HV group than a youngster with only one or two negative background factors. This implies that the two groups require different approaches. The vandalistic behavior of the HV group is a product of their personal problems; typically they have already had several run-ins with the police and the legal system. Finding themselves in a crisis situation, they may initiate vandalistic behavior. The SV group, by contrast, views vandalism as a socially tolerated habit or as acts by which they amuse themselves.

Although the situation can influence vandalism, e.g., an unattractive schoolyard may facilitate vandalistic behavior, we have no reason to believe that deeper causes are responsible for the destructive behavior of this group. In these cases vandalism typically involves nothing more than the normal impulses of the adolescent stage of development, such as playfulness, machismo, or testing social limits.

TABLE 23.4. Percentage of HV youths according to their number of negative background factors

	No interest from parents	Negative school experience	Negative per group	% HV	Total HV
No negative background factor	0	0	0	4%	4
One negative background factor	+	0	0	17%	7
	0	+	0	18%	8
	0	0	+	23%	10
Two negative background factors	+	+	0	34%	15
	+	0	+	44%	19
	0	+	+	51%	21
Three negative background factors	+	+	+	58%	44
Total				24%	128

The Need for a Differentiated Approach by Policymakers

A successful policy for vandalism must take into consideration the two different types of vandal. In fact, this division should play a central role in the formulation of policy. This means that in formulating policy, we should ask ourselves which group will benefit from what sanctions.

The SV Group

Motto: Always catch and punish strongly.

A portion of this group asked for stricter punishment. Further questioning revealed that they in fact meant more consistent punishment. They saw this as the only solution to vandalism. More specifically, they wanted to see more police patrols, so that the risk of being caught would increase, and stricter sentences. Stricter and more consistent punishment must not be translated into aggression. This applies to teaching personnel as well as to police. Aggression only evokes aggression. More consistent punishment means that the youngsters must be convinced that what they destroy they will have to repair themselves. A suggestion could be that vandalistic pupils would have to remain after school everyday and remove graffiti for the duration of the school year. If this were not implemented, the school's compensation for damaged windows would be withheld. Moreover, youths learn to care whether their school is vandalized after school hours because it is they who will have to clean it up the following day. It would actually be even better if the schools were allotted a budget for the reparation of damage and if this budget was only partially used the schools could use the money for something else.

The SV group must do the repair work themselves. This applies not only to the public transport system but to all public buildings, tunnels, streets, and parks. In those cases where compensation for damage cannot be paid by the youngsters themselves, this can be compensated by alternative sanctions such as services, e.g., working for the city. When the work is not done well, fines for the damage should be required after all.

The HV Group

Motto: Big problems need individual coaching.

The HV group needs an individual-oriented approach. Often the members of this group have had bad home lives. A relatively high percentage of the HV group stay up late at night, going out or watching T.V. Such circumstances can only facilitate opportunities for vandalism. As we have already shown, vandalism is less common among youths whose parents are interested and know where their children go, what they do, and when they will be coming home. Generally the HV youngster has many problems, often including relationship problems, and also has had several contacts with the police and the legal system. Obviously something has gone wrong in the earlier stages of the child's upbringing and consequently one may try to bring change into this. But simply making this child restore that which he has destroyed will not be sufficient to bring an end to his vandalistic behavior. These youngsters also need individual help with regard to their personal problems and more attention in the youth centers and the public health services.

Police and justice authorities will have to think twice when punishing HV youngsters in the traditional way. The present system does not seem to deter vandalistic behavior in these children. We believe that in most cases a combination of sanction and counseling will be the only way to reduce vandalistic behavior, and that the results will only be visible after some time.

Untapped Possibilities for a Differentiated Approach

Out of dissatisfaction with the present system regarding vandalism, the city of Rotterdam became interested in alternative punishments. Through the cooperation of the city's public transport services, it was possible to set up an experiment in which youths who had been caught vandalizing streetcars, buses, or subways had to forfeit their free time on Saturdays in order to clean up the streetcars and remove the graffiti from them. In this way the youngsters were made to realize the consequences of their behavior. They saw for themselves how many hours of work it takes to get a wall clean again, while it only took a few minutes to put graffiti on it. Although most of the youngsters – the exceptions being the HV group – did not enjoy the work, they did believe it was an honest form of punishment. Some even felt responsible for the work they had done and this is more than we could expect.

Such sanctions are in the first place directed at the behavior and to a much lesser extent at the person himself. The psychological advantage here is that the self-esteem of the youth is retained; he remains accepted by society and social labeling is avoided. It is therefore not surprising that the experiment as a whole can be considered successful.

The study served as a preliminary to the establishment of an institute in which youths caught for vandalism could undergo alternative treatment. This organization, called HALT (in Dutch: *H*et *ALT*ernatief), should in our opinion function independently of the police and the legal system. Furthermore, we believe that if the HALT program is to be successful, the staff must be experienced with juveniles and be willing to listen to them and their problems in order to build up a trusting relationship with the youths. Tausch and Tausch (1979) assert that the following behavior characteristics are essential in establishing a trusting relationship with youths: real behavior without a false front, openness towards the youths, a positive self-image, and respect for others. These behavior characteristics facilitate better communication with the youths. The developmental stages of puberty and adolescence are characterized by an enhanced susceptibility to model behavior and the youths can just as easily adopt the behavior of the counsellors.

How can we best employ the results of the study and particularly the division between the SV and HV groups in the HALT project?

In the SV group, most cases will effectively be dealt with – since most juveniles in this group do not have major problems – by a combination of two or three consultations with HALT staff and one or, if necessary, two Saturdays of alternative chores.

The story is very different, however, for the HV group. As we have learned, this group consists of youths who have severe problems in one or more areas. In this group, vandalism can be considered the expression of displaced aggression, resulting from dissatisfaction with the situation and the perceived inability to do anything constructive about it. It would be unrealistic to believe that the prescription given above – a few discussions with the HALT staff combined with work – would solve the often deep-rooted problems of these youths. This means that besides this simple approach, long-term counseling will be necessary.

Depending on the specific problem, such treatment may take the form of assertiveness training. In cases where the problematic behavior of the youths is related to their home situation, it may be desirable to include members of the juvenile's direct environment such as parents in the counseling process.

TABLE 23.5. Results of HALT intervention among HV and SV youths

Result	HV	SV	Total
+	5	58	63
–	24	31	55
	29	89	118

$\chi^2 = 10.9$; $df = 1$; $p<0.01$

It goes without question that the employee who works with HV youths must have lots of experience with therapeutic techniques such as role games, and be able to apply these techniques skillfully. In this way the group will receive the attention they need: as experience has shown, this group typically falls outside of things, keeping them in a disadvantaged position. In practice, however, it appeared that right from the start of the HALT program in 1982 the emphasis was placed on treatment of the SV group. The HV group was treated as if they belonged to the SV group. Members of this group require less time per person, whereby more youths can be dealt with in the same amount of time and this scores points with the politicians.

In evaluating the long-term effects of the HALT project on attitude and behavioral change, we asked the youngsters involved in the project for their opinions. The general response was that their visits to HALT had had little influence on their attitudes and behavior. As a rule these visits merely involved the arrangement of tasks. Further, the youngsters felt they received little personal attention and support during these visits, especially since they were rarely received alone and subsequent visits often involved different personnel. Therefore none of the youngsters spontaneously thought to go to the HALT Bureau when they had problems. In part this led to the almost unanimous opinion that the intervention did not lead to later behavioral change. When behavioral change did result, however, and norm-violating behavior ceased, the youngsters attributed this not to HALT but to a change in friends, a change in residence, or simply being too old for vandalistic behavior. The majority of the youngsters involved in the program did continue with norm violations; some committed more serious offenses such as theft and violent crimes and some were picked up by the police after their first contact with HALT.

In Table 23.5 there appears to be a significant difference in the effect of the HALT intervention between SV and HV youth. Our hypothesis that alternative approaches like the HALT program are effective for the SV but not for the HV youngsters appears to be supported. Especially the HV youths believed that there was a lack of communication between the police and HALT, to their disadvantage. Two examples illustrate this point:

1. A police officer sent a youngster to HALT but failed to inform HALT of this. After five futile visits, the case was closed
2. A youngster behaved ideally: he went to HALT and carried out his tasks successfully but a few months later still got charged

Although the differentiated approach of HALT has largely remained merely the ideal of the researchers and directors, and the goal of keeping the project independent of police and the legal system has not been realized, HALT in its present form is considered by many as the example of how vandalism should be approached. The HALT institution has in the meantime expanded to become a kind of status project of the city council of Rotterdam. Hence, a lot of other Dutch communities have been eager to copy the HALT approach. I would strongly advise combining the experience of earlier projects at a local community level into one national integrated approach, including measures for the prevention of vandalistic activities.

Prevention: The Crowning Piece of the Differentiated Approach

As a supporter of the interaction model, I assume that in order to obtain optimal effects, preventive measures must consider the person as well as the situation.

Since I have already mentioned examples of how the situation can be influenced in order to prevent vandalism, I would like in the following to focus primarily on personal elements and how they can be influenced. This is in fact primarily a task for parents. Yet it appears that parents are not always able to do this. Therefore, attempts to influence attitudes and behavior through the school appear necessary: it is obvious that within institutions in which youngsters spend so many hours, they will be confronted with problems typical of adolescence (Rutter, 1979). Up till now, far too little time has been spent on this. Many schools restrict themselves to the traditional curriculum involving the learning of facts and general knowledge. Although we must be careful of generalizations, there is a greater chance that larger school systems will entail impersonal administration based solely on achievement. Small or moderate sized schools are in a better position to use a personal approach with students. In an atmosphere of anonymity, the individual student learns little about his personal responsibility for that which occurs in and around his school. Realistically, it is not a question of a personal or an impersonal approach but rather a more or less personal approach. Thus, we can speak of a continuum with gradations of intimacy.

It was most pleasing that when asked to participate in an experiment regarding vandalism and influencing the attitudes and behavior of the students, almost all the schools we approached reacted positively. Basically, the school intervention consists of two elements:

1. Confrontation with the real consequences of vandalistic behavior via an informative civil servant or a visit to the so-called anti-vandalism center
2. A course in the solving of conflicts

The basic philosophy of this intervention is that some vandalistic behavior can be explained by the inability of youths to deal properly with their problems. Especially when youths come from families in which verbal abilities are underdeveloped, physical aggression towards objects and people tends to be their only solution to conflicts. Therefore we consider the teaching of other possibilities for conflict resolution to be of primary importance to these children. We are convinced that if this works, the displaced aggression released in vandalistic acts will no longer be necessary.

Using the results of research in the German cities of Hannover and Hildesheim (Lerchenmüller, 1983), we developed a course in conflict solving (Van Dullemen and Hauber, 1984). The course consisted of 14 lessons given by the youngsters' own teacher, in which several didactic work forms were used in changing combinations. These were designed to stimulate the active participation of students. Considering both students and teachers were practically undivided in offering a strongly positive evaluation of the preventive school activities, we would like to suggest that such courses be introduced at a national level.

References

Allen, V.L., & Greenberger, D.R. (1978). The aesthetic theory of vandalism. In J. Galvin (Ed.), *Crime and delinquency:* Vol. 7 (pp. 309–319). Beverly Hills: Sage.

Bandura, A. (1977). *Social learning theory.* Englewood Cliffs, NJ: Prentice-Hall.

Bowlby, J., & Salter-Ainsworth, M.D. (1965). Child care and the growth of love. Harmondsworth: Penguin Books.

Christiansen, K.O. (1977). A review of studies of criminality among twins. In S. Mednick & K.O. Christiansen (Eds.), *Biosocial bases of criminal behavior.* New York: Gardner.

Commissie kleine kriminaliteit (1986). *Eindrapport.* 's-Gravenhage: Staatsuitgeverij.

Council of Europe (1976). Report on certain alternative measures to imprisonment. Strasbourg.

Crombag, H.F.M. (1983). Een manier van overleven. Zwolle: Tjeenk Willink.

Eysenck, H.J. (1970). *Crime and personality.* London: Granada.

Hauber, A.R. (1977). *Gedrag van mensen in beweging.* Krommenie: Rotatie.

Hauber, A.R. (1986). Holland, ein Eldorado für jugendliche Straftäter. *Zeitschrift für Strafvollzug und Straffälligenhilfe, 35*(5), 273–277.

Hauber, A.R. (1987). Delinquency and vandalism in public transport. Report for European Conference of Ministers of Transport, Paris.

Herren, R. (1973). *Freud und die Kriminologie.* Stuttgart: Enke.

Lerchenmüller, H. (1983). Soziales Lernen in der Schule. In H. Kury (Ed.), *Interdisziplinäre Beiträge zur kriminologischen Forschung.* Cologne: Heymanns.

Lösel, F. (1975). *Handlungskontrolle und Jugenddelinquenz.* Stuttgart: Enke.

MacCallum, G. C. (1973). Law, conscience and integrity. In N. S. Care, T. K. Trelogan (Eds.), *Issues in law and morality.* Cleveland: Case Western Reserve University Press.
Rutter, M. (1979). *Fifteen thousand hours. Secondary schools and their effects on children.* London: Open Books.
Sutherland, E. H., & Cressey, D. R. (1974). *Criminology.* Philadelphia: Lippincott.
Tak, P. J. P., & van Kalmthout, A. M. (1985). *Dienstverlening en sanctiestelsels.* Staatsuitgeverij, Den Haag: Staatsuitgeverij.
Tausch, R., & Tausch, A. M. (1979). *Erziehungspsychologie.* Göttingen: Hogrefe.
Taylor, I., Walton, P., & Young, J. (Eds.). (1975). *Critical criminology; for a social theory of deviance.* London: Routledge and Kegan Paul.
Van Dullemen, H., & Hauber, A. R. (1982). *Vernielende jongeren, wat bedoelen zij?* Rotterdam: Staatsdrukkerij.
Van Dullemen, H., & Hauber, A. R. (1984). *Omgaan met jezelf; omgaan met anderen.* Leiden: Instituutsrapport.
Wadsworth, M. (1979). *Roots of delinquency.* Oxford: Robertson.
Wise, J. (1982). A gentle deterrent to vandalism. *Psychology Today, 16* (9), 31–38.
Zimbardo, P. G. (1969). *The cognitive control of motivation.* Illinois: Foresman.

24
Relations Between General Attitudes and Personality Traits of Prison Officers and Some Specific Attitudes Towards Prisoners

WILLI SEITZ

Introduction

Modern modes of imprisonment directed towards the prisoner's social re-integration and change of personality confer great importance upon the prison officer (Böhm, 1975; Hohmeier, 1975; Kühne, 1981; Steller & Berbalk, 1974). Thus, prison officers themselves can become "therapists," i.e., they can contribute to changing the prisoner's attitudes and behavior, for of all prison staff they have the most intensive and frequent contact with the inmates and are less separated from them by language barriers than are academically trained therapists. Furthermore, lack of professional therapists may necessitate participation of prison officers in treatment measures in order to guarantee standard treatment (Böhm, 1975, p. 12; Hohmeier, 1975, p. 8).

The attitudes of prison officers are vital for their successful and smooth participation in treatment-oriented imprisonment. Of particular importance are the officer's emotional and cognitive views of the prisoner and of certain behavior towards the prisoner as well as his readiness to practise certain forms of behavior towards the prisoner in accordance with these emotional and cognitive views (Rosenberg & Hovland, 1960; Fishbein & Ajzen, 1975). Such views will be determined by certain characteristics of the prisoner and by the officer's experiences with him. However, Homans' simple "contact hypothesis" (Homans, 1968, pp. 125 ff.), stating that frequent contacts cause mutual sympathy, cannot be maintained in this general form. One should rather consider the specific quality of the contacts and the circumstances under which they take place (Cloerkes, 1986). The different experiences of prison officers and the attitudes resulting from them depend, for example, on the grade of security of an institution (Ziegert, 1982, p. 239). Institutional frames such as rigid role patterns, restrictive behavior of superiors, and overwork caused by too many inmates make it difficult for officers to practise reform-oriented attitudes and behavior (Leky, 1975; Wagner, 1975). Furthermore, ambivalent ideas as to the purpose of imprisonment and ambiguous expectations in the officer's behavior (Hohmeier, 1969, 1975; Ziegert, 1982) give rise to individual balancing procedures of emotional-cognitive consistency and cognitive equilibrium, such as change of attitudes, boomerang effects, differentiation, and padding (Irle, 1975, p. 278 ff.; Stroebe, 1980, p. 180 ff.).

According to Klingemann (1981, p. 51), however, not only the actual material conditions of the institution, but especially the ways in which the situation will be interpreted by the officer (Plake, 1977, p. 123) are decisive for his behavior and the successful social reintegration of the prisoner. In spite of arrangements laid down in the official regulations, there are major differences among prison officers as to behavior and attitudes (Blickhahn, Braune, Klapprott, Linz, & Lösel, 1978, p. 19).

Klingemann (1981, p. 71) reports that individual characteristics such as professional qualification, age, or membership of the general staff (as against specialized staff) have little influence on attitudes (e.g., "custodial orientation") towards prisoners. According to interactional understanding (Mischel, 1973, 1976), the following variables are responsible for different individual reactions to the same conditions: "expectations," "personal constructs," "individual values," and "systems of self-regulation." The general structures of the officer's conditions of activity such as certain ways of experiencing frustration, goal and role conflicts, group conflicts, the balance of power, and institutional organization (Deimling, 1969; Hohmeier, 1973; Klingemann, 1981) will be perceived in different ways depending on the personality of the individual prison officer and will be of varying importance for the attitude towards the inmate. Different officers who so far have gathered the same experiences with the same inmates in the same institution will interpret such experiences according to their own personality and will develop different attitudes towards the inmates.

Relations between general personality traits and specific attitudes towards certain individuals or circumstances have so far been proved in various areas, such as attitudes of police officers towards delinquents (Carlson, Thayer, & Germann, 1971) and attitudes of pupils regarding the punishment of delinquents (Gaensslen, May, & Völpert, 1974). Blickhan et al. (1978) report a significant correlation between attitudes of prison officers towards inmates and the personality trait "intolerance/strictness"; further personality traits, however, have not been examined.

Stable and persistent personality traits (for discussion of the "trait" concept see Angleitner, 1980, p. 37 ff.; Pervin, 1978, p. 20 ff.) can be explained not only by behavioristic learning processes resulting from repeated experiences but also by cognitive processes relating to (corresponding) functions, the (corresponding) profits of (corresponding) reactions in (corresponding) situations ("purposive-cognitive concepts" after Alston, 1970, 1975). Manifold experiences and biographical social influences outside the prison as well as experiences within the institution (with superiors, colleagues, and inmates) may have contributed to the prison officers' establishing stable and persistent tendencies in their reactions (habits, expectations, intentions, attitudes, self-evaluation).

The following investigation will examine whether and to what extent one can empirically establish a relation between prison officers' general personality traits and their attitudes to prisoners. These particular attitudes will be evaluated according to the answers given by prison officers in response to questions regarding their opinions on (traditional vs. progressive) ideas about the origins of delinquency, on possible ways of treating offenders, and on the liberalization of imprisonment (e.g., weekend leave, visits by spouse, payments, co-determination).

It can be expected that the prison officer's interpretation of his own professional role as being predominantly either "custodial" or that of a "social worker" (a consulter, model, and mediator; cf. Klingemann, 1981; Däumling & Possehl, 1970) and his acceptance of the different demands of the public and of the justice policy (demands for law and order, for lowering recidivism, for humane treatment, and for reintegration of inmates) will be related to his individual level of readiness to take an interest in and emphasize with others, to participate in determining their fate, and to accept social opinion leaders and conventional moral principles.

If it is expected that general personality traits will be related to certain attitudes, then expectations also arise about the psychic function of these attitudes. Of the four main functions of attitudes described by Katz (1960), the two that are most important in the present context are the "utilitaristic" function (e.g., to express a repressive attitude satisfies a personal tendency towards "envy") and the function of "value demonstration" (e.g., to express a repressive attitude towards prisoners demonstrates personal "sense of duty").

The question arose as to how many and which fundamental personality traits and reactions should be examined in the present study with regard to their relation to certain attitudes towards prison reform and prisoners. According to Triandis (1975, p. 85; also see Fishbein, 1967, 1979, p. 155; Six, 1980, p. 59), five specific dimensions of attitudinal response towards other persons can be distinguished: (1) intention for (sexual) partnership, intention to marry, (2) intention to admire and to respect, (3) intention for friendship, (4) intention to separate, and (5) intention for dominance-submissiveness. In a previous multitrait-multimethod study (Seitz, 1973), the present author identified the following basic dimensions of attitude towards other persons: (1) aggressiveness based on mistrust and on expectancy of hostility by others vs. friendly agreement with others, (2) benevolence, respect, and social engagement vs. envy or apathy, (3) need for dominant autonomy vs. need for support, and (4) egocentric isolation vs. open-mindedness. Although these studies by Triandis and Seitz came about independently, the results show a high level of similarity, so that the qualities of response identified can be taken as basic transculturally valid qualities. The present study refers to the four dimensions found in the Seitz (1973) study.

The "avoidance" poles of the basic dimensions were expected to be related to restrictive, rejective, and hostile attitudes towards prisoners and negative attitudes towards prison reform. The "approach" poles, by contrast, were expected to be related to liberal and positive attitudes towards prisoners. These expectations were examined by calculation of simple linear correlations between (a) the scores on general social attitudes and personality traits and (b) the scores on attitudes towards certain aspects of prison reform and prisoners. In principle such simple linear correlations cannot indicate causation, in the sense that certain attitudes depend on general personality traits. Nevertheless, with regard to most of the results reported in this chapter it can be expected that general personality traits determine the attitudes towards prisoners rather than vice versa.

Besides the aforementioned four basic dimensions of attitude, the general personality trait "loyalty to traditional values and moral principles" (e.g., orderliness, cleanliness, punctuality) was expected to have a significant effect on attitudes towards prisoners and prison reform. In particular, an effect of the so-called error of contrast might be expected: somebody who for himself is very orderly and scrupulous should be inclined to ignore the corresponding attributes in others (Guilford, 1959, p. 141). It was expected that prison officers with a pronounced "sense of duty" would tend to evaluate prisoners as being indisciplined and as having little loyalty to traditional norms and stable moral principles. Consequently such prison officers should tend to plead for a restrictive way of dealing with prisoners. This assumption corresponds with the aforementioned results of Blickhan et al. (1978), that officers with high degrees of "intolerance/strictness" (in the sense of dogmatic loyalty to traditional norms and to moral principles) perceive a distance between themselves and the inmates, tend to have a suspicious and negative attitude towards prisoners, and regard it as almost impossible to reintegrate them.

On the basis of the preceding reasoning, it was expected that "benevolence" and "sense of duty" would have a contrasting effect on certain attitudes towards prisoners. Benevolence should encourage liberal attitudes towards prisoners, whereas sense of duty should give rise to restrictive attitudes. To disclose this expected effect more clearly, in addition to the simple linear correlations with the attitudes towards prisoners, partial correlations were also calculated, i.e., the "pure" correlations of the trait "sense of duty" were estimated by eliminating the trait "benevolence" and vice versa.

Subjects and Methods

The subjects in the study were 80 male prison officers working in three prisons of the federal state of Hessen. They were all members of the custodial staff rather than of the administrative staff, the social staff, or other special staff. The average age of the subjects was 38 years.

The subjects, in groups of up to ten persons, answered (voluntarily) a bipartite questionnaire. The first part of the questionnaire included 76 items for testing general social attitudes and personality traits:

1. To test “benevolence vs. envy”: 15 items from the set suggested by Seitz (1973, pp. 144, 145), e.g., “I am glad when I see that other persons have attained what they wish.”
2. To test “egocentric isolation vs. open-mindedness”: 15 items from Seitz’s set (1973, pp. 147–149), e.g., “I don’t like to have people around me.”
3. To test “aggressiveness based on suspicion and expectation of hostility by others vs. friendly agreement with others”: 15 items from Seitz’s set (1973, pp. 142, 143), e.g., “Sometimes I feel a need to be offensive to other persons.”
4. To test “need for dominant autonomy vs. need for support”: the 16 items of the subscale “directive attitude” from the “Fragebogen zur direktiven Einstellung (FDE)” of Bastine (1971).
5. To test “sense of duty and loyalty to moral principles”: 15 items from an unpublished scale which in extended former studies by the author proved to be stable across age, sex, and education, e.g., “obedience to and respect for authority are the most important virtues which children should have to learn.”

The second part of the questionnaire contained 21 items for testing certain attitudes towards prisoners and prison practice. These items were formulated by the author owing to a lack of adequate inventories in German-speaking countries. Although a modified and supplemented German version of the Correctional Practice Questionnaire (CPQ) of Kowitz, Graves, Dronberger, Black, and Bishop (1973) was formulated by Klingemann (1981, p. 55), this paper was not published at the time when the present study was planned. The items were formulated on the basis of consultations with prison officers and were grouped into the following categories:

1. “Belief in the therapeutic effect of working,” e.g., “To ensure that after their discharge prisoners will not relapse, it is necessary to provide them with occupational training.”
2. “Outmoded opinions about the origins of criminality”, e.g., “Liberalization of imprisonment is one of the most important reasons for the rise in criminality in our country.”
3. “Intolerance towards personal needs of prisoners,” e.g., “What percentage of payment that is paid for a piece of work by a firm outside the prison should be paid to the prisoners for their work?”
4. “Repressiveness,” e.g., “Letter censorship aids security (as in the prevention of escape). What percentage of all letters leaving the prison do you think contain ideas which the prison authorities should unconditionally know about?”

By contrast to Klingemann’s version of the CPQ, the item set for the present study did not inquire into opinions about the priority of different aims of punishment and treatment.

Results

Intercorrelations Among General Social Attitudes and Personality Traits

It need only be mentioned here that the personality trait "sense of duty and loyalty to moral principles" correlated with the other four personality traits (from $r = 0.251$ to $r = 0.493$), as well as with for example an engaged attitude and a tendency toward isolation from others and lack of respect for others' individuality. This in itself suffices to indicate a potential conflict linked with the personality trait "sense of duty," a conflict which will again be recognized in the results reported later. It could be that subjects with a high score for "sense of duty" are individuals who in their behavior display conflict between on the one hand a tendency not to respect others by virtue of their own strict moral principles, and on the other, a desire to engage in action for others owing to their sense of duty. Alternatively such subjects might be individuals who engage themselves for others and stand up for the improvement of their situation but who will evaluate the well-being of others according to their own personal principles without regard to the specific situation of the individual concerned.

Intercorrelations Among Attitudes Towards Prisoners

According to the correlation coefficients in Table 24.1, attitudes towards prisoners proved largely distinct, though the dimension "repressiveness" may represent an exception. Factor analysis of the intercorrelations revealed three significant factors. One of the three is primarily defined by the dimension "in-

TABLE 24.1. Intercorrelations among attitudes towards prisoners[a]

	Belief in the therapeutic effect of working	Outmoded opinions about causation of criminality	Intolerance towards personal needs of prisoners	Repressiveness
Bel. in the ther. effect of working	–	0.237	0.334	0.454
Outm. opin. about caus. of crimin.		–	0.245	0.393
Intol. tow. pers. needs of prison.			–	0.513
Repressiveness				–

[a] All scores are at a significant level (at least $P = 0.05$)

tolerance towards personal needs of prisoners," while the other two can be defined as subcomponents of "repressiveness," namely "allowance for vs. restriction of information and opinions" and "open-mindedness towards vs. rejection of coresponsibility and codetermination of prisoners."

Relations Between General Social Attitudes and Personality Traits and Attitudes Towards Prisoners

Simple Linear Correlations

A significant correlation coefficient is not seen in each cell of the matrix in Table 24.2, and in addition the reported relations are not very strong. Nevertheless, the results together verify the fundamental assumption that the prison officers' individual differences in specific attitudes towards prisoners systematically covariate with individual differences in general social attitudes and personality traits. The level of the coefficients reported here accords with coefficients reported by Blickhan et al. (1978, p. 26) concerning the correlations between the personality trait "intolerance/strictness" and the professional attitudes of prison officers. According to Table 24.2, in the present study the widest and strongest relations were found for the trait "sense of duty/loyalty to moral principles;" this trait showed an especially close relation to the attitudes "belief in the therapeutic effect of working" ($r = 0.556$) and "repressiveness" ($r = 0.393$). It appears remarkable that the trait "benevolence" shows not one significant coefficient of linear correlation. However, as the following results will show, there are relations between "benevolence" and certain atti-

Table 24.2. Simple linear correlations between general personality traits and attitudes towards prisoners[a]

	Belief in the therapeutic effect of working	Outmoded opinions about causation of criminality	Intolerance towards personal needs of prisoners	Repressiveness
Benevolence	n.s.	n.s.	n.s.	n.s.
Egocentric isolation	0.234	(0.211)	0.368	0.235
Aggression	0.268	0.237	0.257	n.s.
Directive attitude	n.s.	n.s.	n.s.	0.346
Sense of duty	0.556	0.250	0.297	0.393

[a] Except for the coefficient within parentheses, all printed coefficients are at a significant level (at least $P = 0.05$)

tudes towards prisoners, i.e., relations that do not manifest in simple linear correlations.

Above it was hypothesized that regression of the two personality traits "benevolence" and "sense of duty" to the attitudes towards prison practice is impaired by those components of variance which they have in common. Because of that assumption, partial correlations between these two variables and attitudes towards prisoners were calculated, in addition to the simple linear correlations. In this process the influence of the other variable was eliminated.

Selected Coefficients of Partial Correlations

With one exception (second cell in the first line), Table 24.3 shows that the coefficients for the partial correlations between the two personality traits and the attitudes towards prisoners were at a higher level than the simple linear correlations. In the case of "benevolence," two of the four coefficients of partial correlations were at a significant level, whereas with the simple linear correlations (Table 24.2) not one was. These results consequently confirm the assumption that regression of each of the two personality traits to the attitudes towards prisoners is impaired by the other trait. The increase in the partial cor-

Table 24.3. Partial correlations for the general personality traits "sense of duty" and "benevolence" (eliminating the other trait) with attitudes towards prisoners[a]

	Belief in the therapeutic effect of working	Outmoded opinions about causation of criminality	Intolerance towards personal needs of prisoners	Repressiveness
$r_{sdu_{1-n} \cdot be}$ = partial correl. for "sense of duty," eliminating "benevolence"	*0.59* *(0.56)*	0.21 *(0.25)*	*0.38* *(0.30)*	*0.51* *(0.39)*
$r_{be_{1-n} \cdot sdu}$ = partial correl. for "benevolence", eliminating "sense of duty"	−0.16 (0.12)	−0.17 (−0.04)	*−0.25* (−0.10)	*−0.41* (−0.17)

[a] For comparison the corresponding coefficients for simple linear correlations are shown within parentheses. Coefficients at a significant level (at least $P = 0.05$) are italicized.

relations as compared with the simple linear correlations appears most clear in the following cases. For "sense of duty" the correlation with "intolerance towards personal needs of prisoners" rose from 0.3 to 0.38, and that with "repressiveness" from 0.39 to 0.51. For "benevolence" the correlation with "outmoded assumptions about causation of criminality" rose from −0.04 to −0.17, that with "intolerance towards personal needs of prisoners" from −0.10 to −0.25, and that with "repressiveness" from −0.17 to −0.41. Therefore the effect is primarily demonstrated for relations of the two predictors with certain "repressive" attitudes.

So it is valid to conclude that prognostication of high grades for repressive attitudes based on a high score on the predictor "sense of duty" is restricted by the high level of benevolence which is itself linked with the high level of sense of duty. In the other case of a high score for benevolence, the prognostication of liberal and tolerant attitudes is limited by the high level of sense of duty which is linked with a high level of benevolence. The following multiple correlations also serve to illustrate these effects.

TABLE 24.4. Results for multiple regression (beta-weights, multiple correlations) from the general personality traits on the attitudes towards prisoners

	Belief in the therapeutic effect of working	Outmoded opinions about causation of criminality	Intolerance towards personal needs of prisoners	Repressiveness
Benevolence	−0.147	−0.277	−0.267	−0.108
Egocentric isolation		0.032	0.252	0.181
Aggression	0.073	0.193	0.081	
Directive attitude		−0.242		
Sense of duty	0.594	0.345	0.258	0.262
Mult. correl. (r_{mult})	0.576	0.402	0.465	0.358
r^2 mult	0.332	0.162	0.217	0.128
Maximum simple lin. correl. ($r_{simpl.lin.max.}$)	0.556	0.250	0.368	0.305
r^2 simpl. lin. max.	0.310	0.063	0.136	0.093

Results Of Multiple Regression And Multiple Correlation Tests

Table 24.4 contains the beta-weights and the coefficients of multiple correlation for the general personality traits as predictors and the attitudes towards prisoners as criteria. The calculations for the multiple correlations were stopped when the last predictor increased the analyzed variance (r^2 mult. corr.) by an amount that was less than 1%. With respect to the specific criteria this happened after three, four, or five steps of calculation (three, four, or five predictors for which the beta-weights are shown).

From Table 24.4 it can be seen that from 12.8% to 33.2% of the variance for the attitudinal dimensions is cleared up by the predictors. The highest amount of variance (33.2%) is cleared up for "belief in the therapeutic effect of working," the predictor "sense of duty" being primarily responsible for this. The amounts of variance demonstrated by the simple linear correlations lie in the range 6.3% – 31%. The clearest increase from simple linear correlation to multiple correlation was found for "outmoded opinions about the origins of criminality" (an increase from 6.3% to 16.2%, i.e., 9.9%). According to their beta-weights, the predictors "benevolence" (1st line) and "sense of duty" (5th line) are most important for prediction of different attitudes towards prisoners. The results confirm that in spite of being positively correlated, these two variables have contrasting effects upon attitudes towards prisoners.

Discussion of Results

First some possible limitations of the validity of the reported results should be considered.

It may be that individual differences between prison officers in their attitudes towards prisoners are to be attributed to different institutional frames (e.g., different types of prison), and this might also be true of their general traits. A correlation between a general trait and a certain attitude could then be explained by the fact that both variables are confounded by a third variable (quality of institutional frame), without which a direct causal relation would have to exist between the general trait and the attitude.

To clarify this problem, the subjects were divided according to their membership of each of the three prisons. The average scores for the general personality traits and for the attitudes of the three groups of officers were compared. The results demonstrated that correlations between general personality traits and attitudes to prisoners (see Table 24.2) are not to be explained by the fact that two correlated variables are confounded by a third factor relating to the institutional frame. Although significant differences were indeed found between officers of different prisons as regards the general traits "benevolence" and "directive attitude" and the attitudes "outmoded opinions about the origins of criminality" and "intolerance towards personal needs of prisoners," these general traits and attitudes were not mutually correlated.

The results do not provide exact information about the nature of the institutional frame in the different prisons. They varied on any of several criteria: location in the country or a city, kind of prison organization (high security, therapeutic), size, etc.

The reported relations between type of prison and the two aforementioned personality traits ("benevolence," "directive attitude") possibly should not be seen as an indication of the fact that professional attitudes in a certain prison determine the personality development of prisoners. Rather it may be that employment of members of the staff in different prisons conforms to the personality of the prisoners. Either it may be that the administration board assigns officers to different prisons according to their personality, or officers of differing personality may want to work in different prisons. In this way subjects who had high scores for "directive attitude" and low scores for "benevolence" would be found in a prison with a high degree of security rather than in a therapeutically oriented prison where prisoners live in groups.

As reported by Ziegert (1982), within the same prison coexist officers' attitudes which seem to be incompatible. Ziegert found that in a prison with a low grade of security, officers on the one hand accepted relaxing of imprisonment as a measure to reintegrate prisoners but on the other hand regarded this measure as too tender-hearted and complained about inmates having too many rights. The seeming contradiction can be understood as a mechanism of "differentiation" of attitudes in reaction to cognitive imbalance (see Heider, 1958, pp. 176, 177; Stroebe, Thompson, Insko, & Reisman, 1970). Officers in prisons with high grade of security may have traditional, rather restrictive opinions concerning fundamental problems of justice (e.g., concerning prisoners' rights) but through their professional experience know that relaxing of imprisonment is an effective practical measure.

In the present study comparable results were also obtained for officers in the prison with the most relaxed regime. Compared with officers of the other two prisons, these officers had lower scores for the attitude "repressiveness" and higher scores for the general personality trait "benevolence." However, they also had the highest scores for "intolerance towards personal needs of prisoners" and tended to have "outmoded opinions about origins of a criminality" (e.g., in agreeing that "Liberalization of imprisonment is one of the most important reasons for the rise in criminality in our country").

Speculatively the results might be interpreted in the following way. Officers with a high level of benevolence should choose or be assigned employment in a prison with a relaxed regime. Such officers tend to hold nonrepressive attitudes or discern nonrepressive practices as an appropriate way of dealing with inmates. However, they also perceive the negative side of relaxing of imprisonment, especially the higher aspirations that inmates come to hold. As a consequence of such experiences they tend to become intolerant towards personal needs of inmates.

As already mentioned, these considerations are only speculative, because of the lack of exact information about special conditions at the places of work and about the special experiences of the officers. In the case of the present results the differences between officers working in different prisons could also be explained by a difference between ecological conditions in the city and in the country, given that officers who worked in the one prison located in a city showed a higher level of tolerance towards personal needs of inmates and rarely held outmoded opinions about the origins of criminality, in contrast to officers who worked in the two prisons located in the country.

It should also be taken into consideration that the officers' job experiences and the ecological conditions influence not only the general personality traits and the attitudes towards inmates, but also the size of the correlations between general personality traits and different attitudes towards prisoners (see Table 24.2). For example, the correlation coefficients may be influenced by the degree of role fixation at the place of work, by professional qualifications, and by length of employment.

The possibility that within different institutional frames there might exist different relations between general personality traits and attitudes towards prisoners does not render the following considerations concerning the practical value of the present results uncertain in principle. It must only be borne in mind that the results may not be valid in the same way for all institutional frames and for all prisons.

In this discussion of results, it must also be remembered that the personality traits and attitudes were only tested by questionnaires. This does not, however, restrict the validity of the results. It was intended to test such traits and opinions about dealing with inmates as the officers were conscious of. For testing conscious events, the only direct approach is the method of self-evaluation (especially in the form of a questionnaire). Often there is the problem that the contents of two correlated questionnaire scales overlap. In such cases the correlations could be explained by the fact that each of the two correlated scales contains items of similar content. But on the inventories used in the present study this was not the case. The scales for testing general personality traits contained items which concerned only other persons and social matters in general. The scales for testing attitudes towards prisoners, by contrast, concerned attitudes towards concrete prison practices and evaluations of definite behavioral skills of inmates.

From the perspective of basic research in differential and in social psychology, the results confirm the hypothesis that – in spite of the further influences mentioned above – attitudes towards prisoners are determined by general personality traits. Or formulated another way: it is confirmed that general traits realize themselves in certain opinions about concrete decisions and practices. General personality traits and attitudes are linked by the use which they have for the individual. From a functional point of view, the personality construct "trait" can be related with the construct "attitude" in social psychology (for a functional view of "traits" see Alston, 1970, 1975; for a functional view of "attitudes" see Katz, 1960). The size of the correlations reported in Tables 24.2 and 24.3 correspond to the results reported in other comparable studies (see Blickhan et al., 1978; Carlson et al., 1971; Gaensslen et al., 1974; Klingemann, 1981). In the case of the present correlations, about 5% – 30% of the variances in attitudes were ascertained to be covariances with general personality traits. It is true that attitudes towards prisoners are determined by general personality traits only to a limited extent, because of the afore mentioned specific determinants. On the other hand it is to be expected that further theoretical differentiation of the personality constructs employed here would increase their usefulness as predictors. The exemplary partial correlations of the traits "benevolence" and "sense of duty" invite further theoretical analysis of the usual personality constructs and their empirical relations. Of special interest is the interaction of emotionally based behavioral tendencies and regulatory moral-cognitive systems, especially in the area of prosocial motives and prosocial behavior, which nowadays is paid much attention (see Bierhoff, 1980, 1983; Lück, 1975, 1977).

For the practice of imprisonment the results of the present study are meaningful because they demonstrate that the prison officer (in his attitudes and corresponding behavior) is not only a passive object of institutional influences. Rather in correspondence with his own personality, he himself actively forms part of the therapeutic environment.

The results of the study also confirm the value of efforts to develop programs for changing prison officers' basic personality traits and individual behavioral skills (see Blickhan et al., 1978; Kühne, Raschta, & Tausch, 1974; Steller & Berbalk, 1974). In particular it should be pointed out that the two dimensions of officers' behavior which Kühne et al. (1974) found to be changeable by training are also represented in this study in the variables "directive attitude" and "aggressiveness based on suspicion and expectation of hostility" (reactive aggressiveness), and that Kühne et al.'s results were supported. In addition, changes in prison organization and in the regulations regarding the forms of contact between officers and inmates are necessary (see Leky, 1975).

According to theoretical and empirical results about relations between attitudes, behavioral intentions, and actual behavior (Fishbein, 1967, 1979; Fishbein & Ajzen, 1975; see Stroebe, 1980, p. 167 ff.), it can be expected that attitudes towards dealing with prisoners stimulate corresponding behavioral intentions and actual behavior. Whether in the case of given attitudes corresponding behavioral intentions and behavior are indeed realized depends on manifold institutional conditions. Such conditions include the prison officer's former experiences concerning reactions (of superiors, colleagues, and inmates) to his own behavior or to his own decisions, and specific propitious or adverse conditions in an actual situation. So far, knowledge of an individual score on one of the attitudinal scales considered here is not sufficient to predict the individual concrete behavior of an officer reliably. Relations between attitudes and individual behavior (according to Fishbein & Ajzen, 1974; also see Herkner, 1981, p. 257) prove very weak (correlation coefficients about $r = 0.15$). This is connected to the fact that each attitude fits for several behaviors. Which particular behavior actually occurs and which does not depends on the individual's experiences" (Herkner, 1981, pp. 256, 257). If, however, one considers not one single behavior occurring in a definite situation but rather different behaviors by the same person all oriented towards the same object, a significant correlation can be found between attitudes and actual behavior. Knowledge about attitudes does not make possible precise predictions (single behavior criteria) but rather global predictions (multiple behavior criteria). Attitudes are connected with general behavioral tendencies. Pessimism about the relation between attitudes and behavior, which is voiced by some psychologists, cannot be vindicated (Herkner, 1981, pp. 257, 258).

In the present context it should also be mentioned that the possibility of predicting actual behavior from knowledge about the person's attitudes will be moderated by the level of a certain personality trait, by so-called self-monitoring (Snyder, 1979; Nowack, 1985). Self-monitoring means the tendency of an individual in a certain situation to consider what behavior would be adequate in that situation. An individual with a high level of self-monitoring will tend to behave in a way which corresponds to a certain situation and which is less reliable, because it depends on particular social influences and social forces. By contrast, the behavior of individuals who care little about specific adjustment to certain situations tends to correspond to their own inner attitudes. Nevertheless, a study by Snyder and Kendzierski (1982) shows that even in persons with a high level of self-monitoring it is possible to predict behavior from knowledge of the level of a person's attitudes.

Induction of a so-called do it motivation (see Bierhoff, 1984, p. 210) is of considerable importance in encouraging officers to behave in a way which reflects their own attitudes. But the establishing of such a "do it motivation" among members of a prison staff is difficult because of the ambivalent conceptions about the goals and modes of imprisonment which exist between and within institutions of legislation, administration, and execution (see Hohmeier, 1975; Wagner, 1975).

In real life one would expect manifold divergences between an officer's attitudes towards dealing with prisoners as based on the officer's basic personality traits and actual behavior as reflecting former experiences and actual conditions of stimulation and reinforcement. While reforming attitudes may exist, propitious circumstances for their realization in behavior may be lacking. Also the former experiences of such behavior may be rather negative or ambivalent, or because of certain conditions at the place of work, restrictive behavior contrary to the reforming attitudes may be positively reinforced. On the other hand there may be circumstances which permit reforming behavior, but an officer may not be open to these circumstances. Research based especially on the theory of cognitive dissonance (Festinger, 1957) has tried to analyze the effects of divergences between attitudes and behavior. As Festinger (1957, p. 16; 1978) recognizes, it is impossible to make statements of universal validity about the particular events which evoke dissonance and about the individual's ways of reducing dissonance. The importance of a certain event for a particular individual must be taken into account. Dissonance is only caused by events and by information of "private relevance" to the individual. A definite combination of events and information may be consonant or dissonant for one officer but irrelevant for another. Dissonance, consonance, and irrelevance conform to private convictions and intentions.

The matter of convergence/divergence between attitudes and actual behavior was discussed here for the purpose of a holistic consideration but it is not a central theme of the present study. However, the states of psychic balance/imbalance resulting from such convergence/divergence are of considerable importance. The present study reveals that certain combinations of personality traits and attitudes can be expected in many officers. In accordance with the results of Table 24.3 and of Heider (1944, 1946), the following "triads" may be postulated:

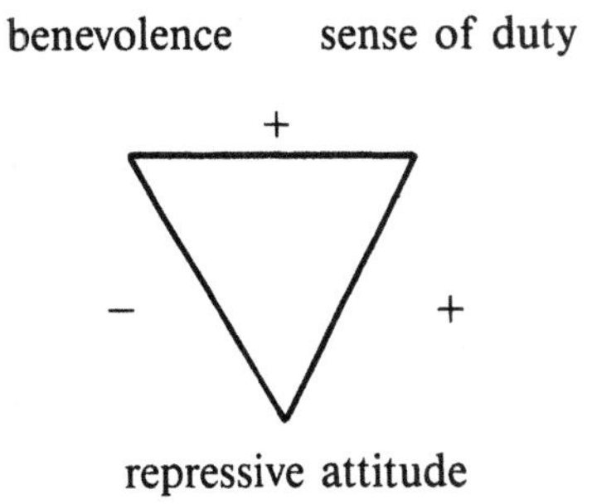

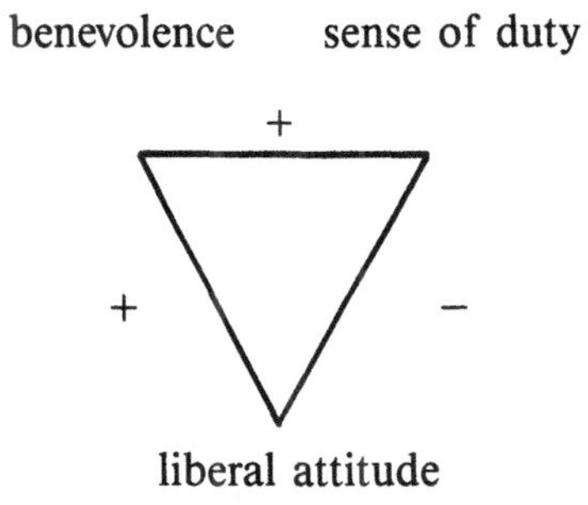

According to the "theorem of multiplication" (Cartwright & Harrari, 1956) these states are imbalanced. In both of the triads, multiplication of the three signs yields a product with a negative sign. Imbalanced combinations are seen by the individual as unpleasant and full of tension. The individual feels unwell and tends to develop mechanisms which balance the whole inner system.

Innerpsychic mechanisms observed as a consequence of imbalance between different attitudes (see Stroebe, 1980, p. 194 ff.) at least hypothetically can also be supposed to be possible consequences of imbalance between attitudes and personality traits. For instance, one could suppose that the two triads depicted above evoke the mechanism "changing the direction of a relation." This can be illustrated as follows: If an officer of high benevolence and with a high sense of duty expresses a liberal attitude, this attitude is consonant with his benevolence. The liberal attitude is, however, dissonant to his sense of duty. To obtain balance in the whole system it would be necessary that he either perceives repressive attitudes to be compatible with his benevolence (and liberal attitudes to be incompatible with his benevolence) or perceives liberal attitudes to be compatible with his sense of duty. In the first case he might perceive repressive measures as effective ways of treating inmates and thus in their best interests, which would be compatible with his benevolence. In the second case an officer might perceive a liberal measure as compatible with his sense of duty because he is convinced that this measure is an effective means of treatment which he feels obliged to support.

According to these considerations it is possible to reduce imbalance by differentiation in the area of the attitudes, especially by differentiation concerning the function of the attitudes, their use for the individual. To fulfill the same purpose (e.g., to satisfy the officer's benevolence), attitudes towards certain ways of dealing with prisoners should thus have other contents than attitudes towards certain ways of dealing with persons other than prisoners. It should be a goal of officer training and counseling to stimulate differentiation between purposes of his attitudes as determined by his personality development outside of prison and before he worked in prison on the one hand, and particular purposes of his attitudes relating to the situation in prison and to the person of the prisoner on the other hand. Such differentiation would promote innerpsychic balance in the officer. The establishment of such differentiation requires pertinent concepts about goals and modes of imprisonment and prison practice which is in accordance with such concepts. As yet, however, such concepts have either not been formulated or are not unequivocally accepted.

There is also another mechanism for reducing imbalance that might be feasible, i.e., so-called padding (Abelson, 1959). For instance, in the case of repressive attitudes dissonance with benevolence could be reduced if the officer were to make himself conscious that his repressive attitude is consonant with more than just one of his personality traits (not only with his sense of duty, but also with his directive attitude and his egocentric isolation).

The mechanisms for regulation of imbalance in an officer that are actually employed depend on the level of his personality development and on the conditions and processes which have caused that development. They depend on his professional socialization and the level of correspondence to his extraprofessional personality development.

It can be expected that a prison officer with a pronounced sense of duty, which the present results suggest should be linked with a high level of benevolence and thus with engagement for other persons, will receive positive feedback from his superiors. But the conflict by which the officer is perhaps bothered will probably not be recognized by his superiors. Any manifestation of that conflict in the officer's behavior or verbal remarks will probably be misunderstood.

Unsolved questions that remain include: On what further conditions does a restrictive or a liberal attitude depend? What consequences (e.g., for the employee's professional contentment) result from the previously mentioned conflicts? What are the barriers to or facilitators of measures to change attitudes? To clear up such questions by means of empirical research lies in the interest of objective programs regarding prison practice, especially in the interest of realistic, unbiased employment of officers and in the interest of the elucidation of their professional self-concept, including ideas about the appropriate kinds of contact with prisoners. Further studies are needed, involving cooperation between research, administrative, practicing institutions.

Nevertheless, the results of the present study also deserve the attention of those persons and authorities responsible for the employment of personnel in prisons. The results point out conflicts which are immanent in expectations placed on a "good" officer and which lead to lasting psychic stress in everyday professional life. Not only discontent with the profession but also psychosomatic troubles may result, causing increased absenteeism or premature retirement.

An empirical relation between innerpsychic tension ("stress") in officers and a large number of diseases and psychosomatic complaints is evidenced by the study by Long, Shouksmith, Voges, and Roache (1986) of prison employees in New Zealand. That study analyzed different sources of professional stress, such as "relations between colleagues," "pressure due to job requirements," and "relations to prisoners." Significant connections were found between the individual officer's perception of the existence of certain stressors and the frequency of illness. The closest connection with illness was displayed by the stressor "relations to inmates." Again, this suggests it would be in the interest of justice administration to pay more attention to individual differences regarding inner conflicts in prison officers, as linked with individual differences in personality.

The importance of self-concept or a feeling of self-worth for job behavior is described in the papers by Super (1951, 1953, 1961) and Korman (1966, 1969, 1970) [see also Scheller and Heil (1979)]. These papers deal with self-concept as a basis of the professional role, with mechanisms for attaining balance between self-concept and professional role, and with the effect of self-esteem as a moderator on the other processes. Increasing the officer's insight into the concepts he holds of himself and of his profession should be a prime goal; counseling of the prison employee and supervision of his behavior in practice should be extended.

References

Abelson, R.P. (1959). Modes of resolution of belief dilemmas. *Journal of Conflict Resolution, 3,* 343–352.

Alston, W.P. (1970). Toward a logical geography of personality: traits and deeper lying personality characteristics. In H.E. Kiefer & M.K. Kunitz (Eds.), *Contemporary philosophic thought, Vol. 2. Mind, science and history* (pp. 59–93). Albany: State University Press.

Alston, W.P. (1975). Traits, consistency and conceptual alternatives for personality theory. *Journal of the Theory of Social Behavior, 5,* 17–48.

Angleitner, A. (1980). *Einführung in die Persönlichkeitspsychologie.* Göttingen: Hogrefe.

Bastine, R. (1971). *Fragebogen zur Direktiven Einstellung (FDE).* Göttingen: Hogrefe.

Bierhoff, H.W. (1980). *Hilfreiches Verhalten.* Darmstadt: Steinkopff.

Bierhoff, H.W. (1983). Motivation prosozialer Aktivität. In H. Thomae (Ed.), *Psychologie der Motive* (pp. 440–504). Göttingen: Hogrefe.

Bierhoff, H.W. (1984). *Sozialpsychologie.* Stuttgart: Kohlhammer.

Böhm, A. (1975). Zur gegenwärtigen und künftigen Situation des Aufsichtsdienstes. *Zeitschrift für Strafvollzug und Straffälligenhilfe, 24*, 10–13.

Blickhan, D., Braune, P., Klapprott, J., Linz, P., & Lösel, F. (1978). Berufliche Einstellungen von Justizvollzugsbediensteten. *Psychologie und Praxis, 22*, 18–33.

Carlson, H., Thayer, R., & Germann, A. (1971). Social attitudes and personality differences among members of two kinds of police departments. *The Journal of Criminal Law, Criminology and Police Science, 62*, 564–567.

Cartwright, D., & Harrari, F. (1956). Structural balance: A generalization of Heider's theory. *Psychological Review, 63*, 277–293.

Cloerkes, G. (1986). Erscheinungsweise und Änderung von Einstellungen gegenüber Behinderten. In K.H. Wiedl (Ed.), *Rehabilitationspsychologie* (pp. 131–149) Stuttgart: Kohlhammer.

Däumling, A.M., & Possehl, K. (1970). *Selbstbild und Fremdbild der Aufsichtsbeamten im Strafvollzug.* Stuttgart: Enke.

Deimling, G. (1969). *Theorie und Praxis des Jugendstrafvollzugs in pädagogischer Sicht.* Neuwied: Luchterhand.

Festinger, L. (1957). *A theory of cognitive dissonance.* Stanford: Stanford University Press.

Fishbein, M. (1967). Attitude and the prediction of behavior. In M. Fishbein (Ed.), *Readings in attitude theory and measurement* (pp. 477–492). New York: Wiley.

Fishbein, M. (1979). Einstellung und die Vorhersage des Verhaltens. In S.E. Hormuth (Ed.), *Sozialpsychologie der Einstellungsänderung* (pp. 148–173). Meisenheim: Hain.

Fishbein, M., & Ajzen, I. (1974). Attitudes towards objects as predictors of single and multiple behavioral criteria. *Psychological Review, 81*, 59–74.

Fishbein, M., & Ajzen, I. (1975). *Belief, attitude, intention and behavior.* Reading, MA: Addison & Wesley.

Gaensslen, H., May, F., & Wölpert, F. (1974). *Die Strafideologie Jugendlicher im Kontext von Einstellungs- und Persönlichkeitsdimensionen.* Unpublished manuscript, University of Munich.

Guilford, J.P. (1959). *Personality.* New York: McGraw-Hill.

Heider, F. (1944). Social perception and phenomenal causality. *Psychological Review, 51*, 358–378.

Heider, F. (1946). Attitudes and cognitive organization. *Journal of Psychology, 21*, 107–112.

Heider, F. (1958). *The psychology of interpersonal relations.* New York: Wiley.

Herkner, W. (1981). *Einführung in die Sozialpsychologie.* Bern: Huber.

Hohmeier, J. (1969). Die Strafanstalt und das Aufsichtspersonal, Dilemma einer Berufsrolle. *Monatsschrift für Kriminologie und Strafrechtsreform, 52*, 218–222.

Hohmeier, J. (1973). *Aufsicht und Resozialisierung.* Stuttgart: Enke.

Hohmeier, J. (1975). Berufsrolle des Beamten mit neuer Zielsetzung. *Zeitschrift für Strafvollzug und Straffälligenhilfe, 24*, 8–10.

Homans, G.C. (1968). *Theorie der sozialen Gruppe.* (3rd ed.). Opladen: Westdeutscher Verlag.

Irle, M. (1975). *Lehrbuch der Sozialpsychologie.* Göttingen: Hogrefe.

Katz, D. (1960). The functional approach to the study of attitude. *Public Opinion Quarterly, 24*, 163–204.

Klingemann, H. (1981). Organisationale Zielkonflikte im Resozialisierungsbereich: Jugendstrafvollzug und öffentliche Erziehung. *Zeitschrift für Soziologie, 10*, 50–75.

Korman, A.K. (1966). Self-esteem variable in vocational choice. *Journal of Applied Psychology, 50*, 479–486.

Korman, A. K. (1969). Self-esteem as a moderator in vocational choice: Replication and extensions. *Journal of Applied Psychology, 53*, 188–192.

Korman, A. K. (1970). Toward a hypothesis of work behavior. *Journal of Applied Psychology, 54*, 31–41.

Kowitz, G., Graves, W., Dronberger, G., Black, R., & Bishop, E. (1973). *Evaluation of an introduction to correctional techniques.* University of Oklahoma.

Kühne, A. (1981). Curriculare und methodische Überlegungen zur Ausbildung des Beamten im allgemeinen Vollzugsdienst (Schwerpunktfach Psychologie). In K. Mai (Ed.), *Psychologie hinter Gittern* (pp. 100–124). Weinheim: Beltz.

Kühne, A., Raschta, F., & Tausch, A. (1974). Fremd- und Selbsttraining von künftigen Vollzugsbeamten. *Kriminologisches Journal, 6*, 105–116.

Leky, L. G. (1975). Der Aufsichtsbeamte als Therapeut. *Monatsschrift für Kriminologie und Strafrechtsreform, 58*, 94–99.

Long, N., Shouksmith, G., Voges, K., & Roache, S. (1986). Stress in prison staff: an occupational study. *Criminology, 24*, 331–345.

Lück, H. E. (1975). Prosoziales Verhalten. *Empirische Untersuchungen zur Hilfeleistung.* Cologne: Kiepenheuer & Witsch.

Lück, H. E. (Ed.). (1977). *Mitleid – Vertrauen – Verantwortung.* Stuttgart: Klett.

Mischel, W. (1973). Toward a cognitive social learning reconceptualization of personality. *Psychological Review, 80*, 252–283.

Mischel, W. (1976). *Introduction to personality* (2nd ed.). New York: Holt & Rinehart & Winston.

Nowack, W. (1985). Self-monitoring – Selbstrepräsentation. In T. Herrmann & E. D. Lantermann (Ed.), *Persönlichkeitspsychologie.* Munich: Urban & Schwarzenberg.

Plake, K. (1977). Sozialer Identitätsanspruch und die Legitimation der Betreuung: Zur Kustodialfunktion der Sozialisationsorganisationen. *Zeitschrift für Soziologie, 6*, 264–278.

Pervin, L. A. (1978). *Current controversies and issues in personality.* New York: Wiley.

Rosenberg, M. J., & Hovland, C. I. (1960). Cognitive, affective and behavioral components of attitudes. In I. Hovland & M. J. Rosenberg (Eds.), *Attitude organization and change* (pp. 1–14). New Haven: Yale University Press.

Scheller, R., & Heil, F. (1979). Berufliche Entwicklung und Selbstkonzepte. In S. H. Filipp, (Ed.), *Selbstkonzeptforschung* (pp. 253–271). Stuttgart: Klett.

Seitz, W. (1973). *Soziale Einstellung und ihre objektspezifischen Differenzierungen.* Unpublished dissertation, University of Würzburg.

Six, B. (1980). Das Konzept der Einstellung und seine Relevanz für die Vorhersage des Verhaltens. In F. Petermann (Ed.), *Einstellungsmessung – Einstellungsforschung.* Göttingen: Hogrefe.

Snyder, M. (1979). Self-monitoring processes. In L. Berkowitz (Ed.), *Advances in experimental social psychology* (Vol. 12, pp. 85–120). New York: Academic Press.

Snyder, M., & Kendzierski, D. (1982). Acting on one's attitudes. Procedures for linking attitude and behavior. *Journal of Experimental Social Psychology, 18*, 165–183.

Steller, M., & Berbalk, H. (1974). Ein Programm zur psychologischen Ausbildung von Vollzugsbediensteten. *Monatsschrift für Kriminologie und Strafrechtsreform, 57*, 88–105.

Stroebe, W. (1980). *Grundlagen der Sozialpsychologie. I.* Stuttgart: Klett.

Stroebe, W., Thompson, V. D., Insko, C. A., & Reisman, S. R. (1970). Balance and evaluation of linked attitude objects. *Journal of Personality and Social Psychologie, 1*, 38–47.

Super, D. E. (1951). Vocational adjustment: Implementing a self-concept. *Occupation, 30*, 88–92.

Super, D.E. (1953). A theory of vocational development. *American Psychologist, 8,* 185–190.

Super, D.E. (1961). The self concept in vocational development. *Journal of Vocational and Educational Guidance, 8,* 13–29.

Triandis, H.G. (1975). *Einstellungen und Einstellungsänderungen.* Weinheim: Beltz.

Wagner, G. (1975). Personalschulung zwischen Traditionalismus und Praxisveränderung. *Zeitschrift für Strafvollzug und Straffälligenhilfe, 24,* 3–8.

Ziegert, U. (1982). Offener Jugendvollzug als Arbeitsplatz des Aufsichtsbediensteten. *Monatsschrift für Kriminologie und Strafrechtsreform, 65,* 230–245.

25
Psychology in Prison: Role Assessment and Testing of an Organizational Model

FRIEDRICH LÖSEL and THOMAS BLIESENER

Introduction

A major object of research in legal psychology is the discrepancy between the abstract legal schemes and the actual functioning of the criminal justice system (Ebbesen & Konečni, 1982). Legal psychology can contribute to the description explanation, prediction and possibly alternation of these discrepancies (cf. Lösel, 1986). One of the fields in which discrepancies between the normative perspective and the social science perspective are particularly apparent is imprisonment. For example, although the goal of special prevention (rehabilitation) is emphasized in the Prison Act of the Federal Republic of Germany, and corresponding formal guidelines have been formulated, there is a broad consensus that it is only partially realized in practice. Nevertheless, when making a realistic appraisal, even critical observers agree that organizational improvements can only be undertaken in small steps (e.g., Wagner, 1984). Despite the international discussion on changing trends in criminal policy (e.g., a renewed interest in general deterrence and incapacitation), some advances in rehabilitative measures can still be seen in West German prison practice (cf. Kaiser, Kerner, & Schöch, 1983; Rotthaus, 1987). Although opposite trends are encouraged by over crowding, unemployment, drug addiction, AIDS, and other present-day prison problems, more favorable conditions for prisons can be foreseen as a result of population changes and particularly the decrease in the especially crime-prone population of young (male) adults (cf. Dünkel, 1987; Hesener & Jehle, 1987; for US trends, see Blumstein, 1983).

The majority of *psychological* research into the organization of prisons has been concerned with the area of treatment. However, the low success rates revealed by outcome evaluation and experiences with process evaluation have shown that the mainly clinical psychological perspective toward the prisoner needs to be supplemented by a more organization-related perspective (Driebold, Egg, Nellessen, Quensel, & Schmitt, 1984; Lösel, Köferl, & Weber, 1987). This can be achieved by more strongly integrating the traditions of prison sociology, as represented by, for example, Clemmer (1940), Cressey

(1959), and Wheeler (1961), into the research and practice of special prevention. In such an approach, it is important not only to focus on the prisoners as a social group but also to include other members of the organization or subcultures in prisons in the analysis. Particularly with regard to prison personnel, an extreme lack of research was noted up to the 1970s (Carney, 1974, p. 130; Hawkins, 1976, p. 85). Since that time, there has been a marked increase in research into prison personnel. For example, empirical studies on prison officers can be found that deal with:

1. Attitudes and personality characteristics (e.g., Blickhan, Braune, Klapprott, Linz, & Lösel, 1978; Farmer, 1977; Jurik, 1985; Kaufmann, 1981; Leky, 1973; Poole & Regoli, 1980; Rosner, 1983; Williams & Soutar, 1984)
2. Role perceptions and role conflicts (e.g., Braune, Klapprott, Linz, Lösel, & Runkel, 1983a; Däumling, & Possehl, 1970; Hephurn & Albonetti, 1980; Klapprott, Blickhan, Braune, Linz, & Lösel, 1976; Rosner, 1983, 1984; Thomas, 1974)
3. Organizational climate (e.g., Moos, 1975; Thornton, 1985)
4. Job stress and job satisfaction (e.g., Braune et al. 1983a; Cheek & Miller, 1983; Lasky, Gordon, & Srebalus, 1986; Long, Shouksmith, Voges, & Roache, 1986; Rosner, 1983)
5. Job activity structures (e.g., Braune, Klapprott, Linz, Lösel, & Runkel, 1980; Hohmeier, 1973; Krüger, 1973)
6. Measures of personnel training (e.g., Blickhan, Braune, Klapprott, Linz, & Lösel, 1980; Braune, Klapprott, Linz, Lösel, & Runkel, 1982, 1983b; Duffee, 1974, 1980; Lindquist & Whitehead, 1986)

Our own previous studies (summarized in Braune et al., 1983a) have revealed, among other findings, that prison officers experience themselves as placed between the role demands of resocialization and security/order. The professional attitudes toward the prisoners, resocialization, their own roles, and further training are fairly consistent and can be characterized by a central dimension of positive versus negative evaluation of prisoners. Correlations exist between the job-oriented attitudes and general attitudes to education or personality characteristics such as authoritarianism. Older or more experienced officers do not show more negative attitudes, but, similar to the findings of Poole and Regoli (1980), there is a U-formed relation which has already been reported in respect of socialization in other institutions. The institutional efficacy of prisons is on average estimated as low. Low personal job satisfaction is, however, less related to discrepancies between desired and actual states in the field of social work than to general professional factors (career perspectives, stress, pay).

Like other investigations, our studies have clearly shown that considerable variations exist both within and between prisons. This does not just apply for organizational climate variables, as reported by Moos (1975), but also for many other variables that are important for organizations. Traditionally, however, the organizational characteristics of prisons have been discussed as if prisons were one homogeneous institution. This can be seen in the classical studies of the "total institution" by Goffman (1972) or the simulated prison by Zimbardo (1972). Although, on the one hand, it is so important to stress the uniqueness of the institution "prison", on the other hand one can scarcely exclude the possibility that this encourages stereotypes and self-fulfilling prophecies that tend toward a reduction in differentiation and changeability. If Goffman's term is modified, one can still assume that, although prison is a *total* organization, it is simultaneously a total *organization* that can be analyzed and changed according to general concepts from organizational psychology.

From such a more general organization-related perspective, it therefore appears plausible to apply to the prison system more concepts from organization development (OD) that have been tried in other contexts (cf. Cascio, 1986; Beer, 1976; French & Bell, 1977). A central but previously uninvestigated group for OD in prisons is prison psychologists. The present study is a continuation of our studies on prison officers that is directed toward the professional role and job structure of prison psychologists.

Conceptual Framing

In the Federal Republic of Germany, Ohler (1977), Braune et al. (1983b), and Kühne (1986) have proposed the use of OD concepts in prisons. According to Braune et al., particular attention should be paid to the following strategies:

1. Assessment Strategies. Diagnostic strategies cover the collection of information on the actual states and processes within the organization or its members. This includes, on the one hand, individual diagnosis approaches. One example of this is the choice or allocation of prison staff. In this field, the institution-specific validation of data and the application of more recent methods (such as assessment centers) still leaves much to be desired. On the other hand, diagnostic strategies are drawn from aggregated individual data (group features) or the organization as a whole. Examples of this are the above-mentioned assessments of the job structure, attitudes, and personality characteristics of prison staff, stress levels and role problems, and "organizational climate."

2. Personnel Development Strategies. This particularly covers measures of professional training, further education, and supervision. Such strategies should advance the ability of the members of the organization to cope with their task by helping them to acquire goal-adequate information, attitudes, abilities, and skills. Examples are the development of psychological training programs, measures to compensate for back-home effects, on-the-job supervision, and also the development of integrated training and further education curricula. More systematic comparative evaluation is needed on all levels. Thus, for example, in our own field experiment we were able to show that single, isolated psychological training courses for correctional officers had only mediocre effects. Within the context of this general limitation, however, relatively structured skill training produced better results than weakly structured T-groups (Braune et al., 1982, 1983a).

3. Job Organization and Environmental Management Strategies. Alterations in work organization particularly relate to the working, informational, and decision-making processes. The management of framing conditions can provide incentives and sanctions to stimulate behavior in accordance with institutional goal settings. Although the legal restrictions impose narrower limitations than is the case in other organizations, there are still concrete possibilities for OD. Examples for organization of work and cooperation are the delegation of responsibility and more autonomy for various departments, improved conference methods, and the establishment of problem-related work groups similar to those found in business organizations. In the organization of incentives and sanctions, one must finally not forget the influence of informal social systems that reflect the individual "spirit of the institution." For example, Marquart (1986) showed that the use of coercion in prisoner control was socialized by informal group-specific reinforcement mechanisms.

Psychologists and other social scientists in prisons can fulfill an important function for the conceptualization, implementation, and evaluation of measures of OD (cf. Böhm, 1981, p. 125; Mey, 1986). Although the psychology services in prisons were greatly expanded in West Germany during the 1970s (cf. Dünkel & Rosner, 1980), it is as yet unclear to what extent these mediator functions are practised. The tasks of psychologists are not clearly stated in the Prison Act (cf. Kühne, 1983; Lösel & Köferl, 1988; Müller-Dietz, 1977), and empirical studies of organization assessment are mostly concerned only with prison officers. For this reason, we have performed a systematic assessment of the role and job structures of psychologists in West German prisons from the perspective of OD (for other German studies, cf. Katein, Kury, & Waldert, 1986; Wagner, 1972). Our study does not just undertake a descriptive analysis but attempts to explain differences between institutions. In order to do this, we chose the "situational approach" developed by the Aston group (cf. Inkson, Payne, & Pugh, 1967; Kieser & Kubicek, 1983). The model is designed for organizations in general and should partially explain variations in staff behavior between different organizations and the reduction of the variance within a single organization. Although it has not previously been applied to prisons, it appears particularly suitable for this field as it stresses the influence of internal and external framing conditions (in business organizations, for example, the size of the organization, public control, and environmental dynamics). In prisons, comparable situational conditions are, for instance, the custody versus treatment orientation, the personnel-prisoner ratio (cf. Bowker, 1982, p. 189ff.), and general trends in criminal policy.

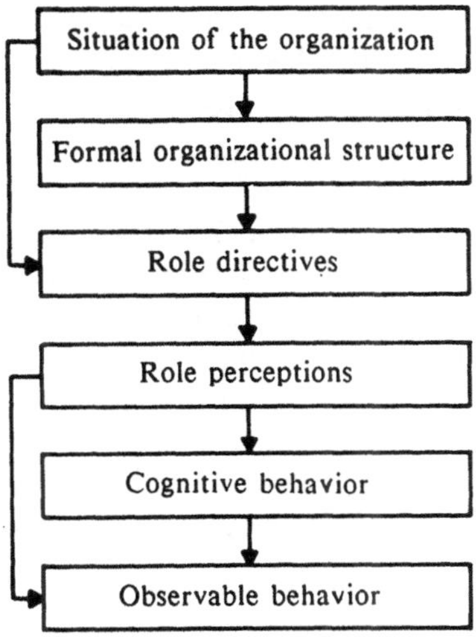

FIGURE 25.1. Inkson et al.'s concept for the analysis of behavior in organizations (Kieser, 1977, p. 121)

According to Inkson et al. (1967), the influence of the "situation" should be mediated by the formal organizational structure, role directives, self-perceptions of roles, and the "cognitive behavior," and find expression in the observable behavior of the members of the organization (see Figure 25.1).

For reasons of research practice, the model from Inkson et al. is generally only investigated on some of the six possible levels. As no comparable applications are available for the field of psychology in prisons, an analysis with the four levels of situational features, role directives, role perceptions, and observable behavior seems adequate. The formal organizational structure can initially be excluded because, on the one hand, it is roughly standardized by the Prison Act and, on the other, as the model shows, the effects of situational variables are also directly connected to the role demands. As regards the differentiation between role perception and "cognitive behavior," we consider that it could be misleading to make a clear distinction, as in both cases we are dealing with attitude constructs that differ only in their degree of specificity.

Method

Ninety-one psychologists participated in the investigation. Data collection was performed anonymously using a structured questionnaire that was distributed in eight different West German states. After permission had been granted by the ministries of justice in each state, the questionnaires were sent to prisons with the request that they be handed out to the resident psychologists. The response rate, related to the number of posts for psychologists in the states involved, reached just over 40%. When considering this response rate, it has to be remembered that it was not possible to make individual contact or send personal reminders. The sample approaches a representative cross-section of the distribution of psychologists in the different types of prison, with a proportion of 44% from closed prisons for adults, 12% from open prisons for adults, 32% from prisons for young offenders, and 12% from social therapeutic prisons.

The questionnaire was partially based on our own previous assessments (cf. Blickhan et al., 1980; Braune et al., 1983a) and was developed in cooperation with prison psychologists. It dealt with the following areas:

Objective Situational Features. Data on the organizational situation were recorded in a structured form. In the present study, only the following variables were considered:

1. The type of prison (open or closed for adults, prison for young offenders, social therapeutic prisons) as an indicator of the degree of custody vs. treatment orientation.
2. The personnel-prisoner ratio (number of officers and other personnel divided by the number of prisoners) as a second important influence on the work structure and relationships within prison.
3. The West German state in which the prison was situated and the governing party (Christian Democratic Party/Christian Social Party; Social Democratic Party) as an indicator of political framing conditions.

Perceived Role Demands. These were assessed with a Q-Sort as in our previous investigations. This contained 21 demands (activities) that had to be ranked on an 11-point scale according to the extent to which they were perceived to be directed at the psychologists. The psychologists had to respond according to a forced distribution, so that the extremes of the scale were used relatively infrequently and the middle of the scale relatively often. They answered the Q-Sort in five different versions: according to how they perceived the demands placed on them by the prison administrators, by the correctional officers, by the social workers, and by the prisoners, and how they viewed the demands they placed on themselves (role self-definition). In a further development of our previous approaches, the 21 role demands were taken from three areas (cf. Braune et al., 1983b; Klingemann, 1981; Rosner, 1983):

1. *Security, order, and smooth day-to-day running* (SO), with items such as "compliance with regulations and orders" and "able to settle disputes."
2. *Prisoner treatment, counseling, and resocialization* (TC), with items such as "counseling and supervision of prisoners" and "training in social competences."
3. *Organization management and development* (OD), with items such as "training and providing further education for the officers" and "organizing teamwork."

The assignment of the individual items to the three content areas proved to be sufficiently objective: The intercoder agreement coefficients (according to Craig 1981) attained $p_{5/6} = 0.81$ for the agreement between five out of six raters.

Activities. The structure of the professional activities was assessed with a questionnaire containing time budget items. Thirty-four activities were listed, and, in addition, the psychologists could also give unstructured answers. They entered how many hours per week or month they actually spent on each activity (actual state). Alongside each activity, they could also enter the extent to which they desired an expansion or restriction of that activity on a 5-point scale (desired state). The activities were also assigned to the above-mentioned three areas by independent raters:

1. *Security, order, and smooth day-to-day running* (SO), with items such as "written correspondence," "office activity," and "crisis intervention."
2. *Prisoner treatment, counseling, and resocialization* (TC), with items such as "individual therapy" and "group supervision."
2. *Organization management and development* (OD), with items such as "training and further education of officers" and "organization of work schedules."

The interrater agreement according to Craig's (1981) index was satisfactory, with $p_{5/6} = 0.77$.

Results

The Structure of the Role Perceptions

Sum scores from the five Q-Sorts of perceived role demands were calculated for the items in each of the three content areas. Table 25.1 gives the corresponding mean comparisons. The results show that there are clear differences in the demands that the psychologists experienced as coming from the various interaction partners. Figure 25.2 illustrates these results. As in our earlier assessments with correctional officers, the most strongly expressed demands perceived as coming from the prisoners were in the area TC, and the weakest in the area SO. The psychologists experienced an inverse weighting regarding the prison administration and the prison officers. As is shown by the standard deviations in Table 25.1, the large group of prisoners were apparently estimated or typified as being relatively homogeneous in their demands. In contrast, the smaller group of prison administrators were considered to be more differentiated. In their self-perceptions, the psychologists were relatively close to the demands of the prisoners in the areas SO and TC. The same finding was also obtained for the psychologists' perceptions of the demands placed on them by

TABLE 25.1. Means, standard deviations, and *F*-tests for the role demands perceived by psychologists

Role sender	Security, order, and a smooth day-to-day running (SO)		Prisoner treatment, counseling, and resocialization (TC)		Organization management and development (OD)	
	Mean	SD	Mean	SD	Mean	SD
Prisoners	25.7	4.3	49.2	4.5	30.3	6.0
Prison officers	43.2	7.2	35.2	7.1	27.1	7.7
Prison administration	41.2	8.0	36.9	7.7	27.8	8.7
Social workers	30.5	5.7	42.0	5.9	32.7	7.1
Psychologist (role self-definitions)	26.2	5.3	43.8	8.4	35.7	8.7
	$F = 204.32$ $P = 0.000$		$F = 80.99$ $P = 0.000$		$F = 26.99$ $P = 0.000$	

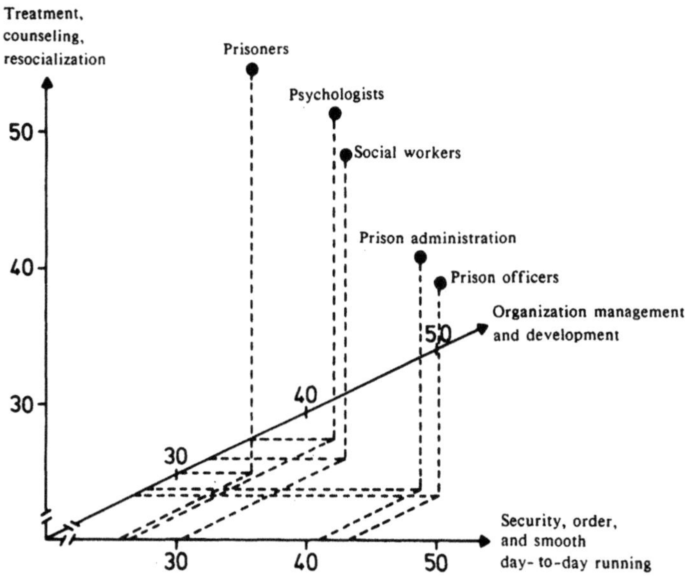

FIGURE 25.2. The self-defined role demands of the psychologists related to the perceived role demands from the other members of the prison community

the social workers. Both results support our earlier findings from the perspective of the correctional officers, and likewise the large similarity observed in the demands placed on them by prison administrators and prison officers (cf. Braune et al., 1983a; Klapprott et al., 1976). However, in their self-perceptions, the psychologists did not place themselves as close to the prisoners' role demands as the prison officers had perceived them to do. It was also noticeable that the strongest demands in the area OD were not experienced as being expressed by the role partners – and especially not by the prison administrators – but were self-imposed by the psychologists.

There were no significant differences in perceived role demands for different types of prison and other formal institutional features. For this reason, we shall not present bivariate findings but only the multivariate structure of relations within the framework for testing the "situational approach" (see p. 432).

The Structure of the Activities

Figure 25.3 presents the results of the time budget assessments made by prison psychologists. It is clear that, in general, there was a predominance of activities in the areas of prisoner diagnosis, management routines, and prisoner counseling and treatment. The more organizational role component was underrepresented in the time budgeting, especially the counseling, training, and further education of officers, improvements in communication, personnel allocation, public relations, and research serving criminal psychology. Alongside the desire for an intensification of the counseling, treatment, and guidance of prisoners, the strongest actual value/desired value discrepancies were found in the area OD.

As far as the discrepancy between actual and desired values is concerned, it can be further seen that almost all of the strongly desired changes required an *increase* in the time budget. The only exceptions were the writing of diagnostic prisoner reports and the mostly routine office work which is often the subject of complaint in many organizations outside of prisons.

In contrast to the role demands presented above, clear differences can be seen in the structure of the actual activities in different *forms of prison* (see Table 25.2). As one might expect, the activities of psychologists in social therapeutic prisons were predominantly in the area TC. In contrast, in "normal" adult prisons a higher proportion was found in the area SO. It is conspicuous that in contrast to the above-mentioned role self-definition, the actual activities that are related to the area OD were relatively infrequent, especially in adult prisons.

As is the case with many aspects of the West German criminal justice system, the activity structures we assessed to some extent varied between different *states*. The mean differences for the SO-related activities were highly significant $F_{(8,70)} = 3.21$, $P < 0.01$. For TC, the *F*-scores only just failed to reach

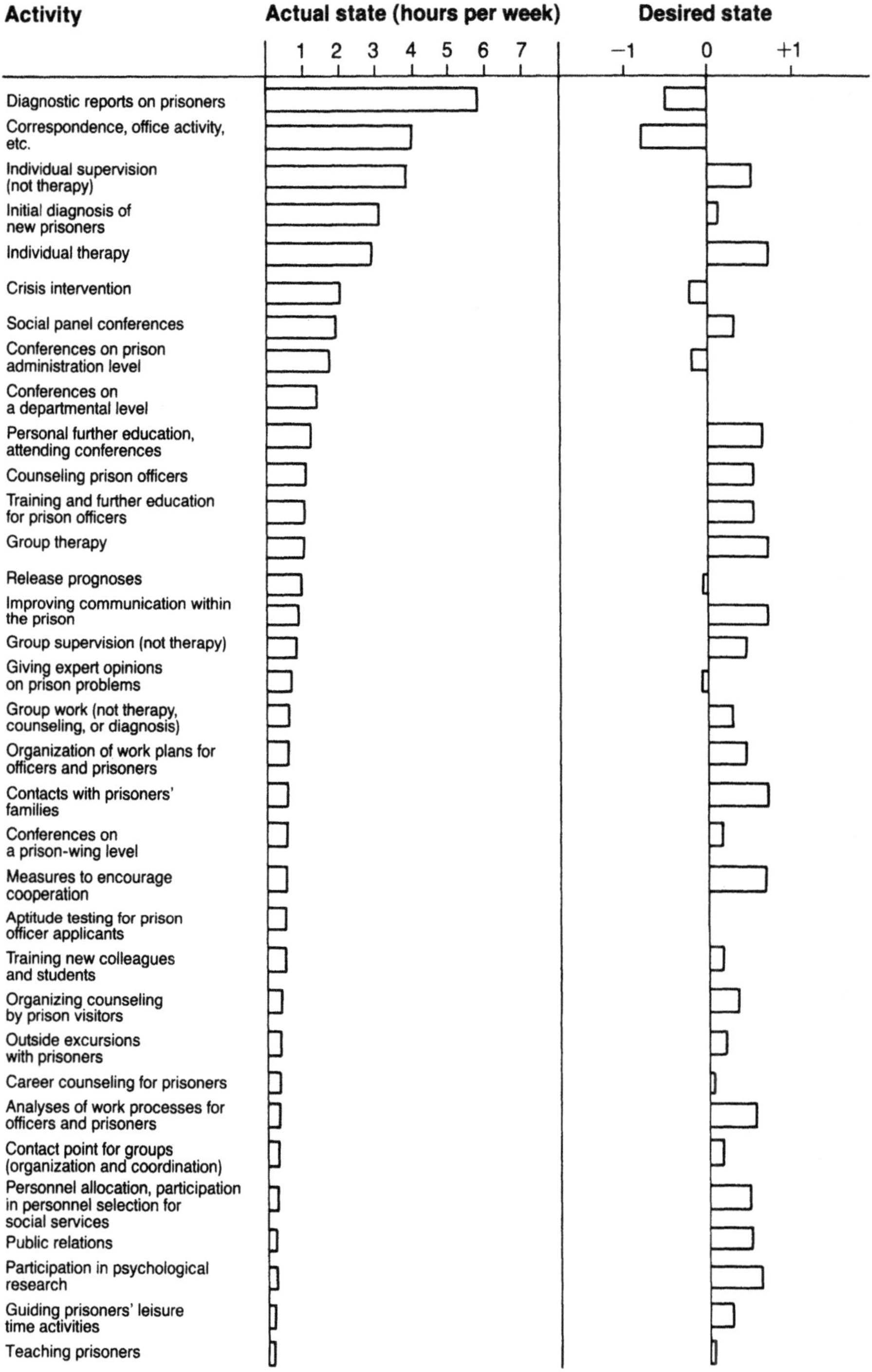

FIGURE 25.3. The time budgets of prison psychologists and the desired states for the single activities

TABLE 25.2. Time budgets for the activities of psychologists in different types of prison

Type of prison	Activities					
	Security, order, and a smooth day-to-day running (SO)		Prisoner treatment, counseling, and resocialization (TC)		Organization management and development (OD)	
	Mean	SD	Mean	SD	Mean	SD
	13.5	7.1	14.1	6.5	12.4	5.9
Social-therapeutic prison	7.2	6.3	18.9	8.9	13.9	4.7
Prison for young offenders	11.2	4.9	14.8	5.1	14.0	4.7
Open adult prison	16.2	7.7	12.8	5.5	11.0	5.4
Closed adult prison	16.2	7.0	12.6	6.4	11.2	6.8
	$F = 7.73$ $P = 0.000$		$F = 3.20$ $P = 0.027$		$F = 1.76$ $P = 0.161$	

TABLE 25.3. Time budgets for the activities of psychologists according to governing political party

Governing political party	Activities					
	Security, order, and a smooth day-to-day running (SO)		Prisoner treatment, counseling, and resocialization (TC)		Organization management and development (OD)	
	Mean	SD	Mean	SD	Mean	SD
CDU/CSU	11.2	5.5	15.5	5.4	13.3	5.6
SPD	16.8	7.1	12.3	6.5	10.9	4.8
	$t = 4.13$ $P = 0.000$		$t = 2.49$ $P = 0.015$		$t = 2.17$ $P = 0.033$	

the 5% level of significance. The states were grouped according to the governing political party as an aspect of criminal policy framing conditions. The results are presented in Table 25.3. The states differed to the extent that in the state governments formed by "conservative" parties, the reported time budget for TC and OD activities was larger, and that for SO lower than in states with social-democratic governments.

TABLE 25.4. Time budgets for the activities of psychologists according to prisons with favorable versus unfavorable personnel-prisoner ratios

Personnel-prisoner ratio	Activities					
	Security, order, and a smooth day-to-day running (SO)		Prisoner treatment, counseling, and resocialization (TC)		Organization management and development (OD)	
	Mean	SD	Mean	SD	Mean	SD
Unfavorable	15.6	7.2	12.2	5.8	12.2	7.2
Favorable	11.6	6.5	15.8	6.7	12.5	4.4
	$t = 2.73$ $P = 0.008$		$t = 2.75$ $P = 0.007$		$t = 0.26$ $P = 0.799$	

The structure of the psychological activities in prisons also varied according to the stress imposed upon the prison by a more or less unfavorable *personnel-prisoner ratio.* If one differentiates the pattern of activities according to prisons with a higher than average versus a low personnel ratio (median split), one obtains the findings presented in Table 25.4. Psychologists in institutions with unfavorable personnel-prisoner ratios spent more time on SO activities and less on TC than their colleagues in institutions with a more favorable personnel-prisoner ratio. In contrast, there were no differences for the OD area of work.

It must, however, be noted that to some extent confounding factors are present for all three differentiating variables. Thus, for example, the prison type and the personnel-prisoner ratio are confounded to the extent that social therapeutic prisons generally have a particularly favorable personnel-prisoner ratio. For this reason, the following path analysis structures must be considered when interpreting the individual findings.

Testing the Situational Model with Path Analysis

In order to avoid confounding factors we specified a path model to test the theoretical assumptions of Inkson et al. (1967) and Kieser and Kubicek (1983). As mentioned at the beginning of this chapter, it is assumed that the influence of situational variables (framing conditions of the organization) on the activities of the psychologists is mediated by the role demands and the role perception. The situational variables listed in the preceding section were entered into the model as alternative data: type of prison (dichotomized into social therapeutic prison/prison for young offenders vs. "normal" adult prison), criminal policy framing (Christian Democratic Party/Christian Social Party state government vs. Social Democratic Party), and personnel-prisoner ratio (low vs. high). On the behavioral level, we included the time budget for the SO, TC, and OD areas of activity; on the role perception level, the corresponding role demands that the psychologists made on themselves (role self-definition). As the external role demands for psychologists are not specified by the Prison Act or other guidelines, they were operationalized in each of the three areas as the sum of the role demands perceived as coming from the prison administration, the correctional officers, the social workers, and the prisoners. This procedure should have a relatively high content validity as, on the one hand, it takes into account the tension between the partially contrary role demands, and, on the other, this polarization has also been confirmed from a different role perspective by our earlier findings.

An analysis of the underlying model using LISREL VI (Jöreskog & Sörbom, 1986) was unable to confirm the theoretical path structure. This was particularly due to the fact that the coefficients of the paths mediated by the role demands and the role self-definition were unexpectedly low. Therefore, in a second step, a descriptive model was developed proceeding from the model parameters. In an optimization process, path coefficients with a low contribution (<0.10) were removed from the model, and, in addition, paths between variables were specified and presented for estimation when their calculated residues and modification indices suggested an error specification (Lomax, 1982). In this way, an improved description of the data should be achieved without aspiring to a model test (cf. Stelzl, 1983). This descriptive model is given in Figure 25.4.

Several criteria can be used to judge the validity of the model (Jöreskog & Sörbom, 1986). The path coefficients made small to medium contributions (0.13–0.44). The squared multiple correlations of all structural equations explained almost 42% of the variance of the entire model ($R^2 = 0.417$). The adjusted Goodness-of-Fit Index, a measure of model validity that is independent of sample size, produced a highly satisfactory value of 0.963. Accordingly, the model describes the empirical data with only negligible error specifications.

The contents show that, in accordance with the original model assumptions, all situational variables have an influence on the psychologists' activities – at times even with relatively high path coefficients. As anticipated, though quantitatively less clear, it could be confirmed that there was a causal ranking proceeding from the influences of the role demands, over the role self-definition, to the activity structure. In accordance with the unconfirmable assumptions of the original model, there were, however, no substantial paths between the situational variables and the role demands, and only two weak coefficients with the role self-definition. Differences between the influences of the three situational variables could be recognized to the extent that the personnel-prisoner ratio related less directly with the activity structure and more through the mediation of the role perceptions. The direct paths of both the other variables showed that the "normal" adult prisons, in contrast to the more treatment- and education-oriented prisons, contributed to more SO activities

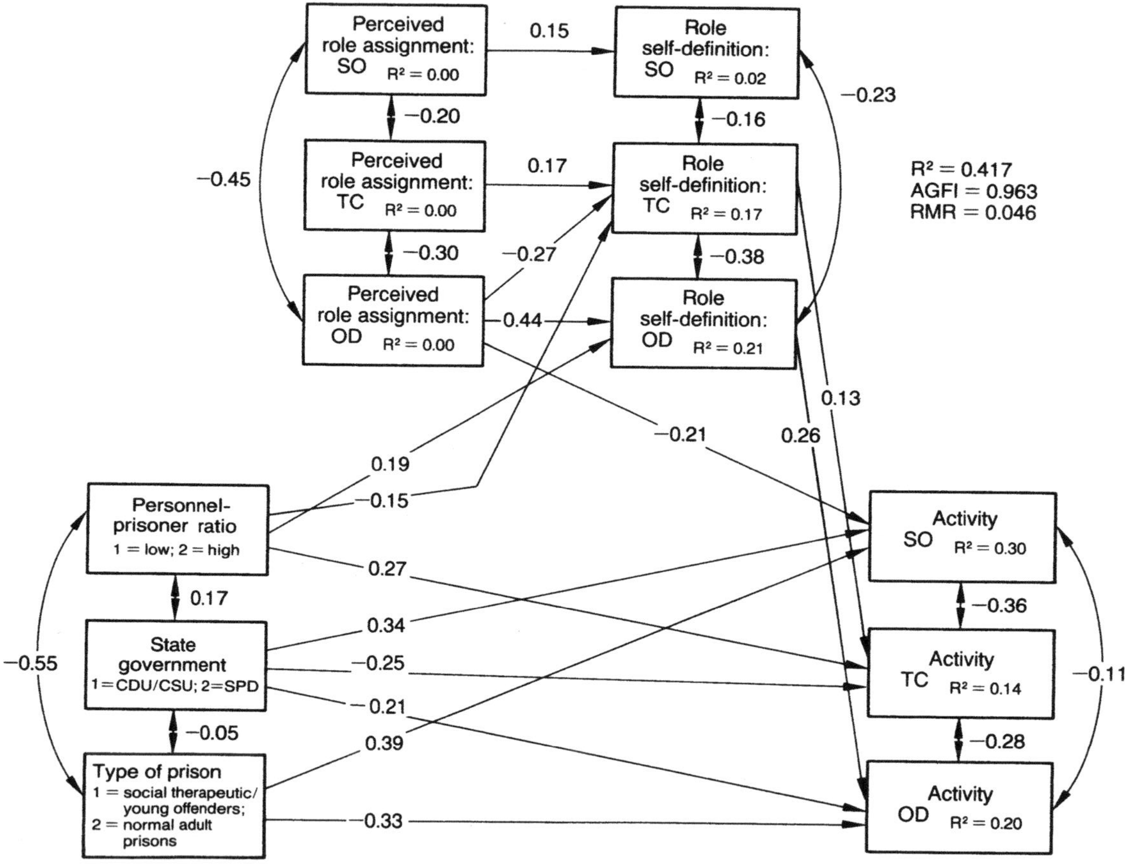

FIGURE 25.4. Path analysis of the relations between situational features of the prison, role definitions, and the activities of prison psychologists. *SO*, security, order, and smooth day to day running; *TC*,

and less OD activities, and that the comparatively rough context variable of criminal policy was reflected in all three areas of activity.

Discussion

Our operationalization of the role features is based on a demand-related role concept in which the perceived content of the tasks imposed on the psychologists is assessed from different perspectives (cf. Kelvin, 1970, p. 149). It is revealed that the structure of the role perceptions within prisons actually presents a more differentiated picture than that suggested by contrasts such as "containment versus resocialization" (cf. also Klingemann, 1981; Rosner, 1984). Although negative correlations exist between each of our three categories of role demands, they are only moderate and primarily due to the methods used (forced choice through the ranking according to a prestructured distribution). The agreement with our previous analyses of prison officers suggests that the role-related perceptions of the psychologists were assessed with a relatively high reliability and validity.

The psychologists above all consider the demands of counseling, treatment, and rehabilitation of prisoners to be important in their role definition. This is in accordance with the traditional understanding of the role of clinical psychology toward prisoners. Alongside this, however, it must be stressed that the psychologists place a relatively high weight on tasks in the areas of organization management and development – especially when this is compared with the perceived view taken by the role partners. This finding possibly relates to the response rate in our study, in that the psychologists who took part are particularly interested in organization psychology, and that this is why they answered our questionnaire on organizational assessment. However, the fact that not only an intensification of the OD area but also of the TC area is strongly desired in the comparison of actual versus desired states in the time budget speaks against such an explanation.

Therefore, our data contradict the stereotype according to which prison psychologists are only interested in treatment concepts. Their role self-definition is more strongly oriented toward organization-related activity than is suggested by their legally relatively undefined role or job description. As the path model shows, although the psychologists orient themselves toward the perceived demands of their role partners, they define their roles relatively autonomously when there are conflicting demands. The achievement of their own role definition, however, appears, to some extent, to be confronted with institutional pressures. This is suggested by the influence of situational variables.

As far as an expansion of OD activities is concerned, it has to be taken into account that an increase in the desired values of the time budget is also considered desirable for most of the other items. Without an (unrealistic) increase in individual working hours or an (at present not very realistic) increase in personnel, there only remains the limited possibility of setting priorities for each individual prison. In this way, an organization psychology perspective would probably be easier to realize if more psychologists were to be placed in high level administrative positions, accompanied by a change in their work structure. According to the present and our own earlier findings, however, the informal level, in which the psychologist clarifies his/her professional role more clearly to the prison officers, is also important. If the prison officers only perceive the psychologist from a TC direction and as an "ally" of the prisoner, which is not in accordance with the psychologist's self-image and work activities, this will result in unnecessary difficulties for organization-related work (for a discussion of similar problems of pluralistic ignorance within prisons, see Kauffmann, 1981; Wheeler, 1961). That OD concepts of prison psychologists should not only be approached through an expansion of personnel is also suggested by the path coefficients of the personnel-prisoner ratio: While a favorable personnel-prisoner ratio correlates with a stronger role self-definition and activities in the TC area, the effects for OD are weaker and show a reverse tendency. It may be possible to explain this through a lower pressure for change when there is a favorable personnel-prisoner ratio. However, this is contradicted by the fact that structurally more favorable framing conditions (especially in the social therapeutic prisons) encourage an OD orientation from psychologists in the actual activity structure.

The clear relations between the recorded situational variables or framing conditions and the reported activity structure of the psychologists is, in our opinion, the most important finding in the study. On the one hand, it underlines the need to pay more attention to the variations between different prisons when analyzing the institution "prison". On the other hand, it supports the assumption of organization psychology, as found in the work of Inkson et al. and Kieser and Kubicek, that the situational features are particularly significant for the explanation of homogenizing or differentiating conditions. Although the multilevel mediation is only partially proven for the role demands and the role self-definitions, this neither contradicts the "situational approach" in general, nor its application to prisons. For, among other factors, the following must be taken into account: Only three indicators are included on each of all the levels, and the situational variables are only dichotomous. As, in addition, it can be anticipated that a high proportion of the variance in the activity and role levels is explained by the methods used, it would be illusory to anticipate high path coefficients. That only negligible paths were observed for the role demands may be due to the fact that we operationalized this construct with the sum of the *perceived* role demands. It is possible that, for example, a scaled weighting of the various role partners would have been more suitable. Nevertheless, an explorative analysis using perceived demands from the prison administration as the single role directive produced nearly the same findings. It is possible that role perceptions or evaluations should not just be calculated with monotone-linear functions, but, for example, with curvilinear ones in order to allow for dissonance or reactance effects.

Because of the unclear formal stipulation of the role of psychologists and the coercive conditions of a total institution, it is plausible that situational structural variables have a fairly direct effect on everyday activities (cf. Jurik, 1985). The findings concerning the personnel-prisoner ratio and the form of prison are also consistent with our expectations: for example, a favorable personnel-prisoner ratio leads to increased activities in the TC area, and in more custody-oriented adult prisons the activities that are related to order, security, and smooth day-to-day running are more frequent than in social therapeutic prisons and prisons for young offenders. In addition, the bivariate analysis clearly shows that, given the framing conditions of a social therapeutic prison, the activities of the psychologists are, in accordance with the goals of such institutions, influenced in the directions TC and OD. Through the combination with prisons for young offenders in the dichotomous variable of the path model, this becomes less clear or is mediated through the covariation with the personnel-prisoner ratio (see Figure 25.4).

In contrast, the paths that proceed from context variables of criminal policy (ruling political party in each state) are somewhat surprising. In states with conservative (CDU/CSU) governments, the activity structure of prison psychologists is oriented more toward TC and OD and less toward SO than in states with social-democratic (SPD) governments. This finding contradicts widespread stereotypes of criminal policy and is not confounded by the effects of personnel-prisoner ratios or the form of prison. It is possible that it can be explained by, for example, nonrecorded features of the institutions that correlate with the state variables, such as prison population, or the training and motivation of the mostly regionally recruited psychologists. Another possible explanation could be that, particularly in the field of prison psychology, conservative-ruled states such as Bavaria have been relatively progressive (cf. Kühne, 1986, p. 18; Wagner, 1972). A similar example is California, where criminal treatment models were particularly encouraged during the time of the conservative Republican government of Ronald Reagan. In our opinion, one should not speculate any further about the causes of this surprising finding without additional data. Nevertheless, we regard it to be a further indication that generalized commonsense theories about the structures and processes in prisons require qualification.

In general, our study has provided information on the previously scarcely researched professional field of prison psychologists, and provides some initial indicators for changes. With the orientation toward general concepts of organization development, we assume that measures should not be designed for too heterogeneous institutions but should, as far as possible, be based on the diagnosis of specific internal features and context variables. Especially after the experiences with the past large-scale trends in evaluations for the treatment of criminals, small-scale measures of organization development, carried out with a close linking of formative and summative evaluation, would seem to be indicated (cf. Lösel et al., 1987). Such strategies should not only lead to a further differentiation of prisons but also to a more differentiated placement of prisoners that would quantitatively relieve prisons and increase their efficacy (cf. Blumstein, 1983).

References

Beer, M. (1976). The technology of organization development. In M.D. Dunette (Ed.), *Handbook of industrial and organizational psychology* (pp. 937–993). Chicago: Rand McNally.

Blickhan, C., Braune, P., Klapprott, J., Linz, P., & Lösel, F. (1978). Berufliche Einstellungen von Justizvollzugsbeamten. *Psychologie und Praxis, 22*, 18–33.

Blickhan, C., Braune, P., Klapprott, J., Linz, P., & Lösel, F. (1980). Förderung individueller Autonomie als Training sozialer Kompetenzen. In F. Ronneberger, H.J. Seel, & M. Stosberg (Eds.), *Autonomes Handeln als personale und gesellschaftliche Aufgabe* (pp. 335–379). Opladen–Wiesbaden: Westdeutscher Verlag.

Blumstein, A. (1983). Prisons: population, capacity, and alternatives. In J.Q. Wilson (Ed.), *Crime and public policy* (pp. 229–250). San Francisco: ICS.

Böhm, G. (1981). *Einführung in die Organisationsentwicklung.* Heidelberg: Sauer.

Bowker, L.H. (1982). *Corrections: The science and the art.* New York: Macmillan.

Braune, P., Klapprott, J., Linz, P., Lösel, F., & Runkel, T. (1980). *Zeitbudget und Erlebensanalyse zur Berufstätigkeit von Strafvollzugsbeamten: eine empirische Erkundungsstudie.* Sonderforschungsbereich 22 der Universität Erlangen-Nürnberg.

Braune, P., Klapprott, J., Linz, P., Lösel, F., & Runkel, T. (1982). Psychologische Fortbildung von Mediatoren als indirekte Resozialisierungsmaßnahme. In W.R. Minsel, & R. Scheller (Eds.), *Rehabilitation. Brennpunkte der klinischen Psychologie*: Vol. 4 (pp. 92–115). Munich: Kösel.

Braune, P., Klapprott, J., Linz, P., Lösel, F., & Runkel, T. (1983a). Ein empirischer Beitrag zur Organisationsdiagnostik und Personalentwicklung im Strafvollzug. In H.J. Kerner, H. Kury, & K. Sessar (Eds.), *Deutsche Forschungen zur Kriminalitätsentstehung und Kriminalitätskontrolle*: Vol. 3 (pp. 1744–1777). Cologne: Heymanns.

Braune, P., Klapprott, J., Linz, P., Lösel, F., & Runkel, T. (1983b). Psychologische Organisationsentwicklung im Strafvollzug. In F. Lösel (Ed.), *Kriminalpsychologie* (pp. 228–238). Weinheim, FRG: Beltz.

Carney, L.P. (1974). *Introduction to correctional science.* New York: McGraw-Hill.

Cascio, W.F. (1986). *Managing human resources.* New York: McGraw-Hill.

Cheek, F.E., & Stefano-Miller, M. (1983). Experience of stress for correctional officers: a double bind theory of correctional stress. *Journal of Criminal Justice, 11*, 105–120.

Clemmer, D. (1940). *The prison community.* New York: Rinehart.

Craig, R.T. (1981). Generalization of Scott's index of intercoder agreement. *Public Opinion Quarterly, 45*, 260–264.

Cressey, D.R. (1959). Contradictory directives in complex organizations: the case of the prison. *Administrative Science Quarterly, 4*, 1–19.

Däumling, A.M., & Possehl, K. (1970). *Selbstbild und Fremdbild der Aufsichtsbeamten im Strafvollzug.* Stuttgart: Enke.

Driebold, R., Egg, R., Nellessen, L., Quensel, S., & Schmitt, G. (1984). *Die sozialtherapeutische Anstalt. Modell und Empfehlungen für den Justizvollzug.* Göttingen: Vandenhoeck and Ruprecht.

Duffee, D. (1974). The correction officer subculture and organizational change. *Journal of Research in Crime and Delinquency, 11*, 155–172.

Duffee, D. (1980). *Correctional management: change and control in correctional organizations.* Englewood Cliffs, NJ: Prentice-Hall.

Dünkel, F. (1987). *Die Herausforderung der geburtenschwachen Jahrgänge.* Freiburg i. Br., FRG: Max-Planck-Institut für ausländisches und internationales Strafrecht.

Dünkel, F., & Rosner, A. (1980). Zur gegenwärtigen Lage des Erwachsenenstraf- und Untersuchungshaftvollzugs der Bundesrepublik Deutschland. In Forschungsgruppe Kriminologie (Ed.), *Empirische Kriminologie.* Freiburg i. Br., FRG: Max-Planck-Institut für ausländisches und internationales Strafrecht.

Ebbesen, E. B., & Konečni V. J. (1982). Social psychology and the law: a decision-making approach to the criminal justice system. In V. J. Konečni & E.B. Ebbesen (Eds.). *The criminal justice system – a social-psychological analysis* (pp. 3–23). San Francisco: Freeman.

Farmer, R. E. (1977). Cynicism: a factor in correction work. *Journal of Criminal Justice, 5*, 237–246.

French, W. L., & Bell, C. H. (1977). *Organisationsentwicklung.* Bern: Haupt.

Goffman, E. (1972). *Asyle: über die soziale Situation psychiatrischer Patienten und anderer Insassen.* Frankfurt/M.: Suhrkamp.

Hawkins, G. (1976). *The prison: policy and practice.* Chicago: University of Chicago Press.

Hephurn, J. R., & Albonetti, C. (1980). Role conflict in correctional institutions. *Criminology, 17*, 445–459.

Hesener, B., & Jehle, J. M. (1987). *Bevölkerungsbewegung und Strafvollzugsbelegung. Die künftige Entwicklung des Strafvollzugs unter besonderer Berücksichtigung der demographischen Entwicklung.* Wiesbaden: Kriminologische Zentralstelle.

Hohmeier, J. (1973). *Aufsicht und Resozialisierung.* Stuttgart: Enke.

Inkson, K., Payne, R., & Pugh, D. (1967). Extending the occupational environment: the measurement of organisations. *Occupational Psychology, 41*, 33–47.

Jöreskog, K. G., & Sörbom, D. (1986). *LISREL VI. Analysis of linear structural relationship by maximum likelihood, instrumental variables and least squares methods* (4th ed.). Mooresville, IN: Scientific Software.

Jurik, N. C. (1985). Individual and organizational determinants of correctional officers attitudes toward inmates. *Criminology, 23*, 523–539.

Kaiser, G., Kerner, H. J., & Schöch, H. (1983). *Strafvollzug* (3rd ed.). Heidelberg: Müller.

Katein, E., Kury, H., & Waldert, H. (1986). Organisationsstrukturen und therapeutische Orientierung im Strafvollzug – eine empirische Untersuchung. *Monatsschrift für Kriminologie und Strafrechtsreform, 69*, 210–220.

Kauffman, K. (1981). Prison officers' attitudes and perceptions of attitudes. A case of pluralistic ignorance. *Journal of Research in Crime and Delinquency, 18*, 272–294.

Kelvin, P. (1970). *The bases of social behaviour. An approach in terms of order and value.* London: Holt, Rinehart and Winston.

Kieser, A. (1977). Organisationsstruktur und Individuum. Probleme der Analyse und empirischer Ergebnisse. In G. Reber (Ed.), *Personal- und Sozialorientierung der Betriebswirtschaftslehre:* Vol. 1 (pp. 111–133).

Kieser, A., & Kubicek, H. (1983). Organisation (2nd ed.). Berlin: de Gruyter.

Klapprott, J., Blickhan, C., Braune, P., Linz, P., & Lösel, F. (1976). Zur beruflichen Situation von Aufsichtsbeamten im Strafvollzug. *Soziale Welt, 27*, 71–86.

Klingemann, H. (1981). Organisationale Zielkonflikte im Resozialisierungsbereich: Jugendstrafvollzug und Öffentliche Erziehung. *Zeitschrift für Soziologie, 10*, 50–75.

Krüger, U. (1973). Die Tätigkeit des Aufsichtsbeamten im Justizvollzug. Dissertation, University of Bonn.

Kühne, A. (1983). Psychologie im Justizvollzug. *Psychologische Rundschau, 34,* 57–71.

Kühne, A. (1986). *Psychologische Aspekte der Organisationsentwicklung in der Strafrechtspflege am Beispiel eines Modells der Weiterbildung in Niedersachsen.* Projektbericht. Hannover: Arbeitsstelle für Unterrichtsforschung der Universität, Hannover.

Lasky, G. L., Gordon, B. C., & Srebalus, D. J. (1986). Occupational stressors among federal correctional officers working in different security levels. *Criminal Justice and Behavior, 13,* 317–327.

Leky, L. G. (1973). Persönlichkeitszüge der Aufsichtsbeamten im Justizvollzug. Dissertation, University of Bonn.

Lindquist, C. A., & Whitehead, J. T. (1986). Correctional officers as parole officers. *Criminal Justice and Behavior, 13,* 197–222.

Lomax, R. (1982). Methods and design. A guide to LISREL-type structural equation modeling. *Behavior Research Methods and Instruments, 14,* 1–8.

Long, N., Shouksmith, G., Voges, K., & Roache, S. (1986). Stress in prison staff: an occupational study. *Criminology, 24,* 331–345.

Lösel, F. (1986). Kriminologische Forschungsperspektiven aus psychologischer Sicht. In H. Kury (Ed.), *Interdisziplinäre Beiträge zur kriminologischen Forschung* (pp. 65–91). Cologne: Heymanns.

Lösel, F., & Köferl, P. (1988). Psychologische Rehabilitation bei Straffälligkeit. In U. Koch, G. Lucius-Hoene, & R. Stegie (Eds.), *Handbuch der Rehabilitationspsychologie* (pp. 742–775). Berlin Heidelberg New York: Springer.

Lösel, F., Köferl, P., & Weber, F. (1987). *Meta-Evaluation der Sozialtherapie. Qualitative und quantitative Analysen zur Behandlungsforschung in sozialtherapeutischen Anstalten des Justizvollzuges.* Stuttgart: Enke.

Marquart, G. W. (1986). Prison guards and the use of physical coercion as a mechanism of prisoner control. *Criminology, 24,* 347–366.

Mey, H. G. (1986). Zur Tätigkeit und zur Berufsrolle des Psychologen im Justizvollzug nach Inkrafttreten des Strafvollzugsgesetzes (StVollzG). *Report Psychologie, 11,* 6–10.

Moos, R. H. (1975). *Evaluating correctional and community settings.* New York: Wiley.

Müller-Dietz, H. (1977). *Strafvollzugsrecht.* Berlin: de Gruyter.

Ohler, W. (1977). *Die Strafvollzugsanstalt als soziales System – Entwurf einer Organisationstheorie zum Strafvollzug.* Heidelberg: Müller.

Poole, E. D., & Regoli, R. M. (1980). Work relations and cynicism among prison guards. *Criminal Justice and Behavior, 7,* 303–314.

Preusker, H. (1987). Erfahrungen der Praxis mit dem Strafvollzugsgesetz. *Zeitschrift für Strafvollzug und Straffälligenhilfe, 36,* 11–16.

Rosner, A. (1983). Die Arbeitssituation der Bediensteten im Strafvollzug – eine empirische Untersuchung zur Situation der Mitarbeiter nach der Strafvollzugsreform. *Zeitschrift für Strafvollzug und Straffälligenhilfe, 32,* 67–73.

Rosner, A. (1984). Berufsfeld Strafvollzug: eine empirische Untersuchung zu einem schwierigen Arbeitsbereich. In H. J. Kerner, H. Kury, & K. Sessar (Eds.), *Deutsche Forschungen zur Kriminalitätsentstehung und Kriminalitätskontrolle:* Vol. 3 (pp. 1682–1718). Cologne: Heymanns.

Rotthaus, K. P. (1987). Die Bedeutung des Strafvollzugsgesetzes für die Reform des Strafvollzugs. *Neue Zeitschrift für Strafrecht, 7,* 1–5.

Stelzl, I. (1983). Zur Uneindeutigkeit von LISREL-Lösungen: Überlegungen und Beispiele. *Psychologische Beiträge, 25,* 315–335.

Thomas, J.E. (1974). Prison officer – conflict in roles. *Journal of Psychosomatic Research, 18*, 259.

Thornton, D. (1985). Intra-regime variation in inmate perception of prison staff. *British Journal of Criminology, 24*, 138–147.

Wagner, G. (1972). *Psychologie im Strafvollzug.* Munich: Goldmann.

Wagner, G. (1984). *Das absurde System.* Heidelberg: Müller.

Williams, T.A., & Soutar, G.N. (1984). Levels of custody and attitude differences among prison officers: a comparative study. *Australian and New Zealand Journal of Criminology, 17*, 87–94.

Wheeler, S. (1961). Role conflict in correctional communities. In D. Cressey (Ed.), *The prison: studies in institutional organization and change* (pp. 229–259). New York: Holt, Rinehart and Winston.

Zimbardo, P.G. (1972). Pathology of imprisonment. *Society, 9*, 4–8.

Author Index

Subject Index

GPSR Compliance

The European Union's (EU) General Product Safety Regulation (GPSR) is a set of rules that requires consumer products to be safe and our obligations to ensure this.

If you have any concerns about our products, you can contact us on ProductSafety@springernature.com

In case Publisher is established outside the EU, the EU authorized representative is:

Springer Nature Customer Service Center GmbH
Europaplatz 3
69115 Heidelberg, Germany

Batch number: 10844669

Printed by Printforce, the Netherlands